SAINT TERESA OF ÁVILA

Saint Teresa at the age of sixty-one, from Friar Juan de
la Miseria's portrait, for which she sat at Sevilla, in
obedience to a superior's command, in 1576.

Saint Teresa of Ávila
A Biography

By

WILLIAM THOMAS WALSH

*"Zelo zelatus sum pro Domino Deo
exercituum."* —3 Kings 19:10

"With zeal have I been zealous for the
Lord God of hosts."
—3 Kings 19:10

TAN BOOKS AND PUBLISHERS, INC.
Rockford, Illinois 61105

Nihil Obstat: H. B. Ries
                   Censor Librorum

Imprimatur: ✛ Moses E. Kiley
                   Archbishop of Milwaukee
                   January 5, 1943

Library of Congress Catalog Card No.: 87-50928

ISBN: 0-89555-325-2

TAN BOOKS AND PUBLISHERS, INC.
P.O. Box 424
Rockford, Illinois 61105
1987

To

Mother Grace C. Dammann, R.S.C.J., President
Manhattanville College of the Sacred Heart
New York City, whose friendship has made so much
of my work possible

WORKS BY WILLIAM THOMAS WALSH

The Mirage of the Many (1910)
Isabella of Spain (1930)
Out of the Whirlwind (novel, 1935)
Philip II (1937)
Shekels (blank-verse play, 1937)
Lyric Poems (1939)
Characters of the Inquisition (1940)
"Gold" (short story)
Babies, not Bullets! (booklet, 1940)
Thirty Pieces of Silver (a play in verse)
Saint Teresa of Ávila (1943)
La actual situatión de España (booklet, 1944)
El caso crucial de España (booklet, 1946)
Our Lady of Fátima (1947)
The Carmelites of Compiègne (a play in verse)
Saint Peter, the Apostle (1948)

ACKNOWLEDGMENT

YEARS ago, when I read an English translation of Saint Teresa's *Autobiography*, as it is improperly called, I wondered whether a woman in whom the divine and the human so strikingly met could really have been as banal, as priggish, as self-consciously "literary" as she often appeared in those pages. Later, when I was able to read the Spanish text, I discovered that the irritating qualities were not hers, but her devout translator's. What a vital book to be embalmed in so much stuffy rhetoric! I resolved that whenever it was necessary to quote that work, I would make my own translations, and as literally as possible, even at some sacrifice of euphony; not excluding the occasional slips in grammar, faulty reference, careless sentence structure, and vigorous colloquialisms of one who wrote with no eye to bookish effect, but just as she spoke, rapidly, tersely, wittily, now and then quite awkwardly. Only thus could one convey, in another language, the characteristic quality, the timbre and rhythm of writings which, whatever their technical faults or peculiarities, were always honest, gusty, human, interesting, and stimulating, often aglow with the beauty and sublimity of genius directed by sanctity. When I came to her letters and later treatises, there were some good translations at hand, notably the excellent ones by the Benedictines of Stanbrook Abbey, England. But having gone so far with my own, it seemed imperative to continue for the sake of uniformity of style — the style being, I hope, Saint Teresa's rather than mine.

The material now available for a new life of this glorious doctor of the science of love is such that the situation seems to call for selection, arrangement, and simplification in a single volume for general use, rather than further research or critical hairsplitting. The chief sources are still the several volumes of letters, treatises, and narratives by Saint Teresa herself, the depositions of witnesses for her beatification and canonization, and the contemporary biographies, of which the most useful is that of Father Ribera, S.J., followed by those of Father Yepes, Father Julian of Ávila, and Fray Luis de León in the order named. Any attempt on my part to go much beyond these would be presumptuous in the light of the vast achievement of Father Silverio de Santa Teresa, O.C.D., who has edited and annotated all of her works in masterly and exhaustive fashion, besides publishing, as the crown of a lifetime of study, a biography of her in five huge volumes.

My first acknowledgment, then, must be to Father Silverio for making the results of his labor available to me in fourteen tomes of the *Biblioteca Mística Carmelitana* (the B.M.C. to be mentioned so frequently hereafter), which he has sent me from Rome at the request of my good friend Dame Beatrice, O.S.B., of Stanbrook Abbey, one of the greatest living Teresian scholars in her own right, to whom also I am indebted for notes, advice, and many other kindnesses, besides her excellent renderings of the Saint's letters, poems, and other writings, which I have so often had occasion to consult when working on my own translations. For the use of books, theological counsel, and other invaluable assistance I must thank the Reverend Father John J. McSherry of New York City; the Reverend Father Ferdinand Pedrosa, O.P., of Letran College, Manila; the Reverend Father Joseph Husslein, S.J., Ph.D., editor of the *Science and Culture Series*, who suggested this work to me; the Reverend Father Eugene A. Moriarty of Bridgeport, Connecticut, and the Reverend Father Leo W. Madden, Lieut. Commander, Ch.C., U.S.M.S.

To my colleague, Miss Mercedes de Arango, M.A., for proofreading; to Miss Carmen de Arango, for scholarly help of the most expert kind in preparing some of my preliminary notes; and to other friends, particularly Miss Angela Williams and Miss Lucille Flagg, I am greatly obliged. I have had unfailing encouragement from Mother Grace C. Dammann, R.S.C.J., and Mother Eleanor M. O'Byrne, R.S.C.J., president and dean, respectively, of Manhattanville College of the Sacred Heart, and all my other associates there. And I have no words to express my thanks for the patience, loyalty, and intelligent criticism of my wife, who has typed the entire manuscript more than once.

No bibliography is furnished here because I could not improve upon the easily accessible ones of Father Silverio, both for Saint Teresa and for Saint John of the Cross.

Finally, it must be obvious that no powers of mine could have brought to a conclusion a task for which I am so ill-prepared spiritually. There have been many discouraging moments, even with such treasures of scholarship as the works of Father Silverio, Dame Beatrice, and others beside me; and I know I should never have completed the book, such as it is, without the prayers of far better persons to aid me. I am especially grateful to several women who, like Saint Teresa, have dared to take the words of Christ our Lord literally, and to accept all the consequences of regarding Him not merely as an historical character, but as the One, together with the Father and the Holy Ghost, in Whose presence and by Whose power and consent we live and breathe: to Mother Saint Mary Catherine, C.N.D., of Notre Dame College, Staten Island, who first introduced me to this marvelous Saint in 1929; to Dame Beatrice, O.S.B., of Stanbrook Abbey; to Sister Mary Ignatia, S.M., editor of the *Magnificat*, Manchester, New Hampshire, and her Teresian household; to Religious of the Sacred Heart at Manhattanville; to the late Sister Mary Boniface Keasey and others of the Missionary Servants of the Blessed Trinity in Alabama; to the late Mother Augustine of the Mother of God, C.D., prioress of the Discalced Carmelites at Santa Clara, California; to the late Sister Mary Gabriel, a Carmelite at Chichester, England (born a Neopolitan princess), who offered Him all the Friday penances of the last year of her life for this my intention; and to my daughter, Sister Mary Concepta, S.M., of the Sacred Heart Convent, Belmont, North Carolina, who has given Him the lovely flower of her youth. If there is any good here besides the human interest of an amazing life story, I have these dear friends to thank.

W. T. W.

Manhattanville College of the Sacred Heart
New York City

December 24, 1942

CONTENTS

SAINT TERESA OF ÁVILA

FIRST IMPRESSIONS OF HOLY ÁVILA

SAINT TERESA of Jesus, popularly known as Saint Teresa of Ávila from the place of her birth, has a double claim upon the interest of posterity, for she not only set the impress of a rare spirit upon the life of her chaotic century and all subsequent history, but she escaped and transcended, in a fashion more than metaphorical, the well-nigh universal laws of death: even the law of decomposition. Today, after more than three and a half centuries, her body remains incorrupt and fragrant, and would seem only to be waiting through a dateless night for the reanimating kiss of the Bridegroom. Science has no satisfactory explanation for this survival. The facile hypothesis that mummies in a very dry air resist decay must yield to the certainty that Teresa's unembalmed remains lay for nine months in moist ground, where the rains broke through her rude coffin and attacked in vain the invisible locks of that mysterious element that said to worms, "You shall not enter here." Yet this was not the proof of her sanctity, nor was it the cause; it merely helped to call attention to it.

What manner of woman was this, who lived sixty-seven most useful and energetic years in spite of diseases and afflictions that would have kept most persons bedridden; who was seen poorly clad on the roads of Spain, mounted on a mule or in a peasant's cart in parching heat or numbing cold; who seldom had enough money to buy a decent meal, yet founded seventeen convents and several monasteries; who slept on bare boards like a beggar, yet expelled a princess, talked to duchesses as an equal, and on one occasion scolded a king? To what principle shall we appeal to explain the levitations and other strange phenomena in the life of one so richly endowed with the more common human qualities? For Teresa had beauty, charm, literary genius of a high order (though uncultivated), an administrative ability second to none; humor and tenderness and common sense; the courage and resourcefulness of a great soldier, with the patient obedience and humility of a saint. With little formal education, she knew more of neurasthenia, for example, than Charcot did three centuries later, and attained such power and clarity as a thinker than even Leibnitz acknowledged his indebtedness to her, and the Catholics revere her almost as a Doctor with Saint Thomas, Saint Augustine, and others of the mightiest minds in the history of man. What was the inner source of so much vital achievement through the medium of a sickly, frail, yet incorruptible body? Consider first the scene.

The world upon which she opened her eyes in the spring of 1515 was a world in the revolutionary agonies of the mighty transition from medieval to modern times. It was only twenty-three years, a single generation, since the fateful 1492, when the Spanish crusade of 777 years ended with the wresting of Granada from the Moors, the expulsion of the Jews, and the discovery of the western hemisphere. Columbus was only nine years in his grave. There were men still living who had sailed with him, some enjoying the gold of the Indies in their native land, others bearing the light of civilization to Mexico or Luzon, none of them much concerned apparently over his prediction of the end of the world in 1655. His patroness, Queen Isabel *la católica*, had been dead eleven years. Charles the Fifth was a boy of fifteen. Pope Leo the Tenth, son of Lorenzo de Médicis, sat on the chair of St. Peter, and in 1514, the year before Teresa was born, had issued a momentous indulgence, under the usual conditions of penance and contrition, to raise funds for the building of the new basilica at Rome, where Michelangelo was at work. And in 1515 a German monk, then thirty-three years old, had just improvised a theological system which he considered an extension of the ideas of Saint Paul and Saint Augustine, but which was so charged with spiritual explosives that it tore asunder the whole fabric of Christian life and culture, and opened the breach for all the conflicts of the modern scene. It was an interesting coincidence, the birth of Teresa of Jesus and the formulation of Luther's dogma of grace in the same year, for she was to regard her lifework as the antidote and expiation for his. Luther, tormented by the disagreement of flesh and spirit, sought to resolve it by embracing the good things of this world, and failed. Teresa trampled them all under her sandaled feet and succeeded.

One of the world's petty revenges was the complete obliteration, oddly enough by pious and friendly hands, of the very scene of her birth. Pilgrims are disappointed when they look for it in Ávila. Her first biographer, Father Ribera, saw the room where she was born and proposed that it be made into a public oratory and shrine, but unfortunately forgot to leave a description of it.[1] There has been some difference of opinion as to when the building was destroyed, and by whom. Some have blamed her friend, Don Diego de Bracamonte, one of a distinguished family of Hebrew Catholics, who purchased it after her death;[2] others the Conde-Duque de Olivares, Philip the Fourth's favorite minister, who acquired the site in 1630, and built on it a church and convent for the Discalced Carmelites.[3]

The primitive scene may be reconstructed in part from certain bits of evidence, including an inventory of household chattels filed by Teresa's father a few years before her birth.[4] The massive solemn bulk of the house rose out of a hillside at the west end of Ávila, near the Moorish quarter, just in front of the Church of Saint Domingo de Silos and alongside the Church of Saint Scholastica. It was called the "money house," for it had once been the public mint, and so probably was plain, severe, and solid, with an official look. The father of Saint Teresa purchased it in 1504, soon after his first marriage, and had it made over into a dwelling. Like most of the residences of the lesser nobility of Castilla, it was heated, even in zero weather, by braziers full of glowing coals; and the spacious hall was furnished with solid hand-carved pieces, some of great antiquity — splendidly carved and inlaid chests and great leather-seated armchairs with majestic lines, all of a severe dignity and restraint, for the Castilian despised vulgar ostentation, and in all things aimed at a rich simplicity.

Everywhere in this house were reminders of the centuries of conflict that had given the Spanish mind a distinctly military

---

[1] Padre Francisco de Ribera, S.J., *Vida de Santa Teresa*, lib. I, cap. III, ed. by P. Jaime Pons, S.J.

[2] P. Silverio, *Vida de Santa Teresa de Jesús* (Burgos, 1937), in five volumes, vol. I, p. 65.

[3] The church has been severely criticized by some architecturalists. See, for example, Quadrado, *España, sus monumentos y artes*, cap. LV; and Father Pons's edition of Ribera's *Life*, cap. III, p. 92, n. 2; also Mrs. Cunningham-Grahame's strictures in her two-volume *Santa Teresa* (London, 1894), vol. I, p. 83. Señor Miguel Mir, *Vida de Santa Teresa* (Madrid, 1912), vol. I, p. 24, does not share the opinion of these writers that the chapel is churrugueresque, and its altars baroque. He calls it a magnificently decorated chapel, containing a room which some say was the one in which Saint Teresa was born.

[4] This inventory is among the documents in *Apuntes para una biblioteca de escritores españolas*, by D. M. Serrano y Sanz, art. *Santa Teresa*, t. II, p. 496.

turn. Here and there, between sculptured images and paintings of ancestors and of saints, the weapons of the head of the family were displayed. There were all kinds of shields, the long oblong sort, both great and little; bucklers, lances, and crossbows, some for war and some for hunting; swords and daggers, complete sets of armor, casques and corselets, armpieces and thigh pieces; and a *poncho* worth, according to the inventory, a hundred *maravedis.* All the trappings of a horse were there, saddles and bridles, breast leather and headpieces, caparisons of silk embroidered with gold, and spurs worked cunningly in filigrain. In the living room one saw a chess table, where doubtless the master of the house sat gravely with a guest or neighbor during long winter evenings, and not a few articles of feminine interest, including a spinning wheel. Of books there were plenty, for those days; great tomes with heavy leather bindings, among which the inventory lists a *retablo* of the life of Christ, a treatise on the Mass, another on the Seven Deadly Sins, and a few works of more profane interest, such as *The Three Hundred* and *The Coronation* by the fifteenth-century poet, Juan de Mena, and some adventurous romances of the order of *Amadís de Gaula* and *Las Sergas de Esplandián.*

In such a house a saint was born at dawn on the morning of March 28, 1515. Two records of the event have been found, with a curious discrepancy in the date. There was the statement of the child's father that "on Wednesday, on the twenty-eighth day of March, of the year 1515, was born my daughter Teresa, at five o'clock in the morning, half an hour before or after (it was just about to dawn on that said Wednesday)." There was a note made by Teresa herself, years later, in her breviary (found after her death) that "on Wednesday, day of San Bertoldi of the Order of Carmelites, on the twenty-ninth day of March, 1515, at five in the morning, was born Teresa of Jesus, the sinner." But it was the father who was right, for the twenty-eighth, not the twenty-ninth, fell on Wednesday.

Teresa's father, Don[5] Alonso Sánchez de Cepeda, traced his descent, through a noble family reduced in circumstances, to Sáncho, King of Castilla and León, and counted two great chieftains, Ximén Blasco and Esteban Domingo, among his ancient kin. His mother, Doña Inés de Cepeda, derived from Vasco

---

[5] So he was called in Ávila. Teresa, as we shall see (Chapter XXVIII), came to have some doubts as to whether her family was entitled to the distinction.

Vázquez de Cepeda, who had fought under Alfonso the Eleventh at the siege of Gibraltar. His father, Juan Sánchez de Toledo, obtained a letter of nobility in 1500. Juan Sánchez' six sons, including Teresa's father, secured another in 1523, thus recovering all the privileges and exemptions of the *hidalgos*, lost during the revolt of the *Comunidades* against Charles V.

It was a truly impressive coat of arms that Don Alonso had carved, in stone above the doorway of the old mint, when he had made it into his home. Various descriptions of it are conflicting. The oldest and perhaps the most authentic tells of the lion of Cepedas in the upper left quarter, of another lion bordered with crosses in the upper right; at the bottom, on the left, six bezants, and to the right of this, three *bandas* or ribbons, and over all, the famous burning tower of the Ahumadas — all reminders of valor in the glorious crusades.[6]

Teresa's family, on both sides, boasted of *"limpia sangre"* — blood "clean" from any Moorish or Jewish taint: an unfortunate distinction growing out of centuries of religious warfare. The Saint herself was annoyed when her friend, Father Gracián, in her old age, inquired into her ancestry. "It is enough for me, Father," she replied, "to be a daughter of the Catholic Church; and it would trouble me more to have committed a venial sin than to be descended from the lowest and vilest men in the world."

Don Alonso himself, though of Ávilese ancestry, had been born in Toledo, probably about 1485, and he was still known, at the time of Teresa's birth, as *El Toledano*. A grave, thoughtful man he was, as patient in adversity as he was modest in prosperity, temperate in his way of life, probably a good horseman and swordsman, and doubtless unfamiliar, like all of his class, even when reduced in fortune, with any sort of useful or profitable work, the very thought of which was distasteful to descendants of chieftains and conquerors. He had married, about 1504, an Ávilese lady named Doña Catalina del Peso y Henao. By her he had two children, Juan and María, who were now approaching maturity. His estate then amounted to some 350,000 *maravedis*, which her dowry increased by 100,000. Doña Catalina died in 1507. Two years later, at Goterrendura, about three and a half leagues from Ávila, the widower of twenty-four or there-

[6] P. Silverio, *op. cit.*, I, p. 40, from Fr. Jerónimo de S. José's *Historia del Carmen Descalzo*, t. I, lib. II, cap. I.

abouts, married a girl of fourteen, Doña Beatriz Dávila y Ahumada, a beautiful and serene daughter of one of the oldest and
noblest families of Ávila, and heiress to considerable property
there and in near-by country places. On her mother's side she
was descended from the illustrious Ahumadas, mighty heroes in
the crusades against the Moors, and from the Tapias. A year
after her marriage to Don Alonso (when she was fifteen) she
bore a son, Hernando; and another, Rodrigo, on March 28, 1511.
She was twenty, her husband thirty, when their third child, Teresa, was born in 1515.

This child's birth, on the fourth anniversary of Rodrigo, was
an occasion for great rejoicing. She was baptized a week later,
on April 4, in the eleventh-century church of Saint John, where
travelers still see in a dim corner the old baptismal font with its
brass rim carved in arabesques, and beside it, the blocks of stone
worn hollow by the knees of thousands of godparents and others
who have knelt there during the centuries. Her sponsors were
two neighbors, Don Francisco de Nuñez Vela (who little knew,
that festive day, of the brutal death that he and his brother, Don
Blasco, were to meet at the hands of Pizarro's men in distant
Peru) and Doña María del Aguila, daughter of Don Francisco
González de Pajares, and a relative of the Marqueses of Villavi-
ciosa, las Navas and Villafranca.

The child was named after her maternal grandmother, Doña
Teresa de las Cuevas.[7] On the origin of the name, her contemporary biographers disagreed. Ribera insisted that it was primitive Spanish, and probably belonged to some early Spanish
saint.[8] Teresa once said that the name was derived from that of
Saint Dorothea,[9] or vice versa, and she venerated that saint as
her patron.

She was a graceful shapely child. Like so many of the Cas-

---

[7] Mir, *op. cit.*, I, p. 21; P. Silverio, *op. cit.*, I, p. 67.

[8] Ribera (*op. cit.*, lib. I, cap. III) believed the name "Teresa" might have belonged to a daughter of the King Don Bermudo, who was compelled by her
brother Don Alonso to marry Abdalla, King of Toledo, against her will, but was
saved by a miracle from the consummation of the marriage, returned home, and
became a nun. Ribera got this from Archbishop Rodrigo's *Cosas de España*, IV,
c. 17. Yepes, like the earlier Latin writers in Spain, believed the name had been
latinized from the Greek as "Tarasia." The Bollandists support Ribera's conjecture, in so far as they mention another Saint Teresa, widow, virgin, sister of Saint
Sancha, both daughters of King Sancho I of Portugal (t. III, June 27, p.
471 *et seq.*).

[9] Gracián, MS. additions to Ribera's *Vida*, vol. 50, c. 6.

tilians, she had the fair rosy skin of the north, and her well-marked brows, straight rather than arched, retained a somewhat reddish tinge even when darkened by time. Her curly brunette hair, on the other hand, suggested a southern strain, while her eyes, which seemed to laugh and dance when she smiled, were almost black, and the small symmetrical nose, with its sensitive nostrils, ended in something like a little hook. Her face was plump and roundish, and marked with three tiny moles that were considered highly ornamental in that day; one below the middle of the nose, the second over the mouth on the left, the third beneath it on the same side. Her hands were small and singularly beautiful.[10]

All the world that this small lovely stranger knew must have consisted of the house and garden on the hill and the people who lived there. When as a middle-aged woman she wrote down her earliest recollections, the person who came first to her mind was her father, whose favorite child she was.

"I had parents," she wrote, "who were virtuous and feared God. . . . My father was fond of reading good books, and he had them also in Spanish, so that his children might read them. These, together with my mother's care to make us pray and be devoted to our Lady and to certain saints, began to wake me up, I believe, when I was six or seven. It helped me, too, that I never saw my parents favor anything but virtue. They had many. My father was a man of much charity for the poor, and compassion for the sick, and even for servants: so much so that he could never be persuaded to keep slaves, for he pitied them greatly; and when a female slave of his brother was in our house he treated her as if she were one of his own children and he said he was so sorry she was not free that he could hardly endure the pain of it. He was of great truthfulness, no one ever heard him swear or murmur. Very pure, too, in everything."[11]

Centuries of war with the Mohammedans had somewhat blunted the Christian conscience of Castilians regarding slavery. The Moors made slaves of men, women, and children, and the Crusaders retaliated in kind. When Málaga fell in 1487, King

---

[10] These details are from Ribera's famous description (*op. cit.*, lib. IV, cap. I) which he got from María de S. José, *Libro de Recreaciones, Recreación* VIII, p. 96. Of the Saint's nose he says, *"tenía la punta redonda y un poco inclinada para abajo."*

[11] St. Teresa, *Libro de su Vida*, cap. I.

Fernando, angry because the Moslems had offered so long and desperate a resistance, scattered many of them through the cities of Spain as slaves, some of whom with their children still endured bondage in Ávila. It was probably a daughter or granddaughter of one of these unfortunates who toiled without hope for one of the Cepeda brothers.

Teresa's recollection of her mother was more brief, but no less affectionate. She remembered a beautiful creature who, like so many well-bred Castilian matrons, deliberately made herself dowdy, even in her twenties, to avoid the dangers of vanity or seduction. Doña Beatriz suffered from ill-health all her life, but never complained; had the purity of an angel, great common sense, and a lovely serenity that consoled and strengthened others while she herself was suffering inward torments. Like a good Catholic mother, too, she welcomed all the children God sent to her; and He sent nine. Lorenzo was born when Teresa was four, Antonio when she was five, Pedro when she was six, Jerónimo when she was seven. Then there was an interval of five years, after which came Agustín, in 1527, and Juana, in 1528. Teresa's favorite was Rodrigo.

The influence that most profoundly shaped her mind, heart, and will during these early years was, of course, the Catholic Faith. In sixteenth-century Spain this was no perfunctory religion, watered down by timidity or desire to please pagan neighbors ignorant of the true content of historic Christianity. The essence of Catholicism is heroism; does not the Church demand nothing less than *heroic* virtue as the first requisite of that complete Christian life which she calls sanctity? The Mass itself, which Teresa attended at one of the near-by churches with her mother, was a re-enactment of the most sublime and sorrowful hours in human history. And one of the invariable customs in the house of Don Alonso was the recital, every evening after supper, of the Rosary, whose mysteries, unraveled before the mind as bead after bead passed through tired fingers, recalled in orderly sequence the whole history of the life of Christ on earth, and the joys, sorrows, and glorious triumphs of His blessed Mother — surely a record of heroism, if ever there was one. In Spain, moreover, circumstances had thrown upon the Christian consciousness a light peculiarly dramatic, militant, and austere. Something of the hardness of the wood of the Cross and its bitter nails seemed woven into the very pattern of Spanish life; these began to enjoy life, says Yepes, this serious child, with whom no one spoke without being captivated, desired to suffer death for the Lord Who had died for her. She talked much of this to her brother Rodrigo, who, though four years older, was dominated by her keener intelligence and stronger imagination. Long talks they had in the patio and the garden, until, when Teresa was seven and Rodrigo eleven, both were convinced that nothing in this world was desirable, save to die a martyr's death and enter immediately into the sight of God and the joys of heaven.

She had heard priests and her mother and father say that these joys would have no end. She had noticed that every pleasure in this life ended with fatigue, or revulsion, or surfeit, or distaste — the cake was soon eaten and the game forgotten. But in heaven it was otherwise. There joy lasted forever — *para siempre.*

"Think of it, Rodrigo," she would say, "forever! *Para siempre!*"

She would make him repeat, *"Para siempre, para siempre, para siempre, Teresa!"*[14] And they would both say the musical words over and over until, in a certain sweet intoxication, they seemed already half in heaven. *Para siempre!*

One day after a solemn conference they came to a momentous decision. Christians were being killed every day by the Moors in Africa. "It seemed to me they bought the vision of God very cheaply," wrote Teresa many years later. Why not go to Africa and be martyred? It was not far to Gibraltar — only a few weeks' walk; and one could get across the straits, somehow, in a boat.

When no one was looking, the children stole out of the house and down the hill to the Gate of Adaja. Hand in hand they went under the ancient stones and out across the bridge, joyfully anticipating the moment when they would have their heads cut off by a Moorish scimitar.[15]

---

[14] Years later, according to a declaration by Sister Isabel de Santo Domingo, in the second *Proceso de Avila* (p. 2), the Saint used to entertain her nuns by telling how she had made her brother repeat these words.

[15] Teresa tells this story herself: *Libro de su Vida,* cap. I. The text used throughout this book is that of P. Silverio, the greatest editor of her works, in the *Biblioteca Mística Carmelitana, t. I* (Burgos, 1915).

people and their ancestors had paid a high price for the truth that was in them.

Ávila itself, when Teresa was first carried through its crooked hilly streets, was a veritable panorama in stone, and in venerated human bones, of the history of Christ's conflict in Spain against the Prince of this world. It was so old, this city, that it probably had stood there high on the hills beside the Adaja, 3000 feet above sea level, when our Lord was working miracles in Palestine. In the first century — in A.D. 63, according to tradition, Saint Peter sent one of the seven apostolic deacons to found a see in Abula, as it was then called, and Saint Segundo shed his blood in one of the earliest Roman persecutions. There, in the fourth century, the arch-heretic Priscillian, who taught a pseudo-Christianity composed of Gnostic and Manichaean ideas from the moribund East, which if accepted would have destroyed all genuine Christian life, was proclaimed bishop by his partisans, but was overthrown and put to death by a Roman emperor no longer pagan. There the Visigoths ruled, as in all of Spain, and first accepted, then betrayed the faith, and were punished by Mohammedan conquerors, whose castle still remains. Not until the eleventh century was the Cross again raised beside the banners of Christian warriors above the lofty city. Between 1090 and 1097, the men of Ávila raised the mighty wall which is among the most remarkable survivals of the Middle Ages. Forty feet high and thirteen feet thick, it rises out of the living rock to girdle the hills on which stand the medieval Cathedral (more like a fortress than a church) and most of the other primitive buildings; it covers a circuit of 9075 feet, and along its machicolated length it thrusts up against the singularly blue sky some eighty-six towers and 2500 merlons. Enclosed by these somber battlements of brownish gray, the houses of the city arise tier on tier toward that fringe of church and convent towers which is a flaming crest in the sunset and the dawn. In the center, facing the walls, stand the palaces of the great lords of Ávila — the Bracamontes, the Verdugos, the Cepedas, the Dávilas, like a cordon of stone around the hillside.

After the reconquest, the community had prospered and pushed its way out beyond the walls into three great suburbs. The one on the almost flat land at the east was destined to play an important part in Teresa's life; but now she knew it chiefly as the section in which stood the Convent of Saint Ann, where

Queen Isabel the Catholic had once refused the crown of **Castile**. At the north, in a narrow glade, lies the suburb of Ajates. There one sees lovely gardens along the slope, and beyond them the mountaintops always white with snow, crowning an infinite variety of shapes and colors. In the south, facing the valley of Ambles, is the suburb containing the convent of the Augustines; toward the east, the great Dominican convent of Saint Thomas, with many other venerated shrines, sanctified by priceless relics of saints. Below, the clear Adaja goes winding through a bed strewn with mighty gray boulders, and along green banks where, in Teresa's time, were many mills, for cloth was the chief product of Ávila, and the waters of the river gave the dyes the quality that made their colors imperishable. From there one looks out on the Vega, eight leagues long and two wide, where the shadows lie in great strips like the waves of the sea, flowing into the mountains.

Everything says here that the conflict for and against Christianity did not end with the expulsion of the Moors and the raising of those ponderous battlements. Within the walls new differences arose, this time between Christian and Jew, and between both and the new class of Catholic Jews called *Conversos, Marranos,* or New Christians. One episode of that struggle was the dethroning, in the midst of Vega, of the effigy of Henry IV, friend of Jews and Moors. In 1491, Isabel the Catholic sent a safe-conduct to the Jews of Ávila, after one of them had been stoned to death by a mob. In the Church of Saint Thomas, where the right arm of the Angelic Doctor was preserved, the little children of Ávila could see the tomb of Torquemada the Grand Inquisitor not far from the beautiful sepulcher of Prince Juan of the Asturias, whom Queen Isabel, after all her triumphs, had had to relinquish in the prime of his youth to death.

To grow up in such a city, where every stone was cursed or hallowed with memories of a bloody and glorious past, was an education in itself. It was a city of passion; and yet, as Don Miguel Mir says, a levitical city. To look at it from the prairie, to see the sun whiten the low square houses as they rose up, tier on tier, above the dark machicolations of the gloomy wall, and gleam fiercely on the golden crest that crowned the churches, convents, and monasteries (where thousands of men and women had crucified their flesh, during the centuries, for the love of God), one could easily imagine this to be Saint Augustine's City

of God, ready to mount into the cloudless sky with a shout of triumph.

All this penetrated, day by day, into the mind and heart of little Teresa de Ahumada. When she was three years old, her father donated a large quantity of wheat to feed the poor, for famine threatened.[12] When she was four (in 1519, the year that Cortés went to Mexico) the Great Plague, something perhaps like the Black Death of the Middle Ages, was laying low thousands in all parts of Spain. To holy Ávila, famous for its health-giving air, the Royal Council of Castile came fleeing; but the plague followed them, and little Teresa began to hear of neighbors who had walked the streets yesterday and were dead today. The clergy, followed by the Royal Council, the city officials, and all the townspeople, then marched in procession, imploring the mercy of God, to the Church of Saint Thomas. They took from its shrine there the famous consecrated Host of La Guardia, stolen and desecrated more than a generation ago, but still intact, and bore it in a gleaming monstrance, to the music of penitential chants, toward the Cathedral; and there the Body of Christ was adored, day and night, for a week. "And the Lord in His mercy heard the fervent prayers of the Avilenses, for the city found itself cleansed in a little while,"[13] though in all the rest of Spain the pest continued for three years.

This must have had a profound influence on the alert mind of such a child as Teresa. Above all, she liked to hear stories of the saints, especially the martyrs, who shared the death of Christ; and she repeated what she had heard until she became one with them in aspiration: she yearned to make the world over as God wanted it to be, to help Christ redeem the souls of all men. She admired heroes and crusaders; but never, at this time or any other time, did she have, apparently, any desire to emulate Saint Joan of Arc or Queen Isabel *la Católica* in defending the City of God with the sword. Sweet, peaceful, generous, serene, loving, harmonious — these are the adjectives that came naturally to the pens of all her contemporaries who described her. Even at the age of six she went straight to the center of the spiritual problem of man, and found its true solution in voluntary suffering undertaken cheerfully in imitation of Christ. Even before

[12] Mir, *op. cit.,* I, p. 30.
[13] Caramolino, *Historia de Ávila* (Madrid, 1873), t. III, p. 196.

Chapter II

A VAIN LITTLE GIRL AND HER FORBIDDEN BOOKS

FIRST a question, then a search, then a wail of anguish filled the house of Don Alonso when the absence of Teresa and Rodrigo was discovered. Doubtless María went one way, Juan another, and young Hernando still another, until there was a cry of "children lost!" through all of Ávila. While Doña Beatriz poured out her heart in prayer, *alguaciles* and *corregidores* ran hither and yon, looking into wells and dark corners and questioning strangers or suspicious looking persons. All in vain. No one had seen the children. Doña Beatriz was sure that they had fallen into a deep well and had been drowned.[1]

Meanwhile the young travelers had crossed the old bridge and turned to the right, taking the rough road along the riverbank. After walking a few hundred yards, they came to a place known as the *humilladero* — a cross set up in the midst of four high pillars of coarse granite, dark with age, on a platform crowning some steps on the shoulder of a little rocky hill. There at the Four Posts, as people called them, they stopped and looked about to determine their course, perhaps to pray at the foot of the cross. They may have glanced back a little regretfully at the sunlit city that sprawled over the hillside, and a little apprehensively at the vast unknown of prairie and mountains that stretched before them. But if Teresa's character had the consistency it appears to have had, she probably said, "Come on, Rodrigo!" and took him by the hand to lead him into the penitential wasteland.

Just then a man happened to pass on horseback. Providentially he was their father's brother, Don Francisco Alvarez de Cepeda.[2]

---

[1] Ribera, *Vida de Santa Teresa*, lib. I, cap. IV, followed as usual by Yepes. Teresa's own account says she ran away with "one of my brothers . . . nearly my own age" (Saint Teresa, *Libro de su Vida*, cap. I). This must have been Rodrigo, as all her biographers agree; he was the next older; Lorenzo, the next younger, was then only three.

[2] Ribera, *loc. cit.* Father Gracián confirms this story, saying, in one of his notes on Ribera's text, that the Saint herself told it to him. See also Mir, *Vida de Santa Teresa*, I, p. 41. Pope Gregory XV was so pleased with this incident that he ordered his secretary to include it in the process of Teresa's canonization. The Church reminds us of it also in the Breviary every October 15: "*Regis superni nuntia Domum,*" etc.

That of course was the end of the journey to Morocco.

The joy of Doña Beatriz, and the alternate scolding and hugging of the children, must be imagined. Rodrigo under cross-examination showed himself a true descendant of Adam. He blamed it all on his sister.[3]

When the two were alone, they talked the matter over, and Teresa, no doubt forgiving the mortal frailty revealed in her brother, decided that since they could not be martyrs they must be hermits. Where did this child of seven learn the secret of all the great mystics, that solitude and detachment are the *sine qua non* of contemplation? Learn it she did, with prophetic insight; and she began looking for places about the house where she might pray alone and, especially, say the Rosary.[4] Deciding to erect several hermitages in various parts of the orchard back of the house, she set Rodrigo to work piling up small stones, one on top of the other, to make the walls. Alas, they fell down immediately and the project had to be abandoned.

Teresa still played, however, at being a nun, making habits out of her mother's old dresses, and organizing her brothers and the other children, cousins and neighbors, in communities of "monks" and "sisters." This was more than play acting. From her earliest years she seemed endowed with a Christian love and pity for the poor. Money was scarce enough in Ávila, but when anyone gave her a few *reales*, she promptly distributed them as alms. With all this, she had her share of that pride of family and pride of race which, carried to an extreme, became faults in the lofty Castilian character. A child who could see memorials to her ancestors all over the city — the sculptured tombs of the Cepedas in the Cathedral and the escutcheons of Ximén Blasco and Esteban Domingo on the romanesque windows of San Pedro — was likely to speak approvingly, even in her last years, of family connections, of good dowries,[5] and even, on one occasion, of "limpia sangre." Yet even in childhood, she was aware of the hollowness of arbitrary distinctions between man and man, and preferred the lowly and simple to the magnificent. When she particularly craved solitude or consolation, she would walk past the beautiful Norman doorway and bell tower of San Domingo,

---

[3] Ribera, *loc. cit.*

[4] Saint Teresa, *Libro de su Vida*, cap. I. Henceforth this book will be referred to as *Vida*.

[5] See her letter to her nephew, Lorenzo de Cepeda, for example, in B.M.C., t. VIII, *Epistolario* II, p. 490.

behind her house, and past the lovely Gothic doorway of Santa Escolástica, from which the Virgin and Child still look pityingly down on all who go that way, and would run down the hill to the oratory of San Lázaro, near the Gate of Adaja, where a house of hospitality was maintained for poor travelers. There she would kneel a long while at the feet of Our Lady of Charity, whose image was uncommonly lifelike and compassionate.[6]

There must have been many anxieties in a family like that of Don Alonso: sickness of the mother and children, clashes of personality, and now and then financial difficulties — he had to borrow 34,000 *maravedis* in 1524, for example, and died without paying it all back.[7] Yet whatever the troubles might be, Teresa would take them to our Lady; or when joy came she would give thanks; and always returned home serene and satisfied. She had a great love for Saint Joseph; to him she carried her most urgent requests, and he never failed her. Another of her favorites was Saint John the Evangelist, perhaps because she had heard that he was beloved of Christ; for it was her Lord and Savior to Whom Teresa gave the warmest and best of her affectionate little heart. The striking scenes of His life were always passing through her mind. In the daily liturgy, as well as in the Rosary, she would contemplate now His birth, now His death, and all the dramatic events in between and after; for thus the Church, to teach her children, weaves His story into the days and months of each revolving year.

One of the scenes that Teresa was fond of picturing to herself at this time was the meeting of Jesus with the Samaritan woman by the well of Jacob, outside the city of Sichar. How unforgettably the hand of Saint John has etched the essential lines of the scene, and suggested the rest, in the fourth chapter of his gospel!

"Now Jacob's well was there. Jesus therefore being wearied with his journey sat thus on the well. It was about the sixth hour. There cometh a woman of Samaria, to draw water. Jesus saith to her, 'Give me to drink.' For his disciples were gone into the city to buy meats.

---

[6] After the destruction of the oratory of San Lázaro, this image was placed in a chapel of the Cathedral, whence it is still carried in solemn procession each October 15 to the church of the Carmelites, and there set facing an image of Teresa.

[7] Doña Elvira Vegil was one of almost 50 creditors who had claims against the estate of Don Alonso after his death. P. Silverio, *Vida de Santa Teresa de Jesús*, vol. I, p. 270, n. I.

"Then the Samarian woman saith to him,

" 'How dost thou, being a Jew, ask of me to drink, who am a Samaritan woman? For the Jews do not communicate with the Samaritans.'

"Jesus answered, and said to her,

" 'If thou didst know the gift of God, and who he is that saith to thee, give me to drink, thou perhaps wouldst have asked of him, and he would give thee living water.'

"The woman saith to him:

" 'Sir, thou hast nothing to draw, and the well is deep: from whence then hast thou living water? Art thou greater than our father Jacob, who gave us the well, and drank thereof himself, and his children, and his cattle?'

"Jesus answered, and said to her:

" 'Whosoever drinketh of this water, shall thirst again; but he that shall drink of the water that I will give him, shall not thirst forever; but the water that I will give him shall become in him a fountain of water, springing into life everlasting.'

"The woman saith to him:

" 'Sir, give me this water, that I may not thirst, nor come hither to draw.'

"Jesus saith to her: 'Go, call thy husband, and come hither.' "*

The deep significance of this apparently casual remark, which cut to the heart of the Samaritan woman and laid bare, as if in the noonday mountain sunlight, the sins of her life; her astonishment, and His gentleness, and His disclosing to her, of all people (according to the thinking of the Pharisees), His divinity; her leaving her waterpot and running to Sichar to spread the news of the coming of the Messias, and the subsequent conversion of many of the people — all the rest of this remarkable incident may have meant little or much to a girl of seven or eight; she was mainly interested in the metaphor of the water, and she penetrated its enormous simplicity and made it her own. Water always seemed to Teresa something delightful and marvelous, something at once so natural and so inexplicable, so definite and so protean in its changes, so clearly an evidence of the power and goodness of God, that she was constantly admiring it and trying to think of ways to describe its properties. Pellucid, crystalline — many beautiful words could be applied to it, but none so splendid, so comforting and refreshing, as water

---

* John 4:6–16.

itself. She never lost this childish wonder and delight at the sight and feeling of it; she was always invoking its memory in figures of speech; it seemed to her poetic mind the most nearly spiritual of all material things. She loved to imagine Christ at the well with the Samaritan woman, and she would say to Him over and over, "Lord, give me that water!" — hardly realizing at the time the tremendous implications of her request.

She was now able to read everything. Nor did she stop with the saints' lives in her father's library, but passed on to the romantic storybooks, which had become so popular since the invention of printing only a few decades before.

Why Don Alonso did not destroy or sell these books is not clear, for he disapproved of them, as did many serious-minded people and most preachers, as tending to make readers vain, flippant, worldly, less disposed to think of the more important concerns of the spirit. From this it appears that he was not much like the romantic type of Spanish gentleman whose somewhat shabby gentility Cervantes was to satirize a few years later. It is true that Don Alonso had on exhibit in his hall "old lances, halberds, morions, and other such armors and weapons." But there the resemblance to Don Quixote ended: it cannot be averred that "his pot consisted daily of somewhat more beef than mutton, a gallimaufry each night, collops and eggs on Saturdays, lentils on Fridays, and now and then a lean pigeon on Sundays," nor is there any evidence that he wore "a jerkin of pine puce, a pair of velvet hose, with pantofles of the same for the holy days." And it is certain, for we have it on the word of Teresa herself, that, far from sharing the taste of the good knight of La Mancha for what we would now call novels, he disliked them, and probably forbade his daughter to read them; for she concealed from him that fact that she did.

Doña Beatriz disagreed with her husband on this matter. She was a great novel reader, and saw no reason why her children should not amuse themselves with the exploits of Don Belianis of Greece and the incomparable virtues and charms of the Princess Oriana of Britain. Indeed, they seemed more like a great blessing than a temptation to a rather frail woman whose privilege it was to bear nine children in the nineteen years of her married life. At a later period Teresa saw her father's point of view, but at this time, naturally, she agreed heartily with her mother, and it appears, from her own account written when she had experienced a complete change of heart on the subject, that the two practised a little feminine deception at the expense of the lord of the house.

"She was fond of books of chivalry," wrote Teresa, "and was not as much injured by this pastime as I was for my part, for she didn't waste time on them at the expense of her work, but we hurried to read in them, and perhaps she did it to keep from thinking of the great troubles she had, and to keep her children busy, so that they would not get into mischief in other ways. This annoyed my father so much that we had to take care that he should not see it."[9]

Possibly Teresa exaggerated the ill effect of these books in later years when, as a nun striving for perfection, she blamed her mother. "I began to form the habit of reading these books," she continued, "and this little fault which I saw in her began to cool my good desires, and to begin to fail in other things; and I thought it was not bad to waste many hours of the day and night in so vain an occupation, even when it was hidden from my father. It got to be so extreme, my passion for reading, that if I didn't have a new book I didn't think I could be happy."

Rodrigo probably shared in her pastime and her deception. The two composed a book of chivalry, which she probably destroyed, for the manuscript has not been found. It would surely be the most amusing if not the most edifying of all her works!

Teresa was so impressed with the harm that all this did her, that she wrote later what seems a rather severe indictment, under the circumstances, of her mother. "I sometimes think how much harm parents do, who do not try to have their children always see things of virtue in every way; for though my mother was so much so herself, as I have said, I didn't take as much of the good on arriving at the use of reason, or almost none, and the evil injured me much."

What were the books that awoke the first fierce struggle in the soul of this young girl? She does not give their names. Doubtless they were extravagant tales on the order of *Amadis of Gaul*, the archetype of hundreds of such works. Originating, perhaps, in the Arthurian cycle, either in France or England, and passing through the none too reverential hands of troubadors in Provence, this romance made its appearance in Portugal, and finally in Spain, where it was first printed in 1519, when Teresa was

---

[9] Saint Teresa, *Vida*, cap. II.

four years old. Its popularity begot a legion of imitations; one of them the *Orlando Furioso*, another, the *Amadis of Greece*, from which Shakespeare borrowed the character of Florizel for *A Winter's Tale*.

Amadis was the illegitimate son of Perion, King of Gaul, and the Princess Elisena of Brittany. Set adrift in a box on a river by his mother, he was picked up at sea by a Scottish knight, and grew up at the Court of Scotland. After marrying Oriana, daughter of King Lisuarte of England, he returned to Gaul, where his astounding adventures began. In all versions of these there is plenty of swordplay, there is hacking and thrusting and the splintering of lances on every page. The noble-minded hero is always seeking adventure, and is constantly in peril of his life from giants, lions, or hateful witches and wizards, as he goes about rescuing damsels in durance, ladies, of course, of matchless beauty and exquisite tenderness.

The number of inferior imitations of this florid tale and the growing concern of thoughtful minds over the effect upon the young are indicated in Cervantes' immortal scene where the curate and the barber burn the books which "wholly extinguished the wit" of Don Quixote, and caused him to fall "into one of the strangest conceits that ever madman stumbled on in this world," until he undertook to go as a knight-errant through the world, revenging all manner of injuries on such caitiffs as the giant Caraculiambro and his like. The good curate passed judgment on *The Adventures of Splandián, Amadis of Greece, Queen Pintiquinesta, Don Olivante of Laura, Florismarte of Hircania, Sir Platyr, Lord Raynold of Montalban,* and *Don Belianis;* but spared *Palmerin of England* and *Tirante the White;* and *Amadis of Gaul,* too, because, as the barber reminded him, it was "the very best contrived book of all those of that kind." Of the others, he damned one for being foolish and arrogant, another for the "drouth and harshness" of its style.

On imaginative Teresa, at nine or ten, such reading was bound to have some effect. "I began to wear gay clothes, and to wish to give pleasure by looking well with much care of hands and hair, and perfumes, and all the vanities there could be in this, and there were plenty, for I was very curious. I did not have an evil intention, for I did not wish that anyone should offend God for me. I continued to have for many years a great desire for too much cleanliness, and things which I didn't think were any sin at all. Now I see how bad it must have been."

This understandable vanity of a little girl becoming aware that she was beautiful, and naturally anxious to be as charming as Oriana in the moated grange, was now encouraged by association with some rather frivolous and worldly cousins of about her own age or a little older, the children of her father's brother, Don Francisco Alvarez de Cepeda — in fact, there was a double relationship, for their mother was Doña María de Ahumada, a niece of Doña Beatriz. Their house on the *plazuela* of San Domingo was connected with that of Don Alonso by a little lane, through which the children ran back and forth. Among the cousins were Pedro, Francisco, Diego, Vicente; Inez, Ana, and Jerónima or Guiomar. These were the only children that Don Alonso, a true Castilian in his strict supervision of the children, would allow in his house.

"We were always together, and they had a great affection for me," said Teresa; "in all that pleased them I kept up a conversation with them, and listened to accounts of their affections and childish tricks, not at all good; and what was worse, my soul began to give itself up to what was the cause of all its misfortune. If I were to give advice, I should say to parents that at this age they should be very careful of the persons who associate with their children; for therein lies much harm, since our nature tends to evil rather than to good. So it was with me."

Instead of imitating her half sister, María, a young woman of great modesty, common sense, and goodness, Teresa, if we must accept her own words literally, "took all the mischief of a relative, who was often in the house. She was so frivolous[10] in her behavior that my mother did her best to keep her out of the house (it seems she foresaw the harm that would come to me through her) and there was so much occasion for her to come in, that this could not be done. With this one I speak of, I de-

---

[10] *Vida.* The Spanish text here reads, *"tomé todo el daño de una parienta que trataba mucho en casa. Era de tan livianos tratos,"* etc. Obviously this passage is open to various interpretations, and needs to be translated with care, in the light of the context and the supporting evidence. In David Lewis' translation, we find *"tomé todo el daño"* rendered as "I . . . learned every evil." This seems to me an unjustifiable exaggeration. To "take all injury" from a flippant person does not denote or connote the learning of "every evil." Mr. Lewis was right in translating *"Era de tan livianos tratos"* as *"she was so light and frivolous."* In Spanish, *livianos* has many shades of meaning, from merely "light" or "frivolous" to "shameful" or even "unchaste." Obviously the more favorable translation is justified here.

lighted to speak. With her was all my intercourse and conversations; for she helped me to all the amusements that I liked, and even put me in them, and let me share her conversations and vanities."

Just what were these conversations and vanities which afterwards appeared so injurious? Her vagueness has made possible the widest latitude of interpretation. Yet it seems obvious that, writing at a time when even the smallest venial sin seemed to her an immense evil, since after all it did offend God, she exaggerated what was probably the natural curiosity of a sheltered little girl about the conversation of a more sophisticated older cousin who enjoyed parading her superior knowledge of the world, and even in shocking her a bit. Many of these dangerous discussions were doubtless of the "He-said-to-me-and-I-said-to-him" variety.[11]

Doña Beatriz was not at all well these days. After the birth of Jerónimo in 1522 she had no more children until Agustin was born in 1527. The next year, 1528, she brought into the world her second daughter, Juana. Teresa was then about thirteen.[12] Her mother was thirty-three, but as she dressed like an elderly lady, she looked much older.

It was probably his wife's condition, and the hope that a change of air would benefit her, that caused Don Alonso to take his family, sometime in 1528, to their estate in Goterrendura, a village of ninety-three inhabitants in the hill country about three and a half leagues north of Ávila. There Don Alonso had owned, for many years, some houses, a garden with a dovecot, two thousand head of cattle in herds, some vineyards, and various meadows and fields — all part of the dowry he had received with his second wife. The country people still remembered the costume and the gems the grave hidalgo had given her at their marriage nineteen years ago. They loved Doña Beatriz, for she was their *castellana*, the richest and most noble woman in the community, to whom the poor never appealed in vain, and to whom the peasants had recourse in their disputes and troubles.

---

[11] The name of this romantic cousin is unknown. There seems to be no solid foundation for the guess of P. Gabriel and others that she was Guiomar. Cf. Silverio, *op. cit.*, I, 92, n. 2.

[12] Teresa is obviously mistaken when she tells us (*Vida*, cap. I) that she was not quite twelve when her mother died. The exact date of Doña Beatriz' death is unknown, but her will was drawn November 24, 1528. Teresa was born in March, 1515.

Probably Goterrendura was very much like home to her, and her health usually improved there.

This time the matter was more serious. Instead of bettering, the condition of Teresa's mother grew worse. When autumn came, there seemed little hope that she could live long. On the twenty-fourth of November she sent for a notary and drew up her will.

Finally — was it a few days later, or the following year? — she received the last sacraments, and died with the same Christian serenity and resignation with which she had lived.

Teresa's reference to this event is brief, almost perfunctory. "I remember that when my mother died I was still twelve years old, or a little less." (Actually she was almost fourteen.) She adds that she was afflicted, and wept much when she began to understand what she had lost. She does not say whether she was in Goterrendura, or (as Padre Silverio considers more likely) in Ávila.

The will of Doña Beatriz was a characteristic one of the period. She committed her soul to God, who had created her and redeemed her with His precious blood, and her body to the earth from which it had been formed; and she requested that if it pleased God to remove her from this present life, her body be buried in the Church of Saint John in Ávila, wherever it might seem good to her husband and lord, Don Alonso Sánchez de Cepeda; that four hundred masses be said for her soul, one hundred at Saint John's, a hundred at Saint Thomas of Ávila, a hundred at the Franciscan monastery there, and the fourth hundred in the Carmelite monastery of Santa María. She concluded by dividing her property among her children, and naming her husband and Teresa's godfather, Francisco Pajares, as executors.[13]

If the disputed date of her death followed, as some have supposed, close upon the signing of the will, winter must have been settling down upon the cold hills and prairies of Castile when Don Alonso and his family left the house in Goterrendura to escort the body of Doña Beatriz to its last resting place. Mir imagines, somewhat gratuitously, that it was probably daybreak or even earlier; that the cold was bitter and penetrating, and the wind shrieked desolately over the Guadarramas and the barren

---

[13] Mir, *op. cit.*, I, pp. 32–35. This author believes Doña Beatriz died a few days after the drawing of her will. Padre Silverio is inclined to think she died in 1529, or early in 1530 (*op. cit.*, I, p. 94, n. 2).

plains, as the body was placed on a cart draped with mourning and drawn by two bullocks, while some of the tenants of the dead woman, with burning torches in their hands (if, as Mir assumes, it was still night), formed a little guard of honor on either side. Whether Don Alonso went on horseback or in the carriage with his children does not appear; but we are asked to imagine the sobs of the little girls, the prayers of María and some of the woman relatives, the groans of the servants as the heavy carts moved slowly down the frozen hill. It was a journey of three or four hours to Ávila. It could have been made, therefore, in the middle of the day.

After the funeral, at all events, there came to Teresa, like the thrust of a sword, the realization of what had passed out of her life. She wept disconsolately, until at last, unable to endure such grief alone, she fled from the house into which so vast an emptiness had come, to the hospice of Saint Lazarus near the gate of Adaja.

There, in the familiar dimness, lighted by the flickering light of votive candles, was the beloved image of Our Lady of Charity, serene and pitiful, holding forth hands of consolation to all the afflicted of earth. Choking with tears, the young girl threw herself on her knees and cried, "Now *you* must be my mother!"

It seemed to her that her prayer was heard. Perhaps through her blurred eyes she saw the gracious head of the Virgin Mother move slightly up and down in assent. At any rate, she never could believe, in the light of later events, that the answer to her prayer was wholly imaginary.[14]

---

[14] *Vida,* cap. I.

Chapter III

ADOLESCENCE, AND THE AUGUSTINIAN CONVENT

A T THIRTEEN Teresa was a very lonely girl. Now she
knew how much she had depended upon her mother, how
immense, even if somewhat taken for granted, had been the
irradiation of love from that self-sacrificing uncomplaining soul.
Don Alonso meant well enough, and Teresa was his favorite; but
how could he have the understanding of a woman? María and
Juan, the children by his first marriage, were grown up. Hernando was eighteen. Rodrigo was at the age when a boy assumes
a rather lofty attitude toward a sister four years his junior. Between these three and the younger children — Lorenzo was nine,
Antonio eight, Pedro seven, Jerónimo six, the remaining two
mere babies — Teresa was thrown pretty much upon her own resources. She began to understand for the first time what loneliness meant. And turning instinctively from human inadequacy
to the infinite resources of Divinity, she found comfort in the
loneliness of Christ on the Cross, and the loneliness of Mary
when the darkness descended upon the dreadful day of her loss.
Perhaps the habit of thinking of Him preferably in the forsaken
moments of His life (she speaks of it in the *Libro de la Vida*,
her "Autobiography")[1] originated at this period. For many years,
before she went to sleep at night, she would remember His
solitary suffering in the Garden, and the mystery of that prayer,
"Father, if it be possible, let this chalice pass away! . . . Nevertheless, not as I will, but as thou wilt."

This fervor was followed, within a few weeks or months, by a
reaction. It was not long before she was reading again, and hid-
ing under her bed for fear of the watchful eyes of her father, the
volumes that kept her delightfully troubled about the woes of
Oriana and the liberty of Andandona; and she must have been
different from other imaginative girls if she did not put herself
sometimes in the place of the lady love of such a hero as Splend-
ian, the lawfully begotten son of Amadis of Gaul, and if she did
not look in her mirror with satisfaction, and begin to think of
better ways of doing her hair. Discovering again that her hands

[1] *Vida,* cap. IX.

24

were singularly beautiful, she began to devote much time to caring for them. Like most girls of her class, she used cosmetics. Even men were addicted to perfumery in that flamboyant century.

She was now old enough to be introduced to the society of Ávila; her mother, at the same age, had been married. Of the details of her social life no record has been found. She had become one of the most beautiful girls in the city, with sparkling black eyes and gleaming teeth, red lips and lovely skin, and one of her modern biographers may be right in supposing that when she appeared at a dance, a *fiesta,* a bullfight, or a *juego de cañas,* she wore some of those jewels that are mentioned in an extant inventory of her father's possessions as having belonged to her mother. There were, for example, a collar worth 30,000 *maravedis,* two gold chains, several gold rings, bracelets, earrings, and other such ornaments; as well as velvet gowns, linen petticoats from Rouen, silks, mourning garments, corsets, girdles of taffeta embroidered with gold, neckcloths such as ladies of fashion wore, and nets of silk cloth or thread to draw over the hair.[2] She rode here and there on the back of a mule, the conventional mount of a Castilian lady, and was noted for her fine seat, even in later life, as Gracián records. She was skillful at chess, a game that appeals more to men than to women, and was delighted when she could checkmate her opponent's king.[3] Doubtless she played with her father on winter evenings, after the younger children were in bed. Like all Castilian ladies, she could spin and sew. Altogether she must have been one of the most desirable maidens of Ávila: beautiful, affectionate, discreet, frank and joyous, reasonably devout, and well dowered from her mother's estate. She was not without some Castilian pride of blood and ancestry, and a share of ordinary feminine vanity, with a profound and

---

[2] Mir, *Vida de Santa Teresa,* I, p. 81.

[3] Teresa herself is our authority for this. She begins Chapter XVI of the *Camino de perfección* with, "You may not think much of all this, as I go on setting up the game, as they say. You have asked me to explain the beginning of prayer to you. . . . Believe, then, that anyone who doesn't know how to arrange the pieces in the game of chess will know how to play badly, and if he doesn't know how to call check, he won't know how to give checkmate. Well, then, you may scold me for speaking about such a thing as a game, which we don't have in this house, and we are not going to have it. Here you see what a Mother God gives you, who knew even this vanity; but they say it is sometimes lawful!" She goes on to explain how to "checkmate" God in the game of prayer. (Valladolid MS., B.M.C., pp. 73–74.)

quite natural desire to be loved greatly, as the ladies in the romances were loved by incomparable lovers. These faults, if such they were, would have enhanced rather than lessened her matrimonial chances. It is likely enough that her father began considering which of the young men of his acquaintance would be a suitable husband for Teresa. Some of her biographers have sought to establish that she herself was contemplating a marriage with some young cavalier; but the evidence for this is of the flimsiest.[4]

About this time she became friendly again with the light-headed cousin whose frivolities had so worried her mother. All their former gossiping and romancing were resumed. Was this sprightly companion Inés or Ana de Tapia, both of whom later became Carmelite nuns? It would be interesting to have a more detailed account of the antics of these two young girls, full of life and fun, who probably thought that they would be committing a daring offense if unchaperoned they exchanged a few words with a handsome young man. It must be admitted that the words of Teresa herself, written thirty-five years later, are susceptible to various constructions:

"Until I conversed with her, which was at the age of fourteen years, and I believe more (to have friendship with me, I say, and to let me in on her affairs), I don't think I had failed God by mortal sin, nor lost the fear of God, although I kept it chiefly on account of my reputation. This prevented me from losing it altogether, nor do I think I could have changed in this for anything in the world, nor was there any person in it whose love could have made me yield myself to this. Would that I had had as much strength in not going against the honor of God, as my nature gave me not to lose in what I thought was the honor of the

---

[4] In her *Vida*, cap. II, Teresa says, after discussion of her "sins," "*Una cosa tenía, que me parece me podía ser alguna disculpa, si no tuviera tantas culpas; y es, que era el trato con quien por vía de casamiento me parecía podía acabar en bien; y informada de con quien me confesaba, y de otras personas, en muchas cosas me decían no iba contra Dios.*" Some writers have understood this to mean a discussion of marriage for Teresa, and Mir is quite censorious of Ribera, who he says (I, 51, n. 2) was the first to "suppress" the incident. Others, including David Lewis, interpret the passage to mean that Teresa was interested in her cousin's prospects of marriage. This view seems to me the correct one. "*El trato*" must refer to the conversations she has been having with her cousin, which, as she has said, were about her cousin's affairs.

world, and I did not notice that I was losing it in many other ways. In vainly seeking this I went the limit. The means that were necessary to keep it, I paid no attention to; but I was very careful not to lose myself altogether.

"My father and sister greatly resented this friendship, and scolded me for it many times. As they could not remove the occasion for her coming to the house, their efforts availed them nothing; for my keen scent for anything evil was considerable. I marvel sometimes at the harm one evil association does, and if I had not passed through it I couldn't believe it; especially in time of youth, the harm it does must be greater. I wish that parents would take warning of me, and look much to this. And so it is, that this intimacy changed me in such a way that of my virtuous nature and soul there remained to me almost nothing,[5] and I think that she and another girl who had the same sort of pastimes, imprinted their habits of mind on me. Hence I understand the great improvement that good company makes, and I hold it certain that if I had conversed at that age with virtuous persons, I should have been flawless in virtue: for if at that age I had had some one to teach me to fear God, my soul would have been gaining strength not to fall. Afterwards, giving up this fear altogether, there remained to me only that of my reputation,[6] which in everything I did kept me tormented. Thinking it would not be known, I dared many things quite against it and against God.[7]

"In the beginning the said things did me harm, as I see it, and the fault must not have been hers, but mine; for afterwards my malice for evil was enough, together with having servants, for I found in them a good disposition for all evil. If any one of them

---

[5] ". . . que de natural y alma virtuoso no me dejo casi ninguno." David Lewis' rendering of "casi ninguno" as "no trace" is a little too free. There is a great difference between "no trace" of virtue, and "hardly any" that the Saint, in her humility, attributes to herself! Cf. Vida, cap. II.

[6] "Quedome solo el de la honra, que en todo lo que hacia me traia atormentada." The "honra" is difficult to translate. It could conceivably mean "chastity"; but the word "honor" is more commonly used in that sense. "Honra" usually connotes the esteem or respect of others.

[7] Again, I find myself at variance with Mr. Lewis, who renders "cosas bien contra ella y contra Dios" as "things that were neither honorable nor pleasing to God." Here "ella" stands for "honra," and "contra honra" means "injurious to reputation" rather than "dishonorable." Cf. also La Fuente, Obras de Santa Teresa de Jesús, p. 25, notes 5 and 7.

had given me good advice, I might perhaps have profited by it;
but interest blinded them, as affection did me.[8] And since I was
never inclined to much evil, for immodest things[9] naturally I
abhorred, but only to the diversions of good conversation;
yet, placed in the occasion, the danger was at hand, and I exposed my father and brothers and sisters to it. From these things
God delivered me, in such a way that I think indeed He managed
against my will that I should not be wholly lost; although it
could not be so secret that I should not have damage enough in
my reputation, and suspicion in my father."

In these pastimes, these conversations, these offenses against
God into which Teresa was led by the influence of her cousin,
each writer who has grappled with these rather vague and self-
contradictory passages has found, one is tempted to say, the reflection of his own spirit. On the one hand sinners have imputed serious sin to a woman canonized by the Church. At the
other extreme are those pious souls who like to think of saints
as almost bloodless abstractions, without the faults and passions
of ordinary human beings.

Of Teresa's contemporary biographers, the two who knew her
best faced the problem courageously. Both of them accepted the
principle that the faults of saints should not be concealed or
glossed over by hagiographers. "I don't think well of those
writers of saints' lives," wrote the Jesuit Father Ribera, "who
wish to cover up the sins and weaknesses in which, as human
beings, they have fallen; for this is to cover up, in part, the
grandeur of the goodness and compassion and wisdom of God,
which suffers these offenses, and rescues them from them, by
means very efficacious, fitting, and admirable. And so, if I knew
more in particular of the sins of Mother Teresa of Jesus, I
would not fail to tell them, for she herself wished them recognized, so that the goodness of God should be known, and His
glory be more resplendent in them. But there is no sense, on the
other hand, in attributing to her offenses she never committed."

---

[8] *"El interés las cegava, como a mí la afeción."* La Fuente's comment on this
(*loc. cit.*) is *"Sin duda en el lenguaje familiar se decía afeción, así como se dice
afecto. Fray Luis de León, como más culto, puso afición. Hoy en día se vuelve a
decir afición, en vez de afición y afecto; pero tiene algo de galicismo.* Mr. Lewis
has Saint Teresa say she was blinded by "passion," obviously too strong a
rendering.

[9] This seems a more accurate rendition of *cosas deshonestas* than Mr. Lewis'
"anything dishonorable."

After Teresa's death and the publication of her "Autobiography," Father Ribera took the trouble to make inquiries concerning her "sins" of persons who knew her intimately. A Carmelite prioress told him that the Saint, discussing the problems of chastity with some of her nuns, when she was an old woman, said in her presence, "I don't understand this matter, for the Lord has granted me the favor of never having to confess anything of the sort during all my life." Ribera's investigations led him to believe that the faults for which she reproached herself were not the sins of the flesh, or any consent of the will to them, but merely light conversations which led her to think of worldly matters, rather than the spiritual ones which afterwards seemed so much more important to her. She seemed to herself to have been guilty of ingratitude, since God had given so much light to her. Ribera suspected that when she wrote, her offenses sometimes seemed mortal to her imagination; but he felt certain they were not.[10]

Father Yepes, who also met her in life, and wrote of her after her death, agreed with all this. God permits His saints to fall into certain weaknesses and faults, he argued, to encourage the rest of us, lest we imagine that sanctity is "something born with, or necessary," instead of the union with Him that anyone who truly wishes it may attain; and he cites the examples of King David, Saint Paul, Saint Mary Magdalen, Saint Mary of Egypt, and others. These saints, in overcoming their faults, conquered the devil and glorified God's mercy. So it was with Teresa; but Yepes believes, that since all impurity was abhorrent to her, she could not have given her consent to, or taken pleasure in, any mortal sin. Later, like other saints, she glossed over her virtues and exaggerated her sins, "making mosquitoes into elephants." Similarly Saint Catherine of Siena wept all her life over her childish vanity.[11]

The real key to the whole difficulty is probably furnished by a casual afterthought which Teresa wrote at the end of the chapter in which she told of her "wickedness." She went on to discuss subsequent events, and at the end reverted, in characteristic fashion, to the former discussion. "There was one thing

---

[10] Ribera, *Vida de Santa Teresa*, lib. I, cap. VIII. In a letter to her brother Lorenzo, Teresa plainly indicated that she had never so much as felt the stirrings of any carnal passion.

[11] Yepes, *Vida de Santa Teresa*, lib. I, cap. VIII.

that I think might have been some excuse for me, if I had not had such faults; and that is, that the conversation was with a person with whom I thought it could end well by way of marriage;[12] and informed by the one with whom I confessed and by other persons, in many things they told me I did not go against God."

These are the words that have led some writers to surmise that Teresa considered a marriage for herself. This is possible, of course, and would detract in no degree from her honor or her sanctity. But a more likely hypothesis, considering the context, is that she was confidante of a girl cousin, who was considering a marriage. Perhaps the older girl told her more than she could comprehend, and so disturbed a lively imagination and a sensitive conscience with fears and scruples that assumed an importance out of proportion to their actuality. No evidence of any wrongdoing on the part of Teresa has ever been offered; and the Catholic Church, bound by the words of Christ, "Whosoever shall look on a woman to lust after her, hath already committed adultery with her in his heart,"[13] has officially declared after the usual careful investigations that she lived in a state of "angelic purity in heart and body" throughout her life.[14]

Perhaps relatives were beginning to notice Teresa's vanity and sentimentality, and to remark about them — or did she only imagine that everyone knew how silly she had been? At any rate, enough was said, after about three months, to alarm her good father, and to make him conclude that it might be well to send her to a convent school for a while. Apparently he did not exaggerate the situation as she did, nor did he blame her in any way. "So excessive was my father's love for me, and so

---

[12] *Vida*, cap. II. The Spanish here could be translated "a person with whom *I* could do well by way of marriage." If this is what Saint Teresa meant, Mir, Bouix, and others would be justified in understanding that she was considering marriage for herself. But taking the context of the whole chapter (II) into account, she seems to me to mean the marriage of her cousin. Besides (and this is decisive) she has previously told us that the person with whom she had the conversations was a girl.

[13] Matt. 5:28.

[14] Gregory XV, in the bull of canonization, said, "*Inter caeteras ejus virtutes, quibus quasi sponsa a Deo ornata excelluit, integerrima effulsit castitas quam, adeo eximie coluit, ut non solum propositum virginitatis servandae a pueritia conceptum usque ad mortem perduxit, sed omnis expertem maculae angelicam in corde et corpore servaverit puritatem.*" Likewise Urban VIII changed with his own hand the words *scelerum suorum*, in the first office submitted for her, to *culparum suarum*, adding "*Sancta Teresia nunquam commisit peccatum mortale.*"

much my dissimulation, that he would not believe so much evil of me, and so he did not remain displeased with me. Although he had some inkling, nothing could be said with certainty, since the time was brief: for as I was so much afraid of my reputation, all my endeavors were that it should be secret, and I did not notice that it could not be so to the One Who sees all."[15]

Don Alonso may have understood his daughter better than she imagined. At all events, he made up his mind to send her to the Augustinian Convent of Our Lady of Grace, where so many of the children of his friends were educated. Yet he shrank from making her a subject of gossip, perhaps at the cost of her reputation. Knowing human nature as he did, the good hidalgo waited for an opportunity, which presently offered itself in the betrothal of his oldest daughter, María, to Don Martín Guzmán y Barrientos, who had an estate at Castellanos de la Cañada. He let it be known that as Teresa's sister was soon to be married, it was not fitting that she should remain alone in the house without a mother.

It may have been fortunate for Teresa that just about this time there occurred at Ávila an event that gave people something more important to discuss than the vanities of a young girl. The Empress Isabel, who in the opinion of some admirers was the most beautiful woman in Europe, arrived on the afternoon of May 24, 1531. She had been recuperating at the gardens of Aranjuez from an illness; now she had come to Ávila to enjoy the bracing air, and to get her two children, Philip and María, away from the epidemics current in the south. The Emperor Charles, absent from Spain for two years, was in Germany, attending to some sort of disturbance created by a monk named Luther. As the Empress meanwhile was ruling the country for him, Ávila was to be the capital of Spain that summer. It was no ordinary occasion, then, when the imperial Portuguese lady was borne on her litter, as the May sun went down, through the east gate. Prince Philip, then four years old, rode like a little man on a small mule, whose bridle was held by the handsome Marqués of Lombay. As many children came dancing down, to the music of all manner of minstrels, and bonfires flamed in the gathering dusk along the crests of the hills, who could have guessed that this boy would be known (unjustly) as the Black Demon of the South, and the Marqués as Saint Francis Borgia?

---

[15] *Vida, loc. cit.*

Teresa must have heard a great deal about that affair. Most likely she was present, and felt as other girls did at the sight of so much splendor. Yet when she wrote the story of her soul, long after the beautiful Isabel was consigned to dust side by side with her glorious namesake and grandmother in Granada, the affairs of the world meant so little to her that she did not even mention the imperial visit, any more than she mentioned the landing of Pizarro in Peru the same year. Yet the Empress and Philip II were to have no small influence, as we shall see, on the course of her life.

On August 24 her Majesty presented the Prince to the notables and populace of Ávila at the historic convent of Saint Ann. Teresa was probably absent. For one hot day in July (the thirteenth, according to one tradition),[16] her father had escorted her through the city gate, and up a winding street to the crest of a hill at the south, overlooking the beautiful valley of Amblés and a breath-taking panorama of prairie and mountains, to a two-story building with tiled roof adjoining the lofty bulk of a church; and there he had said farewell at the door of the Convent of the Augustinians. As Teresa followed one of the nuns, perhaps the Mother Superior, into the quiet interior, Don Alonso returned gravely home, feeling no doubt that he had made the best possible choice.

In this convent there was none of the laxity which had led certain Augustinian communities in Germany to compromise with the fallacies of Luther. On the contrary, the few nuns[17] at Our Lady of Grace in Ávila were noted for the austerity and purity of their lives, their devotion to the Church, and the severe discipline to which they cheerfully submitted. There would be no nonsense, Don Alonso knew, in that convent. It had been founded in 1508, by the widow of a silversmith and her two daughters, all of whom became nuns. In 1520, and for six years thereafter, its director was no less a personage than Saint Thomas of Villanova, who refused to be Archbishop of Granada, and loved the poor so much that he left them his last penny on the day of his death. In 1531, as provincial, he visited the convent, and found the nuns living almost like hermits so

---

[16] A tradition of the Convent of Our Lady of Grace, says Mir, *Vida de Santa Teresa*, I, p. 56.

[17] On one document of the convent, signed May 30, 1532, there are only fourteen signatures.

far as silence, fasting, and prayer were concerned. Don Alonso had some reason, then, to feel satisfied that here his daughter would be safe from all kinds of foolishness, whether books of chivalry, cosmetics, or forbidden conversations.

Teresa's emotions were mixed. As for leaving home and living in the convent, that seems to have troubled her very little, in fact, the novelty of the experience may have had a certain attraction for her, and it was a relief to get away from the miserable situation she thought she created for herself at home. Almost at once, however, she began to reproach herself, feeling that she had offended not only her father, but God Almighty, and that everyone, nuns and students, knew how vain and stupid she had been. As soon as possible, she went to Confession. Perhaps she found a priest skilled in the knowledge of human nature, who saw at once that she was victim of a state of mind common enough in adolescence, and with kind and reassuring words brought her back to a sense of reality and proportion. Perhaps it was the patient, quiet, and irresistible charity of the nuns that broke through the barrier of her fears; perhaps both these influences played their part in the change that was about to come over her. At any rate, she became aware, after about a week, that she was not disliked or distrusted, but on the contrary very popular. Everyone seemed to love her; a great peace descended upon her, and "I was much more content than in the house of my father."[18] She began to forget the miseries that had brought her there, above all, to forget herself, to work, to study, to pray, and to play with the abandon of a healthy girl of sixteen.

From time to time this new tranquillity was disturbed by messages and presents from unspecified people in the world. But the good nuns, who were watching her more carefully than she imagined, noticed the ill effect of such communications and put a stop to them; and from then on she was unhappy no more. As the convent maintained a sort of finishing school for fashionable young ladies, Teresa was there not as a postulant, but as one of the *doncellas de piso* (boarding scholars) who learned to read and to write, to sew, spin, and embroider. She had no intention of being a nun, in fact she tells us that she felt a "great enmity" for the very idea. Nevertheless she conceived a warm love and admiration for the devoted sisters.

She became especially fond of the Mistress of Pupils whose

---

[18] *Vida, loc. cit.*

duty it was to sleep with the lay boarders at night. This *maestra,* Sister María Briceño, was a Castilian lady to her finger tips, descended from one of the illustrious families of Ávila, and so evidently capable of enjoying life that Teresa wondered how she ever renounced the world and all its diversions for an existence of hard work and penance. One day Sister María explained the paradox: "She began to tell me how she had come to be a nun merely by reading what the gospel says, 'Many are called, but few are chosen.' "[19]

It had not occurred to the young *doncella de piso* that nuns do not choose to be nuns, but are chosen by Christ for that particular life. They are free to accept or refuse. If they accept, they must literally, like the merchant who sold all he had to buy the pearl of great price, give up everything, wealth, friends, liberty, everything that is most dear to the people of the world. Christ had made it easy for those who loved Him to do this by giving the example: and those who took Him at His word discovered presently something of the divine paradox of Christianity. They saw that whereas the people of the world, who sought their own gratification, had the discontented and unhappy faces of those who had not found what they sought, the others who asked nothing had received a positive and radiant joy which sustained them even in poverty and pain, and was unlike anything that the fleshpots of the world could offer — to say nothing of the perfect and everlasting joy of the next world which was promised to those who followed Christ.

Sister María loved her Lord most tenderly in the Blessed Sacrament, under which He had hidden Himself that He might better keep His promise to be with His Church all days, even to the consummation of the world. She used to receive Holy Communion every morning; she would go to some other church, at great inconvenience, if there happened to be no Mass in the convent. One Holy Thursday, when she had been unable to receive, and the Host was already reserved in the tabernacle for Good Friday, she wept in great dejection. After some minutes she saw two hands approaching her, holding the Sacred Host, which was placed on her tongue; so Saint Thomas of Villanova reported,[20] adding that Sister María had not volunteered the information, but had admitted the miracle to him when ordered

---

[19] *Vida,* cap. III; Matt. 20:16.
[20] Mir, *Vida de Santa Teresa,* I, 59, from *Divi Thomae a Villanova Opera Omnia* (Manila, 1883), IV, p. 223.

to do so under her vow of obedience. It is recorded also in the annals of the convent that shortly after Teresa went to board there, a light appeared in the presence of all the community, and took the form of a star, which, after floating around the choir, paused over Sister María, and then disappeared into her heart.[21]

The influence of such a woman was bound to make itself felt on a motherless girl. Little by little Teresa began to forget her eyebrows and her hair, the strong arms of Amadís and the woeful sighs of Andandona. Little by little she gave herself to vocal prayer, to the Rosary, the litanies, the beautiful liturgy of the Mass. If she saw someone weeping in prayer, or showing in other ways a complete forgetfulness of self, she began to feel a sort of envy. But the "gift of tears" was not for her. "So hard was my heart in this case, that if I should read the whole Passion, I would not weep a tear. This caused me sorrow." She was an imaginative but not a very emotional worshiper.

After some months in the convent, Teresa was still without any desire to be a nun. Yet there was this difference: she was no longer determined *not* to be a nun. She was able to take an objective view of the problem. "I commenced to say many vocal prayers, and to endeavor that all should commend me to God, that He would give me the state in which I was to serve Him; but I desired, nevertheless, not to be a nun, for this God was not pleased to give me, though I also feared to get married."

Now and then she began to think that perhaps she would be a nun after all, but not in the Augustinian convent, for certain of its devotional practices seemed to her overstrained and unnecessary. No, if ever she became a nun, it would be in the Carmelite Convent of the Incarnation. She had a friend who had professed there, Sister Juana Suárez, whose account of her community evidently made a strong impression. However, she had no intention of being a nun.[22]

One of her own private devotions, practised just before she would fall asleep, was to meditate on the Garden of Gethsemani, cool and silent in the light of the full Passover moon: the three disciples sleeping near by, and there, amid the stones and olive trees, the Savior of the World prostrate in prayer.[23] Again, as before, it was His loneliness that cried out to the motherless

---

[21] *Reforma*, I, 26 *et seq.*

[22] *Vida*, cap. III.

[23] *Ibid.*, cap. IX. She says she formed this habit before she was a nun, but gives no date.

girl; and Teresa knew that it was for her, as for all men, that He underwent the human humiliation of the dread of death, and what was infinitely worse, the anguish of foreseeing that for many souls His sacrifice would be in vain. Nothing moved her so deeply as that cry, "Father, if it be possible, let this chalice pass away!" She could imagine how He looked; she could almost see the pallor of His brow, the drops of sweat that stood out like drops of blood, and rolled down His cheeks. Then she would wish that she could take a cloth, if only she dared, and wipe His brow, cheeks, and lips, and console Him as best a poor girl could. She was under no illusion that she saw or did this. Nevertheless, she knew that Christ had suffered so and that if she could have been present, she would have done just so. Thus, unconsciously, she was beginning to make the sort of meditation that Saint Ignatius had taught his followers to make: to think on some phase of the Passion, and to allow the implications of it to sink into the soul, till all became conformable to the spirit of Christ. And gradually, as she thought of the sublime words of resignation and self-sacrifice — "not as I will, but as Thou wilt" — her own attitude toward the problem of her future began to change. She no longer desired to do this or not to do that. She was ready to do whatever God willed, when He should make known His desires. And so a more solid peace descended upon her, and her days passed so rapidly and delightfully that time seemed hardly to exist any more.

When she had lived in the convent a year and a half (with how many visits home, or visits from her father, she does not state), there occurred the event she had been waiting for to help her decide her future course. A serious illness came upon her. Nothing that was done for her produced any effect. The nuns and Don Alonso decided that she had better go home.

Late in 1532 or early in 1533, Teresa, pale and weak, again entered the door of the house of the Cepedas, high on a hill at the other side of the city. Of the nature and duration of the illness, nothing is known; her cryptic account comprises a single sentence: "God sent me a great infirmity, so that I had to return to my father's house." It was midwinter, and Ávila, gleaming fiercely in the cold sunlight and rising like a silver dream city in the yet frostier radiance of the moon, was almost completely cut off from the outer world by deep drifts that filled the narrow winding roads to Medina, to Madrid, and to Salamanca.

Chapter IV

RUNNING AWAY TO JOIN THE CARMELITES

B Y THE spring of 1533, that terrible spring when the coronation of a scarlet woman in Westminster Abbey symbolized
the defection of England from the Church of Christ and the
disruption of Europe, Teresa was well enough to go out of doors;
and her father decided to take her to the country to recuperate.
As soon as she was able to travel, they set out for Castellanos de
la Cañada,[1] several leagues northwest of Ávila, where María
and her husband, Martín de Guzmán y Barrientos, had their
home. Teresa does not say whether it was spring or summer, or
how they went. Undoubtedly she was mounted on a mule, for
no other transportation was possible on the rocky and often
dangerous defiles of the sierras, and she may have sat, as Mir
conjectures, on one of those ladies' saddles, large and sumptuous
and worth a thousand *maravedis,* that were included in the
famous inventory. The road she took, with her father and perhaps a servant or two, ascended fairly abruptly, until presently,
if she turned like Lot's wife for a farewell glance at her native
city, she must have seen it no longer outlined against the vast
blue dome, but strangely compressed, as if lowered into a great
hollow. Finally, as the narrow trail led them among the cool
hills, they lost sight of lovely Ávila, and went slowly on all
morning through the forest, now skirting the side of a mountain,
now crossing a flat grassy place where a few cattle were grazing,
near some houses of farmers or laborers. Some of the hills were
of terrible and solitary grandeur, huge wastes of gray craggy
rocks, studded with giant pine trees, oaks, juniper, and lab-
danum. Here and there, mammoth boulders were piled pre-
cariously, one on another, as if some giant had balanced them
for his amusement. There were many wild animals in these
forests. It was common enough to see deer leaping from rock
to rock, and one never knew when one might encounter, at a
turn of the road, that fierce and deadly beast, the Spanish wild

---

[1] Mir has a good historical imagination. I have followed, in the main, his re-
construction of this journey. (Mir, *Vida de Santa Teresa,* I, p. 65.)

boar. Sometimes the road wound past a lonely sheepfold, or a little field or vineyard cultivated by poor laborers. This was the way that Teresa and her father must have taken through the vast silence; and toward the end of the day they came in sight of some lofty and sumptuous groves of pine, in the midst of which twinkled the little hamlet of Hortigosa.

This was a suburb of the small town of Manjabalago, which boasted forty-three houses and a church. In Hortigosa there were six houses, the largest and best of which was occupied by Don Pedro de Cepeda, brother of Teresa's father, and was known to the shepherds and laborers of the vicinity as the *palacio*.[2] Don Pedro had married a lady from one of the noble houses of Aguila; but Doña Catalina was now dead, and had left him a son, another Pedro, with whom he lived in the house that probably had once been hers. Don Pedro, according to Teresa, was "a very prudent man, of great virtues," who since his wife's death had turned more and more to thoughts of God and of eternity; in fact, he was already thinking of giving up all his possessions and becoming a monk, as in the end he did.

This grave and thoughtful man was delighted to see his brother and his niece, and insisted that they remain with him for several days. Teresa would have preferred, perhaps, to continue the journey to the house of her sister, whom she had not seen in many months. It was not very exciting for a romantic girl of eighteen to listen to a man whose "speech," she tells us, was "most commonly of God and the vanity of the world." He spent a great deal of time reading, for he had a library full of good books, in Spanish; but if Teresa felt any thrill of interest when he asked her to read one of them aloud to him, she was doomed to speedy disappointment, for it was not one of the novels she had loved before her convent days, but a dusty pious piece of Renaissance rhetoric which she found very dull. In fact, all the books that she read to him one after another bored her to the verge of exasperation. She was too polite, of course, to let him see this. She could never bring herself to hurt anyone deliberately; in fact, she sometimes went to trouble and pain to please those who had no right to exact from her a complacence which afterward appeared to her a waste of good time, if not worse. So she pretended that she enjoyed pages of repetitious

---

[2] *Vida*, cap. III.

verbiage, and read them with a gusto that must have pleased and edified Don Pedro.[a]

She herself, though, was affected by this reading in a way she had little anticipated. For although there were none of the breath-taking, hair-raising moments of the *Amadis of Gaul* stories, the tomes that Don Pedro enjoyed had a quiet something of their own to offer, if one gave them a chance, and the young woman found herself yielding to a sense of peace and security that reminded her of childhood hours when she had liked nothing better than to hear of God and the wonderful things He had accomplished, not merely in nature, but in the souls and lives of men and women. She remembered now that she had been convinced as a small child, without argument pro or con but as an immediate perception, of what her uncle was always saying; that life at best was short and unsatisfying, that loved ones changed or grew old and died, that all things mortal passed away, but that God endured forever; He never changed, nor did His love and providence ever fail those who sought Him with sincerity. Thus Uncle Pedro conquered after all. Perhaps this was just what he had intended.

When she finally left to continue the journey to Castellanos de la Cañada, the same train of thought kept passing through her mind; and with it a sense that she had thus far lived her life to so little purpose that if she were to die, she would not deserve the delightful vision of God, but rather, like callous Dives, would be buried in hell. Perhaps, then, she ought to make a final choice between the world and God. Perhaps she should be a nun. No, she would not. She found the world beautiful and desirable, and she had no intention of giving it up for the restrictions of a cloister. Nevertheless she had come to the conclusion that the religious state was the best, if only one could find courage to embrace it. Courage? Courage she had never lacked for whatever she wanted to do. It was her will that clung to the world and all its alluring possibilities.

It was only a day's journey from Hortigosa to the place where María lived, and Teresa and her father probably made the dis-

---

[a] This seems fairly to be inferred from Teresa's own words: "Though I did not care for them, I pretended that I did; for in this business of giving pleasure to others I have gone to every length, even though it caused me pain; so much so that in others it might have been a virtue, and in me it has been a great fault, for I went many times quite beyond discretion." — *Vida, loc. cit.*

tance before nightfall. Castellanos was a lonely village on the road from Ávila to Salamanca, not far from the *cañada* or sheep walk which the valuable merino flocks used to follow (as they do to this day) to pasture in the northern provinces in summer and southern Extremadura in winter. Except for the shepherds and the migratory sheep, and occasional travelers and couriers on the road, the hamlet, with its ten households, was a little world sufficient unto itself, lying in the midst of a beautifully rolling country, checkered with tilled fields and forests of ancient oaks, extending to distant mountains. The air was clear and transparent, as heady as wine, like that of the mountains; and perfumed with the scents of thousands of flowers. The springs and brooks were cold and crystalline, to the joy, no doubt, of Teresa, for whom water had such fascination. It was a setting of solitary but inspiring grandeur, this panorama on which the two-story house of Don Martín de Guzmán y Barrientos, with its little balconies at the upper windows, and its tiled roofs, looked peacefully out, even as it does to this day.

Teresa's account of her visit to her sister is disappointingly lacking in details. "The love she had for me was extreme, and if she had had her way, I should not have gone away from her; and her husband also loved me much; at least he showed me all hospitality." This is all she says of a visit which must have been, at the time, momentous.

Perhaps the reason for her reticence was that her mind was almost entirely preoccupied by a struggle that had been wakened by the books she had read in Hortigosa, and the sad finality of Uncle Pedro's observations on the futility of human affairs. There had gradually formed in her an opinion, amounting at times almost to a conviction, that he was right; in which case the only fitting course for her was to leave the world and its vanities and be a nun. But just when this thought began to bring a sense of security and peace, the voice of the world (indeed Teresa believed afterwards it was the voice of the devil himself) would raise questions, doubts, and fears. Think, this voice would say, of the rigors and trials of a nun's life, the discipline, the loss of liberty, the separation from loved ones, the hard work, the monotony, the suffering.

Teresa had reached the point where she could answer, "The trials and hardships of being a nun cannot be worse than that of purgatory, and I have well merited hell; it will not be much to live as if in purgatory, and then go straight to heaven, and this is my desire."

"Ah, yes," said the voice, "but think of the delicate way you have been brought up. Think of your health, which has been far from robust lately. You would never be able to stand it."

Teresa retorted that Christ had endured every trial and suffering for her sake, and it would be little enough to suffer something for His sake, in obedience to His invitation and advice.[4]

This went on for three months. "I had plenty of temptations those days!" She was becoming pale and listless again. She began to have serious fainting fits, with fever. "My health was always poor," she wrote. Now it grew worse. The interior conflict was killing her, and she could not make up her mind. Evidently she had some reasons also to believe that her father would not consent; this was an important factor in her hesitation.

Her one consolation, the thing she wrote that "gave me life," was the habit of reading which she formed at the house of Don Pedro. The books of *caballería* had lost their fascination for her, but the writings of the saints more than took their place, and one day, lingering over the epistles of Saint Jerome, she came upon some words which gave her courage. Unfortunately she has not told us what these words were. A reasonable conjecture is that they were in the letter to Heliodorus.[5] "You tell me that Holy Scripture commands us very strictly to obey our parents; it is true, but it also teaches us that if anyone loves them more than Jesus Christ, such a one will be doomed to lose his soul." Teresa made her decision and told her father she intended to enter the Carmelite Convent of the Incarnation.

Parents often exhibit surprising reactions when confronted with this situation: the undevout are sometimes acquiescent, the pious not infrequently resist. Don Alonso, for all his goodness and his reverence for the religious state, was one of these latter. He flatly refused his permission. It was all very well for others to enter the convent, but not for her, and he would not give her up. Was she not the logical person to preside over his house, now that María was married? In vain Teresa entreated, probably

---

[4] *Vida, loc. cit.* She gives the conversation in indirect discourse: I have taken the liberty of making it direct.

[5] This opinion is shared by P. Silverio (*Vida de Santa Teresa de Jesús*, I, 143–145), who quotes at length from the letter, and Mir, *Vida de Santa Teresa*, I, p. 92.

with tears. In vain her friends and relatives interceded. Don Alonso was not to be moved.

"When I am dead," he said with finality, "she may do as she pleases."

Teresa continued to read Saint Jerome, and little by little she approached the second momentous decision. Much as she loved her father, she belonged first to God, Who had made her and died for her; and since God had put it into her heart to leave all things and follow Him, her father had no right to object. At the first opportunity, therefore, she would leave home without his knowledge and enter the convent. Until she did this there would be no rest, no happiness for her. We need not take too literally her later assurance that she had no love of God to overcome her human affection for her family, or Mir's conjecture that she was motivated less by love than by fear of the loss of her soul, and a conviction that the world, which promised so much and gave so little, was a bitter illusion.[6] Various influences, of course, were drawing her toward the final resolution. Among these were Saint Jerome, her own prayers and reflections, the words of an old friend. Very often she was seen making her way through the hilly pass of Ávila — a striking figure in an orange colored skirt bordered with black velvet,[7] which no doubt went very well with her dusky hair — toward the Incarnation, where she told her perplexities to Sister Juana Suárez, and received advice and encouragement.

It was not easy for Teresa to leave her father. He would soon be a very lonely old man in an almost deserted house. His sons were making ready one after another to seek wealth and fame in America. Rodrigo, in fact, had his arrangements all made early in the summer of that year; he had been accepted for the expedition of the Adelantado Don Pedro de Mendoza, whose armada would leave Sanlúcar for Buenos Aires on the twenty-fourth of August. Another resident of Ávila, Juan de Osorio, was going on one of the ships. They would have to ride more than 200 miles to the southern port of embarkation, leaving Ávila late in July or early in August.

The grief of Teresa at the prospect of so long a separation

---

[6] Mir points out rather irrelevantly (*op. cit.*, I, 89) that she never used the word *vocation* in writing of her struggles at this time.

[7] Doña Inés de Quesada, then a nun at the Incarnation, told this to Doña María de Pinel, who recorded it: *Relaciones históricas de los bibliófilos españoles, Relación*, XXVI, p. 328; Mir, *op. cit.*, I, 91.

may be imagined. Rodrigo had always been her favorite brother, and the degree to which he reciprocated her affection is indicated by the fact that before his departure he made a will (June 25) leaving her all his inheritance in case he should never return from the Rio de la Plata. The sad day came, the words of parting were spoken, and Rodrigo, who had once wanted to go with her to Morocco and martyrdom, rode out across the Adaja into the vast wilderness of the world. Teresa never saw him again. He fought valiantly for his king side by side with four of his brothers at the terrible battle of Iñaquito in 1546, and after a distinguished career was killed in 1557.[8]

Now that he was gone, she found herself growing more dependent upon the companionship of Antonio. Lorenzo was nearer her own age, but Antonio (fifteen at this time) had more in common with her, particularly in spiritual understanding. He was so impressed by her eloquent discourses on the vanity of all human affairs and the impossibility of finding real or lasting happiness except in the arms of God that he decided to enter the order of Saint Dominic, and the two agreed that on the day she joined the Carmelites he would go to the Monastery of Saint Thomas. Their plans were made very secretly, and one memorable day in 1535,[9] at the first streak of dawn, they stole out of the house, as if to go to early Mass. Had Teresa slept at all that night? "To the best of my recollection, and I think truly, I don't believe I shall feel it more when I die: for I felt as if every bone in my body were being wrenched apart."

Only the earliest risers in Ávila may have seen an attractive young woman of twenty hurrying through the cool streets, accompanied by a stripling of fifteen, to the gate of Carmen, thence to the bottom of the ravine of Ajates, and up the slope on the other side to the northern suburbs of Ávila, where the lofty bell tower of the Monastery of the Incarnation was already aglow

---

[8] Cf. Silverio, *op. cit.*, I, p. 137 and references there.

[9] The date of Teresa's entry at the Incarnation has been disputed. La Fuente and the Bollandists place it as early as 1533. Yepes says she was 18, which would make it the same year. Ribera gives 1535. Mir, noting that the paper recording her father's dowry to the convent was dated October 28, 1537 believes it was probably November 2, 1536. Doña María de Pinel, Julián of Ávila, and various witnesses in the process of beatification agree on 1535. Finally, Pope Gregory XV, in the bull of canonization, stated that she was 20 years of age, which would make the year 1535. This accords with the statement of the Carmelite historian Father Jerónimo (*Reforma*, lib. I, VII) who says she received the habit in 1536.

with the light of the new day. A pause, the ringing of the porter's bell, a hasty farewell, a question and answer through the grille, and a heavy portal swung open, revealing a nun or a *tourière* in Carmelite attire. Teresa stepped inside and the door closed.

The first intimation Don Alonso had of all this may have been the return later in the day of his son Antonio, very crestfallen and sheepish. For after the disappearance of Teresa in the doorway, the boy, faithful to his promise, had gone to the beautiful monastery where Torquemada had lived and prayed and where the great Isabel la católica had mourned by the tomb of her only son. There he was courteously admitted by a man in white robes; but, alas for the ardor of youth, he found no great eagerness to receive him. Don Alonso was a frequent visitor at Santo Tomás, in fact, for several years he used to go to Confession there. The Dominicans were not likely to accept the son of such a friend without his permission; and when they learned that Antonio had come without his father's knowledge, they sent him home.[10]

About the same time there came a message to Don Alonso from the Mother Prioress of the Carmelites. His daughter was in the convent, but as she had left without his consent, would he kindly come and talk the matter over?

Don Alonso hastened to the convent. It had not occurred to him, perhaps, that Teresa was so much in earnest. But since she felt so strongly about the matter, it must indeed be the will of God. To his daughter's surprise, and to the edification of the good nuns, he gave his consent, and she remained in the convent as a novice.

Her first emotion after the great decision was one of sudden intense joy. "In taking the habit, then the Lord gave me to understand how He favors those who do violence to themselves to serve Him, which nobody understood of me, only a great willingness. At once He gave me a great joy at having that state that has never failed me even to this day," she wrote long afterwards; "and God changed the dryness that my soul had into

---

[10] Antonio later entered a Jeronymite monastery, but was compelled to leave by ill-health. He went to Peru and was killed in the battle of Iñaquito. Cf. P. Silverio, *op. cit.*, I, p. 149; Mir, *op. cit.*, I, 100 *et seq.*; Ribera, *op. cit.*, lib. I, cap. VI; Yepes, *op. cit.*, lib. I, cap. IV; María de San José, *Libro de recreaciones*, No. 9; Serrano y Sanz, *Apuntes*, etc., II, p. 343 *et seq.*

the greatest tenderness. All the things of religion gave me delight, and it is true that I sometimes went about sweeping in the hours I had been accustomed to spend in my pleasure and adornment, and in remembering that I was free from that I found a new joy that astonished me, and I could not understand whence it came."[11]

Life in a Carmelite convent was not what it had been in the beginning. Originally the Carmelites were hermits who never ate meat, seldom spoke, and devoted nearly all their energies to prayer and contemplation, with certain prescribed manual labor. A tradition of the order, making its founders the prophets Elias and Eliseus, is paralleled by history as far back as the twelfth century, when a community of Christian hermits lived under a rule of our Lady on the mountain in Palestine where Elias had confounded the prophets of Baal. Often they were disturbed by the Saracens: and in 1291 the Brothers, singing the *Salve Regina,* were put to the sword, and their monastery burned. The order migrated to Europe, and there, as convents were founded in cities as well as in deserts, several changes were deemed necessary and were permitted in constitutions granted by certain Popes. Inevitably the Carmelites tended, during such times as those of the Black Death and the Great Schism, to become more like the mendicant orders, the Dominicans, Franciscans, Benedictines, and Augustinians. Solitary life was abandoned for community life; abstinence from meat was greatly modified, and silence limited to the night hours, between Compline and Prime. In time the tenure of the prior was extended, and monks were allowed to own private property in spite of their vows of poverty. When communities of nuns joined the order in the fifteenth century, they naturally followed the constitutions observed by the monks. In Spain particularly they flourished and enjoyed great popularity.

The convent of Our Lady of the Incarnation, in which Teresa was now a novice, was founded in 1478. In 1485 it came into possession, through a grant by Bishop Alonso de Fonseca, of the Church of All Saints, which had formerly been a Jewish synagogue. In 1511 it acquired, for the sum of 90,000 *maravedis,* a group of adjoining houses in a pleasant suburb of Ávila, the one called Ajates, looking out among trees and gardens upon the middle of the valley. There a new church was built and con-

---

[11] *Vida,* cap. IV.

secrated in 1515, the year of Teresa's birth; the first Mass was said in it April 28 of that year, when she was a month old.[12]

Adopting the rule of the Carmelite fathers, who had had a monastery in Ávila since 1378, and gaining the protection of powerful personages, the Incarnation became the fashionable convent of the city. It was there that the noblest young ladies usually retired when they decided to give up the world for the religious life. In spite of this it was not corrupted by riches, in fact it suffered from financial stringency from time to time. In certain other respects, such as discipline, it shared in the relaxation that was so widespread before the second Council of Trent. The nuns were not strictly cloistered; they were allowed to go outside for many causes, and to receive visitors almost at will. In entering the convent they did not have to relinquish their private property, nor were they obliged to fast very severely, or to maintain silence long. There were two reasons for this laxity. First, the number of nuns was too great (there were 180 at the Incarnation at one time) for a house of contemplation. Second, there were several *señoras de piso,* "lady boarders," who lived in the convent because they enjoyed its atmosphere, but were not members of the community or subject to its rule; and the fact that they came and went as in a private house, and entertained friends in their apartments whenever they pleased, had its effect naturally upon the life of the nuns themselves. The Incarnation was rather a gay place for a convent.

With so many ladies of noble family in the convent, there was bound to be something of snobbery in the air. Not only were worldly *punctilios* of honor held in much esteem, but social distinctions were made between those of high degree, who, like Teresa, were called *Doña,* and the proletarian souls whose fathers did not happen to be *Dons.* In a community where the Doña Aldonzas, Doña Briandas, and Doña Violantes of fashionable Castilian society came and went, it seemed natural that the Doñas who had taken the veil should enjoy privileges not granted to the others.[13] While many had to share cells, Teresa had one of her own, looking out upon a pleasant field and garden: indeed, it was an apartment which a nun of any order nowadays would consider sumptuous. She had two rooms connected by a flight of steps — an oratory on the first floor, and a bedroom on the sec-

[12] Mir, *op. cit.,* I, 94 *et seq.* See his references, p. 96, note.
[13] P. Gabriel, *La Santa de la Raza,* III, 37; Mir, *op. cit.,* I, p. 97.

ond, and apparently such pictures, statues, and other decorations as she desired.[14] She could receive visits from friends and relatives in her oratory.

She came to have a very healthy dislike, as we shall notice, for the relaxations in the Incarnation: she despised large numbers in an order intended to be contemplative, she despised unnecessary visits and conversations, she despised all snobbery, and especially pride of family or of race. It does not follow, however, that the Discalced Carmelites of the Mitigated Rule in Ávila were morally corrupt, or that they furnished any of the scandals which were too common in those days in some parts of Christendom. If they were lenient, it was only by comparison with the first hermits and the Discalced Carmelites of the Teresian Reform of later days. Compared with some other orders, they led a severe and austere life. The community as a whole was highly respected in a society with a strict standard of feminine virtue, and some of its members managed, in spite of the difficulties indicated, to practise mental prayer and to be reputed as saints. The Carmelite Rule, even as mitigated by Pope Eugene IV in 1432, was severe enough for most nuns. Rubric VI, for example, ordains fasting (that is, one meal a day) from the Feast of the Exaltation of the Holy Cross in September until Christmas, save for three days a week. They could eat no meat in Advent or Lent, and at other times of the year could have it but three times a week. Each nun must take a discipline — that is to say, a scourging — every Monday, Wednesday, and Friday. Their habits were black, of coarse cloth and severe design. On account of the bitter cold of Ávilese winters, they were allowed to wear shoes instead of the primitive sandals, and sheepskins of poor quality, but no gloves. Their beds were simple, without linen sheets or adornments of any kind.

When not in choir or at other devotions, they were expected to do a certain amount of manual labor, at the discretion of the Prioress. They must never be wholly idle. Much attention was paid to communal singing and to great exactness in everything that pertained to the liturgy. With certain slight variations, they observed the rite of the Holy Sepulcher of Jerusalem. Teresa sang very badly, she tells us, when she went to the Incarnation.[16]

---

[14] These rooms were destroyed in the seventeenth century, to make room for a chapel.

[16] *Vida*, cap. XXXI.

The Constitution required that each nun confess at least every two weeks and recommended once a week. Communions were much rarer than now; most of the community received on the first Sunday of Advent, Christmas day, the first Sunday of Lent, Holy Thursday, Easter Sunday, Ascension Thursday, Pentecost, Corpus Christi, All Saints' Day, the feasts of our Lady, and the anniversary of the day of profession. Confessors were to be chosen carefully by the Prioress, and must not be young. Silence was observed from Compline until Prime, that is to say, all night and the first part of the next day, as hours were then arranged. In what was called "the chapter of faults," the Sisters had to accuse themselves humbly of all their shortcomings; novices, however, were excused from this.[16]

Teresa did not find such a life easy by any means. A novitiate is always a time of trial, both outward and inward, for a life which aspires to nothing short of perfection. The novice must always be made over to some extent, and this is bound to be a painful experience at times. Even though Teresa had discovered what Christ meant when He said, "these things I have spoken to you, that my joy may be in you, and your joy may be filled,"[17] and again, "Your heart shall rejoice, and your joy no man shall take from you,"[18] she set down as an afterthought the following revealing admission:

"I forgot to say how in the year of my novitiate I suffered great disquietudes with things which in themselves had little weight, but often enough they blamed me when I was not at fault. I bore it with plenty of sorrow and imperfection; though with the great satisfaction I had to be a nun I endured it all. When they saw me seeking solitude, and saw me weeping for my sins sometimes, they thought it was discontent and they said so. I was devoted to all things of religion, but not to suffer anything that might seem insulting. I rejoiced in being well thought of; I was careful in whatever I did; all seemed to me virtue; although this will not excuse me, for I knew what it was to seek my own satisfaction in everything, and so ignorance does not free me from blame. One is to hold that the monastery was not founded

---

[16] Padre Silverio gives a fairly extended summary of the Rubrics of the Mitigation (*op. cit.*, I, pp. 187–204). I wonder if they were observed as rigorously as he seems to imply?

[17] John 15:11.

[18] *Ibid.*, 16:22.

in much perfection. I, wicked as I was, went to that which I saw wrong and omitted the good."[19]

It is easy to understand the concern of Teresa's superior over what they considered her *"descontento."* Nothing is more likely in any religious order to bring about the dismissal of a novice, with the advice to seek some other vocation for which she may be better fitted, than the discovery that she is melancholy. We shall see what she herself, as a superior, thought of melancholy nuns! And even if we grant, as we must on better acquaintance with her, that this suspicion in her case was unfounded, the fact remains that a novice who thought her convent established "not in much perfection" *was* in a measure discontented, even if she was right in her criticism. Then, too, after all allowance has been made for the humility with which she discussed the short-comings of her early life, it seems plain that her besetting sin was vanity and that this had not disappeared from her character when she stepped over the convent threshold. People do not become automatically perfect on entering a religious order; they have only begun a lifetime of conflict against weaknesses which must be conquered one by one. Even saints, far from being bodi-less abstractions, selfless and sexless, have faults which can be very irritating to those about them. It is unlikely that many of the nuns at the Incarnation applied to their novice the prophecy of a *zahori* who had gone to the convent grounds in search of hidden treasure, and although he failed to find it, predicted that there would be a *beata* there named Teresa. A shrewd mother superior might have had the secret thought that this child, if she had not been a Christian, if she had not such love of God, could in the world have become a beautiful, imperious, voluptuous, perhaps even a ruthless woman, ridden by an in-satiable self-love. Human passions are evil or good, not in them-selves, but in their direction and application. Yet it must have been apparent, too, that this novice had humility, the founda-tion of all the virtues. Some of the sisters noticed that when they left their white mantles in the choir before going to the refectory, she quietly collected and folded them as a voluntary penance.

About this time her duties brought her into contact with one of the older nuns who was dying of the most painful and dis-gusting disorder: as the result of oppilations, she had in her belly open wounds, through which emerged whatever she ate. Some

[19] *Vida,* cap. V.

of the nuns seemed to be afraid of the poor woman's malady; but what impressed Teresa was her remarkable patience. The nun was one of those mystics who had so penetrated the paradoxical secret of suffering at the heart of Christianity that she could endure all pain and humiliation, not merely with resignation, but with a positive joy which no one can understand without witnessing it, as it recurs in convents generation after generation. The face of such a person, offering her sufferings in union with those of Christ on the cross, takes on something of the unearthly beauty, peace, and sublimity of her Master. And so it seemed to Teresa that what she saw in that Christlike face was worth any price that might be paid for it in terms of human inconvenience. It must be paid for, however, and the price was pain. From the magnanimous heart of the novice, vital and alert in the bloom of her youth, there leaped a prayer, a prayer that must be incomprehensible even to Christians who have not penetrated the center of their Faith; she asked God to give her a similar patience, with whatever sickness might be necessary to achieve it. It seemed to her afterwards that she asked this not through love of God, but through a more selfish desire to obtain eternal happiness for herself as soon as possible; however, she did have the courage to make the request. The nun died soon after.

Within a short time Teresa came to the end of her year of probation and was professed, probably on November 2, 1536, in the presence of her father, brothers, and sisters, and many friends and relatives. It was one of the most memorable days of her life, even though she has left no account. A few days before, her father had agreed to give the convent as her dowry either two hundred ducats or twenty-five *fanegas* of bread per year — choosing the latter afterwards. On November 1, Teresa probably made a most careful general confession, for this was usually required. The following day she walked alone with head uncovered to receive Holy Communion at the smaller window, and then received her black veil from the presiding prelate, with his blessing and plenary absolution. Then she joined the procession of all the sisters, singing with them the *Veni Creator,* and carrying her scapular, a leather thong, and a *"Paternoster"* or prayer book. Arriving at where her superior waited near a grated entrance to the chapel, she prostrated herself, with her forehead touching the floor.

"What do you seek, daughter?" asked the prelate, probably Father Provincial.

"The mercy of God and the habit of the Glorious Virgin Mary of Mount Carmel," replied Teresa.

"Will you be able to keep their rule and manner of life?"

"I believe I can, with God's help."

He blessed the veil and other articles she carried, according to the Carmelite rite. She was then clothed, while all intoned the *Veni Creator*. Finally, with her hands on the Gospel and between the hands of her Superior, she pronounced the vows of obedience, chastity, and poverty, and the procession returned to the chapter. The new nun then went to the large grille to be congratulated by her relatives and friends.

Almost immediately after this joyous and tearful day, Doña Teresa (as she was still called) began to discover that her audacious prayer as a novice had been heard on high and was being answered. Her health failed rapidly. This was caused in part, she thought, by the change in her habits of life and in her food.[20] Apparently, too, she undertook excessively severe penances until her superior made her desist. It was evident that her heart was affected, and seriously. She fainted often; some of the seizures were alarming. "It almost deprived me of consciousness always, and sometimes I remained wholly without it." Her father, intensely anxious, sent the best physicians to see her. None could say what was the cause of her sickness, or prescribe a successful remedy. This went on for a year, during which Teresa must have been prostrate a great deal of the time in her apartment.

Finally, after she had been in the convent about two years,[21] her condition grew so much worse, and seemed so unlikely to yield to medical science, that her father suggested taking her to Becedas, several miles from Ávila, where there was a woman noted throughout the province for having cured dangerous illnesses. Teresa's superiors consented and it was agreed that her friend, Sister Juana Suárez, should accompany her.

Who was this wonderful woman of Becedas that could cure all manner of disease? Not even her name remains; we are told only that she had *"mucha fama"* and that persons who professed

---

[20] *Vida*, cap. IV.
[21] Ribera (*op. cit.*, lib. I, cap. VII) says this was in 1537.

to know her work promised confidently that Doña Teresa would be healed. She did not believe this. It was with reluctance that she went to her father's house with Sister Juana late in the autumn of 1537 to prepare for the journey.

Becedas lay about fifteen leagues west of Ávila, almost on the border of the province of Salamanca. The road to it led through Hortigosa and Castellanos de la Cañada, so that Teresa was able to stop, at the end of the first day, to visit her uncle, Don Pedro. How different he must have seemed! It was on his account, after all, that she was now a nun; would she have left the world if his books had not persuaded her of its futility? And on this occasion he introduced her to a little book that was to make another great revolutionary change in her life. It was the *Tercer Abecedario* by Fray Francisco de Osuna, a Franciscan, published in Toledo in 1527 — one of those treatises that worldly people pass by with a shrug of indifference or scorn and mystics press to their hearts in gratitude. It was the third volume of a work intended, as the title implies, to explain the ABC's of prayer: not vocal prayer, the mere recitation of words, either in set or improvised arrangement, but that loftier prayer transcending words, that elevation of the spirit toward an understanding of, and communication with, God, which contemplatives had experienced. Although the various stages of mental prayer had been recognized by many saints, no methodical attempt had been made to analyze and classify them until Osuna wrote this book. It was dangerous, perhaps, for some souls but for others very helpful.

Great, at all events, was the joy of Teresa when, before she departed from Hortigosa, her uncle gave her the third volume of the precious work. It was exactly what she had been longing for without knowing it. She had arrived in the adventure of her soul at the need of something not easily found in the crowded voluble confines of the Incarnation. She wanted to speak to her Creator in higher terms than words: and, although she had received what mystics call "the gift of tears" (tears of joy in the contemplation of the things of God), all efforts to attain mental prayer had failed. In her humility she had attributed this to her "sins." But now Padre Francisco, in the little book with the elaborate coat of arms on its frontispiece, suggested another reason: that mental prayer was hardly possible without both quiet and solitude. "You should not be content," he had written, "with interior recollection without exterior recollection, which is also necessary to you, so that the secret and secluded place may awaken you and invite you to enter into yourself."[22]

These words were like the key to a mystery. She had longed for God and had been asking herself where He was best to be found. By the time she had reached her sister's house at Castellanos, Fray Francisco de Osuna had answered the question for her. God was behind all the wonderful works of His that surrounded her in the majestic solitude that enfolded the house of Guzmán y Barrientos. Mountains and prairies, buds and flowers, clouds and sunshine, and above all, water, beautiful sparkling elusive water — everything she saw was like the pages of a book in which she could read how wonderful and how good was God. This was an intellectual perception; it was as far as the human reason alone could go in the quest for the absolute. Yet that was not enough for Teresa. Her love could be satisfied only by leaping over the gulf that extends from where the light of this world wanes to the pure uncreated Light. In short, she wanted not merely the beautiful works of God but God Himself. Osuna confirmed what she had intuitively felt: that only in man, the greatest of His works — man, whom He had made in His own likeness and image, man, in whose form He had become incarnate — was God to be found indwelling as a personality, a father, a king, a lover, the sum of all the delights for which He had implanted a craving in the human heart. If a person cast off all sin, which is in essence opposition to God, if after being purified by frequent confession and penance, he placed himself quietly at the disposal of God, he might hope to hear God speak to him, deep within the secret recesses of his soul. "Enter into yourself!" For Teresa this was a profound discovery which motivated and will help to explain all the rest of her career.

Circumstances now made it possible for her to put into daily practice the tenets of her new *maestro*. Word had come from Becedas that it was useless for her to proceed there at the beginning of winter: the cure must commence early in the spring, in April. There was nothing to do, then, but spend the winter

---

[22] *Tratado*, VIII, cap. IV, quoted by Mir, *loc. cit.* Padre Silverio does not seem to share Mir's somewhat extravagant admiration of the book. He reminds us (*op. cit.*, I, p. 224) that Maestro Avila, that great director of souls, would not ordinarily allow the third book to be read. It was likely to lead some persons toward the false mysticism of Quietism.

with María and her husband. Whether Don Alonso remained with his daughters or returned to his affairs in Ávila does not appear. Sister Juana undoubtedly stayed. One of those good, placid, unobtrusive souls who can easily accommodate them selves to the ways of others, she left her patient free to seek the recollection which Fray Francisco considered indispensable to prayer. Thus Teresa became a contemplative.

She could hardly have found a better place for the purpose. The fields that surrounded the house of Guzmán Barrientos were enfolded, especially in winter, in a monastic silence and peace that was limitless. It was a splendid and beautiful panorama that extended before her eyes, taking in distant mountains white with snow and studded with greenery, fields and rivulets, wood and plains, domed over with the purest of airy skies. What twilights, what dawns came tinging those marvelous Castilian skies with innumerable colors, shifting daily in an infinite variety of forms! No wonder Mir grows ecstatic over the "serene nights, divinely intoxicating, of the mountains of Ávila and Salamanca — these incomparable nights when the silvery light of the moon illumines the firmament and descends vague, indecisive, over the vast forests and disperses itself among the fields, in which is heard nothing but the sound of the air which moves restlessly in the foliage of the pine forests — ."[23]

Here at last Teresa found the peace she had been longing for. She lifted her heart to God, she became conscious for the first time of achieving mental prayer. It was something different from those meditations on Christ in the Garden which, after the manner prescribed by Saint Ignatius, she had practised at Our Lady of Grace. She now began to be aware of another Personality at work in her meditations. She felt the very presence of Christ as He gave her the prayer of quiet (to use her own phrase) and finally, before she left Castellanos, there came a time when He allowed her the briefest intimation of the highest mystical state known to human experience — the prayer of union. She did not call it so at that period, for she did not know what it was; later she believed it to be such, and wrote that "it lasted such a little while, I don't know if it was as long as an *Ave Maria* but I remained with some effects so great that although I was not twenty at this time, I think I trod the world beneath my

---

[23] Mir, *op. cit.*, I, p. 116.

feet, and so I remember that I was sorry for those who followed it, even though it might be in things lawful."[24]

She had found the method of prayer which she was to practise all her life and to teach as no one else had ever taught it.

"I used to try as much as I could to bring Jesus Christ, our God and Lord, within me present, and this was my manner of prayer. If I thought of some *paso*,[25] I represented it in the interior, although I most enjoyed reading good books, for this was all my recreation. God gave me no talent for meditating with the understanding, nor of availing myself of the imagination, which I have so sluggish that even to think and to bring to represent in myself, as I used to try to do, the humanity of the Lord, I never succeeded." Imaginative and intellectual persons could attain prayer without extraneous help, but persons like her (this is her own explanation) were in grave danger that idle and even sinful thoughts would break in on the meditation and bring it all to nothing, leaving her in a worse state, perhaps, than before. It was different when she aided her imagination by reading of one of the divine mysteries. After a while she found that as soon as she opened the book, mental prayer would begin. Only after Holy Communion could she attain recollection without it. Thus she discovered even in daily suffering a more than human joy. The winter slowly melted into spring, and leaving Castellanos, she followed the path that the sick world had beaten to the door of the famous *curandera*, a long day's journey through glade and over mountain to the west.

---

[24] *Vida,* cap. IV.
[25] Station of the cross; here, some event of His life.

Chapter V

THE QUACK DOCTOR AND THE BEWITCHED PRIEST OF BECEDAS

BECEDAS, a town of some 1500 inhabitants, stood on a piece of elevated ground in the midst of fertile land well watered from three *arroyos;* a land of orchards and wheat fields. It consisted mainly of houses of farmers and artisans, clustered around the church. Somewhere among those roofs was the one to which so many sick persons had come and from which so many had gone (people said) cured. Don Alonso inquired where it was and made his way, with the two nuns and possibly some faithful servant of the family, to its door.

The cure began. Teresa was to take certain medicines, chiefly herbs no doubt, and was to be purged daily. The purges which played so important a part in the therapy of the sixteenth century were no laughing matter. Whether she doubted the efficacy of this method for heart trouble, or whether some distrust of the *curandera* herself crossed her mind, she commenced to feel ill at ease. "At this point the devil began to trouble my soul." She sought out the village priest and asked him to hear her confession.

He was a man of very good family, agreeable, kind, courteous. "He had some learning, although not much," adds Teresa in her naïve account. He had some devotion to our Lady, and never failed to celebrate the feast of her Conception each year. It was his appearance of "some" learning, however, that made her wish to to go to confession to him; for "I was always fond of learning. although confessors who were half-learned did my soul great harm, for I have not had them with as good learning as I should like. I have seen from experience that it is better for them, if they are virtuous and of holy customs, not to have any; for then they don't trust in themselves, but ask someone who really has it, nor would I trust them myself; and a good scholar never deceived me. Not that the others wanted to deceive me, but they knew no better."

Don Fulano (this must serve for his name, since Teresa does not give it) proved to be even less learned than he had appeared at first to be; but he was gentle and kind and showed clearly that he had a great admiration for the purity of soul her confession had revealed. "Then I had but little to confess to what I had afterwards," she explains modestly. He encouraged her to consult him often. Perhaps she began to have some misgivings as to this; at any rate, she seems to have sought to protect herself from too friendly a relation by making it plain to him that she was determined never to offend God. This indeed appeared to be the chief reason why Don Fulano had conceived so strong a liking for her; and he in turn remarked that he was equally resolved not to offend God.

Teresa was far from being a fool. She was beginning to wonder about Don Fulano. It had not escaped her notice that people in Becedas had a certain way of speaking or acting when his name was mentioned. Yes, there was something wrong with this priest. He said nothing offensive, yet his attitude repelled her. "This man's affection for me was not evil, but from too much affection it came to be not good." Nevertheless, because there is something irresistible in purity and sincerity such as hers, a curious change began to take place in their relationship; as if she had become the confessor and he the penitent. This frail woman, young and beautiful, who seemed to live always in the presence of God and could think and talk of nothing but His goodness, His mercy, and His justice, was like a mirror in which, for the first time in many years, he could see his own soul laden with all the black spots his parishioners had in mind when they raised their eyebrows at the mention of his name. Finally the wretched man, overcome with a feeling of shame, dropped all pretense and made what was very much like a confession.

"We talked a great deal. But my conversations then, with the wonder of God that was on me, what gave me most pleasure was to talk of His affairs;[1] and as I was so young, it caused him confusion to see this, and with the great good will he had for me, he commenced to tell me about his perdition. And it was not a small thing, for it was almost seven years that he had been in a very dangerous state through affection and intercourse with a woman of the same place, and with this he used to say Mass. It was a thing so public that he had lost all honor and reputation, and no one dared speak to him against it.

"This hurt me a great deal, for I had much liking for him; for such was my imprudence and blindness that I thought it a

---

[1] The construction here is Saint Teresa's.

virtue to be grateful and loyal to anyone who liked me. Cursed
be such loyalty, which is carried so far as to be against that of
God! It is a madness which is common in the world, and it
maddens me that we owe all the good they do us to God, and
hold it for a virtue, although it may be to go against Him, not
to break off this friendship. Oh blindness of the world!"

So wrote the nun of mature years. But the young Teresa felt
only a great commiseration. She was not the first good woman to
feel the glow of a holy desire to draw a man away from the
influence of a bad woman.

"I tried to know and to inform myself more from persons of
his household; I knew more about his perdition, and I saw
that the poor man was not so much to blame; for the wretch of
a woman kept him bewitched by spells on a little idol of copper,
which she had begged him to wear around his neck for the love
of her, and this no one had been strong enough to be able to
make him give up.

"As for this business of witchcraft, I don't believe it's true,
definitely;[2] but I will tell this that I saw, to warn men to be on
their guard against women who wish to have this intercourse;
and let them believe that when they lose shame before God (for
they more than the men are obliged to keep chastity) they cannot trust anything of theirs. For if only they can have their own
way and that affection which the devil puts in them, they will
pay no attention to anything. Although I have been so wicked,
never have I fallen into anything of this sort, nor did I ever
attempt to do evil, nor even if I could would I wish to force the
will so that they should have it for me, for the Lord saved me
from this: but if He had abandoned me, I should have done the
evil that others do, for in me there is nothing in which to trust.
When I knew this, I began to show him more love. My intention
was good, but the act was wrong; for to accomplish a good, however great it may be, even a small evil is not to be done. I talked
to him very frequently of God. This must have done him good,
although I rather believe that what brought him around[3] was
his liking me much; for, to do me pleasure, he finally gave me the

---

[2] There has been considerable discussion as to just what Saint Teresa meant
here: "Yo no creo es verdad esto de hechizos determinadamente." The Bollandists have attempted to prove that she was not denying a belief in witchcraft.
La Fuente takes the other view. P. Silverio maintains a discreet silence. The
determinadamente certainly weakens the force of the no creo.

[3] "le hizo al caso."

idolillo, which I at once had cast into the river. Rid of this, he commenced, like one who awakes from a long sleep, to set about recalling all he had done those years; and surprised at himself, and grieving over his perdition, he began at last to abhor her. Our Lady must have helped him a great deal, for he was very devoted to her Conception, and on that day held a grand *fiesta.* Finally, he gave up seeing her altogether, and then he could not return enough thanks to God for having given him light. At the end of a year exactly from the first day I saw him, he died."

Teresa was no prude and she did not conceal from herself the danger of this friendship. To help this sinner, a man much older and more worldly wise, she had incurred, she felt, a great spiritual risk; still, she had been the instrument of God's mercy and grace to him in the eleventh hour of life, and she believed that he died a good death. "And it had been very much in the service of God, for that great affection he had for me I never understood to be evil, although it might have been with more purity; but also there were occasions in which, if he had not put himself in the near presence of God, his offenses would have been more serious.[4] As I have said, I would not have done anything then that I understood to be a mortal sin. And I think it helped him to love me, to see this in me, for I believe all men must be more fond of women whom they see inclined to virtue. . . . I hold it certain he is in the way of salvation."

Meanwhile the ghastly quackery of the *curandera* was advancing toward its inevitable conclusion — the complete breakdown of the patient's constitution.

"I was in that place three months with the greatest sufferings, for the cure was more drastic than my constitution required.

---

[4] This passage has been misunderstood, and by no one more unhappily than by Mrs. Cecil Chesterton. In her entertaining but inaccurate *Saint Teresa,* she has the priest of Becedas attempting to seduce Saint Teresa, and supports the charge by mistranslating the sentence, *"Nunca entendí ser mala, aunque pudiera ser con mas puridad; mas también hubo ocasiones para que, si no se tuviera muy delante a Dios, hubiera ofensas suyas mas graves."* (*Vida, loc. cit.*) Here Mrs. Chesterton, translating, makes the Saint speak of an attachment "which might have been of greater purity, as there were occasions wherein *we* might have most grievously offended but for the near presence of God." (*Saint Teresa,* p. 74.) What Saint Teresa wrote, of course, was that *his* (*suyas*) offenses might have been more serious, etc. Ribera omits this episode of the bewitched priest from his life of Saint Teresa (*Vida de Santa Teresa,* I, cap. VII), and thereby incurs the severe censure of the ex-Jesuit Mir. Yepes tells the story, following Teresa's account (lib. I, cap. VI).

After two months, thanks to the medicines, I thought my life was almost finished; and the intensity of the pain in my heart, which I had gone there to cure, was much more violent, and sometimes it seemed to me as if they were seizing upon it with sharp teeth, so much so that it was feared it was madness. With the great loss of my strength (for I could eat nothing, except in liquid form and that with great loathing, fever very continuous, and so wasted away, because they had given me a purge every day for nearly a month) I was so burnt up that my sinews began to shrink, with pains so unbearable that day or night I could get no rest; a sadness very profound."

Her father was now willing to admit that he had been deceived about the *curandera*. There was nothing to do but take his daughter back to Ávila.

The journey must have been extremely painful, but it was accomplished (no doubt with a stop at Castellanos), and soon she was lying emaciated and pierced with pain in the house where she had been born and seemed likely soon to die. All the best physicians of the city, separately and in consultation, agreed that she had tuberculosis in addition to the heart disease, and that it was too late for anything to be done. "This troubled me but little. The pains were what fatigued me, for I was all one [pain] from head to foot; for those of the nerves are intolerable, as the doctors say, and as all mine were shrunken up, certainly, if I had not come to grief through my own fault,[5] it would have been grievous torment."

Three terrible months dragged along. Again it was April, and all the world was in flower and song, but Teresa lay racked with misery, with no consolation but prayer, and no source of patience but the reading, in the *Morals* of Saint Gregory, of the story of Job. "There was a man in the land of Hus, whose name was Job, and that man was simple and upright, and fearing God, and avoiding evil."[6] Wondering at the afflictions that fell upon this good man through no fault of his own, Teresa used to read over and over the words he spoke to his wife as he sat miserably upon a dunghill scraping his sores with a potsherd: "If we have received good things at the hand of God, why should we not receive evil?"[7] And like Job, she thought, "Shall not the fewness

---

[5] *Por mi culpa* does not justify Mr. Lewis' translation, "for my sins."
[6] Job 1:1.
[7] *Ibid.,* 2:10.

of my days be ended shortly? Suffer me, therefore, that I may lament my sorrow a little, before I go, and return no more, to a land that is dark and covered with the mist of death, a land of misery and darkness, where the shadow of death, and no order, but everlasting horror dwelleth."[8]

From April to midsummer she lay in this state, waiting for God to release her.

One day in the heat of August she asked her father if she could go to Confession, intending, apparently, to prepare as usual for the Feast of the Assumption. Don Alonso thought she was making ready for death, and to quiet her vain fears, as he supposed they were, he refused to allow the priest to be summoned. "Oh, the unreasonable love of flesh and blood!"

That night she had a sudden relapse and quickly lost consciousness. When all attempts to revive her had failed, the doctors departed in silence, and the priest came at last with the holy oils to anoint her, while the people at her bedside recited the *Credo* and the prayers for the dying. Poor Don Alonso! His grief and self-reproach were terrible. He kept repeating that it was all his fault, for he had not allowed her to go to Confession.

Teresa, motionless and apparently lifeless, seemed to have stopped breathing. Some of those in the sickroom tried all the ancient tests, such as the mirror and the feather, and all declared her soul had left her body. This word was taken to the convent and a grave was dug. Some Carmelite friars near by held a funeral service.[9] Nuns were sent to escort the body to its resting place.

For a day and a half the fresh grave lay open, waiting for the shrunken body. The nuns from the Incarnation wanted to have her carried there at once and buried. This doubtless would have been done if Don Alonso had not insisted that she was only sleeping, for he could feel her pulse. *"Esta hija no es para enterrar!"* he would cry.[10] They thought him crazed with grief, but no pleading or argument could move him.

During one of those four sepulchral nights when the body was left unattended a little while, a candle burned down, sputtered, and ignited the bed clothes. Young Lorenzo de Cepeda, weary from long vigils, had fallen asleep in a chair beside his

[8] *Ibid.*, 10:20–22.
[9] *Vida,* cap. V.
[10] Ribera, *Vida de Santa Teresa,* I, cap. VII.

sister's body. He awoke with a start just in time to beat out the
fire before it wrapped her in a shroud of flames.

Yet after all this, when even Don Alonso admitted her death,
and the funeral was about to proceed, Teresa opened her eyes
and saw her father and brothers weeping by the bedside.[11]

"Why did you call me back?" she murmured.

What had her soul experienced during that long deathlike
trance? Afterward she remembered something like a vision of
heaven, in which she saw her father and Sister Juana Suárez
among the elect, thanks to her prayers and sufferings. She saw
communities of nuns organized through her efforts, she saw
many souls entering the blessed state on her account, and finally
she saw herself dying and going to enjoy God, and on her sepulcher a cloth of brocade. After telling this to her family, she tried
in humility to make them forget it, saying it was all *disparates y
frenesí,* the embroidery of her fevered brain; but holy and
learned men were convinced by subsequent events that she had
had a supernatural vision and not merely a dream. One of her
confessors affirmed that she had also seen the horrific reality of
hell.[12]

Teresa was in no condition at the time of her strange awak-
ening to discuss such matters in detail. "My tongue bitten to
pieces; my throat, from not having swallowed anything, and
from the great weakness that was choking me, for even water
could not pass. I seemed to be all disjointed, with the greatest
dizziness in my head. All shrunk together in a heap, for to this
end the torment of those days brought me, unable to move arm
or foot, or hand or head, but as if I had been dead, unless they
moved me; I could move only one finger, I think, of my right
hand. Then, as for touching me, not at all! For I was all so sore
that I could not stand it. They used to move me in a sheet, one
at one end and another at the other . . ."[13]

Yet with all this her first thought, on coming to herself, was
to go to Confession, this time with no objection on the part of
Don Alonso! Whatever she had seen during that living death

---

[11] *Loc. cit.*

[12] Yepes, Book I, cap. VI, following Ribera (*op. cit.,* I, VII). Padre Fray Domingo
Bañes, O.P., preaching in the college of the Discalced Carmelites, Salamanca, in
1587, gave the account of Teresa's vision of hell, and told Yepes he "knew it for
certain," presumably from the lips of the Saint herself. Ribera also relates this
of Bañes.

[13] *Vida,* cap. VI.

seared into her soul a conviction of how stained her humanity was in comparison with the immaculate beauty God desired it to wear, so that even years later she would tremble at the recollection. "My pains were unbearable, with which I retained little consciousness, although the confession [was] complete, in my opinion, of everything in which I understood I had offended God. For His Majesty gave me this favor, among others, that never, since I commenced to receive Communion, did I fail to confess anything that I might think was a sin, even though it might be venial, that I should fail to confess it. But without doubt I think that my salvation was in danger enough, if I had died then, on account of my confessors being so little learned on the one hand, and my being so wicked on the other, and for many [reasons]." After Confession she received Holy Communion, "with plenty of tears" over the fact that certain persons had told her that "certain things were not mortal sins, which I have since found to be certainly such[14] — a statement that most Teresian students take to be an exaggeration of humility.

On Palm Sunday, 1537, still in the same helpless and excruciating condition, she was carried across the city to the Incarnation, where the Prioress and the sisters welcomed her as one risen from the dead. All who looked on her were smitten with pity, for she was "nothing but bones." Nevertheless she regained some use of her limbs, little by little, until one day, to her great joy, she was able to crawl a bit on hands and knees and devoutly gave thanks to God. The paralysis continued, however, for three years, and the improvement was so slow that no one imagined she could ever take an active place in her community again. Yet Teresa desired to get well so that she could serve God better by praying in solitude as He had taught her to pray at Castellanos, and as she could not pray in the convent infirmary. Later she was ashamed of this motive, saying "This is our delusion; we do not resign ourselves absolutely to what God does, Who knows better what is good for us." The nuns were astonished and edified by her patience and by her angelic conversation, which was usually about God. They prayed for her, they had Masses said. Finally recourse was had to Saint Joseph. "I wish I could persuade everyone to be devoted to this glorious saint," said Teresa, "for I know from long experience the benefits he obtains from

---

[14] *Ibid.*, cap. V.

God. I have never known anyone who was truly **devoted** to him and performed particular services in his honor, who did not advance greatly in virtue." She always made some special request on his feast, March 19, and invariably obtained it, though not always in the form she had requested. "I only ask, for the love of God, that any who doubts what I say make a test of it himself, and he will see, from actual experience, the great benefit it is to commend oneself to this glorious Patriarch, and to have devotion to him."

At the end of the third year, Saint Joseph answered her prayer. She was completely cured of the paralysis and all the pains that accompanied it. Yet health brought other perils of such a nature that she was sometimes tempted to believe that it might have been just as well if she had remained paralyzed.

Chapter VI

A DARK NIGHT OF DIVINE AND TERRIBLE ADVENTURE

TERESA was able to walk, to pray, to work after a fashion, to resume her part in the routine of the community; but she was not restored to perfect health by any means. Saint Joseph had taken good care, in granting her request, not to deny and cancel that older prayer of her first days in Carmel, when she had deliberately asked for suffering if only it might lead her to the sublime realization of God. The next twenty years were a continual purgatory of physical, mental, and spiritual pain.

Every morning, from about her twenty-fourth to her forty-fourth year, she was seized with fits of vomiting, which sometimes had to be induced with a feather to relieve a suffocating sense of nausea and the almost unbearable pain that pressed upon her heart. Only then could she go about her duties; and she could never take food until after midday.[1]

This was not the worst. Mere physical sufferings to one heroic enough to ask for them were trifles compared to the buffets of that titanic warfare of the soul through which all the saints, sooner or later, have had to pass. "And lest the greatness of the revelations should exalt me," wrote Saint Paul, "there was given me a sting of my flesh, an angel of Satan to buffet me. For which thing thrice I besought the Lord, that it might depart from me. And he said to me: 'My grace is sufficient for thee; for power is made perfect in infirmity.' Gladly therefore will I glory in my infirmities, that the power of Christ may dwell in me. . . . For when I am weak, then I am powerful."[2] And again: "Our wrestling is not against flesh and blood, but against principalities and powers, against the rulers of the world of this darkness, against the spirits of wickedness in the high places."[3]

Teresa was beginning to understand what these words meant. When God invites a soul to follow Him to the heights of love, and that soul acquiesces, it does not become transformed in an instant from a human being, with all its frailties and passions

---

[1] *Vida*, cap. VII; as are all the quotations from Saint Teresa in this chapter.
[2] Cor. 12:7-10.
[3] Eph. 6:12.

of the flesh, into an angel of perfection. On the contrary, it sometimes begins to encounter staggering difficulties and temptations.
To reach the glory of a resurrection which brings a delightful
foretaste even in this world of the eternal heaven, the soul must
know hunger and want, neglect and misunderstanding, the sorrow and loneliness of a Gethsemani even God seems to have
forsaken, and a more or less protracted crucifixion of fleshly
desires, ambitions, and vanities. And so the poor soul struggles
and grows weary, rises to fall and falls to rise again, plunges on
and is driven back from dreadful crisis to more dreadful crisis,
at every moment appearing to be in danger of plummeting into
the abyss of everlasting failure and death. Nor is the only peril
from the treachery and perversity of one's own fallen nature.
The demons of hell, by no mere figure of speech but in the
most sinister actuality, take part against the soul that dares to
climb toward their lost eminence. They spy out its weaknesses
and thrust at them, and if this is unavailing, they flatter its
virtues, seeking to poison them into vices.

And what of God in all this? asks the skeptic; how is it that
when the soul has turned to Him, he allows it to be treated so
shamefully? Undoubtedly the All-Powerful could beat down
every opposition to the soul's aspirations and clasp it triumphantly to Himself. But in this there would be an element of
compulsion against the soul itself; the soul would not be free, and
therefore would not be godlike; and God will have only the
godlike united to His Godhood. He does not deal with souls as
the sculptor does with dumb marble, imprinting His idea upon
and within a dead cold material. Not the dead safety of an
automaton, which is slavery, but the living joyous freedom of a
god, is the destiny of the human soul. Its freedom consists of
perfect union of its will with that of God, Who alone is free.
It may refuse this; but if it freely accepts, it must then advance
along the way of its choice by suffering until all elements of its
enslavement to matter and to evil are purged away.

"The reason for which it is necessary for the soul, in order to
attain to Divine union with God, to pass through this dark night
of mortification of the desires and denial of pleasures in all
things," wrote Saint John of the Cross, "is because all the affections which it has for creatures are pure darkness in the eyes of
God, and when the soul is clothed in these affections, it has no
capacity for being enlightened and possessed by the pure and

simple light of God, if it cast them not first from it; for light cannot agree with darkness. . . .The reason is that two contraries (even as philosophy teaches us) cannot coexist in one person; and that darkness, which is affection for creatures, and light, which is God, are contrary to each other, and have no likeness or accord between one another. . . .

"In order that we may the better prove what has been said, it must be known that the affection and attachment which the soul has for creatures renders the soul like to these creatures; and the greater is its affection, the closer is the equality and likeness between them; for love creates a likeness between that which loves and that which is loved. . . . And thus, he that loves a creature becomes as low as is that creature, and, in some ways, lower; for love not only makes the lover equal to the object of his love, but even subjects him to it. Wherefore in the same way it comes to pass that the soul that loves anything else becomes incapable of pure union with God and transformation in Him. For the low estate of the creature is much less capable of union with the high estate of the Creator than is darkness with light. For all things of earth and heaven, compared with God, are nothing, as Jeremiah says in these words: *Aspexi terram, et ecce vacua erat, et nihil; et coelos, et non erat lux in eis.* I beheld the earth, he says, and it was void, and it was nothing; and the heavens, and saw that they had no light. In saying that he beheld the earth void, he means that all its creatures were nothing, and that the earth was nothing likewise. And, in saying that he beheld the heavens and saw no light in them, he says that all the luminaries of heaven, compared with God, are pure darkness. So that in this sense all the creatures are nothing; and their affections, we may say, are less than nothing, since they are an impediment to transformation in God and the loss thereof, even as darkness is not only nothing but less than nothing, since it is loss of light. And even as he that is in darkness comprehends not the light, so the soul that sets its affections upon creatures will be unable to comprehend God; and until it be purged, it will neither be able to possess Him here below, through pure transformation of love, nor yonder in clear vision."[4]

Teresa's first encounter in the lofty conflict ended in defeat, a defeat so subtle that she was not even aware of it for a long

---

[4] Saint John of the Cross, *Ascent of Mt. Carmel*, Bk. I, Chap. IV, from the text of Father Silverio by E. Allison Peers (London, 1934).

time; and the cause of her disaster was her ignorance of this principle of detachment from creatures. It was the most natural thing in the world that having recovered the use of her limbs, and some degree of health, she should enjoy the faculties so miraculously restored, and should take particular pleasure, as so many of the nuns of the Incarnation did, in the visits of friends and relatives. The conversations in the "speak room" were innocent enough, indeed they often had to do with God and the things of God. How was the young nun to know that if she loved them for her own gratification, and not for the love of God alone, they might lead her away from God? How could she learn, save by bitter experience, that in the contemplative life even the most innocent devotion to creatures might become disastrous?

One of her most frequent visitors was her father. Life had become increasingly lonely for him as one after another of his children left home: first María, to be married; then Rodrigo, to go to Peru; then Teresa to the convent; then two more boys, Antonio and Hernando, to the New World; and finally, by 1540, Pedro, Lorenzo, and Jerónimo also were there — six sons in all, soldiers in daily peril, whom he would never see again on earth. He used to walk often to the monastery of Saint Thomas, to confess to the Dominican father, Fray Vicente Barrón; but the chief delight and consolation of his existence, it is safe to say, was to visit his daughter at the Incarnation. No doubt they had long talks about family affairs and about the absent ones, and certainly, from Teresa's account, they spoke much of God, and of the brief vanity of all worldly things. Don Alonso was so interested in what she told him of her progress in mental prayer, through the aid of the *Abecedario*, that he desired to learn the art himself. It was not long before he was valiantly struggling up the steep and thorny path she showed him, and tasting its incomparable delights and desolations. In the course of the next five or six years he advanced so far that he began to cut short even his visits to the Incarnation, that he might have more time to converse with God.

Oddly enough, while Teresa was encouraging him to continue in the prayer without words, she herself was giving it up little by little, without letting him know, until at last she had altogether ceased. She had become the victim of her friends.

"I began to go from pastime to pastime, from vanity to vanity, from one occasion to another, and to place myself so much in very great dangers of temptation, and to have my soul so corrupted in many vanities, that already I was ashamed to approach God again in such a particular friendship as it is to converse with mental prayer; and what helped me in this was that as my sins increased, my taste for and delight in the things of virtue began to fail. I saw very clearly, *Señor mio,* that this failed me because I failed You. This was the most terrible deception that the devil could practise upon me, under the pretext of humility, to make me begin to fear to pray mentally, on seeing myself so lost; and I thought it was better to do as the many did, since in being wicked I was one of the worst, and to say the prayers I was obliged to say, and vocally, and not to practise mental prayers, and so much conversation with God, she who deserved to be with the devils, and who was deceiving the people; for outwardly I kept up good appearances. And so the house where I was is not to blame, for I managed with my cunning that they should have a good opinion of me, though not knowingly pretending Christianity; for in this matter of hypocrisy and vainglory, glory to God, I never remember having offended Him. . . . This not deeming me so wicked came from their seeing me so young, and in so many temptations, and often retiring to solitude to pray and read much, speaking of God, fond of having His image painted in many places and of having an oratory and of obtaining for it things that would cause devotion, not speaking evil, other things of this sort, which had the appearance of virtue; and how vain I was to make myself esteemed in the things that in the world are usually held dear!"

In spite of her low opinion of her own character, it was so highly regarded in the convent that she was given more liberty than any of the other nuns, even the oldest. In admitting this, she naïvely adds that she never took advantage of it to do anything without permission, or to speak with anybody "through holes, or through walls, or at nighttime." She never even spoke of such things, "for the Lord held me by His hand." What she did for a while, it would seem, was to follow the course of least resistance, to drift with the tide, to do only what she had to do and no more. The danger of this was that there is no standing still in the spiritual life: if the soul is not going forward, it is going backward.

Realistic and objective as always in analyzing her acts and emotions, Teresa does not blame herself alone: she cites the fact that the nuns of the Incarnation were not cloistered. There was no reason, of course, why they should have been, for they had taken no vow of enclosure. She hastens to add that it was not one of the most relaxed houses, but well disciplined, and blessed with many who were seeking perfection. Nevertheless the lack of enclosure was a serious handicap to the more spiritual members of the community. Here again she falls into the hyperbole of a great humility: "As for me, who am so wicked, I should certainly have been carried to hell, if the Lord, with His very especial favors and remedies, had not taken me out of this danger; and so I think the very greatest [danger] is a monastery of women with liberty, and I think it is more like a road to hell, for those desiring to be wicked, than a remedy for their weaknesses. . . . If parents would take my advice, since they won't take the trouble to put their daughters where they may go the way of salvation, but with more danger than in the world, let them look to what touches their honor; and let them marry them very humbly rather than put them in such monasteries — unless they are very well inclined, and please God it may avail them — or else keep them at home. For if she desires to be wicked, she can cover it up only a short time, but there very much, and, in the end, the Lord discovers it; and she hurts not only herself, but everybody; and sometimes the poor little things are not to blame, for they go after what they find. And a pity it is of many who wish to separate themselves from the world, and thinking they are going to serve the Lord and be apart from the dangers of the world, they find themselves in ten worlds all put together, so that they know not how to help or remedy themselves, and youth and sensuality and the devil invite them and incline them to follow certain things which are of the world itself. Behold, they consider it good, so to speak! It seems to me like those wretches of heretics, in part, who try to blind themselves and to make themselves think that what they follow is good, and who thus believe it so, without believing it, for within themselves they have something that tells them it is evil."

This is the middle-aged Teresa speaking. The nun of twenty-six, feeling comparative health flowing through her limbs again, was not capable of such an analysis of her condition. For the temptation that had come upon her was of the subtle kind that assails those who have passed beyond the danger of ordinary carnal offense. When the Enemy of Man cannot conquer a soul through passions and weaknesses, he appeals to the virtues. Teresa was affectionate in the extreme; she loved truth and hated hypocrisy. Very craftily, then, the devil began reminding her of the affection others had for her, and argued that it was her duty to pay them back in the same coin. When he had thus entangled her in vain and useless conversations, he represented that a person given to such pastimes had no right to seek familiar intercourse with God in mental prayer; it was only pride and presumption in her. It was not just, indeed it was false and hypocritical to deceive people by letting them think she was a truly spiritual person, while all the time she was indulging her natural taste for human society and gossip. And after all, why should she give up conversations that were not mortal sins, when she could continue to enjoy them, be a good nun, say her vocal prayers, and keep the law of God?[5]

There was an old nun at the Incarnation, a relative of hers (possibly Doña Juana del Aguila, or Doña María Cimbrón),[6] who felt that the young convalescent's friendships had dangerous possibilities, and begged her, not once but many times, to give them up. She was "a great servant of God, and deeply religious"; yet "I not only didn't believe her, but I was disgusted with her, and I thought she was disturbing herself for no good reason."

The conversations continued, and the number of Teresa's friends increased. One day she was talking with a certain person with whom she had just become acquainted — she does not say whether it was a man or a woman, and there seems to be no evidence for the conjecture[7] that it was Don Francisco de Guzmán, son of Mosén Rubí de Bracamonte — when an extraordinary thing happened. Suddenly she became aware of the presence of Christ in the room, looking at her with great severity, as if to indicate disapproval of her conversing with that person. "I saw Him with the eyes of my soul more clearly than I could see Him with those of the body, and it remained so imprinted upon me, that though this was more than twenty-six years ago, I think I still have it before me. I remained very astonished, and disturbed, and I did not wish to see any more the one with whom I was."

[5] This is the explanation of both Ribera (*Vida de Santa Teresa,* lib. I, cap. VII) and Yepes (lib. I, cap. VII).

[6] Cf. Silverio (*Vida de Santa Teresa de Jesús,* I, p. 304).

[7] Father Gabriel's *Vida gráfica,* t. II, 271–276. Silverio (*op. cit.,* I, 305, n. I) does not agree.

In the days that followed she reasoned herself out of this state of mind in such a way as to furnish proof, without intending to do so, that she was neither a deluded hysterical person, nor a fraud. If she had been the psychopath that some skeptics have tried to make of her, she would have sought to convince herself of the reality of what she had seen, and would have become more and more insistent upon it; and if she had been a pseudomystic, her behavior would have betrayed the fact. But Teresa's conduct was that of a sane, honest, and well-balanced Catholic. This was the first time anything of the sort had occurred to her. She was unaware that it was possible to have an "imaginary vision," or as she puts it, "to see anything except with the eyes of the body." Hence she argued with herself that she must have had an hallucination, that she had not really seen anything. She had heard that the devil sometimes deceives people in such ways, and she resolutely rejected any subjective impression that God had been warning her, as an assumption not capable of proof. Presently she was conversing with the same person again; the friendship became very dear to her, and this went on for some years. And then another strange thing occurred.

She was talking with the same person one day when "we saw coming toward us (and other persons who were there also saw it) something like a great toad, which moved more lightly than they usually do. I could not understand how such a disgusting reptile could have come from where it came from, in the middle of the day, nor had it ever before, and the effect it had on me, I think, was rather mysterious; and this also I never forgot."

Yet once more she persuaded herself that whatever might be the cause of this phenomenon, it had nothing to do with her conversations, since these were not sinful in themselves, and she continued as before. Perhaps a great shock of some sort would be necessary to startle her from her complacency, and to bring her back to the contemplative life for which apparently she had a vocation and a mission. At any rate, the shock was in preparation, and it was to come through one she loved very dearly.

Her father, now in his late sixties, was aging rapidly. This had been noticeable for some time, and his conversations had increasingly concerned the affairs of his soul, and his hopes of the world to come. Under Teresa's instructions he had made great progress in the prayer of quiet, and this delighted her, even after she herself had given up the practice. "He advanced so far that I praised the Lord much, and it gave me the greatest consolation. Very great were the troubles he had, in many ways; all of them he endured with the greatest resignation. He came often to see me, for it consoled him to talk of the things of God.

"Even after I became so ruined, and without having mental prayer, I could not bear to disillusion him when I saw that he thought I was what I used to be; for I was a year and more without mental prayer, thinking it greater humility. And this, as I shall afterwards tell, was the greatest temptation I had, and through it I was on my way to a bad end; for with the prayer I would offend God one day and on others recollect myself again and withdraw myself more from the occasion. When, with this, the blessed man came, thinking that I was conversing with God as I was accustomed to do, it was too much for me to see him so deceived, and I told him I was no longer having prayer, but not the reason. I put forward my infirmities as the obstacle."

Honest Don Alonso had no difficulty in believing that mental prayer was out of the question for one who suffered from daily vomitings, headaches, fevers, sharp pains in the region of the heart. "And my father believed me, for he never told a lie himself. I told him that he might the more believe it, that I had enough to do to be able to serve in the choir." So Don Alonso kept coming to the convent, and telling his daughter, with all the simplicity of a sincere and devout man, of his meditations and their results. Nor was he the only one who confided to Teresa and profited by her instruction. Several others learned the art of mental prayer from her, and she persuaded herself that in this way she was making amends for the neglect into which her false humility had led her.

One day toward the end of 1543, when Teresa was twenty-eight, the old man did not come for his usual visit. She learned that he had been smitten with a sharp pain in his shoulders, which never left him day or night. Was it some rheumatic affliction, or was it *angina pectoris?* Whatever the cause, he took to his bed, and a few days later, although the doctors found his condition much better and thought he would recover, he seemed to have a presentiment that death was at hand. A message was sent to the Incarnation; and Teresa, with her superior's permission, went to stay again at the somber house on the hill.

Her own body was racked with pains and misery as she hastened to her father's bedside to comfort and console him;

moreover, a sense of futility and shame had settled upon her in consequence of her abandonment of mental prayer; but there was much to be done in that house, and she felt that she was re-paying her father, in some measure, for all the trouble he had taken with her during her long illness. He was the human being she most loved in the world — in losing him she would be losing "all the comfort and joy" of her life. When the pain in his shoulder troubled him most, she would encourage him by re-minding him that he had always been especially devoted to that part of our Lord's Passion in which He carried His cross. This must have wounded His shoulder and pierced it with pain; was He not allowing Don Alonso to share in it? Thinking of this, the sick man would lie silent, praying, and from then on he com-plained no more.

The moment for which he had been waiting now seemed im-minent. Fray Vicente Barrón came from the monastery of Saint Thomas to hear his confession, and to give him Viaticum and Extreme Unction. In the serene interval after he had been an-nointed with the holy oil, the old cavalier asked to have his family assembled about his bedside, to hear his last words of advice. It was one of those heroic scenes repeated again and again in the homes of Catholic Spain throughout the ages. María perhaps had come from Castellanos with her husband; and Juan perhaps, the eldest of all. Most of the others were thousands of miles away. But Teresa was there in her black and white robes; and with her, no doubt, the younger children, Agustín, who was eighteen, and Juana, seventeen. It was December 21, 1543.[8]

The dying man began to speak. He had come to the end of his life, and he charged them all to look upon him, and notice how everything in the world comes to an end. Let them commend him to God, and beg for mercy for him when he could not speak for himself, and let them always serve God, for nothing else was of any importance; indeed, he now thought, in the extreme weakness of this hour, that if he had his life to start over again, he would join the most strict religious order he could find, and do nothing all his days but praise and serve God. This he said with tears. If only he had served God better! Well, now he was about to die, and he gave them all his blessing.

After that he lost consciousness, and for three days was either comatose or delirious.

---

[8] P. Silverio, *op. cit.*, I, p. 256.

On the third day he awoke, so lucid in the mind that they were all amazed. They knelt to say the usual prayers. Don Alonso began reciting the Credo:

"I believe in one God, maker of heaven and earth, and of all things visible and invisible, and in one Lord Jesus Christ, the only-begotten Son of God, born of the Father before all ages; God of God, light of light, true God of true God; begotten not made; consubstantial with the Father, by Whom all things were made; Who for us men, and for our salvation, came down from heaven, and was incarnate by the Holy Ghost of the Virgin Mary, and was made man. He was crucified also for us. . . ."

The feeble voice trailed off into a whisper, and then stopped altogether.

"At the middle of the *Credo,* saying the same, he expired," wrote Teresa. "He remained like an angel; and I thought, for my part, he was one, after a manner of speaking, in soul and disposition, for he had a very good one. . . . I thought my soul was wrenched from my body when I saw him finish his life, for I loved him much." It was a consolation to hear Fray Vicente Barrón, her father's confessor, say he had no doubt the good man had gone straight to heaven.

Teresa liked this Dominican so well that she asked him to hear her confession, and she told him not only her sins, or what she considered to be her sins, but her experience with mental prayer, and her reasons for having given it up for a year and a half. He was a man of sense, alert as well as holy; not like some of those well-meaning confessors, who had caused her so much torment by advising her to be content with the minimum her duty required, instead of the heroic effort she felt called to by an interior voice. Possibly he went to the Incarnation to hear her confession after her father's funeral. Or she may have been allowed to go to the monastery of Saint Thomas, where even to this day, in the Chapel of Christ in the Agony, the friars point out an inscription: *"Here Saint Teresa went to Confession."* However that may be, Barrón was the director she had long been looking for. Her first remark about him was that he was *muy gran letrado.* She prized intelligence and learning above all other qualities in her confessors, and she had a peculiar distrust of holy men who were stupid.

"This Dominican father, who was very good and God fearing, did me plenty of good, for I confessed to him and he undertook the direction of my soul with great care, and made me understand the perdition which I had been following. He made me receive Holy Communion every two weeks; and discussing my affairs with him little by little, I told him of my prayer. He told me not to give it up, for in no way could it do me anything but good. I began to resume it, and although I did not give up the occasions of sin, I never left off again."

It was a great happiness to find one who understood her so well, and who could place her feet so securely again on the high road. But if the shock of grief over her father's death, and the wise counsel of Fray Vicente had broken the evil spell that bound her to useless vanities, and left her free to raise her heart to God, the conflict of invisible powers that had so long racked and divided her was not by no means ended. On the contrary, her victory over herself did exactly what anyone with the slightest knowledge of such matters would expect: it incited the enemies of her soul to new and fiercer efforts; it set in motion another phase of conflict that tried her powers of resistance to the last degree, and brought her to an abyss of suffering and persecution in which, humanly speaking, there seemed to be waiting for her nothing but defeat and despair.

Chapter VII

TWENTY YEARS OF CONFLICT

I WAS passing a most miserable life, for in prayer I was getting to understand my faults better. On the one hand God was calling me. On the other I was following the world. The things of God gave me great pleasure. Those of the world held me bound fast. I think I was desirous of reconciling those two contraries, so opposed one to the other as is the spiritual life to the pleasures, satisfactions, and sensual pastimes. In prayer I endured great suffering, because the spirit walked not as master but as slave; and so I was unable to shut myself within myself, which was my whole method of proceeding in carrying on mental prayer, without shutting in with me a thousand vanities. So I passed many years, and now it astonishes me that anyone was able to endure it without giving up one or the other. Well I know that to give up prayer was not in my hand, but in His who wished to do me great favors."

One of the worst of her sufferings was a sense at times of utter loneliness. "A great evil it is for a soul to be alone amid so many perils. I think that if I had someone with whom to discuss all this, it would have helped me not to fall again, if only through shame — since I didn't have any before God. On this account I would advise those who use mental prayer, especially at the beginning, to be friendly and converse with other persons who do the same. It is a thing most important, even though it be but to aid one another with their prayers — how much the more so when there are many more advantages!" Here Teresa observes, in a sentence too awkward and involved for translation, that worldly people have full liberty to compare notes on *their* desires, and asks why, then, the same privilege should not be granted to a lover and servant of God? "For if it is truly friendship that he wishes to have with His Majesty, let him not be afraid of vainglory; and when the first movement assails him, he will come out of the affair with merit. . . . I think the devil has made use of this stratagem, as a thing which is very useful to him, that those who really try to love and please God should so much hide themselves from being understood, while he has incited others of dishonorable intentions to confide in one another, so much so that the offenses thus committed against God, with being so customary, are held to be fashionable and made public. . . . The things that are of service to God are now so neglected that those who serve Him must stand shoulder to shoulder, to go forward, just as it is considered good to walk in the vanities and pleasures of the world, and for these[1] there are few eyes; and if one commences to give oneself to God, there are so many who murmur, that one must seek company to defend oneself, until they[2] become strong enough so that suffering doesn't bother them any more; and if not they will see themselves in a tight fix.[3] I think this must be why some saints go into the deserts. And it is a kind of humility not to trust in oneself, but to believe that God will aid one, with those with whom one converses; and charity grows by being communicated. And there are a thousand blessings which I would not dare to speak of, if I hadn't had great experience of how much there is in this. True it is that I am more weak and good for nothing than all who have been born. Yet I believe that no one will lose who will humble himself, however strong he may be, and trust not in himself but in others who have had experience. Of myself I can say that if the Lord had not disclosed this truth to me, and given me the means to talk very frequently with persons who had mental prayer, I should have gone on falling and rising until I stumbled into hell. For I had many friends who would help me to fall. But when it came to lifting me up again, I found myself so alone that I wonder even now why I did not remain fallen forever, and I praise the mercy of God, for it was only He Who gave me His hand. . . .[4]

"I passed through this tempestuous sea for almost twenty years, with these falls, and with getting up, and [doing it] badly, and then falling again. And in my life [I was] so far from

---

[1] *y para estos hay pocos ojos* (*Vida*, cap. VII, p. 52). The reference of *estos* is not clear. Both Canon Dalton and Mr. Lewis translate it as referring to the "vanities and pleasures," but both take great liberty with the phrase. Canon Dalton: "few see any evil in them." Mr. Lewis: "few there are who regard them with unfavorable eyes." What Teresa wrote was merely, "and for these there are few eyes."

[2] Teresa shifts here from the singular to the plural; it is characteristic of her hasty writing. My translation of this paragraph can be criticized on the ground that it is "not good English." It certainly is not; nor is the original good Spanish. If the reader will be patient, he will be rewarded by his pleasure in following Saint Teresa's improvement.

[3] *"veranse en mucho aprieto"*

[4] *Vida*, cap. VII, p. 53.

perfection that I took almost no account of venial sins; and as for the mortal ones, although I feared them, it was not as it should have been, since I did not keep away from the occasions. I can say that it is one of the most painful kinds of life that I think can be imagined, for neither did I enjoy God nor did I take pleasure in the world. When I was in the diversions of the world, the memory of what I owed God gave me sorrow. When I was with God, the affections of the world disquieted me. This is a warfare so tormenting that I don't know how I could have endured it for a month, let alone so many years. With all this I see clearly the great mercy the Lord showed me, that having to converse in the world so much, I had the courage to keep on with mental prayer. I say courage, for I don't know what in the world could require more [courage] than to plot treason against the King, and to know that He knows it, and never to quit His sight. For although we are always in the presence of God, it seems to me it is otherwise with those who practise mental prayer, for there they are, *seeing* that He observes them, while others can be there [in His presence] for days at a time and never even remember that God sees them."[5]

Thus "the war," as she called it, went on year after year. She never wholly relinquished the thread — and sometimes how fragile it seemed — that bound her to God; yet she was never able to give herself to Him without reserve, as in her heart of hearts she desired to do. She was still shackled by the invisible bonds of friendship, of pity, of charity, perhaps now and then of a sort of vanity. She was the prisoner of a thousand invisible foes — scruples over her past offenses, fears of being presump-tuous, the dread of failure and of hell. Sermons tormented her; for although she delighted in the better ones and never failed to find some benefit in the worst, they always reminded her of her infinite goal and the gulf that still lay before her, until at last she could call herself, in a passage whose words of burning love and humility came tumbling out too fast for rhetorical nicety, "so filthy and stinking a dung heap."[6] She who was summoned to be the bride of eternal Love was still the handmaid of time. Even after she had forced herself, against all the allurements of sense, human perversity, and sly contriving devil, to surrender to

---

[5] *Ibid.*, cap. VIII. My italics.
[6] *"un muladar tan sucio y de mal olor"* — *Ibid.*, cap. X, p. 74.

mental prayer, she found herself listening for the clock to strike, and wishing for something else to do.

All this seems to make "mental prayer" sound like a complex, disagreeable, and dangerous experiment, which only a few intrepid souls should dare attempt. Yet Teresa insists that it is a very simple matter. It is made difficult only by our cowardice and self-love; put these aside, and it is as natural as breathing, something that everybody could do and ought to do. We belong to God. He made us. He loves us. In return let us love Him with simplicity and sincerity. And that, in essence (she seems to say), is true prayer.

"Mental prayer is nothing else, in my opinion, but friendly conversation, frequently conversing alone, with One Who we know loves us." It is attained simply by rising above the pain we feel, imperfect as we are, at being in the presence of a Being Whom we cannot yet love as His perfection deserves. Sometimes she had to drive herself to prayer against an unseen malicious opposition. In such arid moments she would humbly think of her offenses against God, of heaven and hell, of the great debt she owed Him and of the sorrows He had endured for her.[7] And invariably He would come to her aid at last, and give her more peace and joy than when her prayer was easy.

"I had this method of prayer, that since I could not meditate with the understanding, I would try to represent Christ within me. And I used to fare better, in my opinion, in those places where I saw Him most alone. I thought that being alone and afflicted Himself, He was likely to admit me as a person in need. Of these simplicities I had many. Especially in the prayer in the Garden I used to find myself very well — there went I to keep Him company. I used to think on that sweat and agony that He had there. I used to desire, if I could, to wipe from Him that grievous sweat, but I remember that I never dared make up my mind to do it, since my sins stood before me so heavy."[8]

Many years before, in the convent of the Augustinians, the girl Teresa had formed the habit of thinking of Christ in Gethsemani just before she fell asleep. Now, in her thirties, the mature woman still saw Him thus. But it was a different kind of "seeing." She is careful to explain that she did not see Him as in a vision, clearly; nor, on the other hand, did she merely

---

[7] *Ibid.,* cap. VIII, p. 58.
[8] *Ibid.,* cap. IX, p. 64.

imagine Him. "I had such little skill for representing things with my understanding, that unless I saw it before me, my imagination was no help to me. . . . I could think of Christ only as a man; but so it is, that no matter how much I read of His beauty, and saw images of Him, I never could represent Him in myself, except as one does who is blind or in the dark, who, although he speaks with a person, and sees that he is with him, for he knows of a certainty that he is there — I say he understands and believes that he is there, but does not see him."[9]

Teresa was fond of pictures because they helped her imagine the Presence of which she had so positive an awareness. She could neither understand nor condone the Protestant contempt for holy images. "Unfortunate those who lose this benefit through their own fault!" she cried. "Indeed it seems that they do not love the Lord, for if they loved Him, they would rejoice to see His picture, even as here below it gives pleasure to see that of a well-beloved person."

Mental prayer, in her opinion, is for anybody who loves God sincerely enough to try it. One may not succeed at first, but persistence is sure to be rewarded. No matter if the disposition of such a soul is imperfect; "if she perseveres in it, whatever sins and temptations and faults of a thousand kinds the devil may put in her way, I hold it certain that at last the Lord will take her to the port of salvation, as, from present appearances, He has taken me. . . . I can say from my own experience that whoever has begun it, let him not give it up, whatever sins he may commit; for it is the means by which he can make himself whole again, and without it, this will be much more difficult. And let not the devil tempt him, as he did me, to forgo it through humility; let him believe that His words cannot fail; that in truly repenting and being determined not to offend Him, we will again have the friendship we had before, and He will grant us favors as before, and sometimes much greater ones,

[9] *Ibid.*, cap. IX, B.M.C., p. 65. As usual Saint Teresa is precise and objective in reporting and analyzing her own sensations. There is nothing here to support the theory that she suffered from hallucinations! On the other hand, Mrs. Cunningham-Grahame falls into the error, in her brilliant study, of assuming from this passage that Teresa merely *imagined* our Lord near her, and was aware that He was not really there. This opinion fails to notice the careful distinction made by the Saint. Mrs. Cunningham-Grahame did not understand the supernatural in the life of her subject when she wrote her book. Later she became a Catholic, and at the close of her life left many corrections, which her husband refused or neglected to have made.

if the repentance merits it. And whoever has not yet commenced, for the love of the Lord I beg him not to go without so great a blessing! There is nothing here to fear, only to desire; for even if he should not advance, or strive to be perfect, that he may deserve the delights and gratifications that God gives to those people, at the very least he will begin to understand the road to heaven, and follow it; and if he perseveres, I trust in the mercy of God, for nobody takes Him for a friend *without being requited for it.*"[10]

Teresa had not attained this certitude at thirty, nor yet at thirty-five; nor even when she entered upon her fortieth year, with the struggle still raging in the unseen world about her. "My soul began to grow weary," she wrote of that time when, already middle aged, sick almost with despair, she still clung to her pursuit of God without utterly giving herself to Him. Frequently, to bring herself to the right disposition for mental prayer, she would read in some good book. It may have been that *Abecedario* of Osuna, who had first introduced her to mystical theology with such words as these: "Thou, brother, if thou desirest better to hit the mark, seek God in thy heart; do not go outside thyself, for He is nearer to thee and more within thee than thou art thyself."[11]

Yet at other times she found more instruction and delight in the visible creation about her. "It helped me also to see the fields or water, flowers. In these things, and in my ingratitude and sins, I found a reminder of the Creator, something, I mean, that woke me and recollected me and served as a book."[12]

She was devoted particularly to saints who had been sinners before their conversions, thinking, in her humility, that such ought to take more interest in the plight of Teresa the sinner. "It seemed to me that since the Lord had pardoned them, He could me — save that one thing discouraged me: . . . that the Lord had called them only once and they had not fallen again, and mine were already so many that this fatigued me. But thinking on the love He had for me, I again took courage, for of His mercy I never doubted; of myself many times."

One of her favorite reformed saints was King David. Another

---

[10] *Ibid.*, cap. VIII, p. 57. The phrase in italics (*que no se lo pagase*) was inserted by Fray Luis de León, Saint Teresa having left the sentence unfinished.

[11] *Trat.* XXI, cap. VI.

[12] *Vida*, cap. IX, p. 65.

was Mary Magdalen. Ever since she had discovered the generous spirit of the sinner of Bethany in the burning pages of the *Abecedario*, during that memorable winter at Castellanos, she had thought of herself as another such penitent, crouching heart-broken at the feet of Christ, anointing His feet, washing them with her tears, wiping them with her hair. As for Saint Augustine, she had not lived in the convent of his order in Ávila without learning to know him, to love him, and to pray to him. She had never read his *Confessions*, perhaps because she was not sufficiently versed in Latin. Now at last a copy of the famous book was given to her, translated into "Romance" by the Augustinian Father, Sebastian Toscano, and first published in Salamanca in 1554.[13]

Her interest in the two saints most famous for preconversion offenses against the Sixth Commandment has been pounced upon with unholy joy by a certain school of criticism which can think of sin only in connection with sex, even while it commonly denies that any sin is involved. Teresa had a broader understanding of the subject. Sin, she was well aware, is in essence the opposition of the individual will to the will of God. Adultery is a sin not because the act involved is evil in itself (quite the contrary), but because it disturbs the divine harmony that has decreed proper ends for a function, and the sacramental union of one man and one woman. The Church has been even more severe against the four offenses which "cry to heaven for vengeance": willful murder, sodomy, oppression of the poor, and defrauding the laborer of his wages. But in all sin the essential malice is disobedience; and Teresa saw this, of course, not only through the eyes of Catholic sanity, but with the childlike clarity of a pure and virginal soul, with the innocence that penetrates the depths of heaven and hell. She was drawn to Saint Augustine and Saint Mary Magdalen not because they had broken any particular commandment, nor even because in breaking one they had broken all; but because, after resisting the will and the grace of God, they had been forgiven and had become saints. She also had resisted giving up her "vanities and conversations"; she also had resisted the invitation to mental prayer. And it was with no ordinary emotion of recognition and sympathy that she encountered, in the famous *Confessions*, the almost despairing words of Saint Augustine:

---

[13] P. Silverio, *Vida de Santa Teresa de Jesús*, I, p. 336, n. 1.

"And Thou, Lord, till when? Till when, Lord, wilt Thou be displeased? Will there be no end to Thy wrath: Wilt Thou not wish to forget our former offenses? For I felt myself to be in their power, and I used to utter miserable cries. Till when? Tomorrow! Tomorrow! Why not now? Why can I not accomplish in this hour the end of my torpor? Such things I spoke, and wept with bitter contrition of heart. And at that moment I heard a voice from the house that stood near by, with a singing which said and repeated it many times, as if it were a boy or a girl, I don't know which, 'Take, read: take, read': and I suddenly, my face altered, began to think very attentively if by chance the children used to sing such a song in some game, and could not remember having heard it anywhere, and I arose, understanding that it could be nothing else than a divine command to me, that I should open the book and read the first chapter that I encountered. . . ."

Teresa seemed to hear the same voice calling to her. "When I began to read the *Confessions,* I thought I saw myself there, and I commenced to commend myself much to this glorious saint. When I arrived at his conversion, and read how he heard the voice in the Garden, I could not but think, from what my heart felt, that the Lord was speaking to me. For a long time I was wholly dissolved in tears, and within me great affliction and fatigue. Oh what a soul suffers, God help me, in losing the liberty it must have to be mistress of itself, and what torments it endures! I wonder now how I could live in such torment; God be praised, Who gave me life to emerge from so mortal a death."[14]

About the same time — toward the end of 1555, it would seem — there was to be a festival in the Convent of the Incarnation, and some friend of the community donated a painting of Christ, which was set up in the oratory. Teresa went alone one day to see it. It was uncommonly well done and lifelike; it showed the Saviour in His Passion, wounded and bleeding. She looked at His torn hands and feet, His gashed side, His crown of thorns, His patient suffering face. These injuries He had taken upon Himself for her, out of love and pity for her, the wretched sinner who had been dallying and temporizing between His will and the attractions of the world. The thought of her ingratitude, as Yepes says, was like a ray of light from above that pierced her

<hr>

[14] *Vida,* cap. IX, B.M.C., p. 66.

to the heart, and she threw herself on the floor before Him, weeping, and imploring Him to set her free from the chains that bound her. "My Lord and my God," she cried, "I will not get up from here until You grant me this favor!"[15]

It was a decisive moment in her life, that cry from the heart. The last traces of vanity and self-love seemed to have fallen away from her, as the sins of the Magdalen had withered under the searching eyes of Christ. She was free at last, free from herself, free from the world, the flesh, and the devil. Free at last she was, in her own phrase, to be "a servant of love!"[16]

When finally, after many years, Teresa was able to recall these experiences calmly and objectively, and to apply to them her remarkable gift of self-observation and analysis, she jotted down rapidly in the course of her autobiography what is still perhaps the best treatise ever written on mental prayer.[17] She then saw that her own progress in the science of love had led her through four stages or degrees, which she carefully differentiated for the benefit of all who might wish to follow her. With the instinct of a poet she seized for illustration upon the metaphor that had been in her mind ever since, as a girl, she had cried out with the Samaritan woman at the well, "Lord, give me this water, that I may not thirst!" Water, lovely, cleansing, refreshing, life-giving water had been to her, ever since, the symbol of God's grace; so satisfying, yet so ignored and despised; had for the asking, yet so seldom asked for. She thought of her soul as a garden, in which her Lord desired to rest and be loved: the weeds must first be plucked up by the roots, the soil must be prepared, but most of all, water was needed if anything delightful was to grow.

"It seems to me that it can be watered in four ways: either (1) by drawing the water out of a well, which is great labor for us; or (2) with a wheel and buckets for hoisting it with a windlass (I have sometimes done it) is less trouble than the other and brings up more water; or (3) from a river or *arroyo* — this irrigates much better, for the ground remains more full of water and it is not necessary to irrigate so often and it is much less work for the gardener; or (4) with a good rain by which the

---

[15] Yepes, *Vida de Santa Teresa*, lib. I, cap. IX. The Saint says substantially this, in indirect discourse (*Vida*, cap. IX).

[16] Yepes (*op. cit.*, lib. I, cap. X) says that at this point Teresa attained what the doctors of mystical theology call the prayer of quiet.

[17] *Vida*, cap. XI to cap. XXII, inclusive.

Lord irrigates it without any effort on our part, and this is incomparably better than all I have said."[18]

So it is with the four degrees of mental prayer, as Teresa carefully distinguishes them in chapters XI to XXII of her autobiography.

In the *first degree* the soul is seeking for recollection and quiet. Here it can help itself. Memory, understanding, and will are all employed; nor should one try to suspend the understanding, for reading and good resolves are of help. The prayer consists of *loving,* and this is most easily done by placing oneself in the presence of Christ, loving Him in His sacred humanity, and, if possible, thinking of Him *within* oneself, preferably in some phase of His passion, as for example being scourged at the pillar. This requires courage at first. One must grieve for one's sins, weep for them if possible; and above all (for the test of love is sympathy) be ready to share in the sufferings of Christ, to drink His chalice, to help bear His cross. Here Teresa touches upon the mystery Saint Paul referred to in those puzzling words, "I Paul am made a minister, who now rejoice in my sufferings for you, and fill up *those things that are wanting of the sufferings of Christ,* in my flesh, for his body, which is the church."[19] Here is the clear Catholic doctrine of the Mystical Body. Christ asked His disciples to join Him in His sufferings as well as in His peace and His joy. "And he that taketh not up his cross, nor followeth me, is not worthy of me. . . ."[20] "If any man will come after me, let him deny himself, and *take up his cross daily,* and follow me."[21] Plainly it was Christ's teaching that His followers (the members of His Mystical Body, the Church) could and should aid Him in saving themselves and others. Christ is to suffer in His members that thereby the Mystical Body may be built up. Luther completely missed the point — hence his false teaching on the futility of good works. But Saint Paul understood it well; and so did Saint Teresa. "All who wish to follow Christ must walk the way He went."[22]

---

[18] *Vida,* cap. XI, B.M.C., p. 78. I have inserted the numbers for the sake of clarity. Teresa might have found the figure of the garden in the Old Testament as well as in the New. The Prophet Isaias, for example, promised the just: Thou shalt be like a watered garden and like a fountain of water whose water shall not fail (58:11).

[19] Col. 1:23–24. My italics.

[20] Matt. 10:38.

[21] Luke 9:23. My italics.

[22] *Vida,* cap. XI.

Our Lord lets us bear part of the weight of His cross, then, and naturally this means suffering. The beginner in prayer must expect this. He will experience not only regret for his sins and his own unworthiness, but loneliness, disgust, "dryness," a feeling that what he is doing is futile and unprofitable. Did not Christ experience this desolation? The novice, then should be willing to share in the same necessary experience, even if the "dryness" should last all his life, and "not let Christ fall with the cross. . . ." As for the troubles involved, "I know they are very great," adds Teresa, "and I think they call for more courage than many other troubles of the world. But I have seen clearly that God does not leave them without great reward even in this life, for certain it is that one hour of those the Lord has given me in the enjoyment of Himself seemed afterwards, down here, to have paid for all the anguishes I endured in persevering in prayer for a long time. I hold for my part that the Lord wishes to give these torments and many other temptations that occur, often in the beginning and sometimes later on, to try out His lovers, and to find out if they can drink the chalice and help Him to carry the cross before He commits to them great treasures. And I believe that His Majesty wishes to carry us that way for our good that we may well understand the little we are; for the favors of afterwards are so divine that before He gives them He wants us to see our wretchedness through experience, that it may not befall us as it did to Lucifer."[23]

Let the lovers of Christ then embrace the Cross and think nothing of their troubles. Let them not ask for consolations or rewards, but leave such matters in the hands of God.[24] Above all (and this is so important that she repeats it over and over) they should aspire to no higher degree of prayer, but be willing to remain where they are unless it please God to raise them. To attempt to suspend the understanding and induce some higher form of prayer is dangerous, especially for women, "for the devil could cause some illusion."[25]

There is no danger, however, for those who are humble. On the other hand, she warns against cowardice. All the saints aspired to perfection. Saint Paul said, "I can do all things in Him who strengtheneth me";[26] and "Saint Peter lost nothing

---

[23] *Ibid.*, cap. XI, B.M.C., p. 80.
[24] *Ibid.*, cap. XII.
[25] *Ibid.*, cap. XIII.
[26] Phil. 4:13.

by throwing Himself into the sea." There are certain pitfalls, too, for the beginner to avoid. He should be cheerful and free, and not neglect recreation. He should not let the devil keep him from prayer, as befell Teresa, by inciting himself to a false humility, making it seem "a species of pride to have heroic desires, and to wish for martyrdom, and to be anxious to imitate the saints." Married people, of course, must act in conformity with their vocation; but Teresa broadly implied that their progress must of necessity be "but the pace of a hen."[27]

She discovered also that one of the devil's tricks was to discourage mental prayer on the ground that it might be injurious to health; in fact, he "helps a great deal to make them sick when he sees a little fear. He likes nothing better than to give us to understand that everything is going to kill us, or make us lose our health; and if we have the gift of tears, he makes us afraid of going blind. I have been through all that, and so I know about it; and I don't know what better sight or health we could desire than to lose them for such a cause. As I am so sickly, I was always tied up and good for nothing until I resolved to take no account of my body and my health; and now I do little enough. But as it pleased God I should see through this trick of the demon, I would say, when he put before me the loss of my health, 'It little matters if I die. Yes! What, rest!? I don't need rest, but the cross.' And other such things."[28] And the less she thought of her health, the more it improved. There was nothing in her of the hypochondria that often goes with hysteria; she was neither hysterical nor neurotic.

One of the temptations of beginners, she noticed, was the itch to reform others before completely reforming themselves. It was all very well to desire that everyone should become spiritual, but a mistake to let others see that she was teaching them. For they presently discovered their mentor's faults and were confused. "In many years only three people profited by what I said to them." She became convinced that in this stage it was important to care for only one's own soul "until we obtain more solid virtue"; to act as if only God and she existed.

Another manifestation of misguided zeal was the temptation to worry over the sins and defects of others. This temptation to meddle with the affairs of others, which was the vice of the

---

[27] *Vida,* B.M.C., p. 93.
[28] *Ibid.,* p. 94.

Pharisees and the Calvinists, obviously came from the devil. He persuaded beginners in this way to imagine they were grieving because God was offended, when in reality they were indulging a sort of pride or vanity, and neglecting the prayer which could overcome their own faults: "and the greatest harm is to think that this is virtue and perfection, and great zeal for God. I don't refer to the sorrow public sins cause, if they be habitual [ones, or those] of a congregation, or injuries to the Church from those heresies where we see so many souls lost; for that is very good, and since it is good, does not disquiet one. But the safety of a soul that uses mental prayer will be to put everything and everyone out of mind, and mind her own business and please God. . . . Let us, then, always try to look at the virtues and good things we see in others, and mantle their defects with our own great sins. This is a kind of work which, although it cannot be done perfectly at once, comes to attain a great virtue, which is to consider all others better than ourselves. . . . Those who discourse with the understanding should look also to this. . . ."[29]

Teresa is not too dogmatic as to methods of mental prayer. She repeats here that the best way, according to her experience, is to begin by considering some incident of the Passion, "let us say the one in which the Lord is at the pillar. Let the understanding go seeking the causes which are here comprehensible: the great pains and sorrows His Majesty must have had[30] in that solitude, and many other things which can be obtained here, if the understanding is the workman, or if one is learned. This is the mode of prayer in which they[31] all have to begin and to go on and to finish, and [it is] a very excellent and secure road, too, until the Lord raises them to other things that are supernatural.

"I say all, for there are many souls that profit more by other meditations than by the one on the sacred Passion. And so, as there are many mansions in heaven, there are many roads. Some persons profit by thinking of hell, and others of heaven and are afflicted in thinking of hell, others of death. Some, if they are tenderhearted, tire themselves much in thinking always of the Passion, and get pleasure and profit from considering the power and grandeur of God in His creatures, and the love He has for us, which is shown us in all things. This is an admirable way to

---

[29] *Ibid.*, p. 95.
[30] "ternía," for *tendría*.
[31] *Ibid.*, p. 96.

proceed, though we should not often forget the Passion and life of Christ, whence comes and has come all our good."[32]

In any case, it is important not to trust in one's own powers, but to proceed obediently under a good director, a *maestro*. Teresa had suffered so much from the blunders of the well meaning but inept that she never tired of warning her readers against such men. A director, she observed, should have experience, skill, and learning. If he cannot have all three, it is better that he should have the first and second without the third, than the third without the first. For there are always learned men who can be consulted if necessary. Here she is considering beginners; she herself prefers a learned man who does not practise mental prayer, to a holy man without learning, for a well-read man will always understand the principles involved in a situation, even if he has not attempted to apply them to himself. When she speaks of a director, she means something more than a confessor, who hears sins and gives absolution.

"I have met souls who were penned in and afflicted, because he who taught them lacked experience, and they made me sad; and another who didn't know what to do with herself, for when the spirit is not understood, both soul and body afflict one and prevent improvement. One told me that her *maestro* kept her in leash for eight years, and that he would not let her give up self-knowledge, and yet the Lord held her in the prayer of quiet; and so she endured much woe.

"And in any case[33] this matter of self-knowledge is never wholly given up, nor is any soul so gigantic in this business that it doesn't need often to become a little child again and suckle at the breast (and this should never be forgotten, and perhaps I shall speak of it often, for it is highly important) for there is no state of prayer so lofty, that it will not be necessary to return many times to the beginning."[34]

Teresa enumerates a few errors of directors. "A nun begins to have mental prayer: if a simpleton is directing her, and he takes it into his head, he may give her to understand that it is better to obey him than her superior, and without any malice

---

[32] *Ibid.*, p. 97.

[33] I am taking a great liberty here. *Aunque* means "although"; but if so translated it leaves the sentence in P. Silverio's text without an independent clause. Possibly Saint Teresa wrote a sentence so long and involved here that her editors felt obliged to break it up, and not very successfully.

[34] *Ibid.*, p. 97.

on his part, but thinking he is right, for if he is not of a religious order, he may think it is so. And if she is a married woman, he will tell her that it is better to take to prayer (even if it displeases her husband) when she ought to be attending to her house, so that she doesn't know how to arrange her time or her affairs that they may go according to truth. For if he hasn't light himself, he can't give it to others even if he wants to. And although learning may not be necessary for this, my opinion has always been and always will be that every Christian should try to consult if possible with very learned men, the oftener the better; and it is more necessary for those who go by the way of mental prayer, and the more spiritual they are, the more necessary. . . .[35] I am convinced that a person of prayer who deals with learned men will never be deceived by the devil with illusions unless she wishes to be deceived, for I believe they[36] are very much afraid of learning when it is humble and virtuous, and they know they will be exposed and will go away the losers. . . . It will help much to consult with learned men if they are virtuous; and even if they are not spiritual, it will help him, and God will give him understanding of what he has to teach, and will even make him spiritual, that he may profit us: and this I don't say without having experience of it, for it befell me with more than two. I say that a soul who makes herself wholly subject to one master will err much if she does not see to it that he is learned. . . ."

Such were the difficulties with which Teresa wrestled in that first degree of prayer for twenty years until she cast herself at the feet of Christ in the picture and arose comforted and free. Then it was that she received the mysterious gift, beyond any human power to attain, of the second degree, which she calls the prayer of quiet.[37]

---

[35] *Ibid.*, p. 98. When Teresa speaks of "prayer," she usually means "mental prayer." Saint John of the Cross also wrote feelingly of inept directors: "Such persons have no knowledge of what is meant by spirituality, and they offer a great insult . . . to God by laying their coarse hands where God is working" (*Living Flame of Love*, Stanza III).

[36] The devils.

[37] *Ibid.*, cap. XIV. Mir is mistaken in saying she calls the first degree the prayer of quiet (*Vida de Santa Teresa*, I, cap. XXI). She plainly says this of the second. The various degrees of prayer, says Father Adolphe Tanqueray (*The Spiritual Life*, Tournai, 1930, p. 666), "are marked by a greater and greater hold of God on the soul. When He takes possession of the subtile *point of the soul,* letting the lower faculties and the senses free to exercise their natural activity, we have the *prayer of quiet.*"

Chapter VIII

VICTORY IN SURRENDER

BETWEEN 1550 and 1555 — in her late thirties — Teresa had certain transcendental experiences which she could make comparatively clear to others only by returning time and again to her favorite figure.

In the second degree of mental prayer, she says, the soul draws water for its garden with less labor, as with a windless; rather, the gardener Himself intervenes and helps her. She is able to reach the water more easily because the grace is given her to "collect within herself" the three faculties of will, memory, and understanding. The will is "sweetly taken prisoner" by God. The other two faculties assist the will if the latter does not try to influence them. They are "like some doves that don't content themselves with the food the owner of the dovecot gives them without any labor of theirs, and they go to look for something to eat in other places, and find it so bad that they come back; and so they go and they come, to see if the will gives them some of what *she* enjoys. If the Lord wishes, He throws them food, they stay, and if not, they look for it again."[1]

While the Prayer of Quiet lasts, the will, being united with God (though not wholly engulfed in Him), remains calm and quiet, even if the memory or the understanding is distracted, and it can recall these two faculties and make them recollected little by little.

Few souls arrive at this degree of prayer and few go beyond it, says Teresa; some turn back and become very wretched, and

---

[1] *Vida*, cap. XIV, B.M.C., p. 102. Saint Teresa is most herself and therefore most delightful, when she is describing her experiences in mental prayer. I should like to quote *verbatim* and *in toto* the twelve incomparable chapters (XI–XXII). As this is impracticable, some form of condensation is necessary. Father Silverio (I, p. 353) is against fragmentary quotation (1) because the Saint's works are so well known and so accessible that the reader can turn to them for her exact words; and (2) because fragmentary quotation is inadequate. To this I reply that (1) is far less true in English than in Spanish, for our available translations, as I have noted elsewhere, do not do justice to the Saint's vigorous and free expression. There is more force in (2); and I have no doubt that the distinguished Carmelite editor is equal to conveying a true account of her thought (though not of her expression) by summary. I have no such confidence in my own ability to paraphrase some magnificent passages dealing with matters of which I have so slight a comprehension.

she is inclined to attribute this fact to their lack of understanding of themselves and of the high privilege given them. They recognize the quiet and recollection God has bestowed by a satisfaction and peace so complete that they might well think (having progressed no further) that there is nothing more to desire; they might exclaim with Saint Peter, "Lord, it is good for us to be here!" But they are greatly mistaken, and failing to advance, are in danger of falling back.

No matter how long the Prayer of Quiet lasts, it never tires the soul, "for the understanding works here only from time to time, and draws very much more water than it got from the well; the tears God gives here flow joyfully now; although they are felt, they are not procured.

"This water of great blessings and favors, which the Lord gives here, make[2] the virtues increase incomparably more than in the previous prayer; for now this soul begins to rise out of her misery, and now gives herself a little notice of the delights of glory. This I believe makes the virtues increase even more, and to come still nearer to the true Virtue whence all the virtues come, which is God; for His Majesty commences to communicate Himself to this soul and wishes her to feel *how* He communicates Himself. She then commences, on arriving at that point, to lose the lust[3] for the things of this world. And small thanks! For she sees clearly that not a moment of that delight may be had here below, nor are there riches, nor seigniories, nor honors, nor pleasures which suffice to give an eye twinkling[4] of this enjoyment, for it is *real*, and the joy that comes from it truly satisfies us."

In the pleasures the world gives, she adds, there is always a Yes and a No, and people do not even understand wherein lies the enjoyment; but in the Prayer of Quiet there is only a delightful Yes. The No is not part of the pleasure, but comes afterwards, when the experience has passed, and the soul is left with no means of her own to regain it until God so wills.

True, God is always with us, and in all things. But in the Prayer of Quiet "this Emperor and Lord of ours wishes that we understand here that He understands us, and what His pres-

---

[2] *Sic.*

[3] *Codicia* formerly had this meaning; in modern Spanish it is nearer to our "covetousness."

[4] *"Un cierra ojo y abre* — literally, "a shut eye and open."

ence does, and that He desires especially to begin to work in the soul through the great interior and exterior satisfaction He gives it." This delight is in the very intimate part of the soul, "and she does not know whence or how it comes, or often what to do or to ask."

All this Teresa learned from hard experience. "If God should conduct her [the soul] by way of fear, as He did me, it is great trouble unless there is someone who understands her; and it is a great joy to see herself portrayed, and then she sees clearly where she is going. And it is great to know well what she has to do, to go on improving in any one of these states — for I myself have suffered much and have lost plenty of time, by not knowing what to do. And I have great pity for souls who find themselves alone when they arrive at this point. For although I have read many spiritual books, and although they touch on this matter, they tell very little; and if not, the soul is much exercised. For [even] when they tell much, she has trouble enough to understand. . . ."[5]

Then follows a characteristic passage that will not be any easier to read in English than it is in the pungent, individual, and almost untranslatable Spanish:

"What the soul has to do in the time of this quiet, is no more than to be gentle and make no noise. I call it noise to go about with the understanding looking for many words and reflections to give thanks for this benefit, and piling up her sins and short-comings to show herself that she doesn't deserve it. All this moves here, and the understanding begins to act, and the memory boils,[6] and surely those faculties weary me at times, for having little memory, I cannot master it. Let the will quietly and prudently understand that one does not deal successfully with God by any efforts of one's own,[7] and that these [the memory and the understanding] are some great logs laid on without discretion to smother this little spark, and let her know it, and say humbly, Lord, what can I do here? What has the servant to do with the Lord, and the earth with the sky? Or words of love occur to her here, well founded in knowing that what she says is true; and let her pay no heed to the understanding, which is a bore.[8] And if she desires to give it part of what

---

[5] *Vida,* cap. XIV.
[6] *Sic: bulle.*
[7] *"A fuerza de brazos."*   [8] *"Un moledor."*

she enjoys, or labors to make it recollected, she will not succeed, for she will often see herself in this union and repose of the will,[9] and [she will find] the understanding very confused, and it avails her more — I mean the will — to let it alone and not to run after it. But let her rather be enjoying this favor and recollected like a wise bee; for if none entered the hive, but all went about looking for one another, the honey might be made badly.

"Thus a soul will lose much if she does not pay attention to this, especially if the understanding is acute, for once she begins to arrange discourses and to look for reasons, she will think, in short, if they are well put, that she is doing something. The [only] reason that has to be held here is to understand clearly that there is no [reason] why God should do so great a favor, except His goodness alone; and to see that we are so near [Him] and to ask His Majesty for favors, to pray to Him for the Church, and for those who have commended themselves to us, and for the souls in purgatory — not with noise of words, but with a feeling of desiring that He hear us. This is a prayer that includes a great deal, and achieves more than much prating by the understanding. Let the will awaken in herself some reasons which reason itself suggests, such as seeing herself so much better fitted to inflame this love; and let her make certain amorous acts of what she would do for the One she owes so much, without, as I have said, allowing any noise of the understanding in its search for great things. More to the purpose here, and more likely to make it burn, are a few little straws laid on with humility (and they will be less than straws if we bring them ourselves) more than a lot of wood weighted with very learned reasons, which, in our opinion, will smother it in a *credo*. This is good for the learned men who have commanded me to write this, for, by the goodness of God, all may reach this point, and perhaps they will pass the time applying the Scriptures. And although learning cannot fail to be of much use to them before and after [the Prayer of Quiet], here in these stages there is little need of it, in my opinion, unless it is to enfeeble the will; for the understanding itself is so greatly clarified from being so near the light, that even I, being what I am, seem like another person. . . ."

---

[9] *"Muchas veces se verá en esta unión de la voluntad y sosiego.*

Teresa adds that sometimes in this state she is unable to understand the Latin in her Psaltery, or even the verses in Spanish. Then she continues:

"In these times of quiet, then, let the soul repose in her rest. Let learning be put to one side — the time will come when it will be of use to the Lord, and they will prize it so highly that not for any treasure would they wish to be without knowing it, just to serve the Lord, for it helps much; but in the presence of Infinite Wisdom, let them believe me, a little attention to humility and an act of it are worth more than all the science of the world. Here we don't have to argue, but to know fully what we are, and to place ourselves with simplicity before God, who wishes the soul to make a booby of herself (as she really is before His presence), since His Majesty so humbles Himself that He suffers her to be beside Him, we being what we are.

"The understanding, moreover, is moved to give thanks well composed; but the will, like the publican not daring to raise his eyes, quietly makes a better thanksgiving than the understanding is able to make, perhaps by turning rhetoric upside down."[10]

Teresa found that the Prayer of Quiet, like all the other degrees, had its dangers. The devil, jealous of the soul's improvement, might seek to trouble it in two ways. First, he might attempt to deceive it by giving it a false delight, leading toward pride, that is, away from God. But the soul accustomed to prayer should be able to distinguish between the joy that comes from Him and that which is simulated by His enemy. For the devil's pleasure, or that which the soul procures for itself, ends quickly, and leaves no good effect, such as humility or greater love, but only "dryness," restlessness, and disillusionment. A soul can foil this attempt of the enemy by being humble and not curious, by not desiring delights, above all by disengaging herself from all kinds of pleasures, and by resolving "only to help the Lord carry His cross, like brave knights who love to serve their king without pay." Teresa stresses by repetition the need of forsaking all the pleasures of this life. And when the devil finds that a soul thus humble and selfless cannot be deceived by his wiles, he will go away and not often return.

Secondly, "there come times when it is necessary, to save them-

---

[10] *Con trastornar la retórica.*" *Vida*, cap. XV., B.M.C., p. 112.

selves from offending God, those who have already so placed their will in His that to avoid an imperfection they would let themselves be tortured and would endure a thousand deaths — to keep from committing sins (I say), as they see themselves buffeted by temptations and persecutions, it is necessary for them to make use of the first arms of prayer, and to go back to the thought that all things come to an end, that there is heaven and hell, and other things of this sort."[11]

For the childlike humble soul who cheerfully obeys the Saviour's behest to "Take up thy cross, and follow Me," each temptation will pass, and the fruits of the Prayer of Quiet will gradually become evident. She will gain humility, self-understanding, a desire to advance in prayer, and of disregarding any incidental troubles; a "confidence that we shall be saved, united however with fear and humility." Servile fear is now replaced by filial fear and by a great, disinterested love of God. "In short (not to weary myself too much)," concludes Teresa, returning to her favorite figure, "it is the beginning of all the blessings, when the flowers are already in such a stage that they are almost nothing short of budding; and this the soul sees very clearly. . . ."

Passing through these experiences, Teresa arrived, between 1550 and 1555, at what she calls the third degree of mental prayer, the running water from a spring or river of grace that delightfully refreshes the garden of the soul. It is the beginning of the prayer of union. (It might be called the Prayer of Partial Union, to distinguish it from the more complete union she describes later on.) "Here the Lord wishes to help the gardener, so much so that He is almost the gardener Himself, and the one who does everything. It is a sleep of the powers, which are neither wholly lost nor do they understand how they work. The joy and sweetness and delight is incomparably more than what is past. This is because the water of grace goes up to the neck of this soul, who is unable any longer to go forward, nor does she know how, or to turn back; she would like to enjoy the very greatest glory. She is like one who is with the candle in his hand, who lacks little of dying the death he desires. She goes on enjoying that agony with the greatest delight that can be expressed. It seems to me nothing else than a dying almost altogether to all the things of the world, and to be enjoying God. I don't know of any other terms in which to say it, or how to

---

[11] *Ibid.*, cap. XV, B.M.C., p. 113.

make it known, nor does the soul then know what to do, for she doesn't know whether to speak or be silent, to laugh or to weep. It is a glorious folly, a celestial madness, in which the true wisdom is seized upon; and it is the most delightful way of rejoicing the soul. . . .[12]

"I well understood that it was not a *total* union of all the faculties and that it was more than the previous one [the Prayer of Quiet], very clearly. . . . Many times I remained as if out of my mind and intoxicated in this love, and never had I been able to understand how it was. I understood well that it was God, but I could not understand how He worked there; for in very truth the faculties were almost wholly united, but not so engulfed that they did not act. . . ."

One day after Communion, our Lord made it all clear to her in a dazzling moment, and she set it down as well as words would permit:

"The faculties no longer have any power except to occupy themselves wholly with God. Nothing, it seems, dares to stir[13] here, nor are we able to make it move, unless we wish, with a great effort, to divert ourselves from it — and I doubt if that could be at all possible. Here many words are spoken in praises of God, without order, unless the Lord Himself should arrange them — at least the understanding is of no use at all here. The soul wishes to cry out praises, and is not able to contain herself; a sweet restlessness! Now, now the flowers are opening, now they commence to give fragrance! Here the soul would like all to see her and to understand her glory by praises of God, and to help her do it, and to share her joy with them, for she cannot enjoy so much. I think she is like the one the Gospel tells about, who wanted to call, or did call, her neighbors.[14] This is what I think the admirable spirit of the royal prophet David must have felt when he played and sang with the harp, in praises of God. . . . To this glorious King I am very devoted, and wish all were, especially those of us who are sinners.

"Oh, God help me! What a soul is when she is thus! She would like to be all tongues, to praise the Lord. She says a thousand holy extravagances, striving to please the One Who so pleases her. I know a person who, without being a poet, hap-

---

[12] *Ibid.*, cap. XVI, p. 117.
[13] *Bullir.*
[14] Luke 15:6, 9.

pened to make some very feeling verses offhand declaring her sweet pain; not the work of her understanding, but to enjoy better the glory that such delightful pain gave her, she complained of it to her God."[15]

Teresa is speaking here of herself. This was perhaps the first of a series of poems which, making no pretense to polish or elegance, are all the more remarkable for their lyrical passion and beauty. Often thereafter she composed verses without writing them. Some of these are lost, some remain in fragments only, others were taken down by her friends. It is not known which poem she refers to here.[16]

Many truths flashed upon her in her spiritual inebriations. She saw, for example, that "the martyrs did almost nothing on their own account in suffering tortures, for the soul knows well that its strength comes from elsewhere." Her joy at such moments was so great that "sometimes it seems the soul is on the very point of beginning to leave this body. And what a happy death that would be!"

As she wrote this, she could not resist breaking into one of her most passionately beautiful prayers of thanksgiving:

"Be blessed forever, Lord; let all things praise You[17] forever! Please now, my King, I ask it, who when I write this, am not yet out of this holy celestial madness, through Your goodness and mercy, Who have done me without any merits of mine this favor, [I ask] that either all those I talk to, be mad with Your love, or that You let me speak with nobody, or command, Lord, that I take no account of anything in the world, or take me out of it. No longer, God of mine, can this Your servant endure such sufferings as come to her in seeing herself without You! For if she has to live, she does not want rest in this life, nor do You give it. This soul now wishes to see herself free; eating kills her; sleeping afflicts her; she sees that the time of life passes her, to pass in enjoyment, and that nothing can now delight her outside of You; and she seems to live against nature, since she no longer wishes to live in herself, but in You. O my true Lord and glory, what a light and heavy cross You keep prepared for

---

[15] *Vida*, cap. XVI.

[16] Mir (*Vida de Santa Teresa*, I, p. 187, n. I), seems to be wrong in his conjecture that it was the *Vivo sin vivir en mí*. See below, Chapter XXIV.

[17] Kings were addressed with the plural pronoun Teresa usually employs the "You," not the "Thou," in her prayers.

those who arrive at this state! Light, because it is sweet; heavy, for there come times when there is no sufferance that suffers it; and she desires never to see herself free from it, unless it be to see herself now with You. When she remembers that she has served You in nothing, and that she can serve You by living, she desires to burden herself much more heavily, and never to die until the end of the world! . . ."[18]

The Gardener has now given in a moment what the soul could not obtain herself in twenty years. The virtues obtained here remain stronger than in the Prayer of Quiet. The soul, says Teresa, now "sees herself another person, and does not know how she begins to do great things with the fragrance that the flowers are giving of themselves. For the Lord wishes them to open, so that she may see that she has virtues — although she sees very well, too, that she could not obtain them, nor could she do so in many years, and that the celestial Gardener gave them to her in that little moment. Here the humility which remains in the soul is much greater and more profound than in the past degree, for she sees more clearly that she did neither little nor much, except to consent that the Lord do her favors, and to let her will embrace them.

"This kind of prayer seems to me very obviously a union of all the soul with God, except that His Majesty seems to wish to allow the faculties to understand and enjoy the much that He does there. . . ." The soul knows she has much quiet and peace, yet "the understanding and the memory are so free that they can carry on business and attend to works of charity. This, although it seems to be all one, is different in part from the Prayer of Quiet I have mentioned, for there the soul is so that she does not wish to bustle about[19] or stir, taking her pleasure in that holy leisure of Mary. In this prayer she can also be Martha, so that she is almost working in the active and contemplative life together, and can attend to works of charity and business belonging to her state in life, and can read, although they[20] are not wholly masters of themselves, and they understand well that the better part of the soul is somewhere else. It

[18] *Ibid.*, cap. XVI, B.M.C., p. 120.
[19] *bullir* again.
[20] "The faculties," in the opinion of Canon Dalton. While reading the last proofs of this book, I have heard that Mr. E. Allison Peers is about to publish a translation of all the works of Saint Teresa in England.

is as if we were speaking with someone, and another person should speak to us from somewhere else, and we are not wholly in the one [place] or in the other.

"It is something that is felt very clearly, and gives much satisfaction and content when it happens, and it is a very fine preparation, so that when the time comes for solitude and freedom from business, the soul may arrive at a very restful quiet. . . ."

It was through such sublime experiences that Teresa arrived, probably about her fortieth year or a little before, at the fourth degree of prayer, the highest attainable by man or woman in the flesh — which may be called the Prayer of Complete Union, if the word *complete* is rightly understood. It was impossible for her to describe exactly what she had felt; but, having been commanded by her director to set it down as best she could for the benefit of other souls following the same road, she obeyed. These are perhaps the most difficult pages in all her writings to understand. However they may be translated, they are bound to put some strain upon the patience and application of any reader in our tongue. No one who wishes to understand her will regret having made the effort. It was certainly not easy for her to set down these inspired passages.

"May the Lord teach me words in which something can be said of the fourth water!" she implored. "Indeed there is need of His favor, even more than for the previous one. . . . In all the methods of prayer I have mentioned, the gardener labors in something; although in these last the work is attended by such glory and consolation of the soul, that she wishes never to emerge from it; and so it is not felt to be work, but glory. Here one does not have to feel, but to enjoy without understanding what is enjoyed. She understands that a benefit is enjoyed in which all benefits together are comprised, but this benefit is not comprehended. All the senses are occupied with this joy in such a way that they cannot disengage themselves to do anything else, either outside or inside. Before, as I have said, some freedom was given them to show certain signs of the great joy they felt. Here the soul enjoys incomparably more, and can make herself understood much less, for there remains no power in the body, nor does the soul have any that can communicate that joy. At that time anything would be a great embarrassment and a torment and obstacle to her repose; and I say that if it is a union of all the faculties, she cannot [communicate it], being in it, I say, even if she wishes; and if she can, then it is not union.

"This is what they call union, but what it *is*, I do not know how to make clear. It is explained in Mystical Theology, which I don't know how to name the terms of, nor do I know how to understand what is 'mind,' or what difference it has from the 'soul,' or the 'spirit' either. All seems to me one thing — though the soul sometimes goes out of herself, like fire that is burning, and makes a flame, and sometimes this fire increases with impetus. This flame rises far above the fire, but it is not on this account a different thing, but the same flame that is in the fire. Your Reverences, with your learning, will understand this, for I don't know how to say it better.

"What I wish to explain is what the soul *feels* when she is in this divine union. What union is, that is understood already — it is for two separated things to make themselves one. O Lord of mine, how good You are! Be blessed forever! May all things praise You, my God, Who have[21] so loved us that we are able to speak truthfully of this communication, which even in this exile You hold with souls! . . ."[22]

Sometimes, when she received the gift of highest prayer, she would say, "Lord, watch what You are doing, don't forget so quickly such great sins of mine! . . ."

Resuming her description, she promised to tell only what she knew from long experience; and the Lord would have to help her, since her motives were first, to obey, and secondly, to make souls desirous of attaining so high a good. "When I began to write about this last water, it seemed to me more impossible to know what to say, than to talk in Greek, for it is just as difficult; whereupon I gave it up and went to Communion. Blessed be the Lord, Who thus favors the ignorant! O virtue of obedience, which can do anything! God clarified my understanding, sometimes with words, and other times putting before me how it had to be said; and as happened in the former degree of prayer, His Majesty seems to wish to say what I cannot say or know. . . .

"Now, speaking of that water which comes from heaven, to fill and satiate all this garden with its abundance of water, if the Lord never failed to give it when there might be need of

---

[21] *Amastes* was formerly used as a plural form.

[22] *Ibid.*, cap. XVIII. Here and elsewhere in this chapter I have used italics now and then to make the meaning clearer.

it, it is plain to see what rest the gardener would enjoy. And having no winter but being always temperate weather, the flowers and fruits would never be lacking. Then it is clear what delight he would have! But while we live, it is impossible; always must care be taken, when one water gives out, to procure another. The one from the sky comes many times when the gardener is more unconcerned about it. True it is that at first it comes almost always after long mental prayer; and the Lord comes little by little to take this birdling and put her in the nest, that she may rest. When He has seen her flying for quite a while, attempting with her understanding and will and all her powers to find God and to please Him, He wishes to give her the reward even in this life. And what a great reward, one moment of which is enough to repay all the trials that can be had in a lifetime!

"Seeking God in this manner, the soul feels herself almost swooning with sweet and uttermost delight, quite like a sort of fainting, so that the breath, and all the bodily powers, begins to fall away; so that she cannot even move her hands, unless it is with much difficulty. Her eyes close without her wishing to close them, or if she keeps them open, she sees almost nothing; nor, if she reads, can she guess what the letters are, or come close to knowing them. She sees that there *are* letters, but as the understanding does not help, she does not know how to read even if she wishes. She hears, but does not understand what she hears. Thus the senses are of no use unless it is to keep her from enjoying her pleasure to the full, and so they hurt her instead. To speak is too much, for she cannot manage to form a word, nor is there strength, if she could hit upon one, to pronounce it; for all her outward strength is lost, and that of the soul is increased that she may better enjoy her glory. The exterior delight felt is very great and recognizable.

"This prayer does no harm however long it may last. At least it never did any to me, nor do I remember that however ill I was, I felt ill when the Lord gave me this favor, but on the contrary I remained much better. What harm can such a great benefit do? The outward effects are a thing so well known that one cannot doubt there is a great opportunity, when the powers are suspended with so much delight, to leave them stronger than before.

"True it is that at first it passes in such a short time, at least it so befell to me. . . . And let this be noticed, that no matter how long the soul may be in this suspension of all her faculties, it is, in my opinion, very short; if it should be half an hour, it is very much — I think I was never so long. True it is that one can hardly feel what it is, since there is no feeling, but I say it is a very little interval at one time that does not bring some faculty back to itself. The will is the one that carries on the weaving, but the other two faculties quickly come back to tease. As the will is quiet, she suspends them again, and there they are another little while, and come back to life again.

"In this it is possible to pass several hours of prayer, and they do pass; for once the two faculties [of understanding and memory] have began to get drunk on and to enjoy this divine wine, they easily manage to lose themselves again in order that they may be very much better off, and they attend upon the will, and all three enjoy themselves together. But this condition of being wholly lost and without any imagination in anything (for to my understanding this also is wholly lost) — this, I say, is a short interval. Yet they [the faculties] do not return to themselves so completely as to prevent their being for several hours like idiots, while God little by little gathers them together again to Himself.

"Now we come to the interior of what the soul here feels. Let him tell it who knows it, for it cannot be understood, much less said. I was thinking, when I wished to write this (having just received Communion, and having been in this same prayer that I write of) what the soul did at that time. The Lord spoke to me these words:

" 'She wholly effaces herself, daughter, to put herself more in Me; now it is not she who lives, but I. As she cannot comprehend what she understands, it is not to understand, understanding.'[23]

"He will understand something of this who has experienced it, for it cannot be said more clearly, so obscure is that which happens here. I can only say that what is represented is to be joined with God, and that such certitude of this remains, that by no means can one help believing it. Here all the faculties fall away, and are so suspended, that nowise, as I have said, is it understood that they labor. If one is thinking of a station of

---

[23] *Ibid.*, B.M.C., p .135: *como no puede comprender lo que entiende, es no entender entendiendo.* Cf. Saint John of the Cross, *Spiritual Canticle* (Peers), Stanza 28, No. 9, p. 180.

the Cross, it vanishes from the memory as if it had never been held by it; if one reads, there is no memory or consideration of what one reads; no more if one prays. And as that importunate little moth[24] of the memory has her wings burned here, there can no longer be any more fluttering about for her. The will must be quite occupied in loving, but she does not understand how she loves. The understanding, if it understands, does not understand how it understands, at least it does not comprehend anything of what it understands. I don't think it understands, for, as I say, it is not understood. I am not able to understand this. . . .[25]

"In this prayer and union the soul remains in such great tenderness that she wishes to be dissolved, not in sorrow, but in some joyful tears. She finds herself bathed in them without feeling it, or knowing when or how she wept them; but it gives her great delight to see that impetus of the fire appeased by water that makes it grow more — this seems Arabic jargon, and so it goes![26] Several times in this stage of prayer, it has befallen me to be so far outside of myself, that I did not know whether it was a dream or whether the glory I had felt really had happened, and when I saw myself so full of water which distilled painlessly with so much impetus and speed that it seemed yonder cloud of heaven cast it forth, I saw that it had not been a dream — this was at the beginning, which passed briefly.

"The soul remains [so] courageous that if at that moment they broke her into pieces for God, it would be a great comfort to her. That is where the promises and heroic determinations are, the vigor of the desires, the beginning to abhor the world, the very clear seeing of her vanity — and all this much more to the purpose and more profoundly than in the previous degree of prayer, and the humility more increased; for she sees clearly that for that excessive and magnificent favor she had no diligence of her own, nor had it [her diligence] any part in gaining or keeping it. Clearly she sees herself most unworthy, for in a room where much sunlight enters there is not a cobweb hidden from view. She sees her misery. Vainglory flees from her so far that it seems she could never have had it. . . . Her past life and the great mercy of God are then represented before her

---

[24] *mariposilla.*
[25] *Ibid.,* cap. XVIII, p. 135.
[26] *"Parece esto algarabía y pasa ansí."* — Cap. XIX, p. 137.

with great truth, and this without any need of the understanding's going a-hunting for it. . . . She sees that of herself she deserves hell and that they punish her with glory! She dissolves herself in praises of God, and I would like so to dissolve myself now! Blessed be You, Lord of mine, Who thus make so foul a pool of stagnant water as I[27] into water so clear that it might be for your table. Be You praised, O Joy of the Angels, Who have thus been pleased to raise up a worm so vile!

"For some time this improvement remains in the soul; already, understanding clearly that the fruit is not hers, she can begin to share it, and this without losing it for herself. She begins to give signs of a soul that guards treasures of heaven, and to have a desire to share them with others, and to beg God that she alone may not be the rich one. She begins to do good to those nearest her, almost without understanding it or making any account of herself. They understand it, for already the flowers have so much more fragrance that they make people wish to come near them! . . ."

---

[27] *Pecina tan sucia como yo.* — *Vida,* cap. XIX, p. 138.

Chapter IX

THE DEVIL'S REVENGE — FEAR OF THE HOLY INQUISITION

WHILE her spirit was venturing upon that infinite sea of joy and understanding,[1] Teresa was leading a perfectly normal life in relation to her fellow beings. She was performing all the duties of her conventual state. She had some interesting and stimulating friendships. She was a mother to her young sister Juana, who lived at the convent as a *doncella de piso* for about twelve years after the death of Don Alonso, and doubtless she consoled her in such dark hours as when they learned in 1546 that Antonio had been killed and Hernando wounded at Iñaquito.

Six or seven years later (in 1552 or 1553) Juana received a proposal of marriage from a young man of Alba de Tormes, Don Juan de Ovalle, who happened to visit the convent with his brother Gonzalo, husband of one of the daughters of Uncle Pedro in Hortigosa. He seems to have been a youth of no particular talents, rather smug, obstinate, and self-centered, but otherwise of good character and more or less personable. He loved the gentle, affectionate Juana, and his feeling was returned. The only obstacle to their marriage was a large one, his lack of income; but this was removed when his father, on October 31, 1553, made over to him part of his property "for the many and good services that the said Juan de Ovalle, my son, has rendered me, and [he] has been very obedient, like a good son."[2] It was not a large revenue, for the Ovalles were of that fairly numerous class of *hidalgos de gotera* — literally, "gutter noblemen," who enjoyed the rights of nobility in one town only and often were more pinched for money, behind their proud exterior, than many a small farmer with no appearances to keep up.[3] Still, it was enough for a modest beginning.

While Teresa was completing the education of Juana and

---

[1] P. Silverio (*Vida de Santa Teresa de Jesús*, I, p. 356), believes Teresa attained the joys of union in a very few years, but experienced them more briefly and less overwhelmingly at first.

[2] *Ibid.*, p. 324.

[3] *Ibid.*, p. 326, n. 2.

preparing her for the great event of her life, she made some important friends. The one who had the most influence upon her at this time was the elderly Don Francisco de Salcedo, whom she called "the Holy Cavalier."

He was a sort of relation by marriage — his wife, Doña Mencia del Aguila, was first cousin of the spouse of her Uncle Pedro. For forty years he had been given to prayer and study, and for twenty to attending lectures in theology at the Dominican monastery of Saint Thomas. His gentle and courteous bearing and his great charity to the poor made him a popular and revered figure in Ávila and a favorite visitor at the Incarnation, where he formed the habit of conversing with his cousin about God and the things of God. The bent of his mind is indicated by the fact that after his holy wife's death he became a priest.[4] He was not brilliant, but thoroughly dependable, painstaking, and honest. Teresa described him as "so prayerful and charitable that his goodness and perfection shines out in his whole person. And rightly so, for great good has come to many souls through his instrumentality. . . . Much understanding, and very peaceable to all, his conversation not tiresome, but sweet and gracious, together with (its) being upright and holy, which gives a great satisfaction to all with whom he converses.[5] He arranges everything for the great welfare of the souls he deals with, and seems to have no other purpose in life but to do for all what he sees is permitted, and to please all. This blessed and holy man, then, it seems to me was the beginning, with his diligence, of the salvation of my soul."

It was fortunate for Teresa that she had so loyal a friend at that particular time. For with her rapid advance to the highest form of prayer, there had come a new trial, one of the worst she had ever endured — a temptation to believe that her mystical experiences, whose objective reality she never doubted, might have been set before her by the devil as illusions, leading not to heaven but to hell. This fear, which haunted her for weeks, arose from a peculiar historical event. The Spanish Inquisition, so sternly efficient throughout the lifetime of Ferdinand and Isabella, who had established it in 1480, had been almost moribund under Charles the Fifth, but had suddenly

---

[4] *Ibid.*, I, pp. 367–371. See also P. Gabriel, *La Santa de le raza*, III, p. 57.

[5] *Vida*, cap. XXIII. The construction of this sentence is hers.

come to life again in 1544, to uncover a piece of sacrilegious hypocrisy and fraud which, as Ribera remarks, "put fear into all Spain."[6]

There had dwelt for forty years in Córdoba, in the Convent of Saint Isabel of the Angels, of the Order of Saint Clare, a nun on whose growing reputation for holiness the supernatural seemed to have set the seal of approval. Faithful Catholics made long pilgrimages to ask for prayers and to carry away as relics little objects she had touched. Priests and nuns believed in her sanctity. Members of the royal family went to beg for her intercession with heaven. The beautiful and pious Empress Isabel, wife of Charles V, sent her as a gift the robes in which her infant son (Philip II) had been baptized at Valladolid in 1527. Stories were told of her dreadful fasts and long vigils. Finally it got abroad that she had received from our Lord the precious favor of the *Stigmata* — wounds in the hands and feet and side, like His — and Magdalena let it be known that she no longer required any food except the consecrated Host in daily Communion.

Now, such things have happened beyond any doubt in the history of Christendom. The Church has accepted the evidence as to Saint Francis of Assisi[7] and many others, and in our own day is investigating reports of eyewitnesses concerning Teresa Neumann of Bavaria. But it is no secret in Vatican City that in the long conflict between Christ the King and His enemy the Prince of this World there have been true mystics and false mystics; there have been genuine stigmatists and deluded fanatics or paranoiacs; glorified persons who truly subsisted on the Sacred Host as Saint Catherine of Siena did for twenty years, and frauds who for profit or admiration pretended to do so. In all such matters the Church moves slowly and skeptically, sparing no pains to expose hysteria or deceit. And of all the agencies of investigation available for the purpose in that period, one of the most useful was found to be the Inquisition. Somehow this tribunal became suspicious of Magdalena de la Cruz and began making inquiries.

---

[6] Ribera, *Vida de Santa Teresa*, lib. I, cap. IX.

[7] A special feast commemorates the Impression of the Stigmata of Saint Francis, which the Church in her Office describes as a "new miracle, never granted before in past ages." The passage in Saint Paul, Gal. 6:17, does not refer to what today we understand by the term "stigmata."

Arrested and questioned at last, she made a confession so appalling that the Holy Office committed her to prison for life, not only to protect Catholics from being deceived and corrupted, but to help the miserable woman to turn from her crimes and (as finally she did) to die a good Christian. She told the Inquisitors of Córdoba that she was not truly a Catholic but an *Alumbrada,* one of a sect discovered in Spain a generation before when the great Cardinal Ximenes was Inquisitor General. It was one of those secret societies whose anti-Christian activity had undermined for centuries, and made impossible of complete achievement, the life-giving mission of Christianity in European society. This oriental spiritual contagion originated in the Buddistic idea that by pure contemplation the soul, losing its individuality, sinks into the infinite Essence of the All until it arrives at a state of "perfection." Seeking to free itself from the chains of transmigration and from the material world itself, which Buddha and his followers regarded, with profound pessimism, as essentially evil, the soul escapes from all activity until it achieves a state of annihilation, at the end of which, to crown the system, lies Nirvana, the death and extinction of the individual conscience and of human personality. Actually this is a roundabout form of atheism, whose effect is to separate a man from his fellows and from any real communion with God; for communion implies personality, which is denied in this pseudo mysticism to both creature and Creator.

Nearly all the heretical sects which have hampered the Catholic Church in her divine mission to save souls, from Simon Magus to Luther and from Calvin to Mrs. Blavatsky, have been more or less tainted by this oriental poison. The Gnostics, the Manichees, the Cathari (or "Puritans") of the thirteenth century (who under the name of Albigenses were attacked by a Crusade and furnished the occasion for the establishment of the Inquisition), Plotinus and Priscillian, and a host of other heresiarchs, all pretending to be Christians, taught doctrines utterly incompatible with true Christianity, with its communal life stemming from the perfect community of love, the Blessed Trinity. They denied the authority of the Church and the efficacy of her sacraments, the veneration of the Host, sometimes the humanity of Christ, sometimes His divinity. To them the soul's knowledge of God was a matter of intuition, of feeling. Whoever had this *feeling* became one of the Perfect, the Pure, the

Initiate; and it was the common teaching of such sects that these choice and liberated spirits were no longer capable of sin, whatever they might do in the holy state of contemplation. The Beghards of Catalonia and Valencia taught in the fourteenth century that those who had achieved union with God could allow the body all that it desired, since the root of sensuality was dead. Many of these heretics condemned marriage, as an instrument of the devil for the propagation of life, which itself was evil. The result was bound to be a great deal of unnatural vice; and wherever they appeared, these secret societies of Manichaean origin became identified, in the public mind, with certain sins of pagan Rome which the Christian Church had driven into the outer darkness.

The *Alumbrados* were a secret society of this general type. Their tenets are described in a *Memorial* made by one Fray Alonso and sent to the Vatican by the papal nuncio, Ormaneto, with the remark that "this is the greatest and most subtle temptation from which the Church has suffered."[8]

According to Fray Alonso, "The authors of this heresy are necromancers and wizards, and are plainly involved with the devil." They used Christian terms, such as "divine inspiration," "contrition for sin," "the cross of a Christian," but in senses quite different from those understood by true Christians. For example:

"*Sentimiento divino,* according to this doctrine, is a movement of the senses, which comes with a body change and perceptible heat so strong in some persons that it burns them and parches them like a fever. This feeling comes in many ways and shows itself in many parts of the body, generally in the heart, with a movement that makes it palpitate; oftentimes too in the shoulders, in the breast, in the arms, in the palms of the hands, and sometimes the sufferer comes to feel the wounds of Christ. . . .

"*Warmth of God or of the Holy Spirit,* which is the same, is a kind of feeling consisting of only sensible heat which parches and inflames the flesh, so much so as sometimes to cause a breaking out on the face and other parts where it occurs. . . . This phenomenon is often attended by odors, faintings, raptures, sweating, sensible consolations, and sensible grief.

---

[8] P. Silverio (*op. cit.,* I, p. 363 *et seq.*) gives extracts from this *Memorial,* which is in the Vatican archives (*Nunc. Spog.,* vol. 14, p. 187).

"Knowledge of God . . . is a sensible clarity which some call moistening, for when they feel the said knowledge keenly, they feel as if they had been wet. . . .

"Contrition for sin is a sensible grief which breaks the heart and makes them utter shrieks and groans, and sometimes it comes so violently that it makes the patient rabid . . . . and leaves him fatigued and exhausted, and some die of the said griefs when they continue in the patient many days.

"Divine consolation is a sensible joy so powerful and so remarkable that sometimes they begin to dance and to leap about, and it lasts a long time and enthralls the patients in such wise that they eat their hands under that consolation, and go mad seeking for it.

"The mortification and cross of the Christian in this doctrine is plainly felt when the flesh is dead, sick, and exhausted . . . and is experienced by the perfect when the eyes no longer see, nor does the hearing hear, nor does the sense of taste distinguish any flavor in what is eaten; and, truly, the devil begins to bring about this effect in the women, and then there is no danger of the female Illuminates having to do with the males, and moreover, mortification occurs among some of them by touching one another and performing acts of a very unchaste kind which are exchanged between the men Illuminates and the women. . . ."

The members of this sect, continued the *Memorial,* could be recognized by their aversion to friars, "not on account of their lives but their doctrine, although they let it be understood that by the bad example that exists in the religious orders they keep their disciples away from the friars and persuade them to have nothing to do with them." They taught that only God had to be obeyed — a doctrine subversive of both Church and State, assuming as it does that God has not delegated authority to any human being.

Fray Alonso enumerated several signs by which the *Illuminati* (as they were known in Bavaria, two centuries after Philip II expelled them from Spain) could be known:

"If an *Alumbrada* is perfect, she abhors the friars and all confessors who do not share in the said doctrines. If she is married, she abhors matrimony, avoids all communication with people, with persons of other callings or religions. They go about half dead, pallid, and dispirited. . . . When they are in church, they act as if absorbed in thought, and sleepy. Many of them fall on the ground. . . . Some of them utter terrible groans and sobs, and others have sweats and tremblings."[9]

Some of the high priests of this abominable sect were ex-monks, expelled from their monasteries for good reasons; others were astrologers, quack doctors, sellers of charms and love potions, broken down soldiers from the Italian wars, and adventurers of other sorts. They preyed particularly upon emotional women, ill-taught *beatas*, ignorant nuns without vocations. A certain Fray Antonio de Pastrana, the first Illuminate discovered in Spain, under Cardinal Ximenes, made a specialty of seducing impressionable women, "to beget prophets by them," following the example of the notorious Italian *Pseudo-Apostoli* of the thirteenth century.

Much of this would seem too fantastic to believe if we did not have so much evidence in our own time of the grotesque lengths to which the religious instinct, when perverted, can lead human beings. It would seem incredible, too, that men and women could bring themselves to turn their backs on God and worship His adversary; yet satanism or diabolism unfortunately has existed in every age and very often among nonconformists who professed to be too spiritual to belong to the visible Church Catholic.[10]

Magdalena de la Cruz confessed to being a secret devil worshiper. At the age of seven, she said, she was induced by the devil to pretend to be very holy and to simulate the Crucifixion. At eleven, she made a pact with two *demonios incubos* called Balbán and Pitonio, who used to visit her by night under various forms — as a black bull, a camel, a Jeronymite friar, a Franciscan, and so on. Inspired by these foul paramours of darkness, she inflicted wounds on her hands, feet and side, in imitation of those of Christ; she became very skilful at all sorts of legerdemain, and she could feign trances in which she seemed to be insensible to the prick of needles. For ten to twelve years she pretended to live on the Sacred Host, until it was discovered that she had food hidden in her cell.[11]

To one who reads such grotesque revelations of human malice

---

[9] *Ibid.* For other particulars about the Spanish *Illuminati* see my *Characters of the Inquisition*, p. 204 and elsewhere.

[10] See the Espasa *Enciclopedia ilustrada*, etc., vol. 33, p. 724; and my *Characters of the Inquisition*, *passim.*

[11] Menéndez y Pelayo, *Historia de los heterodoxos españoles*, t. II, lib. V, p. 528.

and duplicity, and the naïvely sincere, pure, humble, God-fearing and loving record of Teresa's experiences, it seems incredible that anyone could have confused the two spirits. Yet such an error was possible to a public unaccustomed to making fine distinctions and none too well provided with catechisms.[12] After all, the pseudo mystics did display some of the outward signs of the real ones, just as in the crudest caricature there is some resemblance to the original. And so, as people began to talk more and more about the new *Beata* at the convent of the Incarnation, there were not lacking wise gossips who had it on the best authority that she was probably another Magdalena de la Cruz.

This was bad enough, but endurable, for Teresa had long since got rid of any desire for the good opinion of others. What cut her to the heart was a fear, born of humility, that they might be right.

"His Majesty began to give me very commonly the Prayer of Quiet, and often that of Union, which lasted a good while. But as great illusions had occurred in those times among women and deluded persons, I commenced to fear, since the delight and sweetness I felt was so great and often so irresistible. Granted, I saw in myself, on the other hand, a very great security which was God, especially when I was in prayer, and I saw that it left me very improved and with more strength. But in distracting myself a little, I began to fear again, and to wonder if the devil desired, by making me understand that it was good, to suspend my understanding so that I would give up mental prayer and not be able to meditate on the Passion or avail myself of my understanding. . . ."[13]

Perhaps she had become an *Alumbrada* without knowing it or intending it. What if the devil, who had once got her to give up mental prayer on the pretext of charity and humility, had made her imagine herself God's favored friend, when she was in reality one of the most poisonous of His enemies? She placed the harrowing questions, after a long and painful hesitation, before the Holy Cavalier and other friends.

Now, the very fact that she expressed such fears should have gone a long way to indicate not only her sincerity and humility (qualities for which the *Alumbrados* were never distinguished),

---

[12] *Ibid.*
[13] *Vida*, cap. XXIII.

but the objectivity with which she was able to scrutinize and to test her own experiences and reactions. It is usually a sane person, not a lunatic, who asks himself, "Am I insane?" and an honest man, not an impostor, who wonders whether he is being unfair. But Teresa's friends seem to have been more remarkable for piety and goodness of heart than for acuteness of understanding. After all, they were part of the public that had been horrified by the confessions of Magdalena. Who were they to assert that Teresa's ecstasies came from God and not the devil, when holy and learned men had been deceived by the nun of Córdoba? And Don Francisco, cautious, thrifty, unimaginative soul, had studied enough theology to know how easy it might be for a layman to make a fool of himself in that lofty and dangerous science. When Teresa told him she had faults which she had not been able to overcome, he used to reassure her, in the *locutorio* of the Incarnation, by saying that years ago he had had some very bad habits himself and it took him a long time to get rid of them. Let her not think that she could become perfect in a day. As for her mystical experiences, he could not believe God gave such favors to people still in the clutches of such faults as she imputed to herself. All this disturbed him so much that instead of quieting her fears, he multiplied them. However, he had one helpful proposal to make: he was well acquainted with Don Pedro Gaspar Daza, a *maestro* in theology, whom everyone in the whole province of Ávila knew about and respected. Why not tell him the whole story and abide by his advice? Poor Teresa was only too glad to grasp at this hope, and Don Francisco, at the first opportunity, brought the *Maestro* to the speak room of the convent.

The reputation of Daza must have given her considerable expectation that he would set her harassed soul at rest. He was then archdeacon of the Cathedral of Ávila, having refused a more important post of canon offered him by the Bishop of that place, Don Álvaro de Mendoza. He was a native of the town, well born, and according to all accounts an exemplary priest. He was in great demand throughout the province as a preacher, especially to communities of nuns. He had brought back many sinners to the Faith. He had organized an association of priests dedicated to the practice of evangelical perfection — works of prayer, mortification, penance, charity, frequent recourse to the Sacraments, and so on. He was noted also for his love of the poor: in the summertime he would buy coal and wood, store it until winter, and then distribute it among them. His portrait tells us that he was a grave, kindly, prudent man in middle life, with a bushy beard and moustache, both strikingly black in contrast with the high white cuff that hugged his chin and his long-lobed ears. His head was rather high and somewhat narrow, his brow average. A thoroughly good dependable man one would say, a sound but not a keen intellect, and not much imagination; one of those preachers who, without eloquence or brilliance, have great influence by sheer force of sincerity and goodness.[14]

"When he was brought to speak to me," wrote Teresa, "I was covered with the greatest confusion to find myself in the presence of a man so holy. I told him something about my soul and my prayer, but he did not wish to hear my Confession. He said he was very busy, and so it was."

It is hardly likely that the good *Maestro* had ever had such a soul to deal with before. This did not deter him from proceeding at once with a strong hand. From what she told him of her faults and imperfections on the one side, and the remarkable favors she had received from God on the other, he was inclined to agree with Don Francisco that the two were incompatible. Yet, assuming for the moment that her mystical experiences came from God, he ordered her to give up all her imperfections at once. She must not offend God in any way whatsoever.

"When I saw him so suddenly determined as regards those little things which, as I have said, I did not have courage to forsake at that time with such perfection, I was afflicted, and since I saw him dealing with the affairs of my soul as if it were something that had to be finished all at once, I saw that I needed much more careful attention. In short, I understood that I was not going to improve by the methods he was giving me, for though I was far advanced in the favors of God, I was only a beginner in virtues and mortification. And surely if I had had no one but him to deal with, I believe my soul would never have improved."[15]

Salcedo saw how matters were going, and came to console and encourage her. He told her more of his own battle against imperfection, and of the faults he still had after almost forty

---

[14] See his likeness in P. Gabriel, *op. cit.*, III, p. 57; other details in P. Silverio, *op. cit.*, I, pp. 372 *et seq.*
[15] *Vida*, cap. XXIII.

years of prayer. This prompted Teresa to tell him more about her own difficulties. He was more patient with her than the *Maestro,* and he went to great pains to advise her how to give up this and that *cosilla.*

"I began to have such a great love for him that I had no greater relief from care than on the days when he came, though they were few. When he delayed his coming I was very weary, for I thought he was staying away because I was so wicked."

Yet when he did come at last Don Francisco only made matters worse. Perhaps he had been thinking it over, perhaps he had been talking with Maestro Daza; at all events he now told her flatly that her faults and her favors from God did not agree with each other. Such favors, he said, "belonged to persons very far advanced, and very mortified, and he could not help being much afraid, for there seemed to him to be an evil spirit in some things, although he hadn't fully made up his mind." He asked her to tell him all she could about her prayer.

Teresa burst into tears. There are no words to describe mystical experiences fully, and hers were so recent that she felt utterly unable to give any idea of them. The grave old gentleman looked dubiously at her. A terrible fear took possession of her. Could anything be worse, or more confusing, than to be suspected by the two holiest people she knew of being the dupe of the devil?

Teresa rummaged desperately among her books to see if she could find anything by mystical writers that fitted her own case. Was she the only one who could think of nothing when in the highest state of prayer, or had others found it so as well? Finally, in a book called *"Subida del Monte Sion por la via contemplativa"* by Bernardino de Laredo,[16] she came upon a passage that seemed to describe something of what she had felt. Eagerly she underlined it and showed it to Don Francisco. Would he please talk it over with the Maestro Daza, and would the two servants of God tell her what to do, "and if they thought I should give up mental prayer altogether? For why should I place myself in those dangers . . . if I had had no benefit from it but to be deceived by the devil? It would be better not to do it at all; although this too would be hard for me, for I had proved already what my soul was without mental prayer. Thus I saw misery on

---

[16] Physician to King Juan II of Portugal, who later became a Franciscan lay brother. His book was first published in 1535, anonymously.

all sides, like one who is in the middle of a river, and whichever way he turns he fears greater danger, and there he is, almost drowned. It is a very great trial, that, and I have had many
of them, as I shall say later on; for though it may seem of no
importance, perhaps it will be of some use in understanding how
a soul should be tested. And it is great, surely, the suffering that
is endured, and there is need of circumspection, especially with
women, for great is our weakness, and much harm can be done
by telling them very clearly it is the devil without looking into
the matter very carefully and protecting them from the dangers
that may exist, and advising them to keep everything very secret.
And the men themselves should do the same, for it is only right
they should. And in this I speak as one whom it has cost plenty
of trouble, that certain persons with whom I have discussed my
prayer didn't do so, but asking this one and that one for a good
purpose, have divulged things that should have been very secret,
for they are not for all, and it looked as if I had made them
public. I believe the Lord has permitted it without any fault
on their part, that I might suffer. I don't say that they told what
I discussed with them in Confession, but as they were persons
to whom I told everything on account of my fears that they
might give me light, it seemed to me they should have kept
silence. With all this I never dared to conceal anything from
such persons."[17] Obviously Teresa is referring here to Maestro
Daza. The result of his well-meant consultations all over Ávila
will presently appear.

Meanwhile he and the Holy Cavalier, with the *Subida del
monte* before them, held a solemn conference, while Teresa
waited in great fear, having asked all her friends to pray that
God might show her the truth through them. "The two servants
of God considered with great charity and love what was good
for me." It was Salcedo who finally went to the Incarnation to
deliver the joint verdict.

"He told me that it was the opinion of both of them that it
was the devil, and that what I must do was to confer with a
father of the Company of Jesus, for if I should summon him,
saying I was in need of help, he would come, and I should give
him an account of my whole life in a general confession, and
of my condition and everything with much clarity, and by virtue

---

[17] *Vida*, cap. XXIII.

of the sacrament of Confession God would give him much light, for they [the Jesuits] were very experienced in matters of the spirit. And I must not depart from what he should tell me in anything, for I was in great danger unless I had someone to govern me.

"I was so frightened and pained that I did not know what to do. All I could do was weep."[18]

In this state she went to her oratory, and absent-mindedly picked up a book and opened it at random to a page of the Epistles of Saint Paul. "I thought the Lord had put it into my hands"; for her eyes fell gratefully upon these words of the Apostle to the Gentiles:

"And God is faithful, who will not suffer you to be tempted above that which you are able. . . ."

Teresa took heart again and asked Salcedo to bring a Jesuit father to see her.

[18] *Ibid.*

Image of Saint Joseph guarding a door of the primitive convent of San José at Ávila, which Saint Teresa, by divine command, placed under his protection.

Chapter X

THE ANGEL WITH THE FLAMING DART

S HE waited in an agony of prayer, hope, and fear. A Jesuit! To think of a Father of the Company coming to the Incarnation! How could one so wretched and unworthy dare to face him? What could she tell him? Where could she find words and courage? Imagine her, of all God's creatures, talking to a Jesuit!

Her apprehension reflects not only her own humility but the tremendous reputation that the Company of Jesus had gained in the one generation since Ignatius the soldier had been converted into Ignatius the follower of Christ. The new Order seemed providentially prepared for the necessities of that age of unrest and corruption. Everywhere men talked about the need of reforming the Church, but the task was titanic, and was made more difficult by the opposition of the very critics (not least among them the so-called "liberal" type of Catholic) who inveighed most loudly against the prevailing abuses. Saint Ignatius had the more Christian but rather uncommon idea of beginning, not with the world in general, but with himself. After that he began to dream the splendid dream that had animated the far less practical Ramón Lull two centuries before of converting the Mohammedan world. This, and not Protestantism, was uppermost in his mind when he and nine companions — one descended from originally Jewish stock, another a Basque noble's son — made their historic vow on the hill of Montmartre in August, 1534, either to go to Jerusalem, or if that was not possible, to walk to Rome and ask the Vicar of Christ how they could best serve God and their fellow men. It was not until 1538 that they all met in Rome. Everywhere they were viewed with suspicion, as possible heretics, everywhere they found hostility, persecution, and black slander as they begged money to feed the poor and tend the sick. Ignatius himself, who had been arrested by the Inquisition at Alcalá, had to clear himself from false charges of heresy and even of immorality at various places, and always did so vigorously and triumphantly. At last, having won the approbation of the Pope, the little band went preaching and ministering to the poor through Italy, and then in Spain and France.

The method of Ignatius was not primarily to attack abuses or even heresy, but the more positive course of preaching the truth of Christianity, and of giving good example by practising as perfectly as possible what he preached. In short, these ten men who took the words of Christ literally attempted to do always what they thought He would do under the circumstances. This method was bound to make them hated by the world that hated Him, but it was irresistible, and nothing in the sixteenth century better illustrates His parable of the mustard seed and the paradox of all things truly Christian than the almost incredible success that crowned the sufferings and labors of Ignatius and his friends. The distrust of Charles the Fifth and of the upper classes generally was overcome when the sight of death's havoc on the beautiful face of the Empress Isabel drove Francis Borgia, Duke of Gandia, into their ranks as a humble priest. Now, in 1554, they numbered almost a thousand in twelve provinces and a hundred houses, ruled by Saint Ignatius from Rome. Their original mission had been preaching and ministering to the poor and sick. Now they added the establishment of schools and colleges on a plan carefully worked out by their founder, and besides the ordinary three monastic vows they took a fourth, of absolute obedience to the Pope, binding themselves to go to any part of the world he might designate. Soon they would be laying down their lives beside the Ganges, on the coasts of Florida and Virginia, and in England and Poland. Saint Francis Xavier, whose highest aspiration had once been to have a fat benefice, took the cross to India. Jesuits introduced western science and culture in Japan as Franciscans had in China. The people everywhere called them "the Apostles." Wherever they went, the malignant spirit that tries to "dissolve Christ" found itself checked and repelled.

The first Jesuit in Ávila, it would seem, was Father Miguel de Torres, who journeyed there in 1550 at the request of certain persons to act as peacemaker in a convent of 120 nuns whose dissensions were becoming a serious scandal. His first talk so moved the hearts of his hearers that all of them, commencing with the Abbess, knelt and implored God's pardon, and discipline and harmony were restored. The people were so impressed that several begged the Jesuits to open a house among them.

The order could spare no men at that time, but it happened that Don Fernando Alvarez del Aguila, a relative of the wife of Don Francisco de Salcedo, decided to turn over to them a small college he had endowed and maintained. Becoming a priest he was received into the Company, and three years later returned to his native city to make the Jesuit foundation he had so desired. Early in 1554 the Bishop ceded the parish of San Gil for a Jesuit college.[1]

If the great and bellicose Dominican theologian Melchor Cano really believed, as he said, that the Jesuits were heretics and "precursors of the Anti-Christ," there were others in his and other orders who rose to defend them. Yepes, a Jeronymite, said that Teresa was attracted to them by their great reputation for sanctity and the good they did to souls. Julian of Ávila, who was to be her chaplain, attributed to them the beginning of the tremendous revival of Eucharistic devotion which was to receive its final sanction and universality four centuries later from Pope Pius X. He called them "these holy religious who, just as Jesus Christ sent his sacred Apostles to preach his holy Gospel through the whole world, now, as friends and allies of Jesus Christ and companions and imitators of his Apostles, have been sent to His holy Church to refresh and renew her with the frequenting of the holy sacraments of Confession and Communion, *which were so neglected in Christendom that there were very few persons who confessed and communicated more than once a year.*"[2] Here is trustworthy contemporary evidence of a condition which goes far to explain the scandals of the time, and the importance of the mission of the Society of Jesus.

By 1554 the Jesuits were guiding a considerable number of devout souls in Ávila. One of them was Doña Guiomar de Ulloa, who went to Confession to them at San Gil. Another doubtless was the Holy Cavalier, whose wife was a kinswoman of Father Aguila. Teresa also would have consulted them but for two obstacles. One was her humility, which made her fear she was unworthy to speak to them. The other was the fact that nuns of the Incarnation were allowed confessors only of their own order, and so she had never had occasion to consult the Fathers of the Company. This, together with a certain suspicion if not jealousy on the part of some of her sisters, may be the reason why great secrecy was observed in obtaining the Mother Superior's permission and in making the necessary arrangements at San Gil.

---

[1] Father Pons, S.J., in his edition of Ribera's *Life of Saint Teresa*, p. 122, n. 1.

[2] Julian of Ávila, *Vida de Santa Teresa*, Part I, ch. 10. Saint Ignatius called his institute the *Compañía* de Jesús. "Society" is from the Latin form.

Teresa meanwhile was writing out the sins of her whole life, together with a detailed account of the blessings she had received in prayer.

At last, one morning in March, 1554, there came to the portery of the convent a slender young man in black. No one was supposed to know who he was but the Prioress, the Portress, and the Sacristan. And of course Teresa herself. "I arranged with the Sacristan and the Portress not to tell it to anybody. It did me little good, for when they called me there happened to be someone at the door who told it through the whole convent. But what embarrassments and fears the devil puts in the way of anyone who wishes to attain to God!"[3]

The young Jesuit, it now seems certain (Teresa does not give his name), was Padre Diego de Cetina.[4] His appearance must have been a bit of a shock to her, for he was only half her age, being then but twenty-three, just out of the University of Salamanca, and only three years in the Company. Born in Huete (Cuenca) in 1531, he had been professed in 1551, and had studied at Alcalá before taking his course in theology at Salamanca.[5] In answer to a questionnaire sent him in 1554 (for Saint Ignatius kept closely in touch with all his priests), he made this very modest reply:

"I have half my health, and I am weak in the head. I was always inclined to recite the Hours of Our Lady, and to mental prayer, when they put me to it, and now I am inclined more to mental than to vocal prayer. I always have been partial to sermons, masses, and to speaking about our Lord. . . ." His Spanish superior, in a secret report sent to Rome, said of him eleven years later (two years before he died at the age of thirty-six), "He is a mediocre preacher and hears confessions and is fit for nothing more."[6]

With no striking traits of intellect or personality, then, this rather sickly priest lived his short life and died almost unnoticed by his contemporaries. Laínez thundered the truth at the Council of Trent, Saint Peter Canisius won back huge districts of Germany to the Faith, Saint Francis Borgia became the confidential adviser of kings and Popes, and Blessed Edmund Cam-

[3] *Vida*, cap. XXIII.
[4] Cf. P. Silverio, *Vida de Santa Teresa de Jesús*, I, p. 388, and his references.
[5] *Ibid.*, p. 389; also P. Gabriel, *La Santa de la raza*, III, p. 70.
[6] Silverio, *loc. cit.*

pion shed his blood as martyr on Tyburn hill; but of this poor Jesuit no notice was taken, except the half-contemptuous observation that he was good for nothing but preaching (and hearing confessions) and not much good at that. Yet this same poor Jesuit, humble and self-effacing, was able through his own experience with mental prayer to understand the soul of the great saint who knelt in Confession beside him, and to give her the exact and intelligent direction she had sought in vain from more famous clergymen.

Her relief and gratitude were boundless.

"When I had set forth all my soul before that servant of God (for such he was indeed and very expert too, as one who knew my language well), he told me what it was, and heartened me much. He said it was the spirit of God quite evidently; but that it was necessary to turn anew to [mental] prayer; for I was not well grounded, nor had I begun to understand mortification. And so it was, for I don't think I even knew the meaning of the word. And that I should not give up [mental] prayer by any means, but should exert myself all the more since God had given me such special favors; and who knew but that through my means the Lord wished to do good to many persons? And other things, in which I think he prophesied what the Lord has since done with me. And I should deserve much blame if I did not respond to the graces God had given me. In all this it seemed to me that the Holy Spirit spoke in him to heal my soul, so deeply did he impress it. He caused me great confusion; he guided me in such ways that I seemed wholly changed into another person. What a great thing it is to understand a soul!"[7]

Father Cetina probably made her follow some if not all of the *Spiritual Exercises* of Saint Ignatius,[8] which aimed at drawing the soul gradually nearer to God by contemplation of the sacred humanity of Christ. "He told me to make my prayer each day on a phase of the Passion, and that I should be the better for it, and that I should think only of the Humanity, and that I should resist those recollections and delights as much as I could, so that I should not give in to them until he told me otherwise.

"He left me consoled and strengthened, and the Lord helped

---

[7] *Vida,* cap. XXIII.

[8] Mir goes to considerable trouble (*Vida de Santa Teresa,* I, pp. 754–759) to argue that Teresa never took the Spiritual Exercises. Ribera said she did (*Vida de Santa Teresa,* I, cap. IX), and P. Silverio agrees (*op. cit.,* I, pp. 398–399).

me through him, and helped him to understand my condition and how to govern me. I remained determined not to depart from what he commanded me in anything, and so have I done to this day. Praised be the Lord, who has given me grace to obey my confessors, though imperfectly; and almost always they have been of those blessed men of the Company of Jesus."[9]

Thus she wrote about ten years later, adding that "my soul remained so docile from that confession that it seemed to me there was nothing I would not undertake, and so I began to change in many ways, although my confessor did not press me, but seemed to make little account of everything. And this moved me all the more, for he carried on by the method of loving God, and he gave me liberty and not compulsion unless I did it myself through love. Thus I went on for almost two months, using all my strength to resist the caresses and favors of God. As to my outward life the change was evident, for the Lord already had begun to give me courage to go through with certain things which persons who knew me, and in the same house too, said appeared to them extreme. And considering what I had done before they were right, they were extreme; but considering what I was obliged to do by the habit and profession I had, it still fell short. . . . I began to have a new love for the most sacred Humanity. My prayer began to settle down solidly like a building that already has mortar in it, and to incline me to more penitence, of which I had grown careless, having such great infirmities."[10]

For twenty years now she had had ghastly vomitings, morning and night, along with a chronic weakness of the heart. Father Cetina suggested a diagnosis which the *médicos* of Ávila had overlooked. "That holy man to whom I confessed told me that certain things could not injure me, that perhaps God gave me so much sickness because I did not do penance — His Majesty wished to give me some. He commanded me to do certain mortifications not very delightful to me. I did it all, for it seemed to me the Lord commanded it, and gave him the grace to rule me in such a manner that I should obey him. Now my soul began to feel any offense that I did to God, no matter how small it was, so that if I was wearing something superfluous I could not recollect myself until I put it off."[11] Her health grew better instead of worse under this treatment. Her morning vomitings

---

[9] *Vida,* cap. XXIII.   [10] *Ibid.,* cap. XXIV.   [11] *Ibid.*

ceased about this time, so that she was able to receive Holy Communion without waiting for the painful relief; the evening sickness, however, continued.[12]

What were these certain mortifications which she found "not very delightful"? She passes on, in her matter-of-fact way to more important matters. But Yepes mentions some of them. She wore a shirt of tin plate pierced like a grate, which left the tender flesh of her body streaked with wounds. She very frequently took "disciplines, not with the whips or cords used by ordinary penitents, but sometimes with nettles, sometimes with a bunch of keys," which she laid over her back until the blood flowed. The wounds suppurated, adds Yepes, and "gave out much matter," but the only medication she applied to them was a fresh series of blows. Once she gathered a quantity of blackberry brambles, took them to her cell, stripped herself, and "began to enter them and turn herself about among them as if she were on some luxurious bed, remembering the one that Christ had had on the Cross, and with this thought transforming the thorns into roses." In short she "sought in a thousand ways to imitate the sufferings of Christ." These trifling penances, she said, were a relief from the burning within her of an indescribable love of God, and her sorrow for having offended Him.[13] In this way she attained at last to detachment as complete as is possible to human nature.

When April flowered into the fragrant Castilian May of 1554, the young Jesuit told his penitent a joyful piece of news. Father Francis, he who used to be known in the world as Marqués of Lombay and Duke of Gandia, was in Spain, as Commissary of Saint Ignatius, inspecting the houses of the Company. Having gone to Tordesillas to visit Queen Juana *la loca*, the Emperor's mother, he had declined to stay at the palace where he had once been a page boy, but had lodged more humbly at the Hospital of *Mater Dei*. Now he was coming to Ávila for the formal opening of the new college of San Gil.

Older people of Avila remembered the splendid nobleman with the fine aquiline nose and laughing eyes who had entered the city twenty-three years ago, in attendance upon the Empress (now with God) and her son Prince Philip (now preparing to sail for England to marry Queen Mary Tudor), and all were

[12] *Ibid.*, cap. VII.
[13] Yepes, *op. cit.*, lib. I, cap. XI.

eager to see how the great Borgia would look in his black
soutane, how gray his handsome head had grown, and whether
his eyes were sad since he had trampled the glories of the world
under his feet. When he arrived in the middle of May, he received one of those delirious welcomes which the warmhearted
Spanish people love to give their heroes. Music, dances, proces-
sions, a gorgeous blaze of color, fireworks perhaps — nothing
was too good for the man who had renounced titles, wealth, a
great political career, to be a humble priest; who had declined
to be made a cardinal, and was content to make reparation for
the notorious sins of his family by daily austerities and prayer.
He was a preacher of uncommon eloquence, and when he spoke
at the Cathedral one day during the octave of Corpus Christi, a
tremendous crowd applauded. All the notables of the city, from
the Bishop to the most recent hidalgo, went to visit him.[14]

In the midst of all this he took time to listen to what young
Father Cetina and the Holy Cavalier told him about the nun
at the Incarnation. Would Father Francis speak to her, and hear
her confession? Of course he would; and he did.

"Well, after he had heard me," wrote Teresa, "he said that it
was the spirit of God, and that he thought it was not well to
resist it any further, though up to that time it was well done.
But I must always commence my prayer with a meditation on a
paso of the Passion, and if the Lord then should raise up my
spirit I should not resist it, but let His Majesty raise me up
without doing anything myself to bring it about. He gave
medicine and advice like one who had gone far along the road,
for in this matter experience counts for much. He said it was
wrong to resist any further. I remained very much consoled, and
the Cavalier also."[15]

Even the fears of Salcedo were quieted, then, for the time
being, and when the great Jesuit left Ávila after a few days, the
troubles of Teresa seemed to have fled forever. There followed
a period of daily joy and tranquillity in which she continued to
obey Padre Cetina with childlike trust. Whenever some unusual
doubt or perplexity arose, she would write, no doubt with her

---

[14] Father Pons, *op. cit.*, p. 122, note 1; P. Silverio, *op. cit.*, I, p. 393. Ribera gives
the date as 1557, unaware apparently that Saint Francis made two visits to Avila
(*op. cit.*, lib. I, cap. X). Polanco gives an account of this one in his *Crónica,* of
which Astrain gives a summary in his *Historia de la Compañía de Jesús,* t. I, p. 31.
[15] *Vida,* cap. XXIV.

confessor's permission or at his suggestion, to Saint Francis, and after some weeks would receive a letter of encouragement and advice. Wherever he went he spoke with affection and reverence for her, as if he had some intuition that although he would die first, she would be canonized many years before he would — if indeed his profound humility allowed him to imagine his elevation to the altars of the Church. Their correspondence, continuing after he became third General of the Society of Jesus, must have extended over some eighteen years, from 1554 until his death in 1572. Yet not one of their letters has been found. Were they destroyed, or will they yet be found in the archives of some old convent, or in some Jesuit library? What a lost treasure![16]

Joy, as Teresa often had occasion to notice, is seldom of long duration in this life. It was a blow when Padre Cetina was sent away from Ávila by his superiors in July, 1554. He had been her director for less than four months, yet he had helped her accomplish what she had been striving to attain for twenty years.

"I felt it very much, for I thought I should have to become good for nothing again, and it didn't seem to me possible to find another like him. My soul dwelt as in a desert, disconsolate and full of fear. I did not know what to do with myself."[17]

With his going, some difficulty arose at the Incarnation over permitting her to have an outside confessor. The Jesuits were no longer allowed to come to the Convent, nor was Teresa suffered to go, at least as freely as she wished, to San Gil. She felt this so much that a relative of hers, whose name she does not mention, took her into her own house. How this was arranged more easily than the visits of a Jesuit confessor does not appear. But Teresa states the fact clearly: "A kinswoman of mine arranged to take me into her house, and I was then able to go and get another confessor among those of the Company."[18] She probably confessed to Father Hernando del Aguila and to another Jesuit for a short time until they were sent away on other missions.

Her visits to San Gil led also to an acquaintance with a beautiful young widow who used to spend many hours before the

---

[16]Mother Isabel de Santo Domingo, in her deposition for the process of Saint Teresa's canonization, affirmed that she had seen many letters of Saint Francis, which Teresa had kept until her death (B.M.C., t. 19, p. 78; P. Silverio, *op. cit.*, I, pp. 396–397).

[17] *Vida*, cap. XXIV.

[18] *Ibid.*

Blessed Sacrament in the Jesuit church. Whether they first met there, or whether they were introduced by one of the fathers of the Company, the result was one of the most important friendships in Teresa's life.

A few months previously Doña Guiomar de Ulloa had been one of the gayest, as she was one of the richest and most admired of the young matrons of Ávila. At quite an early age she had married Don Francisco Dávila, lord of Salobralejo, of the illustrious house of Villatoro, whose annual income of a million *maravedis* was colossal for those days. First in Plasencia and then in Ávila they had lived gaily and luxuriously like most persons of their class. When Doña Guiomar went to Mass, for example, a squire or page would carry the costly silk pillow on which she would kneel. She had borne a son, and in 1554 was expecting a second child when her husband died. Like so many of the noble widows of Castilla, she turned from the pleasures of the world to the consolations of religion, gave her substance to the poor and to religious, lived and dressed plainly, and spent many hours in prayer, carrying to church a little piece of corkboard, under her mantilla,[19] to kneel on.

This woman rendered two great services to Doña Teresa. She obtained a second Jesuit director, who was also her own. He was Father Juan de Prádanos, who was sent to the College of San Gil in the spring of 1555, at the age of thirty-seven. He had been a novice with Father Cetina at Salamanca, and although he had been a priest not more than a year, was an adept at mental prayer and the understanding of souls. Under his more sure direction, for he was more intelligent than Father Cetina, Teresa advanced rapidly in the arts of prayer and mortification.

Secondly, Doña Guiomar obtained permission for her friend to go to live with her for a long period, commencing probably in the summer of 1559. This had the advantage of giving more privacy and consideration for the necessities of a contemplative than was possible in a convent of 130 nuns, of whom some had little sympathy for her.[20]

Teresa mentions the fact casually without explaining it. Doubtless a request from so influential a lady as Doña Guiomar would have great weight, all the more so considering the sort of household over which she presided; it was very much like a con-

---

[19] P. Gabriel, *op. cit.*, III, p. 83.
[20] Silverio, *op. cit.*, I, pp. 401–404.

vent. Besides Sister Teresa from the Incarnation, she had living with her a venerable poor woman of sixty, famous through all the province for her holy life and penances — María Díaz del Vivar, popularly called Maridíaz, who spent hours a day in adoration before the Blessed Sacrament. Teresa remained there three years, from 1555 to 1558.[21] She was able now to see her Jesuit director whenever it was necessary, to pray and do penance without being disturbed. Doña Guiomar hardly ever saw her guest, according to her own account, except for a few moments after dinner and supper.[22]

Padre Prádanos set for himself the task of completing the detachment of his penitent from all worldly affairs. She had already given up almost everything that a human being commonly enjoys in this life. All that remained was a lingering fondness for conversations with certain friends. These are not named. Perhaps Father Prádanos considered even the two pious women and the Holy Cavalier distractions to her.

One of the last intimacies that bound her to the world was severed in November, 1555, when her sister Juana, who had left the Incarnation in 1553 to marry Juan de Ovalle, left Ávila with him to live in Alba de Tormes. "She has the soul of an angel," wrote Teresa of this gentle and affectionate girl, and she never ceased to take a lively interest in Juana's family and their affairs. Nor was she less interested, a year later, in the marriage of their brother Lorenzo in Lima to Doña Juana Fuentes y Espinosa, daughter of one of the *conquistadores* of Peru. But if she was still capable of warm and practical devotion to those who had natural claims upon her, she achieved in the house of Doña Guiomar a degree of detachment for which there were some rather startling evidences.

This came about through the advice of Father Prádanos. He said no obstacle between the soul and God, however small, could be considered unimportant if one wished to please the divine Majesty perfectly. To this Teresa objected that it seemed like ingratitude to give up people who had shown her nothing but kindness.[23] Her confessor then told her to ask God for several days what He desired concerning her last few harmless friendships and to recite the *Veni Creator*. One day when she was

---

[21] *Ibid.*, pp. 405–411, and references. Maridíaz lived there until 1563.
[22] *Ibid.*, p. 407.
[23] Pons, *op. cit.*, p. 130.

reciting the hymn after prolonged mental prayer, there came upon her a rapture so sudden and so strong that "it almost took me outside of myself, a thing I could not doubt, for it was evident. It was the first time that the Lord had given me this favor of raptures. I heard these words: 'I desire that you no longer hold conversation with men, but with angels.' I was much frightened, for the commotion of my soul was great, and these words were spoken in my very spirit."[24]

Fear gave way to a deep and steady joy. From that moment she was no longer capable of particular love for anyone, even a relative or friend, who was not a lover and servant of God. "Unless I understand this of a person or know that he is one who practises mental prayer, it is a heavy cross to me to speak to anyone."[25]

There was nothing of oriental quietism in this attitude. On the contrary it inspired her to greater and more fruitful activity in God's service. For example, when Father Prádanos became seriously ill with heart trouble in 1556, from overwork at San Gil, and was given but two hours to live by the doctors, Teresa begged his life of God, and when he was convalescent, she and Doña Guiomar took him to one of the houses owned by the latter in a little place near Toro, and nursed him back to health. They probably went also more than once to Castellanos de la Cañada, for Teresa's brother-in-law, Martín de Guzmán y Barrientos, died suddenly about this time, and to her great sorrow, without the sacraments.[26] She did more than ever for others, but she did it more consciously for the love of God.

During the last of her three years at Doña Guiomar's, she began to have a new experience, at once terrifying and delightful. There came to her an awareness that Christ in His Sacred Humanity stood close to her. Her account of this, written at the command of her confessor, is a perspicuous piece of self-analysis:[27]

---

[24] *Vida*, cap. XXIV.

[25] *Ibid.*

[26] Silverio, *op. cit.*, I, 415–416. Mir, *op. cit.*, I, p. 278.

[27] *Vida*, cap. XXVII. I have kept Saint Teresa's careless construction in the first sentence, as elsewhere, to show how unconscious she was of mere literary effect. Her repetition of words is often confusing: this woman of genius can be redundant, tautological, and turgid. But the reader is entitled to her style, not that of a translator. She never bothered about such trifles as punctuation: sometimes page follows page without a period or a comma. Various editors have had to supply this lack, to make the work at all readable. In the main, I have followed Father Silverio's punctuation, but now and then, for the sake of greater clarity, I have taken the liberty to depart from it. The same applies to paragraphing.

"Being in prayer one day of the glorious Saint Peter, I saw beside me, or felt rather, for I saw nothing with the eyes of the body nor with those of the soul, but it seemed to me that Christ was close beside me, and I saw it was He who spoke to me, as it seemed. As for me, since I was quite ignorant that there could be such a vision, it gave me great fear at first, and I could but weep, although in saying to me a single word to assure me I remained as usual, quiet and joyful, and without any fear. It seemed to me that Jesus Christ was always at my side, and as it was not an imaginary vision, I did not see in what form, but I felt very clearly that He was always at the right side, and that He was witness of all that I did, and that never, when I was recollected a little or was not very distracted, could I fail to know that He was near me.

"Then I went to my confessor, weary enough, to tell him about it. He asked me in what form I saw Him. I told him that I did not see Him. He said to me, how did I know it was Christ? I told him that I did not know how, but that I could not fail to understand that He was beside me, and I saw it clearly, and felt it, and that the recollection of the soul was much greater in the prayer of quiet, and very continuous, and the effects were quite other than I used to have, and that it was something very plain. I could only use comparisons to make myself understood; and certainly, to my way of thinking, there is nothing that squares much with this sort of vision. . . . There are no words to say it here below, we women who know little, but learned men will make it better understood. For, if I say that I do not see Him with the eyes either of the body or of the soul, for it is not an imaginary vision, how is it that I understand and affirm that He is beside me more clearly than if I saw it? For to make it seem that it is like a person in the dark who cannot see another who is beside her, or if one is blind, does not serve. It has some similarity, but not much, for she feels with the senses, or hears her speak or move, or touches her. But here there is nothing of that, nor is any darkness seen; but it is represented to the soul by a sign, more clear than the sun. I do not say that any sun or brightness is seen, but a light which, without being light, illuminates the understanding so that the soul may take joy of such great good. It brings great blessings with it.

"It is not like a presence of God which is often felt, especially by those who have the prayer of union and of quiet, for it seems that in desiring to begin our prayer we find someone to speak with, and it seems we understand He hears us through the spiritual effects of great love and faith that we feel, and other tender resolves. That great favor is of God, and let him to whom it is given hold it dear, for it is a very lofty prayer. But it is not a vision, in which it is understood that God is there, through the effects which as I say, it makes in the soul, for by that means His Majesty wishes Himself to be felt: in this case it is clearly seen that Jesus Christ, Son of the Virgin, is here. In other forms of prayer, certain influences of the Divinity are represented; here, together with those, the Most Sacred Humanity also accompanies us and wishes to give us favors.

"Then the confessor asked me, 'Who said it was Jesus Christ?' I replied that He said so, many times; but before He said it to me, it was impressed on my understanding that it was He, and before this He used to tell it to me, and I did not see Him.[28] If a person whom I had never seen, but had heard of, came to speak to me, and I was blind, or in great darkness, and told me who he was, I should believe it, but I could not affirm it to be that person as confidently as if I had seen him. Here, yes, for without its being seen, a sign is impressed, so clear that it seems impossible to doubt it, for the Lord wishes it to be so graven on the understanding that it cannot be doubted any more than what is seen, or as much; for in that we sometimes suspect that we fancied what we wished to see, but here, although that suspicion may suddenly arise, yet there remains so great a certainty that the doubt retains no force."

At Mass on a feast of Saint Paul, probably January 25, 1558, Teresa became aware of Christ standing beside her in His Sacred Humanity, gloriously resurrected, with indescribable beauty and majesty. This was an intellectual, not an imaginary vision, and therefore, according to doctors of Mystical Theology, of a much higher type. Here Teresa is in exact agreement with Saint Thomas Aquinas[29] as to corporal, imaginary, and intellectual visions. The first, belonging to the purgative stage of mystic experience, comes through the physical senses, and may be a delusion; the second, occurring usually in the illuminative stage, is a positive representation, which exists, however, in the imagina-

---

[28] *"Mas antes que me lo dijese, se imprimió en mi entendimiento que era Él, y antes de esto me lo decía, y no le vía."*
[29] Saint Thomas, *Summa*, I, q. 93, art. 6; I–II, q. 174, art. 1.

tion; the third, experienced in the Prayer of Union, makes itself known directly to the understanding. Teresa's visions belong to this last and highest category. In her attempt to make them clear to others, she gives a long painstaking explanation, in which she struggles for the precise word, repeats frequently and has recourse at last to her favorite analogy of water:

"If I spent many years imagining how to delineate a thing so beautiful, I could not do it or know [how to do it], for it surpasses all that can be imagined here below, even in its whiteness and splendor alone. It is not a splendor which dazzles, but a soft whiteness and the splendor infused, which gives the greatest delight to the vision and does not tire it, nor does the clarity by which one sees this beauty so divine. It is a light so different from ours that the radiance[30] of the sun we see appears something so tarnished in comparison to that clear light that shows itself to the vision, that the eyes would not wish to open themselves afterwards. It is like seeing a very clear water which runs over crystal and reflects the sun [compared] to one very muddy with great cloudiness and it runs along the ground. Not that sunlight is seen, nor is the light like that of the sun: it seems, in short, natural light, and the other an artificial thing. It is light that has no night, but as it is always light, nothing disturbs it. In short, it is such that however great a person's understanding might be, he could not imagine how it is in all the days of his life."[31]

She makes an equally careful attempt to explain how she "heard" Christ's words without the agency of physical sense:

"They are certain words well formed, but they are not heard with corporal ears, but are understood much more plainly than if they were so heard; and not to understand it, however one resists, is out of the question. For when we do not wish to hear in this world, we can stop up the ears or turn to something else, so that even if it is heard it is not understood. In this conversation that God has with the soul there is no remedy, no, none, but they make me listen even in spite of myself, and [make] the understanding be so perfect to understand what God wishes we should understand, that it is not enough to like and not to like it. For He who can do all things wishes us to understand that

---

[30] *Claridad* means a little more here than our "clarity."
[31] *Vida,* cap. XXVIII, B.M.C., p. 219.

that which He wishes has to be done, and shows Himself truly our Lord."[32]

For two years or more she was almost continually aware of the presence of the Sacred Humanity beside her, and during those two years did all in her power to resist, fearing she might be deceived or unworthy. Yet invariably when prophetic words were spoken to her in the manner described, time demonstrated their truth.

It was in the house of Doña Guiomar, in 1558[33] apparently, that she first received the terrifying caress which is called her Transfixion. On several occasions while in rapture she experienced a prayer which she compared to "a certain kind of wounding; for it really seems to the soul as if an arrow were thrust through the heart, or through itself. Thus it causes great suffering, and makes the soul complain, but the suffering is so sweet that she wishes it would never end."[34]

Several times, too, she had this vision:

"I saw an angel beside me toward the left side, in bodily form, something I very seldom see. Although angels are often represented to me, it is without seeing them, except in the sort of vision I have already referred to. But in this one it pleased the Lord that I should see him thus: he was not large, but small, very beautiful, his face so blazing with light that he seemed to be one of the very highest angels, who appear all on fire. They must be those they call Cherubin,[35] who do not tell me their names; but I see plainly that in heaven there is so much difference of some angels to others, and of others to others, that I don't know how to say it. I saw in his hands a long dart of gold, and at the end of the iron there seemed to me to be a little fire. This I thought he thrust through my heart several times, and that it reached my very entrails. As he withdrew it, I thought it brought them with it, and left me all burning with a great love of God. So great was the pain, that it made me give those moans; and so utter the sweetness that this sharpest of pains gave me, that there was no wanting it to stop, nor is there any contenting of the soul with less than God. The pain is not physical but spiritual,

---

[32] *Ibid.*, cap. XXV.
[33] This on the evidence of Doña Guiomar. Cf. P. Silverio, *op. cit.*, I, p. 432.
[34] *Relations*, VIII.
[35] *"Querubines."* Some editors have changed this to *"Serafines."* But Teresa called this angel a Cherub.

although the body does not fail to share in it somewhat, and indeed plenty. It is such a delightful language of love that passes between the soul and God that I beg of His goodness that He give the enjoyment of it to him who may think I lie.

"The days that this lasted I went about as if distracted: I did not wish to see or to speak, but to burn myself up with my pain, which was greater glory to me than anything there is in all creation."[36]

To skeptical minds this vision will appear, perhaps, to be one of the most incredible of the mystical adventures of Teresa. Yet it happens to be one in which her word is supported by objective evidence. After her death her heart was found to be pierced through the center exactly as if it had been stabbed by a dart. More extraordinary still, the heart remains even now whole and untouched by decomposition after 359 years. It may still be seen in its reliquary at the Carmelite convent at Alba de Tormes. Many legends, some of them born of an hysterical devotion, have been invented concerning it, but when these have been discounted, the authentic phenomena remain.

In 1806 one of the nuns at Alba saw what appeared to be two thorns growing out of the heart. A third was noticed in 1864; and in 1870, an affidavit was made by fourteen nuns, affirming that they had seen the "thorns" and witnessed their growth. In 1872 the Bishop of Salamanca wrote to the head of the Carmelite order at Rome that the so-called thorns grew out of the small quantity of dust at the bottom of the tube of crystal, and not out of the heart itself.

In the same year three physicians, professors of medicine and surgery at the University of Salamanca, made an examination of the holy relic at the request of the Prioress, and left an interesting affidavit. They measured the organ. They noted that it was of a bronzed red, and in a state of preservation not to be accounted for by any natural causes. They found the perforation (or as they called it, with superscientific exactness, "a cessation of continuity") on both sides of the heart, above the left and right auricles. They confirmed the bishop's observation that the so-called "thorns" grew out of about half an ounce of dust in the bottom of the reliquary. They could find no scientific reason for their appearance and growth, and therefore set them down

---

[36] *Vida,* cap. XXIX.

as "preternatural and prodigious." Yet in our own time the Carmelite Father Silverio denies that there were any thorns, and deplores all such stories as tending to make ridiculous the true and unquestionable phenomena.[37] What seems certain is that the heart was not decomposed, and is perforated.

Teresa's raptures were becoming frequent, irresistible. She would see Christ in the Host at Mass, and especially after receiving Holy Communion she would be seized with an ecstasy in which sometimes her physical senses seemed no longer existent, while at times her whole body would rise in the air as if lifted by invisible hands or ropes, and would remain there suspended. Many reputable witnesses[38] testified to this phenomenon of levitation. One day when she was kneeling in the choir, waiting for the bell, another nun[39] saw her rise about eighteen inches from the floor. According to Yepes,[40] she once ascended higher than the window through which the Bishop of Ávila had just given her Holy Communion.

When this sort of thing happened in the presence of others, Teresa was much mortified, for she did not wish people to consider her a saint. Once when she felt herself leaving the ground, with the Sacred Humanity beside her, she said to Him, "Lord, for a thing of so little importance as to excuse me from receiving this favor, do not let a woman as bad as I am be esteemed good!" But the Lord evidently desired to draw her closer to Himself in this manner, and to make her sanctity known to others. At such moments her face was singularly youthful and beautiful, and sometimes would shine with light, like that of Moses coming down from the holy mount.

Such was the spiritual eminence at which she arrived during the years 1558–1560. She could now cry out with Saint Paul,

"With Christ I am nailed to the cross. It is now no longer I that live, but Christ lives in me."[41]

---

[37] *Vida*, B.M.C., t. I, p. 234, note 2. The text of the affidavit by the physicians of Salamanca, and of the Bishop's letter, are published by Father Pons, S.J., in his edition of Ribera, appendix, pp. 609 *et seq.*

[38] For example, Ana de los Angeles in the *Proceso de Ávila*, Silverio, *op. cit.*, I, 439, Mir, *op. cit.*, I, 285–286.

[39] Ana de la Encarnación, in the *Información de Segovia*.

[40] Yepes, *op. cit.*, lib. I, cap. 15.

[41] Gal. 2:19–20.

Chapter XI

THROUGH A HELL OF TORMENT TO THE END OF FEAR

WHEN Father Prádanos left Ávila late in 1558,[1] his place as Teresa's director was taken by another Jesuit, Father Baltasar Alvarez.

Like her former confessors of the Company, he was very young — only twenty-four, and in the first year of his priesthood. Born of a noble family in the province of Logroño, he had entered the Company of Jesus in 1555, and had begun his novitiate at Simancas, where Saint Francis Borgia saw him and discerned in him great spiritual qualities. His superiors then sent him to Alcalá for his bachelor's and master's degree in Arts, and then for theology to the Dominican fathers at Santo Tomás in Ávila. He had had rather a short course in scholastic theology when he was ordained in 1558, but was very advanced in mystical theology, subjected himself to great mortifications, and was much given to mental prayer. His cold, rather severe manner concealed an affectionate and understanding heart; and it was not long before he had such a reputation as a director of souls that nearly all the older Jesuits of the Province of Castilla used to consult him. He had hardly said his first Mass when he was made *ministro* of the College of San Gil. During the nine years he remained there, he lived in a room without even a table for his breviary and other books, and had no furniture but some chairs made of rude slats, without backs, for he denied himself even the small luxury of sitting comfortably or leaning against something.[2]

Padre Alvarez, like his predecessors, believed that Teresa's raptures and visions came from God. He must have heard too that Father Francis Borgia had talked with her a second time in 1557, when he had come to Ávila from the deathbed of old Queen Juana the Mad (to whom, in her last hours, he had brought the serenity and peace she had lacked so long) and had once more approved of her spirit. The chief fault of this

---

[1] From Ávila he went to Valladolid, where he remained the rest of his life.

[2] Silverio, *Vida de Santa Teresa de Jesús*, I, pp. 445–447, following La Fuente, *Vida del V. P. Baltasar Alvarez*, caps. 1 and 4. Also Astrain, *Historia de la Compañía de Jesús*, t. II, lib. II, cap. 4.

humble inexperienced young Jesuit was a certain timidity, which made him sometimes too ready to give way to the opinions of those about him. Certain older men of the Company who knew of the impostures of Magdalena de la Cruz and others, were still skeptical about the *Beata* of Ávila, even though few went as far as Padre Avellaneda, S.J., who told his students, "Don't waste time on women . . . but gently and firmly get away from them."[3] Then as today, a certain type of emotional woman who imagines herself to be holy can be a great trial and even a danger to her advisers. Father Alvarez, however, was not likely to err on the side of imprudence. "This great humility of his," wrote Teresa, "brought on me plenty of troubles."[4]

It was no easy task for a young priest, however holy, to direct a nun twice his age, who was likely at any time to be seized with a rapture of divine love that would lift her literally off her feet. Some of her visions at this time were, to say the least, disconcerting. One eve of All Souls, while she was praying at the house of Doña Guiomar with great recollection for those in purgatory, the devil perched himself on her office book and would not go away until she sent him flying with a dash of holy water; and "at that instant," she said, "I saw that some souls were leaving purgatory."[5] On another occasion she saw near her "a very abominable little black creature, snarling as if furious at losing where he had hoped to gain. When I saw him, I laughed and was not afraid, for there were several with me who were helpless, and did not know what remedy to apply to such torment, for great were the blows that he caused to fall upon me[6] without my being able to resist, on the body, head, and arms." She did not dare ask for holy water lest she alarm the others, who did not see the apparition. Finally, as the beating continued, she asked them for some. They got it and sprinkled her. The blows continued, and there stood the fiend, still spitting forth his hatred. Finally Teresa took some of the holy water herself and spattered it on him, whereat he vanished, leaving her sore and exhausted as if she had been beaten all over. More than once as she knelt in the choir or in her oratory the other nuns heard terrific blows raining about her.

---

[3] Silverio, edition of Saint Teresa's *Vida*, p. 224, note 1. See also below cap. 31.
[4] *Vida*, cap. XXVIII.
[5] Deposition of her niece Beatriz of Jesus (Juana's daughter) B.M.C., t. 18, p. 114.
[6] "*Eran grandes los golpes que me hacia dar.*" — *Vida*, cap. XXXI.

Nor was her lot in this respect unique. When Saint Paul speaks of being given an "angel of Satan" to buffet him[7] this is universally understood in a purely metaphorical sense, but there was nothing metaphorical in the modern instance of the Curé of Ars, who in the skeptical nineteenth century was not only thumped and whacked, but had his curtains and bed clothes set on fire by invisible hands.[8] For these happenings there are so many reliable witnesses that the fact must be accepted unless one is prepared to deny the validity of all human testimony. Such events are not pleasant either for the victim or the by-standers, if any; and young Father Alvarez may well have wished that someone else had the direction of a woman who went to him week after week with stories weird enough to raise goose-flesh on the most unimaginative. To make the matter worse, some of the anecdotes about the *beata* at the Incarnation (she went back there at the beginning of 1559, or earlier) had gotten around Ávila. People were beginning to look askance not only at her but at her confessor. Some volunteered the advice that if he kept on hearing the confessions of one so obviously in the power of the devil, he might become just as bad himself, he might go raving mad, he might lose his soul.

Those who warned him most urgently, strange to say, were five or six of Teresa's dearest friends — all of them in fact except Doña Guiomar, who never doubted her. And no one was more firmly convinced that she had been deluded by evil spirits than her old friend Don Francisco de Salcedo. Indeed, the Holy Cavalier went so far as to ask Father Alvarez to have her exorcized; and all this, as Teresa admits, from the kindest motives, for if his fears were true it would be a service of charity to have her rid of so foul a fellowship. A great part of the modern world looks upon possession as a sort of medieval joke. Unfortunately for this theory, there is a mass of evidence to attest the reality of the phenomenon even in our own times. There have been several exorcisms in the United States, for example, during the past ten or fifteen years.[9] Small wonder that Teresa's

[7] 2 Cor. 12:7.

[8] Henri Ghéon, *Secret of the Curé of Ars*.

[9] For example, the one made in Iowa in 1928, by the Rev. Father Theophilus Riesinger, described in the hair-raising pamphlet, *Begone, Satan*, by the Rev. Father Celestine Kapsner, O.S.B., published at Saint John's Abbey, Collegeville, Minn.

friends were in a veritable panic, which was rapidly spreading to a large part of the population of Avila.

This is doubly understandable when one recalls the state of the world in 1559. For two years the Spanish people had been ridden by fear and bewilderment. When Charles V returned ailing and prematurely old in October, 1556, to spend his last days in the monastery at Yuste, he relinquished the crown of Spain to his son Philip II, and with it a sort of fool's paradise of imperial policies. While the Duke of Alba marched on Rome and humiliated Pope Paul IV, Philip raised a great army, with which he inflicted a crushing defeat on the French at St. Quentin. As husband of Mary Tudor he clung to receding hopes of bringing England back into the Catholic fold. He had lost his chance of succeeding Charles as emperor. Still, with all the Spanish possessions — and England — he expected to be the most powerful monarch in the world. And as a sincere Catholic he intended to use all his influence to undo the work of Luther and of Calvin, to bring back unity to Christendom, and to put an end to the threat from the Mohammedans, whose galleys in 1558 scourged the coasts of Italy and took Tripoli from the Knights of Saint John.

From this rosy dream Philip was roused by a series of rude shocks. His war against the Pope was exceedingly unpopular in Spain, where men had dared to cry out against the sack of Rome by the Imperial troops in the year of his birth; and his treasury being bare, he could not follow up his advantage against the French. When his wife died, Philip had some notion of marrying her sister Elizabeth. But he had been outwitted by the rich men from whom he had neglected to take the loot of the Church when he might have done so; now they had the new queen in their hands, and they made sure that England's weight should be permanently on the anti-Catholic side. Meanwhile the Emperor made an appalling discovery in Spain. While he and his son had been defending the Catholic Church in far places, the heresy they were hunting in England, Germany, and (by counsel to the French king) in France, had secretly invaded Spain, and had become a menace to the political and religious unity so dearly won by Ferdinand and Isabella. Hence, although the Inquisition had lapsed into comparative inactivity again after the exposure of Magdalena the Alumbrada, the Emperor ordered it to resume all its original vigor, and to purge Spain of every anti-Catholic conspiracy. The result was the discovery of plots in which even some of his favorite chaplains and court preachers were involved with members of some of the richest and most influential families in Spain.

Philip at the same time was alarmed to find Fray Bartolemé Carranza de Miranda, confessor to his wife, and his nominee for Archbishop of Toledo, suspected of holding Lutheran views: and he allowed him, after a long investigation, to be arrested by the Inquisition. An eloquent court preacher, Doctor Constantino Ponce de la Fuente, was found to be not only a secret Lutheran, but a bigamist, and committed suicide in prison. In Seville, the heresy had roots in the lax Jeronymite monastery of Saint Isadore, whence it spread to nuns and monks elsewhere, and to laymen and women throughout the city. In Valladolid the Lutherans were holding meetings in the middle of the night at the home of Don Agustín Cazalla, doctor of the University of Salamanca and one of the Emperor's most esteemed chaplains, until their activities were discovered by the jealous wife of one of their number.

The political as well as religious danger in all this for a Spain restored to independence and unity only a generation before, is indicated by the grim boast that Doctor Cazalla is said to have made in the prison of the Holy Office: "If they had waited four months to persecute us, we should have been as many as they; and in six months we should have done to them what they are doing to us." The history of Protestant movements elsewhere suggests that when Philip II ordered the Holy Office to take the swiftest and sternest measures against the conspirators in Valladolid and elsewhere, he saved his country from one of those civil wars that devastated France for half a century, and destroyed Germany in the Thirty Years' War.

Philip was still in the Low Countries, but his sister and regent, the Princess Juana, carried out his instructions to cooperate in every way with the Inquisitors. When Cazalla and thirty others were found guilty, she and Don Carlos, heir to the throne, together with Don Juan of Austria, attended a great *auto de fe* in Valladolid on May 21, 1559. Nothing so terrible had happened in Spain in years. A crowd of more than 200,000 assembled to see the brilliant and somber procession, at the end of which, in yellow *sanbenitos*, walked so many persons of high social position, headed by the famous Doctor Cazalla himself. Sixteen who repented or had extenuating circumstances in their favor abjured their errors and were absolved by the Archbishop and reconciled to the Church. Fourteen others were handed over by the Inquisition to the royal officials as impenitent and dangerous heretics; and as heresy was considered a form of high treason (and worse) they were taken outside the city walls after the *auto*, and burned by the secular officials. Thus perished Dr. Cazalla and his brother, Francisco de Vivero, both priests who had secretly betrayed the Faith they professed; their two sisters; a knight of the Order of Saint John; a knight of Zamora; a judge named Herrera; the Bachelor Herrezuelo; and three other women. All but one were strangled before being burned. Some of the women were nuns who, until their hypocrisy was uncovered, had been considered holy.

When King Philip arrived from the Netherlands early in the autumn, one of his first public acts was to attend a second great *auto de fe*, October 8, in the same city. Of the twenty-eight condemned on that occasion, fourteen, including a nobleman named Don Carlo de Seso, were burned after the *auto*. The King did not attend the executions; his supposed love of such spectacles is part of the legend created about him by enemies of Spain and of the Church.

In Sevilla fifty were burned, including a venerable Dominican who under cover of a great reputation for sanctity was found teaching Protestantism to his noble penitents and lending them Lutheran books in Spanish. In the following year, twenty-nine Catholics who had secretly been teaching Judaism were burned.

To the Spanish Catholic, whose ancestors had suffered so much for the Faith, the dogma of Luther on good works was only a new version of the semioriental pessimism underlying the tenets of the Illuminates and other Manichaean heretics. The odium that had been bestowed upon the *Alumbrados* was now transferred, therefore, to the propagators of Lutheranism. An element of race hatred was added when many of them, like Cazalla, were found to be descended from families whose secret attempts to destroy the Catholic Church while pretending to belong to it had led *los reyes católicos* to establish the Spanish Inquisition. All this reacted doubly against Sister Teresa of the Incarnation. She had already suffered from an unjust comparison with the notorious Magdalena the *Alumbrada*. Now people were beginning to suspect her of being one of the new Lutheran sect. Had not the followers of Dr. Cazalla been busy proselytizing in Ávila? They had even approached Doña Guiomar de Ulloa and her friends, knowing from experience that poorly instructed but zealous *beatas* were easily persuaded to take up innovations that wore the garb of reforming piety, and that widows were especially vulnerable; but on learning that they confessed to different priests of various orders, gave up the attempt.[10]

Something of all this became known, no doubt, in Ávila. Very respectable people were saying that it was time the Inquisition looked into some of the goings-on in the house of Doña Guiomar and in the Incarnation, and that if that *beata* did not have care, she would be burned. If distinguished persons in the court had been sent to the bonfire, how could she hope to escape? Some of the nuns in her own convent, especially those who had had no sort of mystical experiences, thought her deluded and possessed, and thus brought the atmosphere of suspicion to the very door of her cell. Acquaintances began to avoid her. Some said she was probably being punished for secret sins in her past life which she had concealed from her confessors.[11] Others said she was a lost soul, beyond hope of redemption. Those who uttered the cruelest slanders were some of the fair-weather friends for whom she had done most.[12] She found it hardest to endure the ill opinion of good people whose distrust of her was perfectly sincere.[13]

Even the consolation of books was now denied her. Unable at this time to read Latin, she had derived satisfaction, and in the first stages of mental prayer much help toward recollection, from a few books in "Romance," that is to say the vernacular Spanish. Her little library included a copy of the *Flos Sanctorum;* the noted *Vita Christi,* by a Carthusian, Ludolph of Saxony, which had been translated into Castilian by order of Ferdinand and Isabella; a translation of the *Epistles* of Saint Jerome; the *Morals* of Saint Gregory; the *Confessions* of Saint Augustine; *The Imitation of Christ* or as it was then called, *Contemptus mundi,* beautifully translated by Fray Luis de Granada; the *Oratorio de religiosos y ejercicio de virtuosos* by Fray Antonio de

---

[10] Venerable Ana of Jesus, deposition for St. Teresa's canonization, B.M.C., t. 18, pp. 471–472.

[11] Yepes, *op. cit.,* lib. I, cap. XII.

[12] *Ibid.*

[13] *Vida,* cap. XXVIII.

Guevara; the *Tercer Abecedario* of Osuna, to which she had owed so much in her youth; and the *Subida del Monte Sion* by Fray Bernardino de Laredo, which she had shown to Salcedo and Daza with such disastrous effect in 1554.[14] All these pious works would seem harmless enough for any nun. But as a great deal of the underhand proselytizing of Doctor Cazalla and his associates had been done by means of religious books in the vernacular, including some by Archbishop Carranza, the Inquisitor General Valdés published an Index in 1559 proscribing many such publications in Spanish. The list was so comprehensive that it included not only heretical works, but such innocent ones as the *Tratado de oración y meditación* by Fray Luis de Granada.

The decree was a great trial to Teresa. "When many books in Romance were taken away, that they might not be read, I felt it much, for some of them gave me recreation to read. . . ." Then she heard the voice of Christ say, "Never mind, I will give thee a living book."[15]

Yet when this moment of heavenly consolation passed away and the hell of conflict raged again about her bowed head, the divine words, more real when spoken than reality itself, seemed to fade in the memory like something heard long ago in a dream, while the sinister voice of a false humility whispered to her exhausted and blunted understanding that perhaps, after all, she had been deceived by her own presumption.[16] Thus there descended upon her, in 1559, the most terrible trial of her whole life. Without books, distrusted and threatened by the public, doubted and feared by her friends and by her sisters in religion, mocked by an all-too-real spirit of evil, which in this final hour of the dark night of her soul's purgation was permitted to take visible shape beside her and to jibe from a foul and terrifying mouth that she would not escape from his hands this time,[17] the poor woman grieved in a Gethsemani where there seemed no hope of solace save from a young confessor who might any day yield to plausible arguments and to his own fears, and abandon her to despair. What would become of her if he forsook her? "I was afraid that I should have no one to hear my confes-

---

[14] P. Gabriel, *op. cit.*, III, p. 122.
[15] *Vida*, cap. XXVI.
[16] *Ibid.*, cap. XXX.
[17] *Ibid.*

sion, but that everyone would flee from me. I did nothing but weep."[18]

Father Alvarez assured her that he would not desert her. He must have been tempted to do so. "My confessor, as I say, was a very holy man of the Company of Jesus. . . . As I was in such fear, I obeyed him in everything, although imperfectly, and so he spent a good three years with me as my confessor, with these trials; for in great persecutions I had, and in plenty of things in which the Lord allowed them to judge me ill, and many without any fault of mine, withal they came to him and he was blamed for me, being without any fault himself. It would have been impossible if he had not had such sanctity and the Lord inspiring him, to be able to endure so much, for he had to make answer to those who thought I was lost and who did not believe him; and on the other hand he had to quiet me and to cure the fear I had, for my greater amendment. On the other hand he had to reassure me; for at each vision, being a new thing, God permitted great fears to stay with me afterwards. All came from my having been such a great sinner."[19]

Father Alvarez was taking no chances. There must not be another Magdalena de la Cruz in Spain, if he could help it. He decided to put Teresa's spirit to every possible test. One of the most excruciating of these was the general confession he insisted on her making at the College of Saint Gil, not through the customary dark grating, but kneeling before him with her face uncovered,[20] while he, no doubt, watched her every expression as a cat watches a bird, for any telltale evidence to confirm the fears of her friends that she might have concealed some sin of her past life.

"I had a confessor," wrote Teresa with great humility, "who mortified me much, and sometimes afflicted me and gave me great trouble, for he disquieted me much, and it was he, as I think, who did me the most good. And although I loved him much, I had some temptations to give him up, and I thought those pains he gave me concerning my mental prayer hindered me. Each time I was determined to do so, I understood at once that I should not, and one reproof would afflict me more than

---

[18] *Ibid.,* cap. XXVIII.

[19] *Ibid.*

[20] Ana de los Angeles and Inés de Jesús so declared in the *Proceso de Ávila,* B.M.C., t. 19, p. 554; see also Silverio, *op. cit.,* I, p. 456. note 1.

the confessor could. Sometimes he tired me out: question on one side and scolding on the other, and I needed all of it, seeing that I had my will so little broken. He told me once that I should not obey unless I was determined to suffer; let me take a look at what He had suffered, and all would be easy to me."[21]

One explanation of the severity of Father Alvarez has been that in addition to being bedeviled by the good people who wanted him to save Teresa from herself, he was undergoing, at this time, some harrowing spiritual desolations of his own, similar to those that afflicted his penitent. Severe at all events he was, both on himself and on others. Ribera, the Saint's first biographer, who knew them both well, says that Teresa remarked to him, laughing, "I love this father of mine very much, though he has a bad disposition." One day Father Alvarez showed Ribera a great pile of spiritual books, and said ruefully, "I had to read all those books to understand Teresa of Jesus!"[22] Doubtless the knowledge that he was enduring a great deal to be of service to her gave Teresa courage to go on. The real proof of her conviction that in spite of everything he was the best possible confessor for her, and the chosen instrument of God for the perfection of her soul, was that she continued to follow his commands for six years, at the most crucial period of her life, even after he left Ávila. "He consoled me with much compassion, and if he had believed in himself I should not have suffered so much, for God gave him to understand the truth of everything, for the Sacrament itself gave him light, as I believe."[23]

He used to discuss her raptures and visions (not her sins, of course) with five or six of her friends, including the Holy Cavalier, and made no bones about reporting to her what they had said. "And my confessor told me that all were convinced that it was the devil, and that I should not communicate so often, and that I should try to divert myself in such wise that I should not be in solitude. I was fearful in the extreme, as I have said, and my heart trouble helped me along, for I did not dare even to be in a room alone, often by daylight, too. I, as I saw that so many affirmed it and I could not believe it, became scrupulous to the last degree, thinking I had little humility, for

[21] *Dijome una vez,* etc. The reference might be to Father Alvarez, but most editors have taken it to mean our Lord. Canon Dalton translates, "Our Lord said," etc., *Vida,* cap. XXVI.

[22] Ribera, *Vida de Santa Teresa,* lib. I, cap. XI.

[23] *Vida,* cap. XXVIII.

all were more of good life beyond comparison than I, and learned too, and so why should I not believe them?"[24]

Her confessor followed the advice of the spiritual *junta* and made her stay away from Communion day after day for nearly three weeks. He even permitted the "five or six" to confront her in a body and cross-examine her. Imagine the scene: Teresa almost at the end of her patience, her friends sadly exchanging glances, the Holy Cavalier more fearful than ever.

"As I used to say some things carelessly, which they understood in a different sense (I loved one of them much, for my soul was infinitely in his debt and he was very holy), I grieved infinitely to see that he did not understand me, and he greatly desired my improvement and that the Lord gave me light: and so what I said, as I say, without reflecting seriously on it, seemed to them slight humility. When they saw some fault in me, and they might have seen many, then everything was condemned. They used to ask me various questions. I replied with sincerity and carelessly. Then they thought I wished to teach them, and that I considered myself wise. All this went to my confessor, for certainly they desired my improvement; he had to scold me."[25]

There came a time when it seemed as if she could not endure one more suspicious word or look. For twenty days of unutterable loneliness and desolation she had gone without the Bread of Life at her confessor's command. Even God seemed to have deserted her as she knelt all alone, trying to pray; and instead of the divine comfort there descended upon her a terrifying and paralyzing helplessness which left her unable to form words or to read them, unable to think any thought except the foul and heavy one that perhaps she was the dupe of the devil and might be lost forever. Tired and sick and tormented, still she rejected this perilous idea. Dimly but tenaciously, in the deepest sanctuary of her struggling soul, she clung to some tenuous thread of hope in this darkest of spiritual nights; and thus she remained kneeling like a statue of agony for four or five hours.

"There was no consolation for me either of heaven or of earth, but the Lord left me fearing a thousand perils, to suffer."

Finally as she stood her ground with the last desperate ounce of strength, the tide of battle turned, the familiar Presence stood

---

[24] *Ibid.*, cap. XXV.
[25] *Ibid.*, cap. XXVIII.

beside her, and the Voice spoke with delightful clarity through the parched and empty places of her soul some of the very words that Moses had heard from the burning bush:

"Have no fear, daughter, for I am, and I will not forsake you, have no fear."

At the recollection of this three or four years later, Teresa wrote: *"Oh Señor mío,* how true a friend you are, and how powerful. . . . Let all things praise You, Lord of the world! . . . Let all the learned men rise against me, let all created things persecute me, let the devils torment me, You will not fail me, Lord, for I have had experience of the gain with which You rescue whoever trusts in You alone. . . . Oh what a good God! And what a good Lord and how powerful! . . ."[26]

This was not the last of her trials, however, by any means. Father Alvarez had assured her at various times that even if some of her experiences were of diabolical instead of divine origin, she need not be afraid, for the devil could do her no harm so long as she did not offend God;[27] all she had to do was to continue to appeal to Him in prayer, and he and her other friends would do likewise. There were days, however, when the young Jesuit had to leave Ávila on some mission or other; and then Teresa had to begin all over again trying to make herself understood by a temporary confessor. There was one substitute, in particular, who subjected her to a trial to which her artless pages have given a grotesque immortality.

Who was the priest who made her drink the last dregs in the cup of her mortifications? Teresa charitably left him nameless. The ex-Jesuit, Mir, assumes without the slightest proof that any substitute for Father Alvarez would necessarily be another Jesuit; he goes even further and suggests that it was Father Jerónimo Ripalda, S.J., one of the most distinguished preachers and writers of his day. Apart from the possibility that Teresa might have confessed to a secular priest in the absence of her Jesuit adviser, it now seems established that this actually happened, and that the anonymous priest was not a Jesuit, but Father Gonzalo de Aranda, one of her best friends in Ávila; for his name was written in the margin of Fray Luis de León's edition of her autobiography in 1588 by no less an authority than Father Gracián, who was her director and confidant during the last seven years

---

[26] *Ibid.,* cap. XXV.
[27] *Ibid.*

of her life. Nor did he necessarily deserve the pharisaical scorn that has been heaped upon his memory. Father Silverio is probably right in concluding, from the fact that Teresa shifts from "he commanded me" to "they commanded me" that her temporary confessor talked the matter over with Salcedo, Daza, and other friends, and was expressing their joint advice — advice which seemed quite natural in that age, however shocking it may seem in ours.[28]

It came about in consequence of a great spiritual favor that Teresa received at this time. Her visions were increasing in frequency, approaching the apogee of their splendor. In that "light that never sets, and has no night"[29] which flooded her whole being with joy, she had begun not only to be aware of the presence of Christ, but to see Him in His sacred humanity. She records this with her usual care and exactness.

"In some things it seemed to me indeed that it was an image that I saw, but in many others, rather it was Christ Himself, judging by the clarity with which He was pleased to show Himself to me. Sometimes it was so indistinct that it seemed to me an image, not like the paintings of this world, very perfect though they may be, for I have seen plenty of good ones. It is nonsense[30] to think that one in any way has resemblance to the other any more or less than a live person has to his portrait, which, however well it may be taken, cannot be as artlessly real, for in short it is seen to be a dead thing. But let us leave this, for here it fits well, and very literally.[31]

"I don't say it is a comparison, for they are never so exact, but truth itself, as different as the living is to the painted, neither more nor less. For if it is an image, it is an image alive; no man dead, but Christ living. And He gives [us] to understand that He is man and God, not as He was in the sepulcher, but as He came from it after returning to life. And He comes at times with such great majesty that there is no one who can doubt but that it is the Lord Himself, especially just after communicating, for we already know that He is there, for faith tells us so. He

---

[28] Mir, *Vida de Santa Teresa*, I, pp. 384–385; P. Silverio, *op. cit.*, I, 469 *et seq.*
[29] *Vida*, cap. XXVIII.
[30] Teresa wrote *"es disbarate"* here for *"es disparate"* — as though one wrote "It is apsurd," etc.
[31] *"Mas dejemos esto, que aquí viene bien y muy al pie de la letra."* — *Vida*, cap. XXVIII.

shows Himself so much Lord of that dwelling that the soul seems all dissolved to see itself consumed in Christ. *Oh Jesús mío, who could make understood the majesty with which You show Yourself?"*

This kind of vision, Teresa goes on to explain, is so over-powering that no one could endure it except in a state of rapture or ecstasy.[32] It was not merely something she had imagined, of that she was quite sure: "for how could we, by any effort of our own, represent the humanity of Christ, or summon up His great beauty with the imagination?" The imagination would have to take time to conceive of one detail after another, until the image was completely fabricated. But in these visions there is no choice for the beholder. She sees what the Lord wishes her to see, and as He desires, and sees it whole, says Teresa, nor can she add or subtract anything.

For two and a half years she frequently enjoyed the sight of His unspeakable beauty, "and the sweetness with which He speaks those words with that most beautiful and divine mouth, and other times with rigor, and I desiring extremely to know the color of His eyes, or what size and shape He[33] was, so that I might know how to tell it, but I have never deserved to see it, nor was I able to do so before the vision was completely lost to me. Sometimes, though, I see Him looking at me with com-passion; but this sight is so overpowering that the soul cannot endure it, and I am seized with such sudden rapture, that I lose this beautiful sight, better to enjoy it all. . . .

"Almost always the Lord has shown Himself to me resusci-tated in this way, and in the Host the same, unless it were that sometimes to encourage me when I am in tribulation He showed me the wounds, sometimes on the Cross, and in the Garden; and with the crown of thorns a few times; and carrying the cross also, sometimes, for my necessities, as I say, and for those of other persons, but always the flesh glorified. Plenty of affronts and trials I have undergone in telling it, and plenty of fears and plenty of persecutions."[34]

Her substitute confessor was one of those who thought that such visions must come from the source that Hamlet feared:

---

[32] *Ibid.*

[33] *U de el tamaño que era.* Teresa plainly uses the singular, referring to His stature, though some editors have made it plural.

[34] *Ibid.*, cap. XXIX.

"The spirit that I have seen
May be the devil; and the devil hath power
To assume a pleasing shape; yea, and perhaps
Out of my weakness and my melancholy,
As he is very potent with such spirits,
Abuses me to damn me."[35]

How could Teresa be sure that the devil was not conjuring up an illusory image of Christ to make her proud and self-satisfied, and so to gain her soul and those of others who might believe in her? Yes, it clearly was the devil, said her temporary director; and therefore she must treat him with the scorn and contempt he deserved. Finding that he was getting nowhere, the foul wretch would soon leave her in peace. Let her make some gesture of scorn whenever the fiend approached her, even in the loveliest guise: *give him the fig*.

This was a gesture of contempt, probably of some obscene origin of which Teresa was ignorant, but very well known in Italy and Spain from ancient Roman times as a protection against witchcraft and particularly against the Evil Eye. It was made by thrusting the thumb between the index and middle fingers. People wore jet or coral amulets representing it. One of these is shown at the Carmel of Medina del Campo as the instrument of the famous "higas"[36] that Teresa was told to give the devil. Some doubt this, but the people of her time would have found nothing strange in her wearing it. It was well known as far away as England. "When Pistol lies," exclaims that worthy in *The Second Part of Henry IV*, "do this; and fig me, like the bragging Spaniard";[37] and in *Henry V* he says to Fluellen, "Die and be damned! and Figo for thy friendship. . . . The fig of Spain!"[38]

There was nothing humorous in this to Teresa as she sadly set about carrying out instructions. It was probably the most difficult and repulsive thing she had ever done in all her life, this business of insulting the Lord God (for she did not doubt it was He during the visions) out of obedience to the Lord

---

[35] Act II, Scene 2. See also *Measure for Measure*, Act II, Scene 2:
"O cunning enemy, that, to catch a saint
With saints dost bait thy hook! Most dangerous
Is that temptation that doth goad us on
To sin in loving virtue."
[36] "*Ficas*" in old Spanish, *la fica* in Italian, *la figue* in French, etc.
[37] *2 Henry IV*, Act V, Scene 3.
[38] *Henry V*, Act III, Scene 6; see also Act IV, Scene I.

God through his minister. Obedience is the cornerstone of all virtues; and so Teresa would bless herself, take holy water, carry a crucifix in her hand, and then, with a tremendous effort of the will, and doubtless often with moans and sobs, make the insulting gesture at the living figure of the suffering Christ.

She tells this painful experience with her usual frank simplicity. "To me this was a great sorrow, for as I could not but believe it was God, it was a terrible thing for me; nor on the other hand could I desire, I have said, that He should leave me; but, in short, I did whatever they commanded me. I implored God much that He deliver me from being deceived; this I always did, and with plenty of tears, and Saint Peter and Saint Paul too, for the Lord told me, since it was on their day He appeared to me for the first time, that they would protect me from being deceived; and so I often saw them on the left side very clearly, though not with imaginary vision. I was very devoted to these glorious saints.

"This business of giving the fig[39] caused me the greatest sorrow when I saw that vision of the Lord. For when I saw Him present before me, I could not believe, if they cut me to pieces, that it was the devil, and so it was a sort of heavy penance for me; and to avoid going around blessing myself so much, I carried a cross in my hand. This I did almost always; the figs not so continually, for it hurt me much. I remembered the insults the Jews had done to Him, and I begged Him to pardon me, since I did it to obey the one He had in His place, and not to blame me, for they were the ministers that He had placed in His Church. He told me not to worry about it, that I did well to obey, but that He would make the truth understood. When they took my mental prayer away from me, it seemed to me He was angered. He told me to tell them that was certainly tyranny. He gave me reasons for understanding that it was not the devil. . . ."

Even this worst and most humiliating of trials passed, and desolation gave way to consolation. Conscious one day of the presence of Christ, but still obedient to her confessor's commands and fears, Teresa knelt clutching the large ebony crucifix at the end of her rosary, holding it up in a moment of final desperation perhaps, between her weary self and the apparition, so that the devil, if indeed he were behind it all, would flee from the sign of contradiction that he hated. She saw the lovely

---

[39] *"Dábame este dar higas,"* etc.

figure approach instead of vanish, and the Lord Himself extend an indescribably beautiful hand. He took the crucifix from her, held it a moment, and returned it.

"When He gave it back to me, it was of four large stones, much more precious beyond compare than diamonds." No, not diamonds, either — a diamond would appear "counterfeit and imperfect" beside this supernatural jewelry. "It had the five wounds very exquisitely wrought. He told me that thus I should see it from then on, and so it befell me that I did not see the material of which it was, but only these stones; but no one saw it but me."[40]

Such favors, though unusual, were not unprecedented in the history of Christianity; and Ribera mentions several. Saint Catherine of Siena saw our Lord place on her finger a ring of gold and pearls which remained there, though none but she could see it. An angel brought two very beautiful garlands from heaven to crown Saint Cecilia, according to Simeon Metaphrastes; she and her husband, Valerian, could see them, but no one else could. When Christ showed His heart to Saint Gertrude and allowed her to place her hand upon it, there remained on each of her fingers a gold ring, and on the middle finger three. One day when Saint Martin was about to say Mass before a great throng, a virgin, a presbyter, and three monks (but no one else) saw over his head something like a ball of fire.

Teresa's jeweled cross passed into the possession of her sister, Doña Juana de Ahumada, who took it to Alba, "and now has it in her keeping, and she has shown it to me several times, and regards it, as she ought, as a great treasure," adds Ribera, who saw it as an ordinary ebony cross, such as nuns wore at the ends of their rosaries. When it was applied to the eyes of Doña Magdalena de Toledo, aunt of Don Francisco de Fonseca, lord of Coca and Alaejos, it arrested the course of cataracts and prevented blindness.[41]

After the saint's death, it seems to have passed from the hands of her sister to those of the Duchess of Alba, and from hers to the Carmelite fathers of Valladolid, who held it in great veneration until it was lost during the persecutions of 1835 and the years following.[42] Wherever it may be now, it served its purpose

---

[40] *Vida,* cap. XXIX.
[41] Ribera, *op. cit.,* lib. I, cap. XI; Yepes, *op. cit.,* I, cap. XIV, follows him in part.
[42] Silverio, edition of Saint Teresa's *Vida,* p. 231, note 1.

for Teresa; and this purpose, in Ribera's opinion, was to reward her constancy in obeying her confessor even to the point of making insulting gestures at the apparitions of our Lord. A subsequent confessor, the Dominican Father Domingo Bañes, told her that the painful act of "giving the fig" had been all wrong in itself, "for it is right to venerate the image of our Lord whenever we see it, even if the devil himself had been the painter — and he is a great painter; on the contrary he is doing us a service." Teresa adds, "This pleased me greatly, for when we see a very good picture, even though we may know it to have been painted by a bad man, we do not fail to respect it, and we make no account of the painter, that we may not lose our devotion; for the good or the evil is not in the vision, but in him to whom it is given, and who does not profit by it in humility; for if he is humble the vision, even if it came from Satan, can do him no harm, and if he is not humble it will do him no good even if it comes from God."[43]

By the beginning of 1560 she had overcome in great measure her fear of being deceived by the devil. Father Alvarez' suggestion that the devil could do no harm to the soul that was resolved not to offend God sustained her in many hours of battle until, like Saint Ignatius before her, she began to realize that demons are generally more troublesome to those who fear them than to those who despise them, and she was able at last to say,

"What happened to me, to make me think of being afraid? What is this? I desire to serve this Lord, and ask no other thing than to please Him; I desire no pleasure nor rest nor any other good, but to do His will. . . . If then this Lord is powerful, as I see that He is, and I know that He is, and that the devils are His slaves, and of this it is not to be doubted since it is of faith, what hurt can they do me, being as I am the handmaiden of this Lord and King? Why shouldn't I have strength to fight with all hell?"

Taking the cross in her hand, she faced the hosts of evil, crying, "Now come all of you, for being the servant of God, I wish to see what you can do to me!"

All her anxieties seemed to vanish in that moment, and the devils with them; and "all the fears I used to have are gone, even to this day; for although sometimes I saw them, as I shall tell later, I have never more, almost, had fear of them, rather

---

[43] *Foundations*, VIII.

it seemed to me they were afraid of me. There remained to me a domination over them, given me by the Lord of all, so that I trouble myself about them no more than about flies. They seem to me so cowardly that when they see that little notice is taken of them they have no strength left. These enemies know how to make a real fight only against someone that they see surrender to them, or when God permits that they tempt and torment His servants for their greater good. May it please His Majesty that we should fear Whom we should fear, and understand that more harm can come to us from one venial sin that from all hell put together, for this is certainly true.

"How frightful we make those devils, for we wish to make ourselves afraid with all our graspings for honors and property and pleasures; and then, allying them to our very selves, who ought to be their adversaries, by loving and desiring what we ought to abhor, much harm they will do us; for we cause them to fight against us with our own weapons, putting into their hands those we have to defend ourselves. This is a great pity; but if we abhor it all for God, and take the Cross to our embrace, and try to serve Him in very truth, he [the devil] flees from those truths as from a pestilence. He is the friend of lies, and a lie himself. He won't play ducks and drakes[44] with anyone who walks in truth. When he sees the understanding obscured, he helps neatly to put the eyes out; for if he sees one already blind, in putting one's rest in vain things, and such vain things — for those of this world seem something that belongs to a child's game — then, seeing that one is a child, he treats one as such, and dares to contend with one, once and many times.

"May it please the Lord that I be not one of those, but that His Majesty do me the favor to let me consider as rest what is rest, and for honor what is honor, and for delight what is delight, and not altogether *vice versa;* and a fig for all the devils, for they will be afraid of me. I don't understand these fears, 'The devil! The devil!' where we could say, 'God! God!' and make him tremble. Yes, for we know that he can't even move unless the Lord permits it. What is this? There is no doubt that I am more afraid of those who are so afraid of the devil than I am of him, for he can't do anything to me, and they, especially if they are confessors, disturb me much, and I have spent several

---

[44] *No hará pato con quien,* etc.

years in such great trouble, that now I wonder how I have been able to endure it. Blessed be the Lord, Who has so truly helped me."[45]

She was free now from fear, but not from persecution. If she no longer dreaded the devil, there were plenty of others in Avila who did, and would continue to do so for her sake. It was still an open question whether the Inquisition would not get her after all.

---

[45] *Vida*, cap. XXV. This passage comes well before the one about the *higas* and the jeweled cross, but Teresa had no very accurate sense of chronology, and psychologically it seems to belong here. It is no easy task to reduce her story to chronological order,

Chapter XII

PETER OF ALCÁNTARA – "TOWN CRIER OF THE LORD GOD"

LEADING a life of Christian perfection almost as rigidly as the primitive Carmelites, Teresa, a year after her return to the convent, was conscious of an immense and growing necessity that recent events had imposed: the need of an *intellectual* certainty that her mental prayer and all the supernatural phenomena that had blossomed out of it like gorgeous flowers from the secret garden of love were indeed the work of the Lord God, and not in any degree that of His enemy; that she was not deceiving herself or others. To complete the purgation of her soul, to fit it for its destiny, there had been need of humiliation from a friendly hand, and this the good Salcedo had dealt out in full measure. She had needed discipline, with patient understanding and *moral* certainty, from men who saw deeply into the significance and the implications of the Passion of Christ, as the Jesuits did. She was grateful to them and to their Company to the end of her life; and if some of her later editors went so far in their hatred and jealousy of them as to leave out of her letters and other writings passages in which she expressed her gratitude and admiration, she was never guilty of any such omission even when certain conflicts and misunderstandings, as we shall see, arose between her and them. Yet there is no doubt that at this time they tried her angelic patience almost to the breaking point (as, according to her revelations, they were intended to do), and that she felt the need of some other direction.

In the vast and complex polity of the Catholic Church, each order has its own special work for which it was called into being; and each has its own bent and character, and the faults of its virtues. The Jesuits have been primarily men of will and of action: teachers, preachers, explorers, missionaries, lovers of God who proved their sincerity by accepting torture and death in every corner of the world. It was in the nature of things that such could rarely devote themselves to the complete life of contemplation, or to the quiet and lonely pursuit of philosophy. And Teresa at this stage needed two things: the reassurance of a contemplative who had progressed as far as she had, as good timid Father Alvarez had not; and the approval of men who knew scholastic philosophy and theology as expertly as only the Dominicans in that day knew them — for it was the especial glory of the order of Saint Dominic to have produced a Saint Thomas Aquinas, and their teaching at Salamanca was then in its heyday.

She found her advanced contemplative not in her own order, but among the Franciscans. It happened, providentially for her, that there came to Ávila in August, 1560, a commissary of the Franciscan *custodia* or district of Saint Joseph, who was noted for sanctity and penance. Having restored his own convent in Alcántara (Extremadura) to the original austerity of the rule of Saint Francis, he had obtained permission from Pope Paul IV to found others of the same sort. For this purpose Friar Peter of Alcántara had come to Ávila, and dwelling at the house of the Lord of Loriana, was ministering to many devout persons who sought his advice and help.

One of his penitents was Doña Guiomar de Ulloa. She had known him years before in Plasencia. It now occurred to her that if any one could bring peace to the mind of her friend Sister Teresa and quiet the scruples of Father Alvarez, the Maestro Daza, and the Holy Cavalier, it was this emaciated friar whose books on mental prayer were so popular among the religious in Spain. Guiomar herself had no need of being reassured. "Such was her faith," wrote Teresa, "that she could not help believing that what all the rest said was of the devil, was the spirit of God; and as she is a person of pretty good understanding, who knows how to keep a secret, and to whom the Lord had given favors aplenty in prayer, it pleased His Majesty to give her light where the learned men were ignorant. My confessors gave me permission to consult her about certain matters. . . ."[1]

This discreet widow went quietly to the Provincial of the Calced Carmelites and obtained permission to have Teresa at her home for eight days, that she might consult Father Peter while he was in Ávila. Teresa knew nothing of this until all was arranged.

The first meeting of the two saints was probably in the church

---

[1] *Vida*, cap. XXX.

of *Nuestra Señora de la Anunciación,* near the north wall of Ávila, between the *Mercado Chico* and the *Arco del Mariscal.* It was one of the ironies of Spanish history that at the time when the Inquisition was seeking out Jewish Catholics of doubtful orthodoxy, this lovely memorial should have been built with Jewish money. The Bracamontes were a prolific and distinguished Jewish family, allied to several of the noble families of Spain — to those of la Cerda y Carvajal, Tellez Giron, Fernandes de Velasco; the Counts of Contamina and of Peñaranda de Bracamonte, the Dukes of Medina de Rioseca.[2] Mosén Rubí, after a long sojourn in Flanders, returned to his native city to carry out the wishes of an aunt, a devout Catholic, who had left a fund for the building of a church; but the chapel he built in 1516 was so singular that the Inquisition ordered the work suspended for several years. Masonic writers find in it a resemblance to a lodge room of the Scottish rite. The Catholic ex-Mason Tirado y Rojas remarks on the pentagonal shape, the two columns at the entrance, the Masonic emblems on the triangular column that upholds the pulpit, the allegories on the chief choir seat, the hammer and compass on the arms of the Bracamontes.[3] It was there, of all places, that Teresa first confessed to Fray Pedro de Alcántara.

Fray Pedro was then sixty-one, but looked older. In 1553, at the age of fifty-four, he had walked barefoot to Rome to get the permission of Pope Julius III to found some poor convents under strict discipline. Almost a skeleton of a man he was, without shoes and wrapped in a wretched old piece of sackcloth. Yet, like Francis of Assisi, he had been seen running through the woods, singing for sheer joy and proclaiming that he was the town crier of the Lord God.

He saw immediately that the woman kneeling beside him was a saint who had the love and courage to attempt to do what he had already done; and to encourage her he told her something of the mortifications by which he had gradually conquered the promptings of self.

"For forty years, I think it was he told me, he had slept only an hour and a half between night and day, and this was the

---

[2] Espasa, *Enciclopedia ilustrada,* t. XXXIII, p. 741; Tirada y Rojas, *La franc-masonería en España,* I, 225–226.
[3] *Op. cit.,* I, pp. 222–223, 225–226. See also Espasa, *loc cit.,* and Carramolino, *Historia de Avila,* II I,p. 114 *et seq.*

hardest penance he had had at the beginning, this overcoming of sleep, and to do it he stayed always on his knees or on his feet. What sleep he had he took sitting, with his head leaning against a little board that he had thrust into the wall. Lie down he could not, even if he wanted to, for his cell, as is known, was no more than four and a half feet long. In all those years he never put up his hood, no matter how strong the sun or the rain might be, or anything on his feet, or any garment at all except a habit of sackcloth, with nothing else over his flesh, and this as scanty as he could endure, and a little mantle of the same stuff over it. He told me that in very cold weather he took it off, and left the door and little window of his cell open so that when he afterwards put on the mantle and closed the door, his body would be glad to be appeased with more shelter. To eat every third day was very usual for him. And he said to me, why was I astonished, for it was very possible for anyone who got himself accustomed to it. A companion of his told me that he had gone eight days without eating. It must have been when he was in prayer, for he had great raptures and impetuosities of love of God, of which I was once a witness.

"His poverty was extreme, and mortifications in youth, for he told me he had happened to be three years in one house of his Order without knowing a single friar, unless it was by his speech; for he never raised his eyes, and so he didn't know the places where he had to go, except by walking behind the friars. This happened to him on journeys. At women he never looked; this for many years. He told me that now he didn't care whether he saw or didn't see; but he was very old when I came to know him, and so extremely thin, that he seemed to be made only of the roots of trees. With all this sanctity he was very affable, although of few words, unless he was asked a question. In those he was quite delightful, for he had a very beautiful understanding. . . ."[4]

In one of their conversations, Peter mentioned casually that for twenty years he had worn a girdle of tin plate without ever taking it off.[5]

Even before Teresa had finished her story, he saw what the situation was. "This holy man gave me light in everything, and explained it all to me, and told me not to be troubled, but to

---

[4] *Vida*, cap. XXVII.
[5] "*Continuo*." *Ibid.*, cap. XXX.

praise God, for it was surely His spirit, that nothing could be found more true and worthy of belief except the Faith itself.[6] And he consoled himself much with me, and showed me all grace and favor, and ever after took great care of me, and confided his interests and affairs to me. . . . He was extremely sorry for me. He told me that one of the greatest afflictions on earth was one he had suffered, and that was the opposition of good men, and that plenty of it was still in store for me; and I always needed someone who would understand me, and there was no one in this city, but that he would speak to my confessor and to one of those who gave me most trouble, who was that married cavalier whom I have mentioned."[7]

Friar Peter, of course, kept his word. He went to see Father Alvarez and told him his opinion of Teresa: that her visions came from Almighty God, and that it was a mistake to make her resist them. The young Jesuit was probably relieved to have his doubts resolved by a man so holy and so much older and more experienced; and from that moment he ceased to harass the soul of his penitent.

Salcedo was not so easily persuaded. "The confessor had little need of it," wrote Teresa; "the Cavalier so much, yet he wasn't wholly convinced; still, it kept him from frightening me so much."[8]

When Friar Peter had finished these kind offices, he made Teresa promise to write him an account of whatever progress she might make in the spiritual life, and to remember him in her prayers; and so he took his departure from Ávila, leaving her "in very great comfort and joy." She promptly gave thanks to her Lord, His Mother, and Saint Joseph, to whose never failing intercession she attributed the coming of her consoler at that crisis — for was not Fray Pedro the commissary of Saint Joseph's *custodia?* What a relief to know that she had not been deceiving herself and others!

Poor Teresa! Had she not learned often enough that there is no lasting heaven in this life? Very suddenly the divine comfort was withdrawn, and she seemed once more defenseless against her old fears and all the desolations of hell. This lasted

---

[6] *Y estuviese tan cierta que era espíritu suyo, que si no era la fe, cosa más verdadera no podía haber, ni que tanto pudiese creer. — Loc. cit.*

[7] *Ibid.,* cap. XXX.

[8] *Vida,* cap. XXX, p. 240.

for two or three weeks.[9] It was bad enough to have physical pains alone, and mental sorrows alone; but when they came together "all favors that the Lord had done for me passed from my memory; there remained only such a remembrance of them as, if I had dreamed them, to give me pain; for my understanding became so torpid that it made me walk in a thousand doubts and suspicions, thinking that I had not known how to understand it, and that perhaps I had imagined it all through desire, and that it was enough that I should deceive myself, without deceiving good people. I seemed so wicked to myself, that I thought all the evils and heresies that had been lifting up their heads were on account of my sins. This is a false humility which the devil invented to disquiet me, and to see if he could drag my soul to desperation."

True humility brings peace and quiet and light to the soul, even though it grieves for having offended God; but "in that other humility which the devil brings there is no light for any good thing, all seems as if God were putting it to fire and blood." Though the soul still believes in God's mercy, she believes without comfort, for the devil, unable to rob her of it, torments her with the thought of how unworthy she is. "It is an invention of the devil, one of the most tormenting and subtle and crafty that I have ever known of him." It was like the temptations of Job. It was as if the devil had been given permission to play *pelota* with Teresa's helpless soul. Prayer became only an additional torment; nothing availed.

"To my way of thinking it is a little bit like an imitation of hell. This is so, as the Lord gave me to understand in a vision; for the soul burns within herself, without knowing who has brought the fire or from where, or how to flee from it, or with what to kill it. Then if she tries to help herself by reading, it is as if she did not know how."

Once, in such a state, Teresa read over part of the life of a saint four or five times without understanding any of it. "To hold a conversation then with anybody is worse, for the devil brings such a hateful spirit of wrath, that I would like to eat everybody up. Then as for going to my confessor, this is certain, for what I am about to say befell me many times, that although they with whom I then dealt and still deal were so holy, they spoke such words to me and 'rebuked me with such harshness,

---

[9] Ribera, *Vida de Santa Teresa*, lib. I, cap. XII.

that when I told them afterwards what they had said, they themselves were astonished, and they told me it was not in their
power. For although they resolved not to do it again, for it afterwards brought them sorrow and even scruples when I had such
trials of body and soul, and they determined to console me with
sympathy, yet they could not. I do not say they spoke evil words
that would offend God, but the most offensive that could be
endured from a confessor. They meant to mortify me, and although at other times I rejoiced in it and was all for enduring it,
at that time it was all torment for me."[10]

Yet she managed to keep herself busy doing good works of the
more humble sort, until at last there came a moment when she
plainly heard the voice of Christ saying, "Don't be wearied:
don't be afraid." It was like the sun rising upon the darkness
of her soul, dispelling all its clouds; and her soul "came forth
again into quiet joy, like refined gold out of a crucible."[11]

This temptation, nevertheless, had reminded her of her need
for theological exactitude. She sought it and found it among
the Dominicans at the Royal Monastery of Saint Thomas, where
she and her father had gone so often to confession. She was
certainly acquainted with the then subprior of the monastery,
Fray García of Toledo, who left a description of her, saying that
her face was "more like that of an angel than that of a human
creature." Scion of the Counts of Oropesa, he had gone to Mexico in 1535 with the Viceroy Don Antonio de Mendoza, had
joined the Dominican Order, and had toiled there until 1545,
when he returned to Spain. He had been subprior at Santo
Tomás since 1555. Just when he became acquainted with Teresa
is uncertain; it is known, however, that he occasionally heard
her confession, and that toward the end of 1560 he introduced
her to one of his *lectors*, Fray Pedro Ibáñez, who was considered
the best theologian in his order and one of the best in Europe.
He was well acquainted with Teresa in the latter part of 1560,
if not before.[12]

It probably took this expert very little time to see that what
he had to deal with was not diabolical delusion, but extraordinary sanctity. However, like a prudent man, he had her write
him out a full account of her method of prayer.

The report completely satisfied him. He gave her the assur-

[10] *Ibid.*, cap. XXX, pp. 242–243.
[11] *Ibid.*, p. 244.   [12] Silverio, *Vida de Santa Teresa de Jesús*, I, p. 495.

ance she desired, that her visions and ecstasies came from God and not from the devil. He was probably the author of the famous memorandum on the state of her soul in 1560:

"1. The end of God is to bring a soul to Himself, and that of the devil to separate it from God. Our Lord never uses means that separate one from Him, nor the devil those that bring one to God. All the visions and other things that take place in her draw her nearer to God, and make her more humble, obedient, etc.

"2. It is the teaching of Saint Thomas and of all the saints that the angel of light is recognized by the peace and quiet he leaves in the soul. Never does she have these things without great peace and joy afterwards, so much that all the pleasures of the earth put together seem to her not like the least of them.

"3. She has no fault or imperfection for which she is not reprehended by the one who speaks within her.

"4. Never did she ask or desire these things, except to accomplish in everything the will of God our Lord.

"5. All the things he tells her go according to the divine Scripture and to what the Church teaches, and are very true in all scholastic rigor.

"6. She has great purity of soul, great sincerity, most fervent desires to please God, and on the other hand, to trample under foot anything there may be of the world.

"7. They have told her that all she should ask of God, being just, she would have. Much she has asked, and things not to be written here, for they would take too long, and our Lord has granted them all.

"8. When these things are of God, they are always ordained for the good of oneself, or the community, or someone. She has experience of her improvement, and of that of many other persons.

"9. No one speaks with her, unless of depraved disposition, without being moved to devotion by her affairs, even though she doesn't tell them.

"10. Each day she goes on increasing in the perfection of her virtues, and they always teach her things of greater perfection. And so, in all her course of time, she has gone on improving, in her visions themselves, in the way Saint Thomas mentions.

"11. Never do they tell her novelties, but things of edification, nor do they tell her nonsensical things. Some persons they have told her were full of devils; but only so she might understand what a soul is like when it has mortally offended God.

"12. It is the devil's way, when he tries to deceive people, to advise them to keep silent about what he tells them; but they have told her to communicate it to learned men who are servants of the Lord, and that if she concealed it, the devil might perhaps deceive her.

"13. The improvement of her soul with these things is great, and the good edification she gives with her example, so that more than forty nuns in her house practise recollection.

"14. These things ordinarily come to her after long mental prayer, and while very absorbed in God and inflamed with His love, or communicating.

"15. These things give her the greatest desire to be right, and not to be deceived by the devil.

"16. They cause the most profound humility in her; she knows that what she receives is from the hand of the Lord, and how little she has of her own.

"17. When she is without those things, things which occur are in the habit of causing her pain and trouble; when that comes, there is no memory of anything, but only a great desire to suffer, and she enjoys this so much that it is astonishing.

"18. They make her rejoice and console herself with trials, murmurings against her, sicknesses, and she has terrible ones, too, of the heart, and vomitings, and many other afflictions, all of which leave her when she has the visions.

"19. With all this she does very great penance, with fasting, discipline, and mortifications.

"20. Both the things of earth that can give her some pleasure, and the trials, of which she has endured many, she bears with equal mind, without losing the peace and quiet of her soul.

"21. She has such a firm purpose of not offending the Lord, that she has taken a vow never to leave undone anything she understands to be more perfect, or anything she is told by any who so understands; and although she holds those of the Company [of Jesus] to be saints, and thinks that through their means our Lord has granted her so many favors, she told me that if she knew it was greater perfection not to consult them, she would never again speak with them or see them, even though it was they who have quieted her and set her feet on the road of these things.

"22. The love she has for God, and her feeling of His presence and being dissolved in His love, is certainly astonishing, and with them she is accustomed to be enraptured almost all day.

"23. When she hears God spoken of with strong devotion, she is often likely to be enraptured, and not to be able to resist, no matter how hard she tries, and then she remains in such a state that it causes the greatest devotion in those who see her.

"24. She cannot endure that anyone converse with her who does not tell her her faults and reprehend her, which she receives with great humility.

"25. With these things she cannot tolerate it when those who are in a state of perfection do not try to live according to their rule.

"26. She is wholly free from affection for relatives, from wishing to speak with people, a friend of solitude; has great devotion to the saints, and on their feasts and mysteries which the Church holds up to view, is filled with the greatest tenderness for our Lord.

"27. If all those of the Company and all the servants of God on earth tell her, or should tell her, that it is the devil, she fears and trembles before her visions commence; but once she is in mental prayer and recollection, she will not be persuaded that it is anyone but God who is with her and speaks with her, even if they cut her into a thousand pieces.

"28. God has given her so strong and valorous a spirit that it is astonishing. She used to be timid; now she tramples all the demons under foot. She is quite beyond the trifles and silly foolery of women. Quite free from scruples. Is utterly honest.

"29. With this our Lord has given her the gift of most happy tears, great compassion for those about her, knowledge of her own faults, much regard for good persons, and abasement of herself. And I say, certainly, that she has helped many persons, and I am one of them.

"30. Commonly keeps God in mind and is aware of His presence.

"31. They have told her nothing [in her raptures] that has not been so and has not come to pass, and this is a very strong argument.

"32. These things cause her an admirable clarity of understanding, and an illumination in the things of God.

"33. That they told her to look into the Scriptures and that it would be found that no soul that desired to please God had been deceived so long a time."[13]

Another very acute analysis of Teresa's mystical states was made during her lifetime or shortly afterward by her Jesuit biographer, Father Ribera. Elaborating on the famous chapter in which Saint Ignatius tells how to discern good and evil spirits,[14] he answers his own question, "What credit should we give to the revelations of Doña Teresa?" by a series of other interrogations:

Are the revelations true? Do they conform to Holy Scripture and the teachings of the Catholic Church? Do they contain any untruth, even if true in general? What effect do they have on the mystic? What is her temperament? Is she discreet, of good judgment? Has she any illness likely to affect her reason? Is she melancholy, impulsive, too passionate in loving and hating, too imaginative? Is she very young, new in the service of God, inexperienced in spiritual matters? Is she proud, desirous of being esteemed, eager to publish her affairs and to talk about them? Does she mention her revelations to many persons? Does she tell about them without being asked? Is she more attached to her own opinion than to those of others? Does she believe what is told her in her revelations and does she follow it, even though learned and spiritual men tell her the contrary? Is she undesirous of asking the opinions of others on the things she thinks have been revealed to her? Does she go to prayer with curiosity, desiring to have these revelations? Does she question our Lord about herself or others, asking for a revelation in reply? In her manner of life and conversation, is she eccentric and different from most others in her state of life? Have her revelations been approved and tested by competent persons?

From all these tests which wise directors had found so useful in trapping impostors, paranoiacs, and *Illuminati,* Ribera finds her emerging triumphant. All the predictions made in her visions were fulfilled, and all were for God's service, and had to do with high and noble things. The raptures made her love God, abhor sin, improve each day in virtue. Her personality had nothing of the *exaltée* in it: she was "very sane and acute and solid of judg-

---

[13] B.M.C., II, pp. 130–133. Formerly this report was attributed to Saint Peter of Alcántara. But as Father Silverio argues, here it is plainly the work of a Thomist, and probably therefore a Dominican; Father Ibáñez, he believes. See his reasons, *op. cit.,* p. 130, n. 1.

[14] *Spiritual Exercises,* Second Week.

ment, with a great discretion, a very good temperament, far removed from melancholy." She never asked our Lord for a revelation but once, and blamed herself much for that; on the contrary, she asked our Lord to lead her by another road. She told her revelations only to persons who might undeceive her, if she was deceived, was very secret, and pained when her advisers betrayed her secret. Finally, her visions were tested and approved as genuine by many learned and spiritual persons. "Some will say," adds Father Ribera rather quaintly, "that she is a woman. Yes, but before God there are no men or women, but only creatures."[15]

Teresa had good reason now to believe that she was safe. Having passed every test, she was ready for whatever God wished her to do. What was it to be?

The answer seems to have come to her by a process of reasoning that began with a vision of hell, the description of which is one of the most vivid passages of her Autobiography:

"After a long time, in which the Lord had given me many of the favors I have described, and others very great, I was one day in prayer when I found myself, without knowing how, in a state where I seemed to be in the middle of hell. I understood that the Lord wished me to see there the place which the demons had prepared for me, and which I merited by my sins. This lasted a very short time, but I think that if I lived many years I could never forget it. The entrance seemed to me like an alley very long and straight, sort of an oven very low and dark and narrow. The ground seemed to me of a water like mud, very filthy and of pestilential odor, and many vile reptiles in it. On the side there was a concavity placed in a wall, like a cupboard, where I saw myself shut up very tightly. All this was delightful to behold in comparison to what I felt there. This that I have said would be hard to exaggerate.

"I wouldn't know how even to begin to exaggerate this, nor could it be understood; but I felt a fire in my soul, which I don't understand how to say what it is like. The most unbearable bodily pains, and I have suffered very grievous ones in this life, and as the doctors say, the worst that can happen here — the shrinking of my sinews . . . and others caused by the devil — all is nothing in comparison with the agonizing of the soul, a sense of constraint, a stifling, an anguish so keen, and with a sorrow

---

[15] Ribera, *Vida de Santa Teresa*, Book I, p. 84 *et seq.*, ed. Pons.

so abandoned and afflicted, that I don't know how to describe it. For to say it is as if the soul were being always pulled up by the roots, is little, for that is as if someone else were putting an end to our life; but here it is the soul herself that seems to be cutting herself to pieces. The fact is that I don't know how to express that interior fire, and that despair over such very heavy torments and pains. I did not see who gave them to me, but I felt myself burn and crumble up into pieces, as it seemed to me; and I say that that interior fire and desperation is the worst.

"Being in such a pestilential place, so helpless even to hope for consolation, there was no sitting down, or lying down, or any room at all, although they had put me in this as in a hole made in the wall; for those walls, which are frightful to look upon, tightened themselves, and everything was suffocating, there was no light, but everywhere the blackest darkness. I do not understand how it can be that without any light everything can be seen that is painful to look upon. . . . I don't know how it was, but I understood it to be a great favor, and that the Lord wished me to see with my own eyes the place from which His mercy had saved me." All the torments she had ever read or imagined about hell were nothing to what she then felt; they were like mere pictures compared to reality itself. "And being burned here is very little in comparison to that fire there.

"It left me so frightened that even now, as I write about it almost six years later, the natural warmth leaves my body, here where I am. And so I don't remember any times since that I have had trouble or pain, without thinking that everything that can be suffered here is nothing, and so it rather seems to me that we complain without cause.[16] And so I say again that it was one of the greatest favors the Lord has done for me, for it has been of much help to me, not only in losing my fear of tribulations and contradictions in this life, but in giving me strength to endure them and to give thanks to the Lord who delivered me, as it now seems to me, from evils so everlasting and terrible."

As Teresa reflected upon the experience afterwards, she began to think of all the miserable souls who had gone there, and were going there, and would go there. This thought filled her with

---

[16] "*y ansi me parece, en parte, que nos quejamos sin propósito*" is difficult to render exactly. — *Vida*, cap. XXXII; B.M.C., I, 265.

grief, and with a burning desire to save them from such a fate, as she herself had been saved. "From then on I had the greatest sorrow for the many souls that condemn themselves to hell, especially those Lutherans, for they were already members of the Church by baptism, and . . . I thought that to save even one of them from such very grievous torments I would endure many deaths very joyfully."[17]

In the heart of a woman who had looked on hell there was no room for that hatred that some of her fellow countrymen had conceived for the misguided wretches of the north who were burning Catholic churches, slaying priests, and desecrating the body of Christ. What Christian could be unconcerned when the Turks reached Malta and made themselves masters of the Mediterranean? And what Spaniard could fail to be alarmed over the great conspiracy in France, involving not only the Queen of England but the Lutherans of Germany, to seize power and set up a Calvinistic government? This so-called Conspiracy of Amboise was the beginning of the long series of eight Huguenot wars; within a year the soil of France would be drenched with the blood of helpless priests and nuns.[18] And even in 1560 Teresa must have heard of the anarchy and depravity that Luther himself noted as consequences of his "reform" in Germany. Yet this woman was so purified of human weakness that she did not share to the slightest degree in that sadistic impulse that gives a sinner pleasure when he can find someone he thinks worse than himself on whom to visit the punishment his secret conscience tells him his own guilt deserves. The worst Catholics could righteously consign the Lutherans to death and to hell. But the best ones, the saints, felt pity and sorrow rather than hatred. And so, instead of denouncing Protestants, Teresa loved them with such utter tenderness that she was willing to die in torments for them, if only it would restore them to the sacraments of Christ's Church. She began to fast, and to keep weary vigils, and punish her poor body in a thousand ways for those Lutherans who had forgotten that Christ came to show men how to do penance.

She made no distinction between Calvinists and other sects. They were all "Lutherans" to her. "Come to know the injuries

[17] *Ibid.*

[18] For details of the Conspiracy of Amboise, see my *Philip II*, p. 279, *et seq.*

of France from those Lutherans," she wrote,[19] "and how this miserable sect went on increasing, I was much fatigued, and as if I could do anything, or were anything, I wept with the Lord and implored Him to remedy so much evil. I think that I would lay down a thousand lives to save one soul of the many I saw being lost. And as I saw myself a woman and wicked and incapable of being of any use for His service, all my anxiety was, and still is, that since He has so many enemies and so few friends, that those be good ones: and so I resolved to do that little bit that I can and that is in me, which is to follow the evangelical counsels with all the perfection I can. . . ." She prayed meanwhile for "the champions of the Church and the preachers and learned men who defend her," and she hoped in this way to "aid in so far as we can this Lord of mine Whom those on whom He has heaped so much good have so afflicted that I think these traitors want to put Him on the cross again today and not to let Him have a place to lay His head."

"O my Redeemer, how can my heart help being much wearied to think of this! How is this now of the Christians? Must they always be the ones who tire You most? Those for whom You do the best works, those who owe You most, those whom You choose for Your friends, those among whom You walk and to whom You communicate Yourself by the sacraments? Aren't they enough, Lord of my soul, the torments the Jews give You?[20] Surely, Lord, anyone who leaves the world now does nothing: since they have so little regard for You, what are we to expect? Do we perhaps deserve that they treat us better? Perhaps we have done more for them, so that Christians may keep friendship? What is this? What do we expect now, we who by the Lord's goodness are without that pestilential scab, when they already belong to the devil? A good punishment they have earned from his hands, and with his pleasures they have won eternal fire. There they go, though I can't help breaking my heart to see so many souls as are lost. . . ."

It was no mere literary hyperbole, this weariness and pain of the heart that Teresa endured. According to Fray Luis de León, she suffered acute physical pain whenever she heard of the

---

[19] *Camino de perfección*, cap. I. Escorial MS., B.M.C., t. III, p. 211.

[20] This sentence appears in Teresa's first draft, the so-called Escorial MS. She omitted it when she made the copy known as the Valladolid autograph, B.M.C., t. III, p. 212

atrocities committed by Protestants against the English or German monasteries. But this was not enough. She must also take upon herself voluntary anguish and privations for those who were unwilling to do their share to "make up the full measure of the sufferings of Christ" of which Saint Paul wrote so mysteriously. She must be perfect, nothing less than perfect.

It seemed to her that perfection for a Carmelite must consist in living up to the spirit and letter of the founders of the Order. The primitive rule observed by the recluses on Mount Carmel had been framed for contemplatives almost eremitical, in groups large enough for the communal life necessary for discipline and small enough for the solitude required for mental prayer; the ideal number was thirteen to sixteen. In Teresa's time the order had departed so far from this ideal that in Ávila, for example, there were 180 nuns, only a few of whom lived as true contemplatives, and that, of course, with the greatest difficulty among the distractions of visits, conversations, and news.

Still, it is a curious fact that without the visits and conversations which she disliked so much, she might never have been able to take the first step toward a remedy. For it was during one of those conversational visits that a concrete plan was first suggested to her. By this time she was much sought after by religious persons who attempted mental prayer and loved to talk of the things of God (she could tolerate no others); and several of them were allowed to meet frequently in her cell, even at night. Most of them, according to Ribera, were her relatives or those of her friend, Sister Juana Suárez. Among them were María de San Pablo, daughter of her friend, Nicholas Gutiérrez; Ana of the Angels, a nun of the Incarnation; Doña Guiomar de Ulloa; two of her own nieces, Isabel and Inés de Cepeda; and a girl of seventeen, Doña María de Ocampo.

María de Ocampo was the daughter of Teresa's cousin Diego, one of the boys who had played in her father's house on the hill, and of Beatriz de la Cruz y Ocampo. Her parents lived in Toledo. When she was five or six years old, she happened to be visiting at Puebla de Montalbán when her aunt, Teresa, returning from a pilgrimage to Our Lady of Guadalupe, happened to arrive, and, greatly taken with her, proposed educating her at the Incarnation. The girl's father refused. By the time she was seventeen, he had plenty of other daughters by a second wife, and so gave his consent. This was in 1559. María at once decided to be a nun. She was much the sort of girl that Teresa had been at a somewhat earlier age, keen witted, affectionate, full of fun and vitality, and overfond (in her own opinion as expressed later) of dress, amusements, and books of chivalry. Her holy desires cooled, however, and when she finally arrived in Ávila, probably at the beginning of 1560, she gave the impression of being rather a worldly young woman, somewhat vain and giddy. Teresa, remembering her own experience, was not exactly pleased with the books of *caballerías;* but instead of taking them away, or administering a scolding, she tactfully remarked that reading was a good habit, and would doubtless lead her in time to good books. It seems likely that she was just as sensible in dealing with María's love for bright ribbons and cosmetics. The result was that the girl became quite at home in the Incarnation, and wholly devoted to the wise and serene woman who was her aunt.[21]

María was in a little group that assembled one evening in Teresa's cell to talk about God and the things of God. One word led to another, as Ribera says, until someone mentioned the difficulty of living a life of perfect contemplation in so large a convent, and the joy it must have been in the olden time to be a Carmelite under the primitive rule. María de Ocampo suggested jokingly that they reform the rule at the Incarnation, and then found some small convents whose members would all be contemplatives. Most of those present took it in the same spirit, and there was much banter and jesting. Perhaps Teresa said nothing. But she could not dismiss lightly an idea that answered so patly a question in her own mind. "Why not?" she must have thought. "Why not?"

The conversation went on. Objections were offered. How could they reform a convent when they had no authority over it? And even if the rest were possible, where could they find the necessary money? Well, as to that, María de Ocampo had a little property that had been set aside as her dowry, and she offered to contribute a thousand ducats.[22]

While they were talking, Doña Guiomar came in, and on hearing what the subject was, hailed it with enthusiasm. "Mother," she cried, "it is a holy work, and I will help you all I can."[23]

---

[21] This substantially is María's account of her going to the Incarnation, and her aunt's treatment of her. Silverio, II, pp. 13–14.

[22] Ribera, *op. cit.*, lib. I, cap. XIII.

[23] Silverio, *op. cit.*, lib. II, p. 16.

Teresa made the reply that might have been expected of her: let them all commit the affair to God in their prayers, and try to learn what was His will.

Little by little, as days went on, she became convinced that He wanted her to found a new monastery under the primitive rule. Finally, after receiving the Host one morning, she was aware of His presence and "His Majesty commanded me plainly to seek it with all my powers, making me great promises that the monastery mustn't fail to be established, and that He would be much served in it, and that it should be called Saint Joseph, and that he would watch over us at one door, and our Lady at the other, and that Christ would go with us, and that it would be a star that would give out great splendor, and that although the religious orders were relaxed, it must not be thought He was little served in them, for what would become of the world if it were not for the Religious; that I should tell my confessor this that He commanded me, and that He would ask him not to go against it or to hinder me in it.

"This vision had such great effects, and such was the manner of this speech that the Lord made to me, that I could not doubt that it was He. I felt the greatest sorrow, for the great fatigues and trials that it was to cost me were shown to me in part, and I was so happy in that house; and although I had already spoken of the matter, it was with no determination or certainty that it would be."[24]

A divine command could not be ignored, however, and Teresa proceeded to inform Father Alvarez, in writing. He took the view that most priests would probably take of so startling a suggestion.

"He did not dare to tell me outright to give it up, but he saw that there was no way of going on according to natural reason, because I had extremely little, and almost no possibility in my companion,[25] who was the one who would have to do it. He told me to talk it over with my Prelate, and that what he should do, that I should do. I did not speak of these visions with the Prelate, but that lady told him that she wished to found this monastery; and the Provincial[26] took it very well, for he is

---

[24] *Vida*, cap. XXXII.
[25] Doña Guiomar.
[26] Father Gregorio Fernández. Both Yepes and Ribera are mistaken in giving the name of Father Angel de Salazar, successor to Fernández.

friendly to every religious order, and gave her all the favor that was needed, and told her he would consent to the house. They talked of the income which had to be had, and we never wished to have more than thirteen, for many reasons. Before we commenced to make arrangements, we wrote to the holy Fray Pedro de Alcántara all that had happened, and he advised us not to fail to do it, and gave us his opinion on everything."[27]

Fray Pedro had written, as usual, on a very small sheet of paper, almost to the edges, setting holy poverty above the etiquette that demanded wide margins. He vigorously urged her to follow in the footsteps of Christ, leading a life of prayer and scorning all worldly goods. Saint Luis Beltrán also sent a warm commendation, but his letter did not arrive for three months. Meanwhile, as the Provincial had given his consent, Father Alvarez saw no reason for not giving his, and the way seemed clear for the founding of the little convent. María's money would make a beginning, and Doña Guiomar, though her generous charities had greatly reduced her estate, was rich in courage and resourcefulness. A serene calm, in which there was almost a foretaste of victory, settled upon the nun of the Incarnation and her devoted group of friends. But it was the calm before a great storm.

---

[27] *Loc. cit.*

Chapter XIII

BEGINNING OF THE REFORM, AND FIRST DEFEAT

THE news got out, and all Ávila was buzzing with it. The *Beata* of the Incarnation was going to leave her convent and found a new one. What, another convent? Were there not enough already in Ávila? And if she had as little money as she appeared to have, the nuns would have to be supported by the town. Who was she to set herself up above everyone else? Were they not good nuns at the Incarnation, yes, and holy ones too? Wherever people met, in houses, at the markets, on all the streets, the thing was talked about. "Have you heard about Doña Teresa de Ahumada's latest?" Thus, says Padre Ribera, the *demonio,* foreseeing some of the harm that the reform would inflict on him and his work, went about the city, raising up a great *borrasca.*[1]

Teresa and Guiomar were subjected to a merciless persecution. Cruel gibes and sarcastic taunts followed them when they went abroad, contemptuous laughter echoed at their heels. Doña Teresa was a nun; let her stay in her monastery and attend to her prayers. Doña Guiomar was a widow and a mother; let her take care of her own house and stop meddling in things that were none of her business. "And so it was that there was hardly a person in the place — people of prayer and all — who were not against us then, and thought it utter nonsense."[2]

Teresa felt it more on her friend's account than her own. Guiomar had to face people, but she was sheltered in the convent. Guiomar was a holy woman, but she (said her humility) was a proud, wicked, presumptuous, meddlesome woman, and they were right in saying so. Guiomar had to depend upon her own reason and conscience, but Teresa had revelations to encourage her. "When I was very weary and commended myself to God, His Majesty began to console me and to encourage me. He told me that here I saw what the saints had endured who founded the religious orders; that I would have to go through much more persecution than I could think of, and not to let it

[1] Ribera, *Vida de Santa Teresa,* lib. I, cap. XIII.
[2] *Vida,* cap. XXXII.

bother us at all. He told me some things to say to my companion; and what surprised me even more was that then we remained consoled for what had happened, and with courage to resist everybody."[3]

People were saying that there was some excuse for the nun because her Provincial had approved of her crazy plan, but there was none for the laywoman, and they avoided her as if she had the pox. Finally matters reached such a pass that when she went to confession on Christmas morning (1560), the priest — "a confessor I know well," said Ribera[4] — refused to give her absolution unless she first promised to give up the plan for the new convent, and so put an end to the scandal she had caused.

Guiomar went to the Incarnation to hold a council of war with her friend. They decided to appeal to the Dominicans before giving up the struggle. Their first impulse, according to Ribera, who added that he got it directly from Teresa herself, was to ask the Jesuits to help, but as these were newcomers in the city, and very poor, "and needed the favor and love of all,"[5] Doña Guiomar, who loved them and did not wish to see their work destroyed on her account, suggested that they have recourse to Fray Pedro Ibánez, prior of Santo Tomás, who had heard Teresa's confessions and had made a favorable report on her.

The two went together to see him. Guiomar spoke first, explaining the whole situation and making it clear that her little estate would provide enough to keep the proposed convent from being a burden to the people of Ávila. She begged him to help, "for he was the most learned man there then in the place," wrote Teresa, "and few more in his Order." Afterwards, "I told him everything we were thinking of doing, and some reasons. I told him nothing of any revelation, but only the natural reasons which prompted me; for I didn't want him to give us any opinion except in accord with them."[6] He listened with grave kindness and patience, and at the end said that he would think the matter over and give his opinion in eight days. Were they determined to do whatever he should say?

"I told him yes," added Teresa in a very feminine sentence, "but although I said this and thought I would do it, I never lost

[3] *Ibid.*
[4] Ribera, *op. cit.*, lib. I, cap. XIII. Teresa also mentions this, *loc. cit.*
[5] *Ibid.*
[6] *Ibid.*

a feeling of certainty about what had to be done. My companion was still more confident; she was determined not to give it up, no matter what they told her." Neither of them knew that Fray Ibáñez had already decided, while listening to them, that their plan ought to be abandoned; but like a good man of God, he wished to pray about the matter before stating a conclusion.

While he was thinking it over, the news had got abroad that his aid had been sought, and people began advising him to have nothing to do with the innovation. Teresa tells us that a certain cavalier (could it have been Salcedo?) took it upon himself to write a letter advising him "to watch what he was doing, and not help us."

After the Dominican prior had considered the matter prayer-fully for eight days, he changed his opinion, and thoroughly approved of the project regardless of what Ávila thought of it. He advised Teresa to go ahead as quickly as possible and trust in God, even if the revenue was scarce; and if others opposed her, let her send them to him, and he would give good reasons.

The two women were very joyful, especially when they learned that "certain holy persons who were usually against us were now more appeased, and some of them helped us." One of these was the Holy Cavalier. Even the Maestro Gaspar Daza, who, in the words of Teresa, was "the looking-glass of all the town," declared that it was the work of God. So the two went ahead with their plans. Doña Guiomar had found a little house in a good section at the north of the city, in the ward called Saint Roch's, not far from her own residence. Very small it was: no one but Teresa believed it was large enough for a convent. Still, it was all their slender means could afford; and Teresa, in a moment of hesitation, heard the Lord say, "Enter it, and you will see what I shall do."[7] Negotiations for the sale were completed. Now nothing remained but the signing of the deed.

This was the moment that the Carmelite Provincial chose for suddenly withdrawing his permission. He had yielded to a storm of indignation that swept through the Incarnation when the nuns there learned that Teresa really meant to leave them and to found another convent. "I was very much detested in all my monastery for wishing to found a more enclosed monastery. They said I was insulting them, that I could serve God just as

---

[7] *Vida,* cap. XXXII.

well there, for there were others better than I, that I did not love the house, that I might better seek income for it than for some other place." Some wanted her put in the dark cell where refractory nuns were sometimes brought to their senses.[8] The Father Provincial decided that it was expedient to put an end to the "scandal."

His action had the opposite effect. It seemed to prove and confirm the worst that had been said about the *Beata,* and tongues wagged more furiously than ever.[9]

Sorrowful, but conscious that she had done all she could, and never for a moment doubting that somehow, sometime, the Lord would find a way to accomplish what He had promised, Teresa remained in her cell, waiting for the next blow. It was not long in coming. It was a letter from Father Baltasar Alvarez. "What fatigued me much was once when my confessor, as if I had done something very much against his will, wrote me that now I would see from what had happened that it was all a dream, and that from then on I should amend myself by not going out of my way in anything or speaking any further about it, for I could see the scandal that had occurred, and other things, all to give pain. This hurt me more than everything else put together, for I thought that if I had been the occasion of giving offense, and was guilty of it, and if those visions were illusion, then all my prayer was a deceit, and that I was then going on very much deceived and lost. But the Lord, who never failed me . . . told me then that I should not be troubled, that I had served God much, and that I did not offend Him in that business; that I should do what the confessor commanded me, being silent for now until it was time to return to it. I remained so consoled and happy that all the persecution that came upon me seemed nothing."

What had caused the young Jesuit confessor to change his mind so quickly? Teresa makes the situation plain: "He who confessed me had a superior, and they[10] have to an extreme degree this virtue of not bestirring themselves except in accord with the will of their superior."[11] A great deal about Father Alvarez, not only on this occasion but in all his well-meant ter-

---

[8] *Ibid.,* cap. XXXIII.
[9] So says Ribera, *op. cit.,* lib. I, cap. XIII.
[10] The Jesuits.
[11] *"El que me confesaba tenia superior, y ellos tienen esta virtud en extremo de no se bullir sino conforme a la voluntad de su mayor." Vida,* cap. XXXIII.

giversations of the past, becomes clear when we discover who his superior was. The rector of the college of San Gil since 1558 had been the Reverend Father Dionisio Vázquez, for many years a thorn in the flesh not only to Father Alvarez but to the entire Society of Jesus.

Like the Benedictines, the Franciscans, the Dominicans, and all other orders, the Jesuits had discovered the general law that in organizations of human beings the first success is followed by a reaction. Their great popularity brought an increase of numbers and their prestige and influence attracted, with many of the desired type, a few whose apostolic zeal had in it some baser alloy of selfishness or ambition. Some of these formed a small but powerful faction which attempted to change the plan of Saint Ignatius, and to make the Society a purely Spanish affair. The caesaropapistic tendencies of Philip the Second seemed to offer an opportunity which they were quick to use; and for years these malcontents, as they came to be known, carried on intrigues at Madrid and at Rome to convert the Society into an instrument of Spanish royal policy, doubtless hoping to dominate it under the King. It is obvious that had they succeeded, the mission of Ignatius would have been brought to an ignominious close; Poland and Bavaria would not have been won back to the Church; the missionary and educational work of the Society all over the world would have been impossible. Fortunately the plot was discovered under the great general Aquaviva, and after a furious conflict which ended in a triumphant vindication of the Society as a whole by Pope Clement VIII, harmony was restored to its ranks by the expulsion of the *malcontentos*. There were only twenty-seven of them, of whom twenty-five were found to be of Jewish or Moorish descent, the ringleaders being all Jews.[12] Saint Ignatius had had no prejudice on this subject. Polanco, his Jewish secretary, was the only person with him when he died. And his friend Laínez, who succeeded him as General of the Jesuits after battling eloquently for reform at Trent, was descended from Jews (though of a family Catholic for generations) and exemplified the noblest qualities of the once-chosen people who had given the world a Mother and a

---

[12] For an account of the *malcontentos*, see Astrain, *Historia de la Campaña*, etc., III, p. 55 *et seq*; also Campbell, *The Jesuits*, I, p. 197 *et seq*. Even to this day a candidate of Jewish descent must have a papal dispensation to be admitted to the Society.

Redeemer. Unhappily a different spirit animated some of the "New Christians" accepted during his administration. Polanco's nephew was one of the malcontents who caused so much trouble that from then on the Jesuits would take persons of Jewish descent only when their Catholic principles had been fully tested and approved.

Now, Father Dionisio Vázquez was not only one of these *malcontentos*, but he was their presiding genius. He had shown great promise in his early days as a Jesuit, in fact he had been confessor to Saint Francis Borgia at one time. Yet he appears in a report sent to Rome by Father Marcelino Vaz as a reserved, somber man, self-centered and proud, who associated with very few persons, and only with those of importance (who presumably could be of use to him). He was very positive in his opinions, which were sometimes strange and ill-founded. He was subject to moods of melancholia during which he was most severe, if not unjust, to his subordinates. He had also the bad habit, fatal to discipline, of showing his likes and dislikes, in short, of playing favorites.[13]

Father Alvarez's treatment of Sister Teresa is now easier to understand. In any case he could hardly be blamed for withdrawing his consent when her own superior had done so. And his harshness and suspicion, so alien to a humble, charitable, and self-sacrificing (though reserved) nature were imposed by Father Vázquez. Not that he was incapable on his own account of treating souls with asperity by way of testing them.[14] Once when he was absent from Ávila and received a letter from Teresa urgently asking his advice, he wrote an answer immediately, but added a command, on the outside of the envelope, that she was not to open it for a month![15] This, however, was what she wanted and she loved him all the more for it, having

---

[13] P. Silverio quotes from this report of P. Vaz (*Vida de Santa Teresa de Jesús,* II, p. 33): "*Primeramente, él es notado de muchas personas de mucho grave, y que no quiere dar parte de sí sino a muy pocos, los más insignes; y los demás, aún en sus enfermedades, no se cura mucho de ellos. Item, de ser mucho confiado en sus opiniones, que algunas veces son extrañas y no muy fundadas a placer de buenos y no poco entendidos. Tiene algunas melancolías, muy graves a sus súbditos. Con el P. Páez ha tenido algunos excesos, aún en presencia de algunos nobles españoles, que desedificaron harto. Otros tuvo en privado con el mismo, de quien no hablo porque no tocan a la edificación exterior, y por ventura que serían acertados, aunque a mí me edificó la paciencia del uno que la aspereza del otro.*" See also the Bollandists, *Acta S. Teresiae,* n. 309, p. 80.
[14] Silverio, *op. cit.,* I, 457.
[15] *Ibid.,* p. 458.

divine assurance in her visions that he was an instrument of good. "Here the Lord taught me what a very great blessing it is to endure trials and persecutions for Him, for the increase I saw in my soul of the love of God and of many other things was such that I was astonished; and this makes me unable to stop wanting trials."[16]

Her confessor and even her own Provincial, then, had lost faith in her mission. But there was one friend who never deserted her, once he had made up his mind she was right. The Dominican prior, Father Ibáñez, had the courage to visit her openly when she was most shunned and gossiped about,[17] and together with Doña Guiomar he wrote to Rome, probably through some prelate of his order, to ask for a papal bull authorizing the foundation of her convent.

At this moment the devil seized upon the opportunity of spreading about from person to person the rumor that she professed to have "had some revelation about the business." This was a dangerous charge in the years following the revival of the Inquisition. Her friends fearfully and secretly warned her of her peril.

"This made me laugh, for I never had any fear on that score, since I well knew of myself that in matters of faith I would expose myself to die a thousand deaths before I would be seen going against the slightest ceremony of the Church or any truth whatever of Holy Scripture; and I told them not to be afraid, for my soul would be in a bad way indeed if there were anything in it of such a sort that I should fear the Inquisition. And if I thought there were any reason to, I myself would go there to ask about it, and if I were taken there, the Lord would set me free and I should be all the better for it."

She told Padre Ibáñez of the fears of her friends, and asked him if there was in her visions, raptures, and prayers that was contrary to Holy Scripture. After reconsidering the whole matter, he assured her she had nothing to fear from the Inquisition.

Five or six months passed, while Teresa obediently kept silence, fasted, prayed, and performed her other duties at the Incarnation. Finally, when the town gossip had subsided, and everyone except Guiomar seemed to have forgotten about the

---

[16] *Vida,* cap. XXXIII.

[17] So says Yepes, *Vida,* lib. II, cap. II. Teresa merely says he talked with her.

Reform, she broached the subject again to Father Alvarez, and found him no more encouraging than before. Nevertheless, she was not left without hope. "Being in great affliction one day because I thought the confessor did not believe me, the Lord told me not to trouble myself, for soon that sorrow would come to an end. I was very happy, thinking it meant that I was going to die soon, and it made me very contented whenever I remembered it."[18]

About this time the Jesuit superiors of Father Dionisio Vázquez decided to remove him from the College of San Gil, and to replace him with Father Gaspar de Salazar. Teresa had no idea what this new rector would be like. Her first intimation of the change was when Father Alvarez told her that a new Rector was coming and would visit her, and she must tell him her whole story "with all freedom and clarity." What would he be? Could there be another Father Vázquez, or would he be more like the typical Jesuits, the "blessed men" that she had known before? When the fatal day came, she entered the confessional at the Incarnation with more than ordinary anxiety. It was probably early in May, 1561.

As soon as she knelt there, all fear left her. No sooner had she knelt there than all her fears passed away. "I felt in my spirit I don't know what, for I don't remember having felt it with anyone before or since, nor shall I know how to say how it was, nor could I by comparisons. For it was a spiritual joy, and my soul's understanding that that soul would understand her and would be in agreement with her, although, as I say, without knowing how. For if I had spoken with him or they had given me great news of him, it would not be much if I took pleasure in understanding that he was going to understand me; but no word had we spoken, he to me or I to him, nor was he one of whom I had previously had any information.

"Afterwards I saw clearly that my spirit did not deceive herself, for it has done me and my soul great good in all ways to deal with him, for his method is particularly good for persons whom the Lord, it seems, already has well along the road, for he makes them run and not go step by step. And his way is to disentangle them from everything and to mortify them; and in this the Lord has given him the very greatest talent, as also in many other things.

---

[18] *Vida*, cap. XXXIII; B.M.C., p. 277.

"When I began to talk with him, then I understood his style, and saw that he was a pure and holy soul, with an especial gift from the Lord for understanding spirits. I was much consoled."[19]

There was an immediate change also in Father Alvarez. "That sorrow never more occurred, because the Rector who came did not go along with the Minister who was my confessor; rather he told him to console me, and that he had nothing to fear, and that he should not lead me by a road so harsh, but should let the spirit of the Lord work."[20]

Soon after the coming of the new rector, Christ urged her again to found the monastery. When she told this to Father Salazar, he believed her. Father Alvarez had a final scruple to struggle with. "Tell your confessor," said our Lord, "to make his meditation tomorrow on this verse: *Quam magnificata sunt opera tua, Domine; nimis profundae factae sunt cogitationes tuae!*"

She wrote a note accordingly to Father Alvarez, and next morning he made his meditation on the beautiful Ninety-First Psalm.

"It is good to give praise to the Lord, and to sing to thy name, O most High; to show forth thy mercy in the morning and thy truth in the night. . . . *O Lord, how great are thy works! thy thoughts are exceedingly deep. The senseless man shall not know; nor will the fool understand these things.* . . . The just shall flourish like the palm tree; he shall grow up like the cedar of Libanus. . . ."

Father Alvarez was freed at that moment from all the doubts implanted in his mind for so many months by the Holy Cavalier, Maestro Daza, and Father Vázquez. From then on he was whole-heartedly on the side of the reform.[21] He told Teresa she was free to hope for it and to work for it.

There were still, however, some formidable obstacles. There was the opposition of her own Provincial. There was the watchful antagonism of many nuns of the Incarnation. And when the brief of authorization came at last from Rome, it proved useless, for it did not specify whether the new convent was to be subject to the Order of Mount Carmel or to the Bishop of Ávila, and a

---

[19] *Vida*, cap. XXXIII; B.M.C., pp. 277–278.
[20] *Ibid.*, p. 277.
[21] Ribera (*op. cit.*, lib. I, cap. XIV) says he got this story from another Jesuit to whom Father Alvarez showed Teresa's note.

new one had to be applied for by Doña Guiomar and her mother Doña Aldonza de Guzmán. It was plain that under the circumstances they must proceed with great secrecy, without disobedience to any superior, and without giving cause for a new commotion among the nuns.

Teresa had recourse to a stratagem. She arranged to have her brother-in-law Juan de Ovalle, who had been living, with his wife Juana and their two children Gonzalo and Beatriz, at Alba de Tormes, go alone to Ávila, quietly buy the house that Guiomar had found, and then bring his family to occupy. They were all established in their new home by August 10, 1561.[22] Teresa was then able to visit them frequently without exciting suspicion, and to give instructions to some workmen who under Juan's supervision began to make the place suitable for a convent. How she was going to pay these men she did not know; but His Majesty told her to continue, and that was enough. Saint Joseph, too, appeared to her, and told her that even if she went ahead without a single *blanca*, the Lord would provide what she needed.

Juana was at the beginning of the last month of her pregnancy when she moved to Ávila; but a Castilian lady, mindful of the heroic example of the great Queen Isabel (who bore five children in between military campaigns and the conduct of international affairs) was not likely to be deterred from doing good by so natural an event as the birth of a child. She set to work cheerfully to make the modest house as habitable as possible, while little Gonzalo, who was five, ran about peering into everything, examining his new surroundings, and watching the workmen who were making repairs and changes. Apparently the neighbors suspected nothing. Ovalle was a *hidalgo*, who, having an income from his estates, however small, could live where he pleased, and it seemed natural enough for him to settle in Ávila, where his wife had grown up.

A few days after they moved in, a part of a wall fell on Gonzalo. His father found him lying motionless on the ground, unconscious, apparently dead. He took him in his arms, called to him, tried to revive him — all in vain.

Carrying the boy's body, Ovalle started toward the house of Doña Guiomar de Ulloa, where Teresa was staying that day. His wife followed him, screaming; she had been talking with a lady visitor in another room when the accident was discovered.

[22] Ribera, *loc. cit.*

Teresa calmly took the child from his father, and laid him out across her knees.

"Be quiet," she said to her sister, "and you others too."

She lowered her veil, and bent her face over the child until it touched his. Then, as Ribera tells it, "silent without, but inwardly like Moses uttering cries to God that he should not discourage those who had come back by reason of the work He wished to do, thus she remained a while, until the boy began to live again, and to put out his hands to touch her face, as if playing with her"; as if he had waked from ordinary sleep.

Teresa gave him to his mother, saying,

"*Oh, válame Dios,* here, you who were so worried about your son, look here, take him."[23]

The boy remained weak for a few minutes, but soon was running about the room, returning every little while to embrace his aunt.

A friend of Teresa used to ask her, "Sister, how was this? This boy was dead." Teresa would only smile and keep silence. In other cases, when she could truthfully deny something, she would do so; hence Ribera was of the impression that the boy was really dead, and that the prayer of Teresa had obtained a miracle.[24]

Not many days after this, Juana was delivered of a second son, whom she called Josepe, after the saint already chosen as patron of the house. At his baptism, September 12, the godfather was the Holy Cavalier, the godmother Doña Guiomar. This child was very dear to his aunt. She would take him in her arms and say, "Please God, boy, that if thou art not to be good, God take thee so, *angelito,* before thou offend Him." This prayer was soon answered. Josepe had been in the world only three weeks when a fatal illness beset him. One day early in October Teresa picked him up and gazed earnestly at him. As she did so, the baby's mother saw her face become "glowing and beautiful, like an angel's." After a few minutes the nun tenderly laid the tiny body on the bed, and moved toward the door.

"You needn't go," said Juana, "for I see that the boy is dead."

Teresa turned back, her face still radiant, and replied, "It is

[23] "*Oh, válame Dios, que estaba ya tan congojada por su hijo, vele ahí, tómele allá.*" — Ribera, *loc. cit.* Yepes in general follows the account of Ribera, but adds the detail about the piece of wall falling on the boy. Ribera says that he got the story from Gonzalo himself, who must have had it from his parents. The boy became very holy in his short life — he died at twenty-four.

[24] Ribera, *op. cit.,* p. 166 (Pons ed.).

something to praise the Lord for, to see what angels come for the soul, when one of these *angelitos* dies."[25]

With all this, the remodeling of the house continued little by little. It was not easy to make so small and badly arranged a building into a convent. There was no room for a refectory, no room for a dormitory, no room for a chapel. A tiny dwelling next door might do for a church, but where was the money coming from? The last of Guiomar's funds had just been spent paying the workmen — and a very expensive job it was — for rebuilding a solid wall of stone and cement. Teresa, in great anxiety, turned to prayer. After Communion she heard Christ say, "I have already told you to enter how you can. Oh, the covetousness of the human race, who worry even about the lack of land! How many times I have slept on the ground because I had no place to stay!"[26]

So Teresa went ahead. Yet there were moments when she could not resist saying, "*Señor mío,* how can you command me things that seem impossible? If I were only free, even if I am a woman! But bound in on every side, without money or any way to get it, without a Brief, without anything, what can I do, Lord?"

One night the Ovalle family heard a great crash, and found that the solid wall put up so laboriously with the last *maravedís* of Doña Guiomar's liquid funds had fallen, its stones scattered as if by some invisible cannonade. When Teresa arrived on the scene, she found Juan angrily berating the workmen for building in so slovenly a fashion. Calling her sister, she said, "Tell my brother not to quarrel with these workmen, for it is not their fault; for many devils joined together to knock it down. Be quiet, and let them build another." Later she said, "What strength the devil uses to prevent this! But it won't do him any good."[27]

The workmen wanted more money before they would continue, and neither Teresa nor her friends had any. Guiomar's valuable lands were all entailed in favor of her children and could not be sold. Nearly all her ready money had gone into a convent for Fray Peter of Alcántara, the remainder into this wall

---

[25] Ribera, *loc. cit.*

[26] *¡Oh codicia de el género humano, que aun tierra piensas que te ha de faltar! ¡Cuántas veces dormí yo a el sereno por no tener adonde me meter!* — *Vida,* cap. XXXIII; B.M.C., p. 280.

[27] Ribera, *op. cit.,* lib. I, cap. XVI.

for Sister Teresa. When she learned of its collapse, she resolved to give up the project. What was the use? If God had wanted the work to go on, so good a wall, so well made, would never have fallen.

Teresa quietly answered, "If it has fallen, raise it up again."

Guiomar finally agreed, though not very hopefully, to send to Toro to ask her mother, Doña Aldonza de Guzmán, for thirty ducats.[28] The friends waited anxiously for their messenger to return. Guiomar was quite dejected after two or three days, but Teresa said, "Sister, rejoice, for the thirty ducats are assured. They are already counted out to him in the lower hall." Their man returned two or three days later with the thirty ducats. He had received them at the hour when she had spoken, and in the place she mentioned.

Some of Teresa's most remarkable visions and raptures occurred between midsummer and Christmas, 1561. She saw Saint Clare in great splendor on her feast day, after Communion, and heard her say, "Be of good heart: go on with the work you have begun, and I will help you."[29] On the Feast of the Assumption, while hearing Mass at the Dominican Church of Saint Thomas, and thinking of the sins she had confessed there in her youth "and of my wicked life," she was taken with such a rapture that she was unable to understand the words that were being spoken or sung, or even to see the Elevation. Suddenly she became aware that she was being clothed in a robe of extraordinary whiteness and splendor. She could not see who was doing it at first. "Then I saw our Lady toward the right side, and my father Saint Joseph at the left, putting that garment on me. I was given to understand that I was now clean of my sins. After being clothed, and I with the greatest delight and glory, then our Lady seemed to take me by the hands. She told me I gave her great pleasure in serving the glorious Saint Joseph, that I might believe that what I sought as to the monastery would be done, and in it the Lord and those two would be much served; that I should not fear there would ever be a failure in this, although the jurisdiction under which it was would not be to my taste, for they would watch over us, and that already her Son had promised us to go along with us, and for a sign that this was true, she gave me that jewel. She seemed to me to have thrown around my neck a very

[28] *Ibid.*

[29] *Vida,* cap. XXXIII.

beautiful collar of gold, with a cross of much value attached to it. This gold and precious stone is so different from that of here below that it has no comparison,[30] for their beauty is very different from anything we can here imagine, and the understanding cannot succeed in understanding what the robe was made of, nor how to imagine the whiteness that the Lord wished to have represented in it, for everything here seems like a smudge of soot, so to speak.

"Very great was the beauty I saw in our Lady, although by form or features I could not make out anything in particular, but all together the shaping of the face, clothed in white with the utmost splendor, not the kind that dazzles, but soft. The glorious Saint Joseph I did not see so clearly, although I saw well that he was there, like the visions I have spoken of, which are not seen. Our Lady seemed to me very much a young girl. Being thus with me a little while, and I with the greatest possible glory and joy, more, I thought, than ever I had had and never did I wish to take leave of it, I thought I saw them go up to heaven with much multitude of angels." Teresa remained incapable of speech or motion for a long time, in a solitude indescribably peaceful and exalted.

In another vision that autumn she saw Saint Peter of Alcántara, many miles away, and conversed with him.

Toward the end of 1561, when the thirty ducats had been spent, and there seemed to be no way of getting any more with which to carry on the work, two merchants from Peru arrived in Ávila with a letter from Teresa's brother Lorenzo, who sent her a lovely gold medal and a considerable sum of money to be distributed among his relatives. Her letter of December 23, 1561, thanking him and telling of her hopes and plans, is so characteristic that I am tempted to quote it all:

"Jhs.
"Señor:
"The Holy Spirit be always with you, sir, amen, and repay you the trouble you have taken to help us all, and with such promptitude. I hope in the majesty of God that you, sir, will be much the gainer thereby; for it is certainly true that the money you sent, sir, to everyone, arrived at such good time that it has

---

[30] This sentence is typical of Teresa's artless method of composition, and I have translated literally: "*Este oro y piedras es tan diferente de lo de acá, que no tiene comparación.*" — *Ibid.*

been consolation enough to me. And I believe that it was God who prompted you, sir, to send me so much; for to a nun like me, who now consider it an honor, glory be to God, to go about patched up, the sum that Juan Pedro de Espinosa has brought, and Parruna (as I believe the other merchant is called), will be enough to keep me from need for some years.

"But as I have already written you, sir, quite at length, for many reasons and causes from which I have not been able to escape, since they are inspirations of God, of such a sort that they are not to be put into a letter, I will only say that persons holy and learned think I am bound not to be a coward, but to put all I can into this work, which is to make a monastery where there shall be only fifteen, the number never to be increased, with the greatest enclosure, so as never to go out and never to be seen without the veil over the face, all of them grounded in prayer and mortification, as I have written you, sir, more fully, and will write by Antonio Morán, when he leaves.

"And this lady Doña Yomar (Guiomar), who writes to you, sir, herewith, is helping me. She is the wife of Francisco Dávila, of Salobralejo, if you remember. It's nine years since her husband died, leaving a million a year; she has an entailed estate of her own, besides that of her husband, and although she was left a widow at twenty-five, she has not married, but gives herself much to God. She is very spiritual. For more than four years we have had a closer friendship than one could with a sister; and although she has helped me enough, for she gave a good part of her income, for the time being she is without money, and as to founding and buying the house I must do it myself; for which, with God's favor, they have given me two dowries beforehand, and I have it bought, though secretly, and to build things that were necessary I had no means. And so it is that wholly on trust (since God wants me to do it, He will provide for me) I hired the workmen. That seemed a crazy thing to do! Enter His Majesty, and moves you, sir, to provide it; and what has most astonished me, the forty *pesos* you added, sir, supplied a very great lack of mine; and San Josepe (for so it is going to be called) I believe would not let it happen, and I know that he will pay you, sir. In fine, though poor and little, very beautiful views and field. This finishes it.

"They have gone for the Bulls to Rome, for although it is of my own Order, we give obedience to the Bishop. I hope to the

Lord it will be for His great glory, for in it go souls fitted to give the very greatest example, who are carefully chosen as much for humility as for penance and prayer. May Your Worships commend it to God, for with His help it will be finished by the time Antonio Morán goes.

"He came here and brought me much consolation, for he seems to me a man of parts and of honesty and good understanding, and knowing so particularly of Your Worships; and surely, one of the great things the Lord has done for me is that He has given you all to understand what the world is, and that you have wished to live quietly, and I understand that you are on the way to heaven, which is what I most desire to know, and always till now was in a flutter about. Glory be to Him who has done it all! May it please Him, sir, that you go always forward in His service, for since there is no limit to His rewarding, we should have no hesitation in trying to serve the Lord, but each day should seek to go a little bit ahead, and with fervor; for it seems, and so it is, that we are always at war, and that until we have the victory we must not be off our guard.

"All those by whom you, sir, have sent money, have been honest men, although Antonio Morán has been the best of all, not only in having the gold sold at a higher price, and without cost, as you, sir, will see, but also in coming himself to bring it here from Madrid, though he was in poor health enough, though today he was better — it was an accident — and I see that he is truly well disposed to you, sir. He brought also the money from Parrona, and all very carefully. Rodríguez also came here, and did well enough. I will write you, sir, by him, for he will be the first perhaps to go. Antonio Morán showed me the letter that you, sir, had written him. Believe me, such thoughtfulness comes not only, I believe, from your virtue, but was prompted by God.

"Yesterday my sister Doña María sent me this letter. When they take her the rest of the money, she will send another. The help reached her just in time. She is a very good Christian and has troubles enough; and if Juan de Ovalle brings suit against her,[31] it will destroy her children. But, of course, Martín de Guzmán carried out his plans (God keep him in heaven) and the

---

[31] Teresa's father, Don Alonso, had died without making any arrangements to divide the properties he had received from his two wives. Litigation followed for years between the children of his second wife (except Teresa) and those of the first. Ovalle made serious charges against Guzmán.

court gave it to him, and unfairly too; and now that they come back to look for what my father sold (may he have glory), I haven't any patience left. And the upshot will be, as I say, to kill Doña María my sister; and God deliver me from any share in property that has to be got doing so much wrong to my relatives; though in this world things are of such wise that it is a marvel to see a father on the side of his son, or a brother for his brother. So I am not surprised at Juan de Ovalle. He did well before, and now, for love of me, he has desisted. He has a good disposition, but in this matter it isn't well to depend too much on it; but when you, sir, send him the thousand *pesos*, make him put it in writing, and send it to me, that the day he resumes the lawsuit there shall be five hundred ducats for Doña María.

"Although the houses of Gotarrendura were not sold, Martín de Guzmán received three thousand *maravedis* for them, and it is just that this be returned. And with the thousand *pesos* that you, sir, have sent, Juan de Ovalle will be relieved, and can live here, as he has been doing, for he came here and is now in need; for if this hadn't come, he couldn't get along steadily, but only at times and badly.

"He is happily married enough, but I tell you, sir, that Doña Juana has proved to be a woman so respected and of such worth that God is to be praised for it — and the soul of an angel. I have turned out to be the most good for nothing of all, whom Your Worships ought not to recognize as a sister, such as I am; I don't know how you all love me so much. This I say in all truth. She has passed through plenty of trials, and has endured them well enough. If without leaving yourself in need, sir, you can send her this, do it soon, even though it be a little.

"The moneys have been given, sir, as you commanded, as you will see by the letters. Toribia was dead. . . . The Masses were said (some of them before the money arrived) for the intentions you named, sir, and by the best persons I could find, and they are good enough. The intention for which you said them, sir, touched me with devotion.

"I am staying at the house of the lady Doña Yomar in all these business matters, which has pleased me, because I am more with those who speak to me of you, sir. And I tell you I am all the more glad to be here — a daughter of this lady came, who is a nun in our house, and the Provincial commanded me to come as her companion — where I am freer to do what I want than in the house of my sister. It is where the talk is all of God, and much recollection. I shall be here until they command me something else, although to carry on the said business, it will be better to be here.

"Now let us speak of my dear sister the lady Doña Juana, who, although last, is not so in my affection. . . . I kiss your hands, sir, a thousand times for doing me such a favor. I don't know how to repay it unless by commending our boy [Lorenzo's son] very much to God, and this is being done, for the holy Fray Pedro de Alcántara, who is a barefoot friar of whom I have written you, sir, has it much in his care, and so have the Jesuits and other persons whom God will hear. May it please His Majesty to make him better than his parents, for although they are good, I want him to be better. Write me always, sir, of the joy and compatibility that is yours, for it pleases me much."

Teresa sent her brother some relics, and once more she kissed his hands a thousand times for the gold medal, adding, "If it had come in the time when I wore gold, I should have coveted the image very much, for it is extremely beautiful. May God preserve you, sir, and your wife too, for many years, and give you good years; for tomorrow is the eve of the year 1562." (In Avila at that time the New Year began with Christmas Eve.) "Be sure you always read my letters, sir. I have taken pains enough to see that the ink is good. This letter is written so hastily, and as I say, at such an hour that I cannot go back and read it over. I am in better health than usual. May God grant yours, sir, in body and soul, as I desire it. Amen.

"To the *Señores* Hernando de Ahumada and Pedro de Ahumada, for lack of time, I am not writing, but I will do so soon. You must know, sir, that several very good persons who know our secret, I mean of this business, have considered it a miracle that you sent me so much money, sir, at such a time. I hope to God that when there is need of more, He will put it in your heart to help me, even if you don't want to.

"Your very true servant, sir,

                    Doña Teresa de Ahumada."[32]

[32] I have translated the text published by P. Silverio, in B.M.C., *tomo* VII, *Epistolario* I, pp. 5-13, from the autograph copy in the possession of the Discalced Carmelites of Santa Ana, of Madrid. For English translations of all the correspondence, see *The Letters of Saint Teresa* by Dame Beatrice of Stanbrook Abbey (London, 1926), 4 vols.

The gift of Don Lorenzo had arrived none too soon for the Reform. People had begun to notice the strange doings in the house occupied by Juan de Ovalle and his wife, and to make a shrewd guess at the truth. Soon the name of Sister Teresa was on the tongues of all the gossips again. One day when she went with her sister and Ovalle to hear Mass at the Church of Saint Thomas, she had the unusual experience of hearing herself preached against, like some notorious public sinner bent on corrupting Christians and destroying the Church; as Ribera says, the preacher did all but name her and point his finger at her. Doña Juana was extremely mortified and wanted to leave, but Teresa only laughed, and appeared to be enjoying the epithets that thundered through the beautiful church.[33]

It was no laughing matter, however, when she began to consider the probability that when the news got to the ears of her Provincial, Fray Angel de Salazar, he would soon make an end of all her work. She had not long to wait for this. On Christmas Eve she received a letter from him, instructing her to leave at once with a companion for Toledo, there to stay at the house of a very rich and noble lady, Doña Luisa de la Cerda. This personage, sister of the Duke of Medina Celi, had been so depressed since the death of her husband that she feared she would go mad. Having heard somehow of the raptures of Doña Teresa and the power of her prayers, she had importuned Fray Angel to let the *Beata* come and stay with her a while to console her. The Provincial had at first refused, but now he gave his consent, finding it convenient to kill two birds with one stone.

Toledo, and in midwinter! Twenty leagues over bad roads, under icy winds, to pamper the whim of some spoiled aristocrat! She could not endure the thought of this journey. She turned to God, and prayed so earnestly that she remained in rapture through all the time of Matins. "The Lord told me I must not fail to go, and not to listen to the opinions of others, for few would counsel me without rashness; and although I should have

<hr/>

[33] Ribera, *op. cit.*, lib. I, cap. XV. Silverio, *op. cit.*, II, 58–60. Mir, with his usual prejudice, conjectures that the preacher was Father Ripalda, S.J. There is no real foundation for this suspicion. As P. Silverio observes, Teresa was on excellent terms at that time with the Jesuits of San Gil and their Provincial, Padre Salazar. The Dominicans also disclaim the imputation that it was one of theirs who preached against the Saint. P. Felix Martín, O.P., insists that the incident occurred in the parish church of Saint Thomas, not in the Dominican monastery of Saint Thomas Aquinas. Cf. his *Santa Teresa y la orden de predicadores*, Avila, 1909, pp. 544–546.

trials, God would be much served, and that it was convenient for this business of the monastery that I should be absent until the Brief arrived, for the devil had armed himself with a great plot against the coming of the Provincial, yet I should fear nothing, for He would help me." She told all this to her friend the Jesuit rector, and he advised that she obey her superior at once. Others, as she had been warned in the rapture, insisted that she must do everything to avoid going if possible; the work would be ruined, it was all another trick of the devil, and so on.[34] Teresa does not mention who they were. Probably those who had done most to hinder her plans.

Preparations were hastily made, and within a few days, early in January, she left the Incarnation with another nun, unnamed — probably her old friend Juana Suárez.[35] Of the mere physical obstacles to such a journey she made no mention, yet they must have been formidable. Stacks of snow, howling winds, cold below zero, wretched and dangerous roads in rough, jouncing, and squeaky carts — this was the prospect a person was likely to face if he was so unfortunate as to have business requiring him to go forth at that time of year across the bridge of the Adaja into a vast treeless wilderness.

---

[34] *Vida*, cap. XXXIV.
[35] Silverio, *op. cit.*, II, p. 70, n. 2.

Chapter XIV

EXILE IN A PALACE AT TOLEDO

IT TOOK three or four days in that season to go from Ávila to Toledo. Travelers had to strike southwest from the frozen Adaja, across a bleak barren land called the Paramera, smitten by a north wind colder than the snow that covered La Serrota at the right, until, having reached the top of a long rise, they would begin to descend into a warmer and more friendly countryside of woods and cultivated fields, now fallow and sometimes blanketed with white, toward the valley of the Alberche. Passing through many villages — El Barro, El Tiemblo, Cadalso, Guisando — they emerged at last into the land of the olive and the vine, and after stopping perhaps at Torrijos or Santa Cruz de Retamar, they would suddenly behold, as if a mirage conjured up by the wand of a magician, the ancient and holy city of Toledo, rising starkly beautiful above its walls in the somber light of the afternoon sun of winter.

Teresa left not a word about this momentous journey: only that she obeyed the Provincial and went reluctantly, her consolation being that "there was a house of the Company of Jesus in that place where I was going, and I thought that by being subject to what they might command me, I should have much safety."[1] She never cared much for Toledo, her father's birthplace. The climate agreed with her, but the people were cold and unresponsive, the general atmosphere depressing and stuffy.[2] Still, it must have been impressive to cross the Bridge of Alcántara into this stronghold that so many men had fought and died for — Romans, Visigoths, Berbers, Christian knights — and to mount the steep crooked streets that clove the tiered semicircles of dwellings until at the very peak she encountered the beetling Alcázar of heroic episodes past and future, and the vast Cathedral where Fernando and Isabel had knelt among bronze and jasper columns lighted by thousands of tapers, to give thanks for victory. If she had arrived two years before, she might have seen King Philip the Second breaking lances with his half

---

[1] *Vida*, cap. XXXIV.
[2] So one gathers from her letters of 1576. She left no comment on the city itself on this first visit.

brother, Don John of Austria, near the statue of Hercules on the plaza, to amuse his French-Médicis bride and a glittering array of notables. But since then the court had moved to the healthier site of Madrid, and a complacent torpor had settled on the old half-Moorish city by the Tagus.

Finally the cart or carriage — whichever it was — pulled up in front of a sumptuous Renaissance palace facing the parish church of Saint Roman. What were the thoughts and feelings of the Carmelite nun in her threadbare habit as she crossed the wide porch with its rare plants, mounted the marble steps, and entered the great doors of solid oak, to follow silent servants through a small corridor into a spacious salon whose walls were hung with mirrors from Venice, tapestries from Flanders and the Orient, paintings by famous masters? She says nothing of all this; but we may be sure that she was not at all abashed by crystal chandeliers, richly carved furniture, or gold and silver plate, nor by the stately woman in widow's weeds who came forward to receive her with the quiet but ceremonious grace in which the Spanish nobility were so well versed. Teresa was equally at home, says Ribera, with all sorts of people; among aristocrats she behaved with a certain natural *señorío,* as of one to the manner born.

After greeting her visitors from Ávila, Doña Luisa de la Cerda gave them apartments where they could have some measure of conventual privacy. It was probably not until the next day that she began to tell Doña Teresa of her incurable grief over the death of her husband, following the loss, one after another, of five of their seven children, and of all her sufferings, the worst of which was the fixed melancholy that now afflicted her. And if she was like a great many widows she probably gave a comprehensive review of the virtues of her late husband.

Don Antonio Árias Pardo de Saavedra, Marshal of Castile and Lord of Malagón, Paracuellos, and Hernán-Caballero, had left her with an enormous fortune with which to provide for the two delicate surviving children. He had been a nephew of Cardinal Tabera, primate of Spain — one of the three men to whom Charles V had committed his kingdom in 1543, and the only one to whom the Emperor accorded unstinted praise. The family of Doña Luisa was quite as illustrious as her husband's. She was related to many of the noblest families in Spain, including the Mendozas; and her cousins included the Prince and Princess of Melito, whose daughter, the fascinating Ana de Mendoza, had been given in marriage by King Philip II to his friend Ruy Gómez, Prince of Eboli.

These and other distinguished persons must have frequented the Cerda palace, for Toledo, in spite of the recent removal of the Court, was still the social capital of Spain. There the most powerful lords still had their permanent residences. A century before, they would have been living at their castles in the country, each ruling like a little king over all he surveyed; but Isabel the Catholic and her great minister, Cardinal Ximenes, had reduced them, in a process of unification and centralization, to the status of courtiers, and they had become mostly city dwellers. While they were at the wars, or on diplomatic errands, or attending His Majesty at Madrid, their ladies enjoyed or endured, as the case might be, a strictly conventional and usually placid and sheltered existence. They would go to Mass, and now and then, on a feast day, hear a sermon or see a procession at some of the various churches or monasteries. They would supervise their complicated households and numerous servants. If they went out in the afternoon, following the *siesta,* it would be on foot, or borne in a litter. (The family coach was a formidable affair, brought forth only for long journeys or occasions of state, as when the King came to the city.) Naturally they spent a great deal of time in the *estrado,* or drawing room, exchanging visits, listening to music, reading or being read to — sometimes hearing the lives of the saints, sometimes the sort of romance that Doña Teresa as a child had hidden under her bed. Now and then there was a flutter when it was bruited about that a company of players had arrived. Queen Isabelle of Valois, the third wife of Philip II, had Lope de Rueda and his comedians and buffoons act before her at least twice, in the fall of 1561; but the Spanish ladies, like the English (and unlike the French) generally did not attend such performances. When there was a tournament on the plaza or on the Vega, however, or when there was an *auto-de-fe* in Zocodover, there was seldom any lack of beautiful faces, or of the glitter of sunlight on old family jewels, rare silks, velvets, and cloth of gold; and when the King or some other personage came in state up the winding streets, the balconies of Toledo were something to behold.

Teresa found all this grandeur a bore, in fact a nuisance. If she was pleased to notice that under her encouragement and by the aid of her prayers Doña Luisa was beginning to shake off her melancholy and to improve in health, she made no effort to conceal her annoyance at some of the results of her hostess's grateful and enthusiastic accounts to her friends: "My dear, you should see her, she is a saint!" and so on. People of fashion began going to the palace in the hope of seeing the *Beata* in an ecstasy. More disgusting still, members of the household used to spy on her at all hours, hoping to catch her in the grip of some strange phenomenon.

So this was how great nobles lived; this was what wealth and social position did to people! Teresa set down her feelings in one of the most human passages in all her writings:

"It pleased the Lord that that Lady should be so much consoled, that she began to show an evident improvement and each day found herself more consoled. . . . The Lord must have done it on account of the many prayers that good persons I knew said for me, that all would go well with me. She was full of the fear of God, and so good that her great Christianity supplied what was lacking in me. She conceived a great love for me; and I had considerable for her, on seeing her goodness; but nearly everything was a cross to me, for the regalements gave me great torment, and their making such a fuss about me put me into a great fear. My soul continued so recollected, that I did not dare to be careless, nor was the Lord without care for me; for while I was there he gave me the greatest favors, and these brought me so much liberty, and made me so despise everything I saw, and the more so the more they were, that I did not fail to converse with ladies so great that I could very honorably have served them, with as much liberty as if I were their equal. I derived a very great advantage, and I told her so. I saw that she was a woman, and as subject to passions and weaknesses as I, and how little the power of nobility ought to be esteemed, and how, the greater it is, the more cares and troubles they have — care to keep the etiquette suitable to their estate, which does not allow them to live; to eat without a fixed time or plan, for everything has to go according to their position and not to their constitutions; many times they have to eat foods more suitable to their position but not to their taste.

"And so I wholly abhorred any desire to be a *señora*. God deliver me from evil etiquette, although I must say I think there are few more humble than this one, even if she is one of the highest in the kingdom, and very simple too. I was sorry for her, and I have seen how many times she acts not according to her inclination but to comply with her station. Then as for servants, the little trust to be put in them is little indeed, though she has good ones; one is not to be talked with more than another, else the favored one becomes disliked. This is a subjection, and one of the lies the world tells is to call such persons lords and ladies, for to me they seem only slaves of a thousand things.

"The Lord was pleased that while I was in that house the persons in it improved themselves in serving His Majesty, although I was not free from trials and the envy certain persons had of the great love that lady had for me. They must have thought, perhaps, that I was seeking some interest of my own. The Lord must have permitted such things to bring me certain trials, and others of different sorts, that I should not drink in the regalement that on the other hand was given to me, and it pleased Him to take me out of it all with betterment to my soul."[3]

In spite of these annoyances and others we are left to imagine — an eye at a keyhole, a servant behind a curtain, a step in a corridor — the six months that Teresa spent under the magnificent roof of Doña Luisa brought blessings not only to her and to the Cerda household, but probably to many others whom she met outside. She spent a great deal of time in prayer in various churches, of which there were at least a dozen within two hundred meters of the Cerda palace. She went often to the college of the Jesuits in the Torno de las Carretas, near S. Pedro Martir, and there found the wise direction she had expected under the Rector, Father Pedro Domenech, a man as learned as he was holy, who heard her confessions all the time she was in Toledo, while other Jesuit fathers probably contributed to the improvement she noted in members of the household whom she sent to them. One of these was a girl, thirteen years old, named María de Salazar, an orphan from Aragon whom Doña Luisa had taken as a servant and was educating. Comely, intelligent, and spiritual, this predestined child was moved by the appearance and conversation of Sister Teresa to desire to follow her example, and probably was promised a place in her convent, if and when it was founded.

---

[3] *Vida, cap. XXXIV*; B.M.C., I, pp. 286–287.

At the Dominican church near the palace, the Carmelite visitor met an old friend, a priest of Saint Dominic who had helped her in Avila, and whom she now was able to help.[4] In one of their conversations, she saw he was in great need of spiritual help — not that he was a bad or lax priest, but that he had become a perfunctory servant of God, content with his routine duties, and making no advance in prayer. Seeing in him a talented man who could do infinite good, she yearned to have him become a saint, as with everyone she particularly liked, and she began to implore God on his behalf. When she received no answer, she wept desolately, and cried, after a night of prayer,

"Lord, You can't deny me this favor! Look how fit this man is to be our friend!"[5]

This cry from the heart brought what she desired. His Majesty stood beside her and told her certain words she was to write out and give to the Dominican. She obeyed, and had the satisfaction — not immediately, but after some time — of noticing a radical change in his life. He devoted himself to prayer with sincerity; he seemed almost a different person.

"These are gifts that God gives when He wishes and as He wishes, and it doesn't depend on time or on services. I don't say that this doesn't matter a great deal, but that often the Lord does not give in twenty years the contemplation that he gives to others in one. His Majesty knows the reason. And it is a mistake for us to think we can understand by years what can be reached in no way save by experience; and moreover, they are very much mistaken, as I have said, who try to understand souls without it. I don't say that one who has not the spiritual life, if he is learned, cannot govern one who has; but let it be understood that in the natural order things go, outwardly and inwardly, by labor of the understanding, and in the supernatural, see to it that they go according to Sacred Scripture. For the rest, let him not kill himself, or think he understands what he does

---

[4] Teresa (*Vida*, cap. XXXIV) tells the incident without mentioning the name of the priest. Yepes said it was Fray Vicente Barrón, who had given the last rites to the Saint's father, and had persuaded her to resume mental prayer, and this was the opinion followed by all the early biographers. But Gracián, in his notes on her Life, says that he was Fray García de Toledo; and this, as Father Silverio observes (ed. of her Life, B.M.C., I, p. 286, note 2) settles the controversy.

[5] *"Señor, no me habéis de negar esta merced; mira que es bueno este sujeto para nuestro amigo."* — *Vida, loc. cit.*

not understand, or suffocate souls who in that respect are governed by a greater Lord, and are not without a Superior."[6]

In one of her visions Teresa saw the immense good that her Jesuit confessor and this Dominican friend would do in their respective orders. Once in an ecstasy she saw the latter carried on high by exultant angels, signifying the great progress he had made in a short time. Even his health improved, so that he could do the penance he had been avoiding for fear of injury. Most significant of all, he was given a heavy cross to bear, when a person he had helped slandered him, and he bore it with meekness and patience.

So much for others. As for her own mission, Teresa discovered that her exile in Toledo had interrupted it only to shape and strengthen it. She had time to pray, to think, to reconsider, to ask the advice of *letrados* and others, and in particular to think her way through the crucial problem, whether to found her convent in absolute poverty, depending on daily charity, or to seek an endowment.

One of the persons to whom she wrote, Father Gonzalo de Aranda, showed her letter in Ávila to Fray Pedro de Alcántara. The holy Franciscan sent her one of those priceless letters of his, on a small piece of paper covered to the edges with his fine handwriting.

"It certainly surprises me," he wrote, "that Your Worship should commit to the opinion of learned men what does not belong to their science. If it were a matter of controversy or a case of conscience, it would be well to take the opinion of jurists or theologians; but in the perfection of life one has to deal only with those who live it, for ordinarily a person has conscience and good sentiment only in proportion as he does good works; and in the evangelical counsels one is not to ask advice as to whether it is well to follow them or no, for this is a limb of infidelity. For the counsel of God cannot fail to be good, nor is it difficult to keep, except for the unbelieving and

---

[6] This is a difficult passage to translate, and Teresa's English translators have not done full justice to her thought. Neither of them will let her say "let him not kill himself." Canon Dalton softens this into "let him not vex or harass himself." Yet the Saint says plainly "let him not *kill* himself" — "*en lo demas no se mate.*" This is one of many examples that could be offered to show how, in translation, Teresa has been robbed by pious persons of a great deal of her vigor and spontaneity of expression, and sometimes made to sound like a prig, though actually no one was less so. *Vida*, cap. XXXIV, B.M.C., p. 289.

those who trust little in God, and those who are guided only by human prudence; for He Who gives the counsel will give the means to follow it, since He can give it, nor is there any good man who gives counsel which he does not intend to have good effect, although by our nature we may be wicked; how much more, then, the supremely Good and Powerful wishes and is able to have His counsels avail those who follow them.

"If Your Worship desires to follow Christ's counsel of greater perfection in matters of poverty, follow it, for no more is given to men than to women, and He will have matters go well with you, as they have with all who have followed it. And if you wish to take the advice of learned men without the spiritual life, seek all the income you please, and see whether they or it will help you more than going without it to follow the counsel of Christ. Oh, if we see something lacking in monasteries of poor women, it is because they are poor against their will, and because they can do nothing else, and not because they have followed the counsel of Christ. I do not glorify mere poverty for its own sake, but poverty suffered with patience for love of Christ our Lord, yes, much more poverty desired, sought for, and embraced with love; for if I felt anything else, or held it deliberately, I should not consider myself sound in the faith.

"I believe Christ our Lord in this and in everything, and I firmly believe that His counsels are very good, as counsels of God, and I believe that although they may not bind under pain of sin, they do bind a man to be much more perfect following them than not following them. I say that they bind him, that they make him more perfect, at least in this, and more holy and more pleasing to God. I hold blessed, as His Majesty tells us, the poor in spirit, who are poor because they want to be, and I have seen the proof of it, although I believe more in God than in my own experience; and that those who are poor with all their hearts with the grace of the Lord live a life of blessedness, as even in this life those live who love, trust, and hope in God.

"May His Majesty give Your Worship light to understand these truths and to put them into practice. Do not believe those who say the contrary, whether through lack of light, or through unbelief, or through not having tasted how sweet is the Lord to those who fear and love Him and renounce for love of Him all the things in the world not necessary for His greater love;

for they are enemies of carrying the cross of Christ, and do not believe in His glory, which comes after it. And, likewise, may He give light to Your Worship, that in the presence of truths so evident you waver not, nor ask opinions except from the followers of the counsels of Christ. Although the others are saved, if they observe what they are bound to, they generally don't have light for more than they do; and although their advice may be good, better is that of Christ our Lord, Who knows what He counsels and gives help to carry it out, and at the end gives payment to those who trust in Him and not in the affairs of the world. — From Ávila and April 14, 1562 — Humble chaplain of Your Worship, Fray Pedro de Alcántara."[7]

Some of Teresa's learned friends advised her not to take this idealistic counsel too seriously. It is not difficult to imagine their arguments — indeed, Teresa indicates what they were: we are living, after all, in a practical world, and more good can be done by making some compromises with this fact than by ignoring it; some religious houses have fallen into great confusion and even relaxation while struggling to get along without an endowment; if she were planning a little hermitage for herself alone the case would be different, but she is dealing with the lives of others who will suffer for her mistakes if she follows the advice of well-meaning but impractical persons like Fray Pedro de Alcántara. And so on. Even Fray Pedro Ibáñez, who had given her such loyal aid and sound advice in Ávila, now took this worldly view. "He sent me two written pages of contradiction and theology as to why it should not be done and also told me he had studied the matter deeply."[8]

Other friends who at first counseled poverty, changed their opinion after considering the difficulties. Teresa hesitated, her heart on the side of Fray Pedro, her head on the side of the others. She had received no direct command from His Majesty on the subject.

God has various ways of teaching His servants. In this instance Teresa's ideas were clarified by a visit, in the spring of 1562, from a remarkable woman in a Carmelite habit so travel stained and patched that it is a wonder the servants admitted her to those aristocratic halls. María of Jesus was forty years of

---

[7] Yepes gives this letter, lib. II, cap. IV, pp. 146–147. P. Silverio quotes it entire in his life of Saint Teresa, Vol. II, pp. 91–92; see also B.M.C., t. 2, pp. 125–126.

[8] *Vida*, B.M.C., p. 297, cap. XXXV.

age, a native of Granada, where her father had been a lawyer. She had entered rather late in life a convent of the Calced Carmelites of Granada, and after several months as a novice, had conceived the idea of founding a small convent of contemplatives. The same thought had occurred to her and to Teresa, and in the same month of the year 1561.

María of Jesus was another of those rare and refreshing souls in whom, by an inner and compelling integrity, feeling, thought, and action are fused into one. No sooner had she concluded that her desire was the will of God than she sold all her inheritance, entrusted part of the proceeds to a friend for the expenses of the monastery she dreamed of, and sewing up the remainder in gold and silver coins in a specially prepared girdle under her rough habit to defray the costs of her journey, she set out with two Franciscan *beatas,* and walked from Granada to Rome. She wore no shoes, and when at last she arrived at Saint Peter's, weary and battered, her feet left bloody prints on the ancient stones as she made her way through a crowd to fall upon her knees before the Vicar of Christ.

Pius the Fourth listened to her plea, looked at the bleeding toes and selfless eyes, and cried, "Valiant woman, be it done as you wish!"[9]

He sent her and her companions for the time being to a Carmelite monastery at Mantua, one of the most rigorous communities in the order, perhaps the only one where the ancient rule of Saint Albert was still observed to a great extent, notwithstanding the mitigation allowed by Pope Eugenius IV in 1432. María made a copy of the rule, and took it with her when she returned to Spain, together with the Pope's brief authorizing her to found a convent under its provisions. While considering ways and means, she learned — possibly from the Jesuit Father Gaspar de Salazar, formerly rector at Ávila[10] — that Doña Teresa de Ahumada had a similar plan, and was then at Toledo; and she went more than seventy leagues out of her way to discuss the matter.

During the fifteen days she remained in the Cerda palace, she showed Teresa her copy of the rule of Saint Albert. A new light began to shine upon the question of poverty versus endowment.

---

[9] *"Varonil mujer! Hágase lo que pide!"* — P. Silverio, *op. cit.,* II, p. 94, following D. Miguel de Portilla, *Historia de Compluto,* t. II, pt. 2, p. 6.

[10] Silverio, *loc. cit.,* p. 95.

"Until I spoke with her, it had not come to my notice that our rule, before it was relaxed, commanded that no private property be held; nor was I for founding it without income, for my intent was that we should not have to worry about our necessities, and I didn't notice the many worries that owning property brings with it. This blessed woman, since the Lord had taught it to her, understood well without being able to read what I, with so much reading of the Constitutions, did not know. And when she told me, it seemed good to me, although I was afraid that they would not let me do it, but would say I had crazy ideas, and that I should not do anything that would make others suffer for me."[11]

María of Jesus left Toledo as quietly as she had come, and went to Madrid, where she found another friend in Doña Leonor de Mascareñas. This Portuguese lady, who had been governess of Philip II in his first years, gave her some houses in Alcalá de Henares, and there at last María founded the convent of her desire, that of *La Purísima Concepción*, popularly called the Convent of the Image, from a famous statue of our Lady donated by the benefactress.

Even after María's departure, and after she had read and copied the rule of Saint Albert, Teresa hesitated to establish a house dependent on alms alone in Ávila. Her learned friends were now citing examples of convents in which the lack of income had caused great distractions. Charity had grown cold, these wise ones said, and nuns could no longer expect that the public would support them; if they did, they would find themselves a prey to anxieties which would choke the life of prayer and thus defeat their own purpose.[12] Their arguments broke in upon the brain of Teresa, almost compelling agreement. Yet thinking of Christ, so poor and homeless as He trod the earth, she could never quite make the surrender to "practical" common sense.

At this critical moment, in June, 1562, who should appear in Toledo but Fray Pedro de Alcántara, so frail that he seemed almost a skeleton in his patched brown robe. How he happened to arrive just then is not clear. Perhaps Teresa, feeling the need of his advice, had asked Doña Luisa to invite him to the palace.

---

[11] *Vida,* cap. XXXV. Chapter VI of the primitive Carmelite rule says, *"Nullus fratrum sibi aliquid proprium esse dicat, sed sint vobis omnia communia."* Pope Gregory IX, in 1229, forbade the Carmelites to own houses, lands or incomes, as opposed to the contemplative life. P. Silverio, ed. of *Vida,* p. 296, n. 1.

[12] Yepes, t. II, lib. IV.

At any rate, there he was for several days, powerfully reinforcing with his luminous words the arguments he had given in his letter. Perhaps this explains why the Dominican, Father Ibáñez, now changed his opinion. Certainly it brought Teresa to a final decision in favor of poverty. "I resolved to go no further in consulting others."

With this her mission at Toledo came to an end. She had done what she had been sent to do, and she had learned the lessons she had been sent there to learn. She had been away from Ávila at a time when her presence there would have done more harm than good. Finally, by her own account, she had completed the spiritual preparation necessary for her lifework. She had come to love not only the ideal of poverty, but Christ's poor themselves. To love the poor in the flesh, unwashed, unsightly, ill-smelling, often ungrateful and perverse — this is the real test of one's love of holy poverty; and Teresa admits that her fastidious soul had never attained the freedom to see and to touch the most miserable of the images of God until gradually in the vast and lonely house of the Cerdas God had revealed to her the hollowness of all wealth, position and power, the misery and futility of those whom this world envies, and the literal truth of Christ's words, "Blessed are the poor in spirit." Formerly she had been glad to give alms to the poor, for the love of Him, but sometimes, as she now realized, with a sort of shrinking from what was soiled or ugly. Now all this was past, and she felt such true sympathy for them (did not the very word *sympathy* mean originally "to suffer with"?) that she ached to give them even the poor and threadbare habit she wore.[13]

It was in those rags, and in the marble halls of the Cerdas, that she wrote: "Until now I thought I had need of others, and had more confidence in what the world could do to help me. Now I clearly understand that they are all little sticks of dried rosemary, and that there is no safety in grasping them, for in having some weight of contradictions or murmurings put on them, they break. And so I know from experience that the true help for not falling is to lay hold of the cross and to trust in Him Who put Himself on it. . . . Though I understood this truth so clearly, I used to be very glad to have people think well of me. Now it is nothing to me, indeed to some extent I think it wearies me, except with those I deal with concerning

[13] *Relación* II, in *Relaciones espirituales*, B.M.C., II, p. 14.

my soul or think I can do some good for. . . . In very great
trials and persecutions and contradictions I have had during
these months, God has given me great courage; the more they
were the greater, and without tiring of suffering." She not only
had no ill-will toward those who spoke badly of her, but loved
them — this was indeed, as she said, a gift from God. It pained
her to think of taking food, especially at times of mental prayer.

"I feel in myself the greatest desire, more than I used to, that
God have persons who serve Him with utter detachment, and
that they be held back by nothing here below, since I see that
it is all mockery — and especially learned men; *for when I see
the great necessities of the Church, I am so afflicted by them
that it seems to me a thing of mockery to be troubled by anything else, and so I do nothing but commend them to God; for
I see that one person wholly perfect, with true fervor of love for
God, will be worth more than many who are lukewarm.*[14]

"In matters of the Faith I find myself, in my opinion, with
much more valor. It seems to me that I could fight all alone
against all the Lutherans to make them understand their error.
I feel deeply the loss of so many souls. I see many improved, and
know plainly that God has wished it to be through my instrumentality; and I know that through His goodness, my soul goes
on increasing in love for Him every day. I think that even if I
tried deliberately to be vainglorious, I couldn't do it, nor do I
see how I could think that any of these virtues is mine, for it is
only a little while ago that I saw myself without any for several
years, and now, for my part, I don't do anything more than
receive favors, without rendering service, but like the most useless thing in the world. . . ."[15]

If there is a note of self-preoccupation here, it must be remembered that Teresa was writing a report under obedience
for her confessor alone, to enable him to judge of her spiritual
condition, and had been told to set down exactly what she felt
and thought. The same is true, of course, of the biography, which
she finished under the roof of Doña Luisa.

Her spiritual apprenticeship was finished. She was ready to
begin the real mission of her life. As if to emphasize the fact,
Juan de Ovalle, her brother-in-law, made his appearance in To-

[14] My italics. This is the heart of Teresa's thought and action.
[15] *Relación* III, *Obras,* B.M.C., t. III, pp. 17–19. In Mr. Lewis' English translation it appears as part of *Relation* II, pp. 349–353.

ledo about this time (June, 1562) to report on the progress of
the work in the house at Avila. His wife Juana had gone to
their home in Alba de Tormes with their children,[16] and he
was anxious to join them there. He begged Teresa to return as
soon as possible.

What ought she to do? Although her work at Toledo was finished, she was not eager to go back to Ávila. There was to be
an election at the Incarnation, and granting it was her duty to
be present to cast her vote, she was dismayed at the news that
her friends intended to nominate her for prioress. "I had never
wanted any office, and had always refused them, for it seemed
to me a great peril for my conscience; and so I praised God that
I was not there. I wrote to my friends not to vote for me."
Furthermore, her election might be fatal to her plans for the
new convent. At this point her provincial, Fray Angel de Salazar,
released her from her obligation to remain at Toledo. As he
did not command her to return, she decided to stay on for a
while. His Majesty, however, had other plans for her. He had
lately confirmed her decision, telling her that "in no way should
I fail to make the house poor, for it was the will of His Father
and His, and He would aid me. Another time He told me that
in endowment there was confusion, and other things in praise
of poverty, and assuring me that anyone who served Him would
never lack what was necessary to live." And now, just as she
was congratulating herself on being, as she puts it, "out of all
that noise" at the Incarnation, "the Lord told me that I was
by no means to fail to go, for since I desired a cross, there was
a good one waiting for me, and I must not avoid it, but go with
courage, and He would help me, and I must go at once."[17]

Her confessor, hearing of this, told her to go, but advised
delaying a few days, for cooler weather. Teresa obeyed as usual.
Besides, courtesy required that before leaving she obtain the
"permission" of Doña Luisa. This proved unexpectedly difficult.
The great lady had grown so accustomed to her companionship
and consolation that she could not give them up, and with the
selfishness that wealth often breeds, made every objection to her
going, even to the point, one infers, of accusing her of ingratitude — and this to a poor nun who had given her what all the
wealth of the Cerdas could never have purchased.

---

[16] Ribera, *op. cit.*, lib. I, cap. XVI.
[17] *Vida*, cap. XXXV, B.M.C., p. 298.

"She felt it so much that I should leave her that it was an additional torment, for it had cost her much to manage it with the Provincial by many kinds of importunities. I took it to be a very remarkable thing for her to give in, considering how she felt about it; however, as she was very fearful of God, and as I told her that a great service could be done for Him, and plenty of other things, and gave her hope that it was possible for me to go back to see her, and so, with trouble enough, she took it in good part."[18]

When the moment came to leave, Teresa's feelings were mixed. She felt sorry for Doña Luisa, who could not conceal her misery. She knew, with a heavy heart, how much she would miss her Jesuit confessor, Father Domenech. Nor was she too spiritualized to feel a certain human repugnance for the sufferings that awaited her in Ávila, even though she had learned to desire suffering for the sake of the suffering Christ. "I saw clearly these two contraries: to enjoy myself, and to console myself and take delight in what weighed me down in the soul, for I *was* consoled and rested, and had an opportunity to spend many hours in prayer. I saw that I was going to put myself in the fire, for the Lord had already told me so, that I was going to carry a great cross, though never did I think it would be as much as afterwards I saw; and with all this, I went away joyful, and I was undone because I could not throw myself into the battle at once, for the Lord wished me to do it, and so His Majesty sent the strength, and put it in my weakness." She was like a person with a jewel that gave rare pleasure to look on and to keep, but she happened to know that someone she loved more than herself wanted it; therefore it gave her more joy to be without it, she said, than to keep it, even though giving it up caused a certain sorrow. So she made her farewells, we may be sure with many tears on the side of Doña Luisa, and set out with her companion on the road to the north.

[18] *Ibid.* The bad construction of this sentence is Saint Teresa's.

Chapter XV

STEALING A MARCH ON SLEEPY ÁVILA

ARRIVING in her native city after a hot and dusty journey whose discomforts she did not trouble to relate, she went directly to the Incarnation, reported to her superiors, and quietly slipped back into the measured routine of the community.

That night a messenger reached Ávila with a brief from the Cardinal of San Angelo, on behalf of Pope Pius IV, granting permission for the founding of a monastery under the Carmelite rule. Dated February 6, it had been nearly five months in transit, and came addressed to Doña Guiomar de Ulloa and her mother — probably in care of the Bishop if the usual custom was observed.

Teresa soon learned of its arrival. Perhaps the Holy Cavalier told her, perhaps the Maestro Daza. It was not Guiomar certainly, for she had gone to visit her mother in Toro to avert suspicion from the work she had been doing on the house.[1] Nor was it Juana, who had gone to Alba, nor her husband Juan de Ovalle, who, living alone, had just caught a cold, with fever. No matter who; Teresa was elated to have the Holy Father's approval. But on the heels of joy came a real anxiety. She was virtually a prisoner in the Incarnation at the moment when she was most needed outside, and she dared not ask to go, lest she arouse suspicion.

It was all the more tantalizing to know that the Bishop of Ávila, Don Álvaro de Mendoza, had arrived on the very night of her return, and that Fray Pedro de Alcántara also was in town, a guest in the house of Don Juan Blázquez, Lord of Loriana.[2] There, however, a little group of Teresa's friends — Don Francisco de Salcedo, Maestro Daza, Father Gonzalo de Aranda, and possibly Doña Guiomar, newly arrived from Toro — met to read the Brief and to discuss what could be done.

The document granted to Doña Guiomar and her mother per-

---

[1] Ribera, *Vida de Santa Teresa*, lib. I, cap. 17.
[2] Not at Salcedo's house, as some editors have inferred from Teresa's reference to a *caballero muy siervo de Dios* — *Vida,* cap. XXXVI. Cf. Silverio, *Vida de Santa Teresa de Jesús,* II, 112.

mission to found "a monastery of nuns, of the number and with the invocation which may seem to you suitable, of the Rule and Order of Saint Mary of Mount Carmel, under the obedience and correction of the venerable Father in Christ, by the grace of God, Bishop of Ávila . . . with a church, belfry, bells, cloister, refectory, dormitory, garden, and other necessary offices . . . within or without the walls of the said city of Ávila, according as it may seem good to you, but without injury to anyone . . . to make lawful and reasonable statutes and ordinances, not contrary to the canon law" and any necessary changes and modifications. Disobedience to the Bishop and other chief Prelates would incur excommunication *ipso facto,* and so on — this was one of the usual conditions imposed by the Holy See to guard against scandals and abuses.

Nothing was said of the Primitive Rule of Saint Albert, or of absolute poverty without endowment. In fact, when the two ladies had asked for it, in 1561, Teresa had not decided upon these two cornerstones. New and unforeseen obstacles now stood in the way. What would the Bishop think of taking under his obedience a monastery which in the ordinary course would have been subject to the Carmelite Provincial? And what would he say when Teresa proposed the primitive rule and absolute poverty?

He said exactly what they feared he would say. If the convent was to have no income, he would have nothing to do with it. There were plenty of convents in Ávila. Why found another which would become a charge to him or to the city, for no apparent good reason? He had never met this nun, Doña Teresa. Perhaps he was somewhat influenced by what her enemies had been saying.

Don Álvaro de Mendoza was a man who seldom changed his mind. The only hope the conspirators had left was that he might listen to Fray Pedro de Alcántara, for whom he had a deep veneration. "It is a little stable of Bethlehem!" the dear old Franciscan had exclaimed when he first saw the poor house that Teresa had chosen; and now, from his bed of sickness in the house of the Lord of Loriana, he wrote the Bishop one of his frugal letters:

"The spirit of Christ fill up the soul of Your Lordship! Your holy benediction received. Sickness has weighed me down so much that it has prevented my speaking of an affair very important to the service of our Lord, and this being the case, and lest we should fail to do our part, in short I should like to give an account of it to Your Lordship, and it is this. A person very spiritual, with true zeal, has for some days been trying to found in this place a most religious and wholly perfect monastery of nuns of the primitive rule and order of Our Lady of Mount Carmel, for which she has desired to take for end and assurance of the said first Rule the giving of obedience to the Ordinary of this place; and confiding in the great holiness and goodness of Your Lordship, since under our Lord you are their prelate, they have carried on the affair until now at a cost of more than five thousands *reales,* and for it they have obtained a brief.

"It is a business that has seemed to me good, and so for love of our Lord I beg Your Lordship to protect it and accept it, for I understand it is an addition to the divine worship and welfare of this city. And since I cannot go to receive your holy benediction and to speak of this, I should take it as a great charity if Your Lordship would direct Master Daza to come, that I might talk with him, or with anyone Your Lordship wishes. But as I understand, this could be entrusted to and discussed with the Master, and that would give me much consolation and charity. I say that Your Lordship could speak of this with the Master Daza, and with Gonzalo de Aranda and with Francisco Salcedo, who are persons known to Your Lordship and have more detailed knowledge of this than I; although I am well satisfied with the first persons who are to enter, for they are people who have been tested, and of their leader I believe that the spirit of our Lord dwells in her; which may His Majesty give to and keep in Your Lordship, for His great glory and the universal benefit of His Church. Amen. Amen. —

> "Unworthy servant and chaplain of Your Lordship
> Fray Pedro de Alcántara."[3]

The aristocratic Bishop did not see fit, for some reason, to grant the request for a conference. He went to his summer place at El Tiemblo, some thirty-two miles from Ávila, and perhaps forgot all about the matter. But San Pedro was not the man to accept defeat tamely. As soon as he was able to drag his emaciated body from his bed, he mounted a mule (or had someone set him

---

[3] P. Silverio, *op. cit.,* II, pp. 124–125; also in B.M.C., t. II, p. 127.

in the saddle) and started for El Tiemblo. Ordinarily he would have walked.

His appearance when he arrived, more dead than alive, more than ever like a skeleton or the gnarled roots of trees in his patched robe, would have touched a stonier heart than Don Alvaro's. And his arguments were such that the Bishop promised to speak with Doña Teresa on his return to Ávila.

She and her friends, who had been praying fervently for Fray Pedro's success, were overjoyed at the good news. Yet it was not clear how she could confer with His Lordship without having her plans prematurely known at the Convent; or how, even if he gave his consent, she could visit the house occupied by Juan de Ovalle, to have the necessary changes made.

While matters were in this state, Ovalle's cold became much worse. He had a high fever, he had gone to bed, and there was no one to take care of him. When the Prioress of the Incarnation learned of this, she instructed Sister Teresa to go at once to her brother-in-law, and to remain with him until he was better.

Teresa hastened with secret joy to the humble residence north of the ancient walls of Ávila. It was not much to look at, this house, a diminutive two-story building still in poor repair despite all she had done the previous year. Yet she could hear echoing in her memory the voice of her Lord saying, "Enter as you can. . . . How often I slept on the ground!" and examining it now, she could see the possibility of a modest convent. This little first floor room would be the chapel. There the altar must stand — the center of the house and the throne of His Majesty. Here she would have a double grille of wood covered with curtains through which the nuns could hear Mass without being seen. Next to this, on the small porch or vestibule, she would have two doors, one giving access to the chapel, the other to the portery; and over the former she would have a statue of Saint Joseph, patron of the house, and over the latter one of our Lady, each in its own niche. She already had the statues, perhaps given by friends, perhaps bought at a great sacrifice, and she was guarding them carefully for the day when they should be put in place — small and lowly treasures speaking the universal language of love, which invariably wishes to set up some likeness of the Beloved to look upon and to enjoy. The Holy Virgin was clad in garments of gold, the gilding painted upon the statue, and held her divine Son in her arms. Saint Joseph, quite ruddy of countenance, was draped with a robe of silk, and characteristically humble and courteous, held his *sombrero* in his hand. He seemed ready to welcome visitors to this new abode, and no wonder, for the convent was to be named for him and placed under his protection.[4]

The second story was to be divided into "cells" for the nuns. Only four would be needed at first, for quality mattered more than quantity, and Teresa had thoughtfully and prayerfully chosen her companions. All were orphans and poor; not a single one had a dowry. The first was Antonia de Henao of Ávila, recommended by her director, Fray Pedro de Alcántara. The second was María de la Paz, who had gone from a poor family in Ledesma to be a servant in the house of Doña Guiomar de Ulloa, where Teresa had formed a correct estimate of her sanctity. The third was another *Avilesa*, Ursula de Revilla y Alvarez de Arévalo, who had been rather giddy as a girl,[5] but at forty-four gave promise of being an exemplary nun. Finally, there was María de Ávila, thirty-seven years old, sister of a good humble priest, Father Julián, whom Teresa meant to have for her chaplain.

The habits for these four and herself she carefully sewed with her own hands. Perhaps the others helped to cut from her patterns the pieces of coarse brown homespun serge that were to form the principal parts of the dresses, and the linen for the toques, and the plain veils in which she would tolerate no unnecessary crimples or pleats or folds or any ornamental superfluities whatever. Anyone who has heard a group of Spanish women talking can imagine the animation of some of these meetings, subdued no doubt to whispers and muffled laughter out of consideration for Juan de Ovalle on his bed of fever upstairs, while carpenters clattered below and all about with no such scruples, and various friends — perhaps the Holy Cavalier, Maestro Daza, Father Julián de Ávila or Father Gonzalo de Aranda — came and went after dark, helped with the work, brought this or that article.

---

[4] It has been said erroneously that San José de Ávila was the first church named for the foster father of our Lord; but there was one in Bologna in the twelfth century. The cult of Saint Joseph had been growing slowly but steadily from very early times. Saint Teresa did not revive it, as some have said, but gave it new popularity.

[5] Yepes, *op. cit.*, II, cap. VIII.

Teresa had not been long at the house when she received word
that Fray Pedro de Alcántara had returned to Ávila and would
see her at a certain chapel of the Cathedral, to discuss the final
details of the assault they were planning upon the strong will of
the Bishop. One day early in August she set forth with a friend
(who later became Sister Isabel de Santo Domingo) for this important rendezvous. Fray Pedro heard their confessions, said his
Mass and gave them Holy Communion. Then they conversed,
and agreed that he should take the Bishop to visit her at the
Incarnation after her return.

Teresa was probably living at the convent again when her
relative, Doña María Cimbrón, was elected prioress for the third
time on August 12.[6] Not long after this the Bishop went with
Fray Pedro to see her. Like most persons, he was captivated by
her simplicity, her sincerity, her quiet intensity of purpose, her
humility without servility, her human (and more than human)
charm and power. Before they had parted he had agreed to take
her monastery under his protection and jurisdiction, and from
that day on he was her loyal and unflinching friend until he
died, requesting in his will that he be buried beside her.

Fray Pedro's lifework seems to have been brought to a close
with this service to another saint. He retired at once to a monastery of his order to await his release, which occurred two months
later.

She made up her mind to found her monastery on the feast
of Saint Bartholomew, August 24, hoping thus to start with the
protection of that apostle, who was especially invoked against
the wiles and assaults of the devil. Much was to be done in the
few days remaining. But at last the cells were partitioned off,
the new doors made, the first floor arranged as a chapel, the
altar set up, the grille installed. Maestro Daza had promised to
say the first Mass. And it is to be supposed that Teresa gave the
most minute attention to the preliminary instruction of her
novices, that they might enter San José with a full realization of
the difficulties before them and the lofty meaning of the austerities they were about to accept for the rest of their lives.

The primitive rule of Carmel, which she was restoring, was
one of the most rigorous in the history of the Church. For-
mulated by Saint Albert in 1209, it had been approved by Pope
Honorius III in 1226 during the turbulent but glorious time

---

[6] Silverio, *op. cit.*, II, p. 135.

when Saint Francis of Assisi and his followers were singing on the roads of Italy, and Saint Dominic was organizing an order for the intellectual defense of Christendom. Twenty years later Saint Simon Stock, General of the Carmelites, then in England, sent a delegation to Lyon, where Pope Innocent IV was, to ask him to clarify certain points in the rule. Innocent referred the matter to two Dominicans, Hugo de San Charo and William, Bishop of Antera, who revised and modified it to suit their own conceptions, which were naturally not identical with those of the first Carmelite hermits. The Pope ratified their work September 1, 1248. Later pontiffs, by dispensation, allowed further relaxations. The result was the sort of convent exemplified by the Incarnation of Avila — not immoral, but too populous for the perfect life of prayer for which the early Carmelites had dedicated their order to the Mother of God.

"According to the teaching of Saint Thomas, and according to truth, the perfection of a religious order does not consist so much in the penances that are done in it, as in having a higher end than another, with the means adapted to such an end," says Ribera;[1] hence, he concludes, the orders which hold the highest rank are those ordained for teaching and preaching. "And next after these come those which are established for contemplation, for as it is greater to illuminate than merely to shine, so it is greater to communicate to others what has been contemplated, than to contemplate only." Since orders of women are not established to preach or teach, he continues, their highest vocation is to aid, by their prayers and penances, the men who labor to propagate or defend the Church in the classroom or the pulpit. And however perfect women in a contemplative order may be in their praying, singing, and other duties, they will not be accomplishing what they are called to do unless they offer their works, including their fasts and other penances, for "those who go into the field, sweating and battling for the glory of God, and the defense and increase of the Church."

The means of approaching this high ideal, in Teresa's opinion, was the primitive rule of Saint Albert. This required, in addition to the usual vows of chastity, poverty, and obedience, that the religious keep silence at certain hours; that they remain in their cells, meditating on the things of God, when not otherwise

---

[1] *Lib.*, II, c. 1, referring to *Summa*, Pars II, q. 188, a. 6, where Saint Thomas regards teaching and preaching as fruits of contemplation.

engaged; that they fast from the Exaltation of Holy Cross (September 14) to Easter, unless prevented by sickness or some other valid excuse; that they never eat meat, unless for health's sake as during an illness; and that they regularly perform some manual labor. In short Madre Teresa — or La Madre, as she was henceforth to be known — was resolved to do away with all the compromises that had changed the most rigorous order of contemplatives into one very like other communities with far different purposes. Was there not more than coincidence in her doing this the very year the Turks destroyed the only convent in the world where the primitive rule was fully observed, the one in Cyprus?[8]

The primitive rule was designed to permit those who desired to follow Christ's counsels of perfection literally to do so with the least possible interference from their own human nature, from friends and relatives, and from the outside world in general. Teresa decreed, therefore, that no nun must ever be seen without her veil, except by father, mother, or sister, or for some good end such as the edification or welfare of the Order. And even then a third person must always be present. The Prioress held the keys of the grille and the portery, and no one could enter or leave without her permission. When it was necessary for a doctor or a priest to visit a nun confined by sickness to her bed, he was conducted by two persons to the door of her cell. No one else could speak to him, nor could he speak with any save the patient; and as he passed through the convent, a nun or lay sister went before him ringing a little bell, to give warning that a stranger was in the house. Novices were obliged to conform to the same strict rule as professed nuns regarding visits and other such matters, on the theory that if they could not be content with the austerities of the life, they might as well find it out in time and depart without taking vows. No member of the community could own any private or personal property. If a nun became strongly attached to anything material — to a book, even to her own bare cell — the Prioress would require that she give it up, lest it interfere with that complete detachment which must be the starting point of the life of contemplation. Finally, no attention was to be paid to the affairs of the outside world, except by permission of the Prioress to give aid or consolation to those in need or distress.

---

[8] Yepes, *loc. cit.*

This Carmelite attitude explains why the writings of Saint Teresa contain so little information about contemporary affairs in one of the most dramatic periods of Spain's remarkable history. Except for a few general statements about the persecution of the Church by Lutherans, the pages she wrote in 1562 and 1563 say nothing of the atrocities perpetrated by the Calvinists against priests and nuns in the fall of 1561, for example, or of the resumption of the Reign of Terror in 1562, when fanatical French Protestants slew 4000 priests, nuns, and monks, expelled or mistreated 12,000 nuns, sacked 20,000 churches, destroyed priceless works of art, manuscripts, and relics; razed 2000 monasteries, old centers of Christian culture, to the ground; exhumed the incorrupt body of Saint Francis de Paula and burned it, cast down the statue of Saint Joan of Arc from the bridge at Orleans, scattered consecrated Hosts in the streets to be trampled on by men and horses, and frequently revealed, underneath a pharisaical pretense of appealing from the Catholic Church to primitive Christianity, a no less fanatical hatred of Christ Himself.

In Spain, too, there were strange and tragic happenings. The Mediterranean had become virtually a Mohammedan lake, and Philip the Second, almost always unlucky at sea, lost fleet after fleet. In April, 1562, his only son and heir, Don Carlos, was at death's gate till the relics of Saint Didacus miraculously restored him. In November the city of Valladolid was destroyed by fire, and Philip gave a large sum for the relief of sufferers and the rebuilding of the town. The next summer he laid the cornerstone of the Escorial and sent a fleet to rescue the heroic defenders of Mers-el-Kebir. Yet of all such matters we find no hint in the pages of Teresa. To her the little house north of the walls of Avila was all the world and something more. "This house is a heaven, if it can be had on earth. For anyone who enjoys only giving enjoyment to God, and pays no attention to her own enjoyment, a very good life may be had; in seeking somewhat more, all is lost, for it can't be had."[9]

With this conception firmly before her, she chose the first nuns from among the most heroic women she knew with an eye to quality rather than quantity. She intended to have no more than thirteen or fourteen in one house; later she added three *tourières* to assume such laborious duties as might keep the nuns from contemplation. She was determined not

---

[9] *Camino de perfección*, Valladolid MS., cap. XIII.

to accept members of other orders or even of the Calced Carmelites. She refused to consider wealth and social position; poverty and low birth must not be obstacles if the candidate was otherwise eligible. Good health and a cheerful disposition were essential. She wanted nothing to do with melancholy women, however holy they might seem to others. Melancholy seemed to her a moral or spiritual sickness, through which the devil could easily find access to a soul and then poison the atmosphere of a whole convent.

Intelligence she prized so highly that she preferred it even to piety. Father Ribera's testimony is conclusive: "She was singularly fond of intelligent people. Next to their having a vocation, what she cared for most in those she received as novices, even if only as lay sisters, was a good understanding. People who knew her holiness and love of prayer were careful to praise the fervor and prayerfulness of the candidates they brought her, thinking this would make her accept them. But she seemed to care to know only whether they were sensible and apt. I myself was among their number, and being greatly surprised, I asked her the reason. She answered, 'Father, our Lord will give her devotion when she enters, and we will teach her prayer. As for those who have practised prayer outside, we very often have to teach them to forget all they have learned — but as for intelligence, we cannot give it to them. Besides, a devout good nun, if she has no brains, is of use only to herself. But I can put a sensible nun at the head of the house and trust her with any of the offices."[10]

What Teresa meant by "intelligence" is indicated by some advice she wrote for her nuns, not long after the founding of San José:

"I certainly believe that the Lord greatly favors anyone who is well disposed, and for this reason it must be noticed what intention she has who enters, that it may not be merely to find a living for herself, as happens to many, although to be sure the Lord can perfect this intention if she is a person of good understanding, and if not, by no means must she be accepted; for neither will she understand how she enters, nor will those who will try afterwards to mend her ways. For, for the most part, anyone who has this fault, it always seems to them[11] they know

---

[10] Ribera, op. cit., lib. IV, cap. XXIV.
[11] Saint Teresa's pleonasm and faulty reference.

what is good for them better than the wisest; and it is an evil that I consider incurable, and very seldom does it fail to carry along some malice with it. It may be allowed where there are many nuns, but among so few it cannot be tolerated.

"A good understanding, if it begins to incline itself to the good, seizes upon it firmly, for it sees that it is the most fitting; and when it does not advance very much spiritually, it will be useful for good advice and for plenty of things, without wearying anybody. When this is lacking, I don't know what good she is in the community, and she can do plenty of harm. This fault is not seen very quickly, for many speak well and understand badly, and others speak curtly and not very exactly, and have understanding for a great deal of good; and there are some holy simplicities which know little for the business and the style of the world, and much for talking with God. For this reason one must have great information to accept them, and long probation before having them profess. Once the world understands that you have the right to throw them out, and that there are many occasions for doing so in a monastery where there are austerities, and what the custom is, they will not take offense at it."[12]

It was just as well, perhaps, that Teresa found only four who measured up to her requirements. Secrecy was so important that she kept even Doña Guiomar out of the house these days, for she was well known in the neighborhood and might arouse suspicion. Meanwhile, as the great day approached, the workmen were discouragingly slow in making the interior alterations, while Juan de Ovalle remained so ill that there was no telling when he could be moved. Yet the house could not be dedicated until it was empty! Teresa lived in continual fear of having to return to the Incarnation before the foundation was made. "I saw to it that everything went off briskly," she wrote, "for many reasons, and one was that every hour I was afraid they would order me to leave."[13]

As the Eve of Saint Bartholomew drew near, a rumor of what was going on got abroad. Fortunately it seemed so far-fetched, considering the size of the house, that people refused to believe it. So the carpenters finished their work, the habits were done, everything was ready except the removal of poor Juan de Ovalle. Almost on the vigil of the feast his fever left him and health and

---

[12] *Camino de perfección*, Valladolid autograph, ch. XIV, B.M.C., t. III, pp. 67–68.
[13] *Vida*, cap. XXXVI.

strength returned so suddenly that Teresa believed his malady had been of supernatural origin. "It was a thing to wonder at that he was ill no longer than was necessary for the business, and when there was need for him to have health again so that I could be disengaged and he leave the house unoccupied, the Lord then gave it to him, and he himself was astonished."

While Ovalle went to fetch his wife and children that they might attend the ceremony, the other friends of the founders were quietly notified that the decisive hour was at hand. Teresa, who had probably had little or no sleep for several days, spent the whole night of August twenty-third fussing about the little chapel, rearranging the altar for the Divine Guest who would soon be enthroned there, thinking of everything, fearing and hoping by turns, seeing to every detail herself like a good captain. Not the least of her final preparations had been the procuring of that indispensable adjunct of conventual life, a bell. Whether she bought one out of the few *blancas*[14] that passed through her hands, or whether some good soul gave it to her, does not appear; but there it was, hanging on the wall near the door, prepared to startle the early morning echoes of sleeping Ávila when its mistress should give the word. Like the house itself and everything in it, it was small and humble, but ready to do what it was made for, valiantly. Hardly three pounds in weight, it had been badly cast, and had come from the foundry with a hole in it which had never been repaired. No matter, it was all the cheaper, and did not Teresa's heart have a hole in it too? Many larger and noisier bells assuredly there were in Spain — great majestic bells that flung their vibrations from hill to hill, old bronze bells, iron bells and silver bells of which the people of various churches and villages were so proud that they sometimes quarreled over their merits, yet this one seemed peculiarly symbolical of the community it was to ring to prayer, to work, and to recreation. Its tone was as high, clear, chaste, and restrained as the love that would be consecrated there to God.[15]

---

[14] A *blanca* was worth but a very small fraction of an American cent of today.

[15] Silverio, *op. cit.*, II, pp. 140–141. Later a Carmelite general had this bell sent to the convent at Pastrana, and there set up in the rooms where the chapters general of the order were held, explaining in a poem that its voice would cause to tremble any religious who had lost his fervor for the primitive rule. When the nuns at Pastrana had to flee in 1835, the townspeople hid all their effects, including the bell, which was finally restored and returned to San José de Ávila.

It was still dark on the morning of August 24 when the little army of the Reform assembled, and began to advance in twos and threes across the dewy fields or through the cool narrow streets. Besides the four young women who were to be received, there were the Maestro Daza, the Holy Cavalier, Juan de Ovalle and his wife and children, Father Julián de Ávila, Father Gonzalo de Aranda, the lovely Isabel de Ortega, and Doña Guiomar de Ulloa and her daughter; besides two nuns from the Incarnation (cousins of Teresa), Doña Ines and Doña Ana de Tapia.

As the dawn came fresh and rosy over the Castilian hills, early risers at the northern fringe of Ávila and in the suburb of Saint Roch must have been rather startled to hear an unaccustomed tinkling from the doorway of the diminutive house where such mysterious activity had lately been reported. Presently all the notable bells of the many churches and convents of the city began to announce, in their various tones, the advent of the new day. But none of them, not even the grandiose chimes of San Gil, Santa Ana and Las Gordillas, conveyed any such emotion as those within the house felt on first hearing the humble voice of the bell of San José.

The ceremony followed quickly lest somone interrupt it at the last moment. Madre Teresa presented her four orphans to Maestro Daza, who in the name of the Bishop gave them their habits, following the old and moving ritual of her own reception twenty-seven years before, and then, putting on the sacred vestments, began saying Mass. Now at last the Blessed Sacrament was enthroned and would remain enthroned for centuries in that humble abode; and the primitive order of the Barefoot or Reformed Carmelites was revived and perpetuated as the four novices in their new robes were formally encloistered and given their names in religion. Antonia de Henao became Antonia del Espíritu Santo; María de le Paz, María de la Cruz; Ursula de Revilla, Ursula de los Santos; María de Ávila, María de San José. By seven o'clock all was finished and the guests were departing.

Madre Teresa and her four daughters were alone at last in the blessed solitude they had desired. All the buffets and pains of so many months and years had been canceled, the prayers of so many days and nights were answered and fulfilled. "In the world you shall have distress; but have confidence, I have overcome the world."[16] It was a glorious moment for Teresa as she fell on her knees before the altar, and became lost in prayer so utterly that three or four hours passed before she returned to her senses.

---

[16] John 16:33.

Chapter XVI

PERSECUTION AND VICTORY

IT WAS nearly noon when Teresa descended from that higher reality, in which she saw and felt things not given to man to utter, to the humdrum world of toil and conflict. "Oh, God help me, what a miserable life this is! There is no lasting joy here, no thing unchanging. Such a little while ago and I did not think I would exchange my joy with anyone on earth, and now the very cause of it tormented me so that I did not know what to do with myself."[1]

There stood beside her now the dark spirit of negation who had tempted Christ in the desert, suggesting that everything she had done was in vain, and worse than vain. Had she not been disobedient in founding a monastery without a command from the Father Provincial of her own order? How could even four nuns be supported in that place? Would they not be hungry? Would they not grow discontented with the austerities she had planned for them? Whatever had put such a foolish idea into her mind when she already belonged to a perfectly good monastery? She, a frail and sick woman, leaving a large and delightful community where she had so many friends, to live penned up in this little place, doing terrible penance! How would she be able to stand it? And these four nuns — perhaps she would begin to dislike them after she had lived with them awhile. Perhaps she had undertaken too much and would have to give it up. Perhaps she would fall victim to despair, and then she would lose peace and quiet and even the power to pray. Perhaps she had been deluded from the beginning by the devil.

All the visions and consolations she had received from Christ began to recede from her mind. "All that the Lord had commanded me, and the many opinions I had got and the prayers I had said almost unceasingly for more than two years, all vanished from my memory as if they had never been. All I remembered was my own opinion, and all virtues and even faith were then suspended in me, leaving me without strength to practise any of them or to defend myself from such blows."[2]

---

[1] *Vida,* cap. XXXVI, B.M.C., p. 307.

[2] *Ibid.* "Y todas las virtudes y la fe estaban en mí entonces suspendidas, sin tener yo fuerza que ninguna obrase," etc.

Teresa is describing here what she felt rather than the actual state of affairs, for she adds immediately that she went to the Blessed Sacrament to throw herself on her knees with an anguish "like that of one who is in the agony of death." It was one of the most severe attacks she had ever endured. "But the Lord did not let His poor servant suffer long; for never has He failed to rescue me in my tribulations, and so it was in this, for He gave me a little light to see it was the devil and to let me understand the truth, and that everything was to try to frighten me with lies; and so I began to remember my great resolves to serve the Lord and my desires to suffer for Him. And I thought that if I was to accomplish them, I was not to go about looking for rest, and if I had trials there would be merit with them, and if displeasure it would serve me for purgatory since I accepted it in God's service. And what was I afraid of, for I had desired trials and these were good ones, and the greater the contradiction the more the gain; and why must I lose courage to serve One to Whom I owed so much? With these and other considerations, doing great violence to myself, I promised before the Blessed Sacrament to do all I could to obtain permission to come to this house, and if I could do it with a good conscience to promise enclosure. As I did this, the devil fled in an instant, and left me quieted and happy, and I remained so and have always been so. . . ."[3]

She was tranquil again but exhausted, "for I had hardly rested all night, nor for several others had I been free from labor and care, and all the days had been very wearisome. . . ." A profound drowsiness came over her, and she retired to her cell to get some sleep.

At this moment she became aware of unusual noises in the city, some sort of hubbub and commotion, shouting and noisy footfalls. It was not long before she learned the cause from a messenger who came hotfoot from the Convent of the Incarnation. The townspeople had heard what she had done and were virtually in a state of riot. They were saying that they would be ruined and disgraced if such things were allowed to happen, and they demanded the instant suppression of San José. The mother superior of the Incarnation wished to see Doña Teresa immediately.

La Madre dragged her aching body from its hard resting place

---

[3] *Ibid.*

and prepared to obey. Before leaving she went to the Blessed Sacrament to ask our Lord and Saint Joseph to help her meet the ordeal that no doubt awaited her, and to bring her back safely if possible to this convent; and she commended to them and to our Lady her four nuns who would now be motherless. Appointing the oldest, Ursula de los Santos, superior in her absence, she departed with Father Julian of Ávila, saying inwardly, "Lord, this house is not mine, it has been made for You. Since now there is nobody to attend it, let Your Majesty do it."

At the Incarnation she found the Reverend Mother, Doña María Cimbrón, waiting in a state of suppressed but mounting indignation as new and more alarming reports continued to come from the city. The Avileses could hardly have been more aroused if a foreign enemy had been discovered within their massive walls. To think that a nun would obtain her liberty on some flimsy pretext, and then use it to set up a ridiculous monastery which was nothing less than a rebuke and an insult to the Incarnation and all its inmates, to say nothing of the townspeople who would have to support her and those who had been foolish enough to follow her! This disobedient, disloyal, conceited, and presumptuous woman had brought disgrace upon the convent and all its members and the whole Carmelite Order. Such things passed from mouth to mouth, and were repeated by relatives outside to nuns inside, and by the nuns to the Superior.

Mother Cimbrón spared Teresa the ordeal of a questioning before the whole community, and scolded her in private. After she had recounted all that had been said, she demanded an explanation. Teresa told her story calmly and humbly. Mother Cimbrón was "somewhat placated," but decided, after some hesitation, to send for the Father Provincial, Fray Angel de Salazar. Meanwhile, instead of committing the culprit to the *cárcel* or prison of the monastery, as some of her sisters demanded, she made her sit down and eat a good supper,[4] perhaps the first food she had tasted that eventful day.

When Fray Angel de Salazar arrived, he summoned Teresa to give an account of her actions before the entire community of 180 nuns. He was very indignant, for he felt that she had gone over his head in placing San José under the jurisdiction of

---

[4] Sister María Bautista, in the *Informaciones* of Valladolid, 1595, B.M.C., t. 18, p. 384. In 1562 she was a boarding student at the Incarnation.

the Bishop of Ávila, and that he had been deceived. What he said may be inferred from Teresa's chronicle:

"I went to trial well pleased enough to see that I suffered something for the Lord, for I didn't find that I had done anything wrong in this matter against His Majesty or the Order; rather I had tried to strengthen it with all my powers, and I would gladly die for it, for my whole desire was that it carry on with all perfection. I called to mind the judgment passed on Christ, and saw what a trifle was this one. I told my fault as one very guilty, and so it seemed to anyone who did not know all the causes. After he had given me a great reprehension, though not with as much rigor as the crime and what many had told the Provincial deserved, I did not try to excuse myself, for I was resigned to it, rather I asked him to forgive me and punish me, and not to be disgusted with me.

"In some things I saw well that they condemned me without cause, for they told me I had done it so that I should be thought well of, and be famous, and other similar things; but in others I understood plainly that they were speaking the truth — for instance, that I was more wicked than others, and that when I had not kept the great devotion practised in that house, how did I expect to keep it in another with more rigor; that I scandalized the people, and was setting up new things. All this gave me no confusion or pain at all, although I gave the impression of having it lest I appear to set small store on what they were saying to me. Finally he commanded me before the nuns to give an account of myself, and I had to do it.

"As I had peace within me and the Lord aided me, I gave my account in such a way that neither the Provincial nor those who were there found anything to condemn me for, and afterwards, in private, I spoke to him more clearly, and he remained quite satisfied, and promised me that if it went well, and the city became quiet — for the uproar of the whole city was as great as I shall now tell — he would give me permission to go there."[5]

The city was not to be mollified so easily. Ávila was not only intensely Catholic but levitical, and nearly every family of importance had one or more members in some one of the many religious communities. It was precisely because the people loved religion, and not because they hated it, that they persecuted

---

[5] *Vida*, cap. XXXVI, B.M.C., p. 310.

Teresa. It was not merely that the new convent would have to be supported by their contributions, but rather that there seemed to be plenty of religious institutions already, under nearly all the great orders; and to the many nuns, and their relatives in nearly every home in the city, the opening of a new monastery appeared not only unnecessary but insulting. The secrecy with which the thing had been done was made to appear highly suspicious in a community still shocked by the revelations concerning Magdalena of the Cross and other *Illuminati*, and the burning of Lutheran priests and nuns after the two famous *autos* of 1559. It was not the mob of the city, but the most learned and respectable persons — those who understood how a single German monk, commencing with a protest against the abuse of indulgences, could be led by pride to attack a fundamental Christian dogma and so to make a fatal breach in the walls of the City of God — it was her own class, in short, who led the attack.

On the morning of August 25, the day after the foundation, the *Corregidor* of Ávila, the *muy magnífico Señor* García Suárez Carvajal, summoned certain of the *regidores,* together with the Procurador General Quiñones, the Mayordomo Flores and the Notary Public Pedro de Villaquirán, to discuss the enormity which all the town was denouncing. They decided that "since it has now just come to our notice that certain women who say that they are Carmelite nuns have taken a house that is subject to a quitrent to this city, and have placed altars and said Mass in it; and being, as there are, many monasteries of friars and nuns, and poor people who suffer need, Resolved, that to remedy the matter and to provide for it, the gentlemen *regidores* who are in this city be called and assembled, to make provision for it, tomorrow, Wednesday, at nine o'clock in the morning, and that the learned men of this city be summoned."

The *Corregidor* went to the new monastery of San José, and knocking majestically on the door demanded entrance in the name of the Republic, while a crowd of other officials and townspeople looked on to see what would happen.

One of the four terrified women inside, probably Sister Ursula, spoke through the door, asking what they wanted. The *Corregidor* replied that the people did not desire another convent in the city, and that they must leave at once and return to their homes.

"We will leave only by command of the one who put us here," said the nun.

"Open the doors or I will break them down!"[6]

The valiant women barricaded themselves in as best they could with pieces of board left over from the recent repairs, and made ready to resist to the last. The *Corregidor* was furious. Undoubtedly he would have forced his way in if he had not happened to see the Blessed Sacrament on the altar near the front entrance. Being a good Catholic, he then desisted and went away, not, however, without a few parting threats.

The *regidores* and *letrados* met on Wednesday morning, appointed Alonso Yera and Perálvarez Serrano to wait upon the Bishop and give him an account of how the city felt about the outrage that had come to light, and resolved if necessary to appeal to Philip II and the Royal Council of Castile. At a third meeting, held on Saturday the twenty-ninth, plans were made for mobilizing all the leaders of public opinion in the city in a *junta magna* to be held in the Council hall the following day. The Bishop also was invited.

It was a solemn and imposing assemblage that came together after Mass that Sunday — indeed, the city could have produced no greater demonstration if menaced by flood, pestilence, or invasion, instead of by five poor women who wanted only to pray and to eat as little as possible. All the ancient nobility, the learning and the religion of Ávila were represented in the colorful throng. There were city officials in brilliant costumes braided with gold. There was the Licentiate Brizuela, acting as provisor for the Bishop. The chapter of the Cathedral was represented by the Canons Pérez and Soria and the Archdeacon Sedano. The Dominican Convent of Saint Thomas sent several delegates, including the prior, Father Pedro Serrano, and the young theologian, Father Domingo Báñez. For the Franciscans there were the Guardian Father, Martín de Aguirre, and Father Hernando de Valderrábano; for the Premonstratensians, the Abbot Father, Francisco Blanco, and a preacher; for the Benedictines, the Abbot, Don Pedro de Antoyano, and one of the monks; for the Jesuit College of San Gil, Father Baltasar Alvarez and Father Jerónimo Ripalda. There were also Maestro Daza and other learned priests and several lay gentlemen from the best families of Ávila.

---

[6] P. Silverio, *Vida de Santa Teresa de Jesús*, II, p. 177.

When all were seated and quiet, the *Corregidor* opened the meeting with a declamation which suggests that he had not read his Cicero in vain:

"We are gathered here, Illustrious Gentlemen and Very Reverend Fathers, for a thing which could easily be decided without the opinion of so many grave men; but the confidence I have from all has made me avail myself of this means so that my actions, approved by persons of such great estimation, may not appear rash or imprudent, and may have greater weight in proportion as those present receive them well.

"Notorious to all is the innovation which dawned upon this city the other day in the form of a Convent of Barefoot Carmelites. And the mere fact of such an innovation is enough to make clear how dangerous and detestable it is. The confusion it causes in a republic, the minds which it disturbs, the tongues which it sets to wagging, the murmurings it foments, the disorders it engenders (for it allows neither order nor quiet in the republic, nor permits good customs and statutes to endure) — of all this, who is ignorant? And this being true of innovations in general, the present one is all the more dangerous since it wears the mask and mantle of greater piety. Allowing convents and religious orders to multiply does not always augment the common welfare and advantage; in this city it is not only convenient but a matter of urgent necessity to prevent new foundations. For although it is among the noblest of Spain, it is not among the richest, and it is as well provided with gentlemen and ladies in all the convents as could prudently be desired. And so it is not just that the devotion of certain women burden the city with what it is unable to bear. Even if the new monastery began with a dowry of income well invested, some of the objections set forth would still obtain, for in the end what is given to a Convent is taken away from the rest of the city, it is alienated forever, it is transferred from the common use and heritage of the citizens. What then will this Convent be, when it is founded without income, without dowry, and with the presumption that it will never have any? This, gentlemen, is to cast upon us a compulsory *alcabala*,[1] to take money out of our purses and food out of our mouths. What heart could endure to see some poor servants of God perishing of hunger? Would we not be com-

---

[1] An excise tax, often very unpopular in Spain. In using this word, the chairman was making a skillful appeal to public sentiment.

pelled to take from our children, to share with them? Furthermore, if the city is the head of all the citizens, and the Convents are its members, how is a foundation made without its authority? What government would endure such activities? If others which are less are not permitted, why this one which is so great?

"And how do we know, gentlemen, that this foundation is not some fraud, or deceit of the devil? They say that this Religious has revelations, and a spirit very peculiar. This very fact makes me fear, and ought to make the most discreet reflect, since in these times we have seen deceits and illusions among women, and in all women it has been dangerous to applaud the innovations to which they are inclined. I do not impute fraud to this Religious, for this is no concern of mine; but I would inspire prudent minds with caution not to admit innovations, not to multiply convents, not to allow them to be established without the permission and knowledge of the city, and that its right be acknowledged to inquire through grave persons whether it is a question of the Lord's service or not. This is my opinion, and I hope it will be approved by all the learning and experience as are here assembled."[8]

When the *Corregidor* had finished, the Licentiate Brizuela, as Provisor for the Bishop, arose to inform the assembly that the foundation had been made with the consent of His Lordship. He then read the brief of Pope Pius IV under which the consent had been given. This duty fulfilled, he discreetly took his leave.

The *Corregidor* stood his ground and asked for other opinions. "Nearly all approved his reasons wholesale, without examining them," continues the *Crónica Carmelitana*. "Others, either doubtful or of contrary mind, kept silent, not daring to defend the truth publicly; a very common weakness in communities where self-interest is ordinarily put before the public good by those who are most bound to defend it, and who receive from it authority to do so."

As one speech followed another, the general indignation against the five Carmelites mounted in a crescendo which at last grew so violent that Teresa was surprised, when she heard of it, that they did not all go then and there to demolish her house. Besides the general accusation that she had injured the

---

[8] *Crónica Carmelitana*, lib. I, cap. XIV, quoted by Padre Felipe Martin, O.P., in his *Santa Teresa de Jesús y la Orden de Predicadores* (Ávila, 1909).

six other convents of Ávila, and through them the whole community and especially the poor, it was alleged that her foundation in poverty violated the spirit of the Pope's brief, which had permitted an endowment; and that the brief had not been presented to His Majesty and the Royal Council for their approval. Practical men observed, too, that the house was subject to a quitrent which the city would now lose. Others pleaded that material damage had been done to the whole community by some little hermitages she had begun to have erected in realization of her childhood ambition, and that one of these retreats would shut off the sunlight from a small arched structure under which were gathered the waters of several springs for public use; therefore the water would freeze in winter and be of no use. Lázaro Dávila, a stonecutter who held the office of Inspector of Wells, had already lodged a complaint on this score against Juan de Ovalle on August 22, two days before the foundation. Altogether the meeting seemed to be, as Julian of Ávila recorded, "the most solemn . . . that could possibly be held in the world, even if the loss or safety of all Spain were at stake. . . . All arrived at the opinion that it was good to have the monastery disestablished, for it was a heavy burden for the city to maintain thirteen nuns, for it was not then claimed there would be more; and they did not notice that these thirteen would go in to serve God, and that in the city many hundreds of men and women were being supported who served the devil with their wicked life; and no order to get out was ever given to all those who were maintained without working, giving bad example to the others — yet they thought the city would be destroyed if they supported thirteen barefoot nuns!"[9] And Teresa remarked, "I was astonished at what the devil could do against a few little women, and how all thought it was a great hurt to the place to have twelve women and a prioress . . . and all living so strict a life."[10] Later she said, laughing, to Father Ribera, "I founded the monastery on the day of Saint Bartholomew, so he would defend me from the demon, and as soon as I did, all his little devils came jumping against me."[11]

There was only one man who dared to raise his voice in that Junta against the hysterical indignation of the community. It

[9] *Vida de Santa Teresa de Jesús,* pt. II, cap. VII.
[10] *Vida, loc. cit.*
[11] Ribera, *Vida de Santa Teresa,* II, lib. V.

seems strange that there were not more, considering that two Jesuits who knew Teresa well and had finally approved her spirit were present. Father Ripalda, S.J., testifying thirty-three years later for her beatification, declared that he had been there and had had a revelation to the effect that her foundation was inspired by God, and that the Jesuits alone defended her against all the other orders and the city officials.[12] But according to Father Baltasar Alvarez, the Jesuits felt obliged to remain silent at the meeting lest they jeopardize their own work, which was comparatively new in Ávila.[13] We have her own word for it, moreover, that her sole defender was a Dominican; and it is now well established that he was Fray Domingo Báñez, *presentado* or teacher of theology at the monastery of Saint Thomas.[14]

Father Báñez, destined to be one of the most famous theologians of his century and to carry on a celebrated controversy with the Jesuit Fathers, Molina and Suárez, on the freedom of the will — a controversy still undecided — was at this time thirty-four years old. Born February 28 at Medina del Campo, of Cantabrian ancestry, he had entered the Order of Saint Dominic at a very early age, and had been professed when he was nineteen, at Saint Stephen's monastery, Salamanca. In 1561, he had been sent to Ávila to teach theology. He was already known in his own order as an acute and profound thinker, humble, discreet, and amiable, much given to prayer and mortification. When he went with other Dominicans to the famous *Junta*, he had not yet met Teresa, but judging her cause on its merits he had the courage to stand alone and defend it, when all the other members of his own order remained discreetly silent. The *Crónica Carmelitana* quotes him verbatim:

"It may seem rash to oppose myself to so many and such grave persons, and to reasoning so well thought out. But if my own conscience gives assurance and puts me under obligation more

---

[12] P. Silverio quotes his exact words, *Vida de Santa Teresa de Jesús*, II, p. 195, and suggests that old age may have blunted his memory when he made this statement.

[13] P. Valdivia, *Historia de San Gil*, in Silverio, II, p. 194.

[14] "*Solo un Presentado de la Orden de Santo Domingo, aunque era contrario, no de el monasterio, sino de que fuese pobre, dijo que no era cosa que ansí se había de deshacer, que se mirase bien, que tiempo había para ello, que este era caso de el Obispo, u cosas de este arte, que hizo mucho provecho.*" — *Vida*, cap. XXXVI, B.M.C., pp. 311–312. Father Báñez wrote on the margin of her original manuscript, "This was the year 1562, at the end of August. I was present and gave this opinion." (Signed) Fr. Domingo Báñez.

than those of others in free discussions such as this, I cannot fail to declare what it dictates to me in favor of the new monastery of Discalced Carmelites. Free at least from passion shall be my testimony, for until this hour I have never spoken with nor met the Foundress, nor discussed her foundation in any way. The thing is new, I admit, and as such has produced the effects that innovation usually does among the multitude. But this is no reason why it should produce them in grave and prudent councils, for not every innovation is reprehensible. Were the other religious orders founded in any other way? Did not the reforms which we see every day, and which our ancestors saw, come to light when they were least thought of? Was not the Christian Church itself reformed anew by Christ? Surely nothing in it, however excellent it may be, could be improved if we all surrendered to the cowardly fear of innovation. What is introduced for the greater glory of God and the reformation of customs ought not be called innovation or invention, but the renovation of virtue, which is always old. And if the trees are not new when they are seen in the spring, nor the sun when it rises each day, why will it be a blameworthy innovation in religious orders to renew themselves? Which is more reprehensible in them: to lose their ancient splendor or to recover it? If the first does not frighten us, why should the second scandalize us? That, gentlemen, is reprehensible innovation which opposes itself to virtue and the greater service of God. The Convent of Carmelites, recently founded, is a restoration of what has been lost, to the great improvement of that holy Order, and the edification of the Christian people. And so on that score this convent ought rather to be favored, and especially by the heads of Christian republics, to whom it belongs to encourage such praiseworthy deeds. May many imitate her! Oh, how much praise would Ávila deserve, and all our kingdoms and the whole Church, if we followed after this heroic virgin! I do not approve of the rash multiplication of religious orders. But it is not easy to determine when this is the case. For if vain and vicious men are not considered rash, however much they multiply themselves, why must those who follow the law of virtue be held and persecuted as such? The cities are full of lost people; these streets swarm with vagrant, insolent, and lazy men, with boys and girls given over to vice; and none of this is considered rash, nor is there anyone who takes the trouble to remedy it — and only four little nuns stowed in a corner, in a hole, commending themselves to God, are held to be a grave injury and intolerable burden to the Republic? And this disturbs and troubles the city, and there are assemblies to look into it? What is this, gentlemen; why do we gather here? What army of enemies breaks down these walls? What fire burns the city? What pestilence consumes it? What hunger afflicts it? What ruin threatens it? Are only four little barefoot nuns, poor, quiet, and virtuous, the cause of so much commotion in Avila? Allow me to say that the prestige of a city so important seems less when it holds so solemn a meeting and convocation for so light a reason.

"I confess that I do not think this foundation should be made without income; not so much on account of the burden thus resulting to the city, for it is very light, as on account of the inconvenience to the religious themselves, who, enclosed and without secure provision, are likely to suffer need. I cannot deny that it pertains to the providence of cities to prevent the mischiefs which can ensue, but that has to do with secular affairs. As for those which by right are ecclesiastic, it is the province of the Bishop to look into them; and if convents are founded by his command, it is for him to arrange them. This new one was established with the knowledge and advice of the Bishop, and what is more, by an especial Brief of the Apostolic See. And so it is wholly outside the secular jurisdiction. And finally, gentlemen and fathers of ours, I cannot in any way agree that the monastery be disestablished by order of the city; but that if there be anything against it, and if it be fitting to undo it, the Lord Bishop, to whom it belonged to establish it, should be informed and consulted."[15]

These bold wise words were bound to have an effect in a gathering of loyal, if excited, Catholics; in fact, they carried the day for reason against almost unanimous prejudice. The *Junta*

---

[15] Martín, *op. cit.*, pp. 275–277. Whether or not these were the exact words of Padre Báñez, they certainly express the sense of his discourse, according to a summary of it which he himself made for the process of the Saint's beatification in 1595: "and then this witness was on her side, without having previously known or seen her, but only through seeing that she had not erred either in her intention or in her means of founding that monastery, since she had done it by order of the Apostolic See; and so this witness said in a public Consistory of Avila, where all the religious orders were opposing her. But then in the same Consistory all came to agree with the opinion of this witness: that they speak to the Bishop, and discuss with him the reasons there were why the monastery should not continue, and so it was done." — B.M.C., t. XVIII, pp. 7–8.

voted to table a proposal that the Blessed Sacrament at San José be consumed and the place closed, and to consult the Bishop before taking further steps.

The Bishop stood by Madre Teresa. Maestro Daza, representing him at a second great meeting, informed the city that the convent had been established by episcopal authority in accordance with the Pope's permission, and that he himself had presided at the opening ceremonies, and had said the first Mass. This did not satisfy the leaders of the opposition, and the City Council sent Alonso de Robledo to Madrid with a salary of one ducat per day to complain to the Royal Council. He left September 12 and was back in Ávila ten days later; whereat the *Consistorio* met at once, and decided to carry on the fight. To this end they sent Diego de Villena to Madrid, where he remained fifty days, presumably looking up the law and arguing for the disestablishment of the convent.

Litigation has always been expensive as well as annoying. Yet Madre Teresa was not wholly friendless. If misfortune had revealed a whole city full of enemies, it had also discovered who her real friends were; and among them were disclosed, in addition to the young Dominican theologian and Maestro Daza, such faithful adherents as Father Julian of Ávila, Father Gonzalo de Aranda, the Holy Cavalier Don Francisco Salcedo, and Doña Guiomar de Ulloa. It is likely that these last two raised a small sum of money out of their shrunken fortunes to defray the necessary expenses of the convent's defense. Father Julian, gentle, loyal, and studious soul, appointed himself *procurador,* and day after day tramped between the Council chamber and the Incarnation, consulting the city fathers and La Madre, and doing all in his power to bring about an agreement whereby the monastery might remain. His companion on many of these trips was the Holy Cavalier, who was too bashful, however, to enter the crowded halls of justice, and usually hid himself near by until Father Julian emerged.[16] Nevertheless Don Francisco helped in his own quiet way, for he was universally respected, and many changed their opinion of Madre Teresa on learning that he was on her side. Father Gonzalo de Aranda went to Madrid to defend her before the Royal Council.

Teresa kept well informed at the Incarnation of everything

---

[16] Julian of Ávila, *op. cit.,* pt. II, cap. VII.

that went on, even though her Prioress showed some displeasure at the frequent visits of her friends. On September 7 she heard that the City Council was willing to allow the convent to remain if she, as a compromise, would have it endowed. Some of her friends considered this a sensible way out of the difficulty and urged her to accept. Some even offered to contribute to the fund.

It was an excruciating temptation. Weary from months of anxiety and trouble, sorry for her friends who had endured so much for her and apparently to no purpose, she began to wonder whether so many good persons could be wrong and she alone right. Humility suggested that perhaps she was being misled by pride, and although she could not forget what the Lord had said during the riots before the great *Junta*, "Dost thou not know that I am powerful? What art thou afraid of?" worldly prudence demanded whether He would be well served if she let His monastery die for lack of revenue.

The Holy Cavalier, who took the "practical" view, wrote an appeal on her behalf to Fray Pedro de Alcántara, and Maestro Daza delivered it at Areñas, where the Saint had gone to die. Presently a reply arrived at the Incarnation, addressed to "The Most Magnificent and Very Religious Lady, Doña Teresa de Ahumada, in Ávila, Whom May Our Lord Make Holy." Ribera saw this epistle and noted that it was written on a piece of paper less than four fingers wide. Unfortunately he did not reproduce the text of what was probably the last letter of San Pedro. Teresa's brief summary of it quotes him as saying that he had heard of her troubles with the foundation, and rejoiced at them, for they were a sign "that the Lord would be much served in that monastery, since the devil tried so hard to have it destroyed, and that I should in no wise agree to have an income." Yet when he died a few weeks later, she was still putting off her final decision.[17] Her friends were arguing that it might be fatal to continue in poverty; and when the Holy Cavalier suggested that if she commenced with an endowment she could easily give it up later and return to her original plan, Teresa agreed to accept the city's compromise and was prepared to sign a contract to that effect the next day.

That night she had one of her several visions of Saint Peter of Alcántara. About a year before his death — during the autumn

---
[17] *Vida*, cap. XXXVI.

of 1561 — she had seen him visibly, though they were many miles apart: and "I understood that he was going to die, and warned him of it."[18] When he died she saw him plainly. "His end was like his life, preaching and admonishing his friars. When he saw that he was now coming to his end, he said the psalm, *Laetatus sum in his quae dicta sunt mihi*, and falling on his knees, died. . . . He told me how he was going to rest. I did not believe it, and told it to several persons, and eight days later came the news how he was dead, or, to say it better, had commenced to live forever. . . . How much good God has now taken from us in the blessed Fray Pedro de Alcántara! The world can no longer endure such perfection. They say that nowadays people are weaker in health, and that these are not the times gone by. This holy man was of this time. He was as sturdy in spirit as in other times, and so he kept the world under his feet. For although people don't go uncovered or do such harsh penance as he, there are many ways, as I have often said, to trample on the world, and the Lord teaches them how when he sees they have courage for it."

Several times after his death Fray Pedro visited her. "It has pleased the Lord to let me see more of him than when he was alive, advising me in many things. I have often seen him in the greatest glory. The first time he appeared to me, he told me that it was a blessed penance that had earned so great a reward, and many other things. . . . Behold here this asperity of life brought to an end with such great glory! I think he consoles me much more than when he was here. Once the Lord told me that people would not ask anything in his name that He would not hear. As many things as I have committed to him to ask the Lord, I have seen them all granted. May He be blest forever."[19]

Once, when a fence was being built at San José, he told her not to have it plastered with cement, but to trust in poverty. "But it will fall down again!" she objected. "If it does," replied Fray Pedro, "there will be someone to put it up again."[20]

He wore a different aspect when he came to oppose her capitulation on the night of indecision, late in October or early in November, 1562, He was a glorified body, as before, "but this

---

[18] *Vida,* cap. XXVII.
[19] *Ibid.,* cap. XXVII.
[20] Ribera, *op. cit.,* lib. IV, cap. XIX.

time he was severe with me, and only told me that by no means must I accept an income, and why had I not been willing to follow his advice? and then he disappeared."[21]

The same night our Lord appeared to her and gave the same advice, adding that if she began with an endowment, she would not be allowed to give it up afterwards.

Her decision was now so firm that no argument could move her again. The next morning she told the Holy Cavalier to reject the contract and to go on with the lawsuit. This the good man did, regardless of his own convictions. When various other attempts at conciliation were made by well-meaning friends, Teresa steadfastly refused every offer of compromise, attributing one of them to "the worst effort of the devil" to undo her work.[22]

The suit dragged on, therefore, through the long winter. In mid-November, Father Gonzalo de Aranda induced the Royal Council at Madrid to appoint a *receptor* to investigate the matter. Pedro de Villaicén was duly appointed and went to Ávila, but was received with distrust by the *corregidores*, who deputed Juan Díaz, a notary public, to accompany him in all his investigations at a salary of six reals per day.

The turning point in the conflict seems to have been the arrival in town of Father Pedro Ibáñez,[23] who as prior of the Dominican monastery of Saint Thomas had tested and approved her spirit in 1560, and had written to Rome for the first bull of authorization. He was so universally loved and respected in Ávila that when it became known that he was on the side of San José, the opposition began to wither away. One objection after another was dropped as public wrath cooled, or was met by compromise. When the city Council, on January 11, 1563, ordered the destruction of the hermitage which cast its shadow on the public fountain, Teresa acquiesced, asking only for an alms with which to construct another, and with this she bought a pigeon house on some adjoining land, and had it made over for the purpose. The dispute over the quitrent was settled by

---

[21] *Vida,* cap. XXXVI.

[22] Mir, anti-Jesuit as usual, tries to pin this on Father Baltasar Alvarez. A more likely guess would point to Father Báñez, O.P., who, in spite of his defense of the convent, thought it should be endowed. (Mir, *Vida de Santa Teresa,* t. I, lib. II, cap. II; Silverio, *op. cit.,* II, p. 213.)

[23] Not Father Báñez, whose name Canon Dalton takes the liberty of inserting in Saint Teresa's *Vida,* cap. XXXVI, p. 337, of his translation.

transferring it to some other near-by houses which were bought by her friends and presented to the Council, April 22. By spring the last opposition had vanished.[24]

Teresa had spent the whole winter meanwhile at the Incarnation regretting her absence from her "orphans," but serenely waiting for the disposition she knew Christ would make of her in His own good time. The Provincial, Fray Angel de Salazar, could not bring himself to let her go to San José, even when the Bishop, Father Ibáñez and others of her friends begged him to do so. He would not even discuss the matter with her until the middle of Lent, 1563. Even then he still hesitated until she said, "Look, Father, we are resisting the Holy Ghost!" in such a way that he could no longer doubt she spoke under the direction of the Holy Spirit.[25] Thereupon he told her to go, with his blessing.

It seemed almost too good to be true. It was not merely that she wished to live in San José for her own happiness, it was rather that the nuns needed her. Ursula de los Santos, excellent woman though she was and trained by Maestro Daza himself, could not teach the primitive rule to the novices, nor could the two chaplains (Maestro Daza and Father Julian de Ávila) who went to hear confessions and to say Mass. The nuns did their best; they would meet in chapter to tell their faults, they helped one another with all charity, they made such mortifications as they could; yet they had to recite the Little Office of Our Lady in the choir, for there was no one to teach them the other.[26] Their small number was another handicap, but this the Provincial now removed by allowing four nuns to go from the Incarnation to San José with La Madre: Ana Dávila, a cousin of the Marquesa de Velada; Ana Gómez and her sister María Isabel; and Isabel de la Peña, daughter of Francisco de Cepeda.

The exact date when Teresa left the Incarnation to realize the dream of so many years is not known. It was in March, 1563; the air must still have been cold, and the ground not wholly clear, perhaps, of snow. She took with her, as her entire worldly wealth, a few articles borrowed from the Incarnation and later repaid: a cheap straw rug, a penitential shirt of chains, a disci-

---

[24] For further particulars about the lawsuit and other matters, see P. Silverio, op. cit., II, pp. 213–230.

[25] Fray Angel de Salazar, in the Informaciones de Valladolid, 1595.

[26] Ribera, op. cit., lib. II, cap. V.

pline or scourge, and an old much-mended habit. With these treasures under her arm, and accompanied by the four new recruits from the Incarnation, she made her way joyfully, according to Carmelite tradition, to the Basilica of Saint Vincent, to prostrate herself in a prayer of thanksgiving before the ancient image of Nuestra Señora de la Soterraña. Then she took off her shoes and went barefooted over the hard cold streets to San José, where the four original nuns were waiting breathlessly for that Teresa de Ahumada who was to be known henceforth as Teresa of Jesus.

Before she would enter the monastery, she opened the grille of the choir and prostrated herself before the Blessed Sacrament. Time and the world fell away, with all her earthly senses, and in the sweet eternity that flowed about her and through her and possessed her utterly, she saw the glorified Christ. He welcomed her with great love and joy, and as He laid a glittering crown upon her head, He thanked her for what she had done for His Mother.[27]

---

[27] *Vida,* cap. XXXVI. Father Silverio believes that Saint Teresa took off her shoes before going to San José, but doubts the tradition that she went barefoot. In her *Constitutions* she provided that her nuns should wear cheap sandals, *alpargatas,* made of hemp. He infers (II, 239) that she did likewise.

LIFE IN THE FIRST CONVENT OF THE REFORM

FROM March until late June or early July Teresa was only a simple nun under obedience to Sister Ana de San Juan, the prioress she had chosen to succeed Ursula de los Santos. For she was there only by the verbal consent of her Provincial, a man of great prudence, who did not give his written permission until August 22, and then only for a year. This uncertainty of tenure did not disturb her happiness in the slightest. Had she not accomplished her desire, that is to say the desire of His Majesty? She was one of the nine chosen women, living in blessed obedience, poverty, solitude, and detachment. It was the beginning of the most serene and untroubled four years of her life; her own word for them is *"descansados."* A few days after her arrival, when all the nine were sitting silent in the choir after Compline, she beheld the Mother of God in great glory holding a white Carmelite mantle over all of them, and "understood how high a degree of glory the Lord would give to those of this house."[1]

Everyone, from the Bishop and the Provincial down, realized that Teresa was the only person capable of teaching the others the primitive rule, but not until about the first of July did they insist on her disregarding humility and accepting the office of prioress. The ill-health of Sister Ana may have furnished the occasion. That excellent woman was sent back to the Incarnation, where the routine was less trying, and dying soon after, appeared to Teresa one morning after Holy Communion, free and glorious in heaven, "like a crystal."

It was not long before the number at San José had reached the limit of thirteen. One of the newcomers was her niece, Doña María de Ocampo, whose casual half-jesting remark had set in motion all the strange adventures now happily crowned with peace and security. Under the gay and flippant exterior of this worldly young woman, who loved cosmetics and dancing and sentimental tales of chivalry, there burned a profound and unselfish piety hidden from nearly all eyes except the shrewd ones of her

---

[1] *Vida,* cap. XXXVI.

aunt. There was great astonishment in Ávila when she entered the convent on the sixth of May, 1563,[2] taking the name of María Bautista, and few could foresee that she would become one of the great lights of the Reform, keeping, amid all the penance and mortification that such a life entailed, a light heart, a quick and witty tongue, and dancing eyes. Her thousand ducats had made the beginning of the work possible; the remainder of her small fortune had helped to purchase the near-by houses with which the quitrent was paid off to the city.[3]

An even more startling vocation, in the eyes of the grave citizens who were beginning to look upon the foundation with approval, and even to contribute alms (somewhat sparingly) to sustain the religious, was that of Doña María Dávila. She was the lovely daughter of another relative of La Madre, Alonso Alvarez Dávila, "a man very noble in lineage and even more so in virtues,"[4] whence he was called Alonso Alvarez *el santo*.

As his heiress, she had had many offers of marriage from rich young cavaliers, but had refused them, waiting perhaps for the Prince of her childish dreams. He did appear finally, but in very different guise from anything that she and her friends had imagined: as the lonely and forsaken Christ. At first she resisted His wooing, reluctant to give up the world, and there followed, in the summer of 1563, a long and bitter *wrestling with God* — "He determined that she should be a nun, and she that she would not," as Ribera has it.[5] In the end she surrendered, and there came upon her such peace and resolution that nothing thereafter, not even the opposition of parents who had no other child, could turn her from the path she had chosen. Madre Teresa accepted her, and it became known that she would enter the convent on the thirtieth of September.

When the day came, María arrayed herself in her most gaudy finery of silks and velvets and cloth of gold, and set out in state for San José, attended by all the splendid young *caballeros* of the city, and many of the older ones, too, for she was related to

---

[2] Ribera, who was her confessor, says she entered about a year and a half after the foundation, on a feast of Saint John by the Latin Gate. (*Vida de Santa Teresa*, lib. II, cap. V.) This would be May 6, 1564: but apparently it was 1563.

[3] *Ibid.*

[4] *Ibid.* María Dávila is not to be confused with María de Ávila, one of the first four nuns at San José. The latter became Sister María de San José, the former Sister María de San Jerónimo.

[5] *Loc. cit.*

nearly all the great families of Ávila. Dismounting at the convent, she bade them and the whole world a joyous farewell. Then entering the small door, she was escorted by La Madre and others to the chapel, where they took off her glittering silken raiment piece by piece, and arrayed her comely limbs with coarse sackcloth; and María Dávila became María de San Jerónimo, bride of the King of Poverty.[6]

There were no lay sisters in the monastery at that time, and the thirteen Carmelites took turns by weeks at the cooking, laundry, and other menial labors. Teresa refused to exempt herself. On the contrary, she brought to the most lowly tasks a desire for perfection, and gave such a memorable example that the nuns, long after, remembered that their food had been most tasty when she had the preparing of it, and that never had the clothes been so immaculate as when she was in the laundry. Nor was she deterred by ill-health, or by the frequency of unexpected raptures, or by her love for prayer. She used to say that God walked among the pots and pans as well as anywhere else. One day when she was standing at the stove with a frying pan in her hand, ready to cook some eggs for the community, Sister Isabel de Santo Domingo saw her become motionless, her face illuminated and beautiful. Fearing that she might fall, for in such states she became wholly unaware of all about her, the nun took her by the arm to steady her; whereupon she, too, became, as it were, electrified by the mysterious divine influence, and both remained inanimate, enraptured, like two statues, while the whole community stole in to gaze and to wonder. The little kitchen where this occurred is still a part of the rambling many tiered modern structure of the Convent of San José of Avila.

However well cooked the food might be when La Madre was in charge, it was none too plentiful. Although the good people of Avila had changed their attitude, they were human enough not to think of giving without being asked, and Teresa was resolved not to beg, but to depend wholly upon the goodness of God. And considering that the thirteen women desired a life of poverty, like that of Christ, their confidence was never disappointed. "His Majesty sent us there what was necessary without asking for it," she recorded simply, "and when this was lack-

---

[6] Ribera tells this story, *loc. cit.* He knew Sister María de San Jerónimo years later when she was prioress of San José.

ing, as it was seldom enough, their joy was all the greater. I used to praise our Lord to see such virtues achieved, especially the disregard they had for everything except to serve Him. I, who was there as superior, don't remember that I ever gave a thought to it; I took it for granted that the Lord was not going to fail those who had no other care but how to please Him. And if sometimes there was not enough sustenance for all, on my saying that it was for those who needed it most, each one thought it was not she, and so we waited till God sent enough for all."[7] Sometimes there would be only an egg or two for the whole convent; but no one complained, and even María de San Jerónimo, who had been the rich María Dávila, rejoiced in these exercises in poverty. Nor were any of them the worse for a meatless diet the year round, and an occasional total abstinence. Teresa found that her own health improved under these hard conditions. One lean day there came some food from the convent of Poor Clares, and she remembered with joy the vision in which Santa Clara had promised to help her.

Now and then the nuns earned a little money by sewing and spinning. Each one would spin, as a rule, five "bundles" of wool a day.[8] La Madre set the example in this, as in everything. When she was not at prayer she was always busy at something. Even if it was necessary to receive a visitor, she would keep occupied with her distaff while she talked, sitting unseen behind the curtain that covered the grille. She always wore an old patched and mended habit, preferably one that had been discarded by someone else, though she was most careful to keep it immaculate, and was noted for the cleanliness of her person and of every house over which she presided.

Her cell (preserved intact until 1722, and then made into an oratory) is still shown to visitors: a tiny room with a small hard bed, on which she slept with no covering except a piece of sackcloth, and no other furniture whatever, unless a little stone ledge jutting out from the wall near the window could be called a bench. There was no chair, there was no table for her few precious books. As for the window, neither this one nor any of the others in San José enjoyed the luxury of glass. Even in the coldest weather — and the temperature in Ávila is often far

---

[7] *Foundations*, cap. I.
[8] Silverio, *Vida de Santa Teresa de Jesús*, lib. III, p. 22, n. 1, and reference.

below zero in winter — they were covered only by pieces of canvas nailed over rude wooden frames. In this poor room Teresa wrote at least two of her masterpieces and a great deal of her voluminous correspondence. Here, too, she had the few hours of sleep she considered necessary. Later on when she was going to start on some journey before dawn, or returned late at night, she would sleep in a trough such as those used for kneading dough, and to avoid disturbing the other nuns would steal out or in by "Saint Ann's Stairway," so called from an image there of that saint holding the Blessed Virgin, who in turn carries the Child Jesus.

The primitive choir, with its very low roof, is still extant. How the thirteenth nun managed to squeeze into it is a mystery, for there was hardly room for twelve. The original chapel no longer exists. What is now called the primitive chapel was actually the second one; and even this is only twelve by eight paces. Poverty was not the only reason. Teresa always preferred small buildings, small chapels, small oratories. She had a distrust amounting almost to contempt for large, ornate buildings; perhaps because she noticed a tendency among the faithful to neglect doing some necessary Christian work on the pretext of the great expense involved, instead of beginning it humbly and inexpensively.

She reminded her daughters that Saint Clare had said, "Strong walls are those of poverty," and added, "True enough, if it is really preserved, it fortifies chastity and all the rest much better than with very sumptuous edifices. Watch out for this, for the love of God, and by His blood I ask it; and if I could say it with good conscience, I would wish that the day you make such [buildings] they will fall down again. It looks very bad, my daughters, to have great houses built with the labor of the poor; may God not permit it, but be poor in all things and little. Let us in something at least be like our King, who had no house except the stable of Bethlehem where he was born, and the cross where He died; those were houses where little recreation was to be had! Those who build them large know what they are about, they have other holy intentions; but thirteen poor little women — any corner will do for them. If there is need to have grounds, on account of the great enclosure and as an aid to prayer and devotion, with some hermitages to go aside to pray, very well; but edifices and a large and curious house, not at all; God deliver us. Always remember that everything will tumble down on the Day of Judgment; how do we know it won't be soon?"[9]

Teresa did enlarge her house, however, to meet the expanding necessities of the community, now having an ell built, now connecting the main building with a newly purchased house near by, now adding an upper story, until in time the whole came to be grouped about a central *patio*, behind which was built the present cloister, with a closed gallery above; and there was a recreation room, about ten paces long by half as wide, besides a refectory, a wardrobe room, garrets, and so on. What delighted her most was adorning various parts of the building with images of our Lord, His Mother, and the saints. Saint Joseph and our Lady, as we have noticed, were at the door to welcome visitors. A beautiful and rare crucifix given to the convent by the Bishop, Don Alvaro de Mendoza, has been venerated there to this day; the nuns called it *el Santo Cristo del Amor*.

Little by little, with the same loving care, she made the scrubby ground about the little houses into a garden where her daughters might find rest, recreation, and above all, the solitude for which they had left the world; and with this last end in mind, she gradually established hermitages at some distance one from another — usually a pigeon house or some such building which was bought and made over into an oratory. These in time came to be known by the names of the saints with whose pictures she adorned them. There was one for example of Saint Catherine the martyr, receiving a ring from our Lord. There was one of Saint Augustine, containing two pictures of him donated by the Augustinian nuns of Our Lady of Grace, and one of his mother Saint Monica. Still another was known as Our Lady of Nazareth, and was dedicated to the mystery of the Annunciation; there Teresa often went to pray, and there she kept her volume of *Los Morales* of Saint Gregory in Spanish, and some others of her favorite books. Of the hermitages she founded, four remain, including the most famous of all, called "Christ at the Column." It was for that little shelter that Teresa got an artist, Jerónimo Dávila, to paint the likeness of His Majesty as she had once seen

---

[9] *The Way of Perfection*, Valladolid autograph, cap. II. This is one of Teresa's delightful digressions. She ends it with, "I don't know what I started to say, for I have digressed. I believe the Lord must have desired it, for I never thought I would write what I have said here."

Him in His scourging. She would stand by the painter as he worked and tell him what to do; the limbs, the wounds, the hair, each line and feature of that sorrowful and bloody face as they were indelibly etched on her memory. It became the most celebrated of the hermitages; the townspeople frequently resorted to it, and miracles were said to have rewarded some of the prayers said there.

As time went on Teresa began covering the barrenness of the surrounding landscape with bloom and foliage. A hazelnut tree that she planted gave abundant fruit for many years; there was also a laurel tree, but this may have been there when she purchased the property. The great obstacle to growing anything in and about Ávila was the scarcity of water. The town, as we have seen, jealously guarded its limited supply for public use; and the only well on the premises of San José was a very deep one on a small field purchased after the foundation, and yielding but a niggardly trickle of vile-tasting liquid. It seems probable that water for the use of the convent had to be fetched laboriously from the public fountain near by.

To one who loved this element as passionately as Teresa did, it was something of a trial not to have plenty of it about; and she resolved to have the well dug out and the water conducted in pipes to the convent, in the hope that it might be improved. To this end she had some *fontaneros* summoned, and told them what she wanted. They replied frankly it would be labor wasted; one of them said that if she could afford to spend money by the bucket,[10] it would be easier to throw it into the well and forget it. Even the nuns laughed when she asked their opinion.

Only María Bautista gave her any encouragement. "Our Lord has to give us someone to bring us water," she said after a moment's reflection. "Well, then, it will be cheaper for His Majesty to give it to us in the house, and so He will not fail to do it!"

Delighted with the childlike faith that motivated this suggestion, La Madre told the workmen to go on with the work. They did so, and were as much surprised as anyone when the *hilito* (little thread) of ill-tasting turgid water became a copious stream, cold and clear, which proved on being tasted to be even better than the waters of the public fonts; in fact, the Bishop used to take his friends there to sample it. "I don't consider it a miracle,"

[10] Ribera, *op. cit.*, lib. II, cap. VI, pp. 204-205.

wrote Teresa, ". . . but to show the faith these sisters have."[11]
Nevertheless the Carmelites were always inclined to see something miraculous in the affair, especially when the well dried
up into a trickle again, eight years later, after the city of Ávila
had granted them in perpetuity a supply from the public
fountains.[12]

The garden was still far too small, and La Madre began to
consider how to extend its limits. On one side there was what
seemed to be a lovely oasis in the midst of a desert — a little
garden where grass and flowers grew inexplicably; and the owner
used to take his ease and recreation in it with great complacency.
As soon as she found the money, Teresa asked him if he would
sell the property. Not by any means, he replied; he had a great
affection for that garden, and would never dispose of it. Not long
afterwards some city officials, examining the public fountains,
discovered that he was secretly piping off part of the water without permission. When this supply was ended, his oasis withered
until it became one with its bleak surroundings. Then he was
only too glad to sell, and Teresa got the ground she wanted.[13]

All this was secondary, of course — the mere stage setting for
the real business of her life. These Spartan women had not left
the world to raise flowers and to watch the grass grow! They were
there to learn the Divine Office, and to follow one of the most
rigorous routines ever devised. Teresa took the greatest pains
to teach everything correctly to her eager pupils. She insisted on
their chanting the office in a low rather than a high voice, for the
sake of greater accuracy and sublimity. For the rest, the routine
probably followed that outlined in the Constitutions that she
drew up for the community in 1565.

Matins were said about nine o'clock in the evening, and none
could leave the choir after the recitation began. An examination
of conscience, lasting fifteen minutes, followed, this, too, while
all were together in the choir. Then the mystery for the next
day's meditation was read. All retired at eleven to beds mat-
tressed with rude bags of straw.

In winter they arose at six, in summer at five; and in the hot
season, to make up for the lost hour of sleep, they were allowed

---

[11] *Foundations*, I.

[12] *Reforma*, lib. I, cap. 53. Silverio, *op. cit.*, III, p. 85.

[13] Silverio, *op. cit.*, III, pp. 74–75, from P. Jerónimo de San José's *Historia del Carmen Descalzo*. Also Ribera, *op. cit.*, II, VI, pp. 205.

an hour's *siesta* in the middle of the day. After arising and briefly
satisfying the demands of cleanliness and decency before making
their appearance in the choir, they were obliged to spend one
hour in mental prayer. They would then recite the Hours —
Prima, Tertia, Sexta, and *Nona.*

The *Nones* could be omitted on a solemn feast of the day of
some saint to whom they were especially devoted, and instead
they would sing. Vespers and Matins were sung on such days;
Lauds also, on the first days of Easter Week, the Feast of Saint
Joseph, and a few other occasions. Teresa directed that the singing be always in plain chant.[14]

After the reading of the Hours, each would go to her own
particular tasks until Mass, which was at eight o'clock in summer, at nine in winter. Those who received Holy Communion
were to remain after reception for a little while, giving thanks.

Teresa encouraged frequent Communion. At the Incarnation,
a representative convent of good repute, it was compulsory only
on the first Sunday of Advent, Christmas, the first Sunday of
Lent, Holy Thursday, Easter Sunday, Ascension Thursday,
Pentecost, Corpus Christi, All Saints', and the feasts of our Lady;
besides the anniversaries of the days on which the nuns received
their habits and were professed.[15] At San José the nuns must
communicate every Sunday and Holy Day, on all the feasts of
our Lord and our Lady, on the feasts of Saint Albert and Saint
Joseph, "and the other days that may seem good to the confessor,
according to the devotion and spirit of the sisters, with the permission of the Mother Prioress."[16] In practice they received
much oftener than this prescribed minimum, and La Madre
herself became a daily communicant. She counted it one of the
greatest favors of her life that one of her two daily vomitings —
the one in the morning — stopped so that she could receive. As
most of her raptures occurred just after she had taken the Sacred
Host, she tried to teach her daughters the right disposition to fit
them for similar favors. For example: "After receiving the Lord
. . . try to close the eyes of the body and open those of the soul,
and look into your heart; for I tell you, and I tell you again, and
I should like to say it many times, that if you adopt this custom

---

[14] *Constituciones,* B.M.C., t. VI, p. 5: *"jamás sea el canto por punto, sino en
tono, las voces iguales."*

[15] Silverio, *op. cit.,* III, p. 296; also B.M.C., t. IX, p. 485.

[16] B.M.C., t. VI, p. 4.

whenever you communicate, and try to have such a conscience as will let you enjoy this Good often, He will not come so disguised that in many ways, as I have said, it will not be made known according to the desire we have to see Him; and it is possible for you to desire it so much that he will discover Himself wholly to you."[17]

Likewise with inexhaustible love she labored to make the little chapel more fit to receive the divine Guest. The corporal and everything else on the altar must be immaculate. She insisted upon having very large Hosts. She perfumed the Tabernacle with essence of roses, the gift of some friend, and paid no attention to the protest of a scandalized clerical visitor. Could anything be too good for His Majesty?

Following the custom of the country at that time, there were two meals daily, the principal one, *la comida,* at ten a.m. in the summer and an hour later in winter, and the supper, *la cena,* at sundown. A little while before dinner a bell would ring, and each nun, wherever she happened to be, would kneel, say a *Pater Noster* and examine her conscience. It goes without saying that the meals were not very sumptuous. Meat was never allowed, except to the sick. (On one occasion when La Madre was ill, the nuns had great difficulty in getting her to take a bite of a piece of chicken.) The strict rule of fast was observed from the Feast of the Exaltation of the Holy Cross (September 14) until Easter, except for Sundays. No communication was permitted at meals. If the Lord prompted some sister to go without some article of food, she might ask permission to do so; otherwise she was to eat what was set before her. No one could eat or drink between meals without the consent of the Prioress. Finally, following Saint Paul,[18] Teresa set down in her Constitutions that "whoever wishes to eat, has to work."[19] On the other hand, there was to be no drudgery that had to be done at a time prearranged, for this might interfere with the life of prayer.

After dinner the nuns had an hour of recreation together. Games were not permitted, "for the Lord will give some the grace to give recreation to the others; when this is taken for granted all is time well spent. They should try not to be boresome to one another but that the jokes and conversation be

[17] *Way of Perfection,* cap. XXXIV, Valladolid MS., B.M.C., III, pp. 165–166.
[18] II. Thess. 3:8–10.
[19] *Vida,* B.M.C., vol. VI, p. 12.

discreet. After this hour of being together, in summer they may sleep an hour; and whoever does not wish to sleep, may keep silence."[20]

Even in talking to visitors, they must avoid the affairs of the world, unless to do good to those who spoke to them, "or to put them in the way of truth, or to console them in some trial." The portress or other third person present at any such conversation must particularly guard against breaches of this rule, and warn any offender. The penalty for a third offense was nine days in prison, with a scourging in the refectory on the third, "for this is something very important to the Order."[21]

At two in the afternoon they attended Vespers. Spiritual reading followed. Work and prayer (and the routine was flexible enough to allow a sister to practice mental prayer or contemplation whenever the Spirit moved her) took up the rest of the afternoon. At five in winter and six in summer they would recite the beautiful office of Compline. Then, after prayer, the Prioress at her discretion might allow general conversation. La Madre was very watchful, however, against those "particular friendships" which could destroy the health and order of a community. "No sister may embrace another, or touch her on the face or on the hands, or have friendships in particular, but all should love one another in general as Christ often commanded His Apostles."[22] Elsewhere she wrote, "Try also to rejoice with the sisters when they have recreation, as it may be necessary, and for the customary time, even though it may not be to your liking, for acting with consideration, all is perfect love."

All the details of clothing, too, were, of course, prescribed. The habit was to be black (not brown, as it is today), of rude sackcloth, with no greater quantity than necessary, and with no extraneous ornamentation. The choir mantles were of the same rough material, but were white. The toque, made of inferior linen, the product of tow, must not be folded or crimpled or plaited; and only the sick could wear a hood or cape even in winter. Mirrors were strictly taboo. The hair must be cut short, "so that no time shall be wasted combing it." Sandals of hemp were worn, with stockings of tow — this is not for warmth but for modesty. There must be nothing of bright color on the garb of a nun, "not even if it be so small a thing as a belt." The bed was to have no mattress, but only a bag of straw with a sackcloth

---

[20] *Ibid.*   [21] *Ibid.*, p. 9.   [22] *Ibid.*, p. 13.

covering. In this, and in other matters, exceptions were made for the sick: they were to have good beds with mattresses. The Prioress was to take great care that the quarters of the sick were clean and comfortable, and that they had everything necessary, though not such luxuries as the rich would enjoy. The other sisters must visit them and treat them with all affection.[23]

Now, if this strict life were considered as an end in itself, or even as a means of escaping the sorrows and labors of the workaday world (as a popular misconception sometimes has it), it would be repellent enough to human nature. To understand something of the joy it gave La Madre and her daughters, one must notice that all their routine was a means to the higher end of Contemplation, and that this itself became a means to still higher ends, and invariably produced still nobler activity.

Oriental mysticism, which has often made its way into the Catholic Church in the form of Quietism only to be cast out again, is as far from this Christian mysticism as hell is from heaven.[24] Commencing with an implied insult to God by despairing of or rejecting in whole or in part His visible and material creation, it goes on logically to repudiate action, authority, and often moral sanity. Buddhism became an elaborate roundabout form of atheism; the Manichees tended to separate the soul from the visible Church, and so, ultimately, from God Himself; the Quietist Molinos led people into an enervating communion with evil under the illusion of pursuing God. Protestantism has eliminated everywhere, to a greater or lesser extent, the heritage Christ bestowed upon His Church, which He promised should remain free from error through the ages.

In Teresa and other Catholic mystics there is none of the sterile false piety, the sensual self-seeking, the self-intoxication of the spirit that appear in all the sects, from the Gnostics to the humanity worshippers of our own age. To her all reality — God Himself, His creatures of every sort and herself — had its value for His sake; and, as we have seen, her exalted state of prayer, far from betraying her into a dangerous stupefaction of indifference or idleness, blossomed continually into beneficent activity. She confided to Saint Francis Borgia that sometimes she was able to accomplish all her usual tasks during the prayer of quiet, and he replied that it was thus also with him. As a mem-

---

[23] *Constituciones*, pp. 11-12, B.M.C.

[24] This is demonstrated, I believe, in my *Characters of the Inquisition, passim.*

ber of the mystical body of Christ (the Catholic Church) she shared its joys and sorrows, its persecutions and triumphs. Having rejoiced with all good Catholics in the struggle the Church had been making since the Black Death in the fourteenth century to cast off the resultant abuses and laxities,[25] she welcomed the completion of the Reform by the Council of Trent in 1563 with inexpressible gladness and thanksgiving.

Even the decrees of a Church Council may remain dead letters, however, if not applied; and although Philip II ordered them enforced in all his dominions, something more than legalistic commands and prohibitions was needed. Teresa made it her mission to show what this something, this spiritual something, was. Surely it was more than a coincidence that she founded her convent in the same year 1563! Better than most, she knew that Christianity was not a penal system, or a code of laws, or a philosophical body of opinion, but the following of Christ along the way of perfection, in short the Christ life assumed by His disciples. It was this Christ life, the spiritual activity of the individual Christian in union with Christ, aided by His grace and conformed to His will, that she wished to oppose to Luther's denial of the Christ life expressed in good works. And she intended to raise up against what she called the fire of Protestantism a veritable wall of prayer — rather, she would quench it with that divine water of grace which was to be sought and found in prayer. The armies of Philip II might do their best in the Netherlands. But "human forces are not enough" wrote Teresa in 1563, "to put out that fire of those heretics."[26] Prayer was the thing; and if thirteen poor little women could do nothing else, they could at least pray. Thus her work became a vital counterpart of the decrees of Trent. And because it was vital, it did not stop with contemplation, but expressed itself in an infinite variety of actions, whose effect is felt in all parts of Christendom today.

Prayer and action: these two aspects of Teresa's life, the inner and the outer, found their expression, and in logical order, in the two books she wrote during her five years at San José. The

---

[25] It is a vulgar error to suppose that no attempts at reform were raised before Luther's protest. Cf. my *Isabella* and my *Philip II*.

[26] *Camino*, cap. III. She added, "As if force of arms could remedy so great an evil!" Two lines are drawn through these words, either by her hand or, more probably, by the hand of one of her directors. B.M.C., III, p. 19, n. 2.

Book of Her Life is not an autobiography in the ordinary sense, but the story of her soul, its troubles and triumphs, up to and including the founding of the monastery. *The Way of Perfection* advises others how to achieve the same difficult self-mastery. These two books explain and complement each other, and together with *The Interior Castle and Mansions*, would constitute a magnificent trilogy embracing all of her ascetical and mystical teaching.

She had composed most of the first draft of the *Vida* in the Cerda palace at Toledo, and had completed it — so at least she thought — in the hot June of 1562, shortly before returning to Ávila; and all this reluctantly, in obedience to Father Ibáñez and other confessors. At the end of 1562 a Dominican confessor, Fray García de Toledo, told her to add an account of the founding of San José, and to revise and rewrite the whole work. She began to do this while still at the Incarnation. She could hardly have accomplished much when she took up her residence at San José in the Lent of 1563, for the rewriting of the book occupied her scanty leisure for the next two years or more, probably until about Christmas, 1565.[27] Besides the vivid and sometimes humorous accounts of trials before and after the foundation, she added several other events, such as the death of Saint Peter of Alcántara and his appearances to her, and divided the whole into forty chapters.

Her own manuscript, which has been preserved in the Escorial, tells much about the authoress and her methods of composition. She wrote clearly and vigorously at great speed, hardly ever erasing or crossing anything out, now and then underlining some words for emphasis, but never leaving any of the blotches, the sudden irregularities of shading, which mark the chirography of neurotics. Hers tells of an intense but well-balanced nature. In the whole manuscript there are only fourteen corrections, of which some were made by her, some by Father Báñez, and the rest by a third person. Sheet after sheet of the yellow parchment, stained and faded by time, is covered with the straightforward unhesitating script of one who knew exactly what she wanted to say, who was so full of her subject that she had no time for the slightest attempt at literary embellishment, who did not even stop for punctuation, except for a vertical line now and then between phrases. There were souls to be saved, and she must

[27] Silverio, *Vida*, B.M.C., t. I, pp. 115–130.

put down what she knew! Yet her *Book of the Mercies of God,* as she first called it, takes its place, with all its imperfections of rhetoric, its redundancy, tautology, pleonasms, faulty reference, careless arrangement, colloquial or slovenly diction, and even bad grammar — among the most powerful, most beautiful, most extraordinary books that have come from the minds of human beings. "The charm of Teresa's style is that she had none," said one of her biographers. "She wrote as she spoke."[28] She can write a polished sentence when she takes the trouble, but she does not scorn the use of some of those vigorous provincial expressions which, in a language in a state of transition, were soon to become obsolete, or at least archaic. She is always getting off the subject, but her digressions, like those of the very greatest poets, are commonly striking and of rarest excellence The remarkable treatise on mental prayer and the prayer of union in her *Vida* (the most fascinating part of the book) is a digression of several chapters. She has besides, another quality that Aristotle rated highly as a test of genius. Her similes and metaphors, seized at random from everyday life and often homely and pungent, are unique, inevitable, speeding straight to the mark.

It was not very easy, writing this book. Imagine a woman of nearly fifty, still suffering from pains and faintness in the heart and a ghastly daily vomiting, sitting clad in coarse sackcloth on the bare floor of her little cell after all the nuns had retired to rest, resting her parchment on the bed or on that little ledge or bench of stone near the unglazed window, while the winter winds howled outside the canvas pane and the cruel cold of a Castilian winter smote her to the bone — imagine her, utterly forgetful of herself, writing on and on, at full speed, page after page, often until two or three o'clock in the morning. Many a person, thinking of this in that barren little room that has become a shrine, and remembering the joy, the good humor, and often the gay wit of that book torn from the heart, must have begun to understand what the fire called sanctity can do. Yet it never occurred to her to mention numb fingers or other physical discomforts, and but for the witnesses for her beatification, we might have heard nothing about them.

She was reading the manuscript over for the first time when Fray García de Toledo sent for it, to submit it to Blessed John

---

[28] Mrs. Cunningham-Graham, I, p. 67.

of Ávila, "the apostle of Andalucía." Teresa obediently sent it off without waiting to revise it, and with it the following note, written on the empty page at the end:

"Jhs.

"May the Holy Spirit be always with Your Worship. Amen. There will be no harm in commending this labor to you earnestly, to oblige you to be very careful to speak to our Lord on my behalf, and considering what I have endured in seeing myself written down and in bringing back to memory so many of my miseries, I might well do so; though I can say truthfully that it has hurt me more to write the favors the Lord has done me than the offenses I have committed against His Majesty.

"I have done what you commanded me in spinning it out, on condition that you will do what you promised about cutting out what you think bad. I had not finished reading over what I had written when you sent for it. There may be some things badly expressed, and others put down twice; for I have had so little time that I could not go back to see what I had written. I beg you to correct it and to have it copied, if it is to be sent to the Father Master Ávila, for someone might recognize the handwriting. I am quite anxious that he be asked to read it, for it was with that intent that I began to write; for if he thinks I am going in the right way, I shall be very much consoled, for I shall have left nothing undone that is in me to do. May you act in all this as you think and see you are obliged to, for the sake of one who thus confides to you her soul. Yours I shall commend to our Lord all my life long; for this please hurry to serve His Majesty by doing me this favor, for you will see from what is said here how well it is to give oneself wholly, as Your Worship has begun to do, to Him who gives Himself without stint to us. May He be blessed forever, and I hope in His mercy that you and I shall meet where we shall see more plainly the great things He has done with us, and that we may praise Him forevermore. Amen. This book was finished in June, 1562."[29]

Instead of delivering the manuscript to John of Ávila, Fray García gave it to Fray Domingo Báñez, who in turn submitted it to the Inquisition at Madrid, and on receiving it back without

---

[29] The letter is undated and unsigned. Father Silverio (B.M.C., t. VII, *Epistolario* I, pp. 13–14) holds it certain that it was written at the end of 1565. For further details and references on the subsequent history of the manuscript, see the introduction to his edition to her *Vida*, p. 117 *et seq.*

any particular censure of its contents, apparently kept it for about twelve years. Meanwhile Teresa, while still at the Incarnation in the winter of 1562–1563, heard that the Inquisitor Don Francisco Soto de Salazar (later Bishop of Salamanca) had arrived in Ávila; and alarmed perhaps by rumors that her book was being investigated by the Holy Office, characteristically took the offensive instead of waiting for the attack. Obtaining permission to visit him, she told him simply the story of her raptures, her visions, and her enforced literary labors, begging him, in conclusion, for a judgment upon her spirit, her works, and her method of prayer, which she assured him she desired to submit, in all things, to the mind of the Church. Salazar replied with kindness that the Inquisition did not concern itself with methods of prayer or the testing of the spirits of mystics, but only with the punishment of heretics. He advised her, as Father Ibáñez had, to send her book to Father John of Ávila, "and with the reply that he will give," he added, "you may rest assured that you shall have nothing to fear."

Teresa then made a laborious copy of her book, which she requested her friend Doña Luisa de la Cerda to have forwarded to the Apostle of Andalucía. Five years later, as we shall see, the copy was still on its tardy way to the unofficial censor on whose verdict the fate of the author and her reform might well depend.

She had not only written this book, she had experienced it very literally, it was the "living book" that Christ had promised her. And so it was fitting that at this time also she attained what seems, from our point of view, the apogee of the divine manifestations of her calling. She had raptures which she could only describe imperfectly by comparing them to the struggles of "one who fights with a strong giant." The very thought of God would fill her with such joy that her face began to shine and to grow strangely young and beautiful; and as her soul waxed strong with the mighty impulse that infused it, her body would become helpless and motionless, remaining in whatever posture it happened to be in, sometimes kneeling, sometimes standing, with the arms extended. When the feet and hands were stiff and cold as in death and the very pulses of her arteries seemed to have ceased, she would see and hear things "which it is not given to man to utter."

This was sometimes embarrassing from a human point of view. Once, for example, a very important Jesuit came to see her at the same hour when a *hidalgo* of Ávila called concerning some business of the convent. When the priest spoke to her of the love of God, she began to feel a rapture coming on, and not willing to have him see it lest he think her holy, she forcibly resisted it by turning away from him while he was talking, and addressing a remark to the *hidalgo*. One of the nuns told her that she ought to be less scrupulous about his thinking her a spiritual person than about giving scandal by breaking off a conversation with him so impolitely.[30] But Teresa could never get over feeling almost ashamed at being caught, so to speak, in ecstasy.

Her niece María Bautista is our authority for many of these occurrences. "One night while we were at Matins in San José of Ávila, this witness saw her body begin to rise like that of a person who stands on tiptoe, and she, on becoming aware that she was going up, threw herself on the floor, for this made her very unhappy." One morning all the nuns saw her rise in the choir, while they were kneeling together before Communion. On one Feast of Saint Joseph, during a sermon, they tried to hold her down, at her instructions. Another time, kneeling at the grille to receive the Host from the Bishop, Don Álvaro, she felt her body growing light and her knees leaving the floor; and desperately clutching at the bars, she kept herself from going higher while the Bishop with great difficulty administered the sacred Body of Christ.

Nothing gave her more distress than to have people see her in such a state. She would pretend sometimes that it was her heart trouble that afflicted her, and would ask for something to eat or drink to carry out the deception.[31] When the nuns finally told her that she need not trouble to dissimulate, for they knew the true nature of her infirmity, she commanded them under holy obedience not to speak of what they had seen. Yet she could not prevent them from storing up memories, and making affidavits for her beatification.[32]

---

[30] Silverio, *op. cit.,* II, pp. 37–38 and references there.

[31] Sister María de San Jerónimo, B.M.C., t. II, pp. 293–294.

[32] In the seventeenth century, Saint Joseph of Cupertino was often seen suspended in the air, and on one occasion at least, arose fully ten yards from the ground. See the very interesting note of P. Silverio on this and similar phenomena, and on some of the solemn nonsense written on the subject by rationalistic scientists — *op. cit.,* III, p. 38. Cf. also Tanqueray, *The Spiritual Life,* p. 711, for levitations of Saint Philip Neri, Saint Peter of Alcántara, and others.

At this period she had several of her most exalted visions. Some of them were terrible, as if to warn people through her of the literal ugliness and wretchedness of sin: as when she saw two abominable little demons astride the neck of a priest who was saying Mass in a state of mortal sin; or when she saw devils tossing to and fro in mockery the body of a person who had died without confession after an evil life, and dragging him about with hooks. "Would to God all in mortal sin might see what I saw!"[33] Again, she saw souls leaving purgatory on their flight to heaven. She saw prophetic representations of the greatness of individual priests and particular Orders.

One Order, which her director and commentator Father Gracián said was the Dominican, was "surrounded by angels, and very near to God; and I was given to understand the great good that an Order would do in the last days, and the fortitude with which its members would sustain the Faith."[34] Not merely once, but on several occasions she saw all the Jesuits together in heaven, with white banners in their hands; "and I have seen other wonderful things of them, and hold this Order in great veneration, for I have dealt much with them, and I see their life conforming to what the Lord has given me to understand concerning them."[35] Her first editor, Fray Luis de León, deleted "all the Jesuits" from this passage, and made it read "a certain order." In another place, where she said that "Saint Francis, Saint Dominic, and Father Ignatius, he who founded the Company" had all received similar favors from God, the famous Augustinian (who like the early Jesuits had suffered from the Inquisition!) committed the inexcusable fault of substituting "Saint Francis, Saint Dominic, *and other founders of Orders.*" Teresa had many revelations, however, about the Jesuits. Once after Holy Communion at their church of Saint Gil, in Ávila, she saw "a very rich pallium over the heads of the Jesuit brothers."[36]

There has been some difference of opinion as to which order she meant by the following:

"Once when I was praying before the Blessed Sacrament, there

---

[33] *Vida,* cap. XXXVIII.

[34] *Vida,* cap. XI; Gracián's note to edition of Fray Luis de Leon, 1588.

[35] *Vida,* cap. XXXVIII. For a good discussion of the mutilation by Fray Luis de León of texts favoring the Jesuits, see Silverio's *"preliminares,"* p. 87 and p. 335, n. 3, of his edition.

[36] *Vida,* cap. XXXIX.

appeared to me a saint whose Order has been somewhat fallen. He held in his hands a large book; he opened it and told me to read some letters which were great and read thus: *In times to come this Order will flourish; it will have many martyrs.* Another time, being at Matins in the choir, there appeared and stood before me six or seven, I thought there were, of that same Order, with swords in their hands. I thought this meant that they were to defend the faith. For another time, being in prayer, my spirit was carried away; I seemed to be on a great field where many were fighting, and those of that Order battled with great valor. Their faces were beautiful and very much inflamed, and they threw many on the ground conquered, others they slew. It seemed to me to be a battle against the heretics. I have seen this glorious saint many times, and he has told me certain things and thanked me for the prayer I made for his Order, and promised to commend me to the Lord."[37]

In spite of Teresa's reluctance to give the name of this Order — "lest the others be aggrieved" — her biographers have had no such scruples, and several have tried to guess her meaning. Gracián thought it was the Dominican. Yepes confidently asserted that it was her own Order of Carmel, and that she meant the Discalced Carmelites of the Reform.[38] Still others have guessed the Jesuits: but to this it has been objected that their order was not "somewhat fallen" in the accepted meaning of the expression, unless the revolt of the *malcontentos* is meant.

Teresa counted as one of her greatest favors a vision in which like a flash she saw and seemed to understand clearly "how all things are seen in God and how He holds them all in Himself. . . . Let us say that the Divinity is like a very clear diamond, much larger than all the world, or a mirror, as I have said of the soul in another vision, save that it is thus in a so much more excellent manner that I would not know how to overestimate it; and that all that we do is seen in this diamond, which is of such sort that it includes everything in itself, for there is nothing that can go beyond this grandeur. A marvelous thing to me it was to see in so short a time so many things together here in this diamond, and a most sorrowful, each time I remember that I have seen such foul things, as are my sins, represented in that

[37] *Ibid.,* cap. XL.
[38] *Vida,* lib. III, cap. XVII. P. Silverio inclines to the view of Gracián — edition of the Autobiography, p. 364, n. 1.

utter purity of splendor.[39] Oh, who will make this understood
by those who commit very lewd and foul sins, that they may remember that they are not hidden, and that rightly God resents
them, since they take place in the very presence of His Majesty,
and we comport ourselves so irreverently before Him! I saw
how well is hell deserved for a single mortal sin; for it is not
possible to understand how very grievous a thing it is to do it
before such great Majesty, and how far removed from Who He
is such things are. And thus His mercy is all the more evident,
since He tolerates us when we understand all this. It has made
me consider that if one thing like this has left my soul so terrified, what will the Day of Judgment be when this Majesty clearly
shows Himself to us and we see the offenses that we have
committed?"[40]

Visions, too, are means to an end. Catholic mysticism always
comes back to the words of Saint Paul: "If I speak with the
tongues of men and of angels, and have not charity, I am become
as sounding brass, or a tinkling cymbal. And if I have prophecy
and should know all mysteries, and all knowledge, and if I
should have all faith, so that I could remove mountains, and
have not charity, I am nothing."[41] Mystical experiences are
always under suspicion among Catholics unless they bring with
them an increase in virtues, especially in charity and humility.
Teresa's raptures invariably stood the test. She prophesied many
future events, revealed to her by Christ; and the fact that they
were always accomplished set up a strong presumption, of
course, for their divine origin.

There was, for example, the vision she had after the sudden
death of her brother-in-law, Don Martín de Guzmán y Barrientos, without confession. It was revealed to her that his wife (her
sister María) would die in the same way, and that she must go
and prepare her. Teresa's confessor did not take this seriously,
but when the warning was repeated, he permitted her to visit
Castellanos, where, without telling María of her vision, she
urged her to confess frequently, and to "take account of her
soul in everything." María followed this advice, lived a holy
life for five years, and then died suddenly, with no one near.

[39] "Limpieza de claridad" is the Saint's phrase.
[40] Vida, cap. XL.
[41] 1 Cor. 12.

Eight days later Teresa saw Christ receiving her into His glory.[42] This was only one of many such instances.

With all these powers she was the more eager, if possible, to observe every devotion that the Church recommended to less favored souls. She had the tenderest love, which has ever since flourished in all Carmelite convents, for Jesus as a child. On one Feast of the Circumcision she came forth from her cell, holding His image in her arms, and dancing gravely as if to unseen music, while the nuns, far from regarding this conduct as odd or humorous, fell in with her mood, and all danced together as King David had danced before the Holy of Holies. The central mystery of Christianity, the fact that God became Man, was the fulcrum of all her thinking and acting; and Mass and Holy Communion were to her, more than to most Catholics, the literal repetition of the Passion, death, and Resurrection of the God-Man. In very deed she had come to live out her own book, to be the living book He had promised her, in these, the happiest years of her life.

---

[42] *Vida,* cap. XXXIV.

Chapter XVIII

"THE WAY OF PERFECTION"

THE nuns were very curious to see what La Madre had been writing all these weeks and months, and were disappointed, naturally, when they were told that no one must see it but the confessor and Blessed John of Ávila. What a book she could write for her own daughters, to console them after she went to heaven, and to make sure that her work would be perpetuated! Knowing that she would never write another for the sake of mere "self-expression," they begged Father Báñez to command her to set down her teachings for their especial benefit. He thought well of the idea, and Teresa, obedient as always, went to work again. In a few months, sitting on the cold floor by the canvas-covered window and leaning upon the stone ledge while all the rest were asleep, she composed the *Camino de Perfeccion*. Just as the *Vida* was the story of her interior conflict, this was the record of her influence upon others, the overflow of that inexhaustible energy with which she had inebriated herself at the waters of prayer, the communal, that is to say the completed aspect of the Christ life within her.

For the average reader, the *Camino* is the book with which to make the acquaintance of this radiant and joyous saint. Teresa had learned a great deal in writing her life story. A mind so keen and creative was bound to overcome certain faults almost unconsciously: to be more concise and pungent, to achieve a more simple and orderly arrangement, to avoid unnecessary repetitions of words and even of sentences. Again, the subject is of more general interest. Much as we admire the beauty and splendor of the best parts of the *Vida*, only advanced contemplatives can understand it. But the *Camino* is for all of us: we can begin to live it by desiring in all sincerity to be Christians. Although it was written for cloistered nuns, the genius of the author and the universal importance of practical Christianity have made it so alive and fascinating that only a very dull person could find it dull.

"The Way of Perfection!" The title itself — taken from a phrase in the *Imitation*, which was widely read in Spain under the name of *Contemptus Mundi* and was one on the little shelf at San José — suggests her purpose. She was not addressing con-

templatives alone, for even in Carmel there were nuns who did not achieve the heights of prayer; she was writing for all who wished to be spiritually perfect, and perfection — which she desired for all the friends of Christ, and especially for priests — was possible without contemplation.

"Saint Martha was holy, although they don't set her down as a contemplative; well, what more would you want than to get to be like this blessed woman who deserved to have Christ our Lord so often in her house, and to give Him food and serve Him, and perhaps to eat at her table, yes and from her own plate? If we are to set ourselves up as inebriated, like the Magdalen, there won't be anyone to give the celestial Guest something to eat. Think then that this congregation is the house of Saint Martha, and that it has to be altogether so, and let not those who may be meant for the active life murmur at those who greatly intoxicate themselves in prayer, for generally it makes them careless of themselves and of everything.

"Let them remember that if they are silent, the Lord is going to make answer for them, and consider themselves lucky to go and prepare the dinner for Him. Let them notice that true humility, I certainly believe, is chiefly in being very quick to be satisfied with what the Lord wishes to do with them, and always to find themselves unworthy to call themselves His servants. Well, then, whether it is to contemplate, or to have mental and vocal prayer, or to cure the sick, or to serve with the housework, or to labor with the desire to be in the very lowest — all is to serve the Guest Who comes to stay with us, and to eat and to refresh Himself. What business is it of ours whether we are in the one or the other?"[1]

Christian perfection was not meant, however, to be limited to nuns. Christ wanted the whole human race to ask for it and to "notice that the Lord invited everybody; since He is truth, there is no doubting it. If it were not general, this invitation, God would not have summoned all men, and even if He did call them, He would not have said, 'I will give you to drink.' He could have said, 'All come and in the end you will lose nothing; and to those who suit Me I will give to drink.' But

---

[1] *Way of Perfection*, Escorial MS., cap. XXXII, B.M.C., p. 266. Father Tanqueray (*op. cit.*, p. 650) defines infused contemplation as "a simple, loving, protracted gaze on God and things divine, under the influence of the gifts of the Holy Ghost and of a special grace which takes possession of us and causes us to act in a passive rather than in an active manner."

I hold it certain that this living water will not be lacking to all, without this condition, as I have said, if they don't linger on the way."[2]

Perfection could be sought and gained, then, without contemplation. Contemplation was a gift of God, it was an awareness of heaven itself, and it would be bestowed on all who desired it. But not necessarily in this world. Some would get it only after death. Perfection, however, was attainable here; and Teresa was sure that it was meant for all who sincerely sought it. "Ask, and you shall receive."

Now, although a person might become perfect without contemplation, she could hardly dispense with mental prayer. This was possible for any Christian; and for a Carmelite it was *sine qua non*, whether she was to be a Mary or a Martha.

How then does one attain success in mental prayer? There are certain helps, says Teresa, such as fasting, penance, and silence. "Prayer and self-indulgence do not go together." Above all, mental prayer requires (1) *love* and (2) *detachment*. Both of these are founded upon (3) *humility,* which in turn requires absolute (4) *obedience.* The whole book, then, is an elaboration of these four points, leading up to a magnificent treatise on the *Pater Noster.* Teresa deals with each of the four in turn, at great length, incisively, wittily, profoundly.

1. *Love.* Here she applies to conventual life the divine command, "Thou shalt love the Lord thy God with thy whole mind, with thy whole heart, and with thy whole soul; and thou shalt love thy neighbor as thyself." The idea that runs through this discourse is that the love of God must always be kept foremost, and must never be sacrificed to any false or deceptive or unspiritual love of one's neighbor. Excessive love of another individual is a great danger in a convent, though careless superiors sometimes think it is a virtue; it prevents one from loving all the sisters equally, and causes factions to form; it saps the will to love God, and it seems to be more hurtful to women than to men; it is a snare of the devil to attempt to ruin convents.

"Let us not consent, O sisters, that our will be slave of any one save Him who bought it with His blood; let them see to it that they don't find themselves trapped, without knowing how, and unable to do anything about it. Oh, God help me! the childish follies that come from this are beyond calculation.

---

[2] *Ibid.,* cap. XXXII, p. 276.

And because they are so petty that only those who see it would understand it or believe it, there is no reason to speak of them here except to say that it will be bad for anyone, and in the prioress, a pestilence. In putting a stop to these partialities, great care is necessary from the very moment when the friendship begins; this more with industry and love than vigor. To remedy this, a great thing is not to be together except at the appointed hours, or to speak to one another, according to the custom which we now observe, which is not to be together, as the Rule commands, but each one separated in her cell. . . .

"As for loving one another, it seems an impertinent thing to recommend it, for what people are so boorish that, speaking always together and being in company, and not having to hold other conversations or other concerns or recreations with persons outside the house, they do not love one another? Especially as virtue always invites love, and this, with God's favor, I hope in His Majesty will always be the case among those of this house. So, not much is to be recommended on this score, in my opinion."[3]

Of particular friendships, however, as snares injurious to true love, she has a great deal to say; and in one of her most striking digressions she includes a vigorous warning against excessive partiality for any one confessor. A certain liking for a priest-director is natural and harmless, like that which exists between relatives and friends. When the devil perceives that a nun has this good and grateful affection for a holy man who understands her spiritual state and is guiding her toward perfection, he tries to make her scrupulous about it, and sometimes torments her so much that she gives him up. In such a case the best thing to do is to consult some other confessor, preferably a learned man, and abide by his advice.[4]

---

[3] Valladolid MS., cap. IV, B.M.C., III, 28.

[4] *Ibid.*, p. 29. The Escorial autograph says here, "What they can do here, is to try not to think of whether they like him or don't like him; but if they like him, let them like him," etc. — B.M.C., III, 225. In the Stanbrook Abbey English translation, the various readings are combined in a sort of mosaic, to give the complete thought of the Saint. P. Silverio has given preference to the Valladolid autograph, printing the text of the Escorial in his appendix. The existence of more than one original in the Saint's handwriting is due to the fact that she laboriously copied the work herself, perhaps several times, to furnish copies for other convents, etc. The Valladolid MS. considerably modifies what she says of confessors in the Escorial. This latter is followed by Fray Luis de León and other editors. It is the oldest, and therefore the one that Teresa wrote first at San José, in 1565–1566.

It is safe to love the confessor, and good for the soul, if he is a holy and spiritual person. If not, there is great danger, especially for enclosed houses. If no levity or vanity is found in the confessor (and "this," wrote Teresa, "is easily seen by anyone who doesn't want to make a boob[5] of herself") pay no attention to the scruple, and the devil will tire of the sport and go away. "But if they understand that the confessor leads toward any sort of levity in what he says to them, let them consider it all suspicious, have nothing to do with him in any way, even if it be conversations about prayer or about God, but make their confession briefly and bring it to an end; and the best way will be to tell *la madre* that the soul is not doing well with him, and to change him." This is highly important, "for it is a dangerous thing and a hell and injury to all . . . it is quite the worst damage the demon can do to convents so enclosed." It is particularly bad in convents where the nuns are allowed only one confessor. "I have seen great affliction in monasteries on this account," wrote Teresa. "But not in mine.

"May the Lord never let anybody in this house experience this trouble . . . of seeing herself distressed body and soul. Or that the superior be so friendly with the confessor that no one dare say anything to him about her, or to her about him. From this comes the temptation not to confess very grave sins because the chickenhearted[6] are afraid of not being left in peace. Oh, God help me! what souls the devil must catch this way, and how dearly their black reserve and concern for their honor cost them, when they think that by not dealing with more than one confessor they are doing a great thing for religion and the honor of their monastery, and so the devil manages in this way to catch their souls, as he could do in no other. If the poor nuns ask for another, there goes the discipline of the order, all lost; and if he is not of their order, even if he were a Saint Jerome, then they are insulting the whole order. Give God much praise, daughters, for this liberty that you have, that although you can't have a large number, yet you can speak with some who, if not your ordinary confessors, can give you light for everything; and I ask this for the love of God of whoever may be your superior, that she always try to deal, and have her nuns deal, with one

---

[5] "*Boba*," from which the English "booby," and our more colloquial United States "boob" derive. Escorial, B.M.C., III, p. 226, cap. VII.

[6] Teresa omitted this word when she wrote the Valladolid MS.

who is learned. God deliver them from being wholly directed by one who is not well taught, however spiritual he may seem to them and in fact may be; meanwhile the more favors the Lord gives them in prayer, the more need have they to be well founded in their devotions and prayers and all their works.

"They know already that the cornerstone must be a good conscience and freeing themselves with all their powers from venial sins and seeking the most perfect. They may think that almost any confessor knows this; but they are much mistaken, for I consulted one who had heard the whole course of theology, and who did me harm enough in things which he gave me to understand were not evil; and I know that he did not mean to deceive me, and that he had no motive for doing so, but that he did not know better.[7] In this having true light to keep the law of God with perfection, all our good consists; on this our prayer is solidly built; without this strong cement all the edifice goes wrong. They have need of talking, then, with people both spiritual and learned." She begs future superiors and the bishop, whoever he may be, to allow the nuns to have more than one confessor, even if the one is suitable in all ways. For one man may be mistaken, and different souls are led by different paths.

The digression finished, Teresa soars to a sublime discourse on the nature of true love, spiritual love, the love that sees the difference between the Creator and His creatures. "Perhaps, sisters of mine, you think this foolishness on my part, and you are saying that you all know this. May it please the Lord that you do, and that you know it in such wise as it has to be known, imprinted on your very bowels. Then, if you know this, you see that I do not lie when I say that whoever comes here has that love. These are the ones whom God has brought to this state, generous souls, royal souls; they are not contented with loving anything so wretched as these bodies, however beautiful they may be, whatever graces they may have (although the sight of this may please them and they may praise Him Who created it), but to dwell on them for more than a moment, to have love, I say, for these things, no!"[8] Such souls cannot allow themselves to be enslaved and ruled by affection for "a nothingness, a shadow." When people wish for the love of others, it is

---

[7] "And it has happened to me with two or three others besides him," she added in the Valladolid autograph, cap. V, p. 32, B.M.C. Escorial MS., cap. VIII, p. 227.
[8] Escorial MS., cap. X, p. 231.

always for self-interest or pleasure; they wish their love to be returned. And by what? "Things of straw and without substance, that the wind blows away"; for when they have loved us a great deal, what is this that remains to us? Chosen souls do not care whether or not their love is returned by others. Yet, loving only God, they love others with a more intense and more beneficent love. Like God Himself, they think more of giving than of receiving. This is true love; other affections, says Teresa, only usurp the name.[9]

It is impossible for such souls to love anyone who has not virtue and the love of God. "I say it is impossible, for even though a person would die for them, and would do them all the good works she could, and might have all the graces of nature combined, her will would not be equal to it, for now it is an educated will, and it has experience of what is now all in all, and they won't throw any loaded dice[10] to her! She sees that they are not meant to be in one, and that it is an impossible thing that their loving one another should last, and she fears that their enjoying themselves will end with life if she does not think the other is keeping the law of God, and that they will go to different places. And the soul in whom God has poured true wisdom doesn't value this love which lasts only here at more than it is worth, or as much." She can love the worldly soul only to draw it nearer to Christ, the captain of love.

"It is a strange thing what an impassioned love this is, what tears it costs, what penances, what prayer, what commending of all whom it thinks to benefit, a perpetual care, a ceaseless discontent. Then if she sees the soul of the one she loves advancing and then falling somewhat back, she thinks there can be no pleasure for her in life, nor eating nor sleeping without this anxiety, always fearful that the soul she loves so much may be lost, that they may have to part forever, for she doesn't give two cents[11] for the death of this life, for she doesn't wish to

---

[9] Valladolid, p. 37, cap. VI. This part of the treatise was much enlarged when she copied it.

[10] Stanbrook Abbey edition (p. 42): "cannot be cheated with false coin." This is an example of how even the best of Teresa's English translators have toned down the vigor of her expression. In both the Escorial and the Valladolid autographs, she very bluntly says "loaded dice" — "no la echarán dado falso." The Stanbrook translation is generally accurate, however, and extremely readable.

[11] Here Teresa was her own censor. In the Valladolid MS. she changed "she doesn't give two maravedis" to "she cares nothing."

grasp at something that vanishes in a puff of wind from between the hands before one can lay hold of it. It is love without self-interest, little or much; all its interest is in seeing that soul rich with the goods of heaven. In short, it is love that conforms to that which Christ has for us; it merits the name of love, not those little tattered putrid affections of the world" — and I don't mean sinful ones, from which God deliver us!"

Earthly affection — the kind that makes one's soul ache if a friend's head aches — is a hell that must be forgotten and never even be mentioned in Carmel. True love considers whether a cross may not benefit our friend, and asks only that she may have patience to bear it and profit by it. We cannot help feeling her trouble, and we would rather endure the pain ourselves than let her bear it (if the merit could be transferred to her); but reason prevails over emotion. Such love never deals falsely with its object, or allows her to remain in error for lack of a needed reproof; it cannot flatter or dissemble faults; "it sees the little motes. O happy souls that are loved by such! . . . O my Lord, will you not grant me the favor that there may be many who love me thus? Surely, Lord, I would far rather have it than to be loved by all the kings and lords of the world. . . ."[13]

Yet friendships are not necessarily to be avoided unless they are "particular" friendships. Indeed, the companionship of God's true friends is a good way to keep near Him. And the nuns must sympathize with the trials and weaknesses of their sisters. Those who are strong must pity others and not be astonished at their lack of strength. They must not judge others by themselves. Any fortitude they have is a gift, and comes through no effort of theirs. It is best to estimate themselves by their weakest moments; this is particularly needful for courageous souls who long for crosses and make little of their own troubles; let them remember what they used to feel when they were weak, and reflect that their improvement is not their doing — otherwise the devil, who is most alert for perfect souls, and uses his subtlest temptations to entrap them, knowing that cruder ones will not succeed, may gradually cool their charity. Prayer is the best means of defeating his ruses and making him disclose him-

---

[12] Escorial MS., cap. XI, p. 233. Her vigorous phrase here is *estos amorcitos desastrados valadies de por acá*. In the Valladolid MS. she omitted the word *valadies*, whose coarse connotation is indicated by its derivation from *"val,"* meaning "a sewer."

[13] Escorial MS., cap. XI, p. 234.

self. A nun should be cordial with her sisters, yes; but particular friendships — never! "Never let such words as 'My life! my soul!' be heard in this house, nor other such things, such as women say to one another. Let them save these choice words to use to the Lord, since they are to be with Him so many times a day, and some of them so intimately that they will have need of them, since His Majesty permits it; and if much used with others, they will not be so endearing with Him, and without this, there is nothing.[14] This is a very womanish thing, and I don't want my sisters to be so in anything, but strong men; and if they do what lies in them, the Lord will make them so virile that they will astonish the men. And how easy it is to His Majesty, Who made us out of nothing."[15]

The best way to show true love for the sisters is to keep the rule perfectly, help them with their labors, and rejoice and thank God for their spiritual progress. If any of them takes offense at "some little word hastily spoken," let her atone for it at once and pray fervently; let there be no offense over the *"punctilios"* which so often caused bloodshed among the proud cavaliers of Castile. "My blood seems to freeze, as they say, when I write this, for I see it is the principal curse of convents." If it should really occur at San José, "let them give themselves up for lost; let them know they have thrown out the Lord of the house. Let them cry out to His Majesty, for if such frequent confession and communion do not prevent this, let them fear there is some Judas among them. The Prioress must be especially watchful on this point. If a nun prove rebellious, send her away to another convent — God will provide her dowry; let them rid themselves of this pestilence"; cut off the branches of it as they can, and if this does not avail, pluck up the roots. If no other way will do, the refractory nun must be imprisoned. "This is much better than that all should be punished by such an incurable pestilence. Oh, what a great evil this is! God deliver us from a monastery where it enters; certainly I would rather have one go into the fire than have all burned."[16]

2. *Detachment*, like love, must be perfect. Perfect detachment "includes everything else"; and Teresa begs any novice who feels that she lacks the fortitude to accept this with all it implies, to

---

[14] *y sin eso, no ay para qué.*
[15] *Ibid.,* p. 235.
[16] *Ibid.,* p. 236.

say so before her profession and to go elsewhere; for "there are other monasteries where perhaps the Lord is served much better." Let her not, however, disturb "these little women whom His Majesty has gathered here for His service."[17]

Relatives are allowed to visit at San José for their own sake, not for that of the nuns. Let a sister consider herself "imperfect, not detached, not healthy, not truly free in spirit, and in need of a doctor" if she does not grow tired of her relatives on their second visit. The only cure for her is not to see them again until after many prayers she has the grace to feel perfectly independent of them, to feel in fact that their visits are a cross; then she may safely see them, now and then, for their own good. So long as she is deeply troubled by their troubles, and delights in their worldly success, she may be sure that she is injuring herself, and is doing them no good. "In this house, my daughters, we must be very careful to commend them to God, after our prayers for what concerns His Church, but beyond that, we must put them out of memory as much as we can. I have been much loved by them, so they say, and I know from my own experience and that of others, that apart from parents (who seldom fail to aid their children, and it is right not to be strangers with them, as detachment sometimes makes us do, when they need consolation, if we see it does not hurt our soul), my relatives, though they have seen me in difficulties, have helped me least of all in them; the servants of God, yes.

"Believe, friends, that if you serve Him as you ought, you will find no better friends than those whom His Majesty will send you. And once resolved upon this, as you are here, seeing that in doing anything else you fail the true friend Christ, you will soon gain this liberty. Whoever tells you that something else is virtue, don't believe it."[18]

Teresa enlarged upon this passage when she copied it later: "You can trust more in those who love you only for His sake than in all your relatives, and they will not fail you, and where you don't expect it you will find fathers and brothers. What these do for us they do expecting pay only from God; the others expect it from us, and when they see us poor and unable to do anything for them, they quickly tire of us. And although this may not be always true, it most often happens here in the world;

---

[17] *Ibid.*, cap. XII, p. 238.
[18] *Ibid.*, cap. XIII, p. 240.

because, in short, it is the world." If a woman can attain detachment from her kin in no other way, it is right for her to go to some other country; however, in Teresa's opinion, detachment is not so much a matter of bodily separation, as of "the soul's resolutely embracing the good Jesus, our Lord."[19]

Detachment from relatives, moreover, is not enough; we must become detached from ourselves. Otherwise we are like one who locks his doors against thieves, and leaves some of them in the house; "and have you not heard that the worst thief is the one inside the house?" Self-love must be got rid of if holy liberty is to be gained. Teresa suggests several ways to achieve this: (1) Constantly remember the vanity of all things, and how quickly they pass. (2) If we become attached to anything, no matter how small, turn the thoughts away from it to God, Who will then give aid with that true humility which is the inseparable sister of detachment — "whoever has these can go out and fight against all hell together and against the world and its temptations, and *against the flesh.*"[20] Finally, (3) we must get rid of the love of these bodies of ours. This last is not easy, for some are "so dainty by disposition" and others are always thinking about their health. "Make up your minds, my daughters, that you came here to die for Christ and not to have a good time for Christ."

The devil suggests that nuns must take care of themselves, if only to be able to observe their rule; the result is that some die without ever having observed it completely for a single month, or perhaps a single day. They need not fear that they will be indiscreet in denying themselves; their confessors will see to that, for "they think penances are going to kill us." The worst offenders are those who go from one extreme to the other; they are seized with a mania to perform penances without rule or common sense, and this lasts two days, after which the devil puts it into their heads that it hurts them, and they give it up altogether, and fail even to keep such elementary items of the rule as "silence, which can do us no harm. As soon as we begin to imagine we have a headache, we stay away from the choir; one day because it aches, another because it has ached, and three more so that it will not ache."

The prioress sometimes is at the mercy of a nun who asks

---

[19] Valladolid MS., B.M.C., cap. IX, p. 48.
[20] Teresa underlined these words in the Escorial MS.

for a dispensation from the rule, especially when some doctor supports the complaining one, and a friend or relative stands by weeping; even if the prioress sees through it, she has a scruple that she may be lacking in charity. "Oh, this complaining, God help me, among nuns – may He pardon me for saying it, but I fear it has become the custom. I once happened to see this: one of them insisted that she had a headache, and complained much of it; come to find out, it didn't pain her much or little, but she had some pain somewhere else."[21]

It is a great imperfection to be always complaining of trifling ailments. Real illness, of course, is different, "Speak about it and take the necessary remedies." Wherever prayer and charity exist, the nuns will note one another's infirmities and insist on caring for them. But the petty indispositions from which women may suffer are often but fancies suggested by the devil. They come and go, and will never end unless they stop talking about them. This habit leads to the relaxation of monasteries. "This body has one fault, that the more people pamper it, the more its wants are made known. It is a strange thing how much it likes to be indulged. How well it finds some good pretext to deceive the poor soul! . . . Remember how many sick people are poor and have no one to complain to; for poor women and pampered women together don't make sense. Remember also the many married women, I know there are some, and persons of quality, who, with serious illnesses, and with heavy trials too, don't dare to complain lest they give annoyance to their husbands. Sinner that I am, no, we did not come here to be better treated than they. Oh, you who are free from the great troubles of the world, learn to suffer a little for the love of God without everyone's knowing it! . . .

"What will happen if this is read outside of this house? What will all the monasteries think of me? . . . But as this is only for my daughters, everything can be excused. And remember our holy fathers of past times and holy hermits whose life we try to imitate; what pains they endured, what loneliness, what cold, what hunger, what burning suns, without having anyone to complain to except to God. Do you think that they were of iron? No, they were as much of flesh as we are; and as soon as we begin, daughters, to conquer this little carcass, it will not bother us so much. . . . If you don't make up your mind to

<hr>

[21] Escorial MS., cap. XV, pp. 242-243.

swallow, once and for all, death and loss of health, you will never do anything. Try not to fear it, and leave all to God, and let come what may come. . . ."[22]

Detachment is not complete with outward mortification — fasting, labor, silence, enclosure, and so on; there must also be interior mortification, what Teresa calls *la vida nonada*, "the nothing life," the life which asks not even for trifling enjoyments, the utter subjection of the body to the spirit. "It seems to me that anyone who really commences to serve God, the least he can offer Him after the gift of his will, is the *vida nonada*. Plainly, if he is a true religious and a true man of prayer, and wants to enjoy the sweetnesses of God, he must not turn his back on the desire to die for him and to undergo martyrdom. Well, don't you know, sisters, that the life of the true religious, or of one who wants to be among the intimate friends of God, is one long martyrdom? Long, because compared to cutting off your head all of a sudden it can be called long, but it is all short, life, and some very short indeed.[23] Well, then, there is no need of bothering about something that has an end, and much less so of life, for we are not sure of a single day; and considering that each day is our last one, who would not toil to make the most of it if he thought he would not live another?"

A good nun must learn to oppose her own will in everything, even in matters of the slightest importance. She may not succeed at first, but little by little, with the help of prayer, she can do so. All desire for possessions and for honor and preference, however slight, must be overcome. "God deliver us by His Passion from saying, 'I am her senior,' or 'I am older than she,' or 'I have done more work,' or 'They treat so-and-so better.' Such weaknesses must be attacked instantly, in their very first movements. If a Prioress allows anything of the kind, let them believe that God has permitted it on account of their sins, to begin their ruin."[24] However, Teresa does not believe the devil will long tempt a truly humble heart. If a nun is troubled in this way, let her tell the Prioress and ask for some "very low office" or busy herself in something that will break her own will.

"God deliver us from anybody who wishes to serve Him, and thinks about her own dignity and fears to be disgraced. . . . No

---

[22] *Ibid.*, cap. XVI, pp. 244–245.
[23] *"Mas toda es corta la vida, y algunas cortisimas." Ibid.*, cap. XVII.
[24] Escorial, cap. XVII, p. 247.

poison in the world so slays perfection as these things do. You may say that these are little things that are nothing at all, that they are not worth noticing. Don't fool yourself with this, for it increases in monasteries like foam, and there is nothing trifling in so notable a danger. Do you know why? Because perhaps it commences in you in some little thing that is almost nothing, and then the devil manages to make it appear much to somebody else, who may even think it charity to ask you how you can tolerate such an affront, and may God give you patience, and you should offer it up to God, and a saint could endure no more. He puts a flute on her tongue[25] which, although you could not have less to endure, makes you tempted even to vainglory, by saying it is a great deal. And this our nature is so utterly weak that even when we get rid of the temptation by saying it is nothing, we feel it all the more on seeing that others feel it for us. It makes our pain increase to think that we are right, and the soul loses all the occasions it had to merit, and remains so weak that the devil may come another day with something worse; and it even happens sometimes, that although *you* don't wish to feel it, they say, 'Are you a beast? for it is right to resent such things.' "

Teresa ended this vigorous passage with the exclamation, *"u, que si ay alguna amiga!"*[26] which she amplified in recopying: "Oh, for the love of God, my sisters, may none of you be prompted by indiscreet charity to show sympathy for another in a matter touching on these pretended insults, for it is like that which the friends of holy Job offered him, and his wife too. . . ."[27]

"I have often told you, and now I write it here, that you in this house, and every perfect person, should fly a thousand leagues from 'I was right,' 'They had no right to do it to me,' 'My sister was not right.' From wrong rights may God deliver us! Do you think it was right for Christ our Good to suffer so many injuries, and for them to be done, and so many unrightful things? She who does not wish to carry a cross, except the one they have a good right to give her — I don't know why she is in a monastery; let her go back to the world where they are not particular about these rights. Perhaps you may have suffered

---

[25] The picturesque idiom *"pone un caramillo en la lengua"* means a little more than this; *caramillo* signifies a flageolet or small flute, but also a deceit or a trick. Escorial, cap. XVIII, p. 249.

[26] Escorial, *loc. cit.*

[27] Valladolid, cap. XII, p. 62.

so much that you ought not to suffer any more? What right is this? I certainly don't understand it. When they give us some honor or enjoyment or good treatment, bring out these rights, for surely it is against right that they give them to us in this life; but when they give us injuries — for so they are called even when they do not injure us — I don't know what there is to talk about. Either we are spouses of so great a King, or no. If we are, what honorable woman is there who does not feel in her soul the dishonor they do to her husband? And even although she may not like to feel this, in short they share honor and dishonor together. To wish to share then in the kingdom of our Spouse and to be His companions in His joy, and yet to remain without any part in His ignominies and His trials, is nonsense. . . .

"Oh, what a very great charity it would be, and what a great service to God, if the nun who sees that she cannot endure the perfections and customs there are in this house, would acknowledge it and take herself off, and leave the others in peace! Nor will all the other monasteries (at least if they believe me) cherish her or grant her profession until she has been on probation for several years to see if they can improve her. I don't mean faults in penance and fasting, for, although they are faults, they are things that do not do such damage; but I mean certain dispositions to be esteemed and respected by friends, and to note the faults of others and never recognize their own, and other similar things, which truly are born of little humility, and if God does not favor her with more spiritual strength until in the course of many years she amends, may He deliver you from having her remain among you. Be sure that she will not be at peace herself or let all the rest of you be at peace."[28]

The primitive rule had called for a year's novitiate. Madre Teresa prolonged this sometimes to four years (in the case, for example, of María de San José, sister of her chaplain, Father Julián de Avila). Even if this were extended to ten years, the humble nun, she said, would not complain, knowing that if she were worthy she would not be sent away; and if she were not, "why should she wish to do harm to this college of Christ?"[29] She advised her daughters to inquire into the motives of those who wish to join them. They must not allow anyone to come merely to find a home — though even that defect might be al-

[28] Escorial, cap. XIX, p. 251.
[29] Ibid., cap. XX, p. 253.

lowed if the candidate had a good understanding; if not, by no means accept her. God would protect the Prioress from error, unless she allowed herself to be swayed by human respect or mere etiquette.[30]

At one point Teresa was interrupted for several days, and resumed thus:

"What a confused thing I am writing! quite like one who doesn't know what he is doing. It is your fault, sisters, for you bade me do it. Read it if you can, for I have written it as I can, and if not, burn it *por mal que va*. It takes leisure, and I have so little time, as you see, that I haven't written anything for eight days, and so I have forgotten what I said, and even what I was going to say.[31] Now look what I have done![32] And I ask you not to do what I have just done, that is, to make excuses for myself; not to do it, I see, is a most perfect custom and of great edification and merit, and I have even taught it to you many times, and by the goodness of God you do it, but His Majesty has never given it to me. May it please Him to give it to me before I die."[33]

From this tactful beginning she goes on to warn them seriously against making excuses for themselves, unless offense or scandal will result from not telling the truth. A truly humble person should be glad to be despised, persecuted, misunderstood, and condemned, even without just cause; for in what better way could she follow Christ, Who was innocent but bore every injustice in silence? Without this practice in humility, it is impossible to reach the summit of perfection. If we are not guilty of a particular fault of which we are accused, we certainly are guilty of others, and we can accept the reproof in atonement for them. Little by little one can thus obtain such liberty of spirit that one can hear oneself ill spoken of with no more concern than if a third person were being discussed.

All that she has thus far written, she explains, is but setting up the pieces on the board for a game of chess: now the real game is to begin. "You must scold me for speaking of a game when we don't have it in this house and ought not. Here you see the sort of mother God gives you; she knows even this vanity! Yet

---

[30] I have quoted this part more fully above, Chapter XVI.

[31] Escorial, cap. XXII, p. 257.

[32] "*Que aora será mal de mí*" seems to have this force; a more literal translation makes little sense.

[33] *Ibid.*

they say it is sometimes permissible." Their game is to checkmate a divine King, and the Queen who will most quickly do
that is humility.

Having thus set up the board, Teresa vigorously comes to
grips, in the next chapters, with the real theme of the book,
which is contemplation. Let them not believe that this means
meditation.[34] Meditation is only a step, and one that all Christians must begin with; but contemplation is quite another thing.
For true contemplation, mental prayer is necessary, and this
demands a striving for the highest virtues. Sometimes God shows
great favors to people whose souls are in an evil state (she is
not thinking here of people in the state of mortal sin), and even
grants them visions; but she cannot believe He would raise
them to contemplation; "for in that divine union, in which
the Lord delights Himself with the soul and the soul with Him,
there is no way for a filthy soul to enjoy the purity of the heavens,
and for the joy of the angels to delight in what is not His."

Yet God sees that he can attract certain souls, still imperfect;
and to such He sometimes grants contemplation, though for a
short time and rarely. They must prepare themselves to enjoy
Him more often. Many, in fact, are called to contemplation, and
only a few respond. Those who do not are left to mental
prayer — these are the servants in His vineyard; but those who
do are His beloved children, and He seats them at His own
table, feeds them, and "even takes food out of His own mouth
to give them." These are safe in His arms. What does it matter
if the world blames and abuses them? He will never permit
them to be spoken against unless for their own greater good.
Why should Christians look anywhere else except to Christ, the
Way? It is not Christian to be wounded over some little point
of honor. Seek nothing less than perfection. "God deliver you,

---

[34] Perhaps Teresa had in mind here the Jesuit "discursive" meditation, which
Saint Ignatius in his Spiritual Exercises called "contemplation," but not in the
sense in which she uses that term. Saint Ignatius seems to use the words *meditate*
and *contemplate* interchangeably. In his second preliminary annotation he speaks
of *"la persona que da á otro modo y orden para meditar ó contemplar,"* etc.
Father Joseph Rickaby, S.J., explains that "we meditate a truth; we contemplate
a scene in our Lord's life" (*The Spiritual Exercises*, New York, 1923, p. 14). "Saint
Ignatius uses the word *contemplation* in quite another sense than Saint John of
the Cross and other mystical writers," says Father Rickaby (*ibid.*, p. 89). "Ignatian
contemplation is not a form of the Higher Prayer: it is what an artist would
call a study of a scene in our Lord's life. We may call such contemplation a
mind painting."

sisters, from saying, when you have done something that is not perfect, 'We are not angels, we are not saints.' Though we are not, it is the greatest help to believe that with God's aid we can be. This sort of presumption I want to see in this house, for it makes humility increase; always have courage, for God gives it to the strong and is no respecter of persons, and He will give it to you and to me."[35]

All nuns, as we have seen, need not be contemplatives. The one who achieves perfection without it may have greater merit, for she has to work harder, and the Lord is treating her like a valiant woman, and is saving for her all she does not enjoy in this life. Let her have courage and continue her mental prayer. One old nun of La Madre's acquaintance could never even attain to mental prayer; the best she could do was to pause a little between the *Ave Maria* and the *Pater Noster* in saying her rosary; yet she was very holy. In a way such souls are safer, for we cannot tell whether spiritual delights come from God or from the devil. If they are not divine, they are a dangerous trap of Satan to incite pride. Nor is it for each one to choose whether she will be a Mary or a Martha. "Let the Lord of the house do that, He is wise, He is powerful, He understands what is suitable for you and what is suitable for Him also." It is well the decision does not rest with us, she adds — we should all become great contemplatives,[36] and there would be no Marthas!

Contemplation is rarely if ever granted without suffering. And if a contemplative is not valiant by nature, the first thing the Lord gives him is courage. "I know that the trials God gives to contemplatives are intolerable; and they are of such a kind that without that food of delight, they could not endure them." He gives the hardest crosses to His favorites. Their way is so steep and rugged that they sometimes imagine they have lost the road and must go back and start over. Then He must refresh them. He gives wine, for water would not be enough; and inebriated with this cup, they forget their sufferings. We must be like good soldiers, not hirelings. The contemplatives are the standard-bearers; they don't fight, but they are exposed to danger like those who do and must hold aloft the standard even if they are cut to pieces, as Christ bore the cross.

"There are persons, it seems, who are ready to ask God for

---

[35] Escorial, cap. XXVI, p. 264.
[36] *Ibid.*, cap. XXVIII, p. 267.

favors as a matter of justice. A fine sort of humility! Hence He Who knows all does well in giving it to them hardly ever; He sees plainly they are not fit to drink the chalice." The best sign of improvement is not rapture, ecstasy, sweetness in prayer — the true value of these will not be known until the next life — but *thinking oneself the most wicked of all;* "this is money that is in circulation, it is revenue that does not fail, these are perpetual annuities." Obedience, she repeats, is essential; without it no one can reach contemplation, or even succeed in the active religious life. To be safe, one must have an experienced confessor, and submit the will utterly to his.

Mental prayer is the way to the living water of contemplative delight; and here Teresa returns with gusto to the figure that had delighted her in childhood. One taste of it, and there is literally no more thirst for the things of this world. Its craving for the next life is stronger than any natural thirst. Water in this world chills, it cleanses, and it quenches thirst. But the water God gives frees the drinker from slavery to material things, cleanses her of all sins, and gives her mastery over the globe and its elements; thus fire and water obeyed Saint Martin, the birds and fishes were subject to Saint Francis. And unlike earthly water, which quenches thirst, this divine cup increases supernatural desire until nature can bear it no more.

"Men have died from this," wrote Teresa with almost prophetic insight, adding, in reference to herself, "I know of one who, if God had not come to her aid instantly with this living water in the very greatest abundance with her raptures, had this thirst so acutely and felt her desire increase so much that she understood clearly that it was quite possible, if unaided, to die of thirst."[37]

God, having no imperfection, never gives this water in excess. It is always wrong to wish for it, and Teresa advises anyone who has an inordinate love for it to be very cautious, lest she be tempted to go beyond reason, and find her health impaired. It is even wise to moderate one's longings. The devil may play a part in these vehement desires that seem almost to drive some imprudent contemplatives mad. Inspirations from heaven always bring prudence, light, and moderation.

There is nothing vague or moonshiny about the mysticism of Saint Teresa. If she walks with her head among the stars, her

---

[37] Escorial, cap. XXXI, pp. 273-274.

feet are always on solid ground, and she is always returning to first principles, to the concrete and the factual, to the real and the visible. Thus, before leading her daughters to the mental prayer which may open infinite vistas of contemplation, she directs their attention to what is very much like an Ignatian meditation. They are to keep Christ near them, to look at Him, to see Him as He was and is. He will accommodate Himself to their mood, asking only for their love. If they are happy, let them think of the Resurrection; if they are sorrowful or beset by trials, consider Him on the way to Gethsemani. Or "watch Him at the column full of pains, all His flesh torn to pieces for the great love He has for you: persecuted by some, spit upon by others, denied by others, without friends, with no one to stand up for Him, stiffened with cold, left in such loneliness . . . And look at Him in the Garden, and on the Cross, and burdened with it, so that they won't even let Him draw His breath; look at Him with His eyes so beautiful and compassionate full of tears, and He will forget His pains to console you for yours. . . . O Lord of the world and my true spouse! . . . If You are willing to suffer everything for me, what is this that I suffer? Of what am I complaining? . . . Let us go together, Lord; wherever You go, I will go, and where You suffer, I will suffer. Daughter, take up that cross. Never mind if the Jews trample on you, pay no attention to what they say to you, make yourselves deaf to murmurings, stumbling, falling with your Spouse — but do not forsake the cross."[38]

With a firm grasp of the central, the *crucial* fact of the world history, the Christian mystic is now ready to set out on the journey to the living water promised by our Lord. Let her pay no attention to those who will warn her of the risks, saying, "There are dangers," "Such a one was lost through this," "The other one, who took to mental prayer, fell," "They injure virtue," "It is not for women, for it brings illusions to them," "It will be better for them to spin," "They don't need these niceties," "The *Pater Noster* and the *Ave Maria* are enough."

Teresa boldly takes up the challenge here flung down by saying promptly that the *Lord's Prayer* and the *Hail Mary* are indeed enough. Nuns do well to found their prayer on the one

---

[38] Instead of the word *cross*, Teresa made the sign here on the manuscript. — Escorial, cap. XIII, p. 294.

that fell from the lips of Christ. There are, however, a few preliminary cautions to be taken:

The first thing is to have in mind Whom you are speaking to, how infinitely great and at the same time how loving and humble He is. We take enough pains to remember who the magnates of this world are when we approach them; we learn who their parents were, and how much income they have, what their titles are, and "there is nothing more to know; for here no account is taken of the persons, however much they deserve, but only of their property.

"O miserable world! Praise God much, daughters, that you have left a thing so corrupt, where they don't pay attention to what people have in themselves, but only to what their tenants and vassals have for them. This is a fine thing to amuse yourselves with in the recreation hour, for it is good sport to remember in what blindness those of the world pass their time. O King of glory, Lord of lords, Emperor of emperors, Saint of the saints, Power above all the powers, Knowledge above all the knowledges, Wisdom itself; You, Lord, are truth itself, riches themselves, do You never cease forever to reign!"[39]

Teresa bridges over the gap between mental prayer and vocal prayer, which has puzzled so many beginners, by saying, in effect, that when the terms are properly understood, they are one and the same thing. When vocal prayer is properly said — with understanding of what we are doing and with complete sincerity — and these are best attained in solitude — it becomes mental prayer. What is mental prayer, then? It is "to think and to understand what we are saying, and with Whom we speak, and who we are who dare to talk with so great a Lord. To think this and other similar things, of how little we have served Him and how much we ought to serve Him, is mental prayer; do not think it is some Arabic jargon, or be afraid of the name. To recite the *Pater Noster* or what you will is vocal prayer, but see what bad music it will be without the former — even the words won't go together sometimes!"[40]

Thus we ourselves, by our own will and determination, can make all our vocal prayer into mental prayer. Contemplation of course is a different matter; it is a gift, she repeats, and must not even be asked for. Yet "it will be possible that while you

---

[39] Escorial, cap. XXXVIII, p. 285.
[40] *Ibid.*, cap. XII, p. 292.

are reciting the *Pater Noster,* God may put you in perfect contemplation, if you recite it well. And in these ways He shows that He hears what you are saying to Him, and His Majesty speaks to you, suspending the understanding and making the thoughts[41] to cease, and taking, as they say, the word out of your mouth, so that you cannot speak, unless with great pain, even if you wish. You understand that without the noise of words the Master is working in your soul, and that her faculties are not at work, and yet she understands. This is perfect contemplation."

The book concludes with the long, glowing, beautiful, inspired meditation on how to say the *Lord's Prayer,* which is the climax and crown of this delightful book. She intended to apply the same method to the *Ave Maria,* but was not permitted to do so; however, she consoled herself with the thought that whoever could say the one could say the other by the same method. Each phrase in the divine prayer becomes the topic of a chapter — indeed, as she remarked, she could have written a long book on the subject without beginning to exhaust it. More than most of her work, it defies quotation and fragmentary citation; and lacking space to give it in full, I must refer the English-speaking reader to the Stanbrook Abbey translation,[42] and content myself with mentioning one or two choice paragraphs. There is, for example, the one on snobbery:

"So goes the world that if the father is of lower station than the son, in two words he will not recognize him for father. This does not happen here, for in this house never, please God, let there be any memory of such things, that would be hell; but she who was greater, let her have her father less in her mouth; all must be equal. O college of Christ! in which Saint Peter, although a fisherman — and so the Lord wished it — had more

---

[41] *Ibid.* The word *thought* — *pensamiento* — is used in an especial sense by the mystics. It is "a deceptive knowledge which, without efficacy, or a determined end of its activity, goes wandering about through various parts. . . . Sometimes it proceeds from the intelligence, by means of species or representations of sensible and corporal things. In both forms it gives trouble enough to the soul." — P. Francisco de Santo Tomás, C.D., quoted by P. Silverio, edition of the *Camino,* p. 119, n. 1.

[42] *The Way of Perfection,* translated by the Benedictines of Stanbrook, etc., third edition, London, 1925. There is a new translation and adaptation of the *Pater Noster* alone by Father W. J. Doheny, C.S.C. (Milwaukee: The Bruce Co., 1942). This is authentic and is not to be confused with the so-called "Seven Meditations on the *Pater Noster,*" which obviously is not the work of Saint Teresa.

authority than Saint Bartholomew, who was son of a king! His
Majesty knew what a to-do would be made over who was of the
better dirt, which is nothing but to debate whether it is better
for mud or for adobe walls. Oh, God help me, what great blindness! God deliver you, sisters, from such discussions, even if they
be in fun, which I hope in His Majesty they will be, if any. And
when anything of this appears in anyone, do not let her stay
in the house, for she is Judas among the Apostles. . . . The good
Jesus gives you a good Father; let no other father be recognized
and spoken of here. . . ."[43]

Again she begs the nuns to realize the importance of the
words, "Thy will be done," and adds, "When I think of this, I
am amused at those who say it is not good to ask the Lord for
trials, for it is small humility. And I have met others so pusillanimous, that even without this refuge of humility, they have not
heart enough to ask for themselves what they think will be given
to them at once. I should like to ask them if they understand
this *will* which they ask the Lord may His Majesty have done in
them, or do they say it only to say what everyone says, but not
to do it; this, daughters, will be very bad. Notice that our good
Jesus seems our ambassador, and that He has wished to mediate
between us and His Father, and at no small cost to Himself;
and it will not be right that what He promises and offers for
us, we should fail to do in truth, and not merely say it. Look,
daughters, take my advice: His will is going to be done in
heaven and on earth, whether you like it or not; believe me
then, and make a virtue of necessity. . . ."[44]

God loves us and will never give us trials without also the
love and strength to bear them. "And I would have you understand with Whom you are dealing, as they say, and what the
good Jesus offers for us to the Father, and what you are giving
Him when you say, 'May His will be done in you,' for it is
nothing else. Don't be afraid, then, that it will be His will to
give you riches or delights or great honors or any of these things
of this world. He does not love you so little, and holds dearly
what you give Him, and wishes to pay you well for it, since He
gives you His kingdom even in this life, as they say. Well, do
you wish to see how He deals with those of whom they truly
say this? Ask His glorious Son about it, Who said it when He

---

[43] Escorial, cap. XIV, p. 299.
[44] *Ibid.*, cap. LIV, pp. 315–316.

made the prayer in the Garden. As it was said there with truth and with all His will, notice how well it was accomplished in what He gave Him of pains and trials and injuries and persecutions, in short, until He had finished His life in death on the cross."[45]

---

[45] *Ibid.*, p. 316.

Chapter XIX

"HAVE CONFIDENCE, I HAVE OVERCOME THE WORLD"

WHEN Teresa finished *The Way of Perfection* early in 1567 and sent it off to Father Báñez at the Dominican convent, she was fifty-two years old, though she looked younger. Her health being what it was, she could expect little more in this world (so little do even saints discern the future!) than time to teach her daughters how to translate what she had written into the harmony of discipline. With this in view, she became her own mistress of novices. It goes almost without saying that she was one of the most successful in the history of asceticism.

Analyzing this success, Father Ribera found that the secret of it was love: she loved them so much that they loved her in return. Her love was like the love of God, which considers not only the present moment, but all eternity. She went to great trouble to provide them with everything necessary for health and well-being, and was particularly anxious that the sick should lack nothing. She wanted them all to be joyful, as she was. (Had she not urged them in the *Camino* to be affable to all persons, that the religious vocation might be esteemed?) When she had to reprehend anyone, she was so grave and impersonal that the culprit felt no irritation, but only gratitude and sorrow. Some little faults she passed over in silence, others she dealt with affectionately, still others with severity, according to the disposition and needs of each nun. When asked why she was sometimes rigorous with a certain sister who was so good and loved her so much, she replied that she understood all that, but that the nature of the woman required such treatment occasionally. Generally she was lenient to the humble and the obedient, but very rigorous with those of contrary mind. Once she had reprehended anyone, she became "joyous and agreeable" when she saw that the reproof was taken in the right spirit.[1]

Like other saints, she had a gift for the discernment of spirits. Ribera tells of a novice who had the votes of the whole com-

---

[1] Ribera, *Vida de Santa Teresa*, lib. IX, cap. XXIV.

munity and seemed in every respect suitable for the Carmelite life. One day La Madre said to her, unexpectedly,

"You will make your profession tomorrow."

"I will wait for my mother," said the startled novice, "if your Reverence commands."

"You will not make your profession in this Order, I tell you," replied Madre Teresa; and no beseeching on the part of the novice or the nuns could make her change her mind. The candidate went home, became ill of "galloping consumption," and died in a few days.

Sometimes she rejected novices for no apparent reason. There was one who, as the time of her profession approached, seemed almost flawless to the nuns; but La Madre dismissed her. When the nuns begged her to change her decision, she refused, alleging that the girl had some physical defect. This did not seem sufficient to the members of the community; they privately agreed, therefore, that she must have had some communication from God concerning the matter. Teresa sent one of her own nieces home to her father, no one knew just why, and resisted all the pressure of relatives for a reconsideration.[2]

Once she stopped abruptly in a discourse and said to a nun who seemed to be listening with all attention and humility, "You don't feel this inwardly." Again she divined a temptation a certain nun was having, without being told about it, and privately wrote her some advice concerning it. Nor was this prescience confined to the convent and to those who were under her eyes. Ribera tells of a "certain rustic man" whom the public generally, and even some learned men, considered a saint. For some reason, probably on the advice of some friend, he went to see La Madre to give her an account of his spirit and of the things he said God told him. Teresa saw at once that his spirit was "not good." She told this to her confessor, but for the sake of charity would not say it to others; instead, she sent the *beato* to certain experienced directors of souls who would "exercise him in bodily labor and in obedience." The holy man refused to submit to this. Not long afterward it became apparent to everyone, says Ribera, that "he was all vanity and madness."[3]

There was a Cistercian nun who seemed very saintly. She fasted so much and took so many disciplines that she became quite weak. Whenever she received Holy Communion or felt

---

[2] *Ibid.*   [3] *Ibid.*, cap. XXV.

some extraordinary impulse of devotion, she would fall on the floor and remain there sometimes for eight or nine hours in what people thought was an ecstasy. The fame of this went through the countryside; but when Madre Teresa was consulted by the nun's confessor, she told him promptly that it was all nonsense: the so-called trances were not true raptures, but came from sheer physical weakness; let him have his mystic stop fasting and using the scourge for a while and he would see what it amounted to. He did so, and the nun, recovering her strength, had no more raptures. Had they been real, they would have continued regardless of her physical condition.[4]

Another confessor told her of a holy woman, a penitent of his, whom our Lady had visited several times, sitting on her bed and speaking to her for more than an hour, in the course of which she revealed to her many things that were to come. Teresa knew that the visions were but delusions, but all she said was, "I will wait and see whether these prophecies come true." None of them ever did.[5]

In one of the Carmelite convents there were two contemplatives, a choir nun, and a lay sister, who had been raised to a very high state of prayer, but in the opinion of La Madre had fallen into a subtle and dangerous temptation. They were beginning to enjoy the sensible sweetnesses of prayer for the sake of the gratification it brought to them, rather than for the love of God, and they both became convinced that if they did not receive the Blessed Eucharist every day they would die. La Madre's cure for this was to suggest that they break their will by giving up Communion for a while. When she saw that they were not inclined to accept this advice, she was more convinced than ever that Satan had a hand in the business, and she insisted. Finally, to give them courage to make the start, she said that she, too, would deny herself Communion the next day.

"But I will die!" protested one or the other.

"Very well, then," said La Madre, "we will all three die together."

The experiment was tried, and with no casualties.[6]

One of the causes of the scandals of the sixteenth century had been the penetration of convents by persons without true vocations. Martin Luther was driven into a monastery by fear. Others

---

[4] Teresa tells this: *Fundaciones*, cap. VI.
[5] Ribera, *loc. cit.*   [6] *Fundaciones*, cap. VI.

entered to gain peace or security, or for some other motive of self-interest. Many such persons, observed Ribera, "enter because they do not have the means with which to marry, or cannot live in the world with the prestige and comfort they desire, and either the vain honor of the world attracts them or the fear of dishonor or labors, rather than the love of God; and if this is so, they are not called by God." It was seldom that such a wolf in sheep's clothing got past the wary eye of Madre Teresa. If she suspected anything of the sort, no amount of wealth or nobility or family connections could keep her from declining or expelling the candidate. "O woman, more than woman!" exclaims her Jesuit biographer. "Valiant woman, made according to the heart of God, renovator of the old age of religion, perfect pattern of sanctity, true despiser of the world and all its shams, lover of God! . . ."[7]

With such a prioress, surrounded by master spirits of her own choosing, the little convent of San José was indeed, as she wrote of it, "a paradise on earth," whose very sufferings had more joy in them than the pleasures of the outside world. Nothing was too difficult for these brave souls, if they were doing the will of God. Teresa delighted in testing them for the necessary virtues, particularly the fundamental one of obedience. One day when there was nothing for dinner except a few cucumbers that had been brought by some charitable soul, it happened that the one placed on her plate was very small and all rotten within. Pretending not to notice this, she called Sister María Bautista, and said,

"I don't feel like eating. Go and plant this in the garden."

"Shall I plant it up and down or sideways, Reverend Mother?"

"Sideways," said the La Madre seriously. It amused her later to record that María Bautista accepted the charge in the same spirit: "She went and planted it; it never occurred to her that it could not possibly fail to decay. The fact that she was acting under obedience made her natural reason blind (in the service of Christ) so that she believed that what she did was perfectly right."[8]

To another nun she assigned six or seven different tasks, all of which could not possibly have been done; but the nun obediently went to work without a murmur.

---

[7] Ribera, *op. cit.*, lib. IV, *prólogo*.

[8] *Fundaciones*, cap. I. The words, "in the service of Christ," were written in between the lines by Father Gracián.

One day Sister Ursula de los Santos, feeling unusually well and happy, was stopped in the cloister in the presence of all the other nuns by La Madre, who with a look of concern took her pulse, felt her forehead, and told her, in tones of great sympathy, to go to bed at once. Sister Ursula quietly obeyed. La Madre sent some of the others to visit her and to ask how she was.

"Very sick," said Ursula.

"What ails you? Where do you feel ill?"

"I don't know, sisters. La Madre says so."

Presently Teresa herself entered the cell, and going to the bedside took the nun's hands in hers. Counting her pulse again with every appearance of concern, she said,

"*Ay, pobre de mi hermana!* Tell them to send for the barber to come and bleed her!"

The barber-surgeon arrived and began to make his preparations. La Madre, drawing him aside, instructed him to bleed the patient only a little, not enough to hurt her. This he proceeded to do. Sister Ursula meanwhile never expressed the slightest surprise or disapproval; perhaps she even agreed that she felt better after the departure of the *barbero*. From that day on, the Saint cherished a particular and tender affection for this nun.

One day, according to Yepes, they had nothing to eat but the leaves of a vine that grew in the garden, but all ate with the greatest contentment. "All that was not God," he adds, "was bitter to them."[9]

So joyously did these women walk the road of mortification that they sometimes got a step or two ahead of the Saint herself. Sister María Bautista heard, for example, that the new Pope, Saint Pius V, wore next to his skin, as a penance, a garment of a very rough sackcloth, known as horsecloth — "which is only a hair shirt," observes Yepes, "in its harshness and its effects." Why not let the Discalced Carmelites wear tunics of this material instead of the coarse wool serge they now had next to their flesh? It would be only a little penance. She spoke to another nun, who agreed with her, and the two went to Madre Teresa, who took the suggestion under consideration and decided to try it out first on herself. Accordingly she put on a tunic of horsecloth; and finding it endurable, gave her permission to the rest.

All went well until the weather grew warm. Then they were

---

[9] Yepes, *Vida de Santa Teresa,* lib. II, cap. XII.

confronted with a difficulty they had not foreseen: horsecloth, it seemed, was a favorite habitation of lice. And a lice-infected household devoted to mental prayer and contemplation is a contradiction in terms. Finally the situation became so intolerable that while La Madre was at prayer one night in the chapel after Matins, between ten and eleven o'clock, the nuns formed a procession, at the head of which they bore a crucifix, and went through the house with burning candles in their hands, singing hymns and psalms, alternated with a stanza composed by one of their number.

Filing into the choir, they prostrated themselves before the Blessed Sacrament, imploring the Lord to deliver them from the unwelcome visitors. La Madre was so touched by their faith that she amplified the verse into chants and responses and joined in the procession and the prayers. She would answer their plea with encouraging words, as follows:

Nuns:
> Since You give us new array,
> O heavenly King,
> Free this serge from denizens
> So threatening.

La Madre:
> Daughters, since you take the cross,
> Be stout of heart,
> And ask of Jesus, Light of yours,
> To take your part.
> He will defend you surely
> In such a thing!

Nuns:
> Free this serge from denizens
> So threatening!

La Madre:
> Ill boots it to be not at ease
> In mental prayer;
> Devotion when the spirit flees
> Is very rare.
> But let your unaffrighted hearts
> To God fast cling.

Nuns:
Free this serge from denizens
So threatening!

La Madre:
Since you have come that you may die,
Be not dismayed,
And do not let such scurvy knaves
Make you afraid.
In all this trouble God will aid
Your suffering.

All:
Since You have given us new array,
O heavenly King,
Free this serge from denizens
So threatening![10]

Not only did the lice disappear from the tunics, but from that time to this the Discalced Carmelite convents have been

---

[10] I have tried to indicate in this rough translation the meter and rhyme scheme Teresa used. "Yours" in the second stanza should have rimed with "cross." In the sixth "scurvy knaves" is not an ideal rendering of *gente tan cevil*, but it must serve for want of a better. La Madre meant "civil," which in modern Spanish means "courteous," but in her day sometimes had the opposite significance, namely, "churlish," "of low origin," etc. The Spanish text, as given in B.M.C., I. VI, p. 117, follows:

Nuns:
Pues nos dáis vestido nuevo,
  Rey celestial,
Librad de la mala gente
  Este sayal.

Saint Teresa:
Hijas, pues tomáis la cruz,
  Tened valor,
Y a Jesús, que es vuestra luz,
  Pedid favor.
El os será defensor
  En trance tal.

Nuns:
Librad de la mala gente
  Este sayal.

Saint Teresa:
Inquieta este mal ganado
  En oración,

El ánimo mal fundado,
  En devoción;
Mas en Dios el corazón
  Tened igual.

Nuns:
Librad de la mala gente
  Este sayal.

Saint Teresa:
Pues vinisteis a morir
  No desmayéis,
Y de gente tan cevil
  No temeréis.
Remedio en Dios hallaréis
  En tanto mal.

All:
Pues nos dáis vestido nuevo,
  Rey celestial,
Librad de la mala gente
  Este sayal.

free from all manner of pedicular intrusion. Ribera says he went to great pains to verify this. He had heard of bugs in only one house, where some nuns of another order stopped for a few days, leaving in the beds a few unwelcome visitors, which, however, departed when they did. If now and then a novice was found with an insect on her clothing, it was taken to be a sure sign that she had not a vocation to be a Carmelite. The crucifix carried in the procession against the lice is still shown at San José, and venerated as the *Cristo de los piojos*.[11]

So the house grew and prospered, now with the addition of a wing, now with a new hermitage in the garden; while vocations became so numerous that La Madre did not know what to say to the excellent candidates who presented themselves. This troubled her not a little. It seemed to her a strange thing that when the world was so much in need of prayers of contemplatives, and when so many were eager to enter under the Primitive Rule, there should be no way to set them to work in an ordered community; for nothing could prevail on her to have more than thirteen at San José. Obviously there was need for a second foundation. But how was this possible? It was difficult enough to maintain one; and what if San José should fail? Teresa wept all the more for the crimes of the northern Protestants and the loss of their souls, and offered her prayers and mortifications for them, thinking, according to Yepes, that the world had sunk to its lowest possible state.[12]

One day in 1566, when the prospect seemed blackest, she had an unexpected visit from a Franciscan, Fray Alonso Maldonado, who had just come back from America, where he had been commissary general of his order. It may be that he brought her news from her brothers — Lorenzo, at least, sent her messages now and then by returning travelers — but Teresa recorded only the part of the visit that made the deepest impression on her.

Fray Alonso, a very learned and holy man, consented to speak to the whole community on what he had seen in the New World; he described it vividly, and dwelt particularly on what they were most curious about, the inhabitants of that inconceivable vastness. He told them that millions and millions of human beings, redeemed by the blood of Christ, dwelt there in a most

---

[11] Ribera, *op. cit.*, lib. IV, cap. XVIII; Yepes, *op. cit.*, lib. II, cap. XII; *Reforma de los Descalzos*, vol. II, lib. VI, cap. XXIII.

[12] Yepes, *op. cit.*, lib. II, cap. XIII.

vile degraded state, often worse than that of beasts, and died, most of them, without knowing that the Son of God had laid down his life for them on the Cross. Think of it — men, women, and children, our brothers and sisters, dying in their sins, and no one to teach them the truth, no one to pray for them. Well, then, this was something the nuns of San José could do and must do. They could offer their sacrifices for the souls of those poor wretches, and beg God to send them apostles.

When he had finished and had given them his blessing and gone away, Teresa sat almost stunned with grief. Then she went, weeping bitterly, to one of the hermitages, perhaps the one where Christ stood at the column, and "I called out to our Lord, begging Him to give me some way to gain some soul for His service, since the devil was carrying away so many, and that my prayer might accomplish something, since I could do nothing else. I had great envy of those who could employ themselves in this work for love of our Lord, even though they might suffer a thousand deaths. And so it befell me that when we read in the lives of the saints that they converted souls, it gives me much more devotion and more tenderness and envy than all the martyrdoms they suffer, because this is the bent our Lord has given me: to think that one soul we gain for Him through His mercy, by our industry and prayer, is worth more than all the services we can render Him."[13]

One night, soon after this, she was praying for the same object when the Christ stood beside her and said, "Wait a little while, daughter, and you shall see great things." She was not to understand for many months what these words meant. Prayers are not always answered immediately, nor is time a thing of great moment to God. Teresa was not even to guess, so far as we know, that three centuries later the nuns of her Reform would pray in Boston, near the Atlantic, in Santa Clara, near the Pacific, and on the plains of Indiana. But God's promises are always kept, and she had not long to wait to discover what the first of the "great things" would be.

There was no little stir at San José one day in April, 1567, when the news came that the Father General of the whole Carmelite Order had arrived at Ávila on his mule, with his inseparable assistant, Maestro Bartholomew Ragusius; and the interest of all must have become intense when they were told that

---

[13] *Fundaciones*, cap. I.

Bishop Don Álvaro was going to bring him to inspect the convent. Even La Madre was in a flutter. She had heard that although he was just, he was very severe, and her humility led her to expect the worst. "I feared two things: one, that he would be displeased with me, and not knowing how things had come about, he would be right; the other, that he was going to order me back to the monastery of the Incarnation, which is of the mitigated rule, and this would be a discouragement to me for many reasons which I need not go into. One was enough: that I could not keep the rigor of the primitive rule there, with the number over 150. . . . When he arrived in Ávila, I contrived that he should come to San José."[14]

There was some reason, perhaps, for apprehension. The Very Reverend Father John the Baptist Rossi of Ravena (whom Spanish writers have always insisted on calling Rubeo) was the first General of his Order to visit Castilla, and he came on no ordinary mission. Noted as a theologian, a canonist, and a preacher since his student days at Padua, he had been summoned to Rome by Pope Paul III, had been elected General of the Carmelites at a Chapter General presided over by Saint Charles Borromeo in 1564, and finally, when Philip II had asked the Holy Father to send someone to Spain to make the Spanish monasteries carry out the provisions of the Council of Trent, he had been ordered to undertake that difficult and thankless labor. He disembarked near Tarragona in the spring of 1566, and proceeded at once to Madrid, where King Philip, who had done so much to make the Council possible, and was now setting a fine example to all Catholic rulers in accepting its consequences (even when politicians warned him of danger to his own prerogatives), received him with the honors accorded only to grandees, and sent him on his errand of reform with every evidence of august approval. Three months later, in September, 1566, Rubeo was in Sevilla, convoking a chapter of some two hundred Carmelite friars of Andalucía.

He proceeded with such severity that it was not long before cries of indignation were mounting to the southern stars, and speeding by letter and word of mouth to the court at Madrid. The Carmelites of Andalucía certainly needed reforming. Although many of the friars were exemplary, and not a few holy, there had been some bad scandals. Rubeo sternly condemned

---

[14] *Fundaciones*, cap. II.

some of the evildoers to the galleys, some to prison, some to exile. Apart from this, there had been a great relaxation in the observance of the rule regarding the vow of poverty. Little by little the friars had been allowed to acquire personal property, money, and sometimes benefices. Many had taken to wearing large ornamental buttons of metal on their shirts, sporting ruffles and collars, and adorning their caps with silk borders of green and yellow, and with colored cords and tassels. Some had flasks of rose water in their cells. Many had musical instruments — and not merely the organ and the harpsichord which were permitted to religious, but such proscribed and profane devices as the lyre (then a sort of mandolin), the *barbyton* or guitar, and another agent of contrapuntal joy called the *adjutum,* of whose exact nature there is some doubt. Rubeo was inexorable about such vanities.

Not content with denouncing them before the chapters he convoked, he would visit each monastery in a city and make a careful examination and cross-examination of every religious, with particular reference to personal property held in violation of the Rule and of the decrees of the Council. Those who possessed anything in private had to renounce it before a notary. A barber was summoned to shave off beards and to encircle heads with tonsures. The account books of the community were carefully scrutinized by one of the General's assistants. While this was going on, Maestro Ragusius made a tour of inspection, carrying with him a huge basket and a pair of scissors. He peered into every cell and cast an inquisitorial eye over the raiment of every friar. Wherever there was a silver or brass button on a shirt or other garment — snip, snip! — the scissors spoke sharply, and the offending object fell into the basket, together with bottles of perfumery, collars, ruffles, and all other abominations which represented, in the eyes of Father Rubeo, just so many compromises with the devil on the part of men who had solemnly vowed to give up all self-love and self-pampering. "This property does not belong to me, it is only for my use," was the only condition under which a Carmelite could have anything. The Father General ruled that a religious discovered in the possession of any goods in his own name at the time of death could not be buried as an ecclesiastic.[15]

---

[15] See the *Vie de Jean-Baptiste Rubeo de Ravenne* of Father Benedictus — Maria a S. Cruce (Zimmerman) — preface to his edition of Rubeo's *Regesta* (Rome, 1936), p. 15; and Father Bruno's *St. John of the Cross* (New York, 1936).

Philip II became aware of all this and much more during one of the most painful winters in his life. In the fall of 1566, when he had been ill a great deal, he had learned of the sacking of the beautiful Catholic churches of Antwerp by agents of the Calvinist synod headed by a Spanish Jew; and he had formed the momentous decision to send the Duke of Alba with an army to restore order in the Low Countries. Regarding himself as the successor of the great Hebrew kings and the anointed champion of the Church everywhere, he was exasperated more than he would ordinarily have been, perhaps, when he heard from the enemies of Father Rubeo that his austerities in Sevilla were unnecessary, tactless, and destructive of the harmony of the Church and of the Realm. Philip had expected a contribution to the unity of Spain, not a virtual revolution among the Carmelites of Andalucía. It was a far different reception, therefore, that awaited Rubeo on his return to Madrid in March, 1567. After seeking an audience with the king for several days in vain, he went to Valladolid, and thence, the second week in April, to Ávila, where he assembled the provincial chapter of Castile and prepared to make his customary inspections. Finally he went to San José.

La Madre found herself face to face on that historic day with a man of about sixty, quiet and self-contained, his face deeply lined under a scanty fringe of beard, and expressive of patience, sadness, and something akin to worry and perplexity; so much his portrait reveals. He had, too, a grave deliberate courtesy that enhanced the judgelike solemnity of his presence. Accustomed to forming accurate opinions of men and women, he looked into the clear black eyes of Teresa as if to read every secret of her soul, while she, with the deeper insight of a contemplative, calmly met the scrutiny, read his mind and soul in turn, and saw in him a friendly spirit. And this man who allowed himself no food but a few herbs and dried vegetables was not long in discovering that she was living the primitive life of Carmel that he himself lived despite the relaxation of his order. A note of kindness and sympathy came into the reserved voice. Teresa found it easier than she had expected to give him an account of her foundation, and indeed of her whole life. He understood, he approved. But how had it happened, he asked, that she had placed herself under the jurisdiction of the Bishop, when she was still a member of the community of the

Incarnation? Teresa explained about the Bull, and at his request, produced the document. Rubeo's keen eye took it all in. He handed it back with the remark that it was of no validity, since he had never been informed of it, nor had his consent been obtained. The Cardinal who had sent it in the name of Pope Pius IV had given her a defective document, and she and her nuns were still subject to his (Rubeo's) jurisdiction.[16] This Bull, it will be recalled, was the second Teresa had obtained. The first had said nothing of leaving the jurisdiction of the Order for that of the Bishop. The writer of the second Bull supposed that the first had done so, and that he was confirming the original permission.[17]

The truth of what the General said was apparent to Madre Teresa as soon as it was brought to her attention. She promptly acknowledged his authority and jurisdiction. The interview ended with his calling her *mia figlia,* and assuring her that her work would not be undone. During the remainder of his three weeks in Ávila, he made several other visits to San José, not by way of inspection, but to talk of spiritual matters, for he saw that she must be a saint.

During one of their conversations she told him of her desire to found other convents, and of the need of discalced friars of the primitive rule to direct the nuns. The first of these objects won his immediate approval. Just before he left Avila, he gave his permission for this by way of a "patent" in which he wrote:

"There is no good merchant or good laborer, or soldier, or scholar who does not take care, and watch, and employ solicitude and undertake great trials, to increase his house, his clothing, his reputation, and all his property. If such men do this, all the more is it demanded of those who serve God in acquiring property to build churches and monasteries and to accumulate all they can for the service of souls and the glory of the divine Majesty." For this reason, he went on to say, he considered the request of Madre Teresa "very religious and holy," and could not refuse to grant it. He gave her permission to take over houses, churches, sites, and other property in any part of Castilla, subject to his jurisdiction, on behalf of the Order. The

---

[16] Julián de Ávila, *Vida de Santa Teresa,* II, cap. VIII.

[17] Fr. Jerónimo de San José, *Historia del Carmen Descalzo,* pt. II, lib. V. cap. XVII. For further details on the misunderstanding that had arisen, see Mir, *Vida de Santa Teresa,* II, pp. 5–8; and Silverio, *Vida de Santa Teresa de Jesús,* III, pp. 146–147.

nuns were to wear brown serge and conform to the primitive rule. Their number was never to exceed twenty-five in any one monastery. Before taking possession of a house, they must first get the approval of the Ordinary (the Bishop or Archbishop) of the diocese; and each convent must include two nuns from the Incarnation. The document was dated April 27, 1567.[18] It was the day when the Duke of Alba left Cartagena to begin a long journey to the Low Countries, from which he would return a sick and broken man.

Teresa's second request (for leave to found a monastery of barefoot friars) was not so readily granted. The Father General knew how bitterly the reforms he had already made were resented by the friars of Castilla, and he felt, with prophetic insight, that this one might contain the seeds of infinite protest and dissension for the Order. Bishop Mendoza, at whose house he was a guest, interceded in vain for La Madre; Father Julian and all her other friends received the same answer, *Non possumus*. Finally the Father General left for Rome without giving them any encouragement. "I had conceived a great love for him," wrote Teresa, "and I seemed to be left in great helplessness."[19]

Perhaps the Bishop gave her a hint that Rubeo favored her project in his heart, and had refused only from fear of opposition. At all events, she wrote a letter which overtook him before he left the country, "putting before him the service he would do to our Lady, to whom he was very devoted. She must have been the one who managed it; for this letter came into his possession in Valencia, and from there he sent me permission for two monasteries to be founded. . . . O greatness of God! And how you show your power in giving boldness to an ant! And how truly, Lord of mine, it is not your fault that those who love You do not do great things, but our own cowardice and pusillanimity!"[20]

It was one thing to have permission, and another to act upon it. There were two reasons why she could not found a monastery of friars. First, she had no house for them, and secondly, she had not a man in prospect to put into such a house. Well, God had brought her thus far; was it like Him to desert her

[18] *Regesta*, pp. 44–45.
[19] *Fundaciones*, cap. II.
[20] *Ibid.*

now? She begged Him to send her just one man. Meanwhile she did have women who were eager to enter a second convent. She had no house for that, either, but she would find one. "Courage did not fail me, nor hope, for since the Lord had sent the one, He would give the other. Everything now seemed possible to me, and so I began to go to work."[21]

---

[21] *Ibid.*

The Very Reverend Father John the Baptist Rossi of Ravenna (called Father Rubeo in Spain), General of the Carmelite Order, who authorized several of Saint Teresa's foundations.

Chapter XX

MIDNIGHT CONQUEST OF MEDINA

H ER choice of Medina del Campo, seventy-five miles from
Ávila, for the second convent, was almost inevitable. If
the community was to exist only on alms, it must be in some
fairly populous town. One of the most prosperous cities in Spain,
with a population of about 16,000 (three hundred or more of
them nobles), Medina then boasted some 1240 streets, fourteen
plazas besides the spacious *Plaza Mayor,* one of the finest in
Spain; twenty-two parishes, two chapters with eighty priests, a
Jesuit college, eighteen convents, and nine hospitals. The principal source of its material greatness was the famous fair to which
merchants came four times a year from every corner of Europe.
There were displayed and sold the rich cloths of Ávila, Toro,
and Segovia, the silks of Valencia and Granada, the fine leathers
of Córdoba; tapestries of Flanders, wool from England, books
and objects of art from Italy, spices from the Indies by way of
Portugal. In the fairs of 1565, more than 150,000,000 *escudos*
were spent in the form of letters of exchange, and in the previous years the sum had been even greater. The ecclesiastical
jurisdiction was in the hand of an Abbot, free and exempt: and
the escutcheon of this proud and independent city, so typically
Castilian, bore the significant boast: *Ni el Rey officio, ni el Papa
beneficio.* All in all, it seemed clear that nuns living a Carmelite life there would not be allowed to starve. This, in turn,
would make it easier to obtain the approval of ecclesiastical authorities. Perhaps the decisive factor in Teresa's calculations was
that she had tried and loyal friends there, who would surely help
to overcome any local opposition. The Jesuits had recently established a college, and the rector was her former confessor, Father
Baltasar Alvarez.

"Being amidst all these cares I remembered how I had been
helped by the fathers of the Company, who were very well regarded in that place — in Medina — and with whom, as I have
already written concerning the first foundation, I had consulted
about my soul for many years, and for the great good they did
to it I always have a particular devotion to them."

She wrote of her plans, accordingly, to Father Alvarez, and "he and the rest said that they would do what they could in the matter, and so they did a great deal to obtain the permission of the people and the prelate, for since it was to be a monastery of poverty, there was difficulty everywhere. . . ."[1] She wrote also to the Carmelite prior, Fray Antonio Heredia, whom she had known in Ávila, asking him to buy her a house, but apparently without much effect.

The next step was to send the chaplain of San José, Father Julian of Ávila, to Medina to look for a place. This most gentle and lovable of men, who was to accompany her on so many journeys and to write her biography, was a protégé of the Maestro Gaspar Daza, and brother of one of the first nuns of the Reform, Sister María de San José. He had been rather wild as a young student at Santo Tomás. One night he returned home so late that he was afraid to face his irascible father, a cloth manufacturer of some means, and decided instead to run away and see the great world. Becoming homesick after a year or two in Sevilla, Córdoba, and other places, he mounted a mule one day in January and set out for the north. He had hardly left Sevilla when the beast threw him, and as he fell, the hilt of his sword was driven violently into his side. He lost consciousness, lying as if dead. After this reminder of the brevity of life, he resolved to become a priest, and on arriving at Ávila went to confession to Maestro Daza, who reconciled him with his father and placed his feet so firmly on the path he had chosen that he was ordained in 1558, and in due course, as we have seen, became chaplain to the nuns at San José. Twelve years younger than Madre Teresa, he was one of the first of her helpers. She knew his limitations: he was not gifted with initiative or executive ability, nor profundity of intellect, and she never even considered him as a Carmelite friar; but he would do faithfully what he was told to do, and he was loved by many for his charity, his patience, and a gentle whimsical sense of humor.

When Father Julian arrived in Medina after a dusty ride of seventy-five miles, the Jesuits received him with great kindness and promptly helped him (as did Fray Antonio the Carmelite prior) to obtain the permission of the Bishop's Provisor. "For, since the most of those fathers knew the Holy Mother, they said their say with right good will, understanding the good that God did to the people among whom she went to plant so good a seed

[1] *Fundaciones*, cap. III.

for the benefit of the souls they dealt with," wrote Father Julian. "For they well understood the mode of proceeding that she and her nuns of those houses had, and that La Madre was desirous of following in many ways, so far as women could, the constitutions and exercises of the Holy Company of Jesus, and so it pleased them that wherever the Company might be, there should be also a house of these discalced nuns; and they also liked to speak with them in particular, because there were always such good souls in these houses of discalced Carmelites, and very much given to prayer and mortification, and as they also dealt with the same, it seemed to them that they were being understood in their own language."[2] One of the Jesuits, Father Juan Hordóñez, testified at a public hearing that the discalced Carmelites "would be a good example for the people, and for reforming them and the other monasteries."[3] Also in Medina at that time, by a happy coincidence, was La Madre's old friend Father Báñez, who once more had the privilege of defending her; and we have it on his word that another Dominican, Fray Pedro Fernández, refuted the arguments of "a religious of a certain Order, a man of authority and a preacher," who "spoke much evil of the said Teresa of Jesus, comparing her to Magdalena de la Cruz, an impostor of times past in Córdoba."[4] Most of the witnesses, however, were on the side of La Madre, and the Provisor granted her request.

The next task of Father Julian was to obtain a house. He now learned that the Carmelite prior had been doubtful about the business when Teresa wrote him, but having been won over by Father Alvarez, had finally "bought" a house on the Calle de Santiago from a friend of his, a pious widow named Doña María Suárez, who lived in Fuente el Sol. In agreeing to sell she had taken his word for it that payment would be made by Madre Teresa in good time.

When Father Julian went to look at this building, he was shocked to find its walls falling into ruins, its *patio* strewn with debris, and the porch, which was to have been the chapel, opening upon the street. This place, surely, would never be fit for a convent by the fifteenth of August, the day on which Teresa had decided to make her foundation!

---

[2] *Vida de Santa Teresa de Jesús* (Madrid, 1881), pp. 249–257.

[3] *Declaraciones*, etc., in B.M.C., vol. V, p. 344.

[4] Silverio, *Vida de Santa Teresa de Jesús*, III, p. 186, note, from B.M.C., t. XVIII, pp. 10, 11.

Father Julian took it upon himself to search for another house. About fifteen days after his arrival in Medina he rented one near the monastery of the Augustinian fathers, for which he promised to pay the owner, Alonso Alvarez, 51,000 *maravedis* per year. In relating all this he naïvely observes that he knew perfectly well La Madre had not fifty-one *maravedis* in the world, let alone 51,000; but her sublime faith was contagious, and he was not aware of having taken any great risk when he hurried back to Ávila to report joyfully that he had obtained the very best house in Medina. Still, as another biographer remarks, the money was more certain to be paid than if she had it in the bank, for banks fail and are robbed, but God never deceives. Father Julian heard her say more than once, "Lord, this business is not mine, but yours; if you wish to do it, you can indeed, and if not, Your will be done."

With no means of paying even for her transportation to Medina, let alone the rent, Teresa proceeded to borrow 9000 reales in childlike confidence that God would send her the means of payment.[5] Now she had (as she supposed) a house, nuns to put in it, and money to get there. Why wait longer?

She had chosen with great care the six professed nuns to be the nucleus of the community. She would take two from San José — Sister María Bautista and Sister Ana de los Angeles, and four from the Incarnation — two sisters, who were cousins of her own (Inés de Jesús and Ana de la Encarnación), Teresa de Quesnada (de la Columna) and Isabel Arias, who became Isabel de la Cruz. These last two had not yet put on the habit of the Discalced, but they had gone to live at San José for a few days to get accustomed to the rule and to be ready for an early leave-taking. All other preparations, including the new habits, were completed during the first ten days of August. By an interesting coincidence, it was during those very days that Philip II was making ready for his long-deferred journey to the Low Countries — the journey that he suddenly and mysteriously abandoned on August 11, after all his luggage had been taken aboard ship.[6]

---

[5] Her faith was not disappointed. A young woman of Ávila, Isabel Fontecha, who had been rejected at San José because the number of nuns there was already thirteen, again came forward and asked to be permitted to enter at Medina. She was the first nun professed there; and her little dowry paid off the loan and part of the rent.

[6] This mystery and its possible explanations are discussed in my *Philip II*, pp. 423–424.

Not so Madre Teresa. On the twelfth, with all her plans made, she gave orders for setting out before daybreak on the morrow.

This was to be the first of a series of missionary excursions without parallel in history save perhaps the voyages of Saint Paul and the peregrinations of Saint Vincent Ferrer. Distance and difficulty were no obstacles to this heroic woman, who had been "dying" of heart trouble and other ailments for more than a quarter of a century, and now, at fifty-three, was only at the start of her active career. She was still a good horsewoman, and on occasion, as we shall see, could ride on a mule, or if necessary, walk any distance. In general she preferred to have her nuns travel in coaches, for the sake of conventual seclusion and recollection.[7] But more often they went in rude peasants' wagons — *carros* — that rattled and thumped and jolted at every rock or rut in the road. So it was, at any rate, on this first adventure. Like an expert general, La Madre disposed of her forces in three or four mule-drawn carts. In one of these she stowed the *impedimenta,* consisting of habits, holy pictures, hangings, articles for the chapel, and so on. In the others she distributed the nuns, all shielded from the gaze of onlookers by curtains stretched upon many poles, behind which they could recite their Office or the Rosary as they slowly jogged along under the mounting Castilian sun. Father Julian, like a marshal in clerical garb, rode alongside the conveyance of La Madre on a mule.

The *mozos* who drove the wagons went on foot, each with a knout thrust in his bright-colored sash. Now they would pass the time by singing, now they would talk in the customary lingo of muleteers, punctuated with oaths and obscenities. This was a sore trial to La Madre. It did not take her long to tell them her opinion of their language, and to beg them for the love of God not to use such words. Nor did she let the matter rest there. Born teacher that she was, she understood the importance of positive as well as negative instruction. It was not long before she began to chat with them, to tell them stories; and although they could not see her lovely face (for like the others she wore a

---

[7] "And for the sake of greater recollection and enclosure, she wanted them always to go in coaches or litters, as decently as they could, so that on the road and in the inns they should not make little account of the nuns, and should not dare to speak words which are commonly said coarsely to other women, seeing them poor and with little authority, and for this reason she desired that outwardly they go as women of importance." — Ribera, *Vida de Santa Teresa,* lib. II, cap. XVIII. Later she changed this policy, for fear of giving scandal.

black veil), they were fascinated by the music of her clear feminine voice, and presently they were all ranged on either side of her cart, listening with rapt enjoyment to stories of God and His wonders and the high adventures of His saints. Soon they had left off swearing and blaspheming. Next, at a hint from her, they would keep silence while the nuns were at prayer. What a power of love was in this woman, to hush the tongue of a Castilian muleteer! Afterwards she never forgot to reward the "boys" with something to eat that she had set aside for the purpose. For the rest, she probably had no objection to their jokes at suitable times, and even enjoyed them. As one of her daughters recorded, "she was no friend of sad people, nor was she one herself, nor did she want those who went in her company to be such. She used to say, 'God deliver me from gloomy saints!' "[8] And it is safe to say that the *mozos de mulas* who "enjoyed hearing her more than all the pleasures of the world" heard many a good jest and witticism from her lips.

Life on the road under Madre Teresa was so well organized that the carts were literally convents on wheels. The day began with Mass and Holy Communion, no matter what need of haste there might be. There was always holy water in each cart, for it was a great thing, she observed, to be able to enjoy so easily the fruits of the blood of Christ! When they came to a church, they all prostrated themselves before it. Even if it was locked up for the night, La Madre would dismount and say, "What a great blessing, that we should find here the person of the Son of God! Unhappy those who drive Him from them!"[9] She would never travel without a priest to say Mass and hear confessions. She always had with her a bell, which she would ring at the appointed hours for the reading of the Office, for prayer and for silence; and a *reloj de arena* to mark the hours. In each cart there was a nun designated as superior, whom the others must obey.

Most of these plans had been thought out when Madre Teresa lay down for a little sleep, or perhaps none at all, on the night of August 12, 1567. Long before dawn she rang the bell for rising. It was still dark when Father Julian said Mass and gave them Holy Communion. Finally, when all were ready to depart,

---

[8] *Santos encapotados* — "hooded" or "shrouded saints." *Relación de la Venerable Madre María de San Jerónimo*, B.M.C., t. II, p. 301.
[9] *Deposition of Mother Ana de Jesús*, B.M.C., t. XVIII, pp. 464–470.

Teresa slipped away through the dewy garden to her favorite hermitage, and falling on her knees before Christ at the Column, begged Him to care for her house and her children in her absence, and to grant that she would find them the same when she returned. By this time there were probably a few curious spectators in front of the convent, for "when it was known in the city there was much murmuring. Some said I was crazy; others were waiting to see the end of that nonsense."[10] Still others said it was all because she wanted to gad about and amuse herself.[11] Impervious to all this, Teresa gave the word to her army. There was a flutter of farewells. Whips cracked, the mules lunged, the clumsy carts creaked, the *mozos* shouted and cursed. The first missionary journey of the Reform had begun.

It must have been a long, hot, tiresome day. They probably stopped in the shade of some little pine grove for the brief *siesta,* which even the saints in Spain will not forego. Toward nightfall, very weary (La Madre admits it) they came within sight of the little town of Arévalo, the girlhood home of Queen Isabel *la católica.* It was about halfway between Ávila and Medina.

A quarter of a league from the place they saw a man approaching on a mule. Presently, on noticing that he wore clerical garb, Father Julian recognized him as Alonso Esteban, one of those who had helped him get the Provisor's consent in Medina. And indeed, when the good man stopped to talk to them, they found he was on his way to Ávila with a letter for none other than Father Julian. Eagerly opening it, the chaplain read it with a face that clearly spelled bad news. It was from Alonso Alvarez, the man from whom he rented the house next to the Augustinian monastery. Alas for human hopes! It said that Madre Teresa must not think of leaving Ávila until she had come to an understanding with the Augustinians; for they were quite displeased on learning what the house was to be used for, and Alvarez felt obliged to cancel his agreement, for they were good friends of his, and he did not wish to become involved in a lawsuit with them.

What a disappointment! Father Julian raised his voice in protest, and the messenger replied so vigorously that Madre Teresa told him to keep quiet, lest he frighten the nuns from the Incarnation — it was bad enough that they had come against

---

[10] *Fundaciones, loc. cit.*
[11] Yepes, *Vida de Santa Teresa,* lib. II, cap. XV.

their will, under obedience and with no faith in the project. What was to be done now? Must they return to Ávila? Father Julian was greatly cast down, thinking of how their critics would rejoice and mock them when they arrived.

Alonso Esteban, having delivered his broadside, went back to Arévalo, expecting them no doubt to turn back. But he did not know La Madre. Quickly surveying the situation, like a good general, she came to a prompt decision. She would not go back. In fact, she was rather pleased that this had occurred, for it showed the devil was opposing her, and that must mean that she was doing something by which God would be well served. She told Father Julian to ride on to Arévalo, and find Alonso Esteban. She even described where he would be found; he would be standing under a certain portico, and the messenger was to ask him to find them all lodgings for the night.[12]

Everything turned out as she expected. Alonso Esteban was where she had "seen" him. He agreed to help; and by the time the carts had rumbled into the ancient village, he had got some rooms for the nuns at the home of a good lady, Ana de Velasco. There a council of war was held at once. And there, to her great surprise and delight, who should appear but Father Báñez, O.P.! How he happened to be in Arévalo that evening is not clear, but there he was — he had a habit of turning up when Teresa had most need of his help — and just as he had saved the day for her in Ávila, so now he encouraged her, almost alone, against all her advisers. He knew what obstacles she had overcome be-fore, he believed she would succeed again. He gave her courage: not that she doubted that the foundation would be made, but she had begun to fear that she could not place it under our Lady's protection on the Feast of the Assumption. "I told him very secretly what had happened. It seemed to him that we could quickly conclude the business with the Augustinians, but to me any delay whatever was irksome, for want of knowing what to do with so many nuns; and so we all spent that night in anxiety, for by that time they had told it to everybody in the house.[13]

While they were still discussing the matter, in the small hours

---

[12] Neither the Saint nor her contemporary biographers mention this incident; it was related years afterward by Sister Inés of Jesus, in the testimony for beatification.

[13] *Fundaciones*, cap. III.

of the morning of August 14, a mule came clattering over the stony pavements of Arévalo, and there dismounted at the door of their lodgings the Prior of the Carmelite monastery at Medina, Fray Antonio de Heredia. Alonso Esteban or some other messenger had gone to Medina the night before to notify him, and he must have ridden some thirty-five kilometers at top speed in the darkness. At any rate, there he was, a great lumbering handsome friar, slightly bent from study, warmhearted, quick to laugh, and looking younger than his fifty-seven years. Never was a man more welcome. For no sooner had he heard of the difficulties about the house rented from Alonso Alvarez, than he offered a solution. What was the matter with the house he had bought, or at least had agreed to buy, from Doña María Suárez? Yes, to be sure, it might need some repairs, but that could always be done after one moved in!

Teresa decided to take the risk, and gave commands accordingly. She sent her two cousins, Inés of Jesus and Ana of the Incarnation, to stay with their brother, Don Vicente de Ahumada, parish priest in the near-by village of Villenueva del Aceral; and with them, under the escort of Vicente Esteban, the two nuns from the Incarnation. Thus the more timorous and less experienced cohorts were spared whatever rigors might be in store, while La Madre and the seasoned veterans of San José (María Bautista and Ana de los Angeles) advanced with Father Julian to find the house of Doña María Suárez at Fuente el Sol, intending afterwards to proceed to Olmedo to enlist the aid of the Bishop of Ávila, Don Álvaro de Mendoza, who was spending the summer there.

Without sleep, and with little if any food, the three nuns of San José jolted along the rough roads as fast as the mules could travel, to Fuente el Sol. Fortunately Doña María was at home and received them with all kindness. She was glad to sell them her house in the Calle de Santiago and to let them pay at their convenience. She even thought of the furnishings, insisting upon their taking along some tapestries and "a very rich counterpane of blue damask." Finally, she gave La Madre a letter to her majordomo, who was living in the house, instructing him to vacate it and turn it over to them. Armed with this, the dusty travelers took their leave as quickly as Castilian courtesy would permit, and hurried to Olmedo. There they had no difficulty in finding the Bishop, who received them with hearty words of encouragement and sent them off in his coach (which must have been not only faster but far more comfortable than the *carro*) under the guidance of his chaplain, Alonso Muñoz.

From Olmedo to Medina is a distance of twenty kilometers, even in a coach. Darkness overtook them on the road, far from their destination. It was evident that when they arrived the majordomo of Doña María would probably be asleep, and the Carmelite Convent, where they must borrow vessels for the altar from Fray Antonio if Mass was to be said next morning, would be locked for the night. Madre Teresa, undaunted, told Father Julian to ride ahead — whether on his faithful mule, or on a fresh mount provided by *El Ilustrísimo* does not appear — and notify those persons that she was on her way. The faithful chaplain spurred his steed and disappeared in the fragrant summer night, while the coach followed ponderously.

It was just midnight when Julian reined in at the gate of the Carmelite monastery on the Calle de Santiago in Medina. Dismounting, he knocked on the door, again and again, as loudly as he could; but the brothers were sound asleep, and it was some while before one of them heard him and got up to find out what all the noise was about. It speaks well for the disposition of the Prior, Fray Antonio, that although roused from profound slumber, he at once made the visitor feel at home, and on hearing that La Madre would soon be there and was resolved to found her convent before daybreak, he had some of his friars assemble things she would need, such as sacred vessels, linens, tapestries, and other furnishings for the chapel and the altar.

While these preparations were being made, the Bishop's coach was heard at the gate, and La Madre descended to receive Fray Antonio's jovial greeting. There was little time now, nor was it the hour for amenities; they must start at once with all their equipment for the house of Doña María. Fray Antonio and two or three other friars insisted upon going along to help carry the equipment. Thus in the first hours of August 15 they set out on foot under the waning stars, a strange procession of friars and nuns laden with vestments, altar cloths, candlesticks, and even more holy objects of gold. Presently they heard voices and the trampling of hoofs, and came upon a street where some spirited bulls, just brought in from the country, were being herded to a corral, for there was to be a *corrida* in honor of our Lady's fiesta next day, and the preliminaries were being watched by a curious crowd of the ragtag and bobtail of Medina — late roisterers and vagabonds, beggars, disreputable women, and here and there a young blade of the town, a little worse for wine, strumming a guitar or a lute. The astonishment of these worthies and camp followers of civilization on confronting so weird a parade of religious, and at such an hour, may be imagined.

"We looked like gypsies who had been robbing some church," said Father Julian, "and certainly, if the police had come upon us, they would have had to take us to the jail until they ascertained where priests, friars, and nuns were going at that hour. And they might not have felt obliged to believe us, considering the appearances, and the hour it was, and the number of people in the streets, for most of those who go about on such an occasion are usually the good-for-nothings and vagabonds of the place. It pleased God that although people stopped us, they were not the police, and they let us pass with saying certain words of the kind that people of that sort are accustomed to say at such an hour. We, not daring to open our mouths, hastened our steps and let them say what they wished."[14] What a picture!

It must have been two o'clock in the morning, or even later, when they roused the caretaker of Doña María and informed him that he must get out at once. "We arrived, thank God and good fortune, at the house where the said majordomo was," continued Father Julian, "and such a bad night we gave him, what with calling him in such haste and our anxiety to get in before some misfortune overtook us, that at last he awoke, and opened the door to us." On reading his mistress's letter, the poor man obeyed, and turned the place over to the newcomers.

"Oh Lord! when we saw the inside —!" wrote Father Julian. It looked even worse, if possible, than when he had given it up as hopeless a few weeks before. The porch was piled with dirt and refuse, its walls foul and scratched, the floor filthy, the roof but a shed cover. Teresa went into the *patio* and ruefully beheld, by the light of a flickering torch and the distant stars, the jagged contours of half fallen walls through which the Castilian night wind was whistling. On the side near the porch there was little left of what had been the partitions of rooms. A stairway leading from a broken door to a diminutive gallery, where the majordomo had lived, and whence he was now removing his few per-

---

[14] *Fundaciones*, cap. III.

sonal effects, was still comparatively intact, as were the porch and one room. The rest, as one chronicler has it, was more like a building lot or mountain site than a lady's house.[15]

"When we arrived at the house, we went into a *patio*," said Madre Teresa. "The walls seemed to me quite fallen, but not as much as when I saw them by daylight. I think the Lord must have wished that that blessed Father be blinded against seeing that it was unsuitable to place the Most Blessed Sacrament there." The porch gave her even more concern, for there the altar was to be; and it was full of earth, while "the walls were without plaster, the night was short, and we had only some square wall hangings — three, I believe — which were nothing for the whole length of the porch. I did not know what to do, for I saw it was not a place to put an altar."[16]

At this point the majordomo, now fully awake and more resigned, came to the rescue with some tapestries that were in the house. These, with the blue damask coverlet of Doña María, would conceal the unsightly walls and shut out the dark street; but there were no nails with which to hang them. Never mind, said Madre Teresa, there must be nails about somewhere, in the walls, in the decayed door, or in the stable that opened off the desolate *patio*. Thanking God for His timely help, she disposed her forces strategically for the final attack. Father Julian and Fray Antonio were to go over the walls looking for nails, and hang the tapestries, while she and the other nuns, having removed the dirt and rubbish from the porch, swept and washed the floor, and tried to remove the dust and cobwebs from the ceilings and walls.

Before the first glint of dawn these labors had been crowned with such a degree of success that the place was as clean as it ever could be, the altar was set up and arranged, and the bell was hung in the little corridor, ready to announce to the world that the sacramental Christ had found within it a new home.

It was probably about five o'clock when some one remembered that to make the foundation legal, a notary public must draw up an account of it. Nothing daunted, Teresa and her companions went to the house of the Provisor to get the necessary permission. The Provisor told them to go and wake the notary. This they did. The notary got out of bed reluctantly, to record

---

[15] P. Francisco de Santa María, *Reforma de los Descalzos*, t. I, lib. II, cap. V.
[16] *Fundaciones*, cap. III.

that they were establishing a convent with the leave and benediction of the Ordinary.

Madre Teresa hurried back to the ruined house, and gave orders for the ringing of the bell for Mass. Fray Antonio vested himself, for he was to be the celebrant. For a moment there was some perplexity over the problem of having the nuns hear the divine Sacrifice from a place of retirement, as the rule provided. La Madre put them in the little stairway, where they watched the priest through the gaping cracks in the old door.

So His Majesty came to San José de Medina. It was all accomplished, just as the Lord had told her it would be. Caesar, observes Ribera, could say, "I came, I saw, I conquered" five days after landing; but Madre Teresa could say it after two.

"I have never seen her so tired," wrote Father Julian. Yet she was supremely happy, too, in the thought that Christ had one more resting place, however humble, in an unfriendly world; and with this in mind, she went out to inspect His property by daylight. She was so eager to see the *patio*, the exterior of the convent and the street that she hardly noticed the curious people who were beginning to stand about, to gape and to ask questions. And then of a sudden all her joy vanished. She saw that in some places the walls were not only broken, but flat on the ground, that it would take weeks to repair the damage, and that meanwhile the Blessed Sacrament could be seen from the street.

This last was particularly serious in an industrial fair town full of merchants from France, the Netherlands, and England, some of them no doubt heretics. Teresa had heard what the Calvinists had done to the Host and the churches that housed It in Antwerp and other northern cities. A great deal of the commerce of Europe at that time was in the hands of men who called themselves Italians, Portuguese, or Spanish, as it might be convenient, and passed as Lutherans, Calvinists, or Unitarians, or even Catholics as they lived in one country after another; but they were no friends of Christ and His Church. They were all "Lutherans" to Teresa. "Oh, God help me, when I saw His Majesty placed on the street, in a time so dangerous as we now have, on account of those Lutherans, what was the anguish that came to my heart!"[17]

With this unexpected fear there came upon her one of the

---

[17] *Loc. cit.*

most violent temptations of her life, a depression of spirit more painful than any bodily sufferings, in whose black depths the enemy struck at her heart with the suggestion that she had made a terrible, yes a blasphemous mistake, that all the prayers leading up to it had been delusions, that all her life had been a wicked farce. Thus beset all day, she endured it in silence, for she did not wish to make her companions any sadder than they were, until, at nightfall, there came a Jesuit from Father Baltasar Alvarez at the college, and "he heartened and consoled me much."[18] She told him nothing of her desolation or any of her troubles, except her concern about the Blessed Sacrament. As it was now plain that the house in its present state was not fit for a convent, he promised to try to find her another while the necessary repairs were being made.

Meanwhile day and night Teresa was haunted by the dread that some injury or insult might be offered to our Lord by one of the foreign heretics or infidels. Day and night she went as often as possible to watch Him in his lonely and shabby home "on the street." She engaged some men to stand on guard all night in the "chapel," and then, fearing that they would fall asleep and neglect their task, she would get up and watch the Sacred Host through a window, "for it was very clear moonlight, and I could see It well."

During the next eight days, while the Jesuit fathers were seeking for a rentable house, many persons came to visit the convent, and went away much edified by the joy and patience with which the nuns endured no common poverty and inconvenience. Such was a lack of space that the stairway opening upon the porch chapel had to be used as choir, confessional, speak room and if need be, "prison," while the small upstairs corridor served as sleeping quarters, community room, and recreation hall. All this La Madre and her daughters were willing to accept because His Majesty had commanded it. And visitors were moved to great devotion, as she noticed, "by seeing our Lord on the porch," while "His Majesty, like one who never tires of humiliating Himself for us, did not seem to wish to leave it." Nevertheless there remained the danger of desecration, and this was intolerable.

---

[18] Why her old confessor and friend did not welcome her to Medina, or go personally to visit her during that long and desolate day, does not appear. P. Silverio conjectures that Father Alvarez "perhaps could not visit her personally on account of the solemnity of the feast." (*Op. cit.*, III, p. 229.) This is Teresa's first mention of him in the account of the actual foundation.

The house must be almost rebuilt; and meanwhile the nuns must find a residence elsewhere.

Finally a rich and devout merchant of the town, Blas de Medina, made a suggestion which temporarily solved the difficulty. Not far away, on the same street, the Calle de Santiago, he and his family lived in a dwelling too large for their needs. It could easily be divided into two apartments, and the nuns at San José de Medina were welcome to the entire second story. Teresa accepted with gratitude. She and her daughters gathered up their poor effects and moved into rooms that were ample for their present needs; and rejoicing to find a large and sumptuous salon decorated with gold, they decided that there should be the chapel and the residence of His Majesty, Christ the King.

Reinforced a week later by the four nuns who had gone to stay at the house of Don Vicente de Ahumada at Villanueva del Aceral, they were now able to follow their primitive rule with all perfection; and there they lived, as quietly and as strictly enclosed as in Ávila, for about two months, through most of the autumn of 1567. Doña María's house, when fully repaired, became the nucleus of the present convent at Medina, where visitors are still shown the little window through which La Madre used to watch His Majesty by the light of the August moon. Money for the alterations and for the purchase of the house began to come from various good people, one of them a resident of the same street — Doña Elena de Quiroga, niece of Don Gaspar Quiroga (the future Cardinal of Toledo, Primate of Spain and Inquisitor General), who not only paid for the house, but built the chapel. Years later she became a nun in that convent, and so, too, did her daughter Jerónima,[19] much to the temporary displeasure of their illustrious uncle.

Presently some houses adjoining the one of Doña María Suárez were donated to the convent, and with them some fine gardens; these were entailed, but Philip II allowed their alienation in 1570. Two years later some other houses were received from the widow of a knight of Santiago; and still others from a tailor named Lázaro Zurdo. So the convent gradually attained its modern proportions, and accumulated its rich traditions. There

[19] Saint Teresa put off the reception of Doña Elena for some years, on the advice of Father Ribera and other Jesuits, including the lady's confessor, for she had several children, and they believed it was her duty to remain in the world until they were old enough to care for themselves. — Ribera, *op. cit.*, lib. II, cap. VII.

travelers may see the cell of Madre Teresa herself (now a chapel) with its painting of angels playing on violins, and a little bench where she took her scanty rest, and on the floor some spots which Carmelites have always believed to be from drops of her blood, scattered by her vigorous "disciplines."

There she was now enjoying a little peace before commencing new labors; and if she had any grief, it was the thought that not once had her Lord spoken to her during all the terrible hours of the foundation. This was unusual, for in most of her worst trials and labors He had given her encouragement. She long wondered about it, until years later, after receiving Holy Communion at Malagón, she reminded Him with childlike directness that during the foundation at Medina He had never once spoken to her.

"Did you not see that the foundation at Medina was miraculous?" replied His Majesty. "What more do you want?"[20]

---

[20] Ribera, *op. cit.*, lib. II, cap. IX.

Chapter XXI

A FRIAR AND A HALF FOR THE REFORM

TERESA was now a celebrity. Laymen and clerics of high and low degree came to invoke her prayers, to ask her advice, to tell her their troubles, or merely to see her out of curiosity. How true it was that "to those who love God, all things work together unto good!" Visitors, once a temptation, were now fitting into the pattern of her work like pieces chosen by an artist for some rare mosaic. This was particularly true of a gentleman who called upon her during the autumn days that followed the turbulent August of 1567.

Don Bernardino de Mendoza, son of the Count of Ribadavia, was a younger brother of Don Álvaro, Bishop of Ávila. The rather vague accounts of his life say nothing of his sharing the piety so generally attributed to his brother, and in the absence of details, one can only conclude that he led the careless and purposeless existence of a young man with more money than was good for him, and took his pleasures as they came without much thought of any life but the present one; for Madre Teresa was assured, in one of her visions, that his soul, at the time he went to see her, was in such a state as to deserve nothing less than hell. Indeed it may fairly be doubted whether he would ever have sought out the conversation of a saint but for the failing of his health and the influence of his older sister, widow of the *Comendador Mayor* of Leon, Don Francisco de los Cobos.

There is extant a pen portrait of Cobos, with a somewhat sketchier one of his wife, Doña María, by no less a student of human nature than the Emperor himself. In a secret memorandum for his son, Philip II, who was ruling Spain as his regent in 1543, Charles described Cobos, then a member of his Council of State and his chief finance minister, as faithful and honest, but old and often in physical misery, and hence not as industrious as formerly. His wife wearied and excited him, wrote the Emperor, and had hurt his reputation somewhat by accepting gifts; these, however, were of small value, and Cobos would no doubt see to it that she discontinued the abuse, now that the matter had been brought to his attention. Cobos knew all the imperial business intimately, and could serve Philip better than anyone, if it pleased God that the cause above mentioned had not tainted the mother's milk of his character. He was ambitious and would try to gain the exclusive favor of the young Regent, even by using women to ensnare him if Philip showed any weakness in that direction — for Cobos had been given to lechery in his younger days. Philip must keep him in his place and make use of him; if Cobos hinted at greater rewards, he was to be told gravely and respectfully that the Emperor would have done more for him, but for the fear of making others jealous and discontented.

Doña María's reputation fares better in the hands of a saint than in those of an Emperor. If she had been overacquisitive during her husband's lifetime, it had been otherwise since his death in 1547; and Madre Teresa may have been recording the prevalent opinion when she wrote, "She is a very Christian woman, and of the very greatest charity, for they tell me she gives alms in great abundance."[1]

One autumn day, then, this lady and her brother, Don Bernardino, went to the house of Blas de Medina to pay their respects to La Madre in her temporary convent on the second floor. It was not their first meeting with her. Through their brother the Bishop they had made her acquaintance in Ávila, where Don Bernardino had given certain gifts to the first convent; and there he had offered her a house he owned about a quarter of a league out of Valladolid, one which had been a "place of recreation" for the Comendador Cobos, and had some very good gardens. He had renewed the suggestion at Olmedo when Teresa stopped there to see the Bishop on her way to Medina, and now he made it for the third time.[2] There were obstacles. She was considering a foundation at Malagón; besides, the Council of Trent had forbidden nuns to live outside cities.[3] She decided to accept, however, for two reasons: once in possession of Don Bernardino's property, she might be able to exchange it for something in town; and "since he was so set on it, I did not wish to keep him from doing his good work, or hinder his devotion."[4]

The suggestion of a foundation at Malagón had come in a

[1] *Fundaciones*, cap. X.
[2] Ribera, *Vida de Santa Teresa*, lib. II, cap. X.
[3] Sess. XXV, *de reg. et mon.*, cap. V.
[4] *Fundaciones*, cap. X.

letter[5] from her old friend, Doña Luisa de la Cerda, the feudal mistress of a little community grouped about one of her ancestral castles, a day's journey south of Toledo. It was far away, compared to Valladolid; still, there was something to be said for scattering the foundations more widely, and as the population of Malagón was too small to support a convent with alms, Doña Luisa was willing and able to provide an annual income. And although Teresa had set her face against this at Ávila, her learned friends, including Father Domingo Báñez, reminded her that the Council of Trent had permitted communities of nuns to accept endowments. Who was she, they asked, to oppose her opinion to a decree of a Council?

While she was considering this matter, a third project was suggested, or rather revived, by a conversation she had with Fray Antonio de Heredia, prior of the Carmelite monastery. She happened to mention to him *"muy en secreto"* that she had Father Rubeo's permission to found a house of discalced friars, and was praying that God send at least one candidate to encourage her. Fray Antonio knew many important people in Medina and all parts of Castilla. Perhaps he might know of one or two who would be suitable. She was quite surprised by the effect this hint had upon the jovial prior.

"When he learned this, he rejoiced much, and promised me that he would be the first one. I took this for a joke, and told him so; for, although he was always a good friar, and recollected, and very studious and fond of his cell, and well educated, I did not think he would do for such a beginning, for he did not have the inner spirit, nor would he carry on with the intensity that was necessary, being delicate and not accustomed to it. He assured me that he meant it, and declared that for many days the Lord had been calling him to a stricter life; and so he had already made up his mind to join the Carthusians, and they were willing to receive him. With all this, I was not very well satisfied, although it made me happy to hear him, and I asked him to let us wait a while, and to exercise himself in the things he must promise to do."[6]

She kept Fray Antonio on probation for a year, during which he bore patiently all sorts of unexpected sorrows, temptations,

---

[5] This letter is not extant, but Yepes says the suggestion was made while Teresa was in Medina (*Vida de Santa Teresa*, lib. II, cap. XVII).

[6] *Fundaciones*, cap. III.

and persecutions. Meanwhile he introduced to her, by what proved to be a happy chance, a young priest of his order named Pedro de Orozco.

Fray Pedro had finished his course in theology at the University of Salamanca when the academic year ended on September 7, and had just returned to Medina with a friend and fellow student, John of Saint Matthias, after an absence of four years. They were ordained at the Carmelite monastery of Santa Ana, probably only a few days before Pedro went to see Madre Teresa. He must have been a good, ordinary friar with no especial gifts of mind or spirit, for Teresa in her brief reference to him does not mention his name and says nothing of him, in fact, except that he told her "great things" about his classmate, Friar John of Saint Matthias. What these great things were she does not say.[7] One of them probably was that he was trying to follow the primitive rule, sleeping but three hours a night, enduring heroic penances, and speaking only of God and the things of God in such a way as to delight all who heard him. Teresa gave thanks to the Lord on hearing this, and begged Fray Pedro to bring his companion to see her.

This was not easy, for Friar John, since taking his vow of chastity, had carefully avoided the company of all women, even if they were holy ones. Why he consented in this instance is not recorded, but consent he did, and one autumn day Madre Teresa looked through the curtain of her grille to see standing outside a friar so short and so slender that he might have been a boy masquerading in Carmelite costume. He was then twenty-five years of age. His dark head was tonsured, his oval face well browned, his forehead high and broad over well-marked brows, his nose long and acquiline. And although he was barely five feet two inches in height, his presence was full of nobility and composure. His folded hands, his ethereal, motionless body, every line of his thoughtful, sensitive face spoke of inner harmony and peace.

A few moments later he had forgotten whether the nun twice his age on the other side of the grille was a woman or not. "In heaven they neither marry nor are given in marriage." And on earth certain great spirits enjoy a comradeship that transcends the accidents of birth, age, or sex. So it was with Fray Juan and Madre Teresa. He talked to her as freely as if he had known

---

[7] *Fundaciones*, cap. III.

her all his life. He told her of his prayer, of his hopes for the future.

He was born Juan de Yepes, at Fontiveros, near Ávila, in 1542. His father, Gonzalo de Yepes, had come from a good family in Toledo; his mother, Catalina Alvarez, was of the humblest origin, and toiled as a silk and wool weaver — a trade that she taught her husband when misfortune reduced him to the same poverty. Shortly after John was born (he had two older brothers, Francisco and Luis) this valiant woman was left a widow; had to feed her boys on black bread when work was scarce; took them to Toledo to seek help from their father's relatives, and in vain; walked five leagues (fifteen miles) to Gálvez, where another relative gave some assistance; and finally returned to Fontiveros to resume the ill-paid drudgery of weaving.

There was never any need for little John to take Lady Poverty as his bride — she was born his sister, and grew up with him. But he loved an even greater Lady. He remembered the altar in the living room of his mother's cottage, with a statue of *La Purísima* on it. Once, the year of the famine and drought, he fell into deep water and saw this same Queen of whom he would one day write, "The angels are mine, and the Mother of God," holding out Her hands to save him — hands so beautiful that he would not extend his own smudgy ones to touch them even to save his life; and then a workman came and fished him out with a pole, while the Lady vanished.

When he was about nine years old his mother, Catalina, took him to Arévalo, where she found employment with a weaver by the river Adaja, almost under the shadow of that five-towered medieval castle in which Isabel *la católica* had lived until she was twelve years old. There his older brother, Francisco, married, and went away to establish himself in a business at Medina del Campo, whence he sent back for his mother and John. This Francisco, though he had several children, asked God for the gift of poverty — a prayer which was answered; nevertheless he managed to send his young brother to be taught by the nuns at the College of the Children of Doctrine, in return for which John would beg alms for the children who lived in wretched poverty in a city where fabulous wealth was exchanged at four annual fairs.

When John was fourteen, he was serving at Mass every morning at the monastery of the Magdalens on the Calle de Santiago, very near the spot where he now spoke with Madre Teresa. Then a *caballero*, Alonso Alvarez de Toledo, offered him work in a hospital of which he was warden, collecting money for the patients and helping to care for the victims of smallpox. The best part of this was that he was allowed time to study grammar at the new college of the Jesuits. There his tutor was the great humanist, Father Bonifacio, and he probably continued his studies for about four years, from 1557 to 1561. In 1563 he became a Carmelite, taking the name of John of Saint Matthias. When he read the history of his order, and discovered that the rule he followed was not the primitive one, he was consumed with a desire to live as the early hermits had, and apparently was resolved to do so as well as he could when he made his profession on August 22, 1563, the very day Fray Angel de Salazar gave Madre Teresa written permission to live at San José de Avila. He was then sent, with other young Carmelites, to the *studium generale* of his order at Salamanca.

"The Athens of Spain" was at the height of its prestige, overshadowing even the University of Paris. In the first years of the sixteenth century the teaching of theology there, and indeed in the whole country, had fallen into disrepute, until the brilliant Dominican, Francisco de Vitoria, by the sheer influence of his lectures and his simple unrhetorical writings, rescued the sacred sciences from what Father Bruno calls "the hopeless speculations of a decadent scholasticism,"[8] by returning to sources — the Sacred Scriptures, the Church Fathers, the definitions of Popes and Councils. Thus the true scholasticism of the Middle Ages restored the tarnished glories of Salamanca; and the first chair of theology, though open to competition, was occupied for two centuries by a series of great Dominican teachers: by Melchior Cano, Dominic de Soto, Pedro de Sotomayor, and, in the time of Juan de San Matías, by Juan Mancio of Corpus Christi, who lectured on the third part of the *Summa* in 1567–1568. Fray Juan had only one year of theology, and never attained his mastership. Perhaps it was natural that a student who selected a room because he could see the Blessed Sacrament from his window[9] should have despised higher degrees and thought more of knowledge itself than of its alphabetical heraldry.

Endowed with literary genius of a high order, this young

---

[8] *Saint John of the Cross* (New York, 1936), p. 37.
[9] *Ibid.*

friar saw the length and the breadth, the height and the depth of things too clearly to write for the sake of glory or his own satisfaction — hence he waited until he knew what he had to say, hence he left no juvenilia, all is mature and of a piece. Having a phenomenal memory, he knew most of the Bible by heart — especially the Canticle of Canticles, the Proverbs and Psalms, Ecclesiasticus and Ecclesiastes. His friend, Juan Evangelista, said he had never known him to read anything but the Holy Scriptures, Saint Augustine *Contra Haereses*, and the *Flos Sanctorum*. His conversation was always of God and the things of God. When his fellow students tried to describe his talks, the word *angelic* always came to their minds; yet they recalled that his explanations were witty, his illustrations humorous, and he constantly made them laugh. This joy of his had a solid foundation. No penance was too heavy for him. He slept but three hours out of the twenty-four. For his retreats and meditations he liked the solitary beauty of nature. He seemed to have acquired the thought of Saint Thomas and the scholastic habit of thinking and writing without much effort; yet he was no slavish imitator of either, and gave evidence, in everything he said or wrote, of a strong and original personality.

"Where there is no love," he used to say, "put love and you will find love."

Though Madre Teresa could have seen none of his writings — indeed, it is not certain that he had written anything at this time — she knew enough about human nature to read him correctly, as she had read Fray Antonio. How could she help finding in him a kindred spirit, she who loved holiness, intellect, penance, and joy so passionately? And how could such a man fail to reciprocate the affection of such a woman? Spiritually, henceforth, they would be mother and son. When Fray Juan told her that he, too, like Fray Antonio, desired a stricter life, she unfolded to him her dream of a monastery of men leading the life of the primitive hermits of Mount Carmel, as she and her nuns were doing, and begged him to wait until she found a house. She would then teach him the observance of the primitive rule, and he and one or two others would be the first friars of the Reform. John consented, and went back to his monastery and his prayers.

Teresa, thinking of big Fray Antonio and of little Fray Juan, burst into the community room, exclaiming,

"Blessed be God, for I have a friar and a half for the foundation of my monastery!"[10]

Such was the beginning of her lifelong friendship with the
glorious little man we now know as Saint John of the Cross.
She used to call him *"mi Senequita"* — "my little Seneca" — a
high compliment considering the exaggerated esteem in which
the pagan philosopher was then held in the land of his birth.
"He is a man after God's heart and mine," she said. His mother,
Catalina, now growing old, also found in her an affectionate
friend. The convent records at Medina show that the sisters
provided shoes and other necessities for her old age, and at last
they laid her frail body among the dead of their own community,
and commended her soul to God. She had been generous with
God, and God, though granting her the poverty she loved,
watched over her to the last.

While her *Senequita* and Fray Antonio were waiting for God
to send them a house, Madre Teresa's practical mind was considering what could be done at once. There was the proposal
of Doña Luisa for a convent at Malagón, and there was an invitation from Doña Leonor de Mascareñas to teach the nuns
of the reformed convent founded by Sister María of Jesus at Alcalá the observance of the primitive rule. Her work at Medina,
at any rate, was done; and while she still revolved in her mind
what the next enterprise would be, she left Sister Ana of Jesus
in charge there as prioress, and departed for Ávila, probably in
mid-October, 1567, taking with her Sister Ana de los Angeles,
who would be competent to take a leading part in another foundation, wherever it might be.

At Ávila she received another visit from Doña María de Mendoza and her brother, Don Bernardino. It happened that they
were about to depart for their estates in Ubeda. They would be
passing through Madrid and Alcalá, and would have room in
their coach for her and one or two companions. It seemed a
providential opportunity for Teresa to help the Carmelites at
Alcalá, and to confer with Doña Luisa regarding a foundation
at Malagón. She agreed accordingly; and one day about the first

---

[10] There has been some disagreement over the meaning of this. Some editors
have thought she was referring ironically to little John as the friar and to big
Antonio as the half friar. Father Gracián took the remark literally: Antonio was
the friar and Juan the half friar. To P. Silverio (*Vida de Santa Teresa de Jesús,*
III, p. 245, note) this is the only plausible interpretation, considering the charity
of La Madre, who would not have held Fray Antonio up to ridicule.

of November, 1567, she set out in the great coach of the late Comendador Cobos with Doña María, Don Bernardino, and two nuns, Ana de los Angeles and Antonia del Espíritu Santo.

When they reached Madrid — it was only a good day's journey by coach — Doña María and her brother doubtless went to stay with some of their aristocratic relatives, of whom there were many, while the nuns stopped at the home of Doña Leonor Mascareñas. Outwardly this seemed a palace, but inside it was a veritable convent. Its owner was an elderly Portuguese lady who had taken a vow of perpetual chastity years before, on arriving in Castilla with the beautiful Princess Isabel, the bride of the Emperor, Charles V. She had been governess (at twenty-four) of Philip II, and no doubt had had a great deal to do with giving an intensely Catholic bent to his mind and character. Later she had served his unfortunate son, Don Carlos, in the same capacity. When that duty was discharged, she wished to become a nun; but the King refused to allow it, believing that she could do more good in the world. From then on she contented herself with being the friend and patroness of religious. The founding of the Carmelite convent at Alcalá for María de Jesús had been only one of her many charities. In her own palace at Madrid she maintained apartments, properly cloistered, where any and all servants of God could find a hospice, with food and rest. Next door, on the Plaza de Santo Domingo, she had established a convent of barefoot Franciscan nuns under the patronage of *Nuestra Señora de los Angeles;* and it was there that Madre Teresa and her two companions spent the next fifteen days, while their hostess was seeking permission of the Ordinary for their visit at Alcalá.

Teresa was delighted with the Franciscan nuns. Though most of them came from luxurious and aristocratic homes, they lived on whatever was brought to their door, and when there was not enough for dinner, went without,[11] and thanked God. Yet she did not find among them the seclusion she had expected. The news had got about the court of Philip II that the famous *Beata* of Ávila was there, and everyone wanted to see her. Pious ladies of noble families wanted to ask for her prayers. Others came out of curiosity, hoping to see her in one of her ecstasies. And her levitations — what fun it would be to see her rising in the air, like a Cupid that was hoisted up by ropes to shoot off

[11] P. Silverio, *op. cit.,* III, p. 258.

fireworks over the heads of the people at Benavente when **King** Philip was leaving for England in 1554! These fashionable ladies wanted a good show, a new sensation to relieve the tedium of a long cold Madrid winter.

Teresa did nothing to gratify their curiosity; on the contrary she defended herself by conversing about the most commonplace and earthly affairs. "What beautiful streets you have in Madrid!" she would say, quite like any other tourist from the country. "What charming parks!" She parried questions about her visions, her method of prayer, her inner experiences in general, by tactfully changing the subject to the mundane things her visitors could understand. Several of them went away saying that she was not a saint after all, but a very ordinary nun, good enough, perhaps, but badly overrated.

One day toward the end of her visit she was invited by Princess Juana, the King's sister, to visit the Royal Monastery of Discalced Franciscan Nuns that she had founded in the house of her birth. Mother of young King Sebastian of Portugal, she had returned to her native land after the death of her husband, had served as Regent for her brother during his absence in England, had devoted herself to poor Don Carlos, and now lived virtually the life of a nun in the convent of her founding. Gentle and sweet, holy and well read was Doña Juana; a lovable and admirable woman. Teresa behaved quite differently with her and the Franciscans of the Royal Monastery. She talked, answered questions, and jested so freely that they were all delighted. "Thanks be to God," they said, "that He has let us see a saint whom we can imitate; one who speaks, sleeps, and eats like us, and talks without ceremony or spiritual prudery!"[12]

The permission of the Ordinary of Toledo having been obtained for the visit to Alcalá, which was in his jurisdiction, La Madre and her companions were rejoined by Doña María de Mendoza and her brother, and all set forth together on November 21, 1567. On the way Don Bernardino signed the deed of gift for his property near Valladolid, and handed it to Madre Teresa. At Alcalá, where they arrived before nightfall, the friends separated, Don Bernardino and his sister to continue their journey to Ubeda, Teresa and the other nuns to go to the Convent of the Image.

---

[12] *Reforma*, t. I, lib. II, cap. X, n. 2, p. 237. The Venerable Ana of Jesus assigns this incident to June, 1569; but P. Silverio gives good reasons for believing it occurred at this visit. *Op. cit.*, III, p. 253, note.

There she remained for two months as acting mother superior, instructing the nuns and even the foundress of the house. It was soon apparent to her where the trouble lay. Madre María of Jesus, for all her holiness, was not highly endowed with executive ability. She had established a routine so severe and inflexible that some of the nuns were on the verge of nervous collapse, all were discontented and unhappy. Teresa's sense of humor, her huge common sense, and her understanding of human nature completely changed the atmosphere in a few weeks. She discouraged extraordinary penances, she established a regimen that even the weakest member of the community could follow without injury to health of mind or body, she restored the note of childlike joy, the true accent of Catholic sanctity.

In the midst of these labors, at the beginning of 1568, she received some very bad news from Doña María de Mendoza at Ubeda. Don Bernardino had become ill a few weeks after arriving there. His condition had grown rapidly worse. When a priest was summoned to hear his confession, he was unable to speak, and could only make signs indicating his repentance. He died without confession.

The urgency of Teresa's prayers for this hapless wretch may be imagined. If she prayed every day for several years for a poor man who had given her a cup of water on the road, what must have been her gratitude for one who had given her a house? What prayers, what penances she must have offered, until, with the faith that moves mountains, she wrung an answer from high heaven. "The Lord told me that his salvation had been in jeopardy enough, and that He had had mercy on him for that service he had rendered to His Mother in that house he had given to make a monastery for her Order, and that he would not go forth from purgatory until the first Mass that would be said there, but then he would leave."[13]

Teresa was inclined to go to Valladolid at once. Yet she had come all this distance to talk with Doña Luisa, who was waiting for her at Toledo, and could hardly leave without seeing her. Again, she must conclude her work at Alcalá. This done, she set out as soon as possible, despite snow and ice and freezing winds, for Toledo, arriving there before Lent.

Don Bernardino was constantly in her mind. What sufferings he must be enduring, sufferings that must continue until the

---

[13] *Fundaciones*, cap. X.

scales of God's outraged justice were tipped by a good deed that she alone could perform! What a responsibility! Yet it was now her duty to discuss all the vexing details of the proposed house at Malagón. Doña Luisa de la Cerda offered to provide the convent, the chapel, and the necessary equipment for thirteen nuns, and to give an annual sum for their maintenance. Thus the problem of revenue came to the fore again. Teresa, as we have seen, had decided upon poverty. But the lack of population at Malagón seemed to call for an exception, and Fray Domingo Báñez, whom she had met at Alcalá, had reminded her again of the decree of the Council of Trent in favor of endowments. Acting on his advice, she accepted the offer of Doña Luisa.

The great lady then took her with the two other nuns to the grim fortress of her ancestors at Malagón. Several remarkable things happened soon after their arrival on Passion Sunday, 1568. Teresa was twice enraptured in the presence of others, to her great confusion. When she was taken to see a certain prospective site for the convent, she said, "This must be left for the barefoot friars of Saint Francis" — who, in fact, did establish a monastery there several years later. At length she found a house that would do; and there, on Palm Sunday, April 11, 1568, the nuns proceeded in their white choir mantles, their faces covered with black veils, each holding a burning taper; and all the townspeople attended the Mass and the installation of the Blessed Sacrament.

San José de Malagón was on the plaza, very near the castle. It was not long before Teresa discovered that she had made a mistake, for the street cries and other noises proved a constant distraction to the nuns. She continued to worry also about the endowment, until her scruples were quieted in an extraordinary vision, probably in 1569 or 1570. "After receiving Communion, the second day of Lent in San José of Malagón, our Lord Jesus Christ represented Himself to me in an imaginary vision, as He was accustomed to do, and while I was looking at Him, I saw that on His head and all about it, where the wounds must have been, He had a crown of great splendor. As I am devoted to this *paso*, I was much consoled, and I began to think what a great torment it must have been, since it had given Him so many wounds, and to grow sorrowful. The Lord told me not to pity Him for those wounds, but for the ones they were giving

Him today. And I asked Him what I could do as reparation for this, for I was resolved to do anything. He said to me that this was not the time to rest, that I must hurry to found these houses, for in the souls within them He would take His rest. And I must take as many as they would give me, for there were many who did not serve Him for lack of where to do it, and that those I should found in small places should be like this one, and that they could merit just as much by the desire of doing the same as in the others, and that I should see to it they were all placed under the direction of a prelate, and that I should take care that interior peace should not be lost through any consideration of corporal maintenance, and He would aid us so that it would never be lacking. Especially they should look well after the sick, for the mother superior who did not provide for and gratify the sick was like the friends of Job — He gave the lash for the good of their souls, and they placed their patience in jeopardy; and I should write the foundation of these houses. . . ."[14]

Teresa was still at work organizing the new community when Doña Luisa left Malagón in April, to take her only surviving son, Don Juan Pardo de Tavera, who was ailing with the stone, to the waters at Horcajo, near Montilla, in Andalucía. She had with her the manuscript of La Madre's autobiography, which she promised to deliver as soon as possible to Blessed John of Ávila, then living at Montilla. The Inquisitor Don Francisco de Soto, to whom Fray García de Toledo had shown it, had suggested that it be submitted to the great preacher whose words had been the occasion for the conversions of Saint John of God and Saint Francis Borgia, and had agreed to accept his verdict. Yet though Doña Luisa spent most of the spring within a day's journey of him, she never found it convenient to send him the book. Teresa's feelings are apparent in her letter of May 18, just before her departure from Malagón.

                    "Jhs.

"May He be with Your Ladyship. I wish I had more time to write at length here; and thinking that I should have it today, I have put it off until the last day, for I am going tomorrow, which is May 19, and I have had so much to do that there has

---

[14] *Relaciones*, B.M.C., vol. II, pp. 44–45. P. Silverio prints this as part of the seventh relation, "*Mercedes de Dios*." Father Burke's English edition (New York, 1911) makes it the third (pp. 354–355).

been no opportunity. I will write you by Father Pablo Hernández;[15] although I have heard nothing from him since you
left here, I will tell him what Your Ladyship commands. I have
praised our Lord that your journey has succeeded so well; we
pray enough for it here. Please His Majesty all the rest may
be the same.

"I am well, and like this town better every day, and so do
all of them; there is no one who is any longer discontented with
anything, and they please me better every day. I tell Your Ladyship, that of the four who came here, three have a high degree
of prayer, and even more. They are of such sort that Your Ladyship can rest assured that although I go away they will not lack
a jot of perfection, especially with the persons who remain in
charge of them. . . .

"I don't understand why Your Ladyship has put off sending
my package to Master Ávila. Don't do it, for the love of the
Lord, but let it be sent at once by a messenger, for they tell
me it is only a day's journey and no more; and this business of
waiting for Salazar[16] is nonsense, for he can't go, if he is rector,
to see Your Ladyship, much less go to see Father Ávila. I implore Your Ladyship, if it hasn't been sent, let them take it
now, for truly it has given me distress, for I think the devil is
doing it. . . . I beg Your Ladyship to send it now at once, and
do what I asked Your Ladyship in Toledo. Believe me, it is
more important than you think. . . ."[17]

The next day Teresa left Malagón on a horse or a mule, for
which she took the liberty of borrowing a saddle she found in
the castle. It was oppressively hot when she reached Toledo, and
she was sick in bed for several days at the Cerda palace, very
stiff no doubt, from the unaccustomed exercise. On May 27 she
got up to celebrate the Feast of Our Lord's Ascension, and to
write a long letter to her benefactress, in which she said, among
other things:

"Jesus be with Your Ladyship. Today, the Feast of the Ascension, the Licentiate brought me Your Ladyship's letter, which
gave me no little anxiety, when I knew he had come, with

[15] The Jesuit confessor of Doña Luisa, a man of such grave aspect that Teresa
used to call him "our Father Eternal" — *Padre Eterno*. Doña Luisa left Madre
Teresa in his care.

[16] P. Gaspar de Salazar, S.J., then rector at Madrid. Apparently Doña Luisa
wished to show him the manuscript before delivering it to Blessed John of Avila.

[17] B.M.C., vol. VII, *Epistolario* I, p. 17.

imagining what it might be, until I read it. Glory be to our Lord, that Your Ladyship is well, and the Señor Don Juan. . . .

"As for the rest, let nothing trouble Your Ladyship. Yet although I say this, I have been troubled by it myself, and so I have told him [the Licentiate] that he has behaved badly, and he is muddled up enough, in my opinion, though certainly he doesn't know what he is about. On the one hand he wants to serve you and says he loves you much, and so he does; on the other hand, he does not know how to make himself useful. Also he is rather melancholy, like Alonso de Cabria. But what differences there are in this world, that this man could be serving Your Ladyship, and doesn't want to, and I, who would like to, cannot. We mortals have to pass through these and worse things, and yet we never manage to understand the world, or to be willing to give it up.

"I am not surprised Your Ladyship is unhappy. Indeed I have been well aware that you would have to endure a great deal, considering Your Ladyship's disposition, which is not the sort that can get along with everybody. But since it is meant to serve the Lord, Your Ladyship must put up with it, and get along with Him Who will not leave you solitary. Here no one is going to think ill of Your Ladyship's going away, except to be sorry for you. Try not to worry about it. Think of what your health means to us. Mine has been bad enough these days. If I had not found the luxury Your Ladyship ordered in this house, it would have been worse; and with good reason, for with the hot sun on the road, the pain I had when Your Ladyship was in Malagón increased so much that when I arrived in Toledo they had to bleed me twice; and I could not stir on my bed with the pain I had from the shoulders up to the brain,[18] and being purged another day;[19] and thus I have been eight days here — at least it will be tomorrow, which will be Friday — and I shall go away weakened, but well. I felt lonely enough when I saw myself here without my lady and friend; may the Lord be served by it all. They have all been very good to me, and Reolin has, too. Indeed it has pleased me the way they have entertained me while you were absent. . . . The sisters are most happy."

Teresa added some details about a curate who was more cap-

---

[18] "*Hasta el celebro*," wrote the Saint, meaning *cerebro*.
[19] "*Y otra día purgar.*"

able than any "except my Father Pablo" and about a "very
theatine" woman (that is to say a "Jesuitical" woman — a
high compliment, signifying one trained by the sons of Saint
Ignatius in prayer and self-sacrifice) who had been brought to
Malagón by the nuns to instruct the little girls of that place
in needlework and Christian doctrine, in which they had been
much neglected. The *teatina* gave free lessons, and was supported in turn by the new convent.

"Now," continued La Madre, "it is very late at night, and I
am worn out. I am taking the saddle that Your Ladyship has
in the fortress (I beg Your Ladyship not to take it amiss) and
another, a good one, that I bought here. I know well that Your
Ladyship will be glad to have me make use of it for these
journeys, for there it was: at least I shall travel on something
of yours. I hope to the Lord to come back on it, and if not, to
send it to you after Your Ladyship returns.

"I have already written to Your Ladyship in the letter I left
in Malagón that I think the devil must be preventing Master
Ávila from seeing this affair of mine;[20] I hope he doesn't die
first, for that would be very awkward. I implore Your Ladyship,
since you are so near, that it be sent to him, sealed, by personal
messenger, and that Your Ladyship write to him, commending
it in particular to him, for he has a mind to look at it, and will
read it if he can. Fray Domingo [Báñez] has just written me
here to have a special messenger take it to him when I arrive
in Avila. It pains me not to know what to do, for it will do me
harm enough, as I told Your Ladyship, to have them know
about it. For the love of our Lord, may Your Ladyship make
haste about this; remember that it is His service, and let Your
Ladyship have courage to travel through strange countries; recall how our Lady journeyed when she went to Egypt, and our
father Saint Joseph.

"I am going by way of Escalona, for the Marquesa is there,
and sent for me. I told her that Your Ladyship had helped me
so much that there was no need for her to do so, but I shall be
going past there. I shall stop half a day and no more, if I can,
and this because Fray García has sent to command me to do so,
for he says he promised it, and it is not out of the way. Señor
Don Hernando and Señora Doña Ana[21] have done me the favor

---

[20] The manuscript of the *Vida*.
[21] Relatives of Doña Luisa.

of coming to see me, and Don Pedro Niño, the lady Doña Margarita, and other friends and people, and some persons have wearied
me not a little. Those of Your Ladyship's household are quite
recollected and secluded . . .

"The unworthy servant and subject of Your Ladyship,

"Teresa of Jesus, Carmelite."

She then added a postscript:

"They have just given our Father Eternal permission.[22] So
it is, and in a way I am sorry; on the other hand I see that the
Lord wishes it to be so, and Your Ladyship to endure trials
alone. . . . May Your Ladyship remain with God, my Lady, for
I don't wish to end; nor do I know how I can go so far from
one I love so much, and owe so much."

Leaving Toledo on May 29 (1568), Madre Teresa and her
companions spent a good part of the next day, Sunday, with
the noble woman referred to in the letter, the Marquesa of
Villena and duchess of Escalona,[23] at her country place of Cadalso, on the way to Ávila. Obedience to the Dominican director who had obliged a great lady at her expense was now satisfied.
Tactfully declining to stay longer, she took to the hot and dusty
road again, and after a journey whose discomforts still remain
untold, arrived at Ávila on the second day of June.

During the next four weeks she rested (comparatively) in
the quiet and holy shelter of San José. On June 23 she wrote
Doña Luisa "for the love of God" to send the manuscript of her
life to Blessed John of Ávila without further delay. But Doña
Luisa was not to be hurried. Like so many of the rich and powerful, she was insulated from the urgencies of the less fortunate
by a complacency which often looked like stupidity, but was
probably at botton plain selfishness.

It was about this time that La Madre received a notable visit
from a relative of hers, Rafael Mexía, who, having heard of
her hope of founding a monastery of discalced friars, came to
offer her a farmhouse he owned in the hamlet of Duruelo, some
eight leagues from Ávila toward Medina del Campo. She gladly
accepted the gift without seeing it. Was it not plain that God

---

[22] To leave Toledo. Doña Luisa would then lose her confessor. The reference is
to Father Pablo Hernández, S.J.

[23] P. Gabriel gives us a portrait of this lady in his *Santa de la Raza*, III, pp.
494–495. Her husband, Don Francisco López Pacheco, was the fourth Marqués,
and a direct descendant of the Don Juan Pacheco who virtually ruled Castile
under Henry IV.

had sent her the house she had been asking Him for, in which to put the friar and a half He had already given? She would at least make a beginning at Duruelo.

Like a good general she planned to combine this stroke with another. She had not forgotten that Don Bernardino was in purgatory, and must stay there until the first Mass was said in his house. She must go to Valladolid, then, as soon as possible. She could stop on the way to see the house of Rafael Mexía at Duruelo; then she would pick up John of Saint Matthias at Medina and take him with her to Valladolid, to train him for his work; then he could go back and open the monastery at Duruelo — that is, if he was still willing, and if the house proved suitable, and if the consent of the proper authorities could be obtained.

All this, one infers, was carefully planned when she left Ávila before dawn on the morning of June 30, accompanied by Father Julian and by Sister Antonia del Espíritu Santo. Yet even the best generals sometimes miscalculate. Teresa and her companions had expected to reach the farmhouse by noon. After traveling all morning under the hot July sun, they found they had taken a wrong road somewhere, and had lost their way. Nobody they met had ever heard of Duruelo. Teresa wrote:

"When we thought we were near it, we had just as far again to go. I shall always remember the weariness and the sense of dizziness we suffered on that journey. And so we arrived a little before nightfall. When we went into the house, it was in such a condition that we did not dare remain there for the night, on account of its extreme lack of cleanliness, and the number of harvesters there were about. It had a reasonable porch, and a double bedroom with its attic, and a kitchenette: our monastery occupied this entire edifice."

In spite of her disappointment, the indomitable lady began to survey this dilapidated bungalow with the analytic eye of a born architect. "I reflected that the porch could be made into a church, and the attic into a choir, for it would do well, and they could sleep in the bedroom."[24]

Sister Antonia was unable to share these optimistic hopes. "Indeed, Mother," she said, "there is no spirit, however good it might be, that could endure this. Do not speak of it."

Fundaciones, cap. XIII.

Father Julian was not quite so discouraging. "Although he agreed with my companion, he did not contradict me." For lack of a lodging, they all spent the night in a country church.

Arriving bone weary at Medina on the following evening, Madre Teresa broke the news of her disappointment to Fray Antonio and Fray Juan. "I spoke with the father Fray Antonio and told him what had occurred, and that if he had the heart to stay there for some time, I held certain that God would quickly mend matters; the whole thing was to make a beginning . . . and that he must believe that neither the former Provincial nor the present one would give us permission . . . if they saw us in a very prosperous house, unless we had no help for it, and in that little place and house they would pay no attention to them.[25] God had given him more courage than me; and so he said that he would live not only there, but in a hogsty. Fray Juan de la Cruz was of the same mind."

Teresa remained at the Medina convent four weeks, making preparations for the two foundations at Duruelo and Valladolid. Father Julian went to Ávila to obtain the help of the Bishop, who sent his secretary with him to Valladolid to ask the permission of the Abbot and Provisor there, while La Madre wrote the Carmelite Provincial for permission to found the monastery at Duruelo. Fray Angel de Salazar, cautious and politic as usual, was very cool to the project. This did not prevent Teresa from telling Fray Antonio to go ahead with his preparations. She felt that Fray Angel would change his mind. And so it turned out; for about this time, she explains naïvely, he needed help on "some great and pressing matter," from Doña María, who took advantage of the opportunity to obtain his consent for the new monastery.[26]

While these arrangements were being weighed, Teresa was giving daily instruction in the Primitive Rule to young Fray Juan, and a very apt pupil he was. The perfections she discovered in him delighted her so much that she could not wait for the foundation to see him in her habit, but had the nuns at Medina make him one of serge sackcloth, and bestowed it on him through the grille of the speak room, no doubt in the

---

[25] *Y que creyese que no nos daría la licencia el Provincial pasado ni el presente . . . si nos viesen en casa muy medrada, dejado que no teníemos remedio de ella. y que en aquel lugarcillo y casa, que no harían caso de ellos. — Ibid.*

[26] *Ibid.*

presence of all the community. Having put it on, her *Senequita* then took off his shoes in token of his resolve to follow the Reform in all its severity.[27] Fray Antonio, who had expected to be the first, accepted the situation with his usual good humor. Yet he was not above twitting his little companion from time to time, about receiving the discalced habit from a woman.[27]

What then of Don Bernardino? Teresa could never forget him very long, and after a vision in which our Lord reminded her to hasten, for the poor soul was suffering a great deal,[28] she could hardly wait for Father Julian to return with the necessary permissions. Finally he appeared with a license from the Provisor, but none from the Abbot. Teresa thought of Don Bernardino, and resolved to wait no longer. At dawn on the ninth of August she began the journey of forty kilometers from Medina to Valladolid, taking with her Fray Juan de San Matías, her faithful squire Father Julian, and six women: Sisters Isabel de la Cruz (Arias) and Antonia del Espíritu Santo, whom she had brought from Malagón; María de la Cruz, one of the first nuns at Ávila; Ana de San José from Medina; two from the Incarnation of Ávila, and a young laywoman named Francisca de Villalpando, who later took the white veil as Sister Francisca de Jesús. She was determined to found the new convent on the next day, the Feast of Saint Lawrence.

There were unforeseen difficulties, as usual, when she arrived at the house of Don Bernardino. "I was filled with dismay, for I saw that it was nonsense to have nuns there, except at great expense; for although it was a great place for recreation, since the garden was so lovely, it could not fail to be unhealthy, being near the river."[29] The property was not sufficiently enclosed to make it suitable for contemplatives, and it was necessary to send to Valladolid for workmen to raise adobe walls about it. Again, it was too far from the city. Finally, she had not yet received the Abbot's permission, and lacking this, could do nothing but stay

---

[27] Declaration of Madre Catalina de Jesús, quoted by Silverio, *op. cit.*, III, pp. 298–299.

[28] *Fundaciones*, cap. X.

[29] This fear of the Saint proved well founded. Most of the nuns became ill. Doña María de Mendoza had them cared for, and finally gave them a new house in a better location. Teresa does not explain why she entered a house outside the city when this was forbidden by the Council of Trent. It is hardly likely she would have done so without some sort of dispensation, which she may have received from the Provisor or the Abbot.

at the nearest convent until it could be obtained. So Teresa and her companions went to the monastery of the Calced Carmelite sisters, a weary distance away, to hear Mass; and there they remained for five days until the walls were finished and the Abbot's license received. It was the morning of the Assumption of Our Lady when Father Julian at last said the first Mass in the house of Don Bernardino.

No doubt it was meant to be on that day; and in deference to the debonair cavalier's desire to do something to please the Mother of God, Teresa called the convent *La Concepción de Nuestra Señora del Carmen*. What a first Mass that was! When the little bell had announced that the mystery of the Incarnation and the Crucifixion had been there repeated, and that the infinite merits of Jesus Christ had been offered to His eternal Father on behalf of a poor sinner who loved His Mother, the nuns all approached the rail to receive their Lord. And at that moment Teresa plainly saw, standing beside the priest, the figure of Don Bernardino, his face resplendent with joy; and "putting his hands together, he thanked me for what I had done to help him go forth from purgatory."[30]

Thus, with a smile never to be forgotten, Don Bernardino vanished into eternal happiness.

---

[30] *Fundaciones, loc. cit.*

St. John of the Cross, whom St. Teresa persuaded to join her in reforming the Carmelite Order.

Chapter XXII

WARNING TO PHILIP II

S HE remained at Valladolid through the whole autumn of 1568, and most of the winter.

Before the end of September she sent Fray Juan de San Matías to Duruelo to prepare and furnish the farmhouse. He was to stop at Ávila and deliver the following letter to Don Francisco de Salcedo:

"Jesus be with you, Sir! Glory to God, that after seven or eight business letters that I could not escape, I have a little time left to rest from them by writing these lines, to let you know, Sir, that I have received much consolation from yours. And don't think that it is time wasted to write to me, for I need it at times, on condition that you don't tell me so often that you are old, for that makes my whole brain ache; as if there were any security in the lives of boys! May God let you live until I die, but afterwards I shall ask our Lord to take you quickly, so that I shall not be without you there.

"I beg you to speak, Sir, with this Father, and help him in this affair, for although he is little, I know he is large in the eyes of God. Certainly he is going to be a big loss to us, for he is discreet and suited to our way of life, and so I believe that our Lord has called him for this reason. There is no friar who does not speak well of him, for his life has been one great penance, though short in time. But it seems the Lord holds him in His hand, for although we have had some occasions of difficulty here in business affairs, and I the chief occasion, for I have been vexed with him at times, yet never have we seen an imperfection in him. He has courage, but since he is alone, he has need of what our Lord gives him. . . . He will tell you how it goes with us here."

Don Francisco had written that he would give six ducats to see her. She would give a great deal more to see him. He was worth a higher price, for "who is going to value a poor little nun? You, who can give metheglin and biscuits, radishes and lettuces, for you have a garden, and I know you are the boy to bring apples — you are to be valued somewhat more highly! That same metheglin is very good here, they say; but as we have no Francisco de Salcedo, we don't know what it tastes like, and have no way of knowing. . . . Remain with God. I kiss the hands of my lady Doña Mencía."[1] Teresa added that the Princess of Eboli was very urgent about a foundation of the Discalced Carmelites at her town of Pastrana, and in a postscript begged the Holy Cavalier to advise Fray Juan as to his mode of life. "He has gone far in prayer and has a good understanding; may the Lord carry it on."

While her *Senequita* was at work at Duruelo, she was looking for a healthier house in Valladolid, for the nuns were sick one after the other, and her own ailments were intensified by the damp air from the frozen river. By the first of November she was greatly relieved to learn that Doña Luisa de la Cerda had at last sent her manuscript to Blessed John of Ávila,[2] who praised it highly and suggested only a few clarifications and changes of expression. Before the end of the year she had decided to found a convent at Toledo.

It was Father Pablo Hernández, S.J. (her *Padre Eterno*) who first suggested this enterprise. He had become her confessor and a devoted friend before she left Malagón, so much so that he used to say, "Madre Teresa of Jesus is a very great woman from the roof down, and from the roof up, much greater."[3] It happened about that time that one of his penitents, a rich merchant named Martín Ramírez, was in his last illness, and wished to do something for God and for the peace of his soul. The Jesuit recommended that he establish a convent for Madre Teresa. Ramírez agreed, but died on the last day of October, 1568, before he could communicate with La Madre, who was then in Valladolid. His brother Alonso wrote her; so did Alonso's son-in-law, Diego Ortiz, with great insistence. Teresa had made up her mind to accept their proposal when she wrote Doña Luisa at Toledo on December 13, asking her to obtain permission from the administrator of the diocese — adding that it might be well not to mention her name, but merely say it was for a convent of Discalced Carmelite nuns. "I have neither time nor strength to

---

[1] Wife of Don Francisco. *Carta* X, pp. 28–32, B.M.C., *Epistolario*, I: "*aloja y obleas.*"

[2] *Epistolario*, I, p. 32; Stanbrook, I, 42. Letter of November 2.

[3] "*La M. Teresa de Jesús es muy gran mujer de las tejas abajo, y de las tejas arriba muy mayor.*" — Ribera, *Vida de Santa Teresa*, lib. II, cap. XIII. This familiar picturesque idiom refers, of course, to the natural and the supernatural; or to "here on earth" and "in heaven."

write much," she said, "for I write to few persons nowadays in my own handwriting. . . . I am wretched. With your Ladyship and in your country my health is better, although the people here don't abhor me,[4] glory to God; but since my will is there, I wish my body were too. What does your Ladyship think of the way His Majesty ordains everything for my tranquillity? Blessed be His name, for He has so pleased to arrange it by the hands of persons, such servants of God, that I think His Majesty is going to be much served in this matter."

Shortly after Twelfth Night she wrote Diego Ortiz more definitely:

"The Father Doctor Pablo Hernández has written me the favor and alms you have given me in offering to found a house of this sacred Order. Indeed, I believe our Lord and his glorious Mother, my patron and lady, have prompted your heart, Sir, to such a holy work, in which I hope His Majesty is to be much served, and you, Sir, to come forth with a great gain of spiritual goods. May it so please Him, as I and all these sisters beg it of Him, and henceforth all the Order will. . . . It has suited our Lord to have my fever pass away. I will make all the haste I can to leave this house as I wish it, and I think, with the favor of our Lord, I shall be through shortly; and I promise you, Sir, not to lose time, or to pay any attention to my illness, should my fever return, in making my departure; for since you, Sir, are doing everything, it is only right that I should do my part, which is nothing, that is, to take some trouble; for there is nothing else for us to do who claim to follow the One Who, without our deserving it, lives always in us. I don't think I shall have but one profit in this affair, for, from what my Father Pablo Hernández writes me of you, Sir, it will be very fine to make your acquaintance, for prayers are what have sustained me until now, and so I beg, for the love of our Lord, that you will not forget me in yours. Unless His Majesty orders otherwise, I think I shall be in that place at the latest after the second week in Lent, for as I shall go past the monasteries it has pleased the Lord to found these years (even though we leave here at once), I must spend a day or two in them. It will be as short a time as possible, since you so desire, Sir; although in a matter so well organized and already accomplished, I think I shall have nothing to do but

---

[4] *"le gente de ésta no me aborrece"* — B.M.C., *Epistolario*, I, p. 35.

look around and praise our Lord. May His Majesty keep you always in His hand, Sir, and give you the life and health and increase of grace I ask."[5]

Teresa and the nuns were ill nearly all winter. In February (1569) they moved into a healthier house within the city, purchased for them by Doña María de Mendoza. Their benefactress then had a serious illness, and La Madre, going to spend a day with her, was snowed in for a week or more. On the nineteenth she wrote Alonso Ramírez, explaining the delay, and asking him not to purchase a house until her arrival in Toledo — "for I wish it to be suitable for us, since you and he who is in glory are giving us the alms.

"In the matter of the licenses, that of the King I take for granted, with the favor of heaven, even though there may be some trouble, for I know by experience that the devil can ill endure these houses, and so always persecutes us; but the Lord can do everything, and he takes himself off with his hands on his head.

"Here we had very great opposition, and from persons of the most important there are here; but that is all over now. Don't imagine, Sir, that you are going to give our Lord only what you now think, but much more; and so His Majesty rewards good works by arranging to have greater ones done, and it is nothing to give a few coppers, for that hurts us very little. When they begin to stone you, Sir, and the gentleman your nephew, and all of us who have anything to do with it, as they almost did in Ávila when San José was established, then the business will be going well, and I shall believe that the monastery will lose nothing, nor will those of us who suffer the trouble of it, but will gain much. Don't worry about it, Sir. I am sorry my Father [Hernández] is not there; if necessary, we shall try to have him come back. In short, the devil has already begun. Blessed be God, Who if we don't fail Him, will not fail us. . . . My health is bad enough, though the fever has not returned. . . ."[6]

When she left Valladolid before the end of February, it was still cold, and the hills were covered with snow; the roads were still icy and in many places impassable. The main one running southwest to Medina, however, was open for travel, and she bravely set out with two nuns from San José de Ávila (Isabel

---

[5] B.M.C., *Epistolario* I, p. 37.
[6] *Ibid.*, pp. 38–40.

de Santo Domingo and Isabel de San Pablo) and Father Gonzalo de Aranda as chaplain. At Medina they were joined by two pious merchants who, bound for the south, escorted them as far as Duruelo.

Teresa had been anxious all winter to see the infant monastery. It had been a keen joy to her to learn that Fray Juan had said the first Mass November 28, 1568, casting off his shoes, and discarding the name of John of Saint Matthias for the one that is immortally his, John of the Cross. All this she had heard from Fray Antonio. "He came here to Valladolid to speak to me with great satisfaction, and he told me what he had got together, and it was little enough; he had provided himself with nothing but clocks — he took five of them, which struck me as very funny. He told me this was so he could keep regular hours, for he did not wish to live carelessly; yet I believe he didn't have anything to sleep on."

Very different from the sleek and well-dressed prior who used to enjoy his familiarity with the "best people" of Medina was the huge man that La Madre saw when she arrived at the Duruelo farmhouse. Fray Antonio de Jesús (for that was the name he had taken) was vigorously sweeping the doorway of the chapel, and seemed to be enjoying it.

"What's this, *mi padre?*" said Madre Teresa. "What has become of your dignity?"

Fray Antonio turned and roared, "I curse the time I ever had any!" as he dropped the broom and went to meet his Mother Foundress, to conduct her into the house. First they went into the tiny chapel, "and I was astonished," said Teresa, "to see the spirit the Lord had put there. And I was not the only one, for two merchants, friends of mine, who had come that far with me from Medina, did nothing but weep. There were so many crosses! So many skulls!

"Never shall I forget a little cross of wood that they had for the holy water. It had attached to it an image of Christ on paper, which I thought caused more devotion than if it had been made of something very well designed. The choir was the attic, which was high in the middle so that they could say the Hours, but they had to stoop low to enter it and to hear Mass. In the two corners toward the church they had two little hermitages, full of hay (for the place was very cold, and the roof almost touched their heads) where they could do nothing but lie down or sit, with two little windows facing the altar, and two stones for pillows, and there, too, their crosses and skulls."[7]

Teresa was deeply moved by the account they gave her of their life. There were four of them who said the Office together: Fray John, Fray Antonio, a Father Lucas of the Calced Carmelites who was not accepted because of ill-health, and a youth not yet ordained, Brother José de Cristo. After they said Matins at midnight, they did not go back to what they called their cells until Prime, but remained so absorbed in prayer that they were not even aware of the snow that had fallen on their habits through the leaky roof. With all this they carried on an active apostolate that was no less than heroic. The Catholics of those tiny hamlets and lonely farms had been greatly neglected spiritually; they had no Mass, no religious instruction, no priestly ministrations of any kind, for there was no monastery near, and no means of maintaining one until the two friars appeared in the old farmhouse, in the habit of Madre Teresa's Reform. After praying all night, Fray John and Fray Antonio would go five or six miles into the countryside to preach to the shepherds and small farmers. They went barefoot, even when the snow was deep, and thus they would toil all day, preaching and hearing confessions, without any thought of food until they returned to Duruelo late in the evening for their evening meal. The people, seeing their holy life and utter disregard of self, soon brought food, more than was needed. Noblemen living miles away heard of their labors and the joy with which they performed them, and would ride over to confess to them. One of these was Don Luis de Toledo, Lord of the Five Towns.[8]

"This gentleman," wrote Teresa, "had built a church for an image of our Lady, surely well worthy of veneration. His father sent it from Flanders to his grandmother or mother (I don't remember which) by a merchant. He was so attached to it that he kept it many years, and finally at the hour of his death commanded them to bring it. It is a large portrait, and I have seen nothing better in my whole life — and many other persons say the same. The Father Fray Antonio de Jesús, when he went to that place at the petition of this cavalier and saw the image, became so fond of it, and with good reason, that he agreed to

---

[7] *Fundaciones*, cap. XIV.
[8] Salmoral, Noharros, San Miguel, Montalvo, and Gallegos. He was a relative of the Duke of Alba.

move the monastery there. This place is called Mancera. Although there was no well water there, or any way it seemed for them to get it, this gentleman built them a monastery suitable to their profession, small, and gave ornaments; he did it very well.

"I don't wish to leave unsaid how the Lord gave them water, for it was held to be a thing of miracle. One day after supper, when the Father Fray Antonio, who was prior, was in the cloister with his friars, talking of the need they had of water, the Prior arose and took a staff that he held in his hands, and made on a part of it the sign of the cross, so at least it seems to me, though I don't remember exactly whether he made a cross, but anyhow, he pointed with the stick, and said, 'Now, dig here.' They had dug very little when so much water came out that it is difficult to draw it off even to clean it out; and very good drinking water, too, which they have made use of there for every purpose, and never, as I say, has it failed. After they laid out a garden, they tried to find water in it, and had a deep well dug, and spent plenty on it; but to this day they have not been able to find any, however trifling.

"Then when I saw that little house, which a little while before no one could stay in, with such a spirit that in every part, wherever I looked, I seemed to find something to edify me, and when I heard the way in which they lived, and their mortification and prayer and the good example they gave (for a gentleman and his wife, whom I knew, who lived in a place near by, came to see me there, and never tired of telling me of their sanctity and of the great good they were doing among those communities) I could not give thanks enough to our Lord. . . . The merchants who had come with me said that they would not have missed coming to that place for all the world. What a thing is virtue, that such poverty should delight them more than all the riches they had. . . .

"After those Fathers and I had talked over certain matters, I asked them especially, for I am weak and wicked, not to be so rigorous in doing their penances, for they went very far in it; and as it had cost me so much in desire and in prayer to have the Lord give me someone to commence it, and as I saw so good a beginning, I was afraid the devil might finish them off before they accomplished what I hoped. Imperfect and of little faith as I am, it did not occur to me that it was a work of God and that

His Majesty was going to carry it forward. They, having those things that I lacked, took little account of my words to give up their works; and so I went away with the very greatest consolation, though I did not give God the praises that such a great favor deserved."[9]

The house at Duruelo fell to ruins after the friars moved to Mancera, and little if anything is now left of it; but the reform established by Saint John of the Cross and Fray Antonio under La Madre's inspiration and direction has continued to this day. From humble Duruelo it spread to various places in Spain, to Italy, and thence quietly but irresistibly throughout the whole world.[10]

Madre Teresa continued her journey toward Toledo, passing through Madrid, and possibly making a short stay there. This must have been the time when, according to a Carmelite tradition, she received a revelation in prayer concerning Philip II. It was certainly the most unhappy year of that misunderstood monarch's life. It was the year in which he began to have the gout that was to plague him to the end. In July Don Carlos, his only son and heir, died in prison. In October his third wife, Queen Isabelle of Valois, was laid in her tomb at the convent of the Discalced Franciscans in Madrid. During that same autumn (1568) Philip borrowed many hundreds of thousands of ducats at high usury in Genoa, and had them sent by sea to pay the troops of the Duke of Alba in the Netherlands. One of the international bankers who had lent the money betrayed the secret to the English government, which, although professing to be still friendly to Spain, seized the gold in transit and never gave it up; hence Alba, after all his brilliant victories, was left in a dangerous situation which he had to meet by levying the taxes which so exasperated the people of the Low Countries, and added immeasurably to the difficulties of the Spanish crown. At Christmas the Moriscos of Granada massacred the Christians, priests and laymen, men, women, and children indiscriminately; and when, in the spring, King Philip sent his brother Don John of Austria to suppress their rebellion, the first rumors were coming from Constantinople, via Venetian spies, of a great fleet that the Grand Turk, influenced by international enemies of Spain in

---

[9] *Fundaciones, loc. cit.* Teresa especially asked the friars not to go barefoot. They persisted, but later were compelled to wear sandals.

[10] Mancera also proved unhealthy. The friars moved to Avila in 1600.

the Netherlands and elsewhere, was going to launch against Christendom the following year. Philip, lonely and bereaved, at odds with the Pope and with his own conscience — for up to this time he had followed the opportunist policies of his father under the guidance of such politicians as Cobos, Ruy Gómez, and Cardinal Espinosa — found himself facing a whole world of enemies; and no man ever needed the grace of God more than he did when he went to a monastery to meditate on Christ's Passion in the Holy Week of 1569. It was the turning point, spiritually, of his life; there is no doubt that whatever his mistakes, he became from then on more and more sincerely Catholic in all his actions until his saintly death in the last years of the century.

This tremendous change in him, with all its repercussions in the history of Europe and the world, is traced by a Carmelite tradition to La Madre's journey from Duruelo to Toledo. Christ in a vision told her that King Philip was in great danger of losing his soul. "Daughter," He said, "I wish him to be saved." He commanded her to deliver a note of warning to Princess Juana, sister of Philip, at Madrid. Teresa, of course, obeyed. Winter must have been just breaking up when she rode wearily into the capital one day in March, 1569, and made her way either to the Franciscan convent where she had formerly stayed, or to the palace; or perhaps to the house of Doña Leonor. At any rate, she found the Princess, delivered the note, and went on her way.

Nothing remains of the missive but a fragment:

"Remember, Sire, that Saul was anointed, and yet he was rejected."[11]

Philip was astonished at this and the other contents of the letter.

"Where is this woman?" he demanded. "I wish to speak to her."

She was already on her way to Toledo. Whether or not this tradition of the warning is true, she often used to refer to Philip as "my friend the King," and asked her nuns to pray for him. To doubt that she helped him in his task and his conflict would be to doubt the efficacy of prayer.

In any case Philip was only an earthly monarch. Teresa was

---

[11] The Benedictines of Stanbrook print this fragment in their edition of the Letters, vol. I., p. 51, with a note by Father Benedict Zimmerman, O.C.D., who apparently considered it authentic. Padre Silverio omits it from his *Epistolario*.

bound on a more important mission for the King of Heaven, who desired a new home in Toledo, when she arrived there on March 24, 1569, and went to the Cerda palace.

"I arrived here, well, on the eve of our Lady," she wrote to Doña María de Mendoza. "My lady Doña Luisa has rejoiced extremely. . . . My founders here are very clever men; we are already at work to obtain the license. I wish to hurry, and if they give it to us quickly, I believe everything will go well. . . ."[12]

On the contrary, everything went wrong. Teresa herself could not have believed (for more than a few hopeful moments) that she would escape the usual mysterious opposition which is the cross and the triumph of all activity truly Christian. One day when a nun asked her how to become a saint, she replied, "Daughter, we are soon going to make a foundation; then you will learn the way." During the foundation this particular sister had many bitter trials, of which she finally complained. "Wasn't it you, daughter," asked La Madre, "who asked me to teach you how to become a saint? This is the way."[13]

Perhaps for the moment she forgot all this, and expected an early realization of her two desires: permission for the foundation, and a suitable house. Neither, however, was obtainable. Alonso Ramírez and his nephew, Diego Ortiz, had failed to obtain the license from the diocesan authority. Ortiz, it now appeared, was a finicky and somewhat cantankerous young man who suggested to his uncle all sorts of provisos and conditions which were a torment to La Madre. Nor was any house to be had. It seems incredible that Doña Luisa and all her wealthy and noble friends could not have found somewhere in the great city of Toledo a residence that would meet the humble requirements of the Carmelites. Yet such was the case. Two months passed. The weather was now uncomfortably hot, the slender treasury of the nuns was reduced to three or four ducats, and nothing had been done.

Teresa decided, after all this disappointment, to go hunting for the license herself. It was out of the question to see the Archbishop of Toledo, Bartolomé Carranza de Miranda, for he had been arrested by the Inquisition, and was now in Rome awaiting judgment on the charge that his works contained

---

[12] Letter of March, 1569, B.M.C., *Epistolario*, I, pp. 38–40; Stanbrook, 1, pp. 51–53.
[13] *Deposition of Isabel de Jesús*, La Fuente, VI, p. 318, n. 20, 21.

heretical propositions of a Lutheran flavor.[14] In the meantime no new Ordinary could be appointed, and the government of the diocese of Toledo was entrusted to a council headed by the Licentiate Don Gómez Tello Girón, a man highly respected for his learning, his wealth, and his descent from an illustrious old family. Thus far he had said no to Doña Luisa, to one of the canons of the cathedral, and to several other personages. Once or twice he had been on the point of yielding, but had been talked out of it by members of the Council. Teresa had an idea that there must be some way to manage him, and she resolved to make the attempt. Going to a church near his house with Sister Isabel de Santo Domingo, she sent him word that she was there and would he have the goodness to come and speak with her? The great man came. He was a "very grave gentleman" (this was the highest compliment that could be paid to a man in sixteenth-century Spain) and no doubt was a model of courtesy to the old woman in the threadbare robe who bowed so modestly before him; but his mind was made up, and he repeated what he had told the others.

"I told him," recorded La Madre tersely, "that it was a hard thing that there should be women who wished to live in such rigor and perfection and enclosure, and that those who did not endure anything of this sort, but kept themselves in luxury, should try to prevent works of so much service to our Lord."[15]

Ribera either expands upon this, or, it may be, sets down what she told him:

"More than two months ago, Señor, I came to this city, not to see it or enjoy it, but to seek the glory of God and the good of souls, and to render to His Majesty in this so illustrious a city the service I have rendered in others of founding a monastery of discalced nuns who keep the first rule of the Order of Our Lady of Mt. Carmel, and for this I brought my nuns with me. It would be a thing worthy of Your Lordship's learning and virtue and dignity to favor a few poor women with such a holy thing, and encourage them to go ahead, since God wishes it done here. I have not seen it so, for all this time neither the importance of those who asked the permission nor the so evident justice of our cause have sufficed to obtain it from Your Lord-

[14] An extended account of this much misunderstood case is in my *Characters of the Inquisition* (New York: P. J. Kenedy & Sons, 1940); and a shorter one in my *Philip II* (New York and London: Sheed and Word, 1937).

[15] *Fundaciones, loc. cit.*

ship. It is indeed a hard thing that some poor women who ask
no more than to live in such rigor and perfection in a cloister
for the love of God should have no one willing to help them,
while those who do not endure any of this, but live in luxury
as they please, try to hinder a work of such service to God. We
have houses to live in, indeed, and if we should return to them
we should risk little, for we have nothing to lose in this world;
but let Your Lordship notice what would be lost in this city,
and how much to your charge it would be. If this is not done
by Your Lordship, consider how you can free yourself from
blame, when you are in the presence of our Lord Jesus Christ,
for Whose love and will we have come, for I do not see how
Your Lordship can acquit yourself if you hinder a thing so
agreeable to the Lord, being appointed by Him to aid with all
your powers in everything that is for His service."

The head of the diocesan council was so moved by this and
other things she said that he gave his permission, but on condition that there be no endowment or patron. Perhaps the snobbery which was one of the faults of Toledo society played a part
there. It was well known that the Ramírez family wished to
sponsor the monastery. They were of lowly origin, and in the
eyes of the aristocrats who ruled the city, nobodies. Teresa, however, was content with her partial victory.

She was no longer bound to consider the Ramírez family, for
they had broken with her, or she with them. "Alonso Alvarez
and I had not been able to agree, on account of his son-in-law,
to whom he gave in a great deal. Finally, we came to disagree
altogether."

As for finding a house, she had never worried much. Indeed
she was so confident, in spite of the failures of Doña Luisa and
others, that she had already bought two somewhat crude but
very devout paintings on canvas for the altar: one of Jesus falling, with the cross on His back, the other showing Him seated
on a stone bench in profound meditation — both still venerated
at the convent in Toledo. Then she obtained two cheap straw
mattresses and a blanket. This was all the "furniture." Nothing
remained now but to find the convent.

Teresa never doubted that God would accomplish this in His
own good time. For a while she thought that His instrument
would be a certain merchant, Alonso de Ávila, a bachelor from
her own city who was noted for visiting men in prison, feeding

the poor, and other acts of mercy. He promised to help but illness prevented him. There was also a Franciscan, Friar Martin of the Cross, who listened to her with great sympathy; but he was in Toledo for a few days only.

She used to go to various churches of the city to pray for hours at a time. One day she heard Mass at the church of Saint Clement with "one of the most important ladies of the city." They went to the altar to receive Holy Communion. As Madre Teresa returned to her seat, a poor woman, crying out angrily against her, began to beat her over the head with an old shoe. She had lost the mate of it in the crowd, and suspected La Madre, as being more shabbily dressed than those about her, of having stolen it. Teresa smiled at her affectionately. What could be better than to bear blows and insults for Christ's sake?[16] "God reward that good woman," she said afterwards, "but I certainly have a headache!"

She had almost forgotten a young student named Andrada, who had introduced himself to her one morning in May when she went to a church to hear Mass, just before her interview with the Governor. Very unprepossessing and ill-clothed he was, one of the many poor tattered scholars who worked their way through the Spanish universities, and she must have been startled when he accosted her, asking if she was Mother Teresa of Jesus. He had come to see her at the direction of the Franciscan father, Fray Martin of the Cross, who just before leaving Toledo had heard his confession, and perhaps discerning in him the simplicity of a great spirituality, had told him of La Madre's difficulty, and had made him promise to help her. He had nothing to offer but his own person, he said; but that was at her disposal. Fray Martin had told him to do whatever she might ask.

Even Teresa was amused at the idea that this lean and ill-clad messenger could accomplish what all her wealthy and powerful friends had failed to do. Her companions laughed outright. Sister Isabel de Santo Domingo took her aside and told her it would not look well for such a disreputably dressed person to be seen talking with Discalced Carmelites.

"Be quiet, now," answered La Madre. "What harm could they think of us, who look like nothing but pilgrims?"[17]

[16] Deposition of M. Isabel de Santo Domingo, B.M.C., t. 19, pp. 491–492.
[17] Ribera, *Vida de Santa Teresa*, lib. II, cap. XIII.

She thanked Andrada graciously, made a note of where he lived, and told him that if there was anything he could do, she would send for him. It seemed unlikely that she would ever do so.

A few days later, when she had the Governor's permission but still no prospect of a house, she found herself thinking about this *pobre estudiante*. After all, he had come to her from a very holy priest, and there was something mysterious about the way he had come to her in the church, so quietly, so directly. Was it not God's way of doing things? She told her companions that she was going to send for him.

They all laughed. They begged her to give up the foolish idea, for Andrada would probably be unable to keep their secret, and everything would be spoiled. Teresa had made up her mind, however; she sent for him and told him she needed a house, and wanted one rented without everyone's knowing about it. He said he would see what he could do.

Within a few days,[18] when she was at Mass in the Jesuit church, Andrada came quietly up to her and showed her a bunch of keys, which he said belonged to a house he had found near by in a little street, probably the present Calle de San Juan de Dios, where the ghetto had been before the expulsion of the Jews in 1492; it was close to what had been the *Sinagoga del Tránsito,* then a priory of the Order of Calatrava.[19] La Madre and her skeptical companions went along with him to inspect it, and found it quite suitable for a beginning. She agreed to accept it, promising to pay the rent with some money she hoped to get from Alonso de Ávila, but actually had to borrow from the wife of the majordomo of Doña Luisa.

"Many times, when thinking of this foundation," she wrote, "I have wondered at the artifices of God. To think that for nearly three months, at least more than two, I don't remember exactly, such rich persons had been going up and down Toledo looking for it, and as if there were no houses in it, had never been able to find it. And then along came this young man, who was not rich but very poor, and it pleased the Lord that he should then find it, and that whereas we might have founded it

---

[18] *Otro día de mañana"* is her expression. This does not necessarily mean the next day, as some editors have inferred.
[19] Cf. Silverio, *Vida de Santa Teresa de Jesús,* III, 384, n. 2, and his long quotation from Don Agustín Rodríguez' *Santa Teresa en Toledo.*

without trouble by coming to terms with Alonso Alvarez, it should not be so, but far otherwise, so that the foundation might be made with poverty and travail.

"Then, as the house pleased us, I gave orders at once to take possession of it before anything could be done in it, so there might be no hindrance; and very soon the said Andrada came to tell me that the house would be empty that very day, and we could move our furniture in. I told him there wouldn't be much trouble about that, for we had nothing but two straw mattresses and a blanket. He must have been surprised; my companions were sorry that I had told him, and asked me why I had said it, for seeing us so poor he would not wish to help us. I paid no attention to this, and as for him, he thought little of it either; for the One Who had given him such willingness was going to carry on with it until he finished his work; and so it is, for what with going about to arrange the house and getting workmen, I don't think we gave him any odds.[20] We hunted up some borrowed furnishings to say Mass, and at nightfall we went with a workman to take possession, with a little bell, one of those rung at the Consecration, for we didn't have any other. And with fear enough on my part, we went about all night getting it ready, and there was no place for a church except in one room, whose entrance was through the little house next door, where some woman lived, and their landlord was the one who had rented to us.

"Having everything ready at the first peep of dawn (and we had not dared to say anything to the women lest they discover us) we began to open the door, which was in a brick partition, and it led to a very tiny *patio*. When they heard the blows, they got up — for they were in bed — terrified. We had all we could do to pacify them, but the hour had come for saying Mass, and although they made a great uproar, they did us no harm; and as they saw what it was for, the Lord quieted them."

Father Juan de la Magdalena, prior of the Calced Carmelites of the city, said the Mass. Early though it was, Doña Luisa de la Cerda and all her household were present, with various passers-by who had been attracted by the tinkling of the little bell. When a little boy cried out, *"Bendito sea Dios!* How pretty it is!" Teresa felt repaid for all her labors.

The end was not yet, however. Presently there appeared the

---

[20] *"No me parece le hacíamos ventaja."*

woman who owned the house, very angry at learning that a church had been established there, for her estate was entailed. Teresa quieted her by promising her a good price for it. Next came members of the diocesan Council, demanding by what right she had dared to found a convent without their knowledge, and asking to see her license. Fortunately perhaps for her, the governor had left town after giving his verbal permission, else they might have prevailed upon him to change his mind. But her old friend, Fray Vicente Barrón, O.P., now a *consultor* of the Inquisition at Toledo, took her part; and one of the canons, Don Pedro Manrique, reminding them that the same thing had been done in other places without disastrous consequences, persuaded them to take no action until the Governor returned.

The poverty of the new convent was pitiful. On the first day, as Teresa recorded, "we didn't have a stick of wood to roast a sardine with, and I don't know whom the Lord impelled, but somebody left a little bundle of wood in the church for us, and we helped ourselves to it." The nights were very cold. La Madre and her two nuns lay on the straw mattresses, all huddled together under their one blanket.

Why did the rich and noble Doña Luisa, who had furnished a whole convent at Malagón, allow her friend to go cold and hungry under her very eyes? Did she feel that she had done enough for the Reform, and that others should take their turn? Or had she perhaps been offended by the frank strictures of La Madre on her delay in sending the autobiography to Blessed John of Ávila? Or did she, like other aristocrats of Toledo, resent the connection of the Ramírez family with the affair? It is a mystery to this day. Teresa delicately drew the wide mantle of her charity over it:

"It will seem impossible that we entered with such poverty, when we were in the house of that lady who loved me so much; I don't know the reason, unless that God wished us to find out for ourselves the blessing of this virtue. I did not ask it of her, for I hate to give trouble, and she did not notice it perhaps, for I owe her more than she could give us."[21]

The fact remains that this very rich woman, so preoccupied with her own sorrows, was present at the first Mass, and must have noticed the poverty of the house.

The community survived and grew notwithstanding. Madre

---

[21] *Fundaciones, loc. cit.*

Teresa sent to Ávila for some nuns from the Incarnation: Doña Antonia del Aguila and Doña Isabel Suárez; and she brought Sister Ana de los Angeles from Malagón to be prioress. Ill-health compelled one of the nuns to return to Ávila. The others embraced the rigors of the life in Toledo with such joy that they were disappointed when the tide of their fortunes turned, and people began showering gifts upon them. Alonso Alvarez Ramírez was one of the first to offer his help, now that he saw the convent established, and to hint at establishing a burial place in it for himself and his family. Someone else gave a chasuble of crimson taffeta and two corporals; others sent blankets and beds. Food became so plentiful that the nuns said in dismay, "What are we going to do, Mother? We don't seem to be poor any more!"[22]

This was only a temporary complaint. The gifts were not so numerous after a while, and it became evident that the house would not be large enough for permanent occupancy. Teresa found herself under the necessity of accepting some sort of endowment. A great nobleman of Toledo offered a sum of money for a new convent, if he could have the chancel for his family. Yet when Alonso Ramírez desired the same privilege, she could not forget that it was he who had first drawn her to Toledo. There was much murmuring in that ancient society over the effrontery of such an upstart. Possibly this had its effect on the Licentiate. In giving his written permission he stipulated that the home must be unendowed — thus apparently excluding the Ramírez family.

If Madre Teresa was not seriously tempted by all this snobbery, she was enough the daughter of her own class to hesitate: "Our Lord was pleased to give me light on this matter, and so he told me once how little these lineages and estates will amount to before the judgment of God, and gave me a great scolding because I had listened to those who were talking to me about this for they were not things for those of us who have despised the world."[23] One day He said to her, "You will be very foolish, daughter, if you pay attention to the laws of the world. Put your eyes upon me, poor and despised by it. Will the great ones of the world perchance be great before Me? Or are you going to be esteemed for lineages or for virtues?"[24]

---

[22] Ibid.   [23] Ibid.   [24] Relaciones. B.M.C., II. p. 44.

She decided that although the terms of the license would not allow the Ramírez family to endow the monastery she could at least let them build the chapel and be buried in it; and so it was arranged despite all the blue bloods of Toledo. Later the money given for the chapel helped to pay for a new house, one of the best in town, worth twelve thousand ducats; and there, from that day to this, many saintly souls have lived and died.

The nuns still point out the small room that was Teresa's cell, its only ornament a statue of Christ at the Column (revered as miraculous), its walls and floor spattered with spots of what is said to be dried blood from the scourgings in which she sought to share His pain. This convent was so noted for the holiness of its members that La Madre devoted an extra chapter of her *Fundaciones* to them. There was, for instance, a very rich but sickly woman who entered at the age of forty, bestowing all her property on the Community, and afterwards enjoyed the best of health in poverty. When Teresa warned her that she might not be accepted, so that she could retain her property if she desired, Ana de la Madre de Dios replied that she would not take back her gift in any case; she had given it for the love of God, and if rejected, would beg her bread for the love of God.

The obedience in that house was so remarkable that the Prioress had to be careful not to speak in jest, lest some nun take her seriously. There was one superior who remarked of a certain one, "What would she do if I told her to throw herself into the pool?" and before the words were well out of her mouth, the sister was in the water up to her neck, and had to be sent off to change her habit. Another who should have been preparing to enter the confessional went up to speak to her superior, who, startled and displeased, said, "Was this a way to recollect yourself? Put your head in the well, and think of your sins." The nun was prevented barely in time from throwing herself into the well. Such was the spirit in that place that learned men had to be brought to restrain the sisters and to point out the dangers of excess even in good things.

It was there, too, that Madre Teresa agreed to accept a certain young woman who appeared to be very holy, yet for some reason she felt ill at ease about her.

"Come tomorrow for your reception," she said suddenly.

"Yes, Mother, and I will bring my Bible."

"Bible, child?" replied La Madre very earnestly. "No, you

shall not come here. We do not want you or your Bible, for we are ignorant women, and do nothing but spin and obey."

It goes almost without saying that she did not object to the Bible as such, for she was always quoting it herself, but to the tendency, very prevalent in the days of Luther, to attack the Church under pretext of appealing to the Scriptures. As Archbishop Carranza once explained, the Church forbade her children to read unauthorized editions of the Bible because her enemies conducted a huge traffic in printing and circulating translations doctored and mutilated to suit their own sinister purposes; thousands of such inaccurate Bibles were printed at Ferrara, for example, and sent secretly to Spain. Hence an excessive preoccupation with the Bible became a symptom of heretical activity. And La Madre was not wrong in suspecting something of the sort in this girl; for after her rejection she consorted with a group of so-called *beatas* and finally appeared with them as a prisoner at an *auto de fe*.

Teresa once knelt before the Blessed Sacrament at Toledo to beg for the grace of a happy death for a dying nun. Then, going to the nun's cell, she saw Christ standing at the head of the bed, His arms outstretched as if protecting her; and He promised that in the same way He would protect all who should die in any of those monasteries, and that they need not fear the temptations of the last moments of this life. Immediately after this, the nun died very joyfully — "like an angel."

The convent was pretty well established and organized two weeks after the foundation. One Saturday, the eve of Pentecost, the Foundress sat down to dine, very tired, yet very happy over the accomplishment of her task — so happy, in fact, that she could hardly eat. Now at last she could rest a little while, now she could relax.

Halfway through the meal a bell rang, and Sister Isabel de Santo Domingo, the *tornera*, came to tell her that a servant of the Princess of Éboli was outside, with a message from his mistress, and insisted upon speaking with her at once.

La Madre got up wearily and went out to meet him.

Chapter XXIII

THE ONE-EYED PRINCESS OF ÉBOLI

LIKE everyone else in Spain, Teresa knew well enough who the great lady was whose gentleman's gentleman faced her at the door. Ana de Mendoza y de la Cerda was the wife of the second most important man in the Spanish Empire. Her father was Diego Hurtado de Mendoza, Prince of Melito, son of one of the viceroys of the Emperor. Her great-grandfather (through one of his early frailties) was the Grand Cardinal and "third King" of Spain, Don Pedro González de Mendoza, adviser of *los reyes católicos* and patron of Columbus. Her great-great-grandfather was the famous fifteenth-century poet and soldier, the Marqués of Santillana. Crusaders, statesmen, prelates, and explorers made her family tree illustrious. She was related by blood to most of the noblest families in Spain, and by marriage to some of those with Jewish strains, such as the Guzmáns, the De Lunas, and others. One of her cousins was Antonio de Mendoza, first viceroy to New Spain; another was Bernardino de Mendoza, admiral of the fleet.

At the age of sixteen this lady had been given in marriage by Philip II to his best friend and lifelong confidant, Ruy Gómez de Silva, a Portuguese by birth, who had come to Spain as a child with Doña Leonor de Mascareñas, to be a page in the court of Charles V. His handsome face and happy lovable disposition so attracted the Empress Isabel that she chose him as the special companion of her son. He had accompanied the Prince to Italy, to the Low Countries, and to England; he had raised the money that had helped to make his victory at St. Quentin possible; now in middle age they were still inseparable friends; and although in foreign affairs Philip was more inclined to follow the advice of the Duke of Alba, Ruy Gómez never lost his confidence, and by his almost universal popularity to the date of his death, seemed to furnish an almost unique exception to the usual fate of ministers. A contemporary historian pays him a high tribute. He was "modest, without artifice, and brief of speech. He spoke only what was necessary, and at the right moment." Though ambitious, he never gained power by evil means, but overcame his rivals by courtesy and generosity.

He was always careful, even when he became very rich, not to dress more brilliantly than the King,[1] who usually wore a plain suit of black, with a simple gold chain at his neck. In political matters he was an opportunist of the school of Charles V; yet the great Papal Nuncio, Ormaneto, once described him as a "loyal and competent minister, very devoted and friendly to the Holy See." He was almost the only person who could control Prince Don Carlos in his last years. And he was the only one capable of restraining the volatile emotions of the lady who had brought him love, wealth, children, and new titles to add to that of Prince of Éboli, which Philip conferred upon him.

His wife retained in her thirties a great deal of the fresh and vivacious charm that so many had remarked when she was married at sixteen. The loss of her right eye in an accident seemed to enhance rather than impair her fascination: the black patch added a touch of mystery, of exotic piquancy to a flowerlike face framed in a wide ruff such as Ann Boleyn made fashionable, and surmounted by a conelike coiffure in four coils of dark hair, one above the other; and her left eye seemed doubly potent to bring young cavaliers to her feet, and to sway the magnanimous heart of Ruy Gómez. Even after the birth of her ninth child, she looked more like a girl than a matron. Her houses in Madrid and in the country were the gayest and most luxurious in Spain, centers of intrigue and gossip, show places of fashion.

She and her husband had probably shed no tears over the departure of Alba for the Netherlands in the spring of 1568. No longer did the Duke's personality and prestige control the foreign and military policies of Philip II. Ruy Gómez alone now had the King's ear, and he was not long in using his influence to bring into the Royal Council a protégé who lived in his house, Antonio Pérez, an adroit, affable, splendidly attired youth whom some called his illegitimate son, though the doubtful honor of siring him belonged, it is now agreed, to Gonzalo Pérez, a secretary to the late Emperor. Antonio soon became the confidential secretary of King Philip, who entrusted more and more of his affairs to him. He had a chivalrous regard for his benefactor's wife, the Princess, whom he described as "a jewel set in the enamels of nature and of fortune." Ana's devotion to her husband, however, was never questioned. It was said that no

---

[1] Cabrera, *Felipe el segundo*, t. II, pp. 140–141.

one less gifted with firmness and gentle understanding could have mastered a woman so proud, vain, and capricious.

Madre Teresa knew even before she reached the turnstile what was wanted of her. The Princess had written her in the autumn of 1568, offering to found a convent for her at Pastrana, five leagues from Guadalajara, where she and her husband had already established hospitals and other public charities, including a beautiful Collegiate Church, and had been generous and intelligent patrons of agriculture. What their town needed now, they felt, was a community of contemplatives; they had heard of the fame of La Madre, and the Princess wished her to come at once and open a house. Accustomed to being obeyed immediately, her Highness had sent the coach for her, and had gone to Pastrana to welcome her.

Teresa replied, as few persons in Spain would have dared to do, that it was then out of the question, for her presence was needed at Toledo. "It pained me, for with the monastery founded so recently, and with such opposition, it would be very dangerous to leave it; and so I determined then and there not to go, and told him [the messenger] so. He told me that this would not be tolerated, for the Princess had already gone there, and had gone for no other reason, and it would be an insult to her. With all this, I had no thought of going, and so I told him to go and get something to eat, and I would write a letter to the Princess, and he could go on his way. He was a very respectable man, and although he took it badly, he accepted it when I told him the reasons I had.

"The nuns who were to be in the monastery had just come; in no way did I see how it was possible to leave so soon. I went before the Blessed Sacrament to ask the Lord to help me to write in such a way that she would not be offended, for we were very badly off on account of beginning just then with the friars, and in every way it was good to have Ruy Gómez, who was in such high favor with the King and with everybody; though as to this I don't recall whether I remembered it, but indeed I know that I did not wish to displease her.

"Being in this plight, it was said to me on the part of our Lord that I must not fail to go, that I would be going to more than to that foundation, and that I should take the Rule and the Constitutions.

"I, when I understood this, though I saw great reasons for

not going, did not dare to do anything but what I was accustomed to do in such matters, which was to be ruled by the advice of the confessor. And so I sent to call him, without telling him what I had heard in prayer (for in this way I am always better satisfied) but begging the Lord to give them light according to what they can know by natural means; and His Majesty, when He wishes something to be done, puts it in their heart. This has happened to me many times. So it was in this case, for considering everything he thought I should go. And with this I decided to go."[2] The confessor on this occasion was Fray Vicente Barrón, O.P.

On the next morning, May 30, 1569, La Madre took her place, with Sister Isabel de Santo Domingo and the Calced Carmelite Father Pedro Muriel, in the magnificent coach of the Princess. They traveled by way of Madrid; and there for some reason, despite the haste of the Princess, they stopped for two or three days with Doña Leonor de Mascareñas at the Franciscan Convent of Our Lady of the Angels, visited the nuns at the Royal Monastery, and perhaps saw the Princess Juana. It was on this occasion that Teresa met a young woman of noble birth who was later to enter one of the reformed convents as Sister Beatriz del Sacramento. She also met two extraordinary men who happened to be staying at the hospice of Doña Leonor: an engineer and a portrait painter, who had left the world to become hermits near Pastrana.

Ambrosio Mariano Azaro, member of a rich and noble Neapolitan family, had been a fellow student of Jacob Buoncompagni, later Pope Gregory XIII, and was a humanist in the best sense, for his curious and versatile mind was equally at home in theology or engineering, canon law or military science. The Council of Trent, which he attended, sent him on a commission of investigation to Poland, then in grave danger of being lost to the Faith. Catherine of Austria, wife of Sigismund II, appointed him general administrator of her palace. He might have made a brilliant marriage had he not chosen instead to become a Knight of Saint John. When he tired of the Polish court, he went to the Low Countries, entered the service of Philip II, and won his esteem by services at the battle of St. Quentin. Subsequently accused of a murder, he was kept

---

[2] *Fundaciones*, cap. XVII.

in prison for two years before his innocence was established.[3] Then he went to Spain, where Philip, a magnificent patron of science as well as of art,[4] set him to work investigating the feasibility of making the River Guadalquivir navigable from Sevilla to Córdoba. Meanwhile Mariano placed himself under the direction of the Jesuits, took the exercises of Saint Ignatius, and on meeting the famous Brother Mateo, a hermit in the desert of the Tardón near Sevilla, decided to forsake the world for the solitude of the Sierra Morena. From there the King summoned him in 1568 to supervise a project for irrigating the *vega* of Aranjuez, the royal pleasure ground, from the waters of the Tajo. This task finished, Mariano was on his way back to his hermitage when he stopped at Madrid to see Doña Leonor, and heard that Madre Teresa also was there.

Mariano's companion was another Neapolitan, of humble origin: John Narduch, who early in life had entered a convent of Observantine Franciscans, but after a pilgrimage to Compostela, and another to the Christ of Burgos, had become a hermit near a famous image of our Lady. When his sanctity attracted attention, he fled from one place to another until at last, in Córdoba, he met Mariano Azaro, with whom he had once traveled from Italy to Poland, and followed him into the desert. Mariano got permission for him through the Princess Juana to study painting under the King's protégé Alonso Sánchez Coello. Narduch had always clung to this ambition; and after a year of instruction he wished to repay the benefactions of Doña Leonor Mascareñas by doing some portraits for her; this was how he happened to be staying at her hospice.

Of the two soldiers of fortune, Teresa found Mariano, with his keen intelligence and burning love of God, by far the more interesting. "When he told me the manner of his life, I showed him our primitive Rule, and I told him that he could observe all that without so much trouble, for it is the same, especially as to living by the labor of his hands, which was what he was much inclined to, telling me that the world was lost through covetousness, and that this caused the Religious to be held in contempt. As I was of the same mind, we agreed at once on this,

---

[3] Teresa is our authority for this. She gives his story of how he was falsely accused, refused to have counsel, and was finally exonerated, like Saint Susanna, when the evidence was found conflicting. *Fundaciones*, cap. XVII.

[4] Cf. my *Philip II*, p. 575. He patronized, among others, Vitoria, Sánchez Coello, Titian, and El Greco.

and in fact on everything; and when I gave him reasons why he could serve God much in this habit, he told me he would think about it that night. Already I saw that he was almost decided, and I understood that what I had heard in prayer, that I was going to something more than a monastery of nuns, was this. It gave me the greatest satisfaction, for it seemed the Lord was going to be much served if he should enter the Order. His Majesty, Who desired it, so moved him that night that the next day he called me, his mind already quite made up, and astonished moreover to see himself changed so speedily, especially by a woman (as even now he sometimes says to me) as if that were the cause, instead of the Lord, who can change hearts."[5]

Mariano not only entered the Order, but handed over to it the hermitage of Saint Peter that Ruy Gómez had given him near Pastrana; and when John Narduch, to whom he read aloud the Rule, agreed that this was what they had been looking for, Teresa had the nucleus for a second monastery of Discalced friars.

She left Madrid well pleased, and after a brief stop perhaps at the Carmelite convent at Alcalá, reached her destination at the end of the same day.

Pastrana was a town of about one thousand souls (there are now but seven hundred) living in houses huddled together in fairly straight parallel rows, on a fertile hillside sloping into green fields where farmers still threshed their grain after the Moorish manner. On all sides Teresa saw beautiful gardens, smelled the fragrance of growing things, heard the happy voices of human beings, until, after lumbering up the last hill, the coach stopped before a ponderous Renaissance palace, with the arms of *Mendoza y La Cerda* over its Romanesque door.

Teresa and her companions dismounted and went in. It was all very magnificent, but she was eager to get into the humble dwelling promised her, looking out upon the beautiful formal gardens of the ducal estate. Her first disappointment was learning that the extensive alterations the Princess had ordered in it were not finished. She must therefore remain in the palace. What a bore! Two weeks passed. The nuns who were to make up the rest of the community arrived from other convents: Isabel de San Jerónimo and Ana de Jesús from Medina, and Jerónima de San Agustín from the Incarnation of Ávila. Five

---

[5] *Loc. cit.*

days more elapsed before they installed the Blessed Sacrament and opened the convent under the name of Our Lady of the Conception.

Mariano and Narduch soon appeared, bringing the Provincial's license for the second monastery of friars. It was a joyful day when they both received the habit of the Discalced at their hermitage of Saint Peter, and in the presence of La Madre and the Princess heard eloquent Fray Baltasar de Jesús, a Carmelite from Medina, welcome them as lay brothers into the Reform, which he also embraced. When the famous engineer became Ambrosio Mariano de San Benito, he declined, like Saint Francis, out of humility, to take holy orders, nor would he do so until his superiors insisted upon it four years later. Juan Narduch took the name of Fray Juan de la Miseria. History remembers him as painter of the most famous portrait of Madre Teresa, who sat for him day after day at the command of her director, as a penance. When the picture was finished, she said, "God forgive you, Fray Juan! To think that after all I have suffered at your hands, you should paint me so bleary eyed and ugly!" Yet the portrait has been defended as a faithful if not flattering likeness.[6]

Teresa remained at Pastrana for almost two months. The whimsical exactions of the Princess and her own faulty sense of time may have made it seem longer, for she wrote, "I was three months in that place, where there were trials enough endured, through the Princess's asking me certain things that were not suitable for our Order, and so I was resolved to go away from there before I would do it. The Prince Ruy Gómez with his prudence, which was much, and being brought to reason, made his wife acquiesce; and I insisted upon certain things, for I had more desire that the monastery of the friars be founded than that of the nuns, through understanding how important it was, as has afterwards appeared."[7] This monastery became, in fact, the most important of the Order in Spain; for two centuries most of the general chapters were held there.

One of the disagreements between the Princess and her guest arose over the old question of endowment. It was obvious to Madre Teresa that so small a population could never support

---

[6] P. Silverio, for example, *Vida de Santa Teresa de Jesús*, I, pp. 129–132. He believes that Teresa's famous remark was playful.

[7] *Fundaciones*, cap. XVII.

the convent if the nuns were left in absolute poverty; and she shrewdly suspected that the Princess's devotion might last only until she became interested in some other novelty. Contrary to her custom, she insisted upon an income, to be fully agreed upon in advance.

The Princess appeared scandalized by the discovery of such a worldly and commercial spirit in one of whom she had expected nothing less than miracles. She had brought the nuns there to lead the primitive Carmelite life, and she would have nothing short of perfection in them — an idealistic attitude not at all uncommon in emotional persons who indulge in religious activity in fits and starts, as a sop to conscience or a relief from the boredom of self-indulgence. Where others were concerned, she would have nothing less than heroic virtue. Ruy Gómez was more reasonable. He was famous for avoiding trouble by adroit compromises. He may have been amused a little by the spectacle of his lovely pampered Ana giving lessons in poverty to a nun who hardly ever ate or slept, or wore anything but a patched robe, or gave a thought to her own convenience. He saw, too, that La Madre was right, and he found a tactful way of making his wife see the wisdom of an endowment.

It was more serious when the Princess insisted that an Augustinian nun, a friend of hers named Catalina Machuca, become a Carmelite and enter the convent at Pastrana — she brought her on from Segovia, in fact, before consulting La Madre, and was highly indignant when the latter refused to accept her. Teresa had always been against taking nuns from other orders, even if they were better fitted for the Carmelite life than Catalina Machuca appeared to be; nor was it like her to allow anyone, even the Princess of Éboli, to choose her novices. Fray Domingo Báñez, who had occupied the chair of theology at the University of Alcalá since 1567, wrote her that she was right and must not consent under any circumstances. Even the Princess could think of no good argument against the judgment of a man who was becoming known as the best Thomist in Spain, and she pressed the matter no further.

Catalina Machuca did not accept the defeat so amiably. An unstable, emotional young woman, she had come to Pastrana to associate herself with a Saint in a novel enterprise that was being talked about everywhere, and she had no intention of being packed off to the Augustinian convent again without at least avenging what she took to be a mortal slight. Her opportunity came when she heard that Madre Teresa had written an astonishing book about herself. She told the Princess about it in such a way as to arouse a keen and perhaps even a prurient desire to read it. The Princess asked La Madre to let her see the *Vida*.

Teresa naturally refused. She had written this intimate and soul-searching document for the eyes of her directors alone.

The Princess insisted. When La Madre again refused, she sent her tactful husband. Perhaps Ruy Gómez pleaded the spiritual good she would gain, and her better understanding of the Reform. Was there any reason why the Princess of Éboli could not see a book that had been shown to the Duchess of Alba? This appeal carried the day, for Teresa must have known that her hostess would never allow herself to be outdone by her rival. With some misgivings, no doubt, she handed over one of the precious copies she had made in her own handwriting, stipulating that the Prince and Princess alone might read it. To this Ruy Gómez agreed.[8]

Ana took the manuscript to her boudoir, or perhaps her garden, and began eagerly to peruse it. It is not difficult to imagine the shrieks of laughter that beat upon the tapestried walls of the palace when her solitary eye (or did she have one of her ladies read aloud to her?) fell upon certain sentences in which La Madre, under orders from her confessors, had sought to imprison the inexpressible within the narrow confines of human speech. So the memory and the understanding were "like some doves that don't content themselves with the food the owner of the dovecot gives them, without any labor of theirs, and they go to look for something to eat, elsewhere, and find it so bad that they come back; and so they go and they come, to see if the will gives them some of what *she* enjoys!" And what a sinner La Madre confessed herself to be! She was always saying so. And listen to this one: "Many times I remained as if beside myself, intoxicated with this love, but I had never been able to understand how it was!" It was not long before nearly everyone in the palace, including the servants and pages, had read the book; and the work which was to be venerated by saints and to earn for its author a comparison to the Fathers of the Church, was

---

[8] *Reforma*, t. I, lib. II, cap. XXVIII, p. 302, n. 6; Silverio, *op. cit.*, III, p. 431.

passed from hand to hand with snickers and titters and ribald guffaws by those who would never begin to comprehend the holy splendor of its truth. Fools and lechers were saying that this was the sort of stuff that Magdalena de la Cruz used to preach to the *Alumbrados* before the Inquisition got hold of her, and that Madre Teresa would probably end on the bonfire.

Such misunderstanding would have been painful to the author under any condition. But to be invited to a lady's house, and then to be insulted and ridiculed and have her confidence betrayed — this must have cut Teresa to the heart, in spite of all her experience of human instability. Yet she was not the one to let personal feelings, however outraged, come between her and the work she had to do for God. She completed arrangements for the convent as rapidly as she could, and when the Blessed Sacrament was installed on June 28, and the habits of the Reform bestowed upon the new nuns — this not in the convent, but in the palace, to gratify the wishes of the Princess — she prepared to depart for Toledo. The Princess made no objection; on the contrary she offered her coach for the journey.

Even this proved a source of embarrassment, for when La Madre arrived in Toledo on the evening of July 21, 1569, many persons observed the magnificence of her equipage, and an unfortunate priest whose mind was deranged followed her to the door of the convent, shouting, "Are you the saint who deceives everybody and travels in a coach?" and many other insults.

Teresa listened in silence without realizing that the man was crazy. Turning to another nun, she said, "There is no one who tells me my faults as well as this man does."[9]

It made no difference when they told her the poor fellow was out of his mind. Sane or insane, he knew that a Religious professing poverty should not be traveling sumptuously, and from that time on she could never be persuaded to ride in a coach if there was any way of avoiding it. Still, with the thrift of a good mother superior, she sent Sister Isabel de Santo Domingo back to Pastrana in the Princess's carriage, to be prioress, remarking that she did not expect the house there to continue, and that if matters did not go well, she would put the nuns in some other convent.[10]

---

[9] Mir, *Vida de Santa Teresa*, II, p. 142, from the *Vida de Isabel de Santo Domingo*.
[10] Deposition of Isabel de Santo Domingo, B.M.C., t. XIX, p. 500.

There was a great deal to be done at Toledo. The tiresome negotiations with the Ramírez family, the organization of the convent and the search for a better house kept her there for more than a year. Of the innumerable letters she wrote during that time — and she was always communicating with her monasteries in Ávila, Medina, Valladolid, Pastrana, Malagón, and Duruelo, and with various friends and benefactors — fewer than a dozen have been found. The most interesting of these were written to her sister Juana and her brother Lorenzo. Juana's seventeen years of married life with small, grasping, jealous Juan de Ovalle, had not been ideally happy. Teresa, who took much to heart all their pecuniary troubles and made them her own, had the tenderest affection for their son Gonzalito, now a page in the household of the Duke of Alba, and she was hurt when she had received no reply from him, October 19, to a letter she had sent him in care of the Inquisitor de Soto. Gonzalito, who was then fourteen, used to twit her about the time when her prayers had restored him to life, saying she must pray especially for him, since she had prevented his entering heaven as a child.[11]

On October 19, 1569, Teresa wrote her sister that their brother Lorenzo was coming home from the Indies. He had done well in Peru, having been *regidor,* royal treasurer, lieutenant governor, captain general, and *alcalde* of Quito, in succession. He had been fairly successful in a monetary way, too, but he cared more for his children's salvation than for amassing a fortune, said Teresa, and their mother having died, he was bringing them to Spain to be educated. This would be doubly good news to Juana, for Lorenzo might help her out of her financial difficulties. "Didn't I tell you that if you left it all to our Lord, He would take care of it? And so I say it now, put your affairs in His hands, and His Majesty will do what is best for us in everything." She added a curiously feminine postscript: "I opened this letter of my brother to . . . I mean I was going to open it, but it gave me a scruple. If there is anything in it about . . ., let me know."[12]

With her Christmas wishes to her sister, early in December, Teresa sent some small gifts purchased with money that had

---

[11] Gonzalo died a holy death in 1585. Three years later his body was found incorrupt.

[12] "*Si hay al(go) de lo que allá no viene, avíseme.*" *Epistolario,* I, 47, B.M.C.; Stanbrook ed. I, pp. 58–59. Part of the postscript was blotted and illegible in the MS.

providentially arrived, probably from Lorenzo. She begged her to go to confession before the great feast, to pray for her, and not to worry about money matters. To forestall any criticism on the score of the articles she was sending, she added, "I have one who directs my soul — not what comes into everybody's head. This I say, so that you can reply when anyone speaks of it; and let Your Grace understand that as the world now is, and in the state in which the Lord has placed me, the less they think I do for you meanwhile, the better it is for me, and this is fitting for the service of the Lord. Certainly if they imagine the slightest sum, even though I am doing nothing, they will say of me what I hear of others; and so, now that you bring me this trifling gossip, we must be careful.

"Believe that I love you well, and sometimes I may do some little thing to please you; but let them understand, when they say anything about it to you, that whatever I have, I have to spend in the Order, for it belongs there — and what business is that of theirs?[13] And believe that anyone who is before the eyes of the world as much as I, has to look to what she is doing even in a matter of virtue. You couldn't believe the trouble I have; but since I do it to serve Him, His Majesty will take care of you and your affairs for me. May He watch over you for me, for I have been a long time at this, and they have rung the bell for Matins. I tell you, truly, that when I see some good thing of those who enter, I have you before me, and Beatriz, yet never have I dared to take anything, even when bought with my own moneys. Yours, Teresa of Jesus, Carmelite."

A few weeks later, January 17, 1570, she wrote Lorenzo, who was still in Peru, a long gossipy letter about the foundation at Pastrana, the new house of friars there, the prayers her nuns were saying for him and for their brother Jerónimo, and the news of various relatives and friends — this one was married, such a one was dead, and so on.

"I have been much better in health this winter," she continued, "for the climate of this country is admirable; and if it were not for other inconveniences (for it would be out of the question for you, Sir, to have accommodations here for your children), I would sometimes wish you could be here, so far as the climate of the country is concerned. But there are places in the vicinity of Ávila where you, Sir, could have them enrolled for the winter,

---

[13] *Y qué tienen que ver en esto?*

for some of them do it. As for my brother Jerónimo de Cepeda, I say, and I rather think, that when God brings him back, he will have better health here. All is as His Majesty desires, and I believe I have not had such good health in forty years, what with observing what they all do, and never eating meat except under great necessity. . . . I have before me the account of the bills they have brought; I will send it herewith, and it is no little advantage that I understand these business matters, and I am such a skinflint[14] and businesswoman that I already know all about it, what with these houses of God and of the Order, and I regard yours, Sir, as I do theirs, and I rejoice to be able to attend to them. . . .

"When I am through here, I wish to return to Ávila, for I am still prioress there, so that I shall not annoy the Bishop, for I owe him much, and all the Order. I don't know what the Lord will do with me, whether I shall go to Salamanca, for they are giving me a house there; and although I am tired, the good these houses do in the communities where they are is so much that my conscience obliges me to found those I can. . . . I forgot to write in these letters the good facilities there are in Ávila for bringing up those children well. Those of the Company have a college,[15] where they teach grammar, and they hear confessions every week, and they make such virtuous men that our Lord is to be praised. They also read philosophy, and afterwards theology at Santo Tomás,[16] so there is no need to go anywhere else for virtue and studies; and in all the town there is so much Christianity as to edify those who come from other places; much prayer and perfection, and secular persons who lead lives of great perfection. . . . I have written you, Sir, how timely was your present to her, for I have been astonished at the financial worries the Lord has given her, and she has borne it so well that He is now pleased in this way to give her some relief. I have no need of anything, but have more than enough of everything; and so what you sent me, Sir, in alms, I will spend some of it on my sister, and the rest on good works, and it will be for you, Sir. Some of it came opportunely enough for me, on account of certain scruples I had; for with these foundations, certain things happen which, however careful I am, and it is all for

---

[14] "Baratona."
[15] The Jesuit college of San Gil.
[16] The Dominican monastery and seminary.

them, leave me able to give less in certain courtesies to learned men, for I always deal with them in the affairs of my soul. In short, in trifles, and so it was quite a relief to me. . . . I would rather be free to tell these gentlemen my opinion, and the world is so greedy for interest that I really hold it in abhorrence to have it; and so I shall keep nothing, but what with giving some to the Order itself, I shall remain free, and I shall give with this intent; for I have as much permission as possible from the General and Provincial, not only to take nuns, but to make changes, and to aid one house with that of others. . . . What makes me sorrowful is to see so many lost; and those Indians have cost me not a little. May the Lord give them light, for both here and there is plenty of wretchedness; and as I go so many places, and many persons speak to me, I often don't know what to say except that we are worse than beasts, since we do not understand the great divinity of our soul and how we debase it with things so debased as are those of the earth. May the Lord give us light. . . ."[17]

Teresa remained in Toledo until August, 1570. Lorenzo had not yet arrived, and that was a disappointment. Bad fortune, however, could always be counted on to be prompt. One day, toward the end of her stay she received a demand from the Holy Office of the Inquisition for a copy of her autobiography. Someone had denounced it. She was not told who. Could it have been some important personage in Pastrana? No matter: her conscience was clear, and she had little time or inclination for recriminations. She was dreaming of new worlds to conquer for His Majesty.

---

[17] *Epistolario*, I, B.M.C., t. VII, pp. 50–57.

Chapter XXIV

SALAMANCA AND ALBA DE TORMES

SALAMANCA was the next venture. The project had been broached to her about the beginning of 1570, in a letter from Father Martin Gutiérrez, S.J., a great scholar and famous preacher who was rector there. She was unwilling at first, believing that the city, for all its scholarship, was too poor to support an unendowed monastery in addition to its many existing foundations. After further correspondence with Father Gutiérrez,[1] however, she decided to make the attempt. She returned to Ávila in August, 1570, to make the necessary preparations.

Through Father Gutiérrez she obtained the permission of the Bishop of Salamanca, Don Pedro González de Mendoza. The next step was to find a house, and for this she enlisted the aid of another friend in Salamanca, a merchant named Nicholas Gutiérrez, who had six daughters in the Incarnation of Ávila (five of whom subsequently became Discalced Carmelites) and who during his visits over a period of years had come to know and admire her. It was not long before he found a house he deemed suitable. It was occupied by students of the University, but they agreed to move out whenever she wanted it.

Teresa left Ávila with only one companion, an older nun of San José, the gentle and holy María del Sacramento. Heavy rains had been pouring for days. The roads were muddy, the rivers swollen and angry. By night it had become intensely cold, and Teresa had a toothache, with a badly distended face. Yet she insisted on pressing on until, toward morning, they sought some rest in a little village (Peñaranda, perhaps) whose name she does not mention. Next day they resumed the journey — it was a hundred kilometers in all — arriving at the famous university town about noon on the vigil of All Saints, October 31.[2]

---

[1] Father Gutiérrez talked over her letters with a young friend of his, Francisco de Ribera, who was so impressed by the spirit of Saint Teresa that he became a Jesuit, and in course of time her biographer. He was 33 years old in 1570. *Vida de Santa Teresa*, lib. II, cap. XVI.

[2] So Teresa says (*Fundaciones*, cap. XIX). Yet one of her letters (to Catalina Hurtado) is dated at Ávila, October 31, 1570. So Father Silverio dates it in his *Epistolario*, but in his life of the Saint (III, 507, n. 2) he makes it October 30, without explanation.

As soon as they had found a lodging, they sent for Nicholas Gutiérrez to inquire about the house. What a disappointment! He had not been able to get the students to leave, nor was he any more successful when La Madre sent him a second time. Finally he appealed to the owner, who ordered the students to vacate before nightfall. After much grumbling they did so, and Teresa went to inspect her new property on the Arroyo of San Francisco, next to the convent of Saint Isabel.

It was a huge, rambling old structure with many garrets, nooks, corners, and unexpected stairways, a rather spooky place as darkness invaded its creaky emptiness. Sister María did not like it at all. La Madre, however, went to work with her customary energy. Father Gutiérrez, on hearing of her arrival, sent two young Jesuits with food and supplies, including two blankets and a table, and instructions to do anything possible to help her. She dispatched one of them, Bartolomé Pérez de Nueros, to find a workman to make alterations, while she and Sister María, and perhaps the other Jesuit, set about cleaning up the house, which was in no little disorder.

Bartolomé Pérez de Nueros found a workman about eight o'clock in the evening at a house in the *Calle de Gordolodo* ("Thickmud Street"), and told him he must come at once on a matter of great importance.

"I have never yet left my house without knowing where I was going," replied the carpenter, Hernández, "and I don't intend to now."

When the errand was explained, he readily consented, "seeing it was a work of charity," and under Teresa's concise orders he labored until four o'clock in the morning, doing the equivalent, by his own account, of four ordinary days' work, and yet at the end feeling as fresh as when he had started.[3]

At the first glint of dawn Teresa rang her little bell, and the first Mass was said, doubtless by one of the Jesuits. Although she had had no sleep for two nights, she spent the day in further sweepings and other arrangements, stopping only to eat a little of the food sent in by some sisters of the Third Order of Saint Francis, next door. When night came the two Carmelites, bone weary, shut themselves up in a room which Hernández no doubt

---

[3] For the account of Bartolomé, see B.M.C., t. 18, p. 375; for that of the *maestro de obras*, Pedro Hernández, t. XX, pp. 28–29. P. Silverio gives some interesting quotations, *Vida de Santa Teresa de Jesús*, III, pp. 512–515.

had made comparatively safe against intrusion, and lying down on some straw (this was always the first "furniture" Teresa installed, in lieu of beds) pulled over them the two blankets donated by the Fathers of the Company, and composed themselves for sleep.

It was a cold, damp house, owing to its nearness to the water of the Arroyo of Saint Francis, and more lugubrious than ever that night, the eve of All Souls, when the city was full of the usual Halloween noises, and all the church bells were tolling mournfully to remind people to pray for the faithful departed. Teresa had to resist a sensation of nausea that her heart condition caused in moments of fear or anxiety. Sister María was not so successful in concealing her feelings. She wondered whether some of the students could have remained hidden in the house. She stirred about, prying here and there for secret intruders. Finally she said,

"Mother, I am thinking that if I should die here now, what would you do all alone?"

Even La Madre was a little disconcerted at the thought of spending the night in such a place with a corpse, but she answered,

"Sister, when that happens, I will think of what I am going to do; now let me go to sleep."

They then slept soundly.[4]

When Teresa remarked upon the hardships of her foundations, it was usually to recall some such amusing incident. Of sufferings as such she made only a general summary, probably at the command of some confessor:

"I don't include in these foundations the great trials of the roads, with cold, with heat, with snowstorms, for once it didn't stop snowing all day long, others we lost the way, others with plenty of illnesses and fevers; for, glory to God, ordinarily I have poor health, but I saw clearly that our Lord gave me strength. For it befell me sometimes when I was busy with a foundation to find myself with such ailments and pains that I was in great distress, for I thought that I was not able even to be in a cell without lying down, and turning to our Lord, complaining to His Majesty, and saying to Him, why did He wish me to do what I could not do; and afterwards, although with suffering, His Majesty would give me strength, and with

---

[4] *Fundaciones*, cap. XIX.

the fervor He put into me and the solicitude I think I used to forget myself.

"As I now remember, I never gave up a foundation for fear of the suffering, although I felt great repugnance to journeys, especially long ones; but once I had started on the way, it seemed but a trifle to me, seeing in Whose service it was being done, and considering that in that house the Lord was going to be praised, and there would be the Most Blessed Sacrament. This is an especial consolation for me, to see one church more, when I remember the many that the Lutherans are destroying. I don't know what sufferings, however great they might be, are to be feared, in exchange for so great a blessing for Christianity, for it must be a great consolation to us, even though many of us, in many places, do not notice that it is Jesus Christ, true God and true man, as He is, in the Most Blessed Sacrament. Surely it is one to me, very often in the choir, when I see these souls so pure in praises to God. . . ."[5]

The community of San José de Salamanca grew and prospered during the ten weeks' stay of its foundress, particularly after the arrival of reinforcements from Ávila and Medina. Yet the lumbering old house was never satisfactory; it was cold, damp, and too large to heat, and in 1573 La Madre felt obliged to transfer the nuns to a new one, though they considered it an "imperfection" to ask for this, and would have gone on enduring the discomfort and ill-health in silence.

Teresa's confessor at Salamanca was Father Gutiérrez. He wept over the manuscript copy of the *Libro de su vida* that she had brought to show him. When he went to the convent he was always accompanied by the young Jesuit Bartolomé, who testified years later that he could overhear their conversations, and that all they spoke of was God. It was one of the most precious friendships in Teresa's life. She grieved deeply when she heard of Father Gutiérrez's death in 1573, as the result of wounds inflicted by Huguenots who attacked him on his way to Rome.[6]

Her raptures became more frequent under the direction of this holy man. It was during the summer of 1571 that she told our Lord in prayer that people quoted Saint Paul at her as an argument against women going about making foundations, and His Majesty replied, "Tell them not to be guided by only one

---

[5] *Ibid.*, cap. XVIII.
[6] Ribera, *op. cit.*, lib. IV, cap. XI.

part of the Scripture, but to look at others. And can they perchance tie My hands?"[7]

She was so abstracted on Easter Sunday, 1571, that by her own account she would hardly have known, except at Communion, what day it was. In the evening, at the recreation hour, a novice called Isabel de Jesús sang a little song she had composed, a charming *cantarcillo* commencing and ending:

Véante mis ojos	"Let mine eyes see Thee,
Dulce Jesús bueno	Sweet good Jesus,
Véante mis ojos	Let mine eyes see Thee,
Muérame yo luego.	And then let me die."[8]

The pain of separation from God, which was the burden of the *letrilla*, so touched the heart of La Madre that her hands became cold and lifeless, and she was seized with an irresistible rapture which lasted for several hours. Three or four nuns carried her to her cell, where she remained in a state of joy paradoxically mingled with a sorrow which, as she described it next day, made her understand better the suffering of our Lady by the Cross. "Until today I did not understand what anguish is," she wrote on Easter Monday with hands that still ached and were numb.[9]

As a result of this experience she wrote the two versions of her famous poem, *"Vivo sin vivir en mí,"* one of which commences:

> "I live with no life in myself,
> And yet I bear a hope so high,
> I die because I do not die."

---

[7] *Ibid.*, lib. IV, cap. XVIII.

[8] The song of Isabel de Jesús continues:

Vea quien quisiere	*Flor de serafines,*
Rosas y jazmines	*Jesús Nazareno,*
Que si yo te viere	*Véante mis ojos*
Veré mil jardines.	*Muérame yo luego . . .*

for the rest of it see B.M.C., t. II, p. 48, note. Dame Beatrice, O.S.B., of Stanbrook Abbey has made an excellent translation of this (Minor Works of Saint Teresa, pp. 60–61) commencing:

O Thou all good and sweet	On *Thee* I gaze and see
Jesus of Nazareth,	A thousand gardens there
Let me but look on Thee,	Thou Flower all seraph-bright
Then send me death.	Jesus of Nazareth,
	Let me but look on Thee,
Let those look who will	Then send me death!
On rose and jasmine fair;	

[9] *Mercedes de Dios*, no. 15, in *Las relaciones espirituales*, B.M.C., t. II, pp. 47–48.

In another rapture the Lord told her that He had visited His Mother at the time of His Resurrection, to console her in her anguish. After His Ascension He had never returned to the earth to communicate with anyone, He said, except in the Most Blessed Sacrament.[10]

With all these celestial experiences, she managed to keep a practical eye upon the progress of the Reform everywhere; and it was no small consolation to her to learn that while she had been establishing the convent at Salamanca, her friars had been founding the first college of the Primitive Carmelite Rule at Alcalá de Henares. This was a logical result of the two monasteries at Duruelo and Pastrana. Hearing that the Calced friars at Alcalá were displeased with their house and would sell it, Fray Ambrosio Mariano and Fray Baltasar of Jesus had made the necessary preparations, had obtained Father Rubeo's permission through the influence of the Prince of Éboli, and had taken possession on November 1, the very day Madre Teresa was founding the convent at Salamanca. Soon, under the name of Our Lady of Mt. Carmel (which was changed later to Saint Cyril of Constantinople) the infant college was playing a vigorous part among the many institutes of religious orders at the university founded by Cardinal Ximenes. After Fray Juan de la Cruz had been brought from his wild retreat at Mancera to be vicar and master of novices, its reputation became such that students from other colleges at Alcalá began going there to take instruction in prayer and to receive the "discipline." He became rector after Father Baltasar returned to Pastrana, in April, 1571. He was not a great administrator, but he was the first intellect among the friars. His maxim for Carmelite education was "*Religioso y estudiante, y el religioso delante.*" Teresa took the keenest interest in all this. She had desired nothing

---

[10] *Ibid.,* pp. 49–50. "The opinion of Saint Thomas, which is generally held, is that after His Ascension our Lord rarely appeared in Person; He merely appeared in a visible form, but not in His real body. His apparitions in the Eucharist may be explained in two ways, says Saint Thomas (*Sum. theol.,* III, q. 76, a. 8): either by a miraculous impression made on the sense of sight (which is the case when He manifests Himself to a single person) or by a form that is real and visible, but distinct from His own Body; for, the Saint adds, the Body of our Saviour cannot be seen in its own proper form except in the one place which actually contains it. What has been said of our Lord applies also to the Blessed Virgin. When she appeared at Lourdes, for instance, her body remained in heaven, and at the spot of the apparition there was but a sensible form which represented her. This explains how she could appear now under one aspect, now under another." — Tanqueray, *The Spiritual Life,* pp. 701–702.

more than the attraction of learned men, doctors of theology, to the Reform.[11]

About the same time, she received an offer of a house at Alba de Tormes from an extraordinary pair, Francisco Velázquez, *contador* of the Duke of Alba, and his wife, Teresa de Layz, whose story is told at length in the *Book of Foundations*.

Teresa de Layz was born of noble parents — of *limpia sangre,* says La Madre. Having had four daughters, they were so disappointed by her sex that they paid little attention to her; in fact, on her third day in the world she was left alone from morning till night. Then a nurse remembered her and ran to see whether she was dead. Picking her up, weeping, she cried, "What, my daughter, you are not a Christian?" The baby raised her head and said plainly, "Yes, I am." It was the last word she spoke, as we can well believe, until she reached the age when children usually speak. Her mother, however, conceived a great love for her from that night. Coming of age, Teresa Layz agreed to marry a man she had never seen, a rich graduate of the University of Salamanca, Francisco Velázquez. He became treasurer of the University, and took her there to live. They had everything life could offer except children. Teresa used to pray passionately to Saint Andrew for this blessing. One night in bed she heard a voice say, "Don't wish to have children, for you will damn yourself." Though frightened, she continued to pray as before until she had a vision — she never knew whether she was asleep or awake at the time — in which she seemed to be in a house, with a corridor leading to a patio, where she saw a well, and beyond that a field, very green and sprinkled with innumerable white flowers of indescribable beauty. Near the well she saw the Apostle Saint Andrew, beautiful and venerable, and knew at once it was he. "These are different children," he remarked "from the ones you desire."

She no longer wanted children. Instead, she was resolved to make her home at Tordillos into a convent.

Her husband having left the University to accept employment as financial factotum for the Duke of Alba, they had to move to Alba de Tormes. Teresa hated this. But when her hus-

---

[11] Silverio, *op. cit.,* III, pp. 491–493. The Discalced College at Alcalá continued its work until it was destroyed by the "liberal" revolutions of the nineteenth century.

The Spanish maxim inserted above may be translated, "Religious and student but religious first," though the effect of the rhyme is thus lost.

band took her into the house he had purchased there, she looked out and saw a patio and a well, and beyond them a green field, exactly as in her dream or vision. From then on she was reconciled, believing that God had brought her there, and more and more desirous of founding a monastery. A Franciscan father to whom she told this related what he had heard of the wonderful Beata of Ávila, who had founded so many convents of perfection. Teresa de Layz was determined to establish one in Alba for Madre Teresa of Jesus, and sent her word to that effect through her sister Juana, who lived there.

Teresa, as usual, was not much impressed at first. Alba de Tormes was not populous enough to support a convent in poverty, and she would not accept an endowment. But when she mentioned the matter to Fray Domingo Báñez, who was teaching theology at the University of Salamanca while she was there, he said she was quite wrong. He once more reminded her that the Council of Trent had permitted endowed houses.[12]

Teresa then consented. She left Salamanca in January, 1571, with María del Sacramento and Guiomar de Jesús, while other nuns set out from Toledo and Medina to join the new community.

Arriving in Alba with an image of the Child Jesus in her arms, she went to live for a while at her sister's house, while the home of Teresa de Layz was being made suitable for a convent. John of the Cross came from Mancera, on his way to Alcalá, to help with the alterations.[13] The people of Alba must have been startled and edified to see a thin small Carmelite friar in his bare feet carrying stones and dirt over snow and ice during that very severe winter! When the work was finished, an agreement was signed whereby the benefactors promised 100,000 maravedis yearly while they lived and half as much thereafter, and the Blessed Sacrament was installed on January 25, 1571. There the convent still stands, looking out upon a little plaza, almost as Teresa left it.

She returned to Salamanca early in March, on learning that the nuns were in distress and needed direction. Next she went to the palace of the Count and Countess of Monterey, probably at the instance of her Provincial, to console them while members of their household were seriously ill. Doña María de Arti-

[12] *Fundaciones*, cap. XX.
[13] Silverio, *op. cit.*, III, p. 547 and his reference.

aga, wife of the tutor of the Count's children, was on the point
of dying of a burning fever. Teresa touched her head, restoring
her to health. And when the little daughter of the Count seemed
to have but a few hours to live, she retired to her room and
prayed earnestly until Saint Dominic and Saint Catherine came
to tell her that God had granted her request, and that it was
His wish that the child wear the habit of their order for a year.[14]

With Teresa's departure from Salamanca, in April, 1571, a
new and disagreeable phase of her conflict began. Soon after
Easter she went to Medina del Campo, for the first time in more
than two years, to settle a dispute over the property of Isabel
Ruiz, who had taken the habit there in 1569, and had bestowed
all her goods as a dowry upon the convent. Some relatives objected, and won over to their side the Carmelite Provincial, Fray
Angel de Salazar. Madre Teresa, on her arrival, concluded that
the nuns were in the right, and became their champion.

This step brought upon her the displeasure of Fray Angel,
who previously had been friendly, on the whole, to her and the
Reform. He was a good, mediocre man who, lacking the genius
of Madre Teresa for sublime conceptions and bold execution,
must have everything running smoothly, always, of course, for
the highest ends; and if he was likely to bend before public
storms, as he had in revoking his permission for San José de
Ávila ten years ago, he would deal severely on the other hand
with any opposition in the organization over which he presided,
for he had no other means of being effective. Human nature
being what it is, his type is common, necessary, and by no means
indefensible. But it is always and everywhere the instinctive foe
of genius, which perplexes and irritates it beyond measure. These
are the good stupid people who persecute poets, heroes, and
saints (except dead ones, whom they honor inordinately, having nothing more to fear from them) and thus unwittingly provide for them the suffering necessary to all great achievement.
Fray Angel de Salazar was one of many such who unconsciously
collaborated, each in his own small way, in perfecting the sanctity
of Madre Teresa of Jesus. He probably felt the strongest conviction of rectitude when he concluded that she was becoming
too independent, and needed to be taught a lesson or two. An
opportunity seemed at hand in the expiration of the three-year

---

[14] Cf. P. Silverio, *op. cit.*, IV, pp. 3, 4 and his references. The little girl lived to
be the wife of the Count of Olivares and mother of the Duke of Sanlúcar.

term of Madre Inés of Jesus as prioress of the Discalced convent at Medina. This cousin of La Madre, one of the first professed at San José de Ávila, had succeeded brilliantly in her task, and in the ordinary course would probably have been re-elected in 1571.

Fray Angel decided otherwise. Without giving the nuns a chance to express their preference, he appointed Doña Teresa de Quesada, a Calced nun of the Incarnation of Ávila. He could hardly have made a worse choice. She was an excellent nun, this well-born lady, with no talent for administration and no vocation to be a Discalced contemplative; in fact, she was one of the nuns from the Incarnation who had gone so reluctantly to the founding at Medina, and had had to return because she could not endure the rigors of the primitive rule. The sandaled nuns at Medina were not likely under any circumstances to welcome a superior who still wore boots and kept the title of *"Doña"* which the *señoras* among them had given up — much less one who had failed to meet their requirements. They held an election, as their constitution warranted, and re-elected Inés of Jesus, with the approval and cooperation of La Madre.

When Fray Angel heard of this, he was so incensed that he ordered Madre Teresa and Madre Inés to leave Medina at once, and to repair to Ávila. It was almost night and very cold when his message was delivered. The nuns wept and begged La Madre, who was ill with the palsy and could hardly drag herself about, to wait a day or two. She replied that since her superior had told her to leave immediately on receipt of his letter, obedience required her to go. When no cart or other conveyance was to be found at that hour, she and her companion, a kindred spirit, mounted a couple of mules and started across the darkening wind-swept countryside. Yepes, who relates this incident[15] gives no further details, leaving us to imagine how the two nuns accomplished the two-day journey under such conditions.

On arriving in Ávila, Teresa went to San José. It was probably a relief to be a simple nun again in that beloved haunt of solitude and peace. Certainly she experienced some of her most notable raptures there during the spring of 1571. On the Tuesday after the Ascension, May 24, she had one of the famous visions of the Blessed Trinity. She had received Communion

---

[15] Yepes, *Vida de Santa Teresa*, lib. II, cap. XXI V. He says it was near Christmas. This must be an error. It was probably late April or early in May.

"with sorrow," she tells us, and had been for some time in prayer, complaining to our Lord "of our miserable nature." As her soul began to be inflamed with love, she understood, in an "intellectual vision," that the Most Blessed Trinity was present, and realized how God could be Three in One; "and so I thought all three Persons spoke to me, and that They were distinctly represented within my soul, saying that from that day on I should see an improvement in myself in three things, for each one of those Persons was granting me a favor; one in charity, and in suffering with joy, and in feeling this charity with fervor in my soul. I understood those words that the Lord said, that the three divine Persons would be with the soul that was in grace. . . ."[16]

About this time she received a visit from one of the two visitors appointed by Saint Pius V to reform the convents of Spain — the Dominican Father Fray Pedro Fernández, who came with a particular mission to the Carmelites of Castilla. A man of about forty, he was one of the best theologians of his time, even among the Dominicans, and Yepes was not alone in considering him "a learned apostolic man." His wise prudent utterances and zeal for the Church had made him a marked man at the Council of Trent. Elected to high office in his order, he was known in it as "the holy provincial." He spoke little, thought deeply, mortified himself rigorously, lived in the presence of God. His first visit in Castilla had been at the Discalced convent in Pastrana. He and his *socius* had entered the ducal city on foot, following a mule laden with their books and other effects. Asked why he did not ride, Father Fernández answered, "A man who is going to visit saints should not travel like a profane person." It was Ruy Gómez, Prince of Éboli, who first told him about Madre Teresa of Jesus. Later he had heard further accounts from Fray Domingo Báñez and other members of his order. With true Catholic prudence, he was inclined to be skeptical of marvels until they were verified beyond question. He had decided to see for himself whether this Teresa of Jesus was a true mystic or a victim of delusions.

After their first meeting he declared, "She is a woman of goodness" — a high compliment from his laconic tongue — and afterwards used to refer to her as "Teresa, the one with the great head," citing her as proof that women could lead lives

---

[16] B.M.C., t. II, p. 50.

of apostolic perfection; as though there had never been a Saint Catherine of Siena in his own Order! La Madre reciprocated his esteem.

When in the course of his "visit" he inspected the convent at Medina, Father Fernández found the nuns discontented and unhappy, and rightly concluding that the cause had been the inept government of Doña Teresa de Quesada, he promptly removed her, and ordered Madre Teresa to take her place. Teresa obeyed as usual. She spent several weeks restoring the discipline and harmony of the convent, before the next thunderbolt fell. One day in July, 1571, Father Fernández arrived to hold a chapter. At the conclusion of it he released her from her office as prioress, informing her that she was to return at once to Avila, to assume command not of her dear San José, but of the Convent of the Incarnation, which was in need of her reforming skill.

For such a catastrophe, as it seemed to Teresa, there had been no apparent preparation, to the casual eye at least, in the foregoing scenes of the drama. When Fray Angel de Salazar visited the ancient convent May 7, he had certified that everything was satisfactory. Nor had Father Fernández found anything wrong, if we may believe the "book of visits" of the Incarnation, when he made his inspection June 27. Yet a few days later he took the unusual step of placing over that community of the mitigated rule a woman who had repudiated it, was obviously out of sympathy with the spirit of the house, and would probably not be very welcome there.

The favorable reports of Fray Angel and Father Fernández are explainable by the fact, on which there seems to be general agreement, that there had been no serious scandals, nothing that could be called moral turpitude, at the Incarnation. There was, to be sure, a dangerous relaxation of discipline. Lady boarders came and went as they pleased. Visits and long conversations with relatives and friends were tolerated, almost as if the place were a fashionable hotel instead of a convent. The true spirit of prayer and recollection having been lost, the income of the house had fallen with its spiritual tone, until there was not even enough to buy food for the nuns. Most of them went to the homes of relatives every day to eat; some were threatening to leave altogether. Nevertheless, except for the shortage of food, there had been no drastic change in the situation since

Madre Teresa left in 1563. Perhaps the authorities of the Mitigated Rule had tolerated what they should have corrected because there were no shocking revelations to wake them from
their lethargy.

Why, then, had Fray Angel suddenly appealed to the Papal
Commissary, as he did, to send Madre Teresa, of all persons,
to reform a convent he had so recently approved? The correct
explanation seems to be the one given by Doña María Pinel, a
nun of the Incarnation, in her history of the institution. Fray
Angel wished to have a certain nun elected prioress there, but
was unable to obtain the necessary votes. Smarting under this
defeat, and the one he had sustained from the Discalced nuns
at Medina, he hit upon a clever scheme to "kill many parrots
with one shot." By having Madre Teresa made prioress of the
Incarnation, he would deprive the Medina nuns of her presence
and snub those of the Incarnation by forcing on them one
who had repudiated their rule. There was not much danger
that they would re-elect her. Meanwhile she would be confined
there for three years, and during that time would be unable
to found any new convents. Thus Fray Angel would be avenged
at one stroke on all who in his opinion had flouted his authority.[17] As for Father Fernández, he had found nothing wrong
with the Incarnation at a single visit, but he was doubtless glad
when Fray Angel called his attention to the laxity he had overlooked, and he must have agreed that Madre Teresa would be
just the person to correct it. In short, the Dominican, unfamiliar
with the circumstances, was taken in by the Carmelite, who
concealed his own purposes under a show of reforming zeal.

It was a sad blow, in any case, to Teresa. It meant an almost
impossible task at the Incarnation, and it might mean the end
of her Reform. She staggered forth from the Chapter among
the novices, weeping and moaning, and in such a state that one
of them had to support her, and heard her exclaim, "Lord God
of my heart and soul, You see me here: I am Yours, my flesh, as
weak, feels it, but my soul is ready. *Fiat voluntas tua!*" With this
she became rigid in the arms of the novice, and remained enraptured for some time, her face glowing and indescribably
beautiful. When she regained the use of her senses, she said,

---

[17] This explanation is accepted by Mir, *op. cit.*, II, p. 200 *et seq.* and Silverio,
op. cit., IV, p. 19 *et seq.*

"Oh, child, what a weak heart I have! Get me a drink of water."[18]

Some weeks passed before Teresa left Medina. The reason is not clear: perhaps she was ill, perhaps her superiors did not set an early date. Late in September or early in October she was kneeling in one of the hermitages in the garden, praying for her brother Agustin, who was in danger, she thought, of losing his soul in America. "Lord," she cried, "if I saw a brother of Yours in such peril, what would I do to remedy it!" Christ stood beside her and answered, "Oh, daughter, daughter, those of the Incarnation are my sisters, and you delay going!"[19]

This rebuke was enough for Teresa. She made her preparations, and as soon as possible — it was in the first week of October, 1571 — took the road for Ávila, to embrace the bitterest task of her life.

---

[18] María de San Francisco, in the *Informaciones de Medina;* Silverio, *op. cit.,* IV, pp. 24-25.

[19] B.M.C., t. II, *merced,* 20, p. 53.

Chapter XXV

PRIORESS OF THE INCARNATION

O N THE eve of the battle of Lepanto, when Don John of
Austria was cruising the Ionian Sea looking for the
Moslem enemies of Christ, Madre Teresa of Jesus, at San José,
was preparing for a struggle perhaps equally important, if we
knew all, in the history of Christendom. She was under no illusion as to what sort of reception she might expect at the Incarnation. It was true that the nuns had accepted her stipulation that
all seculars, boarders, and others be dismissed before her arrival.
Yet this did not mean that they welcomed the enforced authority
of one who had shaken the dust of their corridors from her feet.
Nor did it help matters much that on July 13, 1571, she had
written a formal renunciation of the mitigated rule, in the
presence of Don Francisco de Salcedo (now a priest), the Maestro
Daza, Father Julian of Ávila, and others.[1] To many at the Incarnation this seemed like adding insult to injury. Most of them
protested loudly and bitterly, not only in the convent, but in the
homes of their relatives, where they went every day to get food.
All over the city, *caballeros* and *señoras* were taking their part
and denouncing the outrage in a spirit recalling the demonstra-
tions of 1562.

A large and fashionable audience was probably assembled on
the fine October day when Madre Teresa, bearing in her arms
a small image of Saint Joseph, approached with the Father
Provincial, Angel de Salazar, and possibly a few friends. The
nuns, drawn up as if in battle array before the main portal,
greeted her with an angry chorus of yells which must have
seemed doubly terrifying, coming from long rows of Carmelite
habits. Most of them shrieked defiance at her, if Yepes is to be
believed, and some even cursed her,[2] while the countercries of
her friends, who came bearing a cross to receive her, were
drowned out by the unholy racket which broke into echoes
against the convent walls, and no doubt was taken up by some

---

[1] Father Fernández had ruled that all nuns leaving the Incarnation must make
a formal renunciation of the Mitigated Rule. This was to end the confusion
caused by nuns who left to join the Discalced, and later returned.
[2] Yepes, *Vida de Santa Teresa de Jesús*, lib. II, cap. XXIV.

of the spectators along the street. There actually seemed danger that some might lay violent hands on the new prioress, if she attempted to enter. The *Corregidor* and *Regidor* of Ávila hastened to the scene, fearing a riot. Religion, being a serious matter, has always been taken seriously in Spain.

Fray Angel de Salazar was obviously angry as he conducted La Madre to the door of the chapel, and signified that all the community were to meet in the lower choir. As it happened, the Incarnation had two choirs, the lower one on the same level with the church, with a door between. While the nuns were obeying him, Madre Teresa sat serenely on a stone bench by the chapel door. When all were seated she went in and prostrated herself before the Blessed Sacrament. Then, with Fray Angel, she entered the lower choir. One account has it that she walked absent-mindedly to the seat she had occupied many years before.[3] Be this as it may, Father Salazar took the prioral chair, and read the *patente* of the Apostolic Visitor Fernández, appointing her prioress. He had hardly finished — perhaps he had not quite finished — when the most unearthly clamor arose from the black ranks facing him. This time, in fact, the demonstration became so uncontrolled that several of the nuns fainted.

Teresa went to the fallen sisters, one after the other, and tenderly placed her hands upon their heads, whereat they revived. This must have had a quieting effect upon many of the enraged ladies, and Fray Angel took advantage of a lull in the storm to demand in a loud voice, "Will you have Madre Teresa of Jesus as your prioress?" Catalina de Castro, one of the minority favorable to her, cried out, "We love her and we will have her. *Te Deum Laudamus!*" Others took up the song, "*Te Deum Laudamus!*" and before the opposition could recover its vehemence, they managed to drag her to the prioress's chair, still clasping in her arms the image of Saint Joseph, under whose protection she had placed the issue of the day.

None of this seems to have ruffled her serenity in the slightest. In the midst of the uproar she turned to Fray Angel and remarked with a smile that she did not blame the nuns for being upset under the circumstances. Her calmness undoubtedly helped to quiet the disturbance. In spite of all this, a large faction of the nuns still seemed determined not to accept her governance, and pending the chapter meeting which would be

---

[3] María de San José, in Mir, *Vida de Santa Teresa*, II, 213.

the test of strength next day, they held secret sessions in which they did not scruple to say that if she would not retire voluntarily, they would cast her out bodily.

This was what they had planned; but they had not taken the measure of the great strategist with whom they had to deal. When they entered the chapter room, prepared to see the tyrant enthroned in the prioral seat, they were astonished to find there an image of Our Lady of Clemency (so it is still called) with the keys of the convent in her hand, and in the subprioress's place, a likeness of Saint Joseph. Teresa was sitting humbly at the feet of the Virgin.

Before her enemies had recovered from their astonishment, she began a speech. Learned critics have found Yepes's quotation too rhetorical to be verbatim. To my less practised ear it sounds like her own writings, like something she might have told him:

"*Señoras, madres y hermanas mias:* Our Lord, by way of obedience, has sent me to this house to fill this office, of which I was not desirous, much less deserving of it. This election has given me much sorrow, not only at finding myself in a situation with which I don't know what to do, but because they have taken away from Your Worships your freedom of election, and they have given you a prioress against your will and liking, and a prioress who will do well if she manages to learn the least of the much good there is here. I come only to serve you and to please you in all I can; and in this I hope the Lord is going to aid me much, for in other things anyone can teach and reform me. From this anyone can see, my ladies, what I can do; and though it be to give my blood and my life, I will do it with a right good will.

"I am a daughter of this house, and a sister of Your Worships. I know the disposition and the needs of all of you, or of most of you; there is no reason to be strangers to one who is so much your own.

"Do not fear my government, for although I have lived and governed among Discalced, I know well, by the goodness of the Lord, how those who are not so have to be governed. My desire is that we all serve the Lord quietly, and that we do this little which our Rule and Constitutions demand for the love of the Lord to Whom we owe so much. Well I know our weakness, which is great; but what we don't attain with our works, let us attain with our desires, for the Lord is merciful, and little by little He will bring the works to equal the intention and desire."[4]

This *divino artificio,* as Yepes calls it, was so successful that Teresa was able to begin her administration without serious hindrance. Her common sense prompted her to attack first the temporal but exigent problem of food, the neglect of which had been almost unbelievable. For five years no regular meals had been served. Each of the 130 nuns received a ration of bread every day; for the rest of her sustenance she was obliged to forage as she could, usually at the home of parents or other relatives. Teresa was resolved to put a stop to this. "I shall have need of a few *reales,*" she wrote her sister, "for there is no getting them from the convent — only bread; try to send them to me."[5] She seldom left the house on any errand without bringing back something for her nuns. She was always begging a few *reales* here, a few ducats there from rich persons of her acquaintance: from Doña María de Mendoza; from Don Jerónimo de Guzmán, brother of one of the nuns, Doña Francisca de Bracamonte; from Doña Magdalena de Ulloa,[6] the governess of Don John of Austria until the revelation of his identity in 1559; and from the Duchess of Alba, who gave, for distribution among the convents of the Reform, a hundred ducats, which Teresa employed where there was greater need, at the Incarnation. By such means she managed to give an allowance of one *real* per week to each of many nuns from poor families, some of whom were in dire straits. She was particularly attentive to the sick, and sought delicacies for them. When her brother-in-law Juan de Ovalle happened to mention, one day in March, 1572, that he had a great many turkeys on his place in Alba, she suggested to him a good use for them, and after he had returned home she took care to mention the subject in a letter to her sister.

"Remember, my lady, that in one way or another, those who are to save themselves have troubles, and God does not give us to choose; and perhaps to you, Madam, as more weak, He gives smaller ones. I know better those you are enduring than you, Madam, know how to tell me, or can in a letter, and so, com-

---

[4] Yepes, *Vida de Santa Teresa,* lib. II, cap. XXV. Ribera describes the incident (*Vida de Santa Teresa,* lib. III, cap. I) but does not give the speech.

[5] Letter to Juana, February 4, 1572, B.M.C., *Epistolario,* I, p. 83; Stanbrook, I, p. 93.

[6] After her husband was killed in the 1570 campaign in the Alpujarras, the lady retired to Valladolid, took for her confessor Father Juan de Prádanos, S.J., and devoted her life to charity.

mending you earnestly to God, I think I love you more now than I used to, although it is always plenty. They will give you another letter of mine. I don't believe you are more wicked, although it seems so to you. Go to confession often, I beg, for the love of God and mine. May He be with you, Amen. Send the turkeys, since you have so many. Your unworthy servant, Teresa of Jesus."[7]

To Doña María Mendoza in Ávila she wrote: "As for what concerns the comfort of the body, there has been no lack of sympathy and of someone to take care of me; and in the town they have given me alms enough; and of the house I eat only bread, and even that I'd rather not. We have just finished the alms that Doña Magdalena gave us, and until now we have given a dinner with it (and with the aid of the other alms which Your Ladyship and other persons gave) to the most poor. When I see them now so quiet and good, it hurts me to have to see them suffer, as they certainly do."[8]

It took months to place this cumbersome convent on what might be called a business basis. Teresa was not to be discouraged; she never wavered in her belief that "God never fails anyone who serves Him." Had she not written in the *Camino*,[9] and proved it at San José, that "Whoever serves the Lord will never lack the necessities of life"? And in the *Vida*[10] that "Certain monasteries, from not being recollected, came to be poor"? The implication is clear that the wretched temporal state of the Incarnation was a punishment for its neglect of spiritual affairs, for its compromises with the world in the matter of titles, social discriminations, visits, and conversations. And although La Madre had dealt with temporal difficulties first, she was not long in attacking those spiritual ones which were actually more fundamental. "Seek ye first the Kingdom of God and His justice, and all these things shall be added unto you."

With consummate tact she went about obtaining, one after another, the keys of the front door, the speak room, and other strategic points from careless or incompetent functionaries, and appointed those who would carry out her wishes, particularly in putting a stop to needless conversations and visits. This was

[7] *Epistolario,* I, B.M.C., p. 93.
[8] *Ibid.,* p. 87.
[9] *Ibid.,* cap. II.
[10] *Vida,* cap. XXXV.

not easy, but she soon noted an improvement. About a month after she took office, she wrote Doña Luisa de la Cerda, "My occupations are so great and so unavoidable, both outside and inside of the house, that I have hardly time even to write this. May our Lord pay Your Ladyship for the favor and consolation you gave me with yours, for I tell you I have need of it. Oh, Señora, for anyone who has seen herself in the quiet of our houses, and now sees herself in this hurly-burly, it doesn't seem possible to live, for in every way there is something to suffer. And yet, glory to God, there is peace, which is not a little, as they go about giving up their entertainments and liberty; for although they are so good, and certainly there is much virtue in this house, it is death to change a habit, as they say. They bear it well, and hold me in much respect; but there are one hundred and thirty. Your Ladyship will understand the care that will be necessary to put things in order. Our monasteries give me some; however, as I live here compelled by obedience, I hope in our Lord that he will not allow them to be in need, but will take care of them. I think that my soul is not disturbed with all this Babylon, which I take for a favor of the Lord. Nature is tired of it, but all that is little compared to how I have offended the Lord."[11]

Most of the young noblemen who were in the habit of visiting relatives and friends at the Incarnation desisted when they learned that the new prioress disapproved. There was one, however, a person of some importance in Ávila, who resented giving up what Yepes calls a "somewhat scandalous conversation." Very "blind and *apasionado*" he was; and after he had been told a few times that the nun he wished to see was busy and could not come to the speak room, he demanded to see the Prioress. When she appeared he subjected her to a long, rude, and insolent tirade, the gist of which was that a man of his quality was not to be treated so, and he did not propose to put up with it.

La Madre listened to all this with "much humility and patience." When he had finished, she told him what she thought of him, and promised that if he ever darkened the doors of that house again, she would have the King cut off his head.

"The words that the Saint addressed to him were of such force and efficacy," adds Yepes, "that he made no bones about

---

[11] Letter of November 7, 1572, B.M.C., *Epist.*, I, pp. 79-80.

taking himself off, and determined to give up altogether the conversation he used to have in the monastery." The news got around, and Teresa had no further difficulties with visitors.[12]

During the Lent of 1572 there was not a single visitor at the Incarnation, not even a parent. "My prioress accomplishes these wonders," wrote Teresa, giving all the credit to our Lady.[13] She was not content, however, with such a negative triumph as the elimination of an abuse. Good discipline, after all, was but a means to the higher end of spiritual advancement, and this, in her opinion, could not be obtained under such confessors as the fathers of the Mitigated Rule who were in charge at the Incarnation. She resolved to get rid of these compromising *padres,* and to substitute some of her own Discalced friars. Naturally she thought at once of her *Senequita.* She sent Father Julian of Ávila to Salamanca to explain the situation to the apostolic visitor, Father Fernández, and to obtain his permission, which was readily granted. It was not long before she had John of the Cross and another Discalced friar from Pastrana, Fray Guzmán de San Matías, in Ávila.[14] It was a delicate situation to handle. At first she had only Fray John hear confessions, along with the regular Calced friars.

The nuns, fearing severe and disagreeable penances, sought at first to avoid the little friar from Pastrana by asking when they went into the confessional, "Father, are you Calced or Discalced?"

John of the Cross, sitting in the dark behind the screen on one of his first days in the "box," pulled his habit over his feet and answered "Calced."[15] As soon as he had heard a few confessions the word got about that he was an angelic director, and everyone wanted to consult him. After a while Fray Guzmán also

---

[12] Yepes, *op. cit.,* lib. II, cap. XXIV. Padre Silverio, taking the incident from Fray Francisco de Santa María (*Reforma,* t. I, *lib.* II, *cap.* XLIX, n. 13, p. 371), who was probably the source of Yepes, conjectures, without giving his reasons, that the *caballero* was only a *hidalguete* or country squire, and a mere boy or *muchacho.* Padre Silverio (IV, 122) does not take notice that the contemporary Yepes calls the visitor a *"caballero muy principal"* of the city of Ávila, *"que tenia alli una conversación algo escandalosa,"* and *"andava muy ciego y apasionado."* This makes the unusual severity of Teresa quite understandable; Father Silverio's treatment of the situation as a frivolous trifle does not.

[13] Letter to Doña María de Mendoza, March 7, 1572, B.M.C., *Epist.,* I, p. 87.

[14] Father Bruno, O.C.D., doubts that Fray Guzmán went to Ávila when Saint John did: *Saint John of the Cross,* Ch. XI, n. 14.

[15] P. Silverio, *Vida de Santa Teresa de Jesús,* IV, 130.

began hearing. Thus, by gradual steps Teresa got rid of the Fathers of the Cloth[16] without seeming to do so.

A tremendous spiritual improvement began to manifest itself throughout the community. Many who had most bitterly resented La Madre's coming were now her stanchest friends and supporters. As soon as the Discalced friars had the confidence of the nuns, she had a little house built for them at the end of the garden, with a chapel where they could say their Masses. Her success as prioress of the Incarnation was so evident, in short, that even Fray Angel de Salazar praised her highly, and the Apostolic Visitor Fernandez declined to let her visit the Duchess of Alba, to console her for the long absence of her husband in Flanders, on the ground that she was indispensable.

"The convent of the Incarnation contains a hundred and thirty nuns," he wrote this great lady. "Their life there is as peaceful and as holy as that of the ten or twelve Discalced nuns at Alba, which affords me the greatest wonder and consolation. This results solely from the presence of the Mother, and were she absent for a single day, their former want of restriction is so old established and their present good order so newly rooted, having been instituted only a year, that if the restraint and respect inspired by her sway were removed, they would return to their former state, the foundations being as yet but weak. . . . Besides this, the Mother entered in the face of such opposition and disturbance, and it has cost her so much to pacify the nuns (whom I have penanced), that now she is making progress and her work is in flower, though the seed has not been gathered, it would cause great inconvenience and scruple to remove her. . . ."[17]

The Incarnation was not Teresa's only responsibility during these difficult years. Her own convents and all their problems were constantly in her thought. Ribera compares her to Saint Paul in prison, writing to many disciples in the outer world. She was an industrious correspondent. Her more than 400 extant epistles represent but a third, it has been estimated, of the whole; but there are enough for this period to give us a fairly extensive view of the activity of a tireless mind and a heart infinitely generous. She writes thank-you letters for chickens

---

[16] The friars of the Mitigation were so called because they wore woolen habits, in contrast to the rough serge of the Discalced.

[17] *Letters of Saint Teresa,* Stanbrook Abbey, I, p. 102.

given for the sick. She commiserates with her sister Juana for being in Galinduste; "God deliver me from such a place," she adds, "and from this place too!"[18] She scolds Juan de Ovalle for being so small as to oppose yielding ground for a pathway to the convent in Alba de Tormes, yet she thanks God when he recovers from a tertian fever. Hearing that the fleet from the Indies is at San Lúcar, she hopes for news from Brother Lorenzo. She sends Father John of the Cross to Medina del Campo to exorcize a nun, Sister Isabel de San Jerónimo; but although he has delivered a person at Ávila from three legions of devils, each of whom revealed his name when commanded to do so, he fails at Medina because the poor woman is not possessed, but insane.

She vigorously opposes two candidates proposed by Doña María de Mendoza for the convent at Valladolid, of which the great lady was cofoundress and benefactress. One of the two, recommended by the Jesuit Father Jerónimo Ripalda, has only one eye. La Madre, though suffering with fever and a cruel pain in her jaw, which she has had for six weeks, takes up her pen on the seventh day of March, 1572, and writes Doña María a long letter, saying, among other things:

"Now, that I may suffer in every way, the Mother Prioress of that house of Your Ladyship writes me that Your Ladyship wishes to have a nun accepted in it and that Your Ladyship is displeased, for so they have told me, because I have not wished to take her, and another one that Father Ribalda brings. I have been thinking that they have deceived you.[19] It would pain me if it were true, since Your Ladyship can reprimand me and command me; and I cannot believe that you would be displeased with me without telling me so, unless it is to extricate yourself from them,[20] but that for this very reason Your Ladyship would show it. If this were so, it would give me much consolation, for I know how to settle matters with those Fathers of the Company, for they wouldn't take anybody who was not suitable for *their* Order to do *me* a favor. If Your Ladyship really wants to command it, there is nothing more to be said about it; for it is clear that Your Ladyship can give orders in that house and in all, and

---

[18] *Ibid.*, p. 93.

[19] "*Pensado he que la han engañado.*" This could mean, "I have been thinking that they have deceived her," the novice: but the context seems to indicate that "*la*" stands for "*Vuestra Señoría.*"

[20] "*Ellos,*" referring, probably, to the Jesuits, as it plainly does three lines below.

that I must obey you. I will send to ask permission of the Father Visitor, or the Father General, for it is against our Constitutions to take anyone with the defect she has, and I could not give permission against it, without one of them; and they must learn to read Latin well, for it is the rule that no one is be received without knowing it.

"For the discharge of my conscience, I cannot omit to tell Your Ladyship what I would do in this matter, after commending it to the Lord. I leave aside, I say, the fact that Your Ladyship desires it, for, not to offend you, I am at your disposal in everything, and I shall speak no more about that. Only I beg Your Ladyship to look well to it, and have more care for your house, for if Your Ladyship does not see to its welfare, you will regret it. If it were a house of many, one could better overlook some fault; but where there are so few, they have to be chosen carefully, and I have always seen Your Ladyship with this intention. . . . In my opinion, neither of those two should be received there; for neither sanctity, nor courage, nor such wonderful discretion, nor talents do I see in them, to make the house benefit. Then, if it is to lose, why does Your Ladyship want them accepted? For their own betterment there are plenty of monasteries where, as I say, on account of the large numbers, things can be better overlooked; but when one is taken there, each one has to be fit to be prioress or any office which may present itself.

"For the love of our Lord, let Your Ladyship look well to it, and notice that the common good must always be attended to, rather than the private. . . ."[21]

Teresa may have won this encounter against Father Ripalda and his one-eyed candidate, but not to the permanent injury of their friendship, for within a year he was to be her confessor at Salamanca, and it is to him that we owe the blessing of her *Book of Foundations*, which she wrote at his command.

Another Jesuit, Father Ordóñez, received some sound advice from her concerning a girls' school that some of his penitents were planning at Medina:

"As for having so many, as you say, it always displeases me, for I understand that teaching women and imposing many classes on them is as different from teaching boys as black is from white. And there are so many disadvantages in having many, so far as not getting anything good done is concerned, that I cannot men-

[21] B.M.C., *Epist.*, I, pp. 85–88; March 7, 1572.

tion them now, except that it is best to have a fixed number, and when it passes forty, it is very much and a complete fraud;[22] some will disturb others so that nothing good may be done. In Toledo[23] I have been informed there are thirty-five, and they can't go beyond that. I tell Your Worship that if they have to have so many girls and so much noise, it is not at all right. If some on this account don't wish to give alms, let Your Worship advance little by little, for there is no hurry, and make your congregation holy, for God will aid you, and for the sake of alms we must not damage the thing itself."[24]

Of the extensive correspondence Madre Teresa carried on with Philip II, only a few letters have been found. One of them begged his protection for her convents, tactfully commencing with the assurance that she and her nuns were praying for his intentions, for his fourth Queen, Ann of Austria, and for the infant heir to the throne, Prince Fernando. "Special prayer was offered on the day when his Highness was sworn. This will always be done; and so, the more this Order grows, the more Your Majesty will benefit by it. And for this reason I have dared to beg Your Majesty to favor us in certain things, which the Licentiate Juan de Padilla will mention. May His Divine Majesty guard you as many years as Christendom has need of you. It is a great comfort for the trials and persecutions there are in it, that our Lord God has so great a defender and aid for His Church as Your Majesty is."[25]

Not the least of her trials at the Incarnation was the series of illnesses that continued during most of her term. References to these are scattered through the letters of 1571–73. In the first month her health was somewhat better, but on February 4, 1572, she was writing her sister that she had become ill "almost directly" after she arrived, had the fever several times before Christmas, with a sore throat, and had been "bled twice and purged." She started the new year with a quartan fever, which was still with her in February, with intermittent chills that usually began at two o'clock in the morning. Nevertheless she

---

[22] "Y todo barateria."

[23] The famous *Colegio de Doncellas* founded by Cardinal Siliceo, tutor of Philip II, for poor girls.

[24] "La substancia." — B.M.C., *Epist.*, I, p. 108.

[25] B.M.C., *Epist.*, I, p. 106; Stanbrook, I, p. 119. When little Prince Fernando died at the age of seven, Philip asked his people to thank God that since the boy had to die, He had taken him during the age of innocence.

used to get up every day and attend to her work.[26] In March the wretched weather was very trying. In addition to the quartan ague she had quinsy sore throat, a pain in her side and another in her jaw which lasted six weeks, was bled three times more, and purged.[27] August 27 she felt so much better that "I shall be surprised if it lasts," while in September she had a tertian fever that was epidemic, but soon recovered.[28] In February, 1573, she wrote, "I have very little health during the winters, for this house is very contrary to my ailments."[29]

With all these trials, she had consolations, besides finding a certain joy even in pain and sorrow. If she had made time during the foundation at Salamanca to write the exquisite verses for the profession of Sister Isabel of the Angels, commencing,

> Henceforth I'll joy in wretchedness,
> Let startling fears be my repose,
> And reaping solace from my woes
> Take losses for my sole success,[30]

it is not to be supposed that she wholly relinquished this pleasure at the Incarnation. And who can imagine any more delightful conversations between human creatures than her memorable ones with Father John of the Cross — two poets, two saints — at the famous grille of the convent, he sitting in a chair on one side and she kneeling on the other, until, after a long discourse of God, both became enraptured, and those near by sensed something of the same sort of phenomenon that had been reported of Saint Francis and Saint Clare, at whose meeting a whole house shone with a celestial light?

If her *Senequita* alone approached with her what he was to call "the Living Flame of Love," her other sons at Pastrana did not forget her in her "captivity." It was about this time that they sent her a spiritual challenge couched in all the grandiloquent phrases of the chivalry so dear to her in childhood and still capable of moving her to eloquence and wit. The text of the famous *Desafío,* daring the nuns of the Incarnation to join combat with the powers of evil for the prize of heaven, has been lost,

---

[26] Letter to Juana, B.M.C., *Epist.,* I, 83.
[27] March 7, to María de Mendoza, *ibid.,* p. 85.
[28] *Ibid.,* p. 95, to Juana, August 27 and September 27.
[29] *Ibid.,* p. 100, to P. Gaspar de Salazar, February 13, 1573.
[30] For the rest of this, and translations of Saint Teresa's other poems, see *The Minor Works of Saint Teresa* by the Benedictines of Stanbrook Abbey, p. 28.

but it now appears certain, as La Madre must have learned on inquiry, that the writer was a Father Gracián, who had taken the habit of the Reform at Pastrana on March 25 of that year (1572) and with it the name of Fray Jerome of the Mother of God.

He was one of the twenty children of Diego Gracián de Aldorete and Juana de Antisco, daughter of the Polish ambassador at the Court of Madrid. Several of his sisters were nuns, while one brother became a secretary to Philip II. Jerome, after studying at the Jesuit College at Madrid, took his theology at Alcalá, where he was ordained in 1569 despite his family's preference for the law. An imaginative man, with a flair for the melodramatic, and a streak of vanity which sometimes degenerated into self-pity (judging from the autobiographical *Peregrinación de Anastasio* of his old age), he had extensive learning, genuine piety, a particular devotion to our Lady, and a Christian contempt for the allurements of the world. Going to Pastrana to arrange for a friend to enter the Discalced convent there, he stopped at the monastery, and was so captivated by the life of John of the Cross and the other friars that after several months of horrible temptations from which he was saved by the prayers of Madre Isabel de Santo Domingo, he finally entered their novitiate.[31] Once he made a trip to Madrid, because, he wrote, "I knew a certain thing in secret," and "if I had not gone, the Prince Ruy Gómez would have died" — to which he adds a dark hint of an attempt on the part of unnamed persons to poison the favorite of Philip II.

Father Gracián was twenty-seven years old when he wrote the *Desafío* to the nuns of the Incarnation. Did he mention the food at Pastrana? Many years later his pen was stirred to eloquence by the mere memory that "in Lent we had nothing to eat but turnips and sops of bread, and when at Easter we got a little putrid codfish, we thought it was the fare of kings."[32] Part of Teresa's witty reply seems to touch upon this. There is space here for only a sample of her celestial foolery:

"Having seen the Cartel, we thought we could not muster our forces to enter the field against such valorous and puissant cavaliers, for they had the assurance of victory, and they would

<hr/>

[31] Madre Isabel, prioress at Pastrana, was so taken with Gracián, according to Saint Teresa, that she asked the nuns to pray that he would enter their Order. They "stormed heaven" with prayers, fasts, and scourgings until the favor was granted. — *Fundaciones*, cap. XIV.

[32] *Peregrinación de Anastasio*, Burgos, 1905, p. 23.

leave us wholly despoiled of our goods, and even perhaps too cowed to do that little which we could. Seeing this, no one would sign up, least of all Teresa of Jesus. This is the plain truth, without fiction.

"We agree to act when our forces arrive, and when they have been exercised for some days in these genteel pastimes, it may be that with the favor and aid of those who wish to join us in them we may be able a few days hence to sign the Cartel.

"It has to be on condition that the maintainer does not turn his back, shutting himself up in those caves, but that he sally forth on the field of this world, where we are. It may be that finding himself always at war, where one can never lay down one's arms or be off guard or take a moment to rest with security, he will not be so furious; for there is quite a difference between the one thing and the other, between talking and acting, for we have some understanding of the difference there is in this.

"Come forth, let him come forth from that delightful life, him and his companions; perhaps they will be so quickly stumbling and fallen that it will be necessary to help them rise; for a terrible thing it is to be always in danger, and weighed down with arms, and without anything to eat. Since the champion provides this so abundantly, let him send quickly the maintenance he promises; for if he conquers us by hunger, he will gain little honor or vantage.

"Any *caballero* or daughters of the Virgin who will ask the Lord each day to keep in His grace Sister Beatriz Juárez, that she may not speak without advertence, and always for His greater glory, will be given two years of what she has merited taking care of very tiresome invalids.

"Sister Ana de Vergas declares that if the said cavaliers and brothers will ask the Lord to quit her of a contradiction she has, and give her humility, she will give them all the merit she will gain from it, if the Lord grants it.

"The mother subprioress declares that if the same will ask the Lord to deliver her from her self-will, she will give them what she has merited for two years; her name is Isabel of the Cross.

"Sister Sebastiana Gómez declares that any one of the same who will look at the Crucifix three times a day for the three hours that the Lord was on the Cross, and will obtain that she may conquer a great passion that is tormenting her soul, she will apply to them the merit she may gain (if the Lord grants it) from conquering it. . . .

"Sister María Cimbrón declares that those who each day ask that she have a good end shall have a share in what she suffers; and it is a long time since she has been able to move in her bed, and quite near the end. . . .

"A Knight Errant"[33] declares that if the Master of the Lists obtains for him from the Lord the grace he needs to serve Him perfectly in all that obedience commands of him, he declares he will give him all the merit he shall gain serving in it this year. . . .

"Teresa of Jesus declares that she will give to any cavalier of the Virgin who will make an act every day very resolutely to endure all his life a superior who is very idiotic and spoiled and a huge feeder and ill tempered, the day he does it, she will give him half of what she merits that day, not only in Communion, but in plenty of pains she has; in short, in everything, which will be little enough. He must consider the humility with which the Lord stood before His judges, and how He was obedient even unto the death of the cross. This is for a month and a half, the contract."[34]

Thus La Madre made her reply a two-edged sword, aimed at the improvement of the nuns at the Incarnation as well as that of the friars. Did she have anyone in particular in mind when she wrote of "a superior very idiotic and spoiled and a huge feeder and ill tempered"?[35] She was probably referring to the then master of novices at the monastery of Pastrana, Fray Angelus de San Gabriel, who was giving her not a little concern by his eccentric management of the young men, to whom he often assigned bizarre penances and mortifications that served rather to make people laugh (and thus to bring religion into disrepute) than to accomplish their lawful purpose of overcoming self-love and other faults.[36] Fray Domingo Báñez, to whom she appealed for advice at Saint Stephen's College, Salamanca, wrote her a long letter on the subject on April 23, 1572.

---

[33] *"Venturero,"* probably John of the Cross.

[34] For the rest of this document — some 1500 words — I must refer the reader either to P. Silverio's Spanish text, B.M.C., t. VI, pp. 57–61, or to the good English translation in the first volume of the Stanbrook Abbey Letters, pp. 104–110. One paragraph, asking for long life for Madre Teresa, obviously was not written by the Saint.

[35] *"Un perlado muy necio, y vicioso y comedor y mal acondicionado."*

[36] Silverio, B.M.C., t. VI, Introduction, p. xlv.

He considered the ignorance of those sinning through zeal for virtue worse than that of the victims of passion and obvious wickedness; "for if they fall, they are less corrigible, because they have agreed in their hearts that whoever contradicts them is persecuting virtue, or has little experience in matters of the spirit, or is envious, or has similar faults, so that they won't accept correction from anybody. And what is still worse, they pretend that they are persecuted for virtue, and do not understand that now, it is for their ignorance: and they think that now they are something, since they are persecuted for virtue: and there is created secretly in the center of their heart an idol of self-esteem, and although they appear to humiliate themselves in their thoughts and works, still, at closer view, these are humiliations done not before the majesty of God with the utmost fear of offending Him, but before the secret and hidden idol of their own self-love. Self-esteem is dressed up in virtuous raiment, and then it wishes to be adored by itself and by all the world. And if someone does not adore their statue, they judge him to be a persecutor of virtue, so that they make their designs and deeds the standard of virtue.

"This father master of novices seems to me a man of good zeal and of good desires, and since he wants light, there is no reason to deny it to him. May Jesus Christ give it to him, and teach him the *summa* of perfection. 'Learn of Me, for I am meek and humble of heart.' " After some further remarks about imprudent mortifications, he continues: "This is no way to train novices, in mortifications unrestrained, since their profession is to be one of recollection. To wish to imitate the Padres Teatinos[37] in this is to make another order which is not that of Carmel. They don't have a prescribed habit; their profession is not of recollection and silence, nor of fasting, nor of perpetual choir; they have to go familiarly among the public teaching Christian doctrine; so it is not much if they exercise themselves little in this.[38] The friar and the monk does not need to look for extraneous exercises: let him follow his profession and keep silence; for he will be holy without all the world seeing his mortifications. These zealous desires to edify one's neighbor seem very transparent to me. I adore what they say of Saint Francis, that

---

[37] Silverio and others believe this refers not to the Theatine Order, but to the Jesuits, who were often so designated.

[38] Recollection? *"No es mucho se exerciten en eso poco."*

they held him to be crazy, and he took off his clothes and dressed like a very poor man, because it was from an impulse of the Holy Spirit; but to try to imitate these rare doings without that impulse is only a farce. Saint Francis then had no habit, or Order or profession; on the contrary, he did what in him was prudence. If this father says that he feels there is some spirit to do these exercises, I should like to see them try him out with other exercises more canonically proved. Let them fast like saints, watch like them. . . .

"It amuses me that when dinner is at eleven, this father says they shall eat a bite at nine, since dinner is late! . . . I don't like what this father says, that melancholy will seize him if they deny him what he wants. . . . Let Your Grace console him and advise him to be obedient and keep silent, for the Lord was silent thirty-two years and more, and preached two. . . ."[39]

If Teresa passed on this advice to Fray Angelus, it had no marked effect, for he was of the melancholy type that she considered almost hopeless,[40] and she soon had him replaced by Gracián, who perhaps had taken her delicate hint to learn to rule by learning to obey.

Several visions and locutions of no ordinary sort came to her at the Incarnation. On the eve of Saint Sebastian, January 19, 1572, when all the nuns in the choir had begun to sing the *Salve Regina,* she saw, in an intellectual vision, the Blessed Virgin descend with a great multitude of angels and take the place of her image on the prioress's seat. She remained there all through the *Salve.* Then she said, "You have done quite right to place me here; I will be present at the praises they make to my Son, and I will present them." Teresa remained enraptured, and became aware of the presence in her soul of the Most Blessed Trinity; and she thought that the Person of the Father drew her to Himself "and spoke very agreeable words." Among other things He said, "I gave you My Son and the Holy Spirit and this Virgin; what can you give to Me?"[41]

On Palm Sunday, at Holy Communion, her senses were suspended so that she could not swallow the Sacred Host. While It was still on her tongue, she felt as if all her mouth were filled with blood, and her face and all her body were covered with it,

[39] B.M.C., t. VI, pp. 132–133.
[40] Cf. *Fundaciones,* cap. XXIII.
[41] B.M.C., t. II, *Spiritual Relations, Merced* 25, p. 56.

as warm as if the Saviour had just then shed it. He said to her, "Daughter, I want My blood to benefit you, and have no fear that My mercy will fail you. I shed it with many pains, and you enjoy it with such great joy as you see; I pay you well for the invitation you give Me this day" — referring to the fact that for thirty years she had always communicated on Palm Sunday, after the most careful preparation to receive Him, "for I thought the cruelty the Jews inflicted upon Him was very much after such a great reception, to let Him go to eat so far away, and so I arranged that He should stay with me, and in a poor enough lodging, as now I see. And so I made some silly reflections, and the Lord must have accepted them; for this is one of the visions I hold most certain."[42]

Teresa was fond of large Hosts, and in all her convents had them made so. When Father John of the Cross came to give her Holy Communion on November 18, 1572, he separated the Sacred Particle into two portions, to give one to another sister. La Madre thought he did this to mortify her, knowing her preference for generous ones. "Don't be afraid, daughter, that anyone will be able to separate thee from Me," said the voice of Christ, "giving me to understand," she adds, "that it did not matter.

"Then He represented Himself to me by imaginary vision, as on other occasions, very much in the interior, and gave me His right hand, and said to me, 'Look at this nail, which is a sign that you shall be My wife[43] from today. Until now you have not merited it; from now on, you shall look to My honor not only as Creator and as King and thy God, but as My true wife. My honor is thine, and thine mine.' This favor had such an effect upon me that I could not contain myself, and I remained like a crazy woman, and I said to the Lord, to either raise up my lowness, or not to do me such a favor, for certainly I did not think that nature could suffer it. Thus I was all day very inebriated. I have felt since a great improvement, and greater confusion and affliction at seeing that I did nothing to deserve such great favors."[44]

His Majesty thought otherwise; and one day, about this time, He told her that if He had not created heaven, He would make it only for her.[45]

[42] *Ibid.*, p. 57.
[43] "*Esposa.*"
[44] *Ibid.*, Merced 35, p. 64.
[45] Yepes, *op. cit.*, lib. II, cap. XIX.

Chapter XXVI

STRANGE VOCATION OF THE
PRINCESS OF ÉBOLI

IT WAS Philip the Second who set Madre Teresa free from the Incarnation. Her friends had sought this in various ways, but in vain. Pope Pius V had declined to interfere even at the request of the Bishop of Avila. The Duchess of Alba had had a very positive refusal, as we have seen, from the apostolic visitor; but so great was her desire for the consolation of the *Beata* that she appealed to the King, who may have consented precisely because he was considering the removal of her husband from his command in the Netherlands, and the arrest of her son Don Fadrique for marrying a lady promised to another man. His Majesty made known his wish to Father Fernández in such terms that in February, 1573, La Madre received orders to repair at once to Alba de Tormes. Her visit was brief. She talked with the Duchess till midnight without accepting food or drink; while the great lady likewise refrained, to enjoy the spiritual feast of a saint's conversation.[1]

La Madre had to return to the Incarnation, but the ice had been broken, and it was not long before Father Fernández allowed her to go to Salamanca, at the request of one of the nuns, Sister Ann of Jesus, who offered her dowry to pay the cost of a second foundation in that city. The original house had been always unhealthy and otherwise unsatisfactory. Now, it appeared, a better one was to be had from a somewhat impoverished nobleman, Pedro Rodríguez de la Banda. The property was entailed, but there was every hope that the King, favorably disposed as he was to the Carmelite Reform, would permit the sale.

Teresa left Avila for this adventure in the last week of July, 1573, taking with her Fray Antonio of Jesus, Father Julian of Avila, and only one nun, Doña Quiteria Dávila of the convent of the Incarnation, who, being a cousin of the Marquesa of Velada, was attended by a maid. All went mounted on mules. Father Julian left a droll account of this journey:

"As it was hot, and the sun made our Holy Mother ill, we left

---

[1] Silverio, *Vida de Santa Teresa de Jesús*, IV, pp. 139–154, and his reference.

Ávila almost at dusk, and to start off the journey, before we got to Martin, the Padre Fray Antonio of Jesus, who went along with us, had a great fall from his beast. It pleased God that he was not injured in these and many others he had, going on trips that concerned the Order. A lady's maid went with us. A little further on I saw her fall from her mule and hit her head on the ground, and I thought she must be dead; and God saved her, for no harm was done. And when it had become quite dark, for the night was well along, we lost the ass that was carrying the money and other bundles that were being taken to Salamanca, and he didn't appear all that night; so that, what with falls, and losing the ass, and the thick darkness, I think it must have been past midnight when we arrived at the inn. I did not wish to eat supper, although I believe I needed it, but I made up my mind to get along on fasting so I should not have to miss saying Mass in the morning.

"In the morning a boy went to look for the ass, and found him lying down a little distance from the road, for nobody had touched him, nor was anything he carried missing. So we got up early in the morning to go and say Mass at a hermitage called Our Lady of Parral. We got there in good time, but there was no equipment for saying Mass at the hermitage. I had to go to the village, which was some distance from the hermitage, for equipment, and I did not find the priest in the place; there was no one who could give us equipment.

"Finally, we spent the whole morning going back and forth, and I had to give up saying Mass, much against my will, and supper and breakfast too, and tired enough. And although the Holy Mother had to go without Communion, for she never interrupted a journey on this account, I didn't feel that so much as I did what concerned myself; for although my labor was all wasted on the occasion, still they all laughed at me as they went along, and with reason.

"Another night we had a greater loss than that of the ass, even though they said he carried five hundred ducats: it was this, that since we still traveled by night and in so much darkness, our forces were divided into two parts. The one who went with the Holy Mother, and for the sake of his reputation I don't care to say who he is, left her and the lady Doña Quiteria, who is now prioress of the Incarnation, in a street of a little village, that they might wait there for the other people, that all might be united and not separated; in such wise that in going to look for the rest, well, then, when they appeared, he returned to find those he had left, and never could reach the place where he had left them, and as it was so dark, out of his mind so to speak, for turn where he would he could not find them; and what with saying, 'They must be further on with those who went ahead,' it took us a long while before we were all together again. We would say, one to another,

" 'Is La Madre with you?'

"They would say,

" 'No!'

" 'Isn't she with you?'

" 'Yes! She was with you. What have you done with her?'

"So we found ourselves all in the dark — that of the night, which was plenty, and that of finding ourselves without our Mother, which was much greater. We didn't know whether to go back or go on. We began to shout at random. We had to separate again, some to seek what we had lost, the others to shout to see if she would answer us from any direction. After we had spent a good while in anxiety, and especially he who had left them, we retraced our steps once more, and lo and behold our Holy Mother coming with her companion and a laborer, whom they had taken from his house and had given four *reales* to guide them to the road — and he got the best of it, for he went back to his house very well pleased with them, and we much more so with all our baggage found again, and happy enough to go along relating our adventures.

"We went to put up at an inn where there were so many muleteers, lying on those floors, that there was no place to set one's feet, except on packsaddles or sleeping men. We found a place to put our Holy Mother and the nuns we brought with us, and I believe it was not six feet of floor; so that, to make a long story short, they had to remain standing. The only good thing about those lodgings was that we couldn't wait to get out of them."[2]

Doña Quiteria testified many years later, for the Saint's beatification, that during one of the black nights of the journey to Salamanca, their way was illumined by a mysterious light that

---

[2] Julián de Avila, *Vida de Santa Teresa*, p. 266. Father Silverio gives a long excerpt (B.M.C., t. VI, pp. 147–150), and the Benedictines of Stanbrook publish a translation, *Letters*, I, 295.

seemed to come from behind them. When she wondered what the cause was, Madre Teresa replied, "Ask God about it."[3]

They arrived in the university city at the end of July or the first of August,[4] and immediately notified their friends, including the carpenter Pedro Hernández and the noble Don Pedro de la Banda. La Madre probably took Hernández with her when she went to look at the latter's property. It would cost at least 1000 ducats, she found, to make it over into a convent; but this troubled her very little, for she never doubted that God would send her whatever money she needed for His work; nor was she ever disappointed. A certain student at the University, who bore the distinguished name of Padre Cristóbal Colón, was not a little surprised when she told him that he had 200 ducats, which she wished to borrow. He had just received that sum for his food allowance, but supposed no one knew it. Perhaps he was no less astonished when she repaid him two or three days later, on getting an unexpected alms of the same amount. Money always came to her hand when she needed it. Unfortunately the spending of it, in this instance, had to wait upon the good pleasure of Don Pedro, who had left town and paid no attention to her requests for his return.

"I have come to this place with the desire of seeing to it that these sisters are left in a good place," she wrote him August 2. "I have little time, and as much for this as for the passing of that [time] which will be desirable for building walls, I have been sorry not to find you here, Sir.

"The house seems good to me, although it will need more than five hundred ducats to enter it. Altogether I am content, and I hope in our Lord He will give it to your worship on seeing your house so well employed. May the Lord keep your worship many years. Notice, Sir, that it is a large piece of work that has to be commenced in good time, and these days are passing away.

"For the love of God, Sir, do us the favor of coming quickly; and if you delay, Sir, I beg you to take it in good part if we commence to make the walls, of which we shall need more than two hundred, but this won't hurt the house in any way; but if

---

[3] *Deposición de Doña Quiteria*, B.M.C., t. 18, p. 237; Silverio, *op. cit.*, IV, p. 163.
[4] Padre Silverio tells us (IV, 156) that the whole journey was accomplished "during the first days of August." But in her letter to Pedro de la Banda dated at Salamanca August 2, Teresa says she has seen his house, and has been expecting to see him. She could hardly have arrived, then, later than August 1.

we fail afterwards to come to an agreement about that (though I hope to God it will quickly be settled) we will bear the loss.

"With your coming, Sir, all will be remedied, and may His Majesty give you a very long life, so that you may always continue to gain merit for the eternal one."[5]

Don Pedro did not trouble himself to return to Salamanca until the following month. Teresa meanwhile had the carpenter Hernández go ahead with the alterations, engaging some twenty to twenty-five "workmen and *peones*" for the purpose. He supervised everything; but he was not too busy to spy on the nuns, for he wondered what they had to eat, and found them dining on a piece of bread, a jar of water, and some herbs, as joyfully as if they were feasting on pheasants.[6]

One hot day Teresa looked out of a window on the entresol and said, "Brother Pedro Hernández, these people look very tired; send them something to drink, and I will attend to it."

"Madre," said the carpenter, "there are so many of us, and wine costs so much, that it would take a caveful of money to do it."

"Go and send for it, brother," she replied, "for God is going to take care of everything."

Wine was very dear that year, and cost a *real* and a half for an *azumbre* (about two quarts), but Hernández obediently sent a man to a tavern with about fifty *maravedis* (at least he says he got two *maravedis'* worth for each workman) to buy some. There was so little of it that he poured some water in to make it go further, and handed it to one of the toilers. After three or four had drunk, he looked into the jar again, and found (so he testified for the beatification of La Madre) that there was just as much as before.

Presently Madre Teresa appeared again at the window and said, "Brother Pedro Hernández, have you done what I asked?"

"Yes, *madre,* and I think that the same thing has happened here as at the wedding of the *architriclino,* for the water has turned into wine."

"All right, brother," she answered calmly, "God has done this."

"It surely looks as if there were Good Ones mixed up in

---

this,"[7] said the carpenter. Returning to the workmen, he cried, "Hey, brothers, you can drink hearty now, for this is wine of benediction!"

Although they all drank as much as they wished, they were unable, according to Hernández, to empty the jar.[8]

The work took longer than she had hoped. As Michaelmas approached (the season at which rentals were renewed) it became apparent that she must either pay for another year's rent of the old house, or move into one not fully equipped. Teresa decided on the latter course.

On the eve of Michaelmas there was a terrific downpour of rain. The nuns begged her to postpone the ceremony; indeed, they said, it was out of the question, for the whitewashing of the chapel had not been completed, it was raining too hard to transfer the articles needed, the roof leaked, and the interior was so wet that it would never do to install the Blessed Sacrament until the place was dried and the repairs finished. Furthermore, Don Pedro de la Banda was still out of town, and the business arrangements had not been completed. All their friends, except the merchant Nicholas Gutiérrez, thought it was foolish to make the attempt. The sisters told her this in such peremptory terms that she rebuked them sharply. Then she retired to her cell to pray.

"I found myself very imperfect that day. As it had been announced, I didn't know what to do, but I was in great distress, and I said to our Lord, almost complaining, that either He should not command me to undertake these works, or else He should come to our aid in that necessity. The good man Nicholas Gutiérrez, with his constancy of mind, told me very quietly, as if nothing had happened, not to worry, for God would take care of it. And so it was, for on the day of Saint Michael, at the time when the people were to come, the sun commenced to shine, which gave me devotion enough, and I saw how much better that blessed man had done in trusting in our Lord, than I with my sorrow."

The whole city, except the missing Don Pedro, turned out for the occasion. The chapel dried with miraculous speed, the necessary articles were hastily carried into the house, and at the

---

[7] "Bien parece que andan buenos por medio."

[8] P. Silverio gives this conversation, *op. cit.*, IV, p. 168, n. 2. See also B.M.C., t. 20, pp. 34–35.

appointed hour La Madre and the nuns in their white choir mantles walked in solemn procession behind the Blessed Sacrament, to the strains of glorious music, toward the chosen house. The Countess of Monterey and other notables were present when Fray Diego de Estella, one of the famous preachers of Salamanca, delivered his sermon. The nuns slept that night in their new home, unfinished though it was, and all seemed to have ended happily.

The next day Don Pedro de la Banda returned to the city, and learning what had happened, betook himself to the convent in a violent rage to tell Madre Teresa what he thought of the proceedings. He was "so fierce that I did not know what to do with him, and the devil contrived that he should not be brought to reason, even though we had fulfilled everything that had been agreed upon; it did little good to try to tell him so. When certain persons spoke to him he was placated a little, but afterwards he changed his mind again. I now decided to give up the house; but he didn't want this either, for he wanted us to pay him the money for it then and there. His wife, to whom the house belonged, had asked him to sell it to support two daughters, and it was on this ground that the license had been asked for, and the money had been deposited with a person of his choosing. The situation is, that now more than three years have passed by, and the purchase is not yet completed, nor do I know whether the monastery will remain there. . . ."[9] Don Pedro de la Banda was mean and contentious, and his wife even worse, to the day of Teresa's death and after. In none of her convents had the nuns suffered so much; yet it was a slight matter, she said, to live in a house not their own, considering that the Lord of the world had none.

Don Pedro was not the only thorn in the flesh at Salamanca. There was a dour and testy Dominican Father at the University, Fray Bartolomé de Medina, a brilliant theologian with a great deal of influence, who felt it his duty to warn his students against her, and in a public lecture declared that she was one of those women who went from place to place, and who would be much better off at home attending to their knitting. Teresa refused to take this seriously, though she saw the importance of having him on her side and deliberately set out to win his approval. She

---

[9] *Fundaciones*, cap. XIX. After Saint Teresa's death the nuns gave up the house rather than continue the struggle with Don Pedro.

knew that neither a Padre Medina nor a Don Pedro could destroy a mission such as hers.

Indeed, she was already planning another foundation, this time in Segovia, where Doña Ana Jimena, widow of Francisco Barros de Bracamonte and sister of one of the nuns at Salamanca (Isabel of Jesus),[10] had offered to equip a convent. La Madre was cool to this suggestion at first, feeling perhaps that her founding days were over, until our Lord told her to ask permission of Father Fernández. She did so, and to her great surprise met no opposition at all. She then began to consider ways and means for entering Segovia. It was not long before the enterprise assumed an unexpected importance, chiefly in consequence of certain strange events at Pastrana.

Ruy Gómez, Prince of Éboli, had fallen ill about the time she was leaving Ávila for the second Salamanca foundation, and had died at Madrid on July 29, 1573, in the presence of two Discalced friars, Baltasar of Jesus and Ambrosio Mariano, who had hastened from Pastrana to minister to him in his last hours. Thus ended a life and career that many had envied. The favorite of an Empress and the friend of a King, fortune's darling, the handsome squire of dames, the genial host of diplomats and prelates, the benefactor of saintly friars and nuns, had gone to his reward at last.

At the hour of his death (as afterwards was verified) Ruy Gómez appeared in a vision to the famous hermit, Catalina de Cordona, in her desert cave in the wilds of La Mancha.

This interesting woman was descended on her father's side from the royal house of Aragon, on her mother's from the princes of Salerno; had taken to a holy life at eight after a vision of her dead father in purgatory; had spent her childhood in Italy; had been brought to Spain, and in due course had become lady in waiting to the Princess of Éboli. Attending Mass with the other ladies of the Éboli household in Valladolid, she heard Dr. Cazalla preach in his heyday, long before the Inquisition even suspected him, and horrified her companions by predicting that he would burn as a heretic, for she had seen flames, she said, about his head. Her desire to give up the world completely was encouraged by Saint Peter of Alcántara and by Madre Teresa, to whom she used to write letters signed "The Sinner." Finally she

---

[10] She was the novice whose singing at the first foundation at Salamanca caused the Saint to experience a long rapture.

induced the Prince and Princess to take her with them on a journey to one of their estates near Alcalá de Henares, whence she
made her way, guided by a hermit, Padre Pina, into the barren
desert near the mountain of Vera Cruz.

For the next eight years she lived in a small cave hardly big
enough to shelter her. She ate herbs and roots until a shepherd
began bringing her some meal, which she baked on embers and
ate only every third day; and drank the water of the River Xúcar.
Her mortifications were dreadful, even by comparison with the
many heroic austerities in the history of Spanish mysticism. According to Madre Teresa, she used to scourge herself with a
heavy iron chain for two and a half hours at a time. Once a
woman hermit saw her take off her sackcloth garment to wash it,
and it was full of blood. For a long time the people of that wild
country thought she was a man, for she dressed so to protect herself from molestation. Devils assailed her in the forms of lions,
pards, or huge mastiffs that leaped on her shoulders, or as ser-
pents. She would attend Mass at a monastery of the Mercedar-
ians, a mile or two away, sometimes going the whole distance on
her knees. Gracián tells of an escaped lunatic, so powerful that
he had burst his chains asunder, who appeared at her cave at
midnight and told her she must come with him, for he was God
the Father, and was going to bless all the water in the River
Xúcar, so it would no longer be necessary to make holy water.
She followed him about, praying, for the rest of the night, until
at last he returned to fall exhausted into slumber at the entrance
of her cave, whereupon she went in and took one of her cruel
scourgings for his sake. He awoke perfectly sane, and remained
so for the rest of his life.

It was not strange that in a country so imbued with the love
of the heroic, and especially of that highest heroism which is
sanctity, her solitary cave became a place of pilgrimage. Hundreds went to see her, to implore her prayers. Thus from some
visitor she heard of the friars at Pastrana, and connecting them
with a vision she had had of religious clothed in white, she made
her way there, recognized the choir robes of Fray Mariano as
those she had seen, and resolved to found a monastery of Discalced in the desert. On one of her visits to Pastrana in May,
1571, Ruy Gómez and the Duke of Gandia (son of Saint Francis Borgia) went forth in state to receive her. Mariano took her
to Madrid, where she met the Nuncio Ormaneto, obtained the

permission of Philip II and the Visitor Fernández, **and** spent some time with the Discalced nuns at Toledo, who, like Gracián and others noticed the sweet fragrance of her miserable clothes and of everything she touched. In the end she accomplished her ambition. A house of Discalced friars, of very holy life, kept vigil near her cave. Although she never entered the Order herself, she wore the habit in her desert retreat until her death in 1577.[11]

It was to this woman that the spirit of Ruy Gómez had recourse when the veils of time and mortality fell away and left it naked in the terrible searching light of eternity. In her utterly selfless prayer she saw him standing before her, wretched, sorrowful, forsaken, imploring. Nothing but the alms he had given her, he said, had saved him from hell. Thanks to her he was in purgatory, and in what agony! There were no words to describe the torments that racked him. He begged her in his anguish to help him. Would she please get the prayers of the Carmelite friars for him, above all have two hundred Masses, which his wife had promised, said at once, at once!

The shade of the great man receded into the darkness and littleness of retribution. Catalina seized her heavy chain and scourged herself for his sake, until the whole cave was spattered with blood.

When the vicar of the monastery in whose jurisdiction she lived happened to visit her next day, he saw the stains, reproved her for being excessive in her penance, heard her story of the vision, marked the day and the hour. On the third day a messenger came from Pastrana to announce the death of Ruy Gómez, to give an alms of forty ducats, and to arrange for the two hundred Masses promised by the Princess.

A few days later Ruy Gómez appeared a second time to thank Catalina for the relief he had got from her penance, and especially from the Masses already said for him.[12] If he said anything in either of his apparitions to satisfy the curiosity of historians about the dark insinuations of poisoning in the pages of Father Gracián, the hermit lady died without revealing it.[13]

---

[11] *Fundaciones*, cap. XXVIII; *Reforma*, lib. IV, caps. IV, V, IX, X; Gracián, *Peregrinación de Anastasio*, pp. 206–208.

[12] *Reforma*, lib. IV, cap. XVIII.

[13] Gracián claims to have saved the life of the Prince on a previous occasion: "*Quiso Dios que á este tiempo supe yo una cierta cosa en secreto, fué necesario ir á Madrid . . . y si no fuera, muriera el príncipe Rui-Gómez, que con mi ida se*

Meanwhile the Prince's body lay in state in his palace at Madrid, soon to be wept over by friends and perhaps gloated over by secret enemies. His eyes had hardly been closed when his widow gave an exhibition which, if presented in one of those *comedias de figurón* at the *Corral* in the *Calle del Príncipe,* would have been set down as rank overacting. The Princess declared, in the torrent of her grief, that life held nothing more for her, she would leave this vile world, she would be a Discalced Carmelite nun, she would bury herself in the convent she had founded at Pastrana until merciful death released her. Nor could she wait to get there to put on the habit of the Reform; she made good-natured Fray Mariano take his off, in the presence of her husband's remains, and drape it about her slender shoulders.[14] It seems not to have occurred to her to consult Madre Teresa or any other Carmelite authority about her suddenly discovered vocation. She must enter the convent without a moment's delay. Indeed, the corpse of Ruy Gómez could hardly have been cold when she flung herself into her carriage and ordered the coachman to drive as fast as he could to Pastrana. What tears, what hasty farewells to all her children, what a huge amount of baggage!

Fray Baltasar of Jesus meanwhile bolted ahead on horseback to notify the Prioress at Pastrana that the Princess was coming to enter the convent. It was two o'clock in the morning when he arrived and knocked on the door. Waked out of slumber, Mother Isabel de Santo Domingo listened with growing astonishment, and exclaimed, "What! the Princess a nun? It will be the end of this convent!"

In the morning the great Éboli coach rolled up to the door, and Doña Ana de Mendoza appeared, with the robes of Fray Mariano still hanging loosely about her, followed by her mother, who had come as chaperon and confidante, and two maids, together with so many bags and trunks that the wonder was where they could all be stowed. It was quite a new situation for Carmelite nuns to face. Madre Isabel was truly at a loss. She could not deny that the roof over their heads belonged to the

---

libró su vida" — *Peregrinación,* p. 24. Also, *"Podría ser que le hubiesen dado algún veneno ó ponzoña a comer y descubrírseme á mí en secreto de confesión, y estando enfermo de esto, y no sabiendo la causa, errar la cura, mas como la supieron los médicos mudar el reobarbo en triaca y assí sanó." — Ibid.,* p. 25.

[14] *Ibid.,* p. 25.

Princess. Perhaps she had better admit her, and ask Madre
Teresa what to do next.

The poor nuns! Peace flew out of the window as the Princess
stepped in the door. There is probably not much exaggeration
in La Fuente's sarcastic remark that on the first day she had a
violent "fervor," on the second she mitigated the rule, on the
third she relaxed it, and on the fourth she insisted on having her
visitors admitted to the cloister, all constitutions to the contrary
notwithstanding.[15] After the funeral (the body of Ruy Gómez
was taken to Pastrana) the Bishop of Segorbe and other friends
of the family came to make the customary visit of condolence.
The Princess was so incensed over having to speak with them
through the grille that Madre Isabel permitted them to enter the
cloister, and to facilitate further visits without disturbing the
community, gave Her Highness's mother an apartment opening
on the street. This only caused a more furious scene.

The humility of Doña Ana was such that when a place next to
the prioress was given her in the refectory, she arose in a huff
and took a seat by herself at the other end of the room, finding a
certain solitary grandeur in the lowest place, since she could not
have the highest. She demanded that her two maids be admitted
to the Order. This was a hard requirement, but Madre Isabel
went even that far, and habits were given to the two in the
speak room, while the Princess stood between them, to share in
the blessing, and took a new and better fitting garb for herself.
"The latest news around here about our novice the Princess,"
wrote Fray Antonio of Jesus to the Duchess of Alba, "is that she
is pregnant five months, and is inside the monastery, giving
orders like a prioress, and desires that the nuns speak to her on
their knees, with great obsequiousness."[16]

This sort of thing could not go on indefinitely. There came a
day when the Prioress suggested that if Her Highness could not
accommodate herself better to the Carmelite routine, it might
be just as well if she left the house. The Princess then betook
herself to one of the hermitages in the garden, outside the
cloister and near the street, where she lived for some time, holding court daily to noble ladies and gentlemen from Madrid. It
would be interesting, in the light of later developments, to know

---

[15] Introduction to his edition of the *Vida*, p. 3.
[16] "*Las nuevas que ay por acá de nuestra novicia la princesa son que está pre-
ñada de cinco meses,*" etc. In B.M.C., *Epistolario*, II, appendix, p. 502.

whether Antonio Pérez, the King's confidential secretary, was among the visitors.

One of them certainly was the hermit Catalina de Cardona, who came to Pastrana from her desert cave, and said to her benefactress of former days, "Princess, look what you are doing to these nuns! Do not vex God; for I was at their Matins, and I saw among them angels that protected them with unsheathed swords."[17] Ana appeared frightened by that speech, but not sufficiently to restore the food allowance of the convent, which she had cut off on moving into the garden. "Perhaps you don't know," she said to the Prioress, "that in this world I have been subject to no one but Ruy Gómez, for he was a *caballero* and a gentleman, and I will be subject to no one else, and you are a lunatic."

Madre Teresa heard all this with growing apprehension. "I am very sorry for those at Pastrana," she wrote Father Báñez in January, 1574. "Although the Princess has returned to her own house, they are like captives." After the Prior of Atocha and Fray Angel de Salazar had attempted to bring about a reconciliation, and had failed (for the Princess feigned illness and would not see them), there seemed no alternative to giving up the convent. Teresa's valiant soul did not shrink from this since it was necessary; but she had no place to send the nuns. This made her all the more eager to come to some sort of conclusion with Don Pedro de la Banda, so that she could leave Salamanca and begin the foundation at Segovia. But Don Pedro had an infinite capacity for disagreement; and there was some delay about the permission of the Bishop of Segovia, even after Father Fernández had given his consent. Winter found La Madre still exiled in Salamanca.

Yet the time was not lost by any means. It was about this time that Father Jerónimo Ripalda, S.J., whom she had chosen as her confessor, read her autobiography, with the appended account of the founding of San José of Ávila, and was so impressed that he told her to write similar records of all her foundations. Thus we owe to the famous Jesuit the suggestion for one of the most valuable of her works, and one of the most interesting pieces of narration in any language. It was about this time, too, that she wrote, at the request of the nuns of San José de Salamanca, an analysis of melancholia which is still read with profit, unpedantic

---

[17] Silverio, *Vida de Santa Teresa de Jesús,* IV, p. 207, and his references.

and unpretentious though it is, by modern students of neurasthenia.

"It is so subtle," she wrote, "that it can even play dead when it is necessary, and so we don't understand it until it is past curing." Humble and gentle victims do no harm, except to themselves. In others it may be very dangerous. "Indeed, I believe that in some persons the devil makes use of it as a means to gain them if he can; and if they don't proceed with great care, he will do so. For what this humor chiefly does is to subject the reason, and this accomplished, what will our passions not do?" People without reason are insane, but the neurasthenic does not appear to be so, hence he is all the more dangerous. It is a great hardship, observes Teresa, to have to live as a rational person and treat as rational another who has no reason!

The Prioress must deal firmly with one who has only begun to show signs of melancholy. "I say it again, as one who has seen and dealt with many persons with this malady, that there is no other cure for it save to subdue them by all possible ways and means. If words won't suffice, let there be punishments; if little ones won't serve, there must be heavy ones; if one month of keeping them shut up is not enough, there must be four, for you can do no greater service to their souls." A melancholic in a convent, if not cured, can destroy the discipline of the whole community — hence the importance of restoring her to health. . . . "It seems unjust to punish a sick woman, who can do no more, as if she were well. Well, then, so it would be to tie up maniacs and to whip them, instead of letting them kill everybody." The Prioress who out of pity neglects to deal firmly with such a patient will in the end find her insufferable and demoralizing to the community. "And truly I believe that it often comes, as I have said, from dispositions self-willed and lacking in humility and unbridled, and that the humor itself doesn't give them as much strength as this does. For in some, I say, for I have seen it, tney come under control and can do so when they have someone to be afraid of; why then, can't they do it for God? I am afraid the devil, under pretext of this humor, as I have said, tries to gain many souls."

Yet the Prioress, "without letting them know it, should treat them with much sympathy, like a true mother, and seek what means she can for curing them." Teresa protests that she is not contradicting herself here: under no circumstances must the superior let them have their own way, for that is the root of the evil. However, she should not give them a command that she knows they will disobey. She should manage them by affection so far as possible, and keep them busy in such a way that they will have little opportunity to give rein to their imagination. Nor must they be allowed to spend much time in prayer. They are usually imaginative persons, and their malady lies in a disorder of the imagination. They should not fast as much as others. They should be allowed to eat fish but rarely.

"It may seem superfluous to give advice for this sickness and not for any other, since there are such serious ones in our wretched life, especially in the weakness of women. I do it for two reasons: first, that I think they are good women, for they don't even suspect they have this malady; and since it doesn't compel them to stay in bed, for they haven't any fever, or to call the doctor, the Prioress must take his place; for it is a sickness more prejudicial to all perfection than those that menace life itself in bed. The other is that in other infirmities they either get well or they die; in this they rarely recover or die, but gradually lose all sense, which is to die to kill everybody. They endure in themselves a death enough of afflictions, imaginations, and scruples, even though they always call them temptations, and so they earn great merit; and if they come to understand that it comes from the sickness itself, they will feel greatly relieved, that is if they attach no importance to it. Certainly I have great pity for them, as indeed should all who are with them, considering that the Lord might give it to us, and bearing with them, without letting them know it, as I have said."[18]

If Don Pedro de la Banda proved mulish to the end, Father Medina was beginning to be a little more human. "I am getting on well with Father Medina," wrote La Madre to Father Báñez in January, 1574. "I believe that if I could talk with him often, he would quickly be pacified. He is so busy that I almost never see him. Doña María Cosnez told me she didn't like him as much as she does you."

She kept in mind the importance of placating her enemy even after she left Salamanca. When the Duchess of Alba sent her a beautiful trout at Alba de Tormes, she dispatched it to her prioress at Salamanca, with instructions to take it at once to Father Medina. At Segovia, hearing that he was not yet com-

---

[18] *Fundaciones*, cap. VII.

pletely mollified, she wrote Mother María Bautista at Valladolid, "As for Father Medina, don't be afraid I shall disturb myself about him, even though it were much worse, in fact he has made me laugh instead. I would feel more keenly half a word from Father Domingo (Báñez), for the other one doesn't owe me anything, and I don't care much if he doesn't like me."[19] She could afford to laugh now, for Father Medina was thawing visibly. He was never warmed up to the pitch of friendship, but he was honest enough to admit publicly that he had been unjust to her in his former diatribe. "I have seen her and talked with her," he said, "and without doubt she has the divine spirit and walks by a very sure way."

Teresa finally left Salamanca in January or early in February, 1574, on learning that Doña Ana de Jimena had rented a house in Segovia, and that her brother, Andrés de Jimena, had obtained at least the verbal consent of the Bishop. Despite a fever and other ailments, she set out in the dead of the Castilian winter over the icy wind-swept roads. At Alba she spent two days at the castle of the great Duke. Years later she remembered a certain apartment there, and used it to illustrate a spiritual point.

"Once they left me in one of those rooms in the house of the Duchess of Alba where, on a journey, obedience commanded me to be, since this lady had importuned them. I stood astonished on going in, and wondered what good all the hurly-burly of things could be, and then I saw that it could be to praise the Lord on seeing such differences of things, and now they come handy to me, for I can make use of them here; and although I was there quite a while, there was so much to see that afterwards I completely forgot it all, and I kept no more recollection of those rooms than if I had never seen them, nor would I know how to say what they were made of, but taken altogether, I remember having seen it." Something similar occurred, she remarked — and this was the point of the illustration — when the soul was in union with God.[20]

From the ducal palace she went to her convent at Alba where she probably remained for some days or weeks, for not until mid-March do we find her on the roads again, going toward

---

[19] "Ni se me da mucho que no me tenga esa ley" cannot be translated literally. B.M.C., *Epistolario*, I, p. 125.

[20] *Moradas*, VI, 4, B.M.C., t. IV, p. 126.

Segovia with the intent of opening the convent on the feast of her dear Saint Joseph, March 19. She had with her Fray John of the Cross, Father Julian, Antonio Gaytan, and some nuns who joined the party at Ávila. They arrived at Segovia on the eighteenth, made the final arrangements in the chapel and the cloister, and took possession at dawn on the nineteenth, when Father Julian said Mass.

There were two Masses, in fact, that morning. A young priest, the Canon Juan Orozco de Covarrubias, nephew of the Bishop, happened to notice the new crucifix on the house and to hear the bell as he was going to a church to offer the Holy Sacrifice. Stopping to investigate, he was so charmed with the convent that he asked permission to say his Mass there. It was while he was doing so that the peace of San José de Segovia was disturbed by the arrival of an angry Provisor, who had not heard of the verbal consent, nor could it be verified to him since the Bishop was out of town. Father Julian of Ávila has left an account of the scene:

"Oh, Lord, when they went that morning to tell the Provisor what had happened, he became the most furious man ever seen. Why had we not told him about it? . . . And when he saw him at the altar, he said to him very disgustedly, 'That would have been better left unsaid!' I should think that however much devotion the canon may have had, he would have stopped at that word. Then he went about to try to find out who had done all that, and installed the Most Blessed Sacrament. As the nuns had already been enclosed, and I, on feeling the fury with which he came, hid myself in a stairway that had remained on the porch, he bumped into Fray Juan de la Cruz, who had gone with us, and said to him, 'Who has set up all this, Padre?' I don't remember exactly what he replied; but the Provisor said, 'Take it all out at once; I am certainly going to send you to the jail.' And I believe that he didn't do it since he was a friar, but if it had been I, plainly enough I should have gone there that time. And it would not have been much if, after I had enclosed the nuns so often, they had enclosed me for once, although they don't feel it as much as I would, since they do it of their own free will.

"After all, I didn't run away from the jail, but I hid myself to avoid entering it. The Provisor was in such a hurry to disarrange everything that had been arranged that night of Saint Joseph, that his great wrath did not subside. He sent an *alguacil* to see that nobody said Mass, and sent someone on his own account to say It and to consume the Most Blessed Sacrament. La Madre and the sisters must have been wondering at how thoroughly the fruit of their labors was being undone. I went to the Company as soon as I escaped, to tell what had happened, but although the Rector did all he could to speak at once to the Provisor, he made no impression on him. He was going around looking for the persons who had been present at the giving of the license, and what with the bickering back and forth about the business, it was decided to have a juridical investigation made into how the license had been given.

"With this, then, the affair seemed to be settled. We gave our testimony before the notary with very reliable witnesses, and so the Provisor could not help giving the license to have Mass said, but he would not give it to have the Most Blessed Sacrament put back; and in this he was right, for it was in a rented house and on the porch; and our Mother also agreed to this, for she already knew that to take possession it was enough to say Mass. In all this great fury, the valor our Holy Mother had was splendidly shown, for she was neither disturbed nor overwhelmed nor lacking in confidence, but she spoke to the Provisor with much boldness, and at the same time very politely, so that anyone could see that the Lord was helping her."[21] La Madre was never frightened, once she had made a foundation. "All my fear comes before," she said.[22]

In due course the Bishop returned, everything was explained by the influential members of the Jimena family and their friends, the constable of the Provisor was removed from the door, and the Blessed Sacrament was restored. Finally, some additional houses were bought, and Mother Isabel of Jesus was made prioress.

One of the first acts of Madre Teresa, when the community was established, was to send for the nuns at Pastrana, for there was no longer any hope that the Princess would let bygones be bygones and carry out her agreement to support them. Within two weeks after the first Mass at Segovia, she sent Father Julian and Antonio Gaytán in all secrecy to arrange for the conveyances, to smuggle the nuns from the convent and to get them out

---

[21] *Vida*, p. 273, in B.M.C., t. VI, pp. 194–195; also in Silverio, *op. cit.*, IV, pp. 200–202.
[22] *Fundaciones*, cap. XXI.

of Pastrana without letting the Princess know; for that powerful lady was quite capable of preventing their departure.

Antonio Gaytán, according to Teresa, "was a gentleman of Alba. Our Lord had called him when he was living deeply ensnared in the world some years ago. Now he held it so much beneath his feet that all he thought of was how he could render Him more service. Because I shall have to mention him in the foundations from now on, for he has helped me much and endured much travail, I have said who he is; and if I had to say his virtues, I should not finish quickly. What was most to the point for us is that he is so mortified, that there was not an attendant, of those who went with us, who could do so as satisfactorily. He has great prayer, and God has done him many favors, for all that would be contradiction to others was a joy to him, and he would make light of it, and so indeed in everything that he has suffered in these foundations. And I think surely that God called him and Father Julian of Ávila for this purpose. . . . Their conversation on the roads was to talk of God, and to teach those who went with us and those who met us, and so in all ways they went serving His Majesty."[23]

The two secret emissaries arrived at Pastrana at the end of March or the beginning of April (1574). In a few days they had made all arrangements for the flight of the contemplatives. Five wagons were in readiness in a secluded place outside the village. Mother Isabel de Santo Domingo had all the movables packed, and the nuns prepared to file out at midnight on a certain date. Father Julian even took care to consume the Blessed Sacrament that day at Mass.

It was not easy, however, to keep such activities hidden from the Princess in her own feudal town. In spite of all precautions, the news got to her ears; and toward midnight the *Corregidor* of the village arrived at the convent, with instructions to post guards around it, and to arrest anyone who might attempt to leave.

Negotiations were then in order between the cloister and the palace. The Princess made it known, either through the *Corregidor* or through her own majordomo, that she was willing to discuss terms. She would permit the exodus if they would take along as novices the two maids who had entered the convent with

---

[23] *Ibid.*

her the previous year. Madre Isabel made a counter proposal. She would take one of the young women, who seemed to have the right disposition, but under no circumstances the other. The Princess accepted the compromise, and the preparations continued. Before leaving, however, the Prioress sent for a notary, and in his presence handed over to the custody of the *Corregidor* all the jewels that the Princess had given the convent in happier days — a wise precaution, as it turned out.

It was two o'clock in the morning when the nuns, shepherded by their Mother Prioress and the two men, filed silently into the darkness, formed a procession with a cross before them, and passed to where the five carts were waiting on the farther side of a hill. Thus the journey began, and a weary one it was, lasting several days. When they came to the Henares River, the muleteers advised crossing in a ford instead of by barge. The first wagon reaching the middle of the river was caught in a strong current, and the two mules were unable to pull it across. "The more they were driven, the more they drew back," wrote Father Julian, "or if they went a little more, they were overwhelmed and sank to their knees. I shouted to them to turn around and come back, but although they wished to, they could not return. I was afflicted enough, and all alone, for no one had remained except the waggoners and the nuns. The poor nuns! Some of them seemed to be about to faint. The muleteers cried to the mules and the nuns must have cried out also to God. It pleased the Lord that by dint of shouting and pushing, one wagon got across. When this one was in safety, for it was the strongest, it reached the bank. The mules were unhitched and yoked to each cart, one after the other, so that each could pass over with four mules. And so we got out of this peril, and I with the resolution never, whatever might happen, to believe mule drivers, who, to avoid harnessing and unharnessing, were unwilling to go by the barge, and put themselves in such danger."[24]

This was the very hour when Madre Teresa, miles away in Segovia, knew that her daughters were in danger, and said, "Let us pray for those coming from Pastrana." Meanwhile Father Julian and his "cavalry" as he called it, managed to reach Madrid, where the people stared at them, thinking they were prisoners of the Holy Inquisition of Toledo, being conducted to

[24] *Op. cit.*, part II, cap. VIII.

trial. Finally they arrived at Segovia on the Tuesday or Wednesday of Holy Week, and were joyously welcomed by La Madre and the new community. They hoped they had heard the last of the Princess of Éboli.

This was too much to expect of one who had always had her own way until she encountered Madre Teresa. The Princess sent the Bishop of Segorbe to Segovia to threaten that if they did not accept her other servant, she would sue them for the jewels she had given them. It was fortunate that Madre Isabel had thought of the notary on the night of their flight! La Madre referred her distinguished visitor to the *Corregidor* of Pastrana, and he departed with obvious displeasure.[25]

It is possible that Teresa later accepted the second servant, perhaps on finding in her a better disposition than she had suspected. Toward the Princess herself, despite all the troubles and anxiety she had endured at her hands, she never displayed any feeling but that of compassionate understanding. "As for what pertains to the nuns," she wrote, "the monastery was in much favor with those lords, and with the greatest care of the Princess to entertain them and treat them well, until the Prince Ruy Gómez died, whereat the devil, or perhaps because the Lord permitted it, His Majesty knows why, with the intensified suffering caused by his death, the Princess entered there as a nun. With the sorrow she had, the things of enclosure, to which she was not accustomed, could not give her much pleasure, and on account of the holy Council[26] the Prioress could not give her the liberties she desired. She came to be displeased with her and with all of them in such wise that even while they were still in her house, they annoyed her, and the poor nuns lived in such inquietude that I tried by all means in my power, appealing to prelates, to have them leave the monastery there, founding one in Segovia where they could transfer, leaving behind whatever the Princess had given them, and taking with us some nuns that she had ordered us to take without anything.[27] The beds and little things that the nuns themselves had taken there, they brought away with them, leaving the people of the place very sorrowful. I had the greatest joy in the world at seeing them at peace, for I was very well informed that they had been not at all at fault in the

---

[25] Silverio, *op. cit.*, IV, p. 217.
[26] Of Trent.
[27] Without dowry.

displeasure of the Princess, but rather that they had served her in her habit as much as before she took it. Only in what I have said was the occasion, and in the very sorrow that this lady had, and a servant that she brought with her, who, as it is understood, was entirely to blame. In short, the Lord permitted it; He must have seen that the monastery did not belong there, for His judgments are great and against all understandings. I for one would not have dared do it on my own account, but by the opinion of persons of learning and sanctity."[28]

One good effect, at least, this foundation had had: it tremendously enhanced the growing prestige of the Carmelite Reform at the Court of Madrid. All that had occurred was reported there, no doubt with many exaggerations. It was a nine days' wonder to the courtiers, and most of all perhaps to Philip II, that the invincible Princess of Eboli had at last met her match in the humble woman in sackcloth who was known as Madre Teresa of Jesus.

---

[28] *Fundaciones,* cap. XVII.

Statue of the Queen of Heaven and of the Infant Christ the King, that Saint Teresa placed by one of the doors of her first reformed convent in Ávila.

Chapter XXVII

A DREAM COMES TRUE AT BEAS — FIRST MEETING WITH GRACIÁN

"I NOW have some health, compared with what I have had," wrote Teresa in June to Don Teutonio de Braganza, a descendant of Portuguese kings who was studying at Salamanca, "and if I knew how to complain as well as Your Lordship does, you wouldn't think anything of your pains."[1] This bluntness may have been good for a young man destined to be an illustrious bishop of Évora; but a month later La Madre was writing her niece, María Bautista, "I am so old and tired you would be shocked to see me."[2] She was in her sixtieth year. And this long stay at Segovia — she was there all the spring and summer of 1574 — was anything but a time of rest or relaxation. She carried on her tireless correspondence with friends, relatives, friars, and nuns of the Reform; she predicted future events, such as the elevation of Don Teutonio and the Canon Covarrubias, to the episcopacy — "God makes all my friends bishops and archbishops!" she said to one of them, "and He will you"; she saw persons dying far away, as she had seen the death of Fray Pedro, of Father Gutiérrez, of Pius V; she received notable favors in prayer. It was of this period, too, that Carmelites related the story of her bilocation.

She had left Sister Isabel of the Angels ill at Salamanca. After eight months in bed the poor woman was not only wasted by pain, but tormented by scruples and other agonies of mind and spirit. She seemed weaker than ever on the Feast of Saint Barnabas, June 11, 1574, when the nuns went to Mass. Yet on their return to the infirmary they found her completely changed, alert, happy, and free from all anxiety. Asked how this had happened, she explained that while they were in the chapel Madre Teresa had come to her bedside, blessing her, putting her hands on her face, and saying, "My daughter, don't be silly, or stay in these fears, for great is the glory that God has prepared for you; and believe me, you will enjoy it today."

She remained thus until Matins, when the sisters, except for

---

[1] B.M.C., *Epistolario,* I, p. 135.
[2] *Ibid.*

429

two or three who remained with her, went to the choir to take their regular discipline, for it was Friday. At the first blow of the scourge, they all thought at once of the sick nun, and with one impulse hastened to her cell and began reciting the *Credo,* as was the custom with the dying. At the last word of the prayer she expired, her face and body remaining beautiful and luminous.

The nuns at Salamanca were naturally curious to know what Madre Teresa had been doing at the hour when the dying nun believed she had seen her, and they wrote to Segovia to make inquiries. They were not much surprised perhaps to learn that after Holy Communion that morning she had fallen into a trance so profound that she seemed like one dead. When asked about this afterwards, she was embarrassed, and would say, laughingly, "Get out of here! What things they invent! Strange they are!" Later she admitted to Madre Ann of Jesus, a particular friend, that she had gone in spirit to Salamanca to console the sick sister in her last moments.[3] She admitted having spoken to her of the glory prepared for her, "for His Majesty had showed it to her."[4]

On August 7 that year she saw Saint Albert, whose feast it was, with Christ. After the Lord disappeared, the Carmelite saint told her many things about the order, and warned her that if the Reform was to succeed, the Discalced nuns and friars must be separated from the Calced, under prelates of their own. This was to become a crucial question as time went on. The little group that Teresa had gathered together hardly more than a decade ago had become virtually a new order, of formidable proportions. She had founded convents at Ávila, Medina, Malagón, Valladolid, Toledo, Salamanca, Alba de Tormes, and Segovia. She had monasteries of friars at Mancera, Pastrana, Alcalá, Altomira, La Roda, and Granada, all living such holy

---

[3] Yepes, *Vida de Santa Teresa,* lib. II, cap. XXII; Mir, *Vida de Santa Teresa,* II, pp. 281–282, following the deposition of Ann of Jesus in the *Informaciones de Madrid.*

[4] Accepting this occurrence as a proven fact, Yepes remarks that it is for historians to record such matters, and for theologians to explain them. He suggests that the body of the Saint might by divine power have been in both places, or it might have been in only one truly, while in the other its appearance was supplied by an angel, or by other means. He believes that Teresa went in person to Salamanca to console the sick nun, and that our Lord, wishing her to be seen in Segovia, supplied her presence there "by means material or supernatural." *Loc. cit.*

lives under the primitive rule that their fame had spread through the peninsula, arousing admiration in some and envy in others. Who could fail to see the spirit of God in the preaching of men like John of the Cross, walking barefoot on the icy streets of Alcalá to preach to the rich and to minister to the poor? Was there not a touching reminder of primitive Christian fervor in the lives of the friars at Pastrana, who ate their food — wild cabbage, beet roots, and dried peas — sitting on the ground, took turns in perpetual adoration day and night, and wove linen[5] during recreation to support themselves in their humble necessities? Contemplative souls of all classes of society were beginning to feel the irresistible attraction of this group, and to join it. Teresa knew about every novice, and his qualifications. Nothing pleased her more than when a man of learning applied. "Now we have a man in the house!" she cried, on hearing of the entrance of John (of Jesus) Roca, a bachelor of theology from Catalonia. Although he proved disappointing in the end, for he was too severe and lacked judgment, she continued to look for men with degrees to carry on her work; and when Fray Angelus of Saint Gabriel introduced an excessive zeal for penance that became to certain souls a temptation to something like Illuminism, she had her *Senequita* or some similar apostle of sanity and moderation — some *letrado* — undo the mischief done.

The reputation of the Reform was now such that she had more offers of houses than she could possibly accept. She was promised foundations in Zamora, in Madrid, in Portugal. All these she declined or deferred, to accept one that was to prove very costly to her: a proposal from Beas de Segura, a little town on the border of Andalucía. It probably appealed to her because it came from a woman after her own heart.

Doña Catalina Godínez and her younger sister, María de Sandoval, were daughters of a wealthy nobleman with a large estate in the Sierra Morena. Catalina had been prepared for a brilliant marriage, and had had many offers but had disdained them all when, at the age of fourteen, she happened to read the words over a crucifix, "Jesus of Nazareth, King of the Jews," and went into a rapture from which she emerged with a desire to share

---

[5] Later, at Sevilla and Lisbon, the friars made rigging for the King's navy. Some of the ropes on the great galleons of the Armada were probably woven by some of Saint Teresa's friars.

His sufferings, and a loathing of her proud, pampered self and all the material world. She made a vow of poverty and chastity. She began to wear a plain costume like a nun's. She would wet her face, and turn it up to the sun in the *patio*, so that she would become dark and ugly and undesirable to men. She would pray all night, and kiss the feet of her father's sleeping servants. One Lent she wore his coat of mail next to her skin as a penance.

After four years she became ill with dropsy and heart disease, and had a cancer of the breast which was removed by surgery. These illnesses, which continued for seventeen years, did not prevent her from teaching little girls to work and read. Her sister helped her in this, and after the deaths of their parents, they decided to use their inherited wealth to found a convent in Beas. The permission of the royal Council of Orders was needed, for Beas belonged to the Knights of Santiago. Catalina spent four years vainly trying to obtain it.

When she began corresponding with Madre Teresa, she was almost always bedridden, suffering from a complication of diseases. "She had at this time a continual fever which had lasted eight years, consumption and dropsy, with a fire in her liver which was so inflamed that it could be felt even through her clothing, and it parched[6] her shirt, a thing which seems incredible," added La Madre, "but I informed myself from the doctor of these sicknesses she had at this time, and I was very much astonished. She also had rheumatic gout and sciatica." Finally she promised that if the Lord cured her within a month she would take it as a sign that he wished her to continue with her plan for the convent. She was then miraculously and completely restored to health.

During all the years of her sickness she had cherished the memory of a dream she had had about the year 1553 of walking down a steep narrow path over a precipice, and meeting a barefoot friar, who said, "Sister, come with me," and who led her to safety in a house where she saw many nuns holding candles in their hands. When she asked what order they were, they all lifted their veils and uncovered smiling faces, but made no

---

[6] "*Y le quemaba la camisa*" — literally, "it burned her shirt," but I don't think this, or Mr. David Lewis's rendering, "singed her shifts" accurately expresses the Saint's thought. "To burn the shirt off somebody" is a hyperbolic idiom, not to be taken too literally. The meaning here must be that the heat of the liver parched or dried the lady's chemise, or simply, perhaps, that it was unnaturally hot. — *Fundaciones*, cap XXII.

other reply; while the prioress took her by the hand and saying, "Child, I want you here," showed her the constitutions and the rules of the community — upon which she awoke.

One day when Father Bartolomé Bustamente, S.J., a noted theologian and humanist, was staying at Beas, she told him of her ambition and her dream. He happened to be well acquainted with the family of Doña Luisa de la Cerda in Toledo, through whom he knew of the work of Madre Teresa of Jesus. "The nuns you saw in your dream were the Discalced Carmelites," he said.

Catalina obtained the address of Madre Teresa and sent a messenger to her, offering to found a convent of the Reform in Beas. Teresa, then in Salamanca, was not much impressed: Beas was too far away, and she knew that Father Fernández was averse to her making any more foundations. She mentioned the matter to him, however, and was surprised when he told her to promise the foundation as soon as she could obtain the permission of the Council of Orders — which was so improbable, he added, that she need not count on going to Beas; still, it was not well to discourage such piety as the woman evidently had.

Catalina Godínez betook herself to Madrid during the Lent of 1574 and renewed her application. When Philip II learned that her convent was to be one of Discalced Carmelites, he commanded that permission be granted.[7] La Madre was astonished. So was Father Fernández; but having given his conditional consent, he did not withdraw it.

"I am going at the end of this month," wrote La Madre to María Bautista, September 11, 1574, "and I am afraid that even then I won't leave them [the nuns of Segovia] in their own house; for it was agreed with the Chapter that we should give them six hundred ducats at once, and we have a very good quit-rent of a sister which is worth six hundred and thirty, but we can find no one who will take it or lend on it. Commend it to God, for I shall be very glad to leave them in their own house. If the lady Doña María has given you the money, you were quite right to take it, for it is very secure and good. Let me know if this can be done, or if you know anybody who will take it, or anyone who will lend us on good security, for it is worth more than a thousand; and commend me to God, since I have to go so far away, and in the winter. . . .

---
[7] *Reforma,* t. I, lib. III, cap. XXXII, n. 11.

"If you have anyone there who will lend me a few *reales*, I don't mean give, but until they pay me from those my brother gave me, which they say are already available; for I haven't a *blanca*, and it is out of the question to go to the Incarnation, and here there is no chance, as the house has to be provided for: little or much, get me some."[8]

Toward the end of the month she wrote another gossipy letter to María Bautista, enclosing a message for Father Medina. "I don't want to offend the *Maestro* Medina. Believe me, I have my own ends, and I have already seen some advantage from it; on that account, don't fail to send him the letter, and pay no attention to him even though he may not be so friendly, for there is no reason why he should be, nor does it matter at all what he may say about me. Why don't you tell it to me?"

María Bautista was under the impression that Beas was in Andalucía, where Rubeo's license for foundations did not extend. This displeased Teresa, for she had already made up her mind to go ahead. "God pay you for your advice," she wrote. "I believe I understand what you have erased. Know that Beas is not in Andalucía, but five leagues this side of it, and I already know that I cannot found in Andalucía. . . .[9] I am taking as prioress Ann of Jesus, who is one we took in San José, from Plasencia, and has been and is in Salamanca."

Venerable Ann of Jesus (Lobera) was one of the most loyal and splendid of the many heroic women who followed La Madre in the Reform. Born deaf and dumb, in 1545, she had been miraculously cured by our Lady, and now, at the age of twenty-nine, was noted for her beauty, her intelligence, her sanctity, her good humor, and the "grand manner" with which she walked and talked and did everything.

La Madre loved with great tenderness this tall fair-skinned nun whose hands were so beautiful, and whose face flushed so easily with exertion or emotion; "my daughter and my crown," she used to call her. She shared her cell with her at Salamanca, and liked to watch her when she was asleep and to make the sign of the Cross lightly on her forehead. Father Domingo Báñez considered Ann the equal of Madre Teresa in sanctity and her superior in ability.[10]

---

[8] *Epistolario*, I, *carta* lxii, pp. 144–146.

[9] *Ibid.*, pp. 149–150, *carta* 64.

[10] After Saint Teresa's death, Venerable Ann of Jesus founded the first convents of Discalced Carmelites in France and Belgium.

It was the last day of September, 1574, when La Madre and two other nuns said farewell to Segovia and the grim *alcázar* where Isabel *la Católica* on her white horse had once faced down an angry mob. At the convent of Santa Cruz, where she stopped at the last moment to confess and to hear Mass, she saw Saint Dominic in the chapel named for him, and heard him promise to aid all her future enterprises, after which she remained prostrate before the altar for a whole hour, enraptured. At Communion she saw him again on her left hand, and on her right the Christ, Who said "Rejoice with him," and then disappeared. She asked Saint Dominic why he always appeared on the left, and he replied, "Because the right hand is for my Lord."[11]

Teresa had to be in Ávila for the election at the Incarnation, October 6. It was no small tribute to her administration that the nuns who had so bitterly opposed her three years before now desired, almost unanimously, to re-elect her. This, however, the Provincial would not allow, nor was Teresa sorry to lay down her unwanted office and to return, with his permission, to her own convent of San José. There in mid-October she was joyfully received, and elected Prioress.

Before continuing the journey to Beas, she wished to inspect some of the other convents, and particularly to be at the one in Valladolid for the profession, January 13, of her favorite novice, Doña Casilda de Padilla, a girl of fourteen for whose entry a papal dispensation had to be obtained. She was the third child of a very rich widow, Doña María de Acuña. Her brother, Don Antonio de Padilla, entered the Company of Jesus at the age of seventeen on the advice of his mother's confessor, Father Ripalda, S.J., and in so doing renounced his fortune in favor of his older sister, Luisa. She in turn becoming disgusted with the world, bestowed the whole estate, a huge one, on little Casilda,[12] whose ambitious mother then conceived the idea of marrying her (with a dispensation, of course) to one of her uncles. The child was very fond of this brother of her father, but she loved God more, and at length ran away from home and sought sanctuary in the Discalced convent at Valladolid. Her mother sent officers of justice to bring her back, for she was not yet twelve years old.

[11] This account was given in the *Proceso de Ávila* by her then confessor, Padre Yanguas, O.P.

[12] Saint Teresa devoted all of Chapter XI and part of Chapter X, in her *Fundaciones* to the story of Casilda.

A few months later she fled again to the monastery, apparently on the advice of Father Ripalda, and with the approval of Father Domingo Báñez, and this time the nuns gave her the habit. Her profession in January, 1575, was an event of no small importance to the convent and, judging by the eager interest displayed in her letters, to Madre Teresa. The fortune of Casilda, which she renounced in favor of the convent, provided she remained there, would relieve the nuns of anxiety and probably do infinite good in the years to come. Besides, the example set by a girl whose father had been President of Castilla was sure to encourage other vocations among the rich and powerful. La Madre made no especial appeal to that class, but she was too practical and had had too much experience with want not to see that even the holiest buildings in this world have to be paid for with currency.

Many heroic lives were lived in the convent that had been built with the money of the dissolute Don Bernardino de Mendoza. Teresa tells of another extraordinary nun, Beatriz (Oñez) of the Incarnation, a relative of the Padilla family. Shortly after her profession at Valladolid in 1570, she learned that certain heretics were to be burned in that city, and that they meant to die without being reconciled to the Church. The thought of their going to hell caused her such anguish that she begged their souls of God, promising in return to accept every pain and torment she could endure for the rest of her life. To the surprise of everyone, the condemned repented on the scaffold, made their confessions, and were reconciled to God and to the Church in their last hour. That same night Sister Beatriz became ill of a fever. An interior abscess, very vile and painful, afflicted her. She had another in her throat, which made swallowing difficult. Instead of complaining, she would beg her sisters to ask God to send her more suffering. Often they would go to her cell to gain courage from the sight of her patience and joy in affliction. After three years of every inconceivable pain and misery, she died, in May, 1573. Her body remained angelically beautiful in death, and gave forth a sweet fragrance.[13]

After witnessing, with maternal pride and joy, the profession of Casilda, Teresa set forth at last to make the foundation at Beas. On the way she joined Ann of Jesus, Father Julian, and

---

[13] *Fundaciones*, cap. XII.

Antonio Gaytán at Ávila, while Isabel de San Jerónimo came from Segovia, and Isabel de San Francisco, with five other nuns from Malagón, completed the party at Toledo. The expedition had grown to considerable proportions when it left the imperial city in the first week of February, 1575, for the last long leg of the journey.

The route lay through Daimiel and Manzares, most of it probably on the ancient road that travelers from Castilla to Granada had followed since Roman times. Soon they were in the native country of Don Quixote, surrounded on every side by the lonely, windy, immeasurable plains of La Mancha. Very dusty were the roads in dry weather, and in time of rain full of ruts and mudholes. La Madre and her companions went in rude carts, well covered to protect them from the sun and from the gaze of the innumerable students, merchants, beggars, footpads, officers of the Holy Inquisition or of the Holy Brotherhood, soldiers, friars, and all manner of travelers who passed that way in every season, some on mules, some on foot. Eighty years ago they might have seen Christopher Columbus, walking in the dust or jaunting along on his mule to keep his rendezvous with fame at the Alhambra.

There are many traditions, not very well verified, about Teresa's stops at some of the villages of La Mancha — about her shaking the dust of Manzanares off her sandals, in a most uncharacteristic mood; shocking a cook by eating partridges with the salty observation, not wholly unlike her, that "Penance is penance, and partridges are partridges"; and giving a rosary to a woman who sold her two eggs. Of the latter part of the journey there is an historic account by Sister Ann of Jesus. Even among the wild stony pine-studded slopes of the Sierra Morena, where the Knight of the Ill-Favored Face was soon to encounter the Unfortunate Knight of the Rock in the immortal fantasy of Cervantes, they hardly ever failed to have daily Mass; and whenever they passed a little village church, Teresa would get out and prostrate herself before it, saying as always, "What a great blessing that we should find here the Person of the Son of God! Wretched are those who drive Him from themselves!"

On the last day, high in the mountains, they lost the road, and none of the muleteers could find it. La Madre told the eight nuns to pray to God and their father Saint Joseph. As they were about to advance, they saw on one of the crags a man, who from his voice seemed to be old, crying to them, "Stop! Stop! You will be lost and killed if you go any farther!" They were on the very brink of a high precipice.

In answer to the shouts of priests and seculars, asking where they could go, he pointed to a narrow way, through which they made their way down, and presently, according to Mother Ann of Jesus, the mules seemed not to run, but to fly.

"It was my father Saint Joseph," said Teresa, "and now they won't find him again."[14]

On Ash Wednesday, February 16, they came within sight of a little town lying in the center of a lovely valley encircled by mountains and checkered with green and yellow fields and orchards. It lay on both sides of the Guadalimar, whose scores of brooks and rivulets sparkled in the sun under the limitless blue of the sky. As the travelers rejoiced in the sight, there came forth to meet them a brilliant cavalcade of all the people of the town, high and low. All the other foundations had had to be made by stealth, in the dead of night. This one was a triumph of sunlight and public joy and southern music as all the clergy, in glittering vestments, with a Cross before them, led the procession of *caballeros* in rich Andalusian attire and Carmelites in white robes to the house of the two sisters Godínez.

When Catalina saw La Madre and the nuns, she recognized them at once as those she had seen in her dream twenty-two years before, and a few days later, when Fray Juan de la Miseria arrived, she declared that he was the friar who had led her past the precipice. Both sisters took the habit when the convent of San Josef del Salvador was formally established on the Feast of Saint Matthias, February 24, 1575. They were excellent nuns. The health of Catalina, despite her strange medical history, was strong enough to support all the rigors of the primitive rule.[15]

Teresa had intended to proceed after a few days to Caravaca, in Murcia, and had brought along some nuns with the intention of sending them there; but the permission from the Council of Orders having failed to arrive, she was obliged to remain where she was while Father Julian and Antonio Gaytán went to Caravaca to make the preliminary arrangements. She was still at Beas on April 1. And there, two days later, she met Father Jerome of the Mother of God (Gracián) for the first time.

---

[14] B.M.C., t. XVIII, p. 463; also Silverio, *op. cit.*, IV, p. 316, and Mir, *op. cit.*, II, p. 306.   [15] *Fundaciones*, cap. XXII.

A greatness that he little desired had been thrust upon the young Polish-Spaniard since he had made his profession as a Discalced friar at Pastrana in July, 1573, shortly after sending Teresa the famous *Desafío*. It happened that when the Calced friars of southern Spain resisted the reform of Father General Rubeo, Pope Pius V had appointed two Dominicans as apostolic visitors: Fernández, as we have seen, for Castilla, and Vargas for Andalucía. Of the two, Father Vargas obviously had the more difficult problem. On March 15, 1574, he wrote Philip II of the need of reforming the southern Carmelites, and suggested that it be done by the Discalced Fathers of Pastrana, especially Gracián and Mariano, "who, with their life and doctrine, have much edified this city, though they do not lack persecutions on the part of the Calced fathers."[10] The King acquiesced, and Vargas wrote the Prior at Pastrana, Fray Baltasar of Jesus (Nieto), inviting him to Andalucía. This was an initial mistake, for Fray Baltasar had left Andalucía with a bad reputation in his order for being contentious and contumacious,[17] and was not likely to be welcomed there as a reformer. Nor was it probable that his Provincial, Fray Angel de Salazar, would give him leave to go, particularly at a time when he was displeased with Madre Teresa. It was Prince Ruy Gómez, skilled at political logrolling, who obtained it for him on the pretext that he wished the friar to attend to some business for him. Fray Baltasar went to Granada, lived at the Alhambra as guest of the Count of Tendilla, and founded a Discalced monastery in the city. He made a favorable impression on the Visitor Vargas, who deputed his apostolic powers to him, but later, finding him ineffectual, wrote a letter to his friend, Fray Ambrosio Mariano, asking him to go to Andalucía, and to take some other Discalced friar with him.

Mariano wrote to Fray Angel de Salazar for permission. He was not very candid, this impulsive Mariano, for he told the Provincial he wanted to go to look after some books and property and business affairs that he had left pending before taking the habit. Nor did he say whom he had in mind when he asked leave to take another friar along. This suggests that he may have had reason to believe that the Father Provincial would not approve of the enthusiastic young Father Gracián. At all events, the permission was received, and Mariano and Gracián set forth for the south, soon after the death of Ruy Gómez.

Father Baltasar of Jesus, on returning to Pastrana, delegated to Gracián the apostolic powers he had received from Vargas — very much against the wishes of Gracián, who at first refused, but yielded to the arguments of Mariano. According to the terms of this delegation, signed on August 4, 1574, Gracián was commanded by his superior, Fray Baltasar, to "visit and reform" all the Carmelite convents in Andalucía, and make them conform to their rule.[18] He and Mariano went to Toledo to see Fray Antonio of Jesus, who was now prior of a convent of Calced friars there. They founded a monastery March 7, 1575, at Almodóvar del Campo, where Mariano, at the insistence of Father General Rubeo, was reluctantly ordained a priest. At La Peñuela they visited John of the Cross. Then they went to Granada. Evidently Gracián made a good impression upon Father Vargas, as he did upon most, for he tells us that the Visitor "not only gave me this permission, but handed over to me the original Brief itself, and put me in his place as Apostolic Visitor; and here I was twenty-eight years old, and professed half a year, made Prelate of the Andalusian Calced Carmelites, in opposition to the General, and Protector of the whole order of Calced friars, this province of the Andalusians being the most untamed we have."[19]

Fray Angel de Salazar meanwhile learned of the deception that had been practised upon him, and ordered Gracián and Mariano back to Pastrana. Fortified by the authority of Vargas, they went instead to Sevilla. There Gracián showed his patent for the government of the Discalced friars to Father Agustín Suárez, Calced provincial of Andalucía; but he did not show him the one he had for the Calced, which made him the Provincial's superior; and he made a further bid for his favor by promising to restore the monastery of San Juan del Puerto to the Mitigation. This had been a house of the Calced to which several friars had gone after embracing Madre Teresa's Reform, thus creating an anomalous situation, with two rules, two habits, constant friction, and much public disedification. Gracián kept his word, taking the Discalced novices to the Calced monastery

---

[18] Silverio gives the text, *op. cit.*, IV, p. 271.
[19] *Peregrinación*, dialogue I.

of Sevilla, because, he explains, he had no other place to put them. Thus he created in that large house the very disorder he had removed from San Juan del Puerto.

The unpopularity of this act among the Calced Carmelites, and one is tempted to add, the need of some reforming influence among them, can be inferred from Gracián's pungent account of what happened to a certain novice in a dark hallway just outside the choir. "They gave him a dagger thrust that penetrated his thigh; and perhaps they were aiming at his guts,[20] but God must have lowered the hand of the one who struck it. There were not lacking contemplatives who said the blow was a mistaken one meant for me, for the novice was very good and peaceable and liked by everybody, and his father a great benefactor of the Convent."

The unconscious humor of this last sentence suggests a possible cause of some of the troubles of this holy but rather exuberant young reformer. However this may be, he left the monastery as soon as possible, glad no doubt to have his *tripas* still intact, and with the permission of Cardinal Cristóbal de Rojas, went to live with some Discalced friars at the hermitage of *Nuestra Señora de los Remedios,* where "we had only sardines to eat and had to use slices of bread as plates."[21]

By this time the Calced friars all over Andalucía were indignant, alleging that he had been sent to reform and not to make new foundations. Nor was the Carmelite General Rubeo at all pleased when he learned what had been going on. He had always resented the appointment of the two Dominicans as apostolic visitors, believing that he himself was capable of reforming his own order, and had not taken kindly to the acceptance of their "visit" by the Discalced. Now the revelation of what Gracián had been doing made him so angry that he asked and obtained the revocation by Pope Gregory XIII of the briefs of Pius V making Fernández and Vargas apostolic visitors for Castilla and Andalucía.

When Philip II heard of this, he felt that all his efforts to have the Spanish orders reformed were in jeopardy, and he made such representations to the learned and holy papal Nuncio at Madrid, Monsignor Ormaneto, that the Holy Father revalidated the commission of the two visitors, September 24,

---

[20] "Tripas."
[21] *Ibid.*

1574, thus confirming Gracián in his office as Visitor of both Calced and Discalced friars. To establish his position more securely, Gracián decided to go to Madrid, have a heart-to-heart talk with the Nuncio, and perhaps visit his brother Antonio, secretary to the King. He set forth from Sevilla one spring day in 1575. Beas de Segura lay in his way. Stopping to see the new convent of Discalced nuns, he came face to face for the first time with Madre Teresa of Jesus.

Teresa had heard nothing but good of this young friar. Of the circumstances of his invasion of Andalucía, and especially the legerdemain that he and Mariano had practised upon their superiors, she then knew nothing. She had heard only that they had been extending her reform most marvelously, and that they had been able to carry it into Andalucía by what seemed no less than the intervention of Providence. If she saw the faults and limitations of young Father Gracián, and she was certainly no fool in judging character, her charity drew a mantle over them, while her reason told her that such an energetic and charming youth, with a talent for getting things done, was exactly what the Reform needed at that stage.

"While I was in this town of Beas waiting for the permission of the Council of Orders for the foundation of Caravaca, there came to see me there a Father of our Order, of the Discalced, called the Master Fray de la Madre de Dios Gracián, who had taken our habit while he was in Alcalá a few years before, a man of much learning and understanding and modesty, accompanied by great virtues all his life, and I think our Lady chose him for the welfare of this primitive Order. . . . From the time he began to study, his father wished him to study law. He, though still so young, felt it so much that by force he prevailed upon him to let him take theology.

"When he had taken his master's degree, he talked of entering the Company of Jesus, and they considered him accepted, but for a certain circumstance they told him to wait a few days. He told me that all the luxury he had gave him torment, seeing that that was not a good road to heaven; he always kept hours of prayer, and his recollection and chastity extremely well. . . . Oh, the wisdom and power of God! How unable we are to flee from what is His will! Indeed our Lord saw how necessary it was to commence this work with such a person. I often praise Him for the favor He did us in this; for if I had very much wanted to ask His Majesty for a person who could set all the affairs of the Order in order at these beginnings, I could not have succeeded in asking as much as His Majesty gave us in this one. May He be blessed forever. .

"As a boy in Madrid, he often went to an image of our Lady to which he had great devotion, I don't remember where it was; he used to call her his *enamorada*, and it was quite regularly that he visited her. She must have obtained from her Son the purity with which he has always lived. He says he sometimes thought her eyes filled with tears over the many offenses that were committed against her Son. From this there was born in him a great impulse and desire for the betterment of souls, and a sorrow when he saw offenses against God, very great. To this desire for the welfare of souls he had so great an inclination that any trial became small to him, if he thought he could do good by it. This I have seen by experience in plenty of them that he has endured.

"Then when the Virgin took him to Pastrana, like one misled, thinking he was going to get the habit for a nun, and God was taking him to give it to him himself! Oh secrets of God! And how, without our seeking it, He goes on arranging to do us favors, and to pay this soul for the good works he had done, and the good example he had always given, and the great desire he had to serve His glorious Mother; for His Majesty must always pay for this with great rewards. . . .

"It may seem an impertinent thing that he communicated to me so many particulars about his soul; perhaps the Lord wished it so that I could set it down here, that He may be praised in His creatures; for I know that he has never told so much to his confessor or to anybody else. Sometimes there was reason for it, for he thought that with my many years and what he had heard of me, I might have some experience. . . .

"Although he was not the first, he came at a time when I would sometimes have been troubled over having commenced, if I had not had such great confidence in the mercy of God. I mean the houses of the friars, for those of the nuns, through His goodness, have always gone well until now; and those of the friars didn't go badly, but they were on the point of falling very soon, for since they did not have a Province of their own, they were governed by the Calced. Those who could have governed them, such as Padre Fray Antonio de Jesús, who was the one who began it, were not left free to do so, nor did they have constitutions given by our Most Reverend Father General. In each house they did as they pleased. . . . Our Lord mended matters through the Padre Fray Jerónimo de la Madre de Dios, for they made him Apostolic Commissary, and they gave him authority and government over the Discalced friars and nuns. He made constitutions for the friars, for we nuns had ours from our Most Reverend Father General. . . . The first time he visited them, he put all in such good order and harmony that it seemed indeed that we had been aided by the divine Majesty, and that our Lady had chosen him for the help of her Order. . . ."[22]

Gracián was as powerfully drawn to the spirit of La Madre, during the three weeks he stopped at Beas, as she was to his. "She communicated her spirit to me," he wrote, "without concealing anything, and I declared all my interior to her in the same way; and there we agreed always to work together in all our affairs, and she, besides her vow of religion, made a special vow to obey me all her life, on account of a particular revelation she had."[23]

A strange relationship thus began. Teresa was a mother, in one sense, to this priest less than half her age; in another sense she was his daughter, submitting to his judgment with all the generosity and confidence of a pure and childlike soul. "I rejoiced extremely when I heard that he was there, for I used to desire it much on account of the good news they had given me of him, but I was even more happy when I began to talk with him; for he pleased me so much that I didn't think those who praised him knew him at all. And I was so tired at the time, I thought when I saw him that the Lord was showing me the good that he was going to bring to us, and so for several days I went about with such excessive consolation and pleasure, that it is true I was astonished at myself. Although his commission did not extend to more than Andalucía at that time, the Nuncio sent for him while he was in Beas, and then gave him one for the Discalced friars and nuns of the Province of Castilla. My spirit had such joy that I could not give thanks enough to our Lord those days, nor did I wish to do anything else."[24]

---

[22] *Fundaciones*, cap. XXIII.
[23] *Peregrinación*, dialogue 13.
[24] *Fundaciones*, cap. XXIV.

She wrote in a similar vein on May 12 to Mother Inés of Jesus, prioress at Medina:[25]

"Oh madre mía! how I have wished that you were here with me these days! You must know that in my opinion they have been the best of my life, without exaggeration. The Padre Maestro Gracián has been here more than twenty days. I tell you that as much as I have talked with him I have not begun to understand the worth of this man. He is just right in my eyes,[26] and better for us than anything we could ask of God. What Your Reverence and all have to do now is to ask His Majesty to give him to us as our prelate. With this I can rest from the government of these houses, for such perfection with gentleness I have never seen. God keep him in His hand and protect him, for I wouldn't for anything have missed seeing him and talking with him so much. He has been waiting here for Mariano, whose delay has made us all happy enough. Julian of Ávila is gone on him,[27] and [so are] all. He preaches admirably."

Her good impression was sealed into a lifelong conviction by a vision that came to her one day at dinner, when she had no thought of interior recollection. "I thought I saw beside me our Lord Jesus Christ in the way His Majesty usually represented Himself to me; and toward his right side was the same Master Gracián. The Lord took his right hand and mine, and put them together; and He said to me that He wished me to take this man in His place all my life; and that we must both agree in everything, for so it was fitting."[28]

From then on her obedience to Gracián, as the superior assigned to her by the Lord God, was so complete that test it as he would, he could never find a flaw in it. Yet paradoxically there was nothing slavish in her mastery of the primary Christian virtue. Gracián was not long in discovering the truth of what dour Padre Medina once observed about La Madre: that she never did anything except what her Superior commanded, but that her Superiors never commanded her to do anything except what she desired! "It often happened to me," said

---

[25] B.M.C., *Epist.*, I, letter 72, p. 169.

[26] *"El es cabal en mis ojos."*

[27] *"Julián de Avila esta perdido por el, y todos."*

[28] From a paper in the Saint's handwriting submitted in the *Proceso de Avila* by her niece.

Gracián, "to talk over some matter with her and to be of contrary opinion, and afterwards at night to change my purpose; and going back to tell her it should be done as she had thought, she would smile; and asking her why she did, she would say that, having had a revelation from our Lord that it should be done as she said, though the Prelate told her the opposite, she would go to our Lord saying 'If you want it done, move the heart of my Prelate that he may so command me, for I cannot disobey him.' "[29]

Something of this sort happened now as she began to plan for her next foundation. She had been invited to Madrid and to Sevilla. Which ought she to accept? "I told her to discuss it with our Lord God," says Gracián. "She did so, and in the end He told her it should be at Madrid. I told her to go at once to Sevilla, and so she obeyed. I asked her afterwards why she had not replied to me, since so many learned men had assured her that her spirit was of God, and what I said was only opinion, and moreover I had not commended it to God. She said, 'Nevertheless, faith tells me that what Your Reverence commands me is the will of God, and I have no assurance that revelations are, no matter how many there are.' "[30] Gracián continued to follow his reason, as he had a right to do. He seems to have been influenced by Fray Mariano, who promised to rent a house in Sevilla and sent enthusiastic accounts of how well it could be furnished in that rich city, cluttered with the wealth of the seven seas. According to him, the Archbishop of Sevilla would be delighted, in fact he was anxious, to welcome them.

So La Madre made plans to leave at once for Sevilla, regardless of her vision, her desire to spend the summer in Ávila, her dread of the Andalusian heat, and her Castilian dislike for the people of the South and all their ways. *"Jesús y cruces y pedradas en los Andaluzes"* runs a Castilian proverb: "(The sufferings of) Jesus and crosses and stonings among the Andalusians."

She wrote the Bishop of Ávila on May 11, "Just when I was planning to spend a good summer there in Ávila or Valladolid, there came here Father Gracián, who is Provincial of Andalucía with commission of the Nuncio. . . . In short, we leave for there next week Monday. It is fifty leagues. I am convinced that he

---

[29] Mir, *op. cit.*, II, p. 325, from one of Gracián's notes on the MS. of Ribera, *op. cit.*, lib. IV, cap. XX.
[30] *Ibid.*

would not compel me to do it, but he is so bent on it that if I don't do it, I shall have scruples enough at not complying with obedience, as I always desire. For my part it has been a nuisance, and I certainly have not taken much pleasure in the thought of going in this fire to spend the summer in Sevilla. Please God it may serve Him, for in that case the rest matters little."[31]

Presently, in a second vision, the Christ told her she had done well to obey her superior, regardless of the revelation, and that it was now His will that she make the foundation at Sevilla. As for its being in Andalucía, she had only just discovered that Beas was in that ecclesiastical province. So she had exceeded the authority given her by Rubeo, just as María Bautista had feared! This was an agonizing thought. Reassurance came again, however, when she reflected that Gracián's powers, coming by deputation from the Pope, took precedence. Had not Gracián told her so? What a blessing to live under obedience! She was not even disturbed, at least for very long, when the Bishop of Ávila wrote that officers of the Inquisition were looking about there for a copy of her life. Someone apparently had been denouncing her again.

It seems probable enough that the "someone" was the Princess of Éboli. Certain it is that Teresa and her book were delated in 1574, and we have Gracián's word for it that the delator was "a lady Princess, to injure La Madre, on account of a certain grudge."[32] The power of Ana de Mendoza at that time, about a year after her husband's death, was still such that her intended victim must have been in considerable danger. Several copies of the angelic *Vida* had been in circulation during the twelve years since its completion. The author, as we have seen, had given one to the Duchess of Alba and another to the Princess. The Duke of Alba, on his return from the Netherlands, had several copies made for his friends. It may have been one of these that the Duchess gave to glum Padre Medina, to dissipate his last suspicions. The Bishop of Ávila had another transcribed for his sister, Doña María de Mendoza. For yielding to the importunities of these and perhaps other friends, Teresa incurred the displeasure of Fray Domingo Báñez. "I was annoyed with the said Teresa of Jesus," he recalled years later,[33] "even though I

[31] *Epistolario*, I, p. 165; letter 71.
[32] MS. addition to Ribera's *Vida de Santa Teresa*, t. IV, cap. IX.
[33] In his deposition for her beatification, *Informaciones de Salamanca*.

understood it was not her fault." Nevertheless he gallantly went to her rescue when he learned, in 1574, that a weighty denunciation had been filed against her at the Holy Office in Madrid. To forestall proceedings which might cause her, at the least, a serious inconvenience, he brought forth the copy he had had among his books for a dozen years, ever since the Inquisitors had returned it to him, and writing in the blank pages at the end a vigorous "censure" which was in effect a vindication, sent it off in 1575 to the Holy Office.

"It is a strange thing," he wrote, "to see how lax and worldly people delight in seeing those discredited who have an appearance of goodness. . . . I have always proceeded cautiously in the examination of this account of the prayer and life of this nun, and no one has been more incredulous than I as to her visions and revelations — not so, however, as to her goodness and her desires, for herein I have had great experience of her truthfulness, her obedience, mortification, patience, and charity toward her persecutors, and of her other virtues. . . . I do not, however, undervalue her visions, revelations, and ecstasies; on the contrary, I suspect them to be the work of God, as they have been in others who were saints. . . . I am of opinion that this book is not to be shown to everyone, but only to men of learning, experience, and Christian discretion. It perfectly answers the purpose for which it was written, namely, that the nun should give an account of the state of her soul to those who had charge of it. . . . Of one thing I am very sure, so far as it is possible for a man to be — she is not a deceiver. . . ."[34]

This opinion from the great Thomist who had so brilliantly occupied the first chair of theology at Salamanca must have had great weight with the Inquisitors, and although, with characteristic thoroughness, they had the book further examined by Fray Hernando de Castillo, a favorite preacher of the King, and reviewed even by the Inquisitor General Quiroga,[35] the opinion

---

[34] There is a complete English translation of this "censure" in the Preface to the edition of Saint Teresa's Life by Father John J. Burke, C.S.P., New York, 1911, pp. xxxvii–xxxix.

[35] When Teresa went with Gracián to ask Cardinal Quiroga's permission for a new foundation in 1580, he told her that he had read her book carefully in 1575, approved of it without reservation, and begged her to pray for him. The copy that he had read was, of course, the one that Báñez had sent to the Holy Office. Teresa never saw it again. Gracián had hopes of recovering it, but finally decided to get a copy from the Duke of Alba instead. The copy finally delivered by Doña Luisa de la Cerda to Blessed John of Ávila has not been traced further, or found.

of Báñez constituted in effect the final verdict of the Holy Office on La Madre's spiritual autobiography. She was never again in serious danger from that dread quarter.[36]

Teresa had no human assurance of this happy outcome when the news reached her in the Andalusian heat that she was under investigation. She had something much better, however. Turning to prayer, she heard our Lady say, "Do not grieve, for this cause is mine," and putting aside all fear of the Inquisition, she embraced the cross that Father Gracián had prepared for her. While that young enthusiast, after giving the scapular of the Order to Father Julian (in lieu of the habit the nuns craved for him), continued his journey to Madrid to discuss matters with the Nuncio, she remained at Beas, completing preparations for what her intuition told her was to be one of the most painful experiences of her life: the foundation at Sevilla.

For this enterprise she picked a few choice spirits who were "such souls that I thought I would venture with them into the land of the Turks, and who had the courage, or rather our Lord gave it to them, to suffer for Him; for such were their desires and conversations; much exercised in prayer and mortification, for as they had to stay so far away, I endeavored that they should be those I considered most suitable." They were the women she had intended to take to Caravaca; for prioress, that wise and witty lady María de San José, whom she had first discovered as a maid in the house of Doña Luisa de la Cerda in 1562; besides Sister Ana de San Alberto, Sister María del Espíritu Santo, and Sister Leonor de Saint Gabriel from Malagón; Sister Isabel de San Francisco from Toledo; Sister Isabel de San Jerónimo from Pastrana. Accompanied by Father Julian of Ávila, Antonio Gay-

---

Gracián had several copies made from the one he obtained from the Duke, and distributed them among the convents of the Reform. The Inquisition retained the copy sent by Báñez until after the death of Teresa, when Venerable Ann of Jesus, one of her favorite children, asked for it, and obtained it, to have it edited by Fray Luis de León, at the command of Philip II, in preparation for the first printed edition of 1588. After the death of Fray Luis, it passed through two other hands, and finally arrived at the Library of the Escorial, where it has been venerated ever since. In the Church of the Escorial there is another copy, made by the Saint's niece, Teresa of Jesus, daughter of her brother Lorenzo.

[36] There were, of course, other delations, but the Inquisition never took them very seriously. There was one Dominican father who remained hostile even after her death, and went so far as to carry his denunciations of the *Vida* to Rome, but without effect. A book by the Jesuit Father Hahn, calling her "the patroness of hysterical people," was put on the *Index of Forbidden Books,* and languishes there to this day.

tán, and Fray Gregorio Nacianceno (who had just received the habit from Gracián in Beas) the seven nuns set forth May 18 in "well-covered carts" that jolted and creaked with every movement of the mules, and began to jog along the river valley toward Córdoba. It was a clear hot day, and the countryside was aglow with color and fragrance. If it had been a month earlier! When Columbus wanted to describe the beauty of the calm mid-Atlantic in his logbook, he wrote that it lacked only the song of the nightingale to be like Andalucía in April. But May was delightful enough.

Friar Jerome of the Mother of God, better known as Father Gracián, one of Saint Teresa's favorite confessors.

Chapter XXVIII

THE DEVILS OF ANDALUCÍA

ON THE first day, they stopped for their siesta in a beautiful wood among the mountains, where the sight of so many kinds of flowers and the music of so many lovely little birds so dissolved La Madre in joy over the grandeur of God that the nuns had difficulty in getting her away from the place. Crossing the Guadalquivir on boats, they had a narrow escape from being swept down the swift current, as night fell; and according to Father Julian they almost lost their "furniture," which consisted of "an image and some holy water and some books." The convent at Beas had been too poor to give them anything else, but they consoled themselves with thoughts of the rosy picture Fray Mariano had painted of the endless riches and luxuries they would find in Sevilla, and of the swarm of influential citizens who would hasten to welcome and assist them. On the boat, to pass away the time, they all sang Compline; and La Madre contributed to their consolation by composing some verses, probably the ones with the refrain,

> Vuestra soy, para vos nací:
> ¿ que mandáis hacer de mí?[1]

and such energetic strophes as the following, which Father Julian sang for them with a right good will:

> Dadme muerte, dadme vida;
> Dad salud o enfermedad,
> Honra o deshonra me dad,
> Dadme guerra o paz crecida,
> Flaqueza o fuerza cumplida,
> Que a todo digo que si.
> ¿Qué queréis hacer de mí?[2]

The next day La Madre fell ill of a high fever, and passed so quickly into a lethargy that all her companions were frightened, and decided to carry her out of the blazing sunlight into

---

[1] Mir, *Vida de Santa Teresa*, t. III, p. 334 *et seq.*
[2] B.M.C., t. VI, pp. 79–82. For English translation, see Stanbrook ed., *Minor Works of Saint Teresa*, poem I, p. 3.

the first shelter they could find. What a lodging! It was a small building outside a crowded inn, where people were dancing, singing, and shouting; and when Father Julian went in with Fray Gregorio Nacianceno to get some water, they were foully insulted and cursed at, according to his account, by "the most perverse men I have ever seen in my life." When the gentle priest rebuked them, they became angrier, and heaven knows what would have happened if, quarreling among themselves, they had not all clapped their hands to their swords and rushed out, as to fight. More than forty swords were unsheathed; harquebuses were fired; while some of the loiterers stuck their heads through the curtains of the wagons and greeted the nuns with obscene and blasphemous remarks. Father Julian had to pay two *maravedis* for a jar of water so small that it took several of them to begin to slake the thirst of each of the nuns — it would have been cheaper, he thought, to buy wine.

La Madre, meanwhile, had been taken into the shed and laid on a bed so uncomfortable that she would have preferred being put on the ground. In this shack, whose previous inhabitants, says Mother María de San José, must have been swine, the air was like that of a furnace, the roof so low that they could hardly stand upright; there was no window; spiders and other insects infested the dark hot interior, and the heat of the merciless sun bored through a thousand cracks. As fast as Father Julian and his companion brought water, the nuns threw it on the face of La Madre, but it was so hot that it gave her little refreshment.

The cool of the night revived her, and the fever subsided. As the coming day would be the Feast of Pentecost, and they were desirous of reaching Córdoba, some ten kilometers away, in time to hear Mass, they arose while it was yet dark and resumed their journey. It was dawn when they arrived at the ancient city of the caliphs, entering from the old Madrid-to-Sevilla road by the Ronda Payo near the Convent of the Martyrs on the right bank of the Guadalquivir. The clumsy carts rattled through streets that are no longer there, or have different names (such as the Cruz del Rastro and the Calle del Cardenal González), and through the Calle de las Platerías, the Calle del Mármol Gordo, and the Calle de Ballinas, toward the Puerta del Puente.

Inquiring for a place to attend Mass, they were directed to a church on the other side of the bridge. They were about to cross when they were stopped and told that no one could pass without a license from the governor. After waiting two hours for official Córdoba to awake, they finally obtained one. By that time a large crowd of early loiterers had gathered around them, attracted by the unusual hangings on the carts. When at last they were allowed to cross, they found that the gate of the bridge was too narrow for the carts. Resourceful Father Julian got a saw and pared off the sides of the wagons enough to permit them to squeak through.

When they reached the church, they found it packed with people, for it was dedicated to the Holy Ghost and there was to be a Pentecost sermon by some popular preacher. "When I saw this," wrote La Madre, "it gave me much sorrow, and to my way of thinking it would have been better to go on without hearing Mass than to enter so much hullabaloo. Father Julian of Ávila did not think so; and as he was a theologian, we all had to come round to his opinion. . . ." At the sight of the seven women in their white choir mantles, their faces covered with their black veils, their feet bare, the large congregation fell into as much confusion, she adds, "as if bulls had broken in among them." The nuns, of course, were frightened. La Madre was so shocked that her fever left her.

At this point a good man approached and cleared the way for them to one of the chapels, where Father Julian said his Mass, and they communicated. (A few days later this gentleman inherited a large estate unexpectedly, as a reward, he thought, for helping the servants of God.) "I tell you, daughters, that although this may perhaps seem nothing to you, it was one of the worst experiences I had ever had," wrote Teresa. When they finally got away from the church and the crowd, it was near noon, and they found a shady place under a bridge to take their siesta, first chasing away some pigs that were reposing there.

That afternoon they were on their way to Sevilla. They traveled by night chiefly, for the daytime heat was so intense that La Madre, to help the nuns endure it, bade them think of it as their purgatory, which they might as well get over with; and they even found a certain relief in imagining what the flames of hell must be like. "All this, and many trials that occurred, we bore with the greatest joy," recorded Father Julian, "for the Holy Mother kept up a good and most gracious conversation with us, which encouraged all of us; sometimes saying things of so much weight, other times things to entertain us, still others composing stanzas and very good ones, for she knew well how to do it, but never made use of it except when material from which to make them turned up on the roads, so that with all the prayer she had, it did not prevent her from carrying on a holy conversation, friendly and of great benefit to souls and bodies."[3] On the second day after Pentecost they heard Mass at a hermitage in Ecija, and remained there for the siesta, while La Madre made her vow of perpetual obedience to Father Gracián. Two days later — the ninth since they had left Beas — they came within sight of Sevilla, and saw the Giralda Tower with the sunlight on it, like a signpost by the gates of heaven. It was Thursday the twenty-sixth of May, 1575.

One of the first things they did on arriving at the metropolis, that titanic sieve through which the gold of Mexico and Peru filtered into the hands of international bankers and usurers in all parts of Europe, leaving the generous Spaniards as poor or poorer than before, was to look for Fray Mariano de San Benito, that he might escort them to the house he had rented and furnished so sumptuously, and there allay the pangs of their hunger with the alms of his rich and charitable friends. For they had had nothing to eat for two or three days but a few sardines so salty that they were unable to swallow much of them, lacking water to quench their agonizing thirst. La Madre had in her purse only one *blanca,* a coin worth a very small fraction of a cent. Ah, but there was Fray Mariano at last, handsome, smiling, affable as ever, greeting them courteously, and with him two ladies whom he introduced as friends of his. He was too busy at the moment to take them to their house in the Calle de las Armas, but the ladies would attend to that. So they did, to be sure; but immediately on arriving there they took themselves off, and were seen no more. "Neither they nor anyone," wrote María de San José, "sent us so much as a jar of water."

And now, to climax this miserable adventure, they found that Mariano's house was a small damp place, through which they looked in vain for the luxurious equipment he had promised.

---

[3] *Vida,* part II, cap. VIII, p. 283. The chief authorities for the Sevilla foundation are Father Julian, Mother María de San José (*Libro de Recreaciones*) and Saint Teresa (*Fundaciones,* caps. XXIV–XXVI incl.).

Excitable, forgetful Fray Mariano! Perhaps a hermit who had been so contented in the caves of El Tardón and Pastrana was not the best agent to furnish a house for nuns. Mother María de San José left a memorable description of his "furniture":

"First of all there were half a dozen old hurdles that Father Mariano had had brought from his house of Los Remedios, and they were laid on the floor for beds. There were two or three little mattresses, not very serviceable, like those of Discalced friars, accompanied by a large population of the sort that usually inhabits them. These were for our Mother and some sick nuns. There was no sheet, blanket, or pillow, except a couple that we had brought along. We found a palm leaf rug and a small table, a frying pan, a kitchen lamp or two, a brass mortar and a pail or bucket to draw water." These they borrowed from various people in near-by houses. "And just as we were beginning to think that this, along with a few jars and plates and such things that we found, would at least be the beginning of the house, the neighbors from whom they had been borrowed for that day began to send, one for the frying pan, another for the oil lamp, another for the bucket and table, so that nothing remained with us, neither frying pan, nor mortar, nor even the rope of the well."[4]

As for all the rich charitable people whose aid Mariano had promised, not one appeared. "No one could have believed," wrote Madre Teresa, "that in a city so wealthy as Sevilla, and with so rich a population, we should have had less equipment with which to found than in all the places where we had been. There was so little that I sometimes thought it was not well for us to have a monastery in that place."[5] Father Mariano went looking for some money and bread, but we are not told whether he returned with any. It was Antonio Gaytán who finally borrowed some funds for them from a friend of his in Sevilla. They lived mostly on bread and apples, "sometimes stewed, sometimes raw." One day when there was only bread enough for one, the seven divided it.[6]

All such minor privations they endured, as usual, with jokes and songs and even prayers of thanks. But something harder

---

[4] *Libro de Recreaciones, Recreación* 9, in P. Silverio, *Vida de Santa Teresa de Jesús*, IV, 366

[5] *Fundaciones*, cap. 25.

[6] Madre María, *loc. cit.*

to bear was in store for them. Father Mariano now told La Madre that although there was no difficulty about the Archbishop's consent, it might be just as well for them to wait awhile before attempting to open the house as a convent, in view of certain circumstances that had arisen. For example, it might be expedient, he hinted, to have the monastery endowed, or something of that sort. The shrewd mind of La Madre began to see, through all his evasions, the awful truth. "As his reasons were not sufficient, I understood where the difficulty was — he had not got the license." Finally, under her questioning, he admitted that he and Gracián had not told the Archbishop everything. This prelate, Don Cristóbal de Rojas, noted for his Christian life and his charity to the poor, had a prejudice against new convents, and especially those founded in poverty, and had never once, in all his years of office in Sevilla and before that in Córdoba, granted permission. Knowing this, Mariano and Gracián had said nothing to him of Madre Teresa's founding a house in Sevilla — much less an unendowed one. The good Archbishop, edified by what he had been told of her and her nuns, expected to scatter them among the existing convents of the city, to reform them!

This idea Teresa refused even to consider; it would have been the ruin of her mission. Mariano begged her to be patient, and he would find a way to bring the Archbishop around. He did, in fact, obtain permission for a Mass at the convent on the Feast of the Holy Trinity, May 29, although His Grace was careful to send word that no bell must be rung, or set up — "but this had already been done," adds La Madre innocently. Thus matters stood for a fortnight. Then she decided to take the nuns back to Beas and make the foundation at Caravaca. She could well believe now what she had always heard of Andalucía, that it was the part of the earth where the devils were left most free to tempt and persecute. "Never was I more pusillanimous and cowardly in my life than I found myself there; indeed, I did not recognize myself. Of course the confidence I always had in our Lord did not desert me; but my nature was so different from what it usually was in these affairs, that I understood the Lord withdrew His hand partly from me so He might remain in His being, and I see that if I had had courage, it was not mine."

In all her account of these tribulations — and she suffered

much — there is not one word of reproach for Mariano, much less for Gracián. After all, if they had been frank with her and with the Archbishop, the enterprise could never have been started. No doubt everything had happened as it had by permission of the all-seeing God, for His own good purposes. And when Mariano said she must not think of leaving Sevilla, nor must she write to the Archbishop, as she desired to do, she submitted, and waited patiently. He assured her she had only to leave it all to him. He would win over the prelate by degrees, with the help of Gracián's letters from Madrid.

Strange to say, he finally succeeded. The Archbishop, softened up little by little by eloquent persuasion, finally went to the convent, and was so impressed by Madre Teresa and her daughters that he gave his permission for the foundation. This was soon after some Calced Fathers of Sevilla had visited her, and had gone away supposing that it already had the prelate's enthusiastic support — otherwise, adds La Madre with naïve satisfaction, they would certainly have done all they could to keep him from giving it! So all turned out well after all.

As they became better known, they made some friends, the first of whom was Doña Leonor de Valera, wife of a Portuguese gentleman living in Sevilla. Before the end of 1575 this lady lost her money in the crash that followed the bankruptcy of Philip II, but not until after she had given food, clothing, and money to the convent at Mariano's request; and this was the only one of her investments that survived the panic of 1575, for in later years the community supported her two daughters, when they entered the Order. The Archbishop contributed wheat and money. "Now we are rich," wrote La Madre on July 10 to Gaytán.

Spiritually a great future lay before this house. Madre María de San José, the first prioress, was perhaps the most illustrious woman in the Order, next to Madre Teresa. Born in Aragon, María de Salazar had become a servant in the palace of the Cerdas in Toledo, where La Madre had noticed her at the age of some thirteen years, and had encouraged her to seek a religious vocation. She had finally entered the convent at Malagón, whence Teresa had summoned her for the foundations of Beas and Caravaca. Handsome, spiritual, and keenly intelligent, she was better educated than La Madre herself. Although she never attained the power of Teresa's best writing, she expressed herself with more order, succinctness, and journalistic vividness. Her mind was gentle and feminine, while La Madre's, as Mir has well observed,[7] was more masculine in its vigor and comprehension. Yet far from being jealous of the superiorities of another, Teresa thanked God for them. "This Prioress has a courage that astonishes me," she wrote María Bautista: "much more than I have. I think that since they have me here I have been some help, for the blows fall on me. She has a very good understanding. I tell you she is *extremada* for Andalucía, in my opinion. And how much we need to have them good!"[8]

The first nun to enter San José de Sevilla was Beatriz de la Madre de Dios, a beautiful young woman of such edifying piety that La Madre devoted a whole chapter of the *Fundaciones* to her. At seven she had been sent by her mother to live with an aunt who had no children and wanted her companionship. Two dishonest serving women, to get rid of her, accused her of attempting to poison this relative with corrosive sublimate, and she was sent home. Her mother believed her guilty, and, because she would not confess, whipped and tortured her for a year, making her sleep on the bare floor. (God permitted this, wrote Madre Teresa in her charity, to shape the child's vocation — her mother was actually "a very virtuous woman," who loved her a great deal!) At twelve, reading the life of Saint Agnes, Beatriz conceived a desire to be a Carmelite, and made a vow never to marry. When she refused a man of her parents' choice, they used to throttle her, and all but killed her. Beatriz did not mind much, for she would think of the sufferings of Saint Agnes.

Years later, when she was twenty-seven, she saw Father Gracián preaching in one of the churches of Triana; and the sight of his habit and bare feet attracted her so that she went to confession to him — not without many attempts, for ordinarily he would not talk to women — and thus found her way into the new house of the Discalced Carmelites in Sevilla. Her mother, Juana, that virtuous woman, became a lay sister.

Two other novices were accepted in the first six weeks of the foundation. "Shortly afterwards," wrote Mother María de San José, "we received a great *beata* who was already canonized by the whole city, and through the importunity of many leading

[7] Mir, *op. cit.*, II, p. 359.
[8] Letter of April 29, 1576.

and spiritual people she was received. The poor thing was much more holy in her own opinion than in that of the people; and when on entering she began to miss the praises, and the touchstone of religion commenced to do its work of discovering the number of carats there were in what seemed to shine so brilliantly, she found herself without any, and commenced to be discontented, and we even more so with her, for it would never do to make her accommodate herself to anything religious, and being already a woman of forty years, of high position, and she had an argument ready for everything.[9] She would some-times give the excuse that she was ill, and so did not wish to eat our food, discovering that each thing was unhealthy and would swell one up with wind, as she could read in Galen; other times she would say that the custom and great heat of the country excused her.

"Our Mother, thinking that she would improve with time and to avoid being hard on her, commanded us to bear with her, and gave her permission to confess and talk at times with the clergymen of her acquaintance. In the end, without the knowl-edge of our Mother or anyone in the house, she arranged to leave, after persuading the other novice to go out after her. . . ."[10]

When some of her acquaintances began to criticize this con-duct, and to consider her less holy than before, this *beata* salved her wounded vanity by painting a black picture of conditions in the convent, and finally went so far as to complain to the Holy Office of the Inquisition, with results that will presently appear.

Teresa remained in Sevilla for a little more than a year — the year which saw the beginning of the most furious persecu-tion she had yet to endure. Still, there were compensating joys as usual. One of the greatest was the news that her brother Lorenzo, whom she had been expecting home from Peru for the past five years, had finally arrived at Sanlúcar de Barrameda the first week in August, 1575, with his three children, Fran-cisco, Lorenzo, and Teresita, and his brother, Pedro de Ahumada. This joy, too, had its cross, for Lorenzo wrote that their brother Jerónimo had died in Panama just before they sailed; however, he had had a most holy end, and Teresa, in passing on this in-formation to her sister Juana, reminded her that there was

---

[9] "*Y sabía dar á cada cosa su salida.*"
[10] *Op. cit., Recreación* 9.

nothing to grieve at in such a death. The travelers were on their way to Sevilla, and would be there in about three days.

The arrival of this prosperous brother from the Indies at this particular time seemed plainly the work of God. Teresa was too human not to rejoice in seeing him and his children, and she conceived a particular love for her little namesake, who was said to resemble her even in features. Teresita was then nine, a dark-eyed, lovely, spiritual child, who had already gladdened her father's heart by aspiring to be a Carmelite like her aunt. La Madre's correspondence of that period is full of references to this child. She even sought some way to have her dispensed to enter before the canonical age, until two of her advisers, a Jesuit and a Dominican, convinced her that it would not be lawful to take one under twelve. There was no reason, however, why Teresita could not live in the house, and so it was agreed. She put on a small habit, especially made for her, and became the darling of the community until she was old enough to be a postulant.

Lorenzo was pleased. As for the boys, he was taking them to Ávila, to be educated by the Jesuits, as his sister advised. When they arrived, there seems to have been some unfavorable gossip, which Mother María Bautista heard in Valladolid and promptly reported to Sevilla, about their using the title of "*Don.*" This ancient Castilian honor, once granted so sparingly and so jealously, had been worn, it will be remembered, by their grandparents. One of Teresa's letters suggests that she had come to have doubts as to their rights to use it. There was something more in this than her rule forbidding any of the nuns to call themselves *Doña.* She must have heard that about this time Philip II was beginning a campaign, which he took very seriously, to restrict the title to those whose ancestors had been granted the right by the crown. He used to become quite testy, especially on his gouty days, about those who affected it without what he considered good reason. When a secretary brought him a letter addressed to Don So-and-So of Beetria, he said, "Do it over without the Don — there aren't any Dons in Beetria"; and he struck the "Don" off another address, remarking, "Let him not have it, for his father hasn't it." A few years later he insisted upon this principle in his *premática de cortesías,* which caused so much irritation through Spain and even in Rome.[11]

---

[11] Cf. my *Philip II,* pp. 490, 626.

La Madre was probably not deeply concerned over the discovery that her ancestors had been composed of somewhat more common clay than she had been led to believe, and she had no trouble in persuading Lorenzo to make the boys give up the *"Don."* Not so her brother-in-law Juan de Ovalle. When that small, jealous, grasping bourgeois arrived on October 24 to visit the relatives from Peru, he undid all her good work.

"Let us now come to your counsels," she wrote to her niece María Bautista: "As for the first, about the *Dons,* all who have servants in the Indies call themselves so there. But when they came, I asked their father not to let them use it, and I gave him reasons. So it was done, and they were all calmed down and affable, when along came Juan de Ovalle and my sister, and — why I don't know (perhaps it was to pave the way[12] for their own son to use it), and as my brother was not here, nor was he for so many days, nor was I with them, when he came back they told him so much that nothing I could say did any good. And it is true that now in Ávila nothing else is talked about,[13] which is shameful. And certainly they throw it in my face[14] because of my relation to them; but as far as I'm concerned, never believe that I remember it, or that I care anything about that; for it is nothing compared to other things they say about me. I will speak to their father again for love of you, but I don't think it will be of any use with their uncle and aunt, considering how set they are upon it. Every time I hear of it I am very mortified."[15]

How human a saint can be, even the most angelic of saints! Yet Teresa never forgot to see Lorenzo, fond as she was of him, in the light of eternity. She wanted him to do something for God. When he returned from Madrid — he was there when the Ovalles arrived in Sevilla — she took good care to let him know how inconvenient and inadequate the small convent in the Calle de las Armas was for her nuns, and she soon had him going all about Sevilla, looking for a better house.

Father Gracián, whom we left in Beas taking his departure for Madrid to see the Nuncio, returned to Sevilla in the middle of November. He had spent six months in the capital, doing all he could to avoid the unwelcome and thankless task of reforming

---

[12] Impossible to translate literally: *"por soldar el de su hijo."*
[13] *"Ya en Ávila no hay otra cosa."*
[14] *"Y, cierto, a mí me dan en los ojos, por lo que á ellos toca."*
[15] To María Bautista, April 29, 1576; *Epistolario,* I, pp. 229–230.

the Calced Friars of Andalucía. In spite of his youth, or perhaps because of his youth and zeal, he made a most favorable impression upon the great Ormaneto, to whom in fact his arrival just then may have seemed nothing short of providential. Philip the Second had decided to use the Jesuits as visitors and reformers of the various orders in sunny, happy-go-lucky Andalucía — the Trinitarians, the Minims, *la Merced*, the Calced Franciscans — and had sent Father Olea, S.J., through the province to announce the coming visit. The Jesuits themselves very sensibly objected to this plan, knowing the conflicts and jealousies it would breed, and suggested that His Majesty have each order reformed by one of its own illustrious members. So it was agreed; and while the Papal Nuncio was wondering whom he should appoint for both the Calced and Discalced of Andalucía, who should appear but Gracián. Ormaneto made him visitor. It was a tremendous compliment for a young man in the first years of his priesthood.

It was also a terrifying responsibility, and one that Gracián by no means desired. He was glad, of course, that the Calced, as subject to the Discalced, could no longer prevent their growth, much less destroy them; but he frankly admits that his human weakness made him shrink from the task out of fear. There was nothing of the reforming busybody in Gracián; he had no itch to meddle with others. On the contrary he begged Cardinal Quiroga, the Inquisitor General, to get the King to release him from the job of reforming the Calced friars.

"They will kill us," he said.

"Let them kill us!" cried the old Cardinal with holy wrath. "And to whom can we entrust this except to men of blood and nobility and reputation like you, who don't fear death?"

Gracián agreed, with inward misgivings, that he did not fear death. He returned to Andalucía with every expectation that he would be a corpse before the end of the year.[16]

These fears were not as unreasonable as they may appear, considering what had been happening of late. They were shared by Gracián's brother, the King's secretary, who wrote La Madre a vigorous protest against the dangerous mission; and to a lesser extent, perhaps, by her. Humble as always, she blamed herself for everything. As soon as she heard that Gracián was in town she sent Lorenzo with a letter in which she said, "The grace of the Holy Spirit be with you, *Padre mio!* Oh, if you knew how

---

[16] So he says, *op. cit.*, diálogo I.

unhappy and scrupulous I am today! I tell you I am very wicked, and the worst of it is that I never improve. . . . If someone doesn't come from there to confess me tomorrow, I will not receive Communion. . . . Unworthy daughter of Your Paternity, Teresa of Jesus." In a postcript she added, "In many years I haven't had so much trouble as since these reforms began."

Teresa was not badly informed about the state of tension that had developed that year between the Calced friars and her fathers of the Reform. When such men as Rubeo and Fray Angel de Salazar were angry over the exaggerated reports they had of the activities of Mariano and Gracián, and the foundations of La Madre in Beas and Sevilla, it was not surprising that the indignation of the Calced in general had fairly boiled over at their General Chapter at Piacenza May 21, 1575. They were told that the Discalced had acted disobediently and dishonestly, that they had divided and threatened to destroy the Order with their innovations, that they were actuated by ambition and spite and so on. Unfortunately no defense of the Discalced was presented; the Spanish delegate who might have given it did not arrive in time. Father Rubeo, to be sure, had written twice to Madre Teresa, once in October, 1574, and again in the January following, asking her for a full account of the controversy, that he might submit it to the Chapter. But unhappily his letters did not reach her until June, 1575, after the adjournment of the angry assembly. The delegates therefore voted, with every conviction of their own righteousness, to suppress the three Andalusian priories of the Reform, the friars to leave within three days under pain of being forcibly ejected by the secular arm. Madre Teresa was to found no more convents or monasteries, and was to remain for the rest of her life in some community of her own choosing. It was not until the end of the year that Teresa was formally notified of this by Padre Ulloa, prior of the Calced Carmelites of Sevilla. Perhaps Fray Angel shrank from telling her himself. Yet he certainly shared the prejudice of his brethren against her, for he referred her as "an excommunicated apostate."

Gracián consulted the elder friars of the Reform as to what should be done. He begged them to be conciliatory, as La Madre desired. But after a fiery speech by Mariano, the fathers were in no mood to compromise, and they laid upon Gracián the heavy burden of disregarding her advice and defying the Calced and all the fulminations of Piacenza.

When Gracián returned to Sevilla in November, he was ready to beard the fathers of the Mitigation in their own house; and if anything was needed to add a spark to the explosive feelings left over on both sides from the two chapters, it was his indignation at what he heard they had been saying about him. They made fun of his custom of sleeping with an image of our Lady in his nightgown (no doubt for protection against evil dreams, evil thoughts, evil spirits) in such a way, he wrote, "as to arouse in the hearers the most horrible and cursed blasphemy that could be thought of. And when I was absent on the affairs of the visit, they publicly announced in the pulpit of the Convent of Sevilla that the wickedness and abominations of that evil man had been made known, and that I had been burned, and that they had been given a paper containing my ashes."[17] They were doubtless disappointed when he turned up alive, and their animosity was so apparent that whenever he had occasion to stay at one of their convents, he wore a bezoar stone around his neck as a precaution against poisoning, and would eat nothing but eggs cooked in their shells. One of the lesser offenses they accused him of was the theft of three thousand ducats.[18] But the crowning infamy, the one that made him and must make us burn with indignation, was the foul slur cast upon his friendship with the sick, persecuted, saintly old lady who was his penitent. One of the saddest pages in his book, or in any book, is the one in which he speaks so feelingly of this:

"You must know that she loved me very tenderly, and I her more than any creature on earth, after my mother Doña Juana Dentisco, who also loved me with a more particular love than any other of her sons. But this so great love that I bore Madre Teresa of Jesus, and she for me, is a very different bond from what is usually had in the world, for *that* love is dangerous, vexatious and causes thoughts and temptations that afflict and slacken the spirit, disturb the sensuality. But this love that I had for Madre Teresa of Jesus and she for me produced in me purity, the spirit and love of God, and in her consolation and relief for her trials, as many times she told me, and so I should not want even my mother to love me more than she did. Blessed be God who gave me so good a friend, for now that she is in heaven, this love will not cool, and I can be sure it will be of great benefit!

---

[17] *Peregrinación*, diálogo I, p. 29.
[18] *Ibid.*

But look what a thing is a corrosive tongue, when malicious people judged, from the great communication and familiarity that we two had, that it was not a holy love; and even if she had not been as holy as she was, and if I had been the most evil man in the world, wickedness should not have been suspected of a woman sixty years old, and so cloistered and modest; and with all that we had to conceal this very intimate friendship, so that we should not be maligned."[19]

Incredible as all this sounds, it is confirmed by that well-balanced woman, María de San José, prioress of Sevilla, who recorded that some of the Calced had composed a diatribe against Madre Teresa containing "the most abominable and foul words imaginable, for those that can best be spoken are not fit to be mentioned, but to show the malice of the demon, I will say a few. They said they were going to hand the old so and-so over to whites and blacks so that she could have enough of being wicked; and that she took young girls from one place to another with the pretext of foundations so that they could do it. These and other worse things they said in that *Proceso,* each one declaring what he thought of our Mother."[20]

Teresa had gone so far on the road to perfection that even lies as foul as these could not disturb her much. But she deeply resented the calumnies that were circulated against Gracián. Her anxiety knew no limits on the eve of the Feast of Our Lady's Presentation, the day on which he was to present his credentials to the Calced of Sevilla. There were rumors about that they had locked the door against him, and threatened to do him physical violence. Next day she heard that he had been killed. Throwing herself on her knees, she promised that if his life were spared, she would always have that feast especially remembered in all her convents. "O woman of little faith," said our Lord, "be quiet. All is going to be well."

The friars did no more than give Gracián a very uncomfortable hour or two. "When I presented to them the brief for the visit," he said, "they shut the doors of the convent, and would not obey."[21]

---

[19] *Ibid., diálogo* XVI, p. 309.

[20] Mir quotes this (*op. cit.,* p. 403) from the *Libro de recreaciones, recreación* IX: "*las más abominables y sucias palabras que se pueden imaginar. . . . Decían: aquella vieja tal la habían de entregar á blancos y negros para que se hartase de ser mala,*" etc.

[21] *Peregrinación,* diálogo I, p. 29.

Madre Teresa must have noticed by this time, if not before, that Gracián, with all his virtues, had temperamental limitations capable of doing considerable harm to her Reform — limitations suggested by a portrait revealing him as a plump, baldish man with sad kindly eyes, a rather weak vain mouth, a long nose, a low forehead, and a heavy stubborn chin. Unlike John of the Cross, he had been powerfully attracted, as Father Bruno observes, by the element of the marvelous in the contemplative life. Though charming, he was eccentric, and could be stubborn and unreasonable. His flair for the melodramatic and his lack of the sense of humor that would have prevented many of his blunders are evident in the *chef d'oeuvre* of his old age, the *Peregrinación de Anastasio,* where, although he asserts he has never had nor sought either raptures or ecstasies, he gravely recounts some of his visions, including an intellectual one of a decided Aristotelian and Ptolemaic flavor, in which "the five worlds were placed before me, that is to say, (1) the natural world; (2) the little world or microcosmos which is man; (3) the rational world which is of all the concepts and quiddities or essences of logic and metaphysics; (4) the moral world, of all the virtues and vices; (5) the intellectual or scientific world, of all the arts and sciences, practical and speculative, that exist; and each one of these worlds has twenty orbs. The natural world, for example, has twenty, for under the earth there are four, that is to say, hell, purgatory, limbo, and Abraham's Bosom; and four elements, earth, water, air, and fire; and seven heavens of planets: the Moon, Mercury, Venus, the Sun, Mars, Jupiter, and Saturn; and four major heavens which are called the *Estrellado,* the *Primum Mobile,* the crystalline heaven, and the empyrean heaven; and all these are nineteen, and over all the twentieth orb which is God Who comprehends and includes within Himself all the others." All this, says Gracián, he saw in an instant, while he was a captive of the Moors in Tunis.[22]

A great part of Teresa's energies, during the rest of her life, were devoted to undoing the well-meant blunders of this imaginative young priest, and to trying to make him realize to the full the possibilities for good she had discerned in him. From this time on, to avoid the slanders and calumnies referred to above, they correspond usually in a code in which Gracián is always

[22] *Ibid.,* diálogo XV, p. 283.

referred to as "Paul," La Madre as "Lorenza," or "Angela," and our Lord as "Joseph"; while the Calced friars are "the Egyptians," and the Calced nuns "Night Birds" — "*aves nocturnas.*" Fray John of the Cross is "Seneca"; Fray Mariano is "Elias." This cipher was agreed upon as early as September 27, 1575, when she wrote Gracián an account of the visits the Calced fathers had been making. She told him they were willing to obey him in suppressing any abuse so long as he did not meddle with other matters, and she assured them they would find him lenient and reasonable. "Father Elias is more calm and courageous. I advise Your Paternity to commence without bluster and with suavity, for I believe it is going to be quite a task, and you mustn't try to do it all in a day. Truly I believe there are reasonable people, and so there must be there! You must know that Macario[23] is so terrible, from what they tell me, that I have been quite anxious about his soul. . . . Indeed it makes me fear to see good souls so deceived."[24]

She repeatedly reminded him of the obligation of obedience, and urged him to be gentle and conciliatory, to treat the Calced as erring brothers and not as enemies. His health gave her constant concern. When he was in Toledo at the end of the year 1575, she kept him informed about everything: how Father John of the Cross approved of his work, how Father Mariano was gaining in courage. She begged him under no circumstances to let any nun leave her convent, except to make a foundation. "Your Paternity, *Padre mío,* pay attention to this, and believe that I understand the wrong side[25] of women better than Your Paternity. . . . Believe this truth of me (and if I die, don't forget it) that the devil wants nothing more than to have enclosed people think such a thing is possible."

She was distressed to hear that he had fallen off his mule more than once, and suggested that he have himself strapped on. "I don't know what kind of ass that can be,[26] or why Your Paternity has to travel ten leagues a day, for on a packsaddle it's enough to kill you. I am worried over whether it has occurred to you to put on heavier clothing, for it is now cold. The Lord grant it has not made you ill. Remember (since you like the improvement of

---

[23] Probably Fray Baltasar de Jesús, of whom more anon.
[24] *Epistolario*, I, p. 188.
[25] "*Reveses.*"
[26] No one ever heard of Teresa falling off a mule!

souls) the injury that would befall many if your health fails, and for the love of God, take care of it. Elias is more fearless. The Rector and Rodrigo Alvarez[27] have great hope that everything will be all right. All the fear I formerly had has left me; now I couldn't feel it even if I wanted to. I have had miserable health these days; I have taken a purge, and I am well, which I haven't been in four months or more, and it is unbearable."[28] Nor was Gracián her only maternal care. She worried also about Father Báñez, who had rheumatism, which she was afraid came from sleeping on the floor as a penance during Advent; she wrote Mother María Bautista asking her to find out whether he wore warm enough clothing for the sharp climate of Valladolid.[29]

Of her several letters to Father Rubeo, replying to his criticisms, only two are extant; but they are long and vigorous, and as Mir says, "monuments of wisdom and of holy and apostolic liberty." It was June 17, 1575, when she received his letters of the previous October and January. She replied the next day, tactfully beginning with the remark that although she did not receive them as early as she would have desired, she was much consoled to know that his lordship was in good health, and that all the nuns prayed for him especially every day in the choir, "and apart from this, all are very attentive, for as they know how much I love Your Lordship, and they recognize no other father, they have a great love for Your Lordship, and this is not surprising, for we have no other good on earth. . . ."

She repeated what she had written about her own foundations in Andalucía, and her misunderstanding about Beas. She assured him that she considered all the Discalced friars together as nothing compared to the hem of his garment, and would not cause him the slightest displeasure for anything. She had showed his authorization to the Calced fathers who called upon her, and they had seen that Rubeo allowed her to found "in all parts," and had even commanded her to found, with the result that she had done more than she had strength for, and was now old and worn out. "But my principal concern is what Your Lordship wrote about hearing of the fraud of these fathers,[30] who, although they justify their cause, and truly I hold them to be

---

[27] Her Jesuit confessor in Sevilla.
[28] *Epistolario*, I, 193–196.
[29] *Ibid.*, p. 214.
[30] Gracián and Mariano.

true sons of Your Lordship and to desire not to offend you, yet I cannot help blaming them. And I think they are now coming to the conclusion that it would have been better to have proceeded in another way, so as not to vex Your Lordship. We argue enough about it, especially Mariano and I, for he is very hasty, and Gracián is like an angel, and if he had been by himself, he would have done otherwise, and his coming here was by the command of Fray Baltasar, who was then prior of Pastrana. I tell Your Lordship that if you knew him, you would rejoice to have him for a son, and truly I understand he is one, and even Mariano the same.

"This Mariano is a virtuous and penitent man who makes himself acquainted with everyone through his talent, and Your Lordship may believe, really, that only zeal for God and the good of the order have moved him; still, as I have said, he has been too forward and indiscreet. As for ambition, I don't understand there is any in him, but the devil, as Your Lordship says, stirs up these affairs, and he says many things, for he doesn't know what he is about.[31] I have put up with him often enough, and as I see that he is virtuous, I overlook it. If Your Lordship could hear the excuses they give, you could not fail to be satisfied. This very day he told me that he was not going to rest until he had thrown himself at Your Lordship's feet. I have already written Your Lordship how they both asked me to write Your Lordship, for they did not dare, and to offer their excuses."

She protested against the excommunication of Gracián, and explained that he had fled to his father's house only when the Provincial had ordered him out of the priory in Madrid. After all, he had received his powers from the Apostolic Visitor Vargas and from the Nuncio. And her Discalced friars were considered saints in Spain. They led good lives, were very recollected, and included many holy men of high birth. Twenty or more were studying Canon Law or Theology. There were seventy in all. What would now become of them?

She did not mince matters in discussing the Calced friars of Andalucía. She liked certain ones, especially the Prior, Father Miguel de Ulloa, who was a very good man, but some of the friars of Sevilla led such lives that those of Castilla seemed to her very good by comparison.

---

[31] "Y él dice muchas cosas, que no se entiende."

"Even since I have been here," she went on boldly, "a very painful thing has happened, for in the middle of the day the police found two friars in a house of ill fame, and publicly took them away under arrest, which was very badly done, and weaknesses don't shock me, but I wish their reputation had been looked after. This was after I wrote Your Lordship. All in all, people say it is a good thing they were arrested."[32]

Her letter to Rubeo in early February, 1576, is a moving plea for understanding for herself and forgiveness for Gracián and Mariano. Their story was very different from the ones circulated in Italy, where the Father General then was. The Nuncio had renewed Gracián's commission, and this against the latter's desires. But once he had accepted, La Madre had done all she could to persuade Gracián and Mariano to proceed quietly, and to deal with the Calced as with brothers, "for, as I wrote to Your Lordship, I find here persons of good talent and learning, such as I wish we had in our province of Castilla." She was not surprised that the Calced fathers were tired of "so many visits and innovations." However, as Gracián is a member of the order, she hopes they will accept him as visitor. "And once more I beg Your Lordship, for the love of our Lord and His glorious Mother (for whom Your Lordship has so much love, and this father the same, for it was through being very devoted to her that he entered this Order) to answer him, and with kindness, and let bygones be bygones, even if he is somewhat to blame, and take him indeed for your son and subject, for truly he is, and poor Mariano the same, even if he sometimes doesn't know what he is about. And I am not surprised that he has written to Your Lordship something different from what he really meant, through not knowing how to express himself, for he declares that he never intended, by word or by deed, to offend Your Lordship. . . . Let Your Lordship remember that it is for sons to err, and for fathers to pardon and not notice their faults. For the love of our Lord, I beg Your Lordship to do me this favor." She would not have minded if

---

[32] *"Aun después que aquí estoy, ha acaecido una cosa harto trabajosa, que en mitad del día halló la Justicia dos frailes en una casa infame, y públicamente los llevaron presos, que fué harto mal hecho, que yo no me espantan flaquezas; mas querría que se mirase la honra. Esto es después que a Vuestra Señoría escribí. Con todo, dicen que es bien cogidos que fuesen."* — B.M.C., *Epistolario*, I, p. 176; Stanbrook, I, p. 204. Father Silverio in his monumental five-volume life of the Saint tends to minimize the corruption among the Calced friars in Andalucía, and their violence against the Discalced.

Rubeo had written her directly commanding her to stop foundations and remain in one convent, but "as I had so great a love for
Your Lordship, I could not help being hurt, as a friend, at being
treated as a very disobedient person, so much so that Father
Fray Angel could publish it in the Court before I knew anything about it, thinking it would be a great blow to me, and so
he wrote me that I could have recourse to the Camara of the
Pope, as if it would be a great relief to me! Even if I could not do
what Your Lordship commands me without great hardship, I
would certainly never think of not obeying you. . . ."

Fray Angel de Salazar had given her permission for Beas and
Caravaca, and Gracián for Sevilla; yet the former was now calling her an apostate and excommunicate. "It would have been
fine enough if he had been as hard on Valdemoro. As he is prior
of Ávila, he put the Discalced friars out of the Incarnation, with
very great scandal of the people, and he so treated those nuns
(whose house is such that God is to be praised) that it is pitiful,
the great distress they endure, and they have written me that to
exonerate him they take the blame on themselves. The affliction
of those nuns gives me sorrow enough, for they are given nothing
but bread, and for the rest so much anxiety that it gives me great
grief. God mend all, and keep Your Lordship many years. . . ."[33]

The letters to Rubeo produced no effect. Gracián and Mariano
had never put themselves to the trouble of trying to conciliate
him, despite the wishes of La Madre. Yes, human beings were
disappointing; like little dried bunches of rosemary, as she had
once discovered in Toledo. But God never failed her, and now
and then He allowed her a great consolation. One of these was
the foundation of her convent at Caravaca, in Murcia, on the
first day of January, 1576. Three holy women of that place had
been moved by the sermon of the Jesuit Father Leiva to offer all
their property to God for the maintenance of a convent, and on
his describing the houses of Madre Teresa, they invited her to go
there. After much delay the license was obtained, and at last
some nuns from Malagón, attended by Father Julian and Antonio Gaytán, took possession of a house that had been prepared
for them, and Mother Ann of Saint Albert went from Sevilla to
be prioress. Teresa was well satisfied. To a friend who thought
she had been cheated, she wrote, "As for the price of the house
I am not displeased, nor need you be, for provided the location

[33] *Epistolario*, I, pp. 216–223: Stanbrook, I, 244–252.

is good, I never hesitate to give a third more than it is worth, and I have happened to give even half again as much; for it is so important for a monastery to have it, that it would be an error to stop for that. I would value the water and the view much more highly than what it costs."[34]

Her brother Lorenzo (speaking of houses) had been searching all winter for a new one in Sevilla, and at last finding a good one, in the spring of 1576, lent the nuns money with which to purchase it. It was an old comfortable estate surrounded by fine gardens in the Calle de la Pajería, now the Calle de Zaragoza. By a deed of April 5, 1576, the price was fixed at 6000 ducats, of which Lorenzo put up four hundred on the spot.[35] It had been agreed that the seller was to pay the *alcabala* tax of some three hundred ducats, but by a scrivener's error, the purchaser was made to appear responsible. Subsequently there was a lawsuit, which the convent lost.[36] In the course of the litigation, the blame was cast upon Lorenzo by the angry sellers, with the result that he had to flee to escape arrest, and found sanctuary in the Carmelite monastery with Gracián.

"He has suffered a great deal," wrote La Madre, "both in spending generously, and in carrying the brunt of everything, and he makes one praise God. Indeed these sisters love him with reason, for they have had no other help, except from those who gave us more trouble. Now he is a fugitive on our account; and it was only by good fortune that he was not taken to the jail, which is like a hell here, and all without any justice, for they are asking of us what we do not owe, and want him as surety. It will have to be ended by going to court, which is an endless thing, but he has been glad to suffer something for God."[37]

Never since the foundation of San José de Ávila had she had so many troubles as during this year.[38] It must have been soon after the escape of Lorenzo that Gracián, going one day to visit the Convent, saw the street cluttered with the horses and mules of the *familiares* of the Holy Inquisition, and a crowd of the curious waiting to see the officers bring forth the *beatas* who had

---

[34] Letter to Don Rodrigo de Moya, February 19, 1576, *ibid.*, p. 223; Stanbrook. I, p. 253.
[35] P. Silverio, *op. cit.*, IV, pp. 399–400.
[36] So Teresa wrote Fray Mariano, May 9, 1576.
[37] To María Bautista, April 29, 1576; p. 227.
[38] *Ibid.*

been denounced as heretics. For this was the dreadful climax of all the slanders the devil had been sowing up and down the land about the most glorious of Spanish saints. Father Gracián made his way through the people and the officers of the Tribunal to the interior of the house, where he saw Madre Teresa as serene and smiling as if nothing had happened; it was she, rather, who allayed his fears by saying, "Look, *Padre,* they are burning us all for Christ. But don't be afraid, for no one who has the faith ever suffers anything through the Inquisition."[39]

Whatever the beginning of this *proceso* (it may well have been the vengeful spite of the Princess of Éboli), the immediate cause was a complaint lodged with the Holy Office by the melancholy *beata* who had left the convent in a huff on finding her sanctity so little venerated by the other members of the community. She had reported that the nuns were bound hand and feet and flogged; and that they went to confession to one another and to the Mother Prioress, under the article of the Rule that commanded them to give an account of their spirits to their superior. This last must have suggested Illuminism to the *Padres Inquisidores,* and one of them asked Sister Isabel of Saint Jerome about it.

"Do the nuns tell what is in their heart to the Prioress?"

"Yes," she replied promptly.

He looked severe.

"But the Prioress doesn't give us absolution," she added.

The Inquisitor began to roar with laughter. The situation was beginning to be plain to him, and he did not submit the nuns to the humiliation of being led through the streets like felons, nor did he even hold them for trial. But as the charges were too grave to be dismissed with a mere laugh, they were referred for investigation to two excellent theologians, both Jesuits, one of them Teresa's confessor, Father Rodrigo Alvarez, who asked her to write out for each an account of her spirit.

Besides the vindictive *beata* there was another delator, an unnamed priest who for a time heard the confessions of the nuns. Himself afflicted with melancholy, and not too well gifted mentally and spiritually, he took the accusations of the neurotic novice so seriously that he encouraged her complaint to the Inquisition, and in part corroborated it. Mother María de San

---

[39] One of Gracián's MS. notes to Ribera's *Life,* lib. IV, cap. IX; also *Peregrinación,* diálogo XIII.

José identifies him as none other than the somewhat too genial Father Garciálvarez,[40] who had helped Lorenzo find the new house, and contributed much to its equipment. Why such a benefactor should have called on the heads of the poor nuns the thunders of the inquisitorial examination remains one of the Teresian mysteries. But *todo se pasa,* as La Madre wrote on her bookmark; and the wretched story ended happily with her complete and indeed enthusiastic exoneration by the two Jesuits, whose report was accepted by the Holy Office.

As there was nothing else to hinder the opening of the new house, the nuns took possession of it on May 1, 1576. They wished to do so quietly, but Father Garciálvarez insisted upon a public celebration, which came off on June 3 with *éclat* and general rejoicing. The venerable Archbishop carried the Blessed Sacrament from one of the parish churches through the ancient streets, followed by most of the clergy and many of the confraternities in brilliant procession, while crowds came to admire and to applaud, and salvos of artillery were fired. It was a great feast of justification and exoneration for Madre Teresa. And to cap the climax, when she asked the Archbishop for his blessing, the venerable old man knelt in the sight of all the people, and asked for hers. As night came on, there were fireworks, and rockets flared in the dusk. The Sevillans were enchanted.

Only one untoward incident occurred. A little powder that had been left on a stone bench in the patio, just outside the cloister, somehow took fire. A great flame licked the stone walls, and shot upward through the cloister. Yet although it blackened the masonry to the very edge of some valuable silk tapestries of purple and gold, donated for the occasion, it did not touch them. So much, thought La Madre, for the devil's futile gesture of disapproval.

The house was heavenly, compared to the previous one. "The sisters never finish giving thanks to God," she wrote to Father Mariano. "May He be blessed forever. Everyone says it was a bargain, in fact they insist it could not be had today for twenty thousand ducats. They say the site is one of the best in Sevilla."[41] The cloister and church had been decorated with great care by

---

[40] Father Silverio doubts this (*op. cit.,* IV, p. 391); but if anyone was in a position to know, it was certainly Mother María, the Prioress.

[41] To Mariano, May 9, 1576, B.M.C., *Epist.,* I, p. 233.

Father Garciálvarez, who had even taken the pains of installing a bowl of orange flower water.[42]

It was now time for Teresa to leave Sevilla and to shut herself up forever, as the Chapter General had decreed, in the convent of her choice. She chose Toledo, and on the day after the procession, June 4, 1576, she set out for the north with her brother Lorenzo, Teresita in her Carmelite habit, and a friend named Alonzo Ruiz from Malagón. Very different was this journey from all the others she had made, for Lorenzo as a fairly rich *americano* naturally insisted on traveling in a coach of some grandeur. She really enjoyed this trip. Her health was good, for once; it was a relief to get away from hot Sevilla and the Andalusians, and it was good to think of a future of quiet contemplation of the Divine Majesty, with no more foundations, no more quarrels, no more misunderstandings and slanders. Why should she not be merry? There were many jokes, much laughter, perhaps singing, too, as they rolled through towns with such musical names as Alcolea, Lora, Palma, Posadas, Almodóvar del Río, and Córdoba.

On June 15 they stopped at Malagón, and found the nuns so unhappy in their badly situated house that La Madre seriously thought of discontinuing it, but changed her mind. There was some confusion and much shrieking and laughter one day outside an inn when a large salamander suddenly scrawled upon her arm under her tunic. She probably screamed, as any woman would. Gallant brother Lorenzo plucked it off and cast it away. It landed smack on the mouth of Alonzo Ruiz. Teresa wrote a vivid account of this in a long letter to Father Gracián, remarking especially on the coach, the kindness of Lorenzo and the luxury of traveling at any hour they pleased; together with a little motherly advice on his work and health.[43] The journey continued until, after fifteen days on the road, she entered the grim and lordly city of Toledo, where she imagined she would find not only seclusion, but rest.

---

[42] *Fundaciones*, cap. XXV.
[43] Letter of June 15, 1576, B.M.C., I, p. 237; Stanbrook, I, p. 274.

Chapter XXIX

TERESA IN "PRISON" AT TOLEDO

E L GRECO had been living for a year in Toledo, and his famous painting of a storm gathering over "the gloomy rock on which the gold and violet clusters of palaces, mansions, minarets, and campaniles glows and mellows," as Father Bruno calls it,[1] might have been a symbol and a prophecy of the clash of human and diabolical passions soon to burst above the sexagenarian head of an apostle of love and peace. For Teresa was about to be the center of a conflict almost unprecedented even in the history of the Catholic Church, the beleaguered City of God on earth; a conflict that would rage from Madrid to Rome and back again, from Philip II to obscure little hamlets and convents, pitting Order against Order, friend against friend, making even good men seem (and sometimes act) like demons, and refining, in the indispensable crucible of suffering, the souls of saints. Had she not asked to share the life of Christ on earth? Had she not desired to be mocked, scourged, despised, neglected, bruised, and crucified with His Majesty? Did not Father John of the Cross, on the day of his first Mass, beg two favors: (1) never to commit a mortal sin; (2) to do penance for the sins he might have committed but for the saving grace of God? Prayers from such brave sincere hearts had to be answered! This must be the key to some of those mysterious and often inexplicable conflicts, misunderstandings, and rivalries in the ranks of Catholics. What looks on the surface like the unwisdom of the children of light, if not their incredible stupidity and perversity, may be the evidence of an intense cleansing of the human dross in the mystical body of the Word that leaped from heaven to be the very incarnation of crucifixion and resurrection.

Christlike suffering always has a joy in its heart. Even in crucifixion the Christian soul has a foretaste of resurrection. In its greatest rejoicings it never quite forgets the central paradoxical mystery of the Cross. It was fitting then, that these years of Teresa's retirement should include all the extremes of anguish, and of the highest spiritual exultation.

On the crucifixion side were disappointment, defeat, misun-

---

[1] *Saint John of the Cross* (New York, 1936), p. 162.

derstanding, slander. She had to put off two promising suggestions for new foundations, one from Villanueva de la Jara, the
other from a Jesuit father in Burgos. Her letters to Rubeo had
failed. Malicious gossip converted her journey from Sevilla to
Toledo with Lorenzo and Teresita into an orgy with glittering
damsels and gay cavaliers; even Fray Angel de Salazar believed
it, and was angry. Her enemies said she was planning to establish convents in America. "I have been amused to hear that they
have got me going to the Indies," she wrote to María de San
José. "God forgive them, the best they can do is to say so much
all together, for then people will believe nothing."[2]

Her health that summer was better than it had been in many
years. "I have a pretty cell, with a window looking out on the
garden."[3] Before Christmas, however, she was "out of sorts"
again, following a long fast which began with the Feast of the
Exaltation of the Holy Cross, September 14, and ended with the
following Lent. By February she was quite ill, but recovered in
a few weeks. Then, for the next year or two she had terrific noises
in her head, and was often unable to write. Yet "I think this
sickness is going to be a good thing," she confided to Lorenzo,
"for I am beginning to learn how to write with a secretary."[4]
When she tried to use her own pen, the noises increased.

On the advice of Father Yanguas, O.P., of Segovia, she chose
as her confessor Fray Diego de Yepes, prior of the Jeronymite
monastery of La Sisla, near Toledo. For a time he went regularly
to hear her confessions, then gradually discontinued his visits.
Teresa and the Prioress were mystified, nor could the priest give
any explanation except that he seemed always to be prevented
by some superior power from going. One day in prayer La Madre
learned from our Lord that it was He Himself who detained
Father Yepes because He desired a different confessor for her —
Doctor Velázquez, canon of the Cathedral. Teresa obeyed, on
the advice of Father Gaspar de Salazar, S.J., and managed to do
so without giving offense to Yepes.

For a long while she had had no raptures (though many visions
and other divine favors), but in January, 1577, they returned
with vehemence. "It does not do to resist," she told Lorenzo,
"nor can it be hidden. It leaves me so ashamed that I should like

---

[2] *Epistolario*, I, p. 370; Stanbrook, I, 145, letter of November 26, 1576.
[3] To Lorenzo, July 26, 1576. *Epistolario*, I, 256.
[4] *Ibid.*, February 27 or 28, 1576. *Epistolario*, II, 256.

to stow myself I don't know where. I pray enough to God to free me of this in public; you ask Him too, for it brings many inconveniences with it, and I don't think it is a higher form of prayer. I go about these days like a drunkard in some ways."[5] One day at Matins she remained enraptured so long that Sister Juana del Espíritu Santo had to lead her back to her cell. When she came to herself she said she had made such an effort to prevent the rapture that all her bones ached as if broken. Sometimes when the bell rang for prayer she would shut herself up in the cell and remain two or three hours, silent; if anyone called, she would not reply.[6] Another time the Sacristan found her leaning against a wall, as rigid as stone.

Except in such exquisitely tormenting hours she went about the ordinary duties of a nun so humbly, cheerfully, and perfectly that all the others tried to imitate her. She felt apologetic about having a roof over her head, because Christ had had none. She wore old torn habits, which she carefully patched and darned and kept scrupulously clean, nor could she hide her displeasure if she saw anyone wearing a soiled one; however, the older the better, and she especially liked to wear one that another sister had discarded. Ribera, who knew her and many of the nuns, believed that "the great cleanliness of her soul seemed to have communicated itself to her body," for it was often noticed that toques and tunics she had worn did not have any odor of perspiration, as others did, but retained "a good and agreeable fragrance."[7]

She hated to be idle. If she was not spinning, she was reeling or winding what others had spun, or something of the sort. Even when she went to the grille to converse with confessors or with other "grave" persons — and she was constantly being consulted on spiritual and other problems — she took along some sewing or knitting to do while talking and listening; and she remarked that one excellent thing about enclosed grilles was that they made it possible both to carry on business and to keep one's hands occupied. One of her objections to the books that directors made her write from time to time was that they interfered with her spinning.

Father Gracián had ordered her to finish the book of her

---

[5] To Lorenzo, January 17, 1577. B.M.C., *Ep.*, II, p. 28; Stanbrook, II, p. 215.
[6] So Sister Juana testified: *informaciones de Toledo.*
[7] *Vida*, lib. IV, cap. XIX.

foundations as soon as possible, and to make it tasty — *"sabrosa."*
She had stopped at the end of the account of Alba de Tormes.
Now, working a little at a time — usually early in the morning
and late at night — she bought it down through Segovia, Beas,
and Sevilla to the end of Caravaca (chapter 27).

On the last day of October she reported to Father Gracián,
"The *Foundations* are nearing the end. I believe you will be
glad when you see them, for it is a tasty thing.[8] See whether I
obey well! . . . I don't know how I have had time for what I have
written, and I didn't fail to have some for Joseph,[9] who gives
me strength for everything."

Two weeks later: "It is finished today, the eve of Saint
Eugenius, on the fourteenth day of November, MDLXXVI, in
the monastery of San Josef de Toledo. . . . For love of our Lord, I
beg the sisters and brothers who read this to commend me to our
Lord, that He may have mercy on me, and deliver me from the
pains of purgatory, and let me enjoy Him, if I shall have merited
to be in Him. Since you are not to see it while I am living, may
I have some gain after my death from the weariness I have had
in writing this, and the great desire I have had while writing to
try to say something that will give you consolation, if they should
be willing to let you read it."[10]

A few months later she was hard at work writing *The Interior
Castle and Mansions.* This masterpiece of analysis and exposi-
tion, this crowning arch of the great trilogy on mental prayer
that began with the *Autobiography* and continued through *The
Way of Perfection,* owed its genesis, in the opinion of Father
Gracián, to a suggestion made by him. When they were discussing some question of mystical theology one day, La Madre said,
"Oh, how well that point is written in the book of my life, which
is in the Inquisition!" Gracián replied, "Since we cannot have
it, make a note of what you remember of it and of other things,
and write another book. . . ." When it was finished, he and
Father Yanguas read it over in her presence and pointed out
certain parts that were *malsonantes.*[11] Afterwards he had the
impertinence, as La Fuente rightly calls it, to cross out words,
phrases, and sentences and to substitute in his own handwriting

---

[8] *"Porque es cosa sabrosa."*
[9] Our Lord, in the code. *Epistolario,* I, p. 333; Stanbrook, II, 101.
[10] *Fundaciones,* end of cap. XXVII.
[11] MS. note to Ribera's *Vida de Santa Teresa,* lib. IV, cap. V

what he considered more fitting ones, though Fray Luis de León, who first edited the works of Teresa, found them invariably inferior to hers, which he restored; though he was not so scrupulous about her expressions in praise of the Jesuits!

The effrontery of her director becomes even less understandable in face of all the evidence that this *magnum opus* was written under the direct inspiration of God. Though the occasion may have been furnished by Gracián, the germ of the idea had long been in her mind. Possibly it began years before in a meditation on the words of Christ, "In my Father's house are many mansions."[12] In the last chapter of her *Autobiography* she had set down this thought: "Let us say that the Divinity is like a very clear diamond, much larger than all the world, or a mirror . . . only it is so in such a far loftier manner that I would not know how to exaggerate it; and that all that we do is seen in this diamond, being of such sort that it includes everything in itself, for there is nothing that can go beyond this grandeur. A fearful thing it was to me to see in so short a time so many things together in this clear diamond, and the saddest thing each time I remembered having seen that things as foul as were my sins represented themselves in that cleanness of clarity,[13] and a most piteous thing, too, whenever I think of it, to see such foul things as my sins present in the pure brilliancy of that light."[14] And in *The Way of Perfection* she foreshadowed even more plainly the thesis of *The Interior Castle and Mansions:*

"Then let us consider that within us there is a palace of the greatest richness, all its edifice of gold and precious stones, in short, as if for such a Lord; and you are the one to see that this edifice be such as in truth it really is, for there is no edifice of such beauty as a soul clean and full of virtues, and the greater, the more the stones glow; and that in this palace is this great King, who has thought well of being our Father, and that He is on a throne of the utmost price, which is your heart."[15]

Nevertheless she was dismayed when Gracián told her to write another book. "Why do they want me to write?" she cried. "Let learned men write, who have studied, for I am a fool and won't know what I am saying: I will use one word in place of another,

[12] John 14:2.

[13] This last beautiful untranslatable phrase of Teresa is *"en aquella limpieza de claridad." — Vida,* cap. XL.

[14] *Ibid.*

[15] *Camino,* cap. 28, B.M.C., Valladolid MS., p. 132.

and I will do harm. There are plenty of books on matters of prayer. For the love of God, I wish they would let me spin my flax, follow my choir and duties of religion, like the other sisters, for I am not fit for writing, nor have I health nor head for it."[16] Father Gracián then told her to leave the decision to her confessor, Doctor Velázquez, who ordered her to write the book.

While she was casting about for a suitable form, she had a vision in which this old conception was presented more powerfully and in greater detail. She told Father Yepes how, on the eve of Trinity Sunday, 1577, God had showed her, in a flash, the whole book. It was "a most beautiful gold crystal like a castle in which she saw seven mansions, and in the seventh, which was in the center of it, the King of Glory in the greatest splendor, Who from there beautified and illuminated all those dwellings to the outside of the castle, where the inhabitants received the more light the nearer they were to the center, which was the royal palace where the King was. And she saw that this light did not pass beyond it, but outside of it all was shadows, and the habitat of frogs, vipers, and other animals that were venomous; and while she was admiring this beauty which the Lord communicated to souls from the center, the light suddenly went out, and although the King of Glory did not leave the castle, the crystal was covered with darkness, and remained as ugly and blackened as a coal, with a stench insufferable, and the door was open so that the poisonous animals outside could come in, and this was the state in which the soul remained when it was in mortal sin."[17]

Through this vision, adds Yepes, our Lord revealed to her four things: (1) That God is in all things. An ignorant priest had disturbed her by denying this, saying He was in us only by grace, but Yepes reassured her one day in Toledo. (2) She understood the malice of sin, for since God does not absent Himself from the sinful soul, but remains infinitely present in it, by reason of His immensity, the sin can prevent the splendor of His glory from communicating itself to that soul, and with it all the attendant blessings and treasures. (3) She learned profound humility and self-knowledge, for thereafter she saw that all the beauty of the soul came from His beauty and all virtue

---

[16] Cf. Mir, *Vida de Santa Teresa*, II, 445, and his references.

[17] Yepes, *Vida de Santa Teresa*, lib. II. cap. XX: see also his paraphrase of this in a letter to Fray Luis de León, as translated by Father Zimmerman in his introduction to the revised Stanbrook edition of *The Interior Castle*, p. 17.

from His virtue and power, and all knowledge from His immense wisdom, so that we have little part in the good that is in
us, save by the help of the King. (4) She was moved to obey
Father Gracián's order to write *"El Castillo Interior y Moradas"*[18] — the very title of which our Lord gave her.[19] Teresa told
her future biographer that a flash of light had penetrated her
understanding, so that in the twinkling of an eye she understood "more truths about the highest things of God than if great
theologians had taught her for a thousand years."[20]

So she set to work, and completed the whole marvelous book
in five months' time, writing the *finis* on the eve of Saint Andrew, November 29[21] — though the actual writing time was not
more than four weeks. Never was any book more strangely, more
rapidly composed. One night a nun, waiting at the door of her
cell to give her some message, saw golden rays of light coming
from her face, while she wrote until midnight with tremendous
velocity, covering page after page. When she stopped, the ordinary candlelight, or whatever it was, seemed like darkness in
comparison. Then the watching sister saw her kneel and extend
her arms as if on a cross, and thus she remained, motionless, "for
three hours and more."[22]

Mother María del Nacimiento, who was superior at Toledo in
1577, reported seeing Teresa enraptured over a blank tablet on
which she was about to write; and when she came to herself, the
paper was covered with her vigorous nervous writing. Teresa's
readiness to praise this work more than any of her others came,
no doubt, from her sense that God was the real author, and she
only an amanuensis, who had written it down with comparatively little trouble, as she acknowledged at the end. This jewel,
she wrote Father Gaspar de Salazar, S.J., in a delightful piece of
third-person self-criticism, was better in many ways than the
other one (her autobiography): "for it deals with nothing, except
what is He . . . and with more exquisite enamels and designs; for
she says she was not as well acquainted then with the silversmith

---

[18] *"The Interior Castle and Mansions."* In spite of this editors have insisted on
calling it *"The Interior Castle," "The Mansions," "The Interior Castle or The
Mansions,"* etc.

[19] Yepes, *loc. cit.*

[20] *Ibid.*

[21] Mir tells us (*op. cit.*, II, p. 446) that the date when she finished the book is
unknown, though she clearly gave it at the end of the MS.

[22] Sister Ana de la Encarnación, later Prioress of Granada, as a witness for the
canonization, in Mir, *op. cit.*, II, 447.

who made it, and this is gold of the very highest perfection,
although the stones are not so noticeable at first view as in the
other one. It was made by order of the Glassmaker, and it looks
fine, so they say."[23]

If ever there was a book with the stamp of divinity upon it, it
is *The Interior Castle and Mansions*. In lucidity and sublimity,
in the harmonious marriage of thought, feeling, and phrase it
has been compared to the *Paradiso* of Dante. The plan is as carefully and symmetrically worked out as his, the effect more powerful and unforgettable. Poets have praised its jewel-like similes,
and Thomists have found it in accord at every point with the
lofty teaching of Saint Thomas. Teresa had learned a great deal
about writing since the *Camino,* and even more since the
ponderous, involved, and repetitious paragraphs that clothed the
lovely gems of the Autobiography. Here all is concise, vigorous,
coherent, inevitable.

Where is God to be found? she asks, in effect. And going back
to the illuminating thesis she had got from Fray Francisco de
Osuna's *Tercer Abecedario* the year she went to Becedas,[24] she
answers confidently, "within ourselves."

The human soul, then, is like a beautiful castle, containing
many mansions, in the very center of which the Divine Majesty
is enthroned. Souls in mortal sin cannot enter the palace, but
remain outside among the foul crawling things — servants of the
devil, blackened in their living death, incapable of producing
any good. It was once revealed to her in a vision that anyone
who realized the effects of mortal sin would endure all conceivable torments rather than commit one. These unfortunates are
excluded forever, unless of course they repent and are forgiven.
The castle is entered only by those in a state of grace, and
through the gate of prayer and meditation.

1. In the first mansion are those who, though free from mortal
sin, are deeply entangled in the cares and vanities of the world,
"think about their souls every now and then," pray a few times
a month, and are followed into the building by reptiles that disturb their peace and keep them from seeing its beauty.

2. Here are souls who have begun to have the self-knowledge
necessary for progress, and to practise prayer. They hear our
Lord calling them, through sermons, good works, or words of

---

[23] Dec. 7, 1577, *Epist.,* II, p. 136; Stanbrook, III, 9.
[24] Cf. *supra,* chapter IV.

pious people, through sickness and trouble, yet they do not avoid the occasions of sin, they commit venial sins, and they are fiercely attacked by the devil, so that they suffer more than those in the first mansion — all the more so if the devil sees they are capable of great spiritual progress, for then all hell will league together to stop them. They must associate with spiritual persons, especially with more advanced ones, and resolve never to submit to defeat, but to embrace the Cross of Christ as an invincible weapon, with no ignoble thought of rewards, and to conform their will to the will of God.

3. Now we come to those who try to avoid even venial sins, who love penance, give hours to meditation, spend their time well, perform acts of charity, govern their households well if they have any, are well ordered in dress and conversation. Yet, like the rich young man in the gospel,[25] they still love themselves so much they cannot yet embrace the lonely way to perfection, they are not yet beyond the danger of following that chosen youth who "went away sorrowful, for he had great possessions." Here through our faults we learn the indispensable virtue of humility, which is more necessary even than penance and mortifications. Teresa knew many souls who reached this third mansion and remained there, apparently contented, for many years; yet even under moderate trials they sometimes grew fearful and disheartened, and having practised virtue so long, they felt no need of advice from others. It was no use arguing with them; they thought their conduct holy, and wanted others to agree with them. A person who had enough to live on, and still strove to gain more and more property, could not possibly enter the mansions near the King, however good his intentions and his life; nor could those who could not endure contempt or want of respect. Their penances were as well regulated as their households; they would never be indiscreet in their mortifications, lest they injure their health. "Have no fear that they will kill themselves." Those in this mansion who wish to go further should practise prompt obedience. Even if not in the religious state, they should choose a director, and follow his will implicitly — and not a prudent person after their own minds, but one wholly detached from worldly things. Unless they go forward, they are still in danger of returning, under persecution or temptation, to the first mansions.

---

[25] Matt. 19:21.

4. The fourth mansion is on a distinctly higher plane, and so full of subtle beauties that it is impossible to explain them to those who have not experienced them. The poisonous reptiles rarely enter here, and if they do, they do more good than harm, for the souls are so solidly established in grace that temptations usually make them stronger. Here the prayer of quiet is experienced and with it *sensible* devotion and sweetness, such as Teresa first felt when she began to weep over the Passion and could not stop until she had a severe headache. It is not so important here to *think* much as to *love* much, and this consists not so much in greater sweetness of devotion as in the greater determination to try to please God in everything, "and to endeavor, so far as we can, not to offend Him, and to ask Him that the honor and glory of His Son and the growth of the Catholic Church may always go forward. These are the signs of love, and do not think it is the thing not to think of anything else, and that if your thoughts wander a little, everything is going to ruin."[26]

All involuntary distractions are to be ignored. For example, said Teresa, "while writing this, I am thinking of what is going on in my head from the great noise of it, as I said in the beginning, which makes it almost impossible for me to do what they commanded me to write. It seems as if there were nothing in it but many swollen rivers, and on the other hand that these waters were rushing over a precipice; many little songbirds and whistles, and not in my ears, but in the upper part of the head, where they say is the upper part of the soul.[27] And I have been thinking for quite a long time that [it is because] the great upward movement of the spirit increases with velocity . . .[28] and it will not be anything much if the Lord has wished to give me this head trouble, to understand it better: for with all its hurly-burly, it doesn't hinder me from prayer or from what I am now saying,

[26] *Cuartas Moradas,* cap. I, pp. 48–49.

[27] She may be alluding to Saint Augustine's distinction (*De Trin.,* XIII) between the "higher part" of the reason, intent upon things eternal, and the "lower part," addressing itself to things temporal. Saint Thomas holds that this does not imply two different "powers" of the soul, but merely two different functions. "The lower reason is said to flow from the higher . . . as far as the principles made use of by the lower reason are drawn from and directed by the principles of the higher reason." — *Summa Theol.,* I, q. 79, a. 9.

[28] *Y yo estuve en esto harto tiempo, por parecer que el movimiento grande del espiritu hacia riba subia con velocidad.* Father Silverio says she wrote *riba* for *arriba,* for the sake of euphony. The Stanbrook translation is "I have long thought that this must be so because the flight of the spirit seems to take place from this part with great velocity" (*Interior Castle,* p. 95).

but my soul stays quite complete in its quiet and love and desires and clear understanding . . . and so it is not well that we should trouble ourselves over our thoughts, or pay any attention to them; for if the devil suggests them, it will cease with this; and if it is, as it is, from the misery that remains with us from the sin of Adam, with many others, let us have patience and suffer it for the love of God; since we are also subject to eating and sleeping, without being able to avoid it, which is trouble enough."[29]

5. This is the mansion of the prayer of union. Once more she attempts to explain how this differs from the prayer of quiet. The prayer of quiet seems to touch only the surface of the body, that of union to penetrate to the very marrow. Genuine union is beyond the interference of the devil. The test of it is that while it lasts the senses of seeing, hearing, and understanding are suspended, that God's presence is so manifested that it cannot be doubted, and that the effects are always to increase devotion, detachment, humility, love of God and our neighbor. She distinguishes between various kinds of union, all of which are beyond human power to achieve, a free gift of God. This state is like the preliminaries to a betrothal, a visit to discuss what is to come.

6. Souls in this mansion suffer more than before, but enjoy greater favors. She enumerates some of the afflictions, as she herself endured them, and describes a more than compensating prayer that wounds the soul with exquisite burning love. Here as elsewhere she distinguishes carefully between the false and the true. The divine communications carry power and authority with them; such words as "It is I, be not afraid" will give the soul a *certainty* of being freed from all fears and troubles, and leave joy, peace, and virtue, while locutions proceeding from the imagination or melancholy bring no conviction, peace, or interior joy. Trances, raptures, and ecstasies are all essentially the same. She describes and analyzes them with masterly precision. In true rapture even the breathing sometimes ceases. No one who wishes to understand what raptures are should fail to read this chapter; she covered the subject so completely and admirably that John of the Cross, with all his knowledge of it, said it would be superfluous to include it in his own works. In this man-

---

[29] *Cuartas Moradas*, cap. I. This passage suggests the point of separation between the Catholic Church and Manichaeism, and why Saint Teresa was suspected of being an Illuminate. She would *conquer* involuntary evil thoughts by disregarding them; the Illuminati would make them voluntary bv *surrendering* to them.

sion the soul laments her past sins. In every mansion it is necessary to meditate on the Sacred Humanity of Christ, especially in the Passion. The desire to die and to see God is sometimes so strong as to endanger health and even life. Here the soul is *betrothed* to God, with indescribable joys and trials.

7. This is the most interesting part of the book, not only because it describes the loftiest spiritual experiences known to a human being, but because of its biographical value, for Teresa herself had certainly reached the sublime stage in this, the sixty-second year of her life;[30] and never, perhaps, since the letters of Saint Paul, has a more remarkable personal record been penned. Here the soul enjoys nothing less than a marriage to the Divinity. Previously, in the prayer of union our Lord had united the spirit to Himself by making it blind and dumb, to prevent it from knowing how or why it has such supreme delight. Now He removes the scales from her eyes, letting her see and understand something in an intellectual vision. The Three Persons of the Most Blessed Trinity reveal themselves, following a mysterious illumination that bathes the soul in light. A sublime knowledge is infused into her. What she held by faith, she now understands, so to speak, by sight, though not by the eyes of the body or of the soul. The Three Persons never depart. The effect of this presence is to make the soul far more active in all that concerns God's service. She improves in all the virtues. At last comes spiritual marriage, in which God appears in the very center of the soul, not by an imaginary but by an intellectual vision far more mysterious and sublime than before.

To make clear the difference between spiritual betrothal and spiritual marriage, Teresa resorts again to similes. The union of betrothal may be symbolized by two wax candles whose flames mingle and become one, yet can be separated again. But spiritual marriage is "as if water is falling from the sky into a river or fountain, where it remains all one water, which they can no longer divide, or distinguish which is the water of the river, which fell from the sky; or as if a little brook enters the sea, there will be no way to separate them; or as if in a room there were two windows through which great light enters; although it enters

---

[30] She admitted as much in a letter to María de San José, November 8, 1581; and her mystical marriage had occurred, as we have seen, in 1572. For another remarkable account of "Spiritual Marriage" see Saint John of the Cross, *Spiritual Canticle,* translated from Father Silverio's critical edition by Mr. E. Allison Peers, London, 1934, p. 140.

divided, it is made all one light. Perhaps this is what Saint Paul spoke of: 'He who is joined to and arrives at God, is made one spirit with Him,'[31] referring to this sovereign matrimony, which supposes His Majesty to have come to the soul by union — and he also says: '*Mihi vivere Christus est, mori lucrum.*' This I think the soul can say here, for this is where the little moth we have spoken of dies, and with the very greatest joy, for her life now is Christ."[32]

This marriage has the following effects on the soul: (1) a self-forgetfulness so complete that she appears not to exist; (2) a stronger desire for suffering, with joy when persecuted, and such love of enemies that she grieves at seeing them in trouble and does all she can to relieve them; (3) a desire of serving God and making others do so, instead of a wish to die; (4) a desire to be always alone or occupied on what benefits others. Here ecstasies — and Teresa was astonished to discover this — become rare, and even then they are not like former trances and "the flight of the spirit," and seldom occur in public. Finally (she is always returning to this thought) these high favors were given to help men to imitate Christ, hence they always produce a more intensely active life. It was always those nearest to Christ who bore the heaviest crosses. His Mother, for example, and the Apostles.

"How do you think Saint Paul could suffer such very great trials? We can see by him what effects true visions and contemplation produce, when it is from our Lord, and not imagination or deceit of the devil. Did he perhaps hide himself away with those delights to enjoy them, and pay attention to nothing else? Now you see it: he did not take a day of rest, so far as we know, and he must have taken just as little by night, for then he had to earn his living. . . .[33] This is what prayer is for, my daughters, this is what this spiritual matrimony is for: to bring forth always works, works.

"This is the real proof of its being a thing and favor performed by God; for it does me little good to be very recollected all by myself, making acts with our Lord, proposing and promising to do marvels for His service, if going out of there, when the occasion offers I do just the opposite. . . . I should have said that it is

---

[31] 1 Cor. 6:17. The Douay version gives, "But he who is joined to the Lord, is one spirit."
[32] *Sétimas Moradas*, cap. II, p. 187.
[33] 1 Thess. 2:9.

little in comparison with the much there is when works conform
to acts and words, and that which cannot be done all at once
may be done little by little. . . . Fix your eyes on the Crucified,
and all will be made easy for you. . . . Do you know what it is to
be truly spiritual? To make yourselves slaves of God . . . branded
with His iron, which is that of the cross. . . . And unless you
make up your minds, never fear that you will progress much, for
all this edifice, as I have said, has humility for its cement, and if
you haven't that, our Lord, even for your own good, will not let
you raise it very high, lest it all fall upon the ground."[34]

As examples of action proceeding from contemplation she
cites the works of Elias, Saints Francis and Dominic, and the terrible penances by which Saint Mary Magdalen paid for her
former life of luxury. Both Mary and Martha were necessary,
but Mary had the better part, and paid dearly for it — she was
not always sitting in contemplation at the feet of our Lord.

"And do you think it would be a small mortification for a lady
such as she was to go through those streets, and perhaps alone,
for she did not worry about how she went, and to enter where
she had never before entered, and afterwards to endure the back-
biting of the Pharisee, and many other things that she must
have suffered? For to see a woman like her make such a change
in public, and as we know, among such wicked people,[35] who
needed only to see that she had friendship with our Lord, whom
they held so in abhorrence, to drag out the memory of the life
she had lived, and the fact that she now wanted to lead a holy
one, for it is plain that she must then have changed her clothing
and all the rest; considering what is now said of less renowned
persons, what must it have been then? I tell you, sisters, that the
better part came after plenty of trials and mortifications, and
that even if it were no more than to see her Master so hated, it
was an intolerable trial. And then all those she suffered afterwards in the death of the Lord! I hold for my part that if she did
not receive martyrdom it was because she had suffered it in seeing the Lord die; and in the years she lived, in seeing herself
absent from Him, which must have been a terrible torment, you
see she was not always in the joy of contemplation at the feet of
the Lord! . . ."[36]

---

[34] *Sétimas Moradas.*

[35] *"Entre tan mala gente."*

[36] *Ibid.* Mary Magdalen lived for thirty-two years in a cave in a barren place
near Marseilles, according to St. Vincent Ferrer.

She concludes with some advice of more than contemporary relevance:

"Sometimes the devil proposes to us great desires, so that we shall not put our hand to what we have in hand, and serve our Lord in possible things, but stay content with having desired impossible ones. Granting that you help much in prayer, don't try to benefit all the world, but those who are in your company, and so the work will be better, for you are much bounden to them. . . . Do you say that they don't need to be converted, for they are all good women? What business is that of yours?[37] Well, the better they may be, the more agreeable will be their praises to the Lord, and the more their prayer will benefit those nearest them. In short, *hermanas mías*, what I would conclude with is that we must not build towers without foundations, for the Lord does not look so much to the grandeur of our works as to the love with which they are done; and if we do all we can, His Majesty will see to it that we are able to do more and more every day, if we do not then grow weary, and during the little that this life lasts — and perhaps it will be shorter than each one thinks — we offer to the Lord, inwardly and outwardly, what sacrifice we can, for His Majesty will join it with the one He made to the Father for us on the Cross, that it may have the value which our will would have merited, even though our works may be small."[38]

Here Teresa was setting forth not only the Carmelite ideal, but the actuality realized in the convents she had founded — the primitive Christian life restored, as Fray Luis de León called it. And was she not a living example of the fruition of prayer and rapture in good works? Her activity at this time was almost incredible. Read her correspondence; notice the vast number of persons whose affairs she followed with penetrating interest and love — not to mention the communities she directed so skillfully and watchfully. She had time, or made time, to write her old friend the Holy Cavalier, now Father Salcedo, consoling him for the loss of a large part of his fortune, which he took surprisingly to heart considering what a man of prayer he had been. She sent someone shopping for the Very Magnificent Señor Antonio de Soria, who had forwarded a hundred *reales* for the pur-

---

[37] "*¿Quién os mete en eso?*" p. 207.
[38] *Ibid.*, p. 208.

chase of a bed, some green damask, and other articles.[39] She found the keenest delight in the progress of the two child novices, her niece Teresita, and Gracián's little sister Isabelita; she described them, compared them, prayed for them, and reported regularly on their progress. She stoutly maintained the charms of Isabelita against Mother María de San José, who preferred Teresita, and she was so anxious to have the poor child perfect that she even tried to change the shape and expression of her mouth, which was too prim, especially when she laughed. La Madre would tell her to close it, to open it, to stop laughing. "She says it is not her fault, but her mouth's, and she speaks the truth."[40] This child took the habit November 26, 1576, at the age of ten, by special dispensation. Both the little angels became great lights of the Reform, and prioresses of Discalced convents.

Many of Teresa's longest and most delightful letters are addressed to her brother Lorenzo. Pages from the heart, written for his eyes alone, they furnish invaluable portrayals of both brother and sister in the last years of their lives. Lorenzo is in Avila, placing his boys under the care of the Jesuits, as Teresa advised. He must beware of childish Juan de Ovalle, who has written her a long letter of exaggerated affection for him, but is really jealous of him.[41] "I pity my sister deeply," said Teresa, "but we all have much to suffer."[42] Lorenzo's health is beginning to fail, now that he is back in his own land; in September, 1576, he has a sharp illness, a warning of what is to happen four years later. He begins to pay more attention to his soul, and on her advice consults the Jesuit rector at Avila, and Father Muñoz, S.J. He needs the money he lent the nuns at Sevilla, and Teresa repeatedly writes María de San José urging payment. In October, 1576, he buys an estate at La Serna, consisting of a house, farm lands, and woods, where he plans a serene retirement for his old age.[43] The two are always exchanging gifts. When he is ill she sends him quinces for his cook to make into jam, and a pot of marmalade, which is very cheap in Toledo.[44] He sends her some fish, packed in a pastry, before Christmas,[45] and sweets at various times. She

[39] See her letter to him, end of 1576.
[40] To María de San José, January, 1577, B.M.C., *Ep.*, II, p. 24.
[41] Letter of July 24, 1576.
[42] *Ibid.*
[43] Letter of October 5, 1576, to María de San José.
[44] To Lorenzo, July 24, 1576.
[45] To Lorenzo, January 2, 1577.

sends him some Christmas carols "without either feet or head," reproaches him for not sending one of his own, and quotes to him all she remembers of another poem she has composed, commencing:

> Oh Hermosura que ecedéis
> A todas las hermosuras!
> Sin herir dolor hacéis,
> Y sin dolor deshacéis
> El amor de las criaturas,[46]

and adds, after three stanzas, "I don't remember any more. What a brain for a foundress!" She asks for some sardines for days of abstinence, for fresh eggs are not obtainable in Toledo. She asks him to send her a seal, for she is using one with a death's head on it, which she cannot endure, and she wants one with J.H.S., the name "of the one that I should like to have on my heart, as it was on that of Saint Ignatius."[47]

Naturally it is the soul of Lorenzo that commands her most ardent attention. She has begun to teach him mental prayer, as she taught it long ago to their father, and he is making great progress. He has begun to experience the trials of the purgative way, but generally God is leading him through love, and not through fear as is the case with Father Francisco de Salcedo, who is suffering from melancholy and scruples, she says, and must be treated very kindly. Lorenzo is inclined to be fond of display, and must mortify himself in that regard. Gradually he begins to do more and more penance. He goes without sleep, until Teresa insists that he must get at least six hours a night. "We who are getting old must take care of our bodies lest they weaken the intellect, which is a terrible trial"[48] — this at a time when she herself has a headache from writing letters until two or three in the morning!

The devil has begun to trouble Lorenzo with impure thoughts, but he is to pay no attention to them, since they are not volun-

---

[46] *Ibid:*

> O Beauty, that doth far transcend
> All other beauty! Thou dost reign
> Without a wound, our hearts to pain —
> Without a pang our wills to bend
> To hold all love for creatures vain.
> — Stanbrook translation, *Letters,* II, 199.

[47] *Ibid.*

[48] To Lorenzo, February 10, 1577.

tary; let him keep some holy water by him, and scatter it all around, for the devil will not go unless it touches him — he cannot endure that.[49] Lorenzo wants to give up all luxuries, but she advises him not to part with his plate and rugs, for God expects everyone to live according to his state in life. He has already begun to regret purchasing La Serna, and to wish that he had bought an annuity instead. Teresa, aware that the curse of Spain is the desire to get rich by investment, assures him it is much better to cultivate the land,[50] thus giving his sons honor instead of riches, and she does not want him to take up sheep breeding for profit.[51] Thus contemplatives have their effect even on the so-called practical affairs of nations! Spain might never have experienced her economic decline if more of the *hidalgos* had taken Teresa's advice.

A useful little treatise on prayer could be culled from these letters to Lorenzo. Let him not imagine that if he were free from the cares of his estate, he would pray more. Time well spent, as in looking after his children's inheritance, does not hinder prayer. On January 17, 1577, she sends him a hair shirt to arouse greater love for God in him; he can wear it on any part of the body, so long as it feels uncomfortable — [52] but not after he is dressed for the day, or when he is asleep; and she adds, "Write me how you get on with this little toy. For such it is, I tell you, when we wish to give ourselves some just punishments, remembering what our Lord suffered. I am laughing, for you send me candy, presents, and money, and I send you hair shirts."[53]

The following month she insists that he leave the shirt off if it makes him ill, and on no account wear it more than once a week in Lent, for he is too sanguine to wear it oftener; nor must he take a discipline oftener than twice a week, for it hurts the eyesight. It is a greater penance to be moderate in mortifications at first, for it breaks one's will.[54] At the end of February she sends him another hair shirt, evidently a less grievous one, and bids him wear it for the present instead of the other. She encloses a

---

[49] *Ibid.*
[50] To Lorenzo, January 2, 1577.
[51] Great poverty resulted in England from the avarice of the newly rich, who turned small farmers off the confiscated Church lands to make money raising sheep.
[52] Letter, January 17, 1577.
[53] *Ibid.*
[54] To Lorenzo, February 10, 1577.

hair shirt and a very hard discipline as presents for Teresita, who has asked for them; "give them to her with my love." As for Lorenzo, he must follow instructions very carefully. If the hair shirt reaches all round him, he must wear a piece of linen under it, next to his stomach, to prevent injury; and if it hurts his health in any way, he is to give it up. "God desires your health, and that you should obey, more than your penance." He must not fasten it too tightly over the shoulders. Nor must he wear it every day, for then one becomes used to it, and it ceases to be such a penance. To help him advance in his prayer, she has him read her *Way of Perfection,* especially the meditation on the *Pater Noster.*[55]

Lorenzo's feelings were somewhat hurt by remarks his sister made about him in her "Vejamen" letter to Bishop Mendoza of Ávila, in January, 1577. The term *"Vejamen"* ("taunt" or "scurrilous criticism") came from a ceremony long in vogue at the University of Alcalá, where a candidate for a doctor's degree was seated on a platform, facing the whole student body, while one professor paid him ridiculously exaggerated compliments in bombastic Castilian verse, and another, in a *Vejamen,* accused him of every conceivable fault and folly. Teresa had consulted several of her friends, including her brother, on the meaning of the words *"Búscate in Mí"* ("Seek thyself in Me") spoken to her by our Lord in prayer. Their explanations were to be laid before the nuns of San José for judgment. Hearing of all this, the Bishop entered into the fun with a command that Madre Teresa write a *Vejamen* in reply. Teresa produced a bantering document which was, as one might expect, both wise and witty, and at times fairly devastating, sparing no one.

She accused Francisco de Salcedo of contradicting himself, quoted King David against him, and added "And the worst of all is that unless he recants I shall have to denounce him to the Inquisition, which is near by. For after going through the whole paper saying 'This is a saying of Saint Paul, and of the Holy Spirit,' he says that he has been writing nonsense. Let the correction be made at once; if not, he will see what will happen."

Julian of Ávila "commences well and finishes badly, and so the glory will not be given to him. For here they don't ask him what he says of uncreated and created light, how they are joined, but how we seek ourselves in God. Nor do we ask him what a

---

[55] Letter of January 2, 1577.

soul feels when it is so united to its Creator; and if it is united to Him, how does it have an opinion as to whether there is a difference or not, since there is no understanding there for these disputes? I think that if there were, the difference between the Creator and the Creature might well be understood! . . . But I pardon him his errors, because he was not so long winded[56] as my Father Fray John of the Cross.

Of Father John she made this tart and rather mysterious criticism:

"He speaks good doctrine enough in his reply, for anyone who wishes to do the exercises they do in the Company of Jesus, but not for our purpose. It would cost dearly if we could not seek God except when we are dead to the world. Not so was the Magdalen, nor the Samaritan woman, nor the woman of Cana, when they found Him. Also he has much to say about making oneself one with God in union; and when this comes to be, and God does this favor to the soul, he will not tell them to seek Him, for He has already been found! God deliver me from people so spiritual that all they want is to make contemplation perfect, cost what it may.[57] With all this, we thank him for having explained so well to us what we do not ask. For that matter, it is well to speak always of God, for profit comes to us from where we did not expect it, as has been the case with the Señor Lorenzo de Cepeda, whom we thank much for his stanzas and reply."

Then came Lorenzo's turn:

"For if he has spoken more than he understands, we pardon him his scanty humility in meddling with matters so lofty, as he says in his reply, for the sake of the amusement he has given us, and for the sake of the good counsel he gives, such as, that people may have the prayer of quiet (as if it were in their hand) — and this without our asking him. Now he knows the penalty incurred by anyone who does this!"

In the end she declined to say which of the answers was best: there were defects in all, all of them overshot the mark.

Much of her correspondence had to do with the convents of the Reform, especially with those of Sevilla, Valladolid, and Malagón.

Judging by the number, length, and charm of the letters, her

---

[56] "No fué tan largo."
[57] "Dé do diere."

favorite prioress must have been María de San José. The convent
at Sevilla had a long series of exasperating troubles, which, according to one of Teresa's revelations, God meant to permit for
the perfecting of His saints there. Their poverty, increased by
the necessity of paying usury on their debts, was sometimes so
stark that they had no money for food, and La Madre insisted
that they borrow for that purpose. They were unable for years
to pay back the loan to Lorenzo. When the nuns made fine
linens which they sent her to sell in Toledo at four *reales* apiece,
she found it impossible to get even that low price in such a
miserly city. In spite of all this, the prioress at Sevilla was always
sending her gifts. When María received a present of forty ducats
from San José of Ávila, she forwarded part of it to La Madre,
whose need was the greater. At various times she sent quinces,
dogfish, oranges, butter cakes, coconuts, orange flower water.
Most of these Teresa gave away to the sick prioress at Malagón,
to Doña Luisa de la Cerda, and to others — all except the orange
flower water, which the nuns at Toledo insisted on her keeping.[58] When she could, she sent gifts in return; but she complained that she had never seen a place so devoid of anything
artistic as Toledo.[59]

She was always giving motherly advice to the scholarly María,
usually on matters of health. More than once she urged avoid-
ance of sarsaparilla water. When María had a fever, she thought
it might be "the *ojo*,[60] which often happens in poor bloods,"
and prescribed fumigation in bed with "sulphurwort, maiden-
hair fern, eggshells, a little resin, and some lavender." (We are
not told what effect this had on the patient.) At times she recommended bleeding; for a cold, gum lozenges with essence of roses.

Now and then she sent advice or reproof on other matters. "I
have received your letter of November 3. I tell you they never
bore me, but they rest me from other boredoms. I am amused
that you write out the date in letters. Please God it may not be
to avoid humiliation by not being able to write the ciphers!
Before I forget: your letter to Father Mariano would be very
good, if you did not drag in that Latin. God deliver all my

---

[58] Letter to María de San José, March 2, 1577.
[59] To the same, May 15, 1577.
[60] Literally, "The eye." Apparently, from the context, a colloquial term for
opilation or chlorosis. Cf. P. Silverio's note 2, *Epistolario*, I, p. 398; Stanbrook,
II, 176.

daughters from boasting to be *latinas*. Never let it happen again, nor consent to it. I would much rather have you boast of seeming to be simpletons, which is more like the saints, and not so rhetorical. This is what you get for forwarding me your letters open."[61]

At Father Gracián's orders, Madre María sent two nuns and a lay sister, Margarita de la Concepción, to reform the Calced convent at Paterna, near Sevilla. There had been some scandals there; La Madre even heard that one of the nuns was an unmarried mother,[62] though she could not believe it: and in fact, the rumor appears to have been false. Still, there was plenty of room for improvement at Paterna, as one gathers from the fact that the three terrified visitors had to take refuge one night in a cupboard under the stairs, while the Calced sisters threatened to break open the door and kill them.[63]

One of the three, the lay sister Margarita de la Concepción, gave no end of trouble to her superiors after her return to Sevilla, by supporting Sister Beatriz de la Madre de Dios (the same, alas, of whom Madre Teresa had written a whole chapter) in a conspiracy that almost wrecked the struggling convent. Beatriz had turned out to be neurotic, had false visions and ecstasies, and imagined herself very holy. A wise confessor might have straightened out the tangle in her emotions, but unfortunately she placed her soul in the hands of the genial, but stupid and suspicious Father Garciálvarez. According to Mother María de San José, the devil put it into the muddled head of this priest to ask the two *beatas*, Beatriz and Margarita, to make general confessions, for which purpose he would keep them in the confessional, sometimes together, sometimes singly, from morning till night. "These confessions went on for three or four months, and when I wished to stop such an excess, he went around to all the convents in Sevilla, getting opinions on whether the prioress could interfere with confessions, and according to what he told them, they gave him signatures, and with each one he became more free, disturbing everything and breaking up the harmony of the house by releasing the nuns from their obedience. When it came to this pass, I informed our Mother so that she could correct it. She

[61] Letter of November 19, 1576.
[62] *"Virgen y parida."*
[63] María de San José, *Libro de Recreaciones* quoted in the Stanbrook letters, I, p. 223, n. 3.

told me to put up with it and dissimulate, for it was not the time to do otherwise, since the Lord had given permission to the demons to torment and afflict us."[64]

Garciálvarez poisoned the clergy of Sevilla against the Prioress to such an extent that none of them would believe her. The two *beatas* and their confessor then made many false charges against her, and even against Gracián and Madre Teresa, until at last, when some Calced visitors came to inspect the convent, they managed to have her removed, and Beatriz appointed in her place. But when the Visitor Fernández and the Provincial Angel de Salazar looked into the matter, they restored Mother María, and had Father Garciálvarez dismissed. The two *beatas* then acknowledged that they had lied and submitted to penance. Beatriz is said to have wept herself blind in sorrow for what she had done.

All this was a sad trial for Madre Teresa, considering the hopes she had had of Sister Beatriz. One of the peculiarities of the case was her defense of Garciálvarez, even after his astonishing folly and malice had been exposed. Her lifelong insistence on the freedom of nuns to choose their own confessors may have had something to do with this. Again, she had had a revelation that the troubles at Sevilla were necessary. Gratitude may have been the deciding factor, for she could not think ill of anyone who had ever done her the slightest service; and had not Garciálvarez saved her from being cheated when buying a house? She was well aware that this virtue in her sometimes became a weakness. "I could be bribed with a sardine," she said. Whatever Garciálvarez had done, he had meant well and must not be judged harshly, she insisted to the end, and even begged María not to dismiss him.

Another of her frequent worries during these years was the relaxation in the convent in Malagón. The Prioress, Brianda, had become consumptive. La Madre's letters are full of tender solicitude for her; she was always sending her fruit, medicines, and advice about her health, and it was seldom that any delicacies came from Sevilla or elsewhere without being shared with her. It was inevitable that under one so ill there should be a deterioration of discipline. Teresa was distressed to hear that the Prioress would tell one nun to punish another by slapping or pinching her. "This invention was imported from up this

[64] *Libro de Recreaciones*, R. IX, in B.M.C., *Epist.*, I, p. 369, n. I.

way," she complained to María de San José, referring perhaps to an abuse that had existed at the Incarnation of Ávila in former days. "I think the devil teaches it, under pretext of perfection. . . . They are not slaves, nor should mortification be for anything except their improvement. I tell you, my daughter, one must constantly watch what these little prioresses do with their heads."[65] Had she not forbidden the nuns, in her Constitutions, even to touch one another? Finally she sent a relative of her own, Sister Beatriz of Jesus, to rule Malagón as subprioress, ostensibly assisting Mother Brianda. As to the administrative qualities of "poor Beatriz," she had no illusions; she frankly admitted sending her "for lack of good men" — alluding to a Castilian proverb, "For lack of good men my husband is mayor."[66]

Illness and poverty hounded the community. "They have neither wheat nor money," said La Madre, "but only a world of debts." When Brianda was sent away, the nuns who had so complained of her began to "adore" her, and to dislike Beatriz. Teresa had expected this; she told their chaplain, Father Gaspar, that spiritually they were in a very elementary state.[67] Gradually, however, discipline and harmony were restored.

In her correspondence with the Prioress at Valladolid (her own niece, who, as María de Ocampo had first suggested the Reform) Teresa manifested an occasional asperity contrasting noticeably with her genial supervision of María de San José. With all her virtues María Bautista could be rather irritating at times. She was too ready with criticisms and suggestions, and one wonders whether she did not presume a little, unconsciously perhaps, on her relationship; perhaps her aunt also took much for granted. La Madre wrote her, "If you could only believe what I say you would not be sick so often. It is true that I didn't insist much in my letter the other day that you should not be bled any more. I don't know what this madness is of yours, even if the doctor does say so."[68] She warned her against a certain fair-weather friend, although to expect any more from people, "we shall indeed be boobs."[69] If only María would take "the syrup of

---

[65] Letter to María de San José, November 11. 1576. B.M.C., *Epist.*, I, pp. 353–354.
[66] "*A falta de hombres buenos, mi marido es alcalde.*" Letter to María de San José, November 19, 1576.
[67] Letter of April 17, 1577.
[68] Letter to María Bautista, November 2, 1576.
[69] "*Estaremos bien bobas.*" *Ibid.*

the King of the Medes"[70] when she needed a purge! "For it has
given me life. . . . Of that which you call interior, the more it
troubles you the less attention you are to pay to it, for it is plain
that it is weakness of the imagination and ill humor; and when
the devil sees this, he has to put in his piece.[71] But don't be
afraid, for Saint Paul says that God will not allow us to be
tempted beyond what we can endure; and although you think
you consent, it is not so, but you will gain the merit from this.
Now finish getting yourself well, for the love of God, and try to
eat well and not to be alone, or thinking of anything. Occupy
yourself with what you can and as you can. I wish I were there,
for I have a lot to tell you to entertain you." There are very few
letters to this niece in 1576 and 1577, but more from early 1577
to June 9, 1579, when María Bautista sent her some money to
aid the cause of the Reform in Rome. Doubtless many have been
lost. Even to the end, Teresa inflicted upon this first child of
the Reform the mortifications her nature required, yet she loved
her dearly; and perhaps she was making amends for some of the
asperities of the past when she wrote her toward the end of her
retirement at Toledo, "I don't govern any more as I used to.
Now all goes with love."[72]

---

[70] It is not known what this choice purgative was.

[71] *"Debe de ayudar su pedazo."*

[72] Fragment of a letter which P. Silverio assigns to 1579, the Benedictines of
Stanbrook to 1581.

Chapter XXX

ANGUISH AND AFFLICTION AT TOLEDO

TERESA was not as successful in dealing with men as with women. If her mind had masculine qualities, her heart was too womanly not to be swayed a little toward greater indulgence for the opposite sex: and the weaker a man was (it sometimes appeared), the more vigorously she defended him if there was anything to be said in his favor; particularly if he had ever done her the slightest favor, or if she saw under his frailties some latent spiritual promise. On the other hand, it is true that while she had authority over women, she had none over men, even those of her own choosing. Once she had launched a male vocation on the sea of her Reform, she had to stand more or less helpless on the shore, watching it borne this way and that by winds of circumstance, character, and conflicting spiritual powers.

She was certainly under no illusion that her friars were all perfect. Fray Antonio of Jesus, big and slow and growing old, was prior at Sevilla; and a very poor one, too, wrote La Madre to María de San José: he was timid and pusillanimous; he neglected his work;[1] Gracián must tell him to mend his ways. Some of her letters to the genial Fray Mariano, for whose impulsiveness she had sought the forgiveness of Father Rubeo, are more than a little sharp. "Are you now calling me Reverend and Senora?" she wrote him. "God forgive you, for I think that your Reverence or I must be turning Calced."[2] Again, when he became champion of a well-dowered novice rejected by the nuns at Toledo, she wrote, "Let your Reverence say no more about this, for the love of God. . . . It amuses me, your Reverence's saying you can read her character at a glance. We are not so easy to understand, we women, for they may hear our confessions for many years, and then be astonished at how little they have understood us; and it is because even the women don't understand how to tell their own faults, and the priests judge by what they tell them."[3] She begged him to insist upon

---

[1] Letter of December 7, 1576.
[2] Letter to Mariano, October, 1576. *Epist.*, I, p. 312.
[3] To Mariano, October 21, 1576 — *ibid.*, p. 319.

virtues, not austerities, in the Discalced convents.[4] She urged him to be very careful about being entangled in friendships with those who might wish to use him.[5] She wanted to know why he was in Madrid, and why he was not staying with the Calced friars, in accordance with the Nuncio's wishes;[6] let him speak with more restraint when he complained of anyone, for he was careless and too frank — please God his words had not reached the Nuncio's ears! He had better leave Madrid and retire to Pastrana or Alcalá. "Be careful not to argue with the Archbishop."[7] Again, "In the name of charity, don't call me 'Señora' on the address, for it is not our language." Yet when she heard that he had been ill in January, 1577, she wrote, "Oh what great pleasure it has given me to know that you are well again! God be blessed forever, for it has kept me unhappy these days. Take care of yourself, for the love of God! For when you are well, all will go well. The truth is that when I see you ill or in sorrow, I understand how much I love you in the Lord."[8]

One of the few men who never disappointed her in any way — perhaps the only one — was Father John of the Cross. Yet he is hardly ever mentioned in the correspondence of these years; for every reference to this saint there are a hundred to such men as Mariano and Antonio. True, most of her letters to John have been lost. After her death he destroyed all he had, as a final act of self-denial. This does not explain, however, the infrequency with which his name appears in her letters to others. The tart pleasantries of the *Vejamen* are hardly evidence of a coolness between them. Is it not more likely that he made little or no appeal to a maternal instinct that yearned to spread its protecting wings over the whole world — and this precisely because he did not need her help? How could she mother a bird-like little man who had asked God for only three things, all of which he got: (1) sufferings; (2) that he would not die a prelate; (3) that he would die alone, forsaken and despised? Perhaps La Madre and her *Senequita* were too much alike for human sympathy. There was no conflict between them, no attraction of opposites. If she forgot him, it was almost a self-forgetfulness. She certainly did not underestimate his character.

---

[4] December 12, 1576.
[5] May 19, 1577.
[6] March 15, 1577.
[7] To Mariano, March 15, 1577.
[8] Middle of January, 1577.

Did she not commend him to her Prioress at Beas, two years later, as "a man celestial and divine . . . a great treasure . . . truly the father of my soul, and one of those to whom I have communicated it with most profit . . . for he is very spiritual and of great experience and learning"?

With Gracián it was different. From the start she had seen in him not only many fine qualities, but still better possibilities. She loved his purity (he would rarely talk to women, and tried to avoid even hearing their confessions), his sweetness, his commiseration for the poor and the weak, his courage in answering the strong, his zeal for God and the Reform, his patience under adversity. Such a man, young and eager to learn, might become a saint. Was she blind, then, to his faults? On the contrary, they very quickly revealed themselves to her penetrating and inspired eyes; and this was precisely what summoned all the care and solicitude of her motherly soul to his aid. By September 20, 1576, if not earlier, she was aware of the fatal weakness of his character, though she was probably still in the dark as to the damage it had done to her work. Gracián was evasive, there was a certain lack of honesty and frankness in him. Not that he lied; but he did not always tell the whole truth — which often had the same effect. Teresa wrote him in September, 1576, that his mother, whom she had just met, was a charming woman of "such simplicity and frankness, that I am quite gone on her. She gives long odds to her son in this respect."[9] Father Silverio interprets this as a joke which must have made Gracián smile.[10] Yet it may be that the delicate raillery veiled a serious hint, which we find repeated even more obviously, however tactfully and affectionately, in a letter she wrote him three years later: "I must tell you of a temptation I had yesterday, and it is still with me, concerning Eliscus (code name for Gracián). It seemed to me that he is sometimes careless about telling the whole truth in everything. I see, of course, that they are things of little importance, but I wish he would try to be much more careful in this. For the sake of charity, will Your Paternity please ask him, on my behalf, for I don't believe there will be absolute perfection where this is disregarded. See how I meddle, as if I had no other worries!"[11]

---

[9] "Una llaneza y claridad, por la que yo soy perdida. Hartas ventajas hace a su hijo en esto."

[10] *Epistolario*, I, p. 289, n. 2.

[11] *Epistolario*, II, p. 341.

It is true that La Madre told María de San José and others how holy he was: "Our Father is a Saint!"[12] She admitted to the Archbishop of Evora that Gracián's perfection had her "frightened."[13] But this charitable hyperbole did not prevent her from telling *him* about his imperfection. Nor is there any real contradiction in her letter of November, 1576, urging him to be *less* frank. "Time will relieve Your Paternity a little of the frankness[14] which I hold truly to be that of a saint. But as the devil does not want all to be saints, those who are wicked and malicious, like me, try to avoid temptations."[15] She goes on to complain of his reading her letters to the nuns, lest her expressions of affection ("for I understand whom I am talking to, and can do so on account of my age") be misunderstood. It must have been evident to her that some of her motherly exaggerations had been quoted and distorted by the authors of the foul slanders against them. She begs him not to take offense, "for Your Paternity and I are charged with a very great burden, and we have to render account to God and to the world. Since you understand the love with which I speak, you can pardon me, and do me the favor I have asked of not reading in public the letters I write to you. Notice that people's intelligences are different, and that those in authority must never be too outspoken in certain things; and it might be that I might write them as a third person, or of myself, and that it might not be well for anyone to know it."[16] Here she is reproving him for lack of prudence, discretion, and consideration for her — all of which she sums up in a tactful euphemism as "frankness." But this "frankness" is not the same as the "frankness" she elsewhere accuses him of lacking.

If Gracián's faults were a lien upon her sympathy, his services were almost a deed in fee simple to the gratitude of a woman who could make excuses even for a Father Garciálvarez. He had toiled manfully for the Reform, and he had brought her consolation and peace that she was unable to find in any other confessor.[17] The best reward she could imagine was to help him to become perfect. She was constantly sending him advice. He

---

[12] *Ibid.*
[13] *Ibid.*, II, 150, *"Espantada."*
[14] *"Llaneza."*
[15] *Ocasiones.*
[16] *Epistolario*, I, pp. 359–360.
[17] So she wrote him in September, 1576. *Epist.*, I, p. 267; Stanbrook, II, p. 19.

must ignore this and pay attention to that; beware of one person and not offend the other; judge his prayer by its results and not by the sweetness experienced. She wondered which he loved better, his mother or her. After all, his mother had a husband and other children, but poor Laurencia, as Teresa called herself in the code, had no one on earth but him.[18] She reminded him of the happy days she spent with "Paul" at Beas — never were any happier — and confessed her delight when he signed himself "Your Son."[19] She prayed that since he had so many external troubles, God would give him interior peace; and rejoicing to find in him a resemblance to Moses, she offered him anew to the Lord.[20] She urged him, in dealing with the nuns, to remember that virtues were worth more than austerities.

His health was her constant anxiety. He must get enough sleep. She was pleased to notice that he had gained weight on one of his visits to Toledo. She was so afraid that the Calced friars would poison him that she frequently wrote Mother María de San José asking her to feed him at the convent, and could not thank her enough for so doing.[21] "For the love of God, don't be careless about what you eat in those monasteries!" she begged him.[22] The whole Reform seemed to her at this time to depend upon his health, discretion, and sanctity.

She saw clearly what he must do to be successful. Through the good offices of Philip II and the Nuncio Ormaneto, both friendly to the movement, he must gain the permission of Pope Gregory XIII for a separate province. Nothing was to be expected now from the Carmelite General Rubeo — though Teresa asked the nuns to pray for him when she heard he had broken a leg in a fall from his mule[23] — nor was much to be expected from the King, so far as Rome was concerned, for with all his good will to the Reform, he had been in conflict with several Popes over questions of jurisdiction, and was exceedingly jealous of any recourse to the Papal Court, as a limitation of his own royal power. Meanwhile the Discalced friars were doing nothing, in fact, as Teresa said afterwards, it seemed as if "someone" were always preventing an appeal to Rome; but the Calced

---

[18] September 20, 1576.
[19] Mid-December, 1576.
[20] October 6, 1576.
[21] To María, December 7, 1576, for example.
[22] December 7, 1576.
[23] Letter to María de San José, July 11, 1576.

were taking good care to have their case known there. Her only hope lay in Ormaneto, "the holy nuncio" as she called him — "Matusalem" in the code. But in 1576, alas, his health failed rapidly. "I am afraid we are going to lose Matusalem!" she lamented.[24]

Only one as holy as Ormaneto, perhaps, could have been of real use to such holy work as hers. He was an Italian, a Veronese, seventy-six years of age, and universally respected. In 1553 he had gone to England with Cardinal Pole to effect the reconciliation of that country with the Church; had restored learning and morals at Oxford and Cambridge, where both had suffered at the hands of the "Reformers"; had been present at the true Reform at Trent; and as vicar-general to Saint Charles Borromeo, at Milan, had worked day and night to carry out the decrees of the Council; had been summoned to Rome to reform the churches there; became Bishop of Padua, and in 1572 was sent to Spain as Nuncio, to strengthen the League against the Turks. After many attempts to convert Queen Elizabeth, he had come to the conclusion that she was a lost soul and that England could be restored to its rightful ruler, Queen Mary Stuart, only by a crusade. Now he was old and sick, worn out by his labors and almost penniless through his generosity.

Enter, at this point, the villain of the piece. His very name seemed appropriate for the part he was to play. And yet, in spite of the impression we get even in the letters of Teresa of his cruelty and injustice, the Very Reverend Jerónimo Tostado, a Portuguese by birth, Doctor of the University of Paris, Calced Carmelite Provincial of Catalonia, Consultor of the Holy Inquisition, and Vicar-General and Commissary for Spain and Portugal, was by no reasonable standard a bad man: in fact, he had been selected for all his august offices precisely because he was noted for his learning, his zeal, his intelligence, his virtuous life, his strong will and resolution. He loved the mitigated Carmelite Order, and sincerely believed that it was a mistake to attempt to restore the primitive rule. What he had heard of the work of Madre Teresa, Gracián, and the rest had come from their enemies, and was far from flattering: they were destructive, revolutionary, self-exploiting, deceivers and deceived, victims in some degree perhaps of Illuminism, inspired by the devil to divide and ruin the order to which he had devoted his

---

[24] November 4, 1576, to Gracián.

life. Had not the Council of Piacenza declared them to be rebels, contumacious, and worthy to be dealt with by the secular arm if they continued to refuse obedience? And had not Rubeo sent him to Spain to carry out the decrees of the Council? When he landed in Barcelona in May, 1576, the Calced friars joyfully proclaimed that he intended to shatter all the work of Madre Teresa. If this was an exaggeration, it was one that even she believed, and it was heavy news to her and all the barefoot friars and nuns.

Arriving at Madrid, Tostado found the situation more complicated than he had imagined. Perhaps he had not realized to what an extent the King and the Nuncio had been won over to the Reform. Again, he found himself thwarted by the jealous Caesaropapism of the Spanish court; the Royal Council refused to honor his credentials because they had not been sanctioned by the King's *exequatur*, and he had to send to Rome for new ones. He was helpless, therefore, when he met Gracián for the first time in August, 1576, each claiming to have the superior "powers" — Tostado as visitor for the order, Gracián as apostolic visitor deriving his authority, through Vargas, from the Pope. Tostado refused to show his credentials. It is plain now that he could not. And it is plain also that Gracián claimed to have more authority than he actually possessed, and that he was mistaken in holding that Vargas' powers were superior to those of Rubeo.[25] At any rate, he seemed to have come off well from this first encounter, and as he returned triumphantly to Toledo, La Madre rejoiced in the news that the enemy had departed, bag and baggage, for Portugal. For some time thereafter Tostado would make the most mysterious appearances and disappearances in Madrid and Lisbon. "Now Tostado is coming back, they say," she wrote Lorenzo . . . "it seems like nothing but a comedy."[26]

Gracián confidently proceeded August 26, 1576, to summon a general chapter of the Discalced friars of Castilla and Andalucía — some seventy-five of them — at Almodóvar. He intended to reply in decisive fashion to the General Council at Piacenza, and the confirming chapter of the Calced at Moraleja in May,

---

[25] So says Father Zimmerman in his notes for the forthcoming second edition of Saint Teresa's letters, Vol. I, p. 249, which Dame Beatrice, O.S.B., of Stanbrook Abbey has kindly sent me.
[26] Letter of February 27 and 28, 1577.

1576. When the Discalced fathers met September 8, they voted, at his instance, to set up a separate province, to obey only the General of the Order or a Discalced father delegated by him as visitor, and to send two friars to Rome to explain their position to the Pope, since the opposition had dispatched a similar embassy. They would not accept a visit by the Calced, however, even if the General sent them; and the *Acts* of the Council proclaimed that if he wished to make a visit in person, he must have a Discalced friar as his *socius*.[27]

The fat was in the fire now, with a vengeance. "The establishment of provinces has always been the exclusive right of the General Chapters," says Father Zimmerman, "neither the General in person nor in conjunction with his advisers having the requisite power. Although Gracián believed his powers as Apostolic Visitor or reformer to be superior to those of the General, the only excuse he could offer for such an unprecedented step was that he had heard the Nuncio say that such a separation ought to be made. But if the Nuncio had had the power to make it, he would surely have done so himself."[28]

Teresa had been completely taken in by Gracián's confidence in his apostolic authority. Several times she had begged both him and Mariano to write nice obedient letters to the General. Mariano, it seems, never took the trouble. Gracián wrote one, but it was worse than none,[29] for its truculence ended all hope of conciliation with Rubeo. Nevertheless La Madre was so sure of his "powers" that she supported both of the principal acts of the Council of Almodóvar: the declaration of a separate province and the appointment of two "companions" to go to Rome. This latter, in fact, she had urged upon Gracián while the delegates were still in session, on the ground that "if they set these untruthful statements before the Pope, and there is no one there to reply to them, they will give them as many briefs as they wish against us, and it is highly important that someone be there, for seeing how they live, they will notice the passion [against us], and I believe that until this we shall do nothing."[30]

Two weeks later, when the news of the Council's actions reached Toledo, she assured him, "If it can be done by spending

---

[27] Cf. Father Bruno, *Saint John of the Cross*, p. 149 *et seq.*, and Father Zimmerman's illuminating postscript, p. 370.

[28] *Loc. cit.*

[29] *Ibid.* See also the note to second edition of *Letters*, I, p. 198.

[30] To Gracián, September 5, 1576.

money, God will give it, and let it be given to the companions; and for the love of God, let Your Paternity take care that they do not delay going. Do not take this for a secondary thing, for it is the principal one; and if that Prior of Piñuela knows him [Rubeo] so well, he will be a good one to go with Father Mariano, and when nothing can be accomplished, let it be done with the Pope; but the former would be much better, and this is a most favorable opportunity. And seeing what is happening to Matusalem, I don't know what we are waiting for."[31]

It is clear, then, that she still clung to the hope of conciliating Rubeo, and achieving her ends through him at Rome. She thought he was to be consulted also about the establishment of a separate province, and that the plan would be tentative, pending his decision. This at least seems evident from her letter to Gracián on September 20, 1576, in which she said, "Also I am very glad over the plan that was *discussed* of seeking the province *by means of our Father General*, by as many ways as we can; for it is an intolerable warfare to proceed with the displeasure of one's superior."[32]

Now, from whom could she have obtained this very modified, not to say mendacious, version save from Gracián himself? Did she have an uneasy feeling that he was not telling her everything? This was the very letter in which she twitted him with being less frank than his mother. Bound by obedience to him, she could not question his word; yet she was too shrewd not to have thoughts of her own, and it is likely enough she had begun to find him out. A week later she wrote to Mother María at Sevilla: "For the sake of charity, let your Reverence write me at once, and particularly what is happening; no trust is to be put in our Father, for he will not have the time."[33] Perhaps time was not the only element in Gracián's reticence. Nevertheless he must have sent her, soon after this, an account that satisfied her and quieted her doubts and fears, for she wrote the enthusiastic letter of October 6, comparing him to Moses, and rejoicing over the way things were turning out.

They were not turning out, however, as she had been led to

---

[31] To Gracián, September 20, 1576. The Prior of Piñuela, Fray Pedro de los Angeles, was one of the two *compañeros* appointed at the Council of Almodóvar (1576) to go to Rome; but they never got there. After many delays, two others were named, as we shall see.

[32] *Ibid.* My italics.

[33] Letter of September 26, 1576.

believe. It was the Calced friars who reported the Chapter of Almodóvar at Rome, and the Cardinal Secretary of State wrote to the Nuncio at Madrid demanding an account of the matter. As Ormaneto was too ill to reply, his secretary wrote October 29: "With reference to the complaint of the Carmelites against Father Friar Jerome Gracián who calls himself Provincial of that Order, Monsignore the Nuncio has never made or nominated him Provincial, but only Commissary for the visitation and reform. He calls himself, as far as I know, Provincial because he was nominated Provincial two and a half years ago by a certain Father Francisco de Vargas, of the Order of Saint Dominic, who, being Commissary Apostolic in virtue of a brief of Pius V of holy memory, had power to depose and to institute provincials in the Carmelite Order. . . ."[34]

Ormaneto confirmed this on his recovery, and expressed the opinion that Vargas had had ample faculties. He also wrote to the Cardinal Secretary that "these Discalced fathers are leading a very holy life and are giving the greatest edification and are enjoying great credit with the people; would that it pleased God the others [the Calced] were like them and had as good a reputation. It thus happens that the former are favored and protected both by the authorities and by all good people, which is not the case with the latter."[35] In March, 1577, he wrote that "those who have given wrong information to you about Father Gracián have acted very wickedly, for he is a man of great holiness, leading a very good life."[36]

Why, then, did not Ormaneto, with his influence at Rome and Madrid, bring about a settlement of the dispute? His ill-health is probably the explanation. He had another sharp attack before the end of March, and on June 18 he died, so poor that there would have been no money to bury him but for the charity of Philip II. His passing at that moment was a terrible blow to the Reform.

Teresa had been valiantly trying for months to get the matter before the Pope. Before the end of 1576, she had found support for this plan in her confessor, Father Velázquez, and in "my great friend in the Company," Father Ripalda, S.J., both of whom agreed that the Discalced friars should go to Rome and there

---

[34] Father Zimmerman, in Bruno, *loc. cit.*
[35] Letter of February 5, 1577.
[36] Letter of March 4, 1577.

see Rubeo before appealing to the Holy Father.[37] But the journey of the two companions was postponed again and again, and no appeal was made to Rubeo. "Had we gone to him, it would have been all right. God pardon the one who has always prevented it!" La Madre told Gracián long afterwards: "for I could have arranged it with Your Paternity, although in this you have given me little credence."[38]

It is now fairly evident who the "someone" was. Gracián may have led a holy life, but he had exceeded his powers at Almodóvar. He knew that if the quarrel were thrashed out at Rome, his disobedience (not to mention his duplicity to Madre Teresa) would be exposed and punished. It may be, as some of his apologists have argued, that he weakly gave in to the fury of Mariano. Still, he had motive enough on his own account to prevent the appeal to Rome that Teresa knew was essential. Having gone too far to retreat, he then pinned his hopes upon the secular influence of Philip II, who had browbeaten Popes more than once and would attempt to do so again.

It cannot be merely an accident that while he was thus sacrificing La Madre and the reform to his own reputation and pride, and by indirection supporting the dangerous regalism of Philip II, he was preparing, all unawares, the instrument of his own future punishment and retribution. On March 24, 1577, he handed the Discalced habit to Nicholas Doria, a Genoese banker who had given up the world for the cloister, after setting the bankrupt affairs and currency of Philip II in order and giving all his own huge fortune to the poor. Cold, efficient, unimaginative, ambitious, this friar would one day supersede Gracián, strip him of his habit and drive him out of the Order. Poetic justice, if nothing more,[39] even though Doria was to regret it on his deathbed!

Teresa was probably still unaware of the extent to which she had been betrayed when she left Toledo in the summer of 1577. After the death of Ormaneto she decided to transfer San José de Ávila from the jurisdiction of the Bishop to that of Gracián. The house had somewhat lost its first charity, the discipline had suffered, the nuns were not getting enough to eat. This must

---

[37] Letter to Gracián, late November or early December, 1576.

[38] Letter to Gracián, October 15, 1578. B.M.C., *Epist.*, II, p. 269; Stanbrook, III, p. 162.

[39] In view of all this, Gracián's account of Doria and his virtues, written after his expulsion, is extremely magnanimous: *Peregrinación*, p. 203.

not continue. La Madre, having obtained the necessary permissions, departed for her native city in the heat of July, after sending Doña Luisa a carved coconut from America (one of several presents from Sevilla) which made her rejoice at the wonders of God.

Don Alvaro de Mendoza consented to the change she requested on condition that his body be buried in the chancel beside hers; and there what is left of it lies (but hers does not!) to this day. She asked him to give a canonry to Maestro Daza, who was in need; commended the virtues of Father Gracián to him; and in congratulating him on the marriage of his niece, condoled with him a little on the age of the bridegroom, the Duke of Sesa, remarking philosophically that wives, especially when as lovable as Doña María, were always better treated with husbands somewhat advanced in years.[40] The Bishop took all this in good part. He sent an alms to relieve the hunger of the nuns at San José, which Teresa perhaps had found a way of calling to his attention. She told him she was so anxious to see him free from debt that she would rather have the convent in want than increase his expenses; still, since God had given him such charity, she hoped He would increase his revenues also. "May it please Him to preserve your Lordship many years, and then take me where I can enjoy your company."[41]

Meanwhile the new Nuncio appointed by the Holy Father had landed in Spain on the last day of August, and had proceeded to Madrid. He was Philip Sega, bishop of Piacenza, who had been in Belgium with Don John of Austria when Ormaneto died. An excellent man in many ways, he was full of prejudices against the Discalced, not only because the Calced had got his ear in Italy, but because, as Teresa wrote, he was related to their Cardinal Protector, Cardinal Buoncompagni, the Pope's uncle and secretary of state. If she had any doubt as to what the Reform could expect from him, it must have been dispelled when she heard that on setting foot in Spain he had called her "an unquiet and restless woman, who goes around amusing herself in crazy pranks under pretext of religion."[42] As if to support this view, there appeared, not long after his arrival, a scurrilous

[40] Letter to Don Alvaro de Mendoza, September 6, 1577.
[41] *Fundaciones*, cap. XXVIII.
[42] "*Femina inquieta y andariega que por holgarse andaba en devaneos so color de religión.*" — Yepes, *Vida de Santa Teresa*, lib. II, cap. XXVIII.

pamphlet denouncing her and accusing Father Gracián of every conceivable crime. This did infinite harm; and the sorrow of Teresa was increased when she learned that the authors were Fray Baltasar of Jesus (Nieto), one of her own friars who was traveling about with Tostado, and a lay brother named Miguel de la Coluna.

Father Baltasar, like his two brothers, Melchior and Gaspar, had always been a disturbing element in the Order, and he was intensely jealous of Gracián, who supplanted him in Andalucía. Apparently he wrote the pamphlet, and Miguel signed it, explaining afterwards that he did so without reading it, under duress. Later the two made a complete recantation, admitting they had lied, and did penance for their crime. But the harm had been done, and Teresa was so disturbed in mid-September, 1577, that she wrote an impassioned letter to Philip II, defending Gracián against the calumnies which were already circulating in the Court:

"The grace of the Holy Spirit be always with Your Majesty! Amen. To my notice has come a memorial which they have given to Your Majesty against the Father Master Gracián, and I am astonished at the artifices of the devil and the Calced Fathers; for they are not content with defaming this servant of God (as truly he is, and he has edified us all, and always they write me in the monasteries he visits that he has left them with a new spirit) but they now try to blacken these monasteries where our Lord is so much served. And for this they have availed themselves of two Discalced, one of whom, before he was a friar, was a servant in these monasteries, and has given many reasons to believe he is often not in his right mind;[43] and of this Discalced Father, and others inflamed against the Father Master Gracián (for he is to be the one who punishes them) the Fathers of the Cloth[44] have availed themselves, making them sign absurdities; and if I did not fear the harm the devil can do, it would give me amusement, what they say the Discalced sisters do, for, it would be a monstrous thing for one in my habit. For the love of God I supplicate Your Majesty not to consent that such infamous testimonials be circulated in the courts; for the world is of such a sort that some suspicion of something may possibly remain (however much the contrary

---

[43] "Le falta el juicio."
[44] The Calced who wore wool.

is proved)."[45] She asked the King to investigate the charges him-self, for there were plenty of holy and learned men who were acquainted with her nuns and could tell the sort of lives they lived. She reminded him that Gracián was the son of one of his own secretaries; "and truly, I have thought him a man sent by God and His Blessed Mother, who brought him to the Order for my aid through the devotion he has to her, which is great." She asked God to preserve His Majesty many years, "for we have no other defender on earth."

At this juncture there was an election at the Incarnation, and Teresa, to her great disgust, was elected Prioress by a vote of 55 to 44. She went there with a heavy heart and an aching noisy head.

When the news got out, Tostado sent Fray Juan Gutiérrez, provincial of the Calced Fathers for Castilla, to annul the elec-tion. Teresa's account of the sequel is inimitable:

"I say to Your Reverence that something has happened here in the Incarnation, the like of which has never been seen before. By order of Tostado, the Provincial of the Calced came here to hold the election two weeks ago today, and he threatened great censures and excommunications for those who had voted for me. And with all this it made no impression upon them, but as if nothing had been said to them, fifty-five nuns voted for me; and at each vote they cast, the Provincial excommunicated them and cursed them, and hammered the votes with his fist and gave them blows, and burned them. And he has left them excommunicated for two weeks, and without hearing Mass or entering the choir, even when the Divine Office is said, and nobody speaks to them, neither their confessors nor their own fathers. And what amuses me most is that another day, after this hammered-out election,[46] the Provincial came back to summon them to come and hold an election; and they replied that they had no reason to hold another election, for they had already had it. And thereupon he excommunicated them again, and summoned those who were left, and there were forty-four, and chose another prioress, and sent to Tostado for confirmation. Now they have her confirmed, and the others are brave, and say they are not willing to obey her except as Vice-Prioress.

---

[45] Teresa to Philip II, September 18, 1577. See also her letter to María de San José, end of October, 1577.
[46] "Otro día después desta elección machucada."

Learned men say they are not excommunicated, and that the friars are going against the Council in setting up the Prioress they have, with fewer votes. They have sent to Tostado to tell him they want me for prioress. He says no, unless I want to go there to retire; but that as prioress, they can't even consider it.[47] I don't know how it will end.

"This is, in sum, what has happened till now, and all are astonished to see a thing that offends everybody, as this does. I would gladly pardon them if they would only leave me in peace, for I have no desire to see myself in this Babylon, especially with the poor health I have, and when I am in this house, worse than ever. May God do as best serves Him, and free me from them!"[48]

So matters stood for weeks and months, while Madre Teresa calmly wrote the magnificent last chapter of *The Interior Castle and Mansions*, bringing it to end on the eve of Saint Andrew, November 28. Meanwhile there was an ominous lull which did not deceive her. She knew that another storm was brewing; and while she complimented Gracián on his fortitude under persecution — for he had been not only slandered but at one time cast into prison — she added, "all my anxiety is that Paul (Gracián) do nothing in which he may deviate from the will of God." She begged him not to spend time in prayer that he should be giving to sleep. Lack of sleep might affect the head, and the trouble would not be noticed until it was too late. She urged him "for the love of God," to lay aside his schemes, "however necessary they are," when it was time to sleep; and even prayer. "Please do me this favor, for often the devil, when he sees zeal in the spirit, represents things as of great importance to the service of God, so that, now that he cannot hinder good by one way, he may in another."[49] Several Jesuits, she warned him, had "lost their heads" from overwork.

Scarcely had she finished the last page of her book when the blow fell. This time the victim was Fray John of the Cross, who never wanted to offend anyone, but who, once he had made up his mind that a certain course was right and pleasing to God,

---

[47] *"No lo pueden elevar á paciencia."*

[48] Letter of late October, 1577, to María de San José, B.M.C., *Epist.*, II, pp. 121–122; Stanbrook, II, p. 319.

[49] Fragments of two letters to Gracián, some time in November and December, 1577. B.M.C., *Epistolario*, II, p. 127 and p. 130.

would die rather than forsake it. As a Discalced chaplain at the Calced convent of the Incarnation he had been in an anomalous position, one certain to invite the hostility of the Fathers of the "Cloth." Early in 1576[50] he and his companion, Fray Germán, had been seized by the Calced fathers and carried off to Medina, but the Nuncio Ormaneto had ordered their release. With Ormaneto dead, and a new Nuncio of very different views, the Calced decided to renew the attempt to free the Incarnation from a little friar whose very habit seemed an insult to their rule, and whose voice, like that of Madre Teresa, had affirmed the right of the fifty-five excommunicated nuns to elect a prioress of their own.

Tostado ordered the two friars to leave the Incarnation — they were now virtually confined to a small cottage at the far end of the grounds, across a stony valley — and go to one of their own priories. They refused, despite the death of Ormaneto and the lapse of the powers of the Visitors and the Reformers, alleging that they had been put there by lawful authority, had had no proper notice of the termination of their office, and had no one to replace them. This answer seemed to the Calced Fathers like rebellion against the decrees of the General Chapter.

At this juncture Philip II interfered, and insisted that the fifty-five nuns be released from all censures. Tostado acquiesced, and sent his right-hand man, Father Miguel Maldonado, Prior of the Calced monastery at Toledo, to Ávila.

A most determined and uncompromising man was this Maldonado. He released the nuns in such a way that their plight was worse than before. And he served notice on Father John of the Cross that he must give up the Reform and the Discalced habit in three days or take the consequences. On the other hand, if he proved reasonable and obedient, like a good Carmelite of the Mitigation, he would be entitled, by his well-known erudition, to be made prior of some Calced monastery.

John, of course, refused, knowing what would happen. And happen it did, despite all the watchfulness of his friends. On the night of December 3, 1577, Maldonado and his Calced friars, having appealed to the secular arm as directed by the Council of Piacenza — accompanied, in other words, by armed policemen — broke down the door of the cottage where the two barefoot confessors lived, and dragged them to the old Carmelite mon-

---

[50] Or perhaps late in 1575 — the exact date is unknown.

astery, where they flung them into separate cells, after scourging them twice.

Next morning Maldonado sent for John of the Cross, immediately after Mass. While he was making his thanksgiving, his prisoner slipped away, ran across the fields to the cottage, barred himself in, and managed to tear up some of his papers and swallow the rest — probably letters from Madre Teresa concerning the Reform — before his captors overtook him.

Teresa did not know for many weeks where her *Senequita* was. She heard of the abduction on the morning of December 4, and immediately wrote a vigorous complaint to the King, commencing:

"I am quite convinced that our Lady has desired to avail Herself of Your Majesty, and to take you as defender for the relief of her Order, and so I cannot help hastening to Your Majesty with its affairs. For the love of our Lord, I beg Your Majesty to pardon such daring." After relating all the preliminaries, she came to the seizing of the two friars by Maldonado:

"All the town is quite scandalized (he being no prelate, nor showing whence he does this, for they are subjects of the Apostolic Commissary) that they should be so rash, this place being so near to where Your Majesty is, for it seems they have no fear that there is any justice, nor of God. It gives me great sorrow to see them in their hands, for they have been desiring it for days; and I should think it better if they were among the Moors, for perhaps they would have more pity. And this friar, so much a servant of God, is so frail from all he has suffered that I fear for his life.

"For the love of our Lord, I implore Your Majesty to command that they be rescued soon, and that you give orders that all these poor Discalced shall not suffer so much from those of the Cloth, for they do nothing but keep silent and suffer, and gain much; but scandal is given among the people of the towns. For this same man who is here, for no reason at all took prisoner, at Toledo this spring, Fray Antonio of Jesus, who is a blessed old man, the first of all; and so they go about saying that they have to be abolished, for *el Tostado* has commanded it. . . . If Your Majesty does not order a redress to be made, I don't know where we are going to end, for we have no one else on the earth. Please our Lord you may last us many years. I hope in Him that He will do us this favor, since He finds Him-

self so bereft of anyone who looks to His honor.[51] Continually we
beg for it, all these servants of Your Majesty and I."[52]

Philip apparently sent for her, and she made the journey to
the Escorial, despite winter and age, about the middle of December, 1577. The great Duke of Alba, home to rest and regain
health after his years of heroic labor in the Low Countries, probably had something to do with arranging this visit, for Teresa's
fragmentary account of it is addressed to the wife of his secretary, Albornoz.[53]

The noble palace of San Lorenzo del Escorial was not quite
finished in 1577, but Philip and his family had been living in
it for some time, and the King had his oratory and workshop
there in a little room looking out upon the High Altar of the
Chapel, and spent a great deal of time supervising the architec-
ture, the gardens, the zoo, the scientific laboratories, the art
galleries, and the library. As there is no other record of this
memorable meeting save the letter of Teresa, of which the first
page is missing, the scene cannot be constructed accurately, nor
do we know in which part of the vast edifice the stage was set.
One can imagine the old lady in her patched Carmelite habit
going down the long walk and past the statues of the Kings
of Israel into some lofty room, her head aching and thundering,
her heart thumping with anxiety over what this fateful encounter would bring, and Philip II coming in quietly in his
customary suit of solemn black, with no ornament except perhaps a gold chain at his neck, and turning the penetrating gaze
of his blue eyes upon the deep black ones of the *beata*. Philip
was then fifty, and had been through a great deal — his gout
was beginning to be chronic, his fair hair was darkening, and a
little gray was showing in the beard that covered his prognathous
chin.[54]

---

[51] *"Pues se ve tan solo de quien mire por su honra."*

[52] Letter of December 4, 1577, *Epistolario*, II, pp. 133–134.

[53] This letter was first published, with a photostat of the original, by Don
Bernardino de Melgar, Marqués de San Juan de Piedras Albas, in the *Boletín de
la real academia de la historia* in May, 1919. Although the first page is missing,
the handwriting is accepted as Saint Teresa's by Father Zimmerman, and by the
Benedictines of Stanbrook Abbey, who give an English translation (*Letters*, III,
p. 16). Father Silverio does not include it in the B.M.C., *Epistolario*, II, printed
in 1923. Despite the loss of the first page of the letter, the context indicates that
it was addressed to Doña Inés Nieto, wife of Albornoz.

[54] In my *Philip II*, I referred to Philip's chin as a Habsburg trait, but I have
recently learned from some excellent articles and illustrations in the *Odontología
clínica* (Jan. and March, 1931) and a brochure on *El prognatismo inferior en los*

According to a tradition of the Escorial, La Madre began the conversation by referring to Sega's description of her:

"Sire, you are thinking, 'I see before me this unquiet and restless woman, who goes about amusing herself with *devaneos* under pretext of religion.' "[55]

Most persons who met Philip for the first time were speechless in his self-contained majestic presence until he set them at their ease with a curt, "Calm yourself — *sosegaos.*" Even Teresa, by her own account, was confused for a moment before that soul-piercing gaze, and cast down her eyes. When she raised them again, the King's expression had become mild and benevolent. She then told him her story, and begged his aid.

"Is that all you want?"

"I have asked a great deal."

"Then be at peace," said Philip, "for all shall be as you wish."

Teresa fell on her knees to thank him. He bade her rise, made her a courteous bow, and gave her his hand to kiss. She went away praising God for the help "this Caesar" had promised.

"As I left the other building where the Duke was, your kind husband, to whom I owe so much, came up to me and told me that the King our Lord had ordered him to write out my petition so that my wishes might be carried out without delay. This was done: I dictated and Señor Albornoz noted down my words."[56]

Returning to Avila, she went not to the Incarnation, but to her old cell at San José, where, in spite of the King's encouragement, the year ended dismally. It had been an unlucky year for Spain, 1577 — a year of poor crops, costly bread, much sickness and suffering among the poor, strange astronomical phenomena. For Teresa, on the human side, it had been a nightmare of anxieties. She was still in the dark as to where John of the Cross was. And on Christmas Eve, as if to make the cup of her afflictions run over, she fell as she was lighting her way to the choir with a little oil lamp for Compline. She had reached the top of the narrow way when she grew dizzy and tumbled

---

Borbones de España, both sent me by the Marqués de Villa-Alcázar, that in spite of the popular belief, the prognathous chin came from the Castilian royal house, ·ot from the Austrian.

[55] *Letters*, Stanbrook, III, p. 17, n. 2.

[56] *Ibid.*, Stanbrook translation. Suggestion for some Ph.D. candidate: find the MS. of the memorandum Teresa dictated to Albornoz. It may be among the inexhaustible records, still unpublished, in the Spanish Archives.

down the stairs, breaking her left arm. She always insisted that the devil had done it. "God help me," she cried as she lay at the bottom, "he tried to kill me!" and she heard a voice say, "He did, but I was with thee."

The pain was intense, and there was no one on hand who could set the bone. A *curandera* near Medina was unable or unwilling to come, and instead sent some advice which was worthless. Months later this quack arrived with a male assistant to break and reset the arm, while the nuns prayed in the choir, and Teresa endured excruciating torments. After that she moved her hand a little, but the arm was never much good, and to the day of her death she was unable to dress or undress without help.[57]

Could anything more happen to this tired old woman? Yes, it could and it did.

---

[57] Ribera, *Vida de Santa Teresa*, lib. IV, cap. XVII. Also her letters to Gracián, February 16, and March 7, 1578.

Chapter XXXI

DE PROFUNDIS

IF SHE was to drink to the full the chalice of Christ, who in His human nature experienced the desolation of seeming to be forsaken even by His Father, it was necessary that she stand wholly alone. Her Lord had been deserted on the night of darkness even by the saints who were His friends and apostles. And perhaps it was fitting and inevitable that His bride, Teresa of Jesus, should suffer the pain of feeling herself abandoned even by "those blessed men of the Company" who, together with the Dominicans, had been her stanch and almost indispensable champions.

As this situation has been grossly exaggerated by the ex-Jesuit Mir,[1] and minimized by some overzealous Jesuits,[2] it may be well to ask what are the known facts before attempting a conclusion.

The little tiffs La Madre had with Father Ripalda and Father Olea over some novices cannot be made into major issues even by those who are resolved to build up a case against the Jesuits. Such differences occur between friends everywhere, in and out of convents.

The famous affair of Casilda de Padilla left deeper and more lasting scars, at least on the Carmelite side. Casilda was one of the five children of the *Adelantado* of Castilla and his wife Doña María de Acuña. The eldest, Antonio, entered the Company of Jesus, renouncing his father's property and the vast wealth that went with it. His oldest sister, Luisa, in turn renounced it to take a vow of perpetual virginity; later, being dispensed, she married, had several children, and after her husband's death became a Discalced Carmelite. The next daughter, María, entered the Dominican Convent of Saint Catherine at Valladolid. The whole estate, together with what she could expect from her mother's, then passed to Casilda, who, as we

---

[1] Mir, *Vida de Santa Teresa*, and elsewhere.

[2] P. Juan Antonio Zugasti, S.J.: *Santa Teresa y la Compañia de Jesus, discurso pronunciado en Salamanca*, etc., Bilbao, 1914; and P. Jaime Pons, S.J.: notes, and in particular Appendix No. 2 to his edition to Ribera's life of the Saint, p. 578 *et seq.* See also Father Zugasti's longer work, *Santa Teresa y la Compañía de Jesús*, Madrid, 1914, which amplifies the arguments in the *Discurso*.

have seen, was received into the Discalced Convent at Valladolid at the age of eleven, under a dispensation. To this her mother, a pious but volatile woman, never became reconciled, and she and certain relatives made every effort to prevent the child from taking her vows, threatening, if she insisted, to cut off her inheritance.

"Certainly this angel owes little to her mother," wrote Teresa to Mother Brianda at Malagón in December, 1576. "On account of the girl's grief, and she feels a great deal of it, I should like to see it over and done with; and thus I have written her asking it, and if they won't give her anything, not to mind at all."

At this point we learn that certain Jesuits are somehow involved in the case. La Madre wrote to Mother María Bautista to be careful what she said to Casilda, who would surely tell her mother. After some obscure remarks about a Don Pedro, whose identity has been the subject of much controversy,[3] La Madre went on to say, "I don't know what to tell myself about this world, for as soon as profit is involved, there is no sanctity, and this makes me want to abhor the whole thing. I don't know why you resorted to a Theatine[4] (as Catalina tells me this Mercado is) knowing how they are concerned in it. Prádano has pleased me much; I believe he has great perfection, that man. God give it to us, and their money to them."[5]

There is certainly some resentment here against the Jesuits. Yet only a short while before Teresa had told María de San José at Sevilla to enlist their help as confessors. "It might be well if our Father Garciálvarez spoke to them. . . . It is well, in spite of all that, to get some one of the Company sometimes to hear

---

[3] Mir insists (*op. cit.*, II, 720) that he is Casilda's uncle, Pedro Manrique de Padilla, S.J., and this view is shared by the Benedictines of Stanbrook and by Padre Silverio (B.M.C., *Epistolario*, I, p. 405, n. 4 and p. 409, n. 1). Father Zugasti (*op. cit.*, p. 76) points out, however, that this Jesuit was ill most of the time, and died January 12, 1577, about the time he has been supposed to have been busy in the Casilda intrigue, but the extant correspondence is too incomplete to justify a very positive opinion. I wonder whether Don Pedro could be Pedro Xalame, chaplain of the convent at Valladolid, whose name appears among the witnesses to Casilda's act of renunciation (cf. *Epistolario*, I, appendix, p. 424)?

[4] A Jesuit or a disciple of the Jesuits.

[5] In this same letter (to María Bautista, late December, 1576) the Stanbrook translation has, "The fathers of the Company, hurt at seeming to be actuated by self-interest, have approved his (Don Pedro's) line of conduct. . . ." (*Letters*, II, p. 185.) The Spanish reads: *Es tanto lo que les parece mal lo que piensan que tienen los de la Compañía de interesales, que por esto les pareció lo hiciese ansí,* etc. (B.M.C., *Epistolario*, I, p. 409), which might be interpreted differently.

Confessions, for it will have the good effect of doing away with fear.[6] It would be fine with Father Acosta, if possible. God pardon them, for with that [novice] all your troubles would be over, if she is so rich; however, since His Majesty does not bring her, He will assume the care. Perhaps she was more needed where she was." This was October 5, 1576. On November 26 she made another reference to the Jesuits of Sevilla: "It would be no small benefit if the Rector there were willing to take charge of you, as you say, and so for many things he would be a great help. But they wish them [their penitents] to obey them, and you should do so, and although what they say may on occasion be not so good for us, it is well to overlook that, for the great importance of having them. Think of some things to ask them about, for they are very fond of this; and they are right, for if they undertake a thing, they do it well; and thus they do wherever they assume this care."[7] This certainly does not indicate any prejudice against the Company; quite the contrary. The clause, "what they say may on occasion be not so good for us," proves very little; for two years later, in advising Mother María to have only Discalced Carmelite friars as confessors, Teresa wrote, "Never mind if they sometimes make mistakes."[8]

Teresa was naturally much pleased when Casilda made her

---

[6] It is interesting to notice what different meanings various translators will find in the same words. The Stanbrook version here is, "It would do much to destroy their fear of us" (II, p. 69). But the original does not say whose fear, or fear of whom. The Spanish is, *"que hara mucho al caso para perder el miedo."* Could this not refer to fear by the nuns — of Garciálvarez, for instance, who about this time was beginning to manifest his idiosyncrasies as a confessor?

[7] Again, compare the Stanbrook translation: "It would be no small thing if the Father Rector of Sevilla took charge of you as he says he would like to do: he would be a great help in many ways. But these fathers wish people to obey them; this you would have to do, and although their directions do not always quite suit us, we must overlook that because it is very important to keep on good terms with them. Think of some questions about which you might consult them — it pleases them, which is quite right, for when they undertake a charge they do it thoroughly, as is their custom in whatever they do" (II, p. 145). This seems to me to introduce a subtle overtone which I am not conscious of in reading the words of Saint Teresa: *"No será poco bien si el Retor de ahí se quisiese encargar, como dice, y ansí para muchas cosas sería gran ayuda. Mas quieren que los obedezcan, y ansí lo haga, que, aunque alguna vez no nos esté tan bien lo que dicen, por lo mucho que importa tenerlos es bien pasarlo. Busque cosas que los preguntar, que son muy amigos de esto; y tienen razón, que si se encargan de una cosa, de hacerlo bien; y ansí lo hacen adonde toman este cuidado."* — B.M.C., *Epistolario*, I, p. 370: letter to María de San José, November 26, 1576.

[8] To María de San José, July 22, 1579.

profession a few weeks later (January 13, 1577) after renouncing her father's estate and the inheritance due from her mother in favor of the convent, with the proviso, however, that it would be void if she left. And when at last she did leave, by papal dispensation, in 1581, to become prioress of the Mitigated Franciscans — a step she later regretted — La Madre accepted the disappointment cheerfully, as one might expect. "At first the news gave me a shock," she told Gracián, "but then I considered that the judgments of God are great, and that, in fine, He loves this Order, and that He is going to draw some good from it, or avert some evil that we do not understand. For love of our Lord, let Your Reverence not be troubled."[9]

The letter goes on to say that the Jesuit confessor of Doña María de Acuna had advised the nuns not to vote for a subprioress who would not agree to renounce Casilda's property. Still, the Discalced should remain on friendly terms with the Jesuits, for most of the postulants at Valladolid were sent by them, and would not enter if they could not consult them. "God deliver us from such intrigues!"[10]

Madre Teresa suspected clearly, then, that some Jesuit had played a part in getting Casilda to leave the Reform, and that Casilda's mother wanted her money for a "college." Considering her friendship for the Jesuits, and the fact that her son was one of them, it would be reasonable to suppose that any college she founded would be for them — particularly if they were interested in helping her to recover the necessary funds. But did she found a college? Not even Mir offers any proof that she did. He implies, and the Benedictines of Stanbrook Abbey state[11] that it was for "the college" at Valladolid. To this Father Zugasti, S.J., replies that the Jesuits had three colleges in Valladolid, all of them founded before the Discalced Carmelite Reform[12] — though he does not discuss the possibility that one of the three may have used the Padilla fortune for expansion! Still, if the Jesuits wanted the money, so did the Carmelites, both intending to use it for a holy purpose.[13] The only indisputable moral to

---

[9] To Gracián, September 17, 1581.

[10] The text is in *Lettres de Sainte Thérèse*, by Father Grégoire of Saint Joseph, t. III, number 390. The Benedictines give a translation, Vol. IV, pp. 216–219. The date is September 17, 1581.

[11] *Letters*, Vol. II, p. 183, n. 2.

[12] *Op. cit.* (*Discurso*), p. 77.

[13] "There was some litigation between the Jesuits and Carmelites, with no gain

be drawn from all this seems to be that Jesuits and Carmelites are human beings.

Although Casilda and her money were gone, the incident was not without advantage to the Reform. Her profession, following the melodramatic entrance of the Princess of Éboli, made the Discalced in a sense fashionable, and attracted to them the services and the property of many rich young women. This, however, did not appeal much to La Madre. "Please don't send me any more *señoras*," she wrote Father Yepes.[14] And to Gracián: "His Majesty must want us not to honor ourselves with ladies of the earth, but with poor little people such as the Apostles were, and there is nothing to worry about. And since they have taken the other daughter from Santa Catalina de Siena, to keep her company, it turns out that nothing is lost there, I mean in the eyes of the aforementioned of the world; for to God, as I say, perhaps it is better that we place our eyes on Him alone. May she be with God. And may He deliver me from those gentlemen (*señores*) who can do it all and have strange whims."[15]

Teresa had a more serious encounter with the Jesuits early in 1578, when the fate of the Reform still hung in the balance, over Father Gaspar de Salazar, S.J. Since his rectorship in Ávila in 1561, when his understanding of her spirit played so decisive a part in her life, this friend of hers had been rector in Madrid, Marchena, Cuenca, Belmonte, and Toledo, whence he had kept up a desultory correspondence with her. A man of contemplation, taciturn and aloof with most persons, he had the reputation in the Company of being an able administrator, but quarrelsome at times and very hard on those under him. In 1562 his Provincial removed him from Ávila for certain differences he had with the Bishop, Don Álvaro:[16] and in 1575 he was deposed from his rectorship at Cuenca for undue severity to his subordinates.[17] This side of his character seems to have escaped Madre Teresa. He had once done her a great service. That was enough to make her see only his virtues, which were considerable, through the magnifying glass of her gratitude.

---

for the latter," says the editor of the Stanbrook *Letters*, II, p. 183, n. 2, giving no explanation of the vague statement, or of another on the same page: "In the end Don Antonio received a large share of it, which came to the Jesuit College at Valladolid." Perhaps the next edition of the *Letters* will clarify the matter.

[14] Yepes, letter to Fray Luis de León, in Mir, II, *op. cit.*, p. 478.
[15] Letter of September 17, 1581.
[16] Astrain, *Historia de la compañía*, etc., t. II, lib. I, cap. VIII.
[17] *Ibid.*, t. III, lib. I, cap. IV.

The fact that he was one of several Jesuits who sought, through the Nuncio and Philip II, to have changes made in the Constitutions of the Company, in 1577,[18] makes it plain that he certainly followed, if he was not actually a member of, the small but dangerous group called the *malcontentos*, who gave so much trouble to their fellow Jesuits at this period,[19] and who, if they had succeeded, would have made the Company subservient to the Crown, and have limited its influence to Spain.

About 1577, also, it was bruited about that Father Salazar wished to leave the Company of Jesus and to become a Discalced Carmelite. When this came to the ears of the Jesuit Provincial for Castilla, Father Juan Suárez, he was not at all pleased. A learned and holy man, though of a cold, reserved, and sometimes obstinate nature (in the judgment of his brethren),[20] he knew that the Reform of Madre Teresa had made a powerful appeal to certain Jesuits of contemplative habits of mind. Gracián had refused to receive eight of them at Alcalá without the consent of their superiors, which apparently was not forthcoming — so at least Fray Juan de la Miseria wrote in his autobiography. And after several Jesuits had gone over to the Carthusians, Father Alonso Román complained that the *Cartuja* of Valencia was "eating into the Society like a moth."[21]

The commotion aroused in the Company by the news that Father Gaspar de Salazar desired to leave was commensurate with the many high offices he had held. Father Suárez, the Provincial, was so disturbed that he wrote Madre Teresa a letter whose contents and tone may be inferred from her reply:

"The Father Rector gave me a letter of Your Paternity which certainly has surprised me much, since Your Paternity tells me in it that I have spoken about Father Gaspar de Salazar's leaving the Company of Jesus and going over to our Order of Carmel, because our Lord so desires and has revealed it.

"As for the first, His Majesty knows, and this will be found to be true, I have never desired it, much less attempted it with

---

[18] *Ibid.*, t. III, lib. I, cap. V.

[19] *Ibid.*, t. III: also Campbell, *History of the Jesuits*, p. 197 *et seq.* Cf. also *supra*, Ch. 13.

[20] Astrain (*op. cit.*, t. III, lib. I, cap. IV) says he was noted "*de ser algo cerrado y esquivo en su trato.*"

[21] *Ibid. Cartuja* is the Spanish for the Italian *Certosa*, the French *Chartreuse*, the English "Charterhouse."

him; and when anything of those matters came to my notice, and it was not by your letter, it so disturbed me and gave me such great sorrow that it did nothing to improve the poor health I had at that time. And this so recently, that I must have learned of it considerably after Your Paternity, as I think.

"As for the revelation that Your Paternity mentions, since he has not written me nor have I known anything of that determination, neither would I know if he had had any revelation in that matter.

"If I had had the false revelation that Your Paternity mentions in it, I am not so wicked that for such a thing I should desire so great a change to be made, nor to give him an account of it; for, glory to God, I have been taught by many persons the value and credit that is to be given to those things; and I do not believe that Father Salazar would pay any attention to that, if there were nothing more in the affair, for he is very sensible.

"As for what Your Paternity says of the prelates investigating it, that will be quite proper, and Your Paternity has the power to command it; for it is quite clear that he will not do anything without the permission of Your Paternity, and as I think, giving you notice of it. The great friendship there is between Father Salazar and me, and the honor it does me, I will never deny, although I am convinced that the service of our Lord and His Blessed Mother has influenced him more than any other friendship in what he has done for me, for I well believe it has happened that neither of us has written to the other for two years at a time. As I am a very old woman, it will be understood that in other times I have found myself in greater need of his aid, for this Order had only two Discalced fathers, and I could better have attempted this change than now, when, glory to God, there are, as I think, more than two hundred, and among them persons competent for our poor way of proceeding. Never have I thought that the hand of God would be more shortened for the Order of His Mother than for the others.

"As for what Your Paternity says, that I have written that it may be said that you prevented it, may God not write me in His book if such a thing even entered my mind. . . . And never will I believe that even for very grave reasons will His Majesty allow His Company to go against the Order of His Mother, since He made use of it to restore and renovate it, much less for so trifling a thing; and even if He does permit it, I fear that it will be possible to lose in other directions what it is hoped to gain in another.

"Of this King we are all vassals," she continued, borrowing a figure from Saint Ignatius. "Please His Majesty that those of the Son and of the Mother be such that like strong soldiers, we may look only where the banner of our King goes, to follow His will; and if the Carmelites do this in truth, it is plain that those of the name of Jesus cannot draw apart, as so many times I am threatened.[22]

"May it please God to preserve Your Paternity many years.

"Indeed I know the favor you always show us, and so, although miserable, I commend you much to our Lord; and I beg Your Paternity to do the same for me, for this half year troubles and persecutions have not stopped raining on this poor old woman; and now this business, which I don't hold to be the least. With all this, I give Your Paternity my word that he shall not be told to do it, nor shall it be done by any person on my behalf, nor has it been said."[23]

To this noble and touching appeal, Father Suárez replied by sending a note to the rector of Ávila, Father Gonzalo Dávila, to the effect that "if Madre Teresa of Jesus judges that it is proper for Father Salazar to be received into her order, let her communicate with the others [of the Discalced], or by writing to the Superior of each house all can be advised within fifteen days, and it is more than fifteen since Madre Teresa and the Prioress here have known it. This would be efficacious diligence with the aid of God."[24]

Father Dávila forwarded this with a note saying the Father Provincial would soon be in Ávila and would discuss the matter with her; meanwhile he begged her holy prayers. He suggested that if she would read the Provincial's note again, she would find it less offensive than she had supposed. In conclusion he urged her to do as Father Suárez had said; and would she let him know what she intended to do, "for I believe it will be of no small importance to you to do what we ask, in charity."[25]

Teresa's reply to this thinly veiled threat was at once frankly respectful and finely ironic:

[22] "De que tantas veces soy amenazada."
[23] B.M.C., Epistolario, II, pp. 156–160, February 10, 1578.
[24] Epistolario, II, p. 161, n. I; Stanbrook, III, p. 41.
[25] Ibid., p. 162; Stanbrook, p. 42.

"Jhs. The Holy Spirit be with your worship. I have read the letter of the Father Provincial again more than twice, and always I find in it so little consideration for me, and such assurance of what has not even crossed my mind, that His Paternity will not be surprised that it should give me pain. This matters little, for if I were not so imperfect I should have to consider it a pleasure that His Paternity should mortify me, since, as I am his subject,[26] he can do it. And since Father Salazar is one also, it occurs to me that it would be a better remedy for him to put a stop to it than for me to write what you want me to do, to those who are not mine;[27] for it is the duty of his prelate, and they would be right in paying small attention to what I might tell them.

"And surely, I see no other way, nor do I grasp what are these truths you tell me, Sir, that I should write; for unless it is to say that news has come to me from heaven that he is not to do it, nothing else has been left for me to do. However, as I told you, Sir, I don't have to give an account of everything, and it means offering a great insult to one whom I owe good friendship . . . and I would be offering an insult to a person so important[28] and so much a servant of God, by defaming him in all our monasteries (even if they had to pay attention to me), for it is a great infamy to say that he would be willing to do what he cannot do without offense to God.

"I have spoken to you, Sir, with all truth, and in my opinion, I have done what I was obliged to do in courtesy[29] and Christianity. The Lord knows I speak truth in this, and to do more than I have done I think would be going against the one and the other.

"I have already told you, Sir, that when I do what I think I ought in anything, God gives me courage to endure, with His help, all the evil results that may come. At least I cannot complain that they were not prophesied, nor that I have failed to do what I could do, as I have said. It may be that you, Sir, are more at fault in having commanded it to me, than I am for not obeying.

"Also I am quite sure, that if the affair should turn out other-

---

[26] Teresa had consulted Father Suárez about her spirit, and had great affection for him as a director.
[27] Under her authority, referring to the Discalced friars.
[28] "Grave."
[29] "Nobleza."

wise than as you, Sir, desire, I should be just as much blamed as if I had done nothing; and that the mere fact that I have said anything will be enough [to have it said] that the prophecies[30] are beginning to be fulfilled. If there are trials in store for me, let them come when they will.[31] I have committed offenses against the Divine Majesty which merit more than they can bring.

"Furthermore I don't think I deserve to have the Company inflict them upon me, even if I had had a hand in this business; for it neither makes nor breaks what concerns you. Your principles are of more lofty origin than that.[32] Please the Lord it may be mine never to deviate from doing His will, and may He give you, Sir, the light always to do the same. It will be a great pleasure to me to have our Father Provincial come here, for it has been a long time since our Lord has wished to let me have the pleasure of seeing His Paternity.

"Your unworthy servant and daughter, Sir,

"Teresa of Jesus."[33]

Father Dávila called upon her at San José, a day or two later. Teresa's letter to Father Gracián, forwarding one from Father Salazar and giving an account of the interview, makes her innocence of the charges of Father Suárez quite clear. First she begged "Paul," for the love of God, to be careful not to fall on the rough roads where he was traveling, for her own accident had taught her what a tumble could do. It was very cold, the first hard frost of the winter, but she did not feel it as in Toledo. Her left arm and hand were still bound up in a poultice or plaster of saffron, "which seems like a coat of mail, and it is of little use to me." Nevertheless she wrote the letter herself, for the autograph of most of it is extant:[34]

"I send Your Paternity herewith a letter that the Provincial of the Company sent me on the affair of Carrillo,[35] which so disgusted me that I should like to have replied to him worse than I did reply to him. For I know that he has been told that I had nothing to do with this change, which is the truth, and

[30] The "false revelations" attributed to her regarding Father Salazar. P. Silverio, *Epistolario*, II, p. 163, n. 1.

[31] "*En hora buena.*"

[32] "*De más alto vienen sus fundamentos.*" Another possible rendering is, "Your foundations are deeper than that."

[33] *Epistolario*, II, 161–163; Stanbrook, III, 42–44.

[34] In the convent of the Discalced at Madrid.

[35] Code name of Father Salazar, S.J.

when I learned of it, it gave me sorrow enough, as I wrote Your Paternity, and with a great desire that it should proceed. I wrote him[36] a letter as emphatically as I could, just as I took my oath in that one to the Provincial, for they are of such a sort that I thought they would not believe it if it were not said with so much emphasis. And it is highly important that they believe it, on account of what he[37] says of the fake revelations; let them not think that I have persuaded him in this way, for it is such a big lie.[38] But I tell Your Paternity that I have so little to fear of their fierce threats,[39] that I am amazed at the liberty God gives me. And so I told the Rector that in anything I understood to be for His service, the whole Company and all the world would not keep me from carrying it out, and that as I had had no part in this business, I would have just as little in making him give it up.

"He asked me, even if I wouldn't do this, to write him a letter in which I would tell him what I say in that one, that is that he cannot do it without being excommunicated.

"I said to him, 'Does he know these Briefs?' He said, 'Better than I.' I said, 'Then I am sure of him, that he will do nothing in which he thinks there is any offense to God.' He said, 'Nevertheless his great affection might deceive him and lead him astray'; and so I wrote him[40] a letter by the messenger by whom he wrote me that one.

"What foolishness, Your Paternity! For I was well aware from indications that they saw it;[41] although I didn't let him[42] know it. And in it I told him not to trust in his brethren, for those were brethren that Joseph had,[43] for I know they must have

[36] Father Salazar.
[37] The Provincial.
[38] *"Pues es tan gran mentira."*
[39] *"Sus fieros."*
[40] Father Salazar.
[41] The Jesuits saw her letter to Father Salazar.
[42] The Rector.
[43] Father Zugasti believes that these words were interpolated by some hand unfriendly to the Jesuits. He argues that Teresa with her illuminated mind could not have said this, for Joseph's brothers did not accuse him, but he accused them. As Father Silverio remarks (*Epistolario*, II, p. 166) the learned Jesuit apologist seems to have misunderstood the Saint here. She was not referring to the Jesuits accusing Salazar of wishing to be a Carmelite, but to their betraying his confidence to the Father Provincial, as Joseph's brethren sold him into slavery. Father Silverio believes this part of the letter authentic, with the rest. He adds, "Zugasti has a mania on interpolations," and invites him to see the words in the handwriting of Saint Teresa at the Carmelite Convent of Saint Ann, in Madrid.

seen it; for his own friends must have been the ones who ex-posed him, and I am not surprised, for they felt it much too much. They must be afraid of his starting a precedent.

"I said to him, 'Didn't some of them become Discalced?' He said, 'Yes — Franciscans; but they threw them out first, and after-wards they gave them permission.'[44] I said they could do that now. But they are not ready for that, any more than I am to tell him not to do it, but to inform him, as I do in that letter, and to leave it to God, for if it is His work they will desire it. For otherwise (as I tell him there) I have asked about it, and surely, it is not likely that he can do it;[45] and those men must be citing the common law, like that other lawyer who persuaded me, at the foundation of Pastrana, to take the Augustinian,[46] and he was wrong. As for the Pope's giving permission, I don't believe it, for they will have all the doors blocked against him. Will Your Paternity please make inquiries, and advise him, for it would give me much sorrow if he should commit any offense against God. I well believe, as I understand it, that he will not do it.

"It has given me much anxiety, for if he stays with them after they know the inclination he has elsewhere, he will not have the prestige he usually has. To be here is out of the question, unless it can be done properly. And I keep thinking of what we always owe to the Company. Not to receive him if we can, through fear of them, would be to do wrong to him, and to ill pay his good will. God set it right, for He will direct it, though I fear lest those matters of prayer he talks about may have influenced him, for he gives too much credit to them. I have often told him so, but in vain.

"It also gives me sorrow that those [nuns] of Beas must have said something to him about that, judging by the disposition that Catalina of Jesus showed. The good thing about all is that he, certainly, is a servant of God, and if he deceives himself, it is in thinking that He desires it, and His Majesty will look after him. But he has got us into trouble,[47] and you may believe that if I had not heard from Joseph[48] what I wrote Your Pater-

---

[44] The Jesuits threw them out, and the Franciscans gave them permission.

[45] "No se debe de poder hacer." Stanbrook: "He certainly ought not to take the step."

[46] Catalina Machuca.

[47] "Ruido," literally "noise."

[48] Code name for our Lord.

nity, I should have done all in my power to put a stop to it. Yet, although I don't believe as much as he does in these matters, it goes very much against me to oppose it. How do I know but I should be keeping some great good from that soul? For Your Paternity may believe that in my opinion he doesn't have the spirit of where he is; I always thought he would enter. . . .

"As quickly as Your Paternity can, send the letter of Father Salazar by way of the Prior of Granada, who is to give it to him privately, and impress this well upon him; for I dread being written to again by the Company, either myself or any of these sisters — and they don't write in code.[49] Or by the way of the Court, commending it strictly to Roque, and if he gives a good tip and gives it to the same muleteer, it ought to go safely. Don't be careless about this, *mi Padre,* for it ought to be sent to him, so that he will do nothing, if he has not already done it, and Your Paternity should put off giving him the license, in my opinion, for all is for his greater good. . . . That letter of the Father Provincial and the reply may be useful sometime. Don't tear them up, if you think so."[50]

Gracián never forwarded the letter to Father Salazar. Later Teresa was glad of this[51] and she was already frightened by the thought of the possible consequences of "Carrillo's" (Father Salazar's) breaking with the Jesuits. It was an extraordinary letter she wrote to Gracián on March 2, 1578:

"Carrillo is right in saying that I have little courage, for he has answered the first letter I wrote him, telling him it was the devil and many other things. He says I make him laugh, and that it changed him neither little nor much. He says I am like a rat that is afraid of the cats, and that he has promised it while holding the Most Blessed Sacrament in his hands, and that the whole world will not be enough to prevent it. I tell you he frightens me, for his brothers say that he and whoever gives him that habit are excommunicated. He says he already has permission from his Provincial, and that Your Paternity wrote him a letter, and that although you fear like a man, you write like an angel; and he is right, for such it was.

"It is a hard thing his own ask, that he be not received; it

---

[49] *"Y sus cifras vienen bien claras,"* literally, "their ciphers come very clear."
[50] Letter to Gracián, February 16, 1578, B.M.C., II, pp. 164–170; Stanbrook, III, pp. 45–51.
[51] Letter to Gracián, May 22, 1578.

must be because they believe it cannot be done. Judging by their usual diligence, I believe they must have written to Your Paternity to notify the convents. They have pressed me so hard that I told them I had written to Your Paternity.

"For certain, if it is going to be done, and if it can be done as he says, it would be better to have it over with than to raise such a hullabaloo here by sending out notifications to ourselves, for I don't know how Your Paternity can do that; for if it can be done, it seems [against?] conscience not to admit him. I well believe from the way he pictures it that nobody will stop him, and so it would be better to wait, if it is not already done. May the Lord direct it, for the more they object, the more I think it is going to serve God, and the devil wants to prevent it. They must be afraid that he will not be the only one; yet they are so numerous that they would hardly miss them, even if they were those Your Paternity mentions.

"I should like to send Your Paternity the letter from the Prioress of Valladolid[52] in which she tells about the hullabaloo that has arisen over the affair of Carrillo. In short, she says they[53] are very well pleased with me and the Discalced; that all the threats seem fierce to me, but will not amount to anything.[54] What makes me pause, and what makes me afraid, and what I want Your Paternity to look into and be very frank about, is whether he can do what he says without offense to God or excommunication, for if what those others[55] say is true, Your Paternity can in no way do it. . . .

"Unworthy daughter of Your Paternity, and how truly one! How little I find myself so with other fathers!

"Teresa of Jesus."[56]

Finally, on September 3, 1578, Father Salazar wrote his gen-

---

[52] María Bautista.

[53] The Jesuits, apparently.

[54] *"Ello me parece todo los fieros de manera, que no han de ser nada."*

[55] The Jesuits.

[56] *Epistolario,* II, pp. 171–176, Stanbrook, III, pp. 52–56. Father Zugasti, following an earlier Jesuit scholar, Father Montoya, has challenged the authenticity of this letter (*Discurso,* pp. 51–52) alleging that Saint Teresa must have been taken in by a forgery which she considered a message from Father Salazar. Father Silverio replies, conclusively it would appear, that the whole letter is unquestionably in her handwriting and may be seen at the convent of the Discalced Carmelites at Sevilla. If she was deceived, he argues, it was by Father Salazar. See his note 1, p. 171; also notes 2 and 3 on p. 173, and the one on p. 174.

eral, Father Everardo Mercuriano, S.J., a smug letter which makes it clear how much Teresa had overrated him:

"If it has been a question of my speaking with Discalced friars or nuns — there are none in this city — I have neither seen them, nor written to them, nor ever spoken of them among ours, nor even in preaching ventured to quote a Saint of their Order." He pleaded that he had kept the rule as well as he could. He usually prayed for five or six hours at a time, he said, being a poor sleeper and having few duties at Córdoba. He was considered a good and loyal son of the Company — "blessed be God, blessed be God. Never have I asked for a dispensation; and if the devil ever did tempt me, I held the road more firmly, for several months ago Father Bernal, Provincial, told me that if I wanted it, His Paternity would give it to me. If . . . any have asked for it, seeing that on their account they think I am humbled and persecuted, never would it please God that I should ever leave what I have loved so much and my mother that has nourished me, which is the Holy Company . . . or that for all the world I would insult my flesh and blood which loves and esteems the Company and favors it much, and receives so much in a spiritual way. They have told me that I wish to command; (yet) in the time of Cardinal Espinosa, who was like my father, they gave me — to my shame and confusion I tell it — a good bishopric, and in the Company I have always resisted being Rector; I don't know how they can say that I desired to command *someone who has more lice than order of life.*[57] Your Paternity may rest assured that I am and will be a son of the Company forever, and do me this charity, that although I am so wicked and deserve to have whatever evil may be said of me believed, you will not believe it until you know it of me. . . ."

This letter, in the opinion of Father Zugasti, clinches what he calls the "innocence" of Father Salazar. "*The document* attributed to Carrillo (P. Salazar) in the letter Saint Teresa wrote to Father Gracián March 2, 1578, *is not Father Salazar's;* for Father Salazar clearly and definitely affirms that in the years he was in Córdoba (1578–1579) he wrote no letter to any Dis-

[57] "*A quien tiene más piojos que orden de vida.*" Father Silverio observes, "What a phrase for a man of so many hours of prayer!" (*Loc. cit.*, II, p. 156, n. 1.) The words that I have italicized are omitted by Father Zugasti in his *discurso*, p. 48, and in his longer work, *Santa Teresa y la Compañía de Jesús*, p. 278. They do not lend much support to his theory that Father Salazar could not have made the coarse comparison of Saint Teresa to a rat.

calced friar or nun. Therefore, he did not write to Saint Teresa."[58]

In his eagerness to prove his point, Father Zugasti neglects to tell us the date in 1578 when Father Salazar went to Córdoba. To sustain his point it would have to be in January or February. But he himself on the previous page has said that *"toward the end of* the year 1578," the Jesuit Visitor, Father Antonio Ibáñez, arrived in Toledo from Aragon to look into the doings of the *malcontentos;* that he was not the man to speak to Father Salazar without investigating, but probably told the Provincial, Father Suárez, to sound him out; and that Father Suárez transferred Father Salazar to the college at Córdoba. "He was there," then adds Father Zugasti, *"for the space of two years* (1578–1579)";[59] but nowhere does he give the all-important date, without which we may still take the word of Saint Teresa that she had a letter from Father Salazar, asserting in the strongest terms his intention of leaving the Jesuits for the Carmelites.

Father Zugasti is on firmer ground when he explains the conduct of the Provincial Father Suárez in the light of the conspiracy of the *malcontentos.* It was the first great internal danger the Jesuits had had to face. They were not afraid of the external foes of whom their Lord had warned them. They could confront the harquebuses of the Huguenot pirates, or (as Father Campion did) the instruments of torture in the tower of London, with serene courage. But this intrigue took them unawares, and it is not surprising if, in dealing with a hidden menace in their own house, some of them were victims for the moment of frayed nerves, false rumors, ill-founded suspicions and fears. And of course there were all sorts of temperaments among them, as in every other order.

It must also be noticed, as La Madre confessed to Gracián, that the nuns at Beas had something to do with the business. It is not at all improbable that Father Suárez got his idea of a false revelation from some mistaken or exaggerated remark of one of these sisters. Believing it, he would naturally take the view he did; and if he thought his brother, Father Salazar, had been the victim of some piece of pseudo mysticism, it was his duty to try to protect him from it. The mind of the Church had always been against transferals from one Order to another: the

---

[58] *Ibid.,* p. 51.
[59] My italics.

Canon Law had forbidden it, making the Carthusians a sole exception for a Jesuit. Father Suárez was but doing his duty. His mistake was his failure to understand the woman he addressed, and perhaps some lack of consideration and courtesy. Again, as Father Silverio suggests, it is likely that both Madre Teresa and his superiors in the Company took Father Salazar too seriously.[60] He had the defects of character and the emotional instability that one might expect to find in one of the *malcontentos*. Yet he served the Church and the Company until his death, and may have expiated whatever faults he had by untold suffering.

Some Jesuit Father whom La Madre refers to as "the cat" — was it Father Suárez? — appears to have spoken disparagingly of Father Salazar to Father Gracián. Teresa wrote the latter on May 22, 1578: "God forgive him, for if he were as bad as he says, you may be sure they would not have taken so much trouble not to lose him. I am very glad Your Paternity did not send the letter to Sevilla; for I deem it better to conduct ourselves toward them with all humility. For truly we have owed them much, and we are still indebted to many of them. . . .

"I have also heard from Toledo that they are complaining a great deal of me. Yet it is true that I did all I could, and even more than justice called for; and the only reason they have to complain against Your Paternity and me is, I have thought, that we have been so careful not to displease them. And I believe that if God alone had been considered, and if what so good a desire demanded had been done only for His service, that peace would now be restored and they more contented, for the Lord Himself would have smoothed things over. But when we follow human respect, the end it seeks is never attained — rather, the reverse, as now appears; as if what he wanted to do were a heresy! As I have told them, they resent its becoming public. Surely, my Father, they and we have had enough of dirt in the business.[61] Withal, I am glad it has happened as it has; I hope our Lord will be pleased."

This, too, after all, was a tempest in a teapot. Only a month

---

[60] *Vida*, IV, p. 483. It is possible, too, that María Bautista was right in her opinion, cited above, that Teresa exaggerated the resentment of the Jesuits against her.

[61] *"Cierto, mi Padre, que ellos y nosotros hemos tenido harto de tierra en el negocio."* — *Epistolario*, II, p. 215; letter of May 22, 1578. Montoya challenged the authenticity of the second paragraph of this letter, but not very successfully. Cf. Silverio, *loc. cit.*, p. 215, n. 2.

later (June, 1578) we find Teresa writing most affectionately and confidentially about her soul to Father Gonzalo Dávila, S.J., the rector at Ávila, whose direction she was apparently following; and more than once she wrote Fray Mariano, who was an engineer, urging him to help the Jesuits there with their water supply. There was nothing vindictive in this magnanimous soul.

What of the sons of Saint Ignatius? Mir would have us believe that the bickering over Salazar became a serious feud, leading to a definite and permanent breach between them and Saint Teresa; and that all the Jesuits were ordered to have nothing more to do with her and her Discalced nuns, "in a manner official and public and obstreperous."[62]

It was so public and obstreperous that Mir himself had not found the official document after more than three centuries. It was Father Zugasti, S.J., who first published, in 1914, the text of the circular letter of the Provincial, Father Suárez, to all the houses and colleges of Castilla, dated January 23, 1579:

"At various times I have informed Your Reverence, by word and by letter, that it was the will of Father General that the communication of ours with the Carmelite nuns is all to be given up, in so far as it is found to exceed the method of our Institute, and only that is to be continued which was in accord with what was recommended to Your Reverence. . . .

"I have now learned that His Holiness has so instructed the Carmelite Fathers of the Cloth, so called, through their superiors, and so I trust that the said nuns will find in the said friars of their own Order superiors, preachers, and confessors quite sufficient to give them doctrine and counsel and to administer the Holy Sacraments to them, as much as necessary for their salvation and perfection; and since the said Fathers are masters of the new Order and know the theory and practice of ends and means and method which God our Lord wishes to be used in it, and which His Holiness has approved for the said nuns, and since ours have not the said theory and practice, and our ends and means and method is neither given for the said nuns by God nor approved by His Vicars, I have come to the conclusion that ours will not be as successful as the said Fathers in helping them to their perfection by their method; and I have confidence in God and in His Providence that through the teaching, counsel, and example and administration of Sacraments of the said religious Fathers in their Order, the said religious Mothers will better pursue the end they seek of their salvation and perfection by their method. . . ."

To this Father Suárez added a significant notation: "the intention is to reduce the communication to the precise form of our Institute."[63]

This letter is not as damaging to the Jesuits as Mir expected (not to say hoped) it would be. It is obviously not a piece of personal spite or revenge on the part of Father Suárez. He was acting under orders from his General in Rome, and in accordance with a ruling of the Pope. The policy decided upon was so natural that the only wonder is that it was not adopted before. The Jesuits were under no obligation to do the work of another Order with a mission very different from theirs. They had an active apostolate to assist in the regeneration, the re-education, and the extension of Christendom. Addressing themselves not to a few chosen souls, but to thousands and millions of laymen, they made it their chief aim to draw men from heresy and mortal sin to a good Christian life. It might even be said, then, that their mission *had* to take in as many persons as possible, and therefore must consider primarily beginners in the spiritual life. In this they succeeded brilliantly and on a scale that no human wisdom could have foreseen half a century before. This is not to say that they taught people to remain beginners. Any Christian might go on indefinitely, as Madre Teresa did, and as John of the Cross probably did, from the *Spiritual Exercises* of Saint Ignatius. Some Jesuits, like Father Baltasar Alvarez, attained a high degree of contemplation; and if his brethren looked askance at this in a day when even Teresa was mistaken for an Illuminate, they did not prevent his persevering to the end in a prayer different from the discursive method, the prayer of "composition of a scene" taught by Saint Ignatius; nor did the Inquisitors interfere, although they investigated him. Still, he was bound to be, in the nature of the case, an exception. For all the Jesuits to become contemplatives like John of the Cross would have been to ruin and betray their own divine mission. Teresa would have been the first to acknowledge the folly and danger of imposing a counsel of perfection on all Christians. She did not attempt to make a contemplative of any good woman who might apply. She was displeased, on the other hand, when

---

[63] Zugasti, *op. cit.* (*discurso*), pp. 79–80.

Gracián gave much time to preaching that he might have devoted to prayer. In the vast divine polity of the Catholic Church, no one Order can be all things to all men; it does well if it accomplishes the thing for which it was brought into being; if it tries too much, it may fail.

The Jesuits, after countless acts of generosity to the Carmelite Reform, were rudely reminded by the turmoil of the *malcontentos* that it was time to draw in their lines and attend more strictly to their own particular mission. Had it not been Teresa's aim for a long time to have only Discalced friars as confessors to the nuns? With some 200 barefoot friars available, there was certainly little need of Jesuits, whose services were urgently required for the growing enterprises of their own Company. As a human being she naturally resented having the break come from their side. But she had no right to resent it, nor did she waste much time in doing so. In a few weeks we find her again begging Mariano, as we have seen, to help the Jesuits of Ávila with their water supply. On the Feast of Saint Michael she asked Gracián to enlist the aid of "one of the Company, a great friend of mine," Father Paul Hernández — the *Padre Eterno* of the old days in Toledo — who was then in Madrid;[64] and in writing a long appeal to the latter, she recommended Gracián to him on the ground that he had been trained by the Jesuits all his life.[65] Only the malice of those who hate the Jesuits more than they love the Church — or those who hate the Jesuits precisely for having done so much for the Church — can make much of a mountain out of the molehill of this controversy.

Nowhere have I found the suggestion — but is it not worth considering? — that some of Teresa's difficulties with the Jesuits, as with others, may have resulted from the strange character of her champion, Father Gracián. If he was charming to her, he could be very irritating to others. She thought he was a Jesuit in temperament, but the Jesuits seem to have taken a different view. Superficially, yes, he had their energy and zeal, but he lacked the stamina and good judgment that they sought in their postulants. This may have been the reason why they did not take him in his youth, as it certainly helps to explain why they would not accept him later, when he was expelled from his own Order.

[64] Letter to Gracián, September 29, 1578.
[65] Letter to Father Hernández, October 4, 1578.

Poor Gracián! He meant so well, he strove so earnestly, yet he made so many mistakes! The history of the Reform would have been quite different if he had had the qualities of John of the Cross. They were unlike in almost everything save in their love for God. John taught that it was wicked to seek for supernatural illumination, for reason and revelation were enough to save a man's soul. He was distrustful of visions, raptures, locutions, spiritual feelings, what he called "spiritual gluttony." He would admit no special virtue in any special statue or crucifix. He was calm and self-possessed under all circumstances. When a woman held out a baby to him in Granada in 1583 and cried that he was the father and must support it, he quietly asked where the mother lived, and learning that she had never been outside of that city, demanded how old the child was. "Almost a year!" said the woman. "Then," said John pleasantly, "its birth must be a miracle, and one of a high order, for I have not yet been a year in Granada, and I never was here before."[66] Gracián on the other hand was moody and excitable, sentimental almost to the verge of superstition, enamored of the marvelous in religious experience, quick to believe signs, omens, and feelings, sometimes more fluent in words than cogent in thought. An instinctive dislike between two such men was to be expected. It seems certain that Gracián, at least, felt an aversion — or was it jealousy? — for little John of the Cross. He does not even mention him in his account, in the *Peregrinación*, of the founding of monasteries in which John played so important a part!

This perhaps explains why Gracián had done nothing to rescue or even to find him, during the months that had elapsed since the two friars had been dragged from the cottage near the Incarnation on the night of December 3, 1577. Teresa appealed to "Paul" time after time, but in vain. She wrote in fact to everyone who might have any influence. Where was "Seneca"? It was as if the earth had swallowed him. In January,

---

[66] Bruno, p. 278, and his reference. There is no real contradiction between Saint John's distrust of raptures and visions, and the fact that he was favored with many. Like Saint Teresa and all true mystics, he knew that those who sought such rare gifts of God might be deceived by the devil, or by their own pride and self-love. He approved of the use of images and pictures, of course, to arouse love and devotion, but discouraged a *sensual* attachment to them. (*Ascent of Mount Carmel*, Book III, ch. 15 and ch. 34.) See the letters, documents, and depositions about him in Peers, *Complete Works of Saint John of the Cross*, Vol. III, appendix.

1578, she heard a rumor, instigated perhaps by the Calced, that Tostado had sent him to Rome. "All consider him a saint," she wrote the Bishop of Évora, January 16, 1578. "In my opinion he is a great article;[67] and placed there by the Apostolic Visitor, a Dominican, and by the late Nuncio, and subject to the Visitor Gracián, it is a madness that has been astonishing. . . . I am afraid they are treating him severely, and I fear some misfortune."

In March she wrote Gracián, "I grieve a great deal for Fray John, lest they bring some other charge against him. God treats His friends terribly; yet in truth He does them no wrong, for He dealt likewise with His Son."[68] This thought was much in her mind during that terrible year. "You know," she wrote Mother María de San José, "that if you are going to enjoy the Crucified, you have to bear a cross . . . and those whom His Majesty loves, He treats like His Son."[69] And to Father Báñez she wrote, "I well understand that the Lord wants me to have in this life nothing but cross and more cross."[70] Yet when Gracián wrote her of his longing for more crosses, she begged him, for the love of God, to give them "a few days' rest," for any trials he had would surely involve others.[71]

Here perhaps she was thinking of Father John of the Cross. No doubt he was suffering for all of them, wherever he was. But where was he? She urged Gracián to have Fray Antonio see his friend the Duchess of Alba, and Fray Mariano to see his friend the King. Finally Philip sent for the friar-engineer,[72] but the mysterious silence at the Escorial remained unbroken. Gracián was visiting many influential people in Madrid; could he not get some of them to do something? Lady Guiomar and all the nuns were weeping constantly. "I am astonished at this enchantment of Fray John of the Cross."[73] Even as late as August 19 she had not learned the truth, for she wrote to Gracián, "I tell you, I am sure that if some person of note should ask the Nuncio for Fray John, he would at once order him to go to [one of] his houses, if he were told what that father is, and how unjustly they detain him. I don't know how it happens that nobody ever remembers this Saint. The Princess of Éboli would do it if Mariano told her to."[74]

[67] "Gran pieza."
[68] March 11, 1578.
[69] June 4, 1578.
[70] July 28, 1578.

[71] To Gracián, April 21, 1579.
[72] To Gracián, April 17, 1578.
[73] To Gracián, May 22, 1578: "encantamiento."
[74] To Gracián, August 19, 1578.

Not until the latter part of August, 1578, did she learn that John of the Cross had been taken to Toledo and shut up in the convent of the Calced Carmelites on the east side of the city, looking down on the Bridge of Alcántara and the swift reddish Tagus that coils like a great watery snake along the base of the somber rock. There, within the gloomy ocher-colored walls of the old three-story building (nearly three feet thick, judging by what remains of them) he was led before Tostado the day after his arrival, was informed of the decision of the Council of Piacenza, and was asked to obey and give up the Reform. Both men had wills of steel; both thought they were right. When John calmly refused, pleading obedience to the authority that had placed him at the Incarnation, Tostado ordered him punished according to the rules prescribed for recalcitrant friars by Blessed Soreth.

For nine months he was locked up in a narrow cavity in a wall, six feet wide by ten long. The only opening was a small dormer window in one corner, looking out into a gallery, where a little ray of sunlight sometimes glittered, so that John could see it when he stood on a stool to read his office. Every evening he was taken to the refectory to eat his meal of bread and water on the floor (later, this happened only three times a week, and finally only on Fridays). In the refectory, too, he was scourged by the whole community. As he knelt half-naked, the Calced friars would walk about him in a circle, each lashing at his bare back until it was raw and bloody with wounds that would scar it till the day of his death. He was silent, thinking of the scourging of Christ at the pillar. In vain they cried, "Senseless block!" and struck harder blows. Afterwards his tunic stuck to the wounds and became clotted with blood.[75] He wore it the whole nine months without a change.[76]

Yet out of the black misery of that cell, as he stood on tiptoe to see a ray of God's sunshine through the aperture in the corner, there burst from his brave unconquerable heart some of the imperishable poems that later became texts for his great doctrinal works in prose. He composed orally, without paper, and memorized as he went along: seventeen stanzas (perhaps thirty) of the *Spiritual Canticle;* the poem with the refrain, *"Although 'tis night,"* the one beginning, *"In principio erat Verbum";* and

[75] Bruno, *op. cit.*

[76] Saint Teresa to Gracián, end of August, 1578.

possibly *"Dark Night."*[77] Nothing in Spanish, as Menéndez y Pelayo says,[78] can compare with these passionate and exquisite cries from a soul given utterly to a deathless love; "so sublime is this poetry that it scarcely seems to belong to this world at all."

Even in unrhymed translation his stanzas retain some of the qualities that make them great:

> Whither hast thou hidden thyself,
> And hast left me, O Beloved, to my sighing?
> Thou didst flee like the hart
> Having wounded me:
> I went out after thee, calling, and thou wert gone. . . .

> O woods and thickets
> Planted by the hand of my Beloved,
> O meadow of verdure
> Enameled with flowers,
> Say if he has passed by you.

> Scattering a thousand graces
> He passed through these groves in haste,
> And looking upon them as he went
> Left them, by his glance alone
> Clothed with beauty.[79]

Not since the Canticle of Canticles, perhaps, had anyone sung more ecstatically of the spiritual marriage of the soul with God:

> *Oh noche, que guiaste,*
> *Oh noche amable más que la alborada!*
> *Oh noche, que juntaste*
> *Amado con amada,*
> *Amada en el Amado transformada.*

---

[77] Bruno, *op. cit.*, p. 173; see also Father Silverio's introduction and notes to the *Spiritual Canticle*, in B.M.C., Vol. III; and the translations by Professor E. Allison Peers, 1934, London.

[78] *Historia de los heterodoxos españoles*, Madrid, 1887, t. II, p. 583.

[79] Peer's translation, *Spiritual Canticle*, p. 26 *et seq.* For the Spanish text see Father Silverio's edition, B.M.C., III, p. 7 *et seq:*

> *A dónde te escondiste,*
> *Amado, y me dejaste con gemido?*
> *Como, el ciervo huiste,*
> *Habiéndome herido:*
> *Salí tras tí clamando, y eras ido,* etc.

Finally, on the fourteenth of August, 1578, the vigil of the Assumption, Father Maldonado went to his cell and found him lying motionless on the floor, exhausted and emaciated. Prodding him with his foot, he asked why he did not stand up. John, who had thought it was only the jailer, arose as quickly as his weakness would permit, and asked pardon.

"What were you thinking about, that you were so absorbed?"

"I was thinking that tomorrow is the feast of our Lady, and that it would be a great consolation for me if I could say Mass."

"Not in my time," said Maldonado.

It certainly seemed as if nobody, as Madre Teresa wrote, even remembered the little man of God. But there was one who never forgot. The next night our Lady appeared to him in a vision, clothed in beauty and glory indescribable, and told how to make his escape: how to loosen the bolts on the lock of his room, which window of the gallery to climb through, how to make a rope out of two old coverlets torn up. One dark night he followed instructions. The rope was too short and he fell nine feet, unhurt. He dropped from a rampart, rolled down a steep riverbank, followed a dog that was eating garbage, leaped over a wall into a courtyard, found himself in a space between two convents, saw a mysterious light and heard a voice say "Follow me," and when he came to a high wall, felt himself lifted over it, to land without injury on a narrow street. While the Calced friars pursued with hue and cry, he made his way to the convent of the Discalced nuns, who concealed him in their infirmary. Finally, weeks later, he managed to get to Almodóvar, where he arrived just in time to attend the second General Chapter that Gracián had called.[80]

Gracián was about to take the fatal step that Teresa had so long feared. She had been warning him for months against the danger of provoking the Nuncio and the Calced fathers by having an election without permission from the Pope or the General. In April she had quoted to him the opinion of learned theologians that it could not be done. It was a *cosa mal sonante*. If they held it, they would have more trouble getting it confirmed than in obtaining the papal permission for a separate province, which, after all, could be accomplished by a letter from the King to his ambassador at Rome. But Gracián would

[80] For a more detailed account, see Father Bruno, *Saint John of the Cross*, pp. 178–185, and the documents in Peers, Vol. III, appendix.

be only giving new ammunition to the Calced if he carried out his rash intention.[81] She begged him not to come to Ávila, where he meant to escort his mother and sister, lest he be seized on the way.[82] Besides, there were no accommodations for receiving his mother; workmen were putting a new roof on the choir and were very noisy. "What a life!" wrote Teresa.

Gracián disregarded all her counsels, and proceeded to Ávila, where he apparently quarreled with her, and used indefensible language, if we may judge by her letter of April 26, after his departure:

"Jesus be with Your Paternity, my Father and my Prelate as you say, which has caused me no little laughter and rejoicing; but each time I remember it, it amuses me to think how earnestly you told me not to judge my Prelate.

"Oh, *mi padre!* How little need there was for Your Paternity to swear, and not like a saint either, but more like a mule driver, for I quite understand it. . . . I will say no more now except to remind Your Paternity that you gave me permission to criticize you and to think what I please. . . ."[83]

In May, when she was enduring agony from the resetting of her arm by the quack *curandera,* she earnestly found fault with him for sending doddering Fray Antonio to straighten out the affairs of the convent at Malagón, without adequate instructions, for he had only made matters worse; and she made some unflattering remarks about Father Mariano, which however she crossed out before sending the letter.[84] "Commend me much to God, for I am old and tired, but not in my desires."[85] One of her constant desires was that he should do nothing that would offend God. At this period she usually worked until one or two in the morning,[86] and of course got up before sunrise.

In midsummer a fresh blow fell upon the Reform. On July 23, the Nuncio Sega solemnly revoked all of Gracián's powers. Two weeks later the Royal council forbade the Discalced friars to obey the Nuncio. It was now plain, however, that Gracián's authority was at least questionable, and he barely escaped arrest at Valladolid, where he heard that Sega had excommunicated

[81] To Gracián, April 15, 1578.
[82] *Ibid.,* April 17.
[83] To Gracián, April 26, 1578.
[84] To Gracián, May 8, 1578.
[85] *Ibid.,* May 14.
[86] Letter to Father Dávila, S.J., June, 1578.

him. He then visited La Madre at Ávila, and left her most anxious about his future course. On August 14 she wrote him a letter full of earnest advice: Let him not offend the King, whatever Mariano might advise. If he spoke with the Nuncio, let him justify himself, but make plain his desire to be obedient, and the fact that he had delayed his submission only because he knew Tostado was determined to destroy the Reform. Let him seek a separate province on any terms the Calced might require, for on that depended the very existence of the Reform.[87]

When some visitors saw him on behalf of Sega, Gracián, then at Pastrana, was tempted to defy them, but finally submitted on the advice of a holy lay brother to whom it was revealed that in no other way could the Reform be saved. He then proceeded, however, to Almodóvar, where he convoked the Chapter of October, 1578, and did exactly what La Madre had been fearing: he held an election, and had old Fray Antonio, of all persons, chosen Provincial. Father John of the Cross raised his voice in vain against this folly; nor was he pacified when the Chapter delegated two "companions" to go to Rome: Fray Juan de Jesús Roja and Fray Pedro de los Angeles. John's prediction that they were going to Rome barefoot but would return shod was literally fulfilled. Arriving in Italy, Fray Pedro handed over his papers to one of the Calced and allowed himself to be entertained in a palace; when he reappeared in Spain, it was as a friar of the Mitigation. Gracián had carried out Teresa's wishes too late and had chosen the wrong man.

The Nuncio was furious, of course, when he heard of the election, which was tantamount to a defiance of his authority and an unlawful proclamation of a separate province. On October 16 he annulled the acts of the Chapter, declared the election illegal, and ordered Antonio to appear before him. (It did not help matters, either, when the old friar put off his appearance until November 13.) He dissolved the separate province. He incorporated the houses of friars with those of the Calced in Castilla and Andalucía. Sending for Gracián, he reproved him with great sternness and refused to listen to anything he might say in his own defense.

The King and Royal Council instructed the Discalced friars and nuns not to obey the Nuncio, since he had not shown any authority to interfere with religious houses in Spain. Sega re-

---

[87] To Gracián, August 14, 1578.

taliated by excommunicating all who had taken part in the Chapter.

It is doubtful whether Gracián realized, even then, how he had gone from blunder to blunder in his pious obstinate way. On hearing of the death of Rubeo, in October, Teresa wrote that she could do nothing but weep when she remembered that recourse to him would have saved them all their troubles. "I am glad that you are going to learn from experience to carry on affairs the way they must go, and not against the stream, as I have always said." She advised him not to send the friars to Rome, now that Rubeo was dead and the whole situation worse.

This advice was wasted. Gracián stubbornly went ahead until the Nuncio had him "imprisoned" at Alcalá. Did he maintain there the unflinching spirit of John of the Cross? He tells us that his enemies told his mother, Doña Juana Dantisco, that he intended to give up the Reform, hoping that she, out of maternal love, would persuade him to do so. Apparently Teresa heard the report and believed it, for we find her urging him, November 15, to stand firm in his tribulations. "I am not surprised that Your Paternity wants to get free from them, and looks for means, but it would not be right to forsake the Virgin in a time of such need. Surely Doña Juana would not advise it, nor would she consent to such a change."[88]

As for Doña Juana, that valiant Polish mother of twenty children wrote him at once,[89] "They have told me that you wish to leave the Order of our Lady, and if such a thing has passed through your mind, never speak to me again, or write to me, or consider me your Mother, for I don't want a son who has so little courage that persecutions make him leave such a Mother as the Virgin Mary, and turn his back on the Order to which he gave himself so willingly and I afterwards dedicated him." The Count of Tendilla, a great friend of the Reform at Court, promised to stab Gracián if he left. Cardinal Quiroga, the Grand Inquisitor, had once told him he did not have the courage of a fly, and that he ought to go to the King and lay the whole matter before him.[90] If Gracián remembered that now, it was too late to do anything about it.

---

[88] Letter of November 15, 1578.

[89] *Peregrinación*, Diálogo 9, p. 141. The Nuncio ordered Gracián to remain at the Priory at Alcalá until further notice, to fast three days a week, to be scourged once a week, and to have nothing more to do with the Discalced.

[90] Saint Teresa, to some unknown person, August 10, 1578.

As another year drew to its close, the Reform seemed almost at its final gasp. Teresa had fought the good fight to the end, she had never faltered, she had encouraged everyone. But the day before Christmas, when she might have expected a little peace, she received a letter of such a discouraging sort from Gracián that even she seemed to be breaking down. It had been rumored that she was to be sent to some other convent — one of the Calced, no doubt — to be incarcerated. Gracián may have told her also some of the worst slanders that were being circulated against the Discalced nuns and friars. Whatever the letter contained, the sick tired old lady burst into tears, crying, "God give me patience!" and continued to weep all day like an unconsolable child. "Now, Lord, Thou art granting my desire for suffering!" the nuns heard her say as she shut herself in her cell, refusing food or drink. There she stayed till evening, when Blessed Ann of Saint Bartholomew knocked at the door and begged her to come to the Refectory.

Teresa went, but was unable to eat any of the food. A lay sister told afterwards of seeing Christ appear beside her, take up a piece of bread, bless it, and place it in her mouth, saying,

"Eat this for love of Me."

Even after that she was seen to weep bitterly all through midnight Mass.[91]

---

[91] Deposition of María de San José, in Stanbrook Letters, III, p. 171.

Chapter XXXII

TRIUMPH OF THE REFORM

THE first sign of any turning in the tide of misery was barely perceptible just after Christmas. On the morning of Saint John's day a postman stopped at the convent with a letter from Madrid containing the only good news Teresa had received in many a long week. Gracián and Mariano were to be freed.[1] Thus she began the year 1579 with a ray of hope that was soon to be confirmed, on the vigil of the Feast of Saint Joseph, with a vision in which she saw her Patron and our Lady praying to Christ for the Discalced, and heard Him say that she would be freed from her "prison" in twenty days: that she should have recourse to Philip II, who would be a father to the Reform; and that her Order would continue, despite the joy of hell and many people of the world at its persecution, for at the very moment when the Nuncio ordered its destruction, God confirmed it.[2]

All these prophecies came to pass. The Duke of Alba had already won over the Royal Council to the cause of the Reform. One of Teresa's most valorous champions at Court was the Count of Tendilla, who had threatened to let Gracián taste his poniard if he deserted her; in fact, it was another of this choleric nobleman's outbursts, this time to Sega, that led to the King's intercession. The Nuncio was so offended that he went to the Escorial and demanded an apology. Perhaps in doing so he cast some reflection upon Madre Teresa and her Discalced. King Philip, who had been convinced of their sanctity since the Apostolic Visitor Fernández had told him of their way of life — Philip II, "who was always the father of truth and justice, and champion of reform and virtue,"[3] treated his visitor to

---

[1] Teresa to Roque de Huerta, December 28, 1578; Stanbrook *Letters*, III, p. 177. Teresa speaks of "the two fathers," evidently referring to Gracián and Mariano. Silverio gives a shorter version of this letter, the original of which has been missing since the eighteenth century.

[2] To Fray Juan de Jesús, March 25, 1579. La Fuente doubted the authenticity of this letter on the ground that the style was unlike Teresa's. Father Silverio evidently agrees, for he does not print it in his *Epistolario*. The Benedictines of Stanbrook accept it (III, p. 205), citing the statement of P. Grégoire that he had seen the signature, and found it undoubtedly Teresa's.

[3] Yepes (*Vida de Santa Teresa*, lib. II, cap. XXIX), who heard Philip's deathbed general confession. If this is a prejudiced opinion, it is far nearer the truth than

one of his rare exhibitions of anger. There was such a terrible quality in the wrath of this patient self-disciplined man that when he gave the lie to Cardinal Espinosa, for example, that ecclesiastical politician went home heartbroken and died the next day. Now, in the same deadly tone he said to the Nuncio, "The Count owes you satisfaction, and I will see that he gives it, for no one in my kingdom is allowed to show disrespect to the representative of the Holy Father with impunity. But I am aware of the hostility of the Mitigated friars against the Reform, and this looks bad, for the Discalced lead austere lives of perfection. *See that you favor virtue, for people tell me you are no friend of the Discalced.*"

The Count, at the King's command, wrote an apology to Monsignor Sega, who then, at the end of his patience, declared that he would be only too happy if His Majesty would appoint some persons in whom he had confidence to investigate the whole matter with him. Philip seized upon the suggestion and named four assessors: Don Luis Manrique, his almoner; Canon Villavicencio, an Augustinian court preacher, and two Dominican fathers, Fray Pedro Hernández and Fray Hernando del Castillo. These four, after some stormy sessions with the Nuncio, finally pointed out to him that he had formed his prejudiced opinion of the Discalced without reading all the evidence, and asked him to examine certain testimonials. Sega consented, and had the surprise of his life. A good and honest man at heart, though not of a judicial temperament, he saw at once that he had been misinformed, acknowledged the error, and set about making amends. On April 26 the assessors formally declared in favor of setting up a separate province for the Reform. On July 3 the Nuncio joined with them in petitioning the King to request this of the Pope. It was almost a foregone conclusion that an appeal from both the King and the Nuncio would find a favorable reception at Rome, and on June 22, 1580, Pope Gregory XIII issued the bulls making the Reform permanent, and establishing it as a separate province in Spain.

This victory for La Madre, after so many years of conflict and suffering, was crowned by the assembling of the first legal Chap-

---

the popular caricature created by the enemies of Spain and of the Church. Even so good and so scholarly a man as Father Bruno, O.D.C., is both unfair to Philip and inaccurate when he refers, in the Prescott manner, to "the impassive monarch, who could be distracted only by the buffooneries of his duenna" (*Saint John of the Cross*, p. 161).

ter General of the Reform at Alcalá on February 1, 1581. Gracián was elected Provincial, and the new province was established on March 3 by the Apostolic Commissary Juan de las Cuevas. Teresa went to great pains to see that the new Constitutions would be such as to protect and perpetuate the Reform. She read the Pope's brief for the first time Wednesday in Holy Week, 1581, at Palencia. Now at last, as she wrote Mother María de San José, she could say with holy Simeon her *nunc dimittis:* let them not pray that her life be prolonged, for her work was done.[4]

As one of many legacies to her sons, she wrote a memorandum of four things our Lord told her in prayer at the hermitage called Nazareth in the garden of San José de Ávila — four counsels whose observance would make the Reform flourish, and whose neglect would cause its failure:

1. There must be suitable superiors.
2. Have many houses, but few friars in each.
3. Have little to do with seculars, and this only for the good of their souls.
4. Teach rather with good works than with words.[5]

With these celebrated *Avisos,* which were placed at the head of the *Constitutions,* Teresa committed the future of her Order to God. There was no longer any doubt that the Reform would survive. The Nuncio Sega, now that his eyes were open, did not stop at half measures, but appointed Father Angel de Salazar Vicar-General and Visitor of the Discalced, with instructions to show the nuns and friars every consideration.[6] Fray Angel, being in ill health, made Gracián his deputy in Andalucía, while he himself "visited" in Castilla. One of his first acts was to give Madre Teresa permission to leave San José, in fact he ordered her to inspect several of her convents, commencing with the one at Malagón, where the illness and departure of Mother Brianda had left matters in a sorry state.

Teresa was not much pleased. She sent Fray Angel's letter of instructions to Gracián, asking him to tear it up afterwards, and remarking, "By this letter Your Paternity will see what has been

---

[4] Stanbrook *Letters,* IV, p. 155.
[5] This vision was on June 6, 1579.
[6] Sega did this April 1, 1579, revoking the powers he had previously given the Provincials.

arranged for the poor old hag.[7] According to the indications (though it may be only a suspicion) it is more a matter of the desire of these my Calced brothers to see me far away from them than the necessity of Malagón. This has hurt me a little, I mean the rest of it, not the thing itself, the going to Malagón; though I should be sorry to go as prioress, for I am not up to it, and I am afraid of failing in the service of our Lord."

The "poor old hag" may have been wrong about the motives of Father Salazar. As if aware of this herself, she said in another letter, "Truly he is of such a very good disposition that he doesn't know how to say no."[8] It was true that the convent at Malagón needed attention. Furthermore, the fame of La Madre was now such that many important people were asking her superiors for her companionship and spiritual help; among others the Bishop Don Álvaro de Mendoza, his sister Doña María, and the Duchess of Alba, grieving because her husband and son had been imprisoned by Philip II. It was Alba that Teresa had chiefly in mind when she left Ávila on June 25, 1579, for Malagón; and not the Duchess so much as a postulant, the daughter of a benefactor, the Lawyer Godoy, who seemed to be out of her mind, and used to scream at the top of her voice, pretending to be sick.

La Madre was not to see Alba, however, for more than three years. After a few days at Malagón, she proceeded to Valladolid, where she spent most of the month of July. Her correspondence of that time is full and various. We learn that Casilda's family are withholding her dowry, and begin to expect the inevitable. Father Gracián's sister, now a nun in the convent, is a "little saint." La Madre has met Fray Nicholas of Joseph-Mary Doria, and likes him very much, though he has not Gracián's charm and sweetness; however, he is talented, humble, and sincere, and will be a great help to her Paul, who has chosen him for his *socius*[9] — Doria, who is to be his nemesis. She sends two of her books to the Bishop of Évora. The two friars have arrived in Italy. Brother Lorenzo should not worry about the pranks of his son Francisco; boys will be boys. She plans to stop at Alba on the way to Salamanca. There is not a word about the most sensational

---

[7] *"La pobre vejezuela."* Letter to Gracián, June 10, 1579. She wrote the same suspicion to María Bautista at Valladolid, June 8.

[8] To María Bautista, June 9, 1579.

[9] To Gracián, July 7, 1579.

event of that year in Spain: the arrest, on July 28, on King Philip's orders and under his personal direction, of the Princess of Éboli and her paramour, Antonio Pérez.[10]

Teresa arrived in Salamanca about the middle of August, 1579. She was there until the end of October, repairing the harm done by an inefficient prioress and seeking to liberate the nuns from the house of Pedro de la Banda. When she found another, the prospective sellers changed their minds. "There is no trusting these Sons of Adam," she lamented to Gracián, in a letter in which she also complained that he did not return her affection. No other place was to be found. If these sisters only had as good a house as the one in Sevilla! And yet Mother María de San José was dissatisfied, and had committed the blunder of telling the nuns at Sevilla that their home was unhealthy: that was enough to make them ill. Teresa then made some surprising criticisms of her former protégé. "She has lost much credit with me. I fear the devil has begun with that house, and that he wants to destroy it altogether. . . . I see the childishness[11] of that house, and I can't endure it, and this Prioress is more clever[12] than her estate calls for. And so I have been afraid[13] . . . as I told her there, that she has never been frank with me. . . . I tell you I have put up with a great deal from her in that place. As she has written me several times with great repentance. I thought she had amended, since she acknowledged it. . . . I have written her terrible letters, and I might as well have been hitting an anvil." It was three o'clock in the morning when Teresa finished this letter,[14] on the Feast of Saint Francis, 1579. A few days later she departed for Salamanca, for the last time.

November found her once more at San José de Ávila, but not for long. She had a stroke of *perlesía*,[15] and a heart attack; but before she had fairly recovered she was on the roads again, in a downpour of rain that continued for three days. After a brief stop at Toledo, she pressed on to Malagón, arriving there November 25. This time, though still so ill and aching that she was hardly able to get out of bed, she made certain reforms that

[10] Cf. my Philip II, p. 599 *et seq.*

[11] "*Rapaceria.*"

[12] "*Sagaz.*"

[13] Two or three indistinguishable words in the MS. here omitted.

[14] To Gracián, October 4, 1579.

[15] This can be either paralysis or palsy. From the fact that Teresa had several attacks, I take it to be the latter.

she had postponed on her last visit. She found it hard to replace Mother Brianda, and the difficulty was increased by the interference of certain unidentified priests. Fray Antonio had caused much mischief by his visit the previous year.

The house at Malagón, looking out upon the noisiest street in the town, had always been unsatisfactory, and Doña Luisa de la Cerda had agreed to build another, which was to have been finished in the latter part of 1579. When Teresa arrived unexpectedly on Saint Catherine's day, November 25, she was planning to have the nuns move in at once, only to learn from the workmen that the building would not be ready for occupancy for six months.

She replied that she would give them thirteen days, for she intended to open the new convent on the Feast of the Immaculate Conception, December 8. Then, taking a broom and a basket, she went to work herself cleaning up debris; it was eleven o'clock at night before she stopped to read her office. At sixty-four she seemed as active as in the old days at San José or Medina. She gave orders like a sea captain, performed prodigies of labor, fell on her knees and asked pardon if her sharp tongue offended anyone. Perfect health seemed hers those busy days; it was not until all was done that her fever and pains returned. When the eve of our Lady's feast came, only eleven of the nuns' cells were ready, but it was enough to accommodate the community for the present, with some doubling up; and on the eighth, as she had planned, Teresa and the sisters went in procession to the new house, behind the splendor of the Blessed Sacrament.

She wrote an enthusiastic report of all this to Father Gracián. "The change was made with great rejoicing. . . . It made them very happy, and they seemed like nothing but little lizards coming out into the sun in the summertime. . . . Oh *mi Padre*, how necessary my coming here has been!" Sister Jerónima del Espíritu Santo (Acevado), who was later to establish the mother house in Italy, was made prioress, and charged with rectifying the errors of poor Brianda. All seemed well. "God grant it may always be so," said Teresa.[16]

Of all her convents this was her favorite. Here alone she was free to create, not merely to adapt. The two-story building of

---

[16] Letter to Gracián, December 12, 1579, *Epistolario*, II, p. 364, Stanbrook dates it December 8 (*Letters*, III, p. 279).

stone and cement was built around a central patio surrounded
by a cloister, upon one of whose wings the confessionals still open,
with their tiny screened windows designed by Teresa herself.
The garden is large and beautiful, shaded by trees. The refectory is well lighted and ventilated, and still contains the tables
chosen by her; and adjoining this are the kitchen and laundry.
The cell she occupied on the upper story is said to be just as she
left it. This, as Padre Silverio says, is the ideal Teresian convent.[17] It was a daily joy for her to see it assume its final shape,
to find the life of prayer she planned for all her daughters made
easier by the position of every window, every stairway, and every
stone and stick. "How well I remember," she wrote Gracián,
December 18, "what a letter from your Paternity made me
suffer on Christmas Eve a year ago! God be praised that times
are so much better." Yet there was no complete satisfaction in
this life. She was learning more and more from the nuns of the
laxity and disorder which prevailed under her cousin Sister
Beatriz of Jesus, who had administered the convent for Mother
Brianda. "She has never said a word to me, even now, though
she sees that they all tell me about it and that I know it. I have
decided that she has very little virtue or discretion."[18]

When Mother María de San José took the part of the nuns at
Malagón, Teresa reproved her vigorously. She hoped that God
would make her a saint, "for wicked as you are, I wish I had
several like you, for I wouldn't know what to do if a foundation
were to be made now, for I don't find anyone fit to be prioress,
though there ought to be; and since they are not experienced
and I see what has happened here, I have felt great fear that the
devil may trick us with good intentions into doing his work.
And so it is needful to walk always in fear, and close to God, and
trust little in our understandings; for, however good they may
be, if this is not so, God will forsake us to go astray in the very
thing we think we are most sure of. . . . Some of the things Your
Reverence wrote me about astonished me.[19] Where was your
understanding? . . . O, God help me, the silly things that letter

[17] P. Silverio, *Vida de Santa Teresa de Jesús*, t. III, p. 283 *et seq.*

[18] To María de San José, early in January, 1580. All such expressions by La
Madre must be taken not in the ordinary sense, but in the light of the perfection that was so dear and so clear to her. To her a little disobedience would be
a "scandal," and an evasion that the world considers slight would be "wicked."

[19] She refers to Mother María's taking the part of the nuns at Malagón. — P.
Silverio, *Epistolario*, II, p. 384, n. 1.

contained, all to get your own way! The Lord give us light, for without it there is no having strength or skill, except for evil. I am glad Your Reverence is so disillusioned, for it will help you in many things; for to improve, it is useful to have made mistakes, and so experience is gained. God keep you — I didn't think I could write so long a letter."[20]

On the day after opening of the new house, her maladies all returned and she had another attack of *perlesía*. At Christmas, however, her joy was such that all the nuns felt and shared it; and when, after making a slip in reading the lesson for the day, she prostrated herself on the floor of the choir, they were all dissolved in tears, and none could speak a word.[21]

She left Malagón on February 13, 1580, to found a house at Villanueva de la Jara, in La Mancha of Toledo, where a priest had told her he had assembled in a hermitage nine holy women who wanted to adopt her rule and obedience. She was not much interested until our Lord told her to go; then she departed in such good health that it seemed as if she had never been ill in her life. As her cart rumbled through the frozen countryside, crowds gathered everywhere to see her, for her reputation was now secure, and the news of her coming had spread everywhere. In a house at Villarrobledo, where she stopped to eat, people broke through the windows and the walls to get a glimpse of her, until the police arrested a few. In another town she had to depart three hours before dawn to escape the crowd. She was asked to bless people, and in one place a herd of cattle. At the Discalced Monastery of *Nuestra Señora del Socorro*, all her friars came forth in procession to receive her, and after kneeling to ask her benediction, escorted her to the church, singing the *Te Deum*. This was the monastery that Catalina de Cardona had caused to be built in the midst of a desert, and though she had died in 1577, the fathers were still called "the Friars of the Good Woman," by the people round about, and many pilgrims visited the cave where she had lived, at the entrance of the Church. When Teresa received Communion there, she saw the hermit woman in her glorified body attended by angels, rejoicing, and heard her say that she must continue her foundations.[22]

Teresa was clutching an image of the Child Jesus to her breast

---

[20] *Ibid.*
[21] Deposition of Ana de San Bartolomé, B.M.C., t. II, p. 300.
[22] Ribera, *Vida de Santa Teresa*, lib. III, cap. IX.

when she arrived at Villanueva, a short distance away, just before High Mass on the first Sunday of Lent, February 21, 1580. The whole population, headed by their clergy, assembled in procession to receive her and to follow the Blessed Sacrament with her to the new convent, where she gave the habit to nine women weeping with joy.[23]

While she was superintending the digging of a well some days later, a workman dropped a windlass, which struck her with tremendous force and knocked her flat on the ground. She got up uninjured; everyone said that Saint Joseph — it was on the eve of his feast — had protected her,[24] though afterwards a painful abscess resulted. But Teresa was well pleased with the new community at Villanueva, and well she might be, for under her rule the nine holy women led a heavenly existence, of which many miraculous details were reported and believed. Although food was very scarce following the sterile year 1579, and money was even scarcer, the nuns trusted in God so completely that they got along with six *fanegas* of wheat instead of the sixty they ordinarily required, and seemed none the worse for it; for like the widow of Elias, they found their wheat bin always full. Their one little pear tree bore enough fruit for two months to supply their needs, with plenty left over to sell and give to the poor. Money was mysteriously found lying about, especially when the nuns had recourse to the *Niño* that La Madre had carried in the procession. A broken pot would stay together whenever cooking was to be done, and then fall apart again.[25] All the accepted laws of economics and even of nature seemed to yield before the love and trust of these simple souls.

Teresa was ill again when she left the hallowed place March 20, accompanied by Sister Beatriz of Jesus, Fray Antonio of Jesus, and a nurse. They arrived in Toledo on Saturday in Passion Week, March 25. On Maundy Thursday she had another stroke of *perlesía,* which left her prostrate for a month. She still had a fever and was very weak when she went with Father Gracián to see Archbishop Quiroga, the Inquisitor General. The Holy Office was examining her autobiography again, but the Archbishop assured her there was nothing to worry about.

[23] Yepes, *Vida de Santa Teresa*, lib. II, cap. XXIX.
[24] Ribera, *loc. cit.* See also Blessed Ann of Saint Bartholomew, *Autobiography,* Book II, ch. 8.
[25] Yepes, *op. cit.*, lib. II, cap. XXX.

Several copies of the famous book had been read and approved by various personages of deeper spiritual discernment than the Princess of Éboli. The Duke of Alba, for example, was reading it in his prison at Úbeda. Teresa had a profound influence on this great soldier and opportunist statesman. He took with him on his last campaign (the conquest of Portugal, for which the King released him) a picture of Christ that she had given him, and he used to say later that by looking at it he was able to practise mental prayer even in the confusion of war.

When Teresa left Toledo June 7, she was attended by a nurse who was to be her companion for the remainder of her days and to leave some of the most interesting data concerning her. This was the kind and gracious Ana de San Bartolomé whom we now call Blessed. Born Ana García, the child of poor village laborers, she had entered San José de Ávila as the first lay sister in 1572. Now twenty-eight years old, with little or no formal education, she had so good a mind and such sound judgment that she became Teresa's confidential secretary as well as nurse, learning to write miraculously by merely copying La Madre's letters. It was she who dressed the old lady in the darkness before dawn, and helped her off with her tunic in the small hours of the next morning; she who wrote out most of the last energetic letters; she who went foraging for an egg or two or a piece of bread as they passed through villages impoverished by famine and drought.[26]

From Villanueva they went to Medina, where Sister Ana de la Trinidad was cured of a violent erisipelas by the caressing touch of Teresa's hand on her swollen face; then to Valladolid, and thence to Segovia, stopping on the way in inns which were hot and stifling even at night.

At Segovia, where she stayed from about June 13 to July 8, La Madre had the great sorrow of learning of her brother's death. Lorenzo's health had been failing gradually since his return from America in 1575. Generous to a fault, he found himself hard pressed at times for money, and constantly bedeviled by his younger brother Pedro de Ahumada, who had followed him

---

[26] She wrote a delightful autobiography. She helped to introduce the Reform into France in 1604, took the black veil there, became a prioress, and founded the house in Antwerp in 1612. She was beatified by Pope Benedict XV on May 6, 1917. There is an English translation of her Life, published by the Carmelites of St. Louis, Mo., in 1916.

back from the Indies, a penniless wreck of a man, a hopeless neurotic who, on being denied a pension by Philip II, became so embittered that he went about grumbling at everything and everybody. Teresa thought he was insane in his attachment to Lorenzo. She sent the latter long letters begging him have patience with their unfortunate brother, who could not help his infirmity, and to give him money in installments, instead of the lump sum that Pedro had let slip through his hands in 1580. This was the state of affairs when Lorenzo became acutely ill on June 26, 1580. His heart had been weakened by the high altitudes in the Andes, and it probably did him no good to live so near Ávila, which is half a mile above sea level. In six hours he was dead, of what would probably now be called coronary thrombosis.[27] Teresa, many miles away, turned pale at that moment, and told the nuns at Segovia that she had seen him die, and pass through purgatory into heaven. A few days later she saw him with Saint Joseph, both very radiant, beside the priest at Mass.

Many of her friends died in 1580, the terrible year of the *catarro universal*, a virulent form of influenza. The Holy Cavalier, Father Francis de Salcedo, was one of them. Philip II might have died in Portugal if his young fourth wife had not knelt by his bedside and offered her life in place of his, so necessary to Spain and to the Church; and God took her at her word.

The death of Father Baltasar Alvarez occurred at Belmonte a month after Lorenzo's, on July 25, 1580. Since 1574 he had been rector at Salamanca and visitor for the Jesuit houses in Aragon. His last years were saddened by suspicions of certain other Jesuits that his high state of contemplation, in which he had followed the lead of Teresa, was a delusion of the devil. There was talk of sending him to Peru in 1579, but nothing came of it. Although his death grieved Teresa, she saw him in glory and splendor, and wrote, "I rejoice that he has left this life of misery and is now in safety. Life passes so quickly that we ought to think more of how to die than how to live. . . . I am four years older than my brother, yet I never manage to die."[28]

---

[27] Silverio, t. IV, p. 569.

[28] To María de San José, July 4, 1580. It was in this letter that Teresa reported a rumor that the Moriscos were plotting to assault Sevilla, and congratulated the nuns there on the prospect of being martyrs.

Lorenzo having named her his executrix, Fray Angel de Salazar gave her permission to go to Ávila to look after the interests of her nephew Francisco. (The younger son, Lorenzo, had returned to Peru in 1578.) After a brief stay there, she took the young heir to Valladolid by way of Medina, for the signing of some papers concerning his father's estate. Gracián went with her to help with the business matters, which were very distasteful to her.

Soon after their arrival in August, Teresa was stricken by the epidemic *catarro*. She was so ill that the nuns at Valladolid felt sure she was going to die. Heretofore, although she had passed her sixty-fifth year, she had always retained an appearance of the bloom of youth; illnesses, fasts, vigils, scourgings, and incredible labors had left her cheek unwrinkled and her black eyes youthful. Now, as she slowly mended, María Bautista and the nuns noticed for the first time that she looked like an old woman.

During the long slow convalescence that kept her in Valladolid until after Christmas, 1580, she had many anxieties. Some relatives were beginning to grumble about a bequest Lorenzo had made for a chapel at San José de Ávila, to be paid for out of the money still owing to him from the convent at Sevilla. "Oh my daughters, what weariness and contention these temporal possessions bring with them!" she wrote to the nuns at Ávila, October 7. Lorenzo's son Francisco was one of her chief worries. At first he seemed to have a vocation, and Gracián took him to Pastrana. But the young man left in a month, finding the life far too strenuous. Teresa wrote Gracián that he seemed to have been transformed into a different creature. He would have nothing to do with any Discalced friars or nuns, least of all with her. He intended to marry, and take care of the property his father had left him. His digestion was ruined, he had headaches, and something was wrong with his heart.[29] Happily these afflictions were but temporary, for only three months after he left the monastery, he married a lovely girl of fourteen, Doña Orofrisia de Mendoza y de Castilla. La Madre was delighted with this match. Her letter to her nephew in Peru, informing him of his brother's good fortune, is very Spanish, very bourgeois, and very feminine:[30]

---

[29] Letter to Gracián, November 20, 1580, obviously dictated by Saint Teresa but signed "Ana de San Bartolomé."

[30] To Lorenzo de Cepeda, December 27, 1580.

"Her mother is first cousin of the Duke of Albuquerque, niece of the Duke of Infantazgo, and other very important titled people. In short, as for father and mother, they say there are none better in Spain. In Ávila she is related to the Marqués de las Navas, and to him of Velada, and very much to the wife of Don Luis, the one descended from Mosén Rubí.[31] They gave her four thousand ducats. He writes me that he is very happy, which is the main thing. I am told that Doña Beatriz, her mother, is of such worth and discretion that she will be able to manage them both, and that it will be arranged, from what they say, that it won't cost much. Doña Orofrisia has only one brother, heir of an entailed estate, and a sister is a nun. If the heir has no son, he will inherit it. A thing that may possibly be."

Before the end of 1580 Teresa had made up her mind to found two more convents. She desired three, in fact, but the one at Madrid had to wait upon the return of Philip II from Portugal, and he was there until 1583. Burgos and Palencia, however, were within the bounds of possibility. "More than six years ago," she wrote, "some very religious persons of the Company of Jesus, old men and learned and spiritual, told me that our Lady would be much served if a house of this sacred Order were established in Burgos, giving me certain reasons for it that moved me to desire it."[32] The suggestion for Palencia had come from her old friend Don Álvaro de Mendoza, who was now bishop of that place. When she hesitated during her convalescence, expecting to die, Father Ripalda, S.J., told her that old age was making her cowardly. "I saw plainly that that was not true," she said, "for now I am older and I am not cowardly."[53] When our Lord said, "What are you afraid of? When have I ever failed you?" she resolved to essay both foundations, commencing with Palencia.

She was pleased when this foundation was made on the Feast of King David, to whom she had great devotion (because, she explained, he, too, was a sinner!). It was fitting, too, that the advance preparations should have been made by a holy priest of Jewish descent, the Canon Francisco Reinoso, nephew of Father

---

[31] Mosén Rubí de Bracamonte, the Hebrew Catholic who built the famous chapel of Masonic design and symbols in Ávila, referred to above.

[32] *Fundaciones*, cap. XXXI.

[33] *Fundaciones*, cap. XXIX.

Jerónimo Reinoso, friend of Saint Pius V and afterward bishop of Córdoba. He had already rented and prepared a house, and unlike Fray Mariano in Sevilla, had even the beds made up and all necessities on hand on the cold foggy twenty-ninth of December when six tired nuns and the lay sister Ana arrived. Everyone was happy, for there was no opposition anywhere, the Bishop was greatly loved, and "the population," added Teresa, "is the best and noblest I have seen."

Since the house was only rented, it was necessary later to find another. She was offered two adjoining the famous hermitage called the Church of Our Lady of the Street, in the most populous part of the town. This she disliked so much that Canon Reinoso found her one that seemed far more attractive, although the owner asked a stiff price, and she agreed to take it. Next day at Mass she began to feel uneasy. As a thought of the humble house near *Nuestra Señora de la Calle* came to her mind, she heard the voice of our Lord saying in reference to it, "This is the one for thee." She went to confession to Father Reinoso, "a most prudent and saintly man, and endowed with the gift of good counsel in everything," who naturally was somewhat perplexed. While he and his friend Canon Salinas were hesitating, Christ said to her, "They don't understand how much I am offended there, and this will be a reparation." At this juncture, the owner of the house she had agreed to take raised his price by 300 ducats, thus giving her the right to withdraw. She then took the house next to the hermitage. Afterwards she wondered why she had not preferred it from the start. She learned, too, that its dark and lonely rooms had been used by men and women as an all-night rendezvous. The Carmelites put an end to that scandal when they took possession on the Feast of Corpus Christi, in the presence of most of the townspeople. Gracián traveled all night to be present.

It was at Palencia that Teresa first heard that Pope Gregory XIII had decreed the permanence of her Reform by setting up a separate province for the Discalced. The future of the Order being now assured, the friars resumed their foundations. John of the Cross had already made one at Baeza; Valladolid, Valencia, and Salamanca soon followed. *"Nunc dimittis!"* she could well say with a full and grateful heart, *"nunc dimittis."* A sister who entered her cell unnoticed saw her write in complete absorption, and sigh profoundly as she laid down her pen; and was frightened when there came from her mouth rays of something like the splendor of sunlight.[34]

Having had an unexpected offer of a house and its upkeep from a widow in Soria, Teresa left Palencia for that place at the beginning of June, 1581, but not without regrets. She had found the people of Sevilla cold and unfeeling. Toledo was ugly and barren of taste. But Palencia — "I don't want to omit saying many praises of the charity I found in Palencia, in particular and in general. Truly it seemed to me like something of the primitive church, at least not very often found nowadays in the world, to see that we were not getting an income, and that they would have to give us our food, and not only not forbidding it, but saying that God was doing them the very greatest favor. And if it be examined with light, they spoke truth; for even if it was no more than to have another church where the Most Blessed Sacrament was multiplied, it was much."[35] No other city ever drew such a tribute from her.

She went to Soria with Father Doria (Gracián was busy founding a college at Valladolid) and seven nuns. The house being well equipped, they made the fifteenth foundation without difficulty, calling it the Monastery of the Most Blessed Trinity. The first Mass was said on the Feast of the Prophet Eliseus, June 14, 1581, and the first sermon preached on the Feast of the Transfiguration by Father Francisco de la Carrera, S.J.

At Soria that summer La Madre had her last conversation with Father Francisco de Ribera, S.J., who was to be her first and one of her best biographers. And on the day after she left the place, she had a strange encounter, at dusk, in the little town of Burgo de Osma, with the Jeronymite Father Yepes, her second biographer, whom she delicately warned of a great penance he would have to endure.[36] The following day she pressed on toward Ávila. The roads were uncommonly bad, and the muleteer incompetent, so that the nuns had often to get out and walk past a dangerous cliff or a defile, and barely escaped being dumped into the mud and over a precipice. When they reached Segovia on Saint Bartholomew's Eve, August 23, 1581, Teresa was in such a state that the sisters prevailed on her to stay and rest for eight days before resuming the journey.

---

[34] Ribera, *op. cit.*, lib. III, cap. X.
[35] *Fundaciones*, cap. XXIX.
[36] Yepes tells of this, *op. cit.*, lib. II, cap. XXXII.

It was a sad situation that confronted her when she finally arrived at San José, September 5: the first fruit of her sacrifice and prayer now relaxed and undisciplined, the nuns discontented and half starved, the debts piling up, the buildings unrepaired. At the bottom of the physical misery there was, as always, a spiritual negligence. She was not long in tracing this to Father Julian of Ávila, who, in his dotage, had become what she feared most, an overindulgent and overfriendly confessor. He had dispensed the nuns from this rule and that rule until the Constitutions seemed hardly in force, and God, being no longer well served, had stopped providing.

The nuns were so glad to see their Madre that they elected her prioress, saying there was never any lack of food where she presided. This confidence was not in vain. As soon as Teresa had restored the harmony of discipline and prayer, during the autumn of 1581, the rest seemed to take care of itself; God fed them as He fed the birds of the air.

"I am astonished at what the devil can do," she reported to Gracián, "and almost all the blame belongs to the confessor, though he is such a good man; but he has allowed them all to eat meat, and this was one of the petitions they made. What a life!"[37]

The affable old chaplain did not enjoy the reforming process.

"How peevish Julian goes about these days. One can't growl at *la Mariana* every time she wants to see him. . . . It is all holy, but God deliver me from confessors of many years. We shall be lucky if we succeed in rooting this up. What would happen if they were not such good souls! After I had written this, certain things happened here with one nun that displeased me very much, and so I have mentioned it, and I didn't mean to speak of it. . . . The remedy . . . will be to send the two away from here; for although it is holy, it cannot be tolerated. . . ."[38]

Teresa's health was better that fall, but she was never without some suffering. In September she had the grief of hearing that Casilda had left the convent at Valladolid. In October she was profoundly disturbed by a scandal of which her twenty-one-year-

[37] From Palencia, February 27, 1581. Padre Silverio insists (*op. cit.*, t. V, p. 151, note) that Mir exaggerates the crisis at San José (*Vida de Santa Teresa*, II, pp. 643–645). Perhaps so, but P. Silverio has a tendency to minimize.

[38] To Gracián, October 26, 1581. "*Oh, mi Padre, que desabrido anda Julián! A la Mariana no está para regañársele cada día que le quiere, sino para rogarle con él. Todo es santo, mas Dios me libre de confesores de muchos años.*

old niece Beatriz (daughter of Juan de Ovalle and Juana) appears to have been the innocent victim. A certain Don Gonzalo, a frequent visitor to their house, had a jealous wife who proclaimed everywhere that her husband was "carrying on a wicked friendship" with the young woman.[39] "And she affirms and says this so publicly," continued La Madre,[40] "that for the most part they must believe it. And so, as for the girl's reputation, it must already be so lost that there is no use talking about it, but of the many offenses that are committed against God. I am so sorry that a thing of mine should be the occasion of this, and so I have tried to get her parents to send her away, for certain learned men have told me they are obliged to do so; and even if they weren't, it seems to me common sense to flee, as from a wild beast, from the tongue of an impassioned woman. Others tell them that this would make what is a lie seem true, and they should not make any change. They tell me husband and wife are living apart." Juana de Ahumada insisted that her daughter was wholly innocent, and Teresa believed this, for she offered to take the girl into one of her convents. Finally the parents sent her to stay with an uncle. Don Gonzalo's wife soon died, whereupon he made a proposal of marriage to Beatriz, which she refused. In 1585 she entered the convent at Alba, and became an exemplary nun.

Alba was always in La Madre's thoughts, but somehow she never managed to get there. Life was so full of crosses. Her relatives had begun a lawsuit over the estate of Lorenzo. She suspected Father Nicholas Doria and Mother María de San José of having agreed to keep her in the dark about a certain money transaction.[41]

It must have been a relief from such sordid interludes when John of the Cross made his appearance in Ávila on the seventh of November. It was the first time she had seen him since his arrest in 1577, and it was the last time they were to meet in this world. As prior of *Los Mártires* at Granada, he had come to beg her to found a convent there, to combat the vicious immorality of the Moorish city. This was out of the question, for she had promised to go to Burgos. However, when he left on November

---

[39] She was not a *"muchacha,"* as Father Silverio calls her. She was born in 1560.
[40] To Sancho Dávila, October 9, 1581.
[41] For the ramifications of this puzzling affair, see P. Silverio, *op. cit.,* V, p. 160 *et seq.*

28, she sent two nuns with him to make the foundation. It was January 21 when they reached Granada. How the stubborn Archbishop opposed them, and how a thunderstorm set fire to his library and jolted him out of bed, leading him to change his mind, are told at length in the pages of Ribera and Yepes.[42]

One of the last thoughts of John of the Cross before leaving Ávila had been to try to save money from his scanty travel allowance to send to Gracián, who was in need — Gracián, who had never lifted a finger to get him out of prison and who did not put in an appearance on this occasion until "Seneca" had departed. Was Teresa contrasting the two in her mind when she wrote Gracián, just before he came, "O Jesus! How few people in this world are perfect!"?

As if to exemplify the fact, she drew back, in a final moment of hesitation, from the thought of the bitter cold of Burgos in winter, and her own infirmities.

"Never mind the cold," said Christ. "I am the true warmth. Satan is exerting all his strength to hinder the foundation: do thou exert thyself on My behalf that it may be made, and go thyself without fail, for the fruits of it will be great."[43]

Gracián gave a grudging consent to go with her. He reminded her that she had only the verbal permission of the Archbishop, and secondhand at that, through the Bishop of Palencia.

"Now look, Padre," said Teresa, "the affairs of God have no need of such prudence. . . . The foundation is going to be a great service to Him, and if we delay it any longer it won't be done. Let us make the attempt, and do you keep silent, for the more we suffer the better it will be; and you must know, *Padre*, that the devil is making a great effort to keep it from being talked about; but in spite of this, let Your Reverence command what you will, for that will be the best thing."[44]

As usual he commanded what she had made up her mind to do.

---

[42] Ribera, *op. cit.*, lib. III, cap. XII; Yepes, *op. cit.*, lib. II, cap. XXXIII.
[43] *Fundaciones*, cap. XXXI.
[44] Yepes, *loc. cit.*

Chapter XXXIII

"ARISE, MAKE HASTE, MY LOVE, MY DOVE, MY BEAUTIFUL ONE, AND COME"

THE expedition left for Burgos as soon as Gracián returned from a hasty trip to Salamanca. Besides him and La Madre, there were Sister Ana de San Bartolomé and two nuns from Alba; four more were to be picked up at Palencia on the way. It was cold, and snow was beginning to fall dismally on roads still muddy from recent heavy rains. If Teresa turned in the squeaky cart to look back at the jagged sky line of Ávila, darkening against a gray sky, it was the last glimpse she had in this life of the city of her birth. She passed through Medina, stopped four days at Valladolid, was received by a great crowd at her beloved Palencia, and after sending a man ahead to see whether the roads were passable (for many of them were deep under water) she heard our Lord say, "Indeed you can go, and don't be afraid, for I shall be with you"; and she went.

The rest of the journey to Burgos was the most dangerous she had ever made. The rains that year were terrible. There were floods everywhere. Roads were washed out, or under water. Wagons sank in the mud up to the hubs. At one place they had to get out and walk along a riverbank. Then, going up a hill, Teresa saw the cart ahead turn over, and it looked as if the nuns were going to be spilled into the river, when a boy who was with the muleteers seized one of the wheels and held on — miraculously, as it seemed to her — until help came. Then she insisted that her cart go first; if anyone was going to be drowned, it must be she.

That night there was no bed to be had when they arrived at an inn.

As they approached Burgos, they had to cross the River Arlanzón on some pontoons which were almost submerged in the deep black icy water and so narrow that if the carts deviated but a trifle, they would slip off. The nuns all went to confession to Father Gracián or the other priest, and asked La Madre's blessing before making the perilous attempt. Teresa showed no sign of fear, in fact she seemed joyful as she said, "Hey, my daughters, what more could you ask than to be martyrs here, if need be, for the love of our Lord? Let me by, for I intend to be the first, and if I am drowned, you can return to the inn." So the valiant old lady took her place in the first cart, and passed safely across.[1]

She had left Palencia with a quinsy sore throat which became so much worse with fatigue and exposure that she was unable to move her tongue, and had difficulty taking even liquid food. On the last day of the journey, as she opened her mouth for Holy Communion, her tongue was loosed. She still had a fever, however, when they approached the historic city where the Cid Compeador lies buried, and Alfonso V swore he was not his brother's murderer; the city whose inhabitants say of their climate, "Burgos has nine months of winter and three months of hell."

Father Gracián insisted that before looking for their lodgings they go to the celebrated Holy Crucifix, the *Santo Cristo de Burgos* in the convent of the Augustinian fathers, to give thanks for their journey and to ask a blessing for the foundation; besides, he explained, it would be better to enter after dark, unseen. It was well after nightfall when Teresa, more dead than alive, reached her destination in the house of Catalina de Tolosa, the benefactress who had suggested the foundation; and she was so wet and chilled that she sat up all night by the fire without being able to get warmed through. The smoke made her ill; her head grew dizzy, and she began to vomit and spit up blood with such violence that a wound opened in her throat. One of her most disgusting trials from then on was the frequent emergence of her voice, not through her half-paralyzed mouth, but through the gaping aperture in her neck.

The next day she was unable to get out of bed. When she learned that Doctor Manso and other important persons were coming to welcome her to Burgos, she had herself carried on a couch to a window opening on a corridor, and there through a curtain, she carried on her business as usual. Very little, apparently, had to be done. The house was fine and spacious, suitable in every way. The donor, Catalina de Tolosa, was a widow, a Viscayan of the middle class, four of whose eight children had already entered the Discalced convents, two at Alba, the others elsewhere, while a younger daughter, Elena, was asking for the habit. And she had not only given the house, but had promised

---

[1] Ribera, *Vida de Santa Teresa*, lib. III, cap. XIII; Yepes, *Vida de Santa Teresa*, lib. II, cap. XXXIV.

to pay for its upkeep. What more could be desired? Only the
formal license of the Archbishop, Don Cristóbal Vela; and as he
was the son of the famous viceroy of Peru, Don Blasco Vela
Núñez, whose brother Francisco, it will be remembered, was
Teresa's godfather, it seemed as if nothing remained but to call
on him, inform him of the arrival of the party from Ávila, and
bring back the license.

Yet when Father Gracián went to see him, he was received
with marked coldness, if not aversion. Yes, the Archbishop remembered having said something to the Bishop Don Álvaro in
Palencia about Madre Teresa's visit to Burgos, but he had supposed she meant to come to discuss the matter with him, not to
bring eight nuns, a lay sister, and a couple of priests to set up a
new house in a city of poor people, who already had too many
convents and monasteries to support.

To poor Teresa, lying on her couch in expectation of good
news, this was a dreadful blow. What a blunder to bring the
nuns! So at least it seemed at first glance. On further reflection
she saw that it was a blessing, for without them she would have
had to return defeated to Ávila, while now she had the excuse
that it was not easy to take so many back in midwinter. She resolved to stay and see what Don Álvaro and other friends could
do with the Archbishop. He might at least permit them to have
Mass, so that the nuns would not have to walk across the city in
foul weather.

Don Cristóbal would not yield an inch, even after Gracián reminded him that the Jesuits, on first going to Burgos a few
years before, had said Mass in that very house. Someone, it
would seem, had brought about a powerful change in the kindly
Ordinary's attitude toward La Madre and her Reform. Father
Ribera, S.J., explains that he really loved her and admired her
work, but felt some doubt as to whether she would actually make
the foundation — in which case a decree of the Council of Trent
forbade him to give his permission.[2] Mir attempts to put the
blame on the Jesuits.[3]

For three weeks the nuns were able to hear Mass only on Sun-

        [2] Ribera, *op. cit.*, lib. III, cap. XIV.
        [3] Mir, *Vida de Santa Teresa*, II, p. 749. Mir gives a secondhand quotation of
Gracián to this effect, cited by Palomino, *The Letters of St. Teresa*, Vol. III, note
to letter 40, from a lost MS. note of Gracián to Ribera's *Life*, the last page of
which is missing.

days and holydays, and then by going very early through muddy streets to a distant church. When at last La Madre, having recovered some of her strength went to see Don Cristóbal, they all took a scourging, one after another, while she was gone. What a disappointment when she returned! The Archbishop had received her courteously enough. She had found him a gentle, quiet, somewhat indolent man with a sad and weary face. But he could be very stubborn, and he had given her not the slightest hope.

Gracián was ready to abandon the fight and return to Ávila. Even Teresa was tempted for a moment.

"Now Teresa, be strong," said the voice of His Majesty beside her. She refused to listen to the counsel of defeat.

It was well that she had this encouragement, for there was worse to come. Only gradually did the horrible truth dawn upon her. But alas, alas, it was true. Good Catalina de Tolosa in her generosity had previously promised her property to "certain fathers" who directed her conscience, and were now filling her with scruples over the transfer of the gift to the Carmelites. Teresa could see that she was very unhappy. She wanted to keep her agreement, but she feared a lawsuit if she did.

When this became clear, La Madre freed the woman from her promise and renounced all rights to the house, while Gracián and the canon, Doctor Manso, found temporary quarters for them in the Hospital of the Conception. It was not a very attractive residence. The old building had a most unsavory reputation among the superstitious. Some said it was bewitched, and weird women visited the place by night. Teresa could well believe it in that city; she used to say that the devil of Burgos was a *diablejo tonto,* for of all her foundations, this seventeenth gave her the most trouble and sorrow. Still, it was good to have even temporary shelter, and it was priceless to have the Blessed Sacrament, and to hear Mass daily; so she took possession of the gloomy old place on the eve of Saint Matthias, February 23. Well, there they were, for better or worse, and there, indomitable, they set about storming heaven in earnest, having recourse particularly to Saint Joseph, whom they implored to find them a home not later than his feast day, March 19.

On March 18 Teresa discovered a suitable house, but the price seemed exorbitant. "What, does money stop you?" asked our Lord. She then rented the place, and afterwards she found it so desirable that she considered the cost very cheap. Ah, that good Saint Joseph, who had never failed her! It was with happier hearts that they established themselves in their third home in Burgos in as many months. Teresa was not even disturbed on Holy Thursday when some rough men, impatient to pass her when she was prostrate in a church in prayer, gave her several kicks to make her move over.[4]

Something — perhaps the story of all this heroism, perhaps some letters from such influential friends as Don Álvaro de Mendoza, perhaps the good offices of the Canon, Doctor Manso, who said, "I would rather argue with any number of theologians than with Madre Teresa" — something began to soften the Archbishop's heart a little. He went twice to visit the old lady in the new home, and spoke kindly to her. Still, he would not give his permission. It was not until another whole month had passed that he finally capitulated, on April 18. The convent was formally inaugurated on the twenty-second.

Within a month (May 20, 1582) Teresa wrote her friend Canon Reinoso of Palencia a letter which leaves little doubt that the rift between her and the Jesuits had become a serious breach during the foundation at Burgos, despite the fact that they had first suggested the enterprise to her. Perhaps feelings on both sides had been inflamed by the repetition of such expressions as the advice Father Avellaneda, S.J., gave his students in 1577: "Don't waste time on women, especially Carmelite nuns, either in visits or by letters, but gently and firmly get away from them." But some new friction had occurred at Burgos, as the following to Reinoso indicates:

"By the enclosed letter . . . you will see something of what is going on as regards the Company, for truly I think they are commencing a deliberate hostility,[5] and the devil bases it on casting at me faults for which they ought rather to thank me with very great testimonies which some of their own could give. It all comes down to these black money matters . . . and as I believe that they will tell a lie,[6] I see clearly that the devil must be involved in this plot. Now they have told Catalina de Tolosa that because our prayer doesn't impress them, they don't wish to have

---

[4] Ribera, *loc. cit.*

[5] "*Enemistad formada.*"

[6] "*Todo va á parar en estos negros intereses que dice que quise y que procuré y harto es no decir que pensé y como yo creo que ellos dirían mentira,*" etc. There is a small blot after the word "*ellos.*"

anything to do with the Discalced. The devil must go to great trouble to disconcert us, since they are so urgent. They also told her that their General was coming here, that he had disembarked, and I recall that he is a friend of the Señor Don Francisco.[7] If in this way this intrigue could be unraveled, and silence imposed by acquainting themselves[8] with the truth, it would be a great service to God, for it is a pity for people so important to deal in puerilities[9] of this sort."[10]

This letter, like the ones concerning Father Salazar, has been the subject of lively controversy. Carmelite scholars — both Zimmerman and Silverio, for example — accept it as authentic. La Fuente, a stanch friend of the Jesuits, questions its reference to them, while others, notably the Bollandists[11] and Father Montoya, S.J., have sought to prove that the Calced Carmelites were meant. Father Zugasti, S.J., believes the Company of Jesus is in question, but argues that Madre Teresa said that the Jesuits would *not* lie, and that the word *not* was deleted by a blot.[12] The Jesuits all resent, naturally, the imputation of untruthfulness. Father Pons, S.J., has in like manner denied the authenticity of a fragment of a letter of Saint John of the Cross to Mother Ana de San Alberto, Prioress at Caravaca, the manuscript of which is cherished by the Carmelite Discalced friars at Duruelo, advising her to be wary of the Jesuits in a certain business matter and adding, "I am sorry you didn't have it put in writing with the Fathers of the Company, for I have never noticed that they are people who keep their word. And so I understand that they will not only deviate in part, but if there is a sharing of jurisdiction, they will make a complete about-face if it suits them."[13] Father Felipe Martín, O.P., vigorously retorts[14] that Father Pons offers only his own denial against the manuscript at Duruelo.

---

[7] Francisco de Reinoso, according to Father Zimmerman. — Stanbrook *Letters,* IV, p. 316, note.

[8] Or "himself."

[9] *Niñerias.*

[10] Mir, *op. cit.,* II, 750; Stanbrook, IV, 316.

[11] *Acta Sanctae Theresiae a Jesu,* párr. 84.

[12] *Discurso,* p. 89. Mir publishes a facsimile of this letter, blot and all. The blot does not appear large enough to have covered a "no," judging by the size of that word in Teresa's handwriting in other parts of the letter (Mir, *op. cit.,* II, p. 750).

[13] "*Pesádome ha de que no se hizo luego la escritura con los Padres de la Compañía, porque no los tengo yo mirado con ojos que son gente que guarda la palabra. Y así entiendo que no solo se desviarán en parte, mas si se defiere, se volverán de otra en todo si les conviene.*"

[14] *Op. cit.,* p. 559.

So the controversy has raged, and to no good purpose. Every-one knows that the Jesuits, like the Dominicans and the Carmel-ites and all other orders, have the faults of their virtues, and that some of them at times carry loyalty and *esprit de corps* too far. But no one acquainted with them will believe that they all lie, even if the charge was made by a saint in a moment of tension. They can boast among their assets that in spite of so much pro-vocation, they have seldom if ever attacked other orders as mem-bers of other orders have attacked them; and that the opposition they have inspired, even among Christians, has always been tainted by the appearance of unreasonable hatred. What seems clear in the affair of Catalina de Tolosa is that the good silly lady promised her house to both orders; that the Jesuits, having the prior claim, felt justly aggrieved; that one word led to another, until even saintly Carmelites, in the heat of the con-troversy and disappointment, may have made some rash general-izations about them. Instead of a denial, Father Zugasti could well afford to laugh and say, "What of it?"

As for Teresa's letter to Reinoso, the two Carmelite scholars have made some sensible remarks. "It is clear from the whole tenor of the letter," says Father Zimmerman, "that the Society (Com-pañía) aimed at is the Society of Jesus, and not, as has sometimes been supposed, the Mitigated Carmelites. . . . Catalina de Tolosa had promised her large fortune to the Jesuit College at Burgos, but transferred the legacy to a convent founded by herself. Fear-ing that she might suffer and the nuns be involved in a lawsuit, Father Gracián and Saint Teresa renounced the property, but had to act cautiously on account of the Archbishop. The Jesuits, not knowing how much they owed Saint Teresa, resented her presence at Burgos."[15]

Father Silverio remarks that it was quite logical for the Jesuits to object to the decrease in the alms promised to them. "Neither the Company nor any other religious Order is exempt from hav-ing some of its members commit imprudences in these and sim-ilar affairs. It would be to ask a continuous miracle of virtue and of social ethics. Let us not be pharisees. . . ." Those most scan-dalized by the conduct and resentment of the Jesuits would have done exactly the same themselves, in his opinion.[16] Had not

---

[15] Stanbrook *Letters*, IV, p. 314, prefatory note to letter of May 20, 1582. Cata-lina de Tolosa later became a Discalced nun at Palencia.
[16] P. Silverio, *Vida de Santa Teresa de Jesús*, t. V, pp. 314–315.

Teresa and the Carmelites resented the loss of Casilda's estate at Valladolid?

There is no sense in exaggerating this controversy. The inevitable separation between two orders with different missions had occurred. It is unfortunate that the breach had to come in the last years of Teresa's life: for thus it acquired an appearance of importance out of all proportion to the reality. The saints of both orders, who cooperated so often after La Madre's death, could testify that there could be no true and lasting quarrel, as she had once intimated, between the Society of Jesus and the Order of His Mother. But in these last months of her life she was clearly enduring the veritable Calvary which she had so earnestly desired, and perhaps we should not be too much surprised to find her apparently separated from the best of her friends of other years, and buffeted by the last temptations endurable to human nature. Furthermore, it must be remembered that the disputed charge was written in strictest confidence to a director, and was never intended to have the publicity it has since attained.

Just after Teresa dispatched this explosive letter, there was another heavy rain, and on Ascension Thursday, May 24, a dangerous flood from the River Arlanzón began to swirl around the convent and the whole section in which it stood. Houses were destroyed, trees uprooted, dead bodies washed from their graves. As the swift and muddy water rose over the doors and windows of the first floor, the lower rooms began to fill. The nuns begged La Madre to flee to safety while there was still time, as people in the neighboring houses and in several monasteries were doing. Teresa refused, and taking the Blessed Sacrament from the chapel to the upper story, she assembled them all to say litanies for their safety.[17] They remained there from six o'clock in the morning until midnight without food or rest. At length Teresa, feeling very weak, asked for a bit of bread. A strong novice went downstairs, waded in the water up to her cincture, and fished out a floating loaf, from which a soaked piece was broken for La Madre.[18]

The next day some divers swam under water and broke the doors and windows, letting the water pour out as the flood sub-

---

[17] Ribera, *loc. cit.* Yepes follows him in the main.
[18] Blessed Ana de San Bartolomé's account, *Autobiography*, Book II, ch. 8.

sided. "They seemed like angels of God," said Blessed Ana de San Bartolomé.[19] Eight cartloads of debris were left on the lower floor by the receding torrent. The rickety old house shook and rattled in the wind that shrieked through the gaping cracks in the roof, just over the bed of the undaunted Foundress. Sister Ana stayed up all night watching her, and, when she fell asleep, covered her with a blanket from her own cot.

Thus the last of Teresa's convents was established, like all the others — even more so — in tribulation and pain. When the time came to return to Ávila late in July (for she was still Prioress there) she committed the new establishment to our Lord with no little anxiety, for she had only twenty *maravedis* to leave the sisters for their food, and the damage from the flood was yet unrepaired. "Why should you doubt that this is now finished?" said His Majesty. "You may go indeed." Teresa then made her farewells, and followed the road westward toward Palencia, after sending a note to tell Gracián to be sure not to go to Sevilla, for the plague was raging there.[20]

Arriving at Valladolid on a hot day in mid-July, she had an opportunity to drink a few of the last bitter lees of human ingratitude. Her relatives had always gone to her with their difficulties, as to a court of appeal. Now they gave her the reward that human beings often bestow on a mediator. It was all over her brother Lorenzo's bequest to San José de Ávila to build a new chapel. For some reason, her niece, the critical Mother María Bautista, sided with the family, and induced young Teresita to do likewise. There must have been furious scenes about the old lady with the crippled arm, the weak heart, and the gaping neck, and it is not unlikely that she expressed her opinion to them very frankly. Finally their lawyer told her no lady would behave as she did.

"Thank you, sir," replied La Madre, "and may God reward you for this favor."

It was one of the saddest moments in her life, perhaps, when she took her last leave of the house that Don Bernardino's money had bought. María Bautista escorted her and her companion to the door — it seems almost incredible, but we have the word of Blessed Ana de San Bartolomé for it — and said,

"Get out of my house, both of you, and don't ever come back!"

[19] *Ibid.*
[20] Letter of June 25, 1582.

So "the poor old hag" took to the roads again, sick of body and heart. She had written from Medina that she would be in Ávila by September 1. That hope was never to be fulfilled. There was discontent at Alba de Tormes; she must go there and restore peace. "I know more or less which sisters are disquieting the rest," she wrote Doña Teresa de Layz, the foundress of the convent,[21] "and if God gives me health I shall try to go to Alba as soon as possible to unravel the plots." And at this juncture, who should meet her on the road but white-haired Fray Antonio, venerable as Father Time with his scythe, in the coach of the Duchess of Alba, who was in great trouble and had sent for her. She must therefore to Alba at once. Alba at last! When she had wanted to go there she had been sent to Ávila. Now, when she wanted to go to Ávila, she must go to Alba. Such was the way of this world. Obedience was everything. Her chief disappointment was that Gracián refused to go with her.

It had not occurred to the Duchess to send any provisions in her luxurious coach. On the way, at Peñaranda, Teresa fainted out of weakness. When she revived, she asked for some *cosilla* to eat. Sister Ana went around the village trying to buy an egg, but not a single one was to be found; all she could get was a couple of figs, which she gave, weeping, to La Madre. Teresa munched on them and said, "Don't be sorry for me, daughter, for these figs are very good; many poor people don't have such luxury." Another day she had only some cabbage and onion stew, which was very bad for her condition. With this she continued the journey, and at nightfall, on the vigil of Saint Matthew, she reached Alba de Tormes, quite exhausted, too exhausted, in fact, to visit the Duchess.

The prioress, Mother Juana del Espíritu Santo, insisted on her going to bed at once. She did so, saying, "God help me, how tired I am; but I haven't been to bed this early in twenty years."

Next morning she got up, walked about the convent, heard Mass, received Holy Communion with great devotion, and took a severe discipline. Thus she went on, getting up and resting in turn, attending Mass each day, until the Feast of Saint Michael, September 29. Then, after Mass, she had a hemorrhage which left her so weak that she had to be helped back into bed in the infirmary. She had asked to be placed there so that she could

---

[21] Letter of August 6, 1582.

look through a certain window and see the priest saying Mass in the chapel beyond.

All that summer the sisters at Alba had noticed strange lights shining in the choir, and sometimes at night heard something like a hushed but very distinct sigh passing through the corridors and cells. Now they began to understand the significance of all this. It was evident that Madre Teresa was going very soon to meet His Majesty face to face.

Sister Ana was with her continually, day and night. The Duchess of Alba was allowed in the cloister, and forgetting all those troubles which Teresa had come to assuage, fed her with her own ducal hands, and probably spoke futile words of consolation.

One day the great lady was announced at the door of the infirmary just after some medicine of a peculiarly vile odor had been spilled on the bed.

"*Cubra, cubra!*" moaned Teresa, "Don't let the Duchess come in yet. It smells terrible, and she will be offended."

Sister María de San Francisco told her not to worry. It smelled very good — indeed it was like *agua de ángeles*. The Duchess, too, commented on the delightful smell, which she thought must be some rare perfume — yes, it was like *agua de ángeles*.

Teresa spent all of the first night of October in prayer, and at dawn asked to have Fray Antonio of Jesus hear her confession. The first friar of her Reform was evidently much moved as he went in to hear the last self-accusation of a pure and virginal soul. The word went around the house that Christ had told her she was about to die. Some sisters told her afterward they had heard Fray Antonio say he would ask our Lord not to take her yet. "Never mind about that," said Teresa. "I am no longer needed in this world."[22] The nuns all gathered at the bedside that day, and received her last counsels.

On October 3, the eve of Saint Francis, at about five o'clock, she asked for *Viaticum*. The nuns dressed her in her veil and white choir mantle, and lighted holy tapers in the infirmary. She was so weak that they had to turn her in the bed. While they waited for the priest, each holding a lighted candle, La Madre began to speak:

"*Hijas mías y señoras mías,* for the love of God I beg that you

---

[22] Yepes, *op. cit.,* lib. II, cap. XXXVIII. In the main he follows Ribera, as usual.

will take great care with the keeping of the Rule and Constitutions, and pay no attention to the bad example that this wicked nun has given you, and pardon me for it."[23]

When the priest arrived with the Blessed Sacrament, and she became aware that her Lord was entering the room, she raised her body on the bed without any help, as though to throw herself on the floor. The nuns who held her down noticed that a change had come over her countenance: it was beautiful and illuminated beyond description, much younger than her age warranted. "And clasping her hands, full of joy," says Ribera, "this swan of utter whiteness began to sing at the end of her life more sweetly than they had ever heard her sing, and spoke lofty things, amorous and sweet. Among others she said, 'Oh my Lord and my Spouse, now the desired hour is come. Now it is time for us to go. Señor mío, now is the time to set forth, may it be very soon, and may Your most holy will be accomplished! Now the hour has come for me to leave this exile, and my soul rejoices at one with You for what I have so desired!' "[24]

She gave many thanks for having been a daughter of the Church and for dying in it. Over and over she repeated it: "In short, Lord, I am a daughter of the Church. . . . I am a daughter of the Church." She spoke again of pardon for her sins, asked the nuns to pray for her, and again begged them to keep her Rule. Several times she repeated the words, "Sacrificium Deo spiritus contribulatus: cor contritum et humiliatum, Deus, non despicies. Ne projicias me a facie tua, et Spiritum Sanctum tuum ne auferas a me. Cor mundum crea in me, Deus."

At nine o'clock that evening Teresa asked to be anointed. When Fray Antonio brought the holy oils, she joined in the psalms and prayers. He asked her then whether she wished to lie in Ávila or in Alba.

"Do I have to have anything of my own?" she answered. "Won't they give me a bit of earth here?"

She was in great pain during the night, but from time to time could be heard praying and singing. The next morning, October 4, she turned suddenly on one side "like Mary Magdalen in the paintings," and holding a crucifix tightly in her hand, remained perfectly still, as some of them had seen her in the prayer of

---

[23] Ribera, op. cit., lib. III, cap. XV.
[24] Ibid.

union or in rapture; and thus she lay, motionless, ecstatic, until evening, except at one time when she made little signs as if speaking earnestly with someone. At nine o'clock in the evening she breathed forth her soul so gently that it was difficult to tell the precise moment; it was just as they had often seen her in the highest prayer. Her face was gloriously young and beautiful. The little sigh that escaped her lips was like the sound they had heard so many nights during the summer.

Many strange things occurred at her passing. A brilliant star had been noticed just over the church every evening between eight and nine. Crystal rays of colored light passed the window of the infirmary cell where she was to die. Shortly before she went, Blessed Ana de San Bartolomé saw our Lord at the foot of the bed in majesty and splendor, attended by myriad angels, and at the head, the Ten Thousand Martyrs who had promised Teresa, in a rapture years before, to come for her in the moment of death. When she sighed her last, one of the sisters saw something like a white dove pass from her mouth. And while Sister Catalina de la Concepción, who was very holy and had less than a year to live, was sitting by the low window opening on the cloister by La Madre's cell, she heard a great noise as of a throng of joyful and hilarious people making merry, and then saw innumerable resplendent persons, all dressed in white, pass the cloister and into the room of the dying Saint, where the nuns gathered about her seemed but a handful in comparison; and then all advanced toward the bed. And this was the moment when Teresa died.

* * *

The *médicos* said, of course, that her death was caused by old age, fatigue, and hemorrhage. The mystics admitted that these played some part, but denied that they were the principal cause. Long ago Teresa had felt certain that if the joy of her prayer, or on one occasion a celestial song, lasted a moment longer her soul would leave her body. She certainly had all the appearances of death in many of her raptures. In the *Moradas* she said that she would die of an impetus of love.[25] And this, in the opinion of Father Yepes[26] and others, is just what happened.

Sister Catalina de Jesús, who, being very ill, was not informed

---

[25] Cf. *Morada* VI, c. 10 and *Vida*, cap. XX.
[26] Yepes, *op. cit.*, lib. II, cap. XXIX.

that La Madre had died, knew it nevertheless, and told Father Gracián that the Saint had appeared to her in glory, and said she was going to the enjoyment of God, and had had a great impetus of love for Him, with which her soul had passed. Pope Gregory XV, in the bull of canonization, accepted and confirmed this view. The Roman Breviary likewise has it: *"intolerabili divini amoris incendio potius quam vi morbi, Albae cum decumberet . . . purissimam animam Deo reddidisse."*

Skeptical materialists who reject the mind of the Church have some very embarrassing facts to explain. After all her illnesses, the body of this woman of sixty-seven remained as white and smooth as alabaster — like that of a child of three, says Ribera. All the wrinkles that had gathered since her illness of 1580 had vanished. A sweet smell which nobody could describe or identify came from the body and everything that had touched it — towels, garments, even Teresa's fingerprints on a plate. It became so overpowering in the cell where she died that the windows had to be opened to prevent headache and faintness.

She was buried on the day after her death, October 5, with due solemnity, but without embalming, under an arch adjoining a wall of the lower choir of the convent. Clad in the habit she herself had made, she was carried there on a simple bier; and according to Ribera, the grave was piled with rocks, quicklime, and bricks, this at the instance of Doña Teresa de Layz, "who thought thus to make the body more secure."[27]

During the ensuing months the sisters often went there to pray. If they happened to fall asleep, a sudden noise would wake them, and sometimes they could smell the same sweet fragrance, especially on the days of saints to whom La Madre had had a particular devotion. This made them very curious to see the body, and when Father Gracián arrived in Alba nine months after her death — it was July 4, 1583 — they persuaded him to exhume it.

The casket was found broken and full of moist earth and "the smell of dampness," for the grave had evidently been saturated by some underground spring close by. Yet when the body was undressed and cleansed of mud, it was discovered to be intact and incorrupt, just as on the day of burial; "for as our Lord in life protected her from all impurity with the most perfect virginity," explains Ribera, "so after death He kept her from all

---

[27] Ribera, *op. cit.*, lib. III, cap. XVI.

corruption, and would not allow worms to touch what the flames of lust had spared."[28]

The whole convent was filled with the sweet odor that came from the firm unrotted flesh when, clothed in a new habit, it was laid in an open coffin in the chapel. In 1585 it was taken secretly to Ávila, one arm being left at Alba for the consolation of the nuns there. There were many supernatural occurrences and miracles, and ailing persons were cured by touching the holy remains. Ribera saw them in 1588 and left a minute description of them. Small portions in time were sent as relics to various parts of the world — a finger to Paris, another to Brussels, a bit of flesh to Rome, another to the Carmelites of La Puebla, in Mexico. Ribera deplored the dismemberment of her body as a desecration by man of what God had left intact, and Father Silverio agrees. But whether in her relics, or more commonly in the prayers and sacrifices of her children, Teresa still preaches, teaches, and heals nearly four centuries after her death; her sound has indeed gone forth to the far corners of the earth. In 1586, after much controversy inspired by the local emulations of Alba and Ávila, the body itself was taken back to the former place,[29] where it still reposes. The heart, too, in its closed reliquary, is there intact, save for the hole visible in the center, where Teresa felt the angel's fiery dart of love.

If all this created a sensation in Carmelite circles in 1583, there was equal rejoicing throughout Spain three years later, when physicians and ecclesiastics made a public record of the condition of the remains. The miracles wrought through her intercession (and they have continued to our day) led Lope de Vega, Cervantes, and several European monarchs to swell the mighty ranks of those urging her cause, until Pope Paul V declared her blessed in 1614, and Pope Gregory XV canonized her in 1622. Great was the joy in Spain when Pope Urban VIII, at the request of King and Cortes, declared her patron of the country, after the Apostle Saint James. Of all the magnificent saints of that fervent land, she has always held the highest place in the hearts of the people. In 1922 the University of Salamanca conferred on her the degree of Doctor of Theology, *honoris causa*, while Queen Victoria placed an academic cap and insignia on her statue. Even greater distinctions have testified to her high rank among those

---

[28] *Ibid.*, lib. V, cap. I.
[29] *Ibid.*, lib. V, cap. II.

"learned and holy men" for whom she had such respect. Although she has never been proclaimed a doctor of the Church, the Church commends her "celestial teaching" to the faithful in the Breviary and in the collect of her Mass, October 15; while Pope Pius X, in a letter to the General of the Discalced Carmelites in 1910, remarked that "what the Fathers of the Church taught without system and confusedly, this Virgin has reduced, with such mastery and elegance, to a body of doctrine."

Meanwhile the Reform had spread to France, to Italy, and ultimately to every part of the world, to be an example and an expiation, the salt of a corrupting humanity. Teresa hoped that in times of persecution her convents would supply His Majesty with martyrs whose blood would be the seed of the Church. Remembering this, the sixteen Carmelites of Compiègne, now beatified, offered their lives to God at the height of the Great Terror in 1794, and went singing to the guillotine; and the bloody reign stopped in a few days with the execution of Robespierre.[30] And all over the world there are Carmelites ready to follow this high example if need be.

In her own country the power of her name has been so great that even Communists who could burn churches, desecrate altars, slay nuns and priests, and fire bullets into an image of the Crucified have been unable wholly to shake off a veneration bred into the bones of their ancestors. It is said that during the war of 1936 a force of them, advancing to attack Ávila, saw coming to meet them a woman in Carmelite robes who cried, "Don't you dare touch my city!" Someone shouted, *"Es Santa Teresa,"* and the Reds broke and fled as if for their lives. I cannot vouch for this story, but its acceptance in Spain is a tribute to the Saint's hold upon the hearts of her countrymen, even when they think they hate (God forgive them) all that she held most dear. In the first months of the war, the Communists took her severed arm from its sanctuary; yet not even in their hands did it receive the treatment the Huguenots had given the intact remains of Saint Francis de Paula, and on being recovered by Nationalist troops, it was escorted with great veneration through the remainder of the war by Generalissimo Franco.

Most of her physical entity may still be seen at Alba de

---

[30] Cf. *Les Seize Carmélites de Compiègne* by Dom Louis David, O.S.B., Paris, 1906, and *Les Bienheureusses Carmélites de Compiègne* by Victor Pierre, Paris, 1913. Gertrude von le Fort's *Song From the Scaffold* is highly fictionalized.

Tormes. Yepes had knelt there in 1606, and smelled the good odor of paradise he had noticed at their last meeting at Burgo de Osmo in 1581, when he had suspected her of indulging in *pastillos* to sweeten her breath.[31] And there, as recently as 1914, when the sepulcher was last opened, a photograph was made of the darkened flesh[32] that still defies all the known laws of time and decomposition, waiting to be awakened by the kiss of her Bridegroom's mouth when He comes again to an earth of sin and folly. For the madness that ruled her life, as the low market place sees it, has turned out to be the one true sanity; and the little girl who thrilled at the words *para siempre* has thrown away a world to gain all heaven. If that smiling mouth, still more like a woman's than a skeleton's, could speak to the anguished hearts of our bloody days, it might well repeat what she once wrote for the nuns of San José:

"Let those who are to come after us be afraid and read this: and if they don't see what now exists, let them not cast the blame upon the times, for it is always a good age for God to give great favors to those who truly serve Him."[33]

---

[31] So he admitted to Blessed Ana of San Bartolomé. See also his *Vida de Santa Teresa*, lib. II, cap. XXIX.

[32] Padre Silverio published this photograph as the frontispiece of the fourth volume of his life of Santa Teresa.

[33] *Fundaciones*, cap. IV, B.M.C., p. 33.

INDEX

If you have enjoyed this book, consider making your next selection from among the following . . .

Born in 1891 in Waterbury, Connecticut, William Thomas Walsh, prominent historian, educator and author, gained international attention for his Spanish historical biographies, *Isabella of Spain* and *Philip II*, both of which have been translated into Spanish, as have *Saint Teresa of Avila* and *Characters of the Inquisition*. These works represent a contribution to historical literature unsurpassed in the twentieth century. *Isabella of Spain* was a great success in Spain just before and during the Spanish Civil War, and it was also translated into French and German; *Philip II* received favorable attention from both the *New York Times* and the *London Times*. Mr. Walsh also wrote a perennially popular little book entitled *Our Lady of Fátima*, as well as several other works, and for two decades he contributed short stories, articles and poetry to national magazines. William Thomas Walsh's educational background included a B.A. from Yale (1913) and an honorary Litt.D. from Fordham University. In 1914 he married Helen Gerard Sherwood, and the couple had six children. For 14 years Mr. Walsh directed the English department of Roxbury School in Cheshire, Connecticut; he did newspaper reporting during World War I; and he held the position of Professor of English at Manhattanville College of the Sacred Heart, New York City, for many years. In 1941 he received the Laetare Medal, which is awarded by the University of Notre Dame in recognition of distinguished accomplishment for Church or nation by an American Catholic, and in 1944 he was awarded two honors: Spain's highest cultural honor, the Cross of Comendador of the Civil Order of Alfonso the Wise, and the 1944 Catholic Literary Award of the Gallery of Living Catholic Authors. William Thomas Walsh died in 1949.